# THE FAMILY
## AN INTRODUCTION

## SIXTH EDITION

# J. Ross Eshleman
### WAYNE STATE UNIVERSITY

ALLYN AND BACON
Boston   London   Toronto   Sydney   Tokyo   Singapore

Managing Editor: Susan Badger
Series Editor: Karen Hanson
Production Administrator: Susan McIntyre
Editorial-Production Service: Kathy Smith
Photo Research: Lisa Feder/Susan McIntyre
Cover Administrator: Linda Dickinson
Composition Buyer: Linda Cox
Manufacturing Buyer: Megan Cochran

**Photo Credits:** 12, © Susan Lapides 1980; 25, Mark W. Richards; 55, North Wind Picture Archives; 58, The Granger Collection; 79, © Susan Lapides 1981; 91, U.S.D.A. Photograph; 119, The Christian Science Monitor/R. Norman Matheny; 126, Paul Conklin; 141, The Picture Cube, Francie Manning; 147, The Christian Science Monitor/R. Norman Matheny; 168, © Frank Siteman MCMLXXXIII; 175, Neal Menschel; 200, © Frank Siteman 1986; 209, The Christian Science Monitor/Melanie Stetson Freeman; 232, The Picture Cube © Spencer Grant; 249, The Picture Cube © Spencer Grant; 265, © Frank Siteman, MCMLXXV; 274, The Christian Science Monitor/Robert Harbison; 297, H. Clark; 305, © Susan Lapides; 324, The Picture Cube © Nancy Bates 1984; 332, The Picture Cube © Frank Siteman MCMLXXXI; 360 EKM–Nepenthe, Frank Siteman; 368, © Frank Siteman MCMLXXXIII; 386, © Susan Lapides 1980; 408, T. A. Hoffman; 439, AP/Wide World Photos; 448, Frank Siteman; 462, © Frank Siteman MCMLXXXIII; 473 © Frank Siteman MCMLXXXI; 499, UNICEF Photo by Lazzopina; 511, © Frank Siteman MCMLXXXI; 539, © Frank Siteman; 544, The Picture Cube © Nancy Bates; 552 © Frank Siteman MCMLXXXVI; 564, Ken Karp.

**Library of Congress Cataloging-in-Publication Data**

Eshleman, J. Ross.
    The family : an introduction / J. Ross Eshleman. -- 6th ed.
      p.    cm.
    Includes biographical references and index.
    ISBN 0-205-12629-4
    1. Family.  2. Marriage.  3. Family--United States   I. Title.
HQ515.E83 1991
306.85′0973--dc20

90-37625
CIP

Printed in the United States of America

10  9  8  7  6  5  4  3  2      95  94  93  92  91

This textbook is printed on
recycled, acid-free paper.

# Contents

## PART II   FAMILY LIFE-STYLES: CULTURAL AND SUBCULTURAL VARIATIONS

## 5   *LIFE-STYLES AMONG CHINESE FAMILIES*   136

## 6   *LIFE-STYLES AMONG AFRICAN-AMERICAN FAMILIES*   158

## PART IV    SEXUAL NORMS AND RELATIONSHIPS

**10    SEXUAL RELATIONSHIPS IN PREMARITAL AND NONMARITAL
CONTEXTS    290**

---

# PREFACE

What should an introductory family textbook try to do? First, I believe it should provide a thorough and objective coverage of the basic concepts and ideas in marriage and the family. The ideas should be presented clearly and intelligibly. The coverage should include specific factual data as well as abstract principles, and empirically supported findings as well as hypotheses for testing. Since many students will find this introduction to the family to be their terminal course as well, the text should arouse a curiosity toward, and include tools for, an ongoing process of observation, understanding, and analysis of marital and family relationships and organizations.

Second, and equally important, I believe an introductory family textbook should capture the interest of the student. This should not be done at the expense of accuracy but should convey realistically the processes and organization of marital and family behavior in an understandable, readable, and interesting way. From this, the student should be able to relate personal and familial values and behaviors to differing life-styles and patterns both within his or her own society and in relation to others. In other words, the student should be made to see more clearly his or her place in the United States or in the world picture.

I have tried to write a text that is both interesting and highly readable, to be relatively comprehensive in the coverage of topics, to emphasize the family in the United States and supplement it heavily with historical and cross-cultural referents, and to be accurate, yet contemporary—including nontraditional marital and family life-styles, yet keeping them in a realistic perspective relative to the more common traditional family forms. I have tried to document extensively in presenting the study of the family as a scholarly discipline and have tried to encourage further thought and reading by concluding each chapter with questions for discussion and an annotated bibliography for further reading. Extensive use of the latest census material has been made and illustrative selections have been inserted (note the boxed panels).

Each of these attempts was an outgrowth of several major objectives: (1) to present an objective description and analysis of contemporary U.S. families within a world perspective, (2) to examine without condemnation or praise nontraditional family and marital life-styles, (3) to apply general theoretical schemes and frames of reference to family issues, (4) to present basic concepts and descriptive materials clearly and intelligibly, (5) to suggest questions and supplemental sources to stimulate discussion and reading beyond the textual materials, and (6) to cultivate in the student an increased awareness of his or her particular niche in the family and general social order.

*The Family* basically follows a sociological and social-psychological approach. Chapters 1–4 deal with understanding the family irrespective of time or place. They summarize basic issues in families in the United States; examine approaches to the study of families; establish five basic frames of reference or theories central to understanding family groups and systems; illustrate the boundaries of marital, family, and kinship organization; and look at the linkages between the family and other institutions with a major focus on marriage as related to the world of work. Chapters 5–7 look at cultural and subcultural variations in family life-styles: between traditional and contemporary mainland Chinese families, among African-American families in the United States, and, finally, by social class. Chapters 8 and 9 bring structure and process to the creation of a marital and family status by examining the who, why, and how of mate selection in contemporary U.S. society. Chapters 10 and 11 single out sexual norms and relationships as a major and significant social fact of the nonmarital, marital, and family system. Chapters 12–15 deal with the family life cycle: marriage, parenthood, child rearing or socialization, and middle and later years, including dying, death, and the post-marital family. Chapters 16 and 17 examine the nature of crisis, domestic violence, divorce, and remarriage. The book concludes with a chapter on the family and social policy.

As a result of an extensive review of the literature, as well as selected feedback from faculty and students who used previous editions, various changes and additions appear in this sixth edition. Considerable changes in reorganization have occurred within chapters. Extensive new and updated material will be evident throughout the text: there are more recent census data, many new inserts, and significant new research findings on topics ranging from AIDS and the homeless to intimate relationships beyond traditional marriage/family boundaries, and from latchkey children to the abuse of parents. As in the previous edition, five basic frames of reference (structural-functional, interactional, developmental, exchange, and conflict) are described and applied at various points throughout, extensive use is made of recent census data and research findings, and selected inserts (boxed panels) are provided to supplement the basic textual material. All chapters end with a summary, key terms and topics, discussion questions, and annotated further readings.

It is my hope that you will find the ideas stimulating and clearly explained. Where you find errors, where you disagree with particular points, when you can supply supplemental material or observations, please inform me. I hope the book will be readable and interesting, will present an accurate portrayal of family systems, will be flexible in its use, will stimulate thought and discussion, and, perhaps most important, will change behavior by expanding our awareness of, and sensitivity to, self and others.

It is difficult to know where to begin or end in expressing a deeply felt sense of gratitude and appreciation to many people. Surely, the most sacrifices were made by my wife and children. I also want to acknowledge my Ph.D. advisor, A. R. Mangus, and my department chairman for the nine years I was at Western Michigan University, the late Leonard Kercher. Both men had a major influence on my life, my interest in the family, and my professional achievement.

To single out others would require a lengthy list. But several should be mentioned. Professionals in the field who were users of the last edition and the reviewers for this edition's manuscript—John Bedell, California State University at Fullerton; Ruth Busch, Auburn University; Sylvan Clavan, Saint Joseph's University; David Klein, University of Notre Dame; and David Kent Lee, Sacramento State University—provided valuable reactions, comments, and suggestions for changes in this edition. Friends and colleagues who provided encouragement and support in areas other than textbook writing should be acknowledged as well. Finally, individuals such as Karen Hanson and Susan McIntyre at Allyn and Bacon, each fulfilling their professional tasks, were influential in getting this book into its final form. Kathy Smith provided excellent editorial and production assistance. To each of these individuals I extend my thanks and appreciation.

# THE FAMILY

# CHAPTER ONE

# AN INTRODUCTION TO THE FAMILY: ISSUES AND CHANGE

© Frank Siteman.

*The Family?* What is this family? Is *the* family the one with one female legally married to one male? Does this couple have two children (one of each sex, of course) born within wedlock, a husband employed full time serving as the primary provider and ultimate authority, a wife as a full-time mother and housewife, and a cohesive, loving, sexually exclusive unit bound until death do they part? Or is *the* family one with a single parent who has a child born outside of wedlock? Does *the* family include a wife who is employed full time, a husband who chooses to be the primary child rearer, a childless couple, or a less than cohesive, conflict-ridden, abusive unit that experiences divorce?

Is the word **family** a meaningful concept? Does it imply images of married couples, love, permanence, children, sexual exclusivity, housewives, legal unions, and intergenerational continuity? If so, are these images more than a perceived idealism that is inconsistent with the realities of today's relationships: remarriages, dual careers, childless couples, one-parent households, same-sex unions, gender inequalities, abusive partners, or intergenerational disruptions? Some writers are asking if it is time yet to begin thinking about "families" less in terms of structure and stability than in terms of process and change, and less in terms of traditional images and forms by which everything else is judged than in terms of close relationships or sexually bonded primary relationships.[1] The former terms suggest a traditional ideal existing among a small segment of the population, while the latter suggests a broader, more comprehensive, more accurate portrayal of the reality of human, close, primary, sexually bonded relationships.

It is difficult to find terms or concepts that differentiate family from nonfamily relationships and experiences. The term *sexual bond* has just been suggested. Others have suggested *family realm* as a term that differentiates familial aspects of the human experience from nonfamilial realms such as the political, economic, medical, educational, military, or artistic arenas, among others.[2] The family realm, created by the birth process, establishes ties across generations and includes characteristics of permanence, a concern with "total" persons, a process orientation that grows out of caregiving, a unique and intense emotionality, an emphasis on qualitative purposes and processes, an altruistic orientation, and a nurturing form of governance.

This book is entitled *The Family*, and will continue to use that concept, but with the recognition that marriages and families have many forms and behaviors that do not fit traditional notions. Many relationships that are close, primary, and intimate are family-like, but do not fit traditional definitions. This book proposes to examine a wide range of family and family-like patterns that exist in North America and around the world. Current research findings have

---

1. John Scanzoni, Karen Polonko, Jay Teachman, and Linda Thompson, *The Sexual Bond: Rethinking Families and Close Relationships* (Newbury Park, CA: Sage Publications, Inc., 1989).

2. Ivan F. Beutler, Wesley R. Burr, Kathleen S. Bahr, and Donald A. Herrin, "The Family Realm: Theoretical Contributions for Understanding its Uniqueness," *Journal of Marriage and the Family* 51 (August 1989): 805–816.

been incorporated in an effort to understand the uniformities, regularities, and consistencies as well as the differences, irregularities, and changes that exist in norms, values, and behaviors associated with what is recognized as marriage or family type relationships.

Similarities and most differences in attitudes, behaviors, and organization create little conflict or controversy. Most of these similarities and differences are not even obvious to the majority of persons who never undertake a systematic study of the family. Do parents, teachers, or businesspeople get disturbed over higher divorce rates in the West, employment rates of mothers, or the failure of Amish-Americans to use electricity or drive automobiles? Generally not. However, social controversy does arise when Amish buggies present a highway danger to fast-moving automobiles, when children of working parents are not provided adequate care, and when property settlements and child placements cannot be agreed upon by divorced couples. This introductory chapter alerts us to selected major issues brought about by social change and to selected characteristics of families and family type relationships in the United States. Chapter 2 discusses approaches used to examine issues such as these.

## IDEAL-TYPE CONSTRUCTS

Many concepts, illustrations, and ideas used in this book are treated in "ideal-type" terms. Ideal types are *not* what are implied in the common usage of the word: that which is ideal, good, best, valuable, perfect, or desirable. Rather, ideal types are hypothetical constructs based on "pure" characteristics.

Ideal types always represent the end, the extreme, or the pole of a continuum. Created hypothetically, they provide contrasting points with which to compare any social phenomenon. Patriarchal/matriarchal, nuclear/extended, primary/secondary, individualism/familism, or rural/urban are examples of ideal types. The "pure" characteristics of rural might include geographical and social isolation, homogeneity, agricultural employment, sparse population, and a subsistence economy. Characteristics of urban are likely to include social heterogeneity, industrial employment, dense population, and impersonality. Any community in the world could be placed along this ideal-type continuum, but none is likely to include all characteristics to their maximum degree. These terms accentuate, even exaggerate, reality rather than describe it accurately. On a rural/urban construct, Chicago would fall toward the urban end of the continuum. However, New York may be more characteristic of urban than Chicago, and Tokyo more characteristic than either. Few would argue against the residents of Rough Creek, Arizona, or Mud Lick, Kentucky, being classified as rural, but compared to tribes living in the rain forests of Brazil or the Philippines, both are quite urban.

The concept "ideal type" was systematically developed by the German sociologist Max Weber.[3] He was careful to point out that, first, value connotations should be avoided. The prefix *ideal* denotes a constructed model, not evaluation or approval. It makes no suggestion as to what ought to be or what norm of conduct is approved or disapproved. Second, an ideal type or ideal construct is not an average or model characteristic. An average denotes a central tendency, whereas an ideal type is a representation derived from the extreme instances. Third, as mentioned, the ideal type is not reality. It is an abstraction, a logical construct, and by its very nature is not found in reality in its pure form.

### The functions of ideal-type constructs

An ideal-type construct performs several basic functions: (1) it provides a limiting case with which concrete phenomena may be contrasted; (2) it provides for the analysis and measurement of social reality; and (3) it facilitates classification and comparison. In short, the ideal type provides a means to clarify what any phenomenon would be if it always or ever conformed to its own definition. Thus, ideal types enable social scientists to make valid and precise comparisons between societies, institutions, or families separated in time and place. It enables we who are studying the family to have a methodological tool that provides assistance in examining the upper or lower classes, African-American or white-American families, or arranged or free-choice mate selection. At this point, it is used to examine selected issues in the American family.

## ISSUES IN U.S. FAMILIES

There is little dispute that "the family" in United States society is changing. This is widely acknowledged in the mass media and is documented by empirical research. Arland Thornton, for example, examined three decades of changing norms and values concerning family life from the late 1950s through the middle 1980s.[4] Using data from a broad range of data sets, documentation was provided to show a weakening of the imperatives to marry, to remain married, to have children, to restrict intimate relations to marriage, and to maintain separate roles for males and females.

Changes such as these are not necessarily "bad" or disruptive, nor do they always present a conflict of interest between groups or persons. Not all changes occur at an equal rate, nor do all segments of a society adjust equally to the changes taking place. Thus it would be possible to deal with nearly any

---

3. Max Weber, *The Methodology of the Social Sciences*, trans. and ed. Edward H. Shils and Henry A. Finch (New York: The Free Press, 1949).
4. Arland Thornton, "Changing Attitudes toward Family Issues in the United States," *Journal of Marriage and the Family* 51 (November 1989): 873–893.

issue in the family by noting what predominant patterns existed at some point in the past and then comparing them with present patterns. Similarly, it would be possible to establish a series of **ideal-type constructs** (extended family/conjugal family, patriarchal family/matriarchal family, arranged marriages/free choice of mate, homogamy/heterogamy), place any aspect of a given family system at different points of time on the continuum, and observe the changes or trends that seem to be taking place.

The selected issues in the family that will be discussed in this chapter follow this procedure. This type of dichotomization into two classifications (*see* Table 1–1) is not meant to perpetuate myths such as that traditional patterns were monolithic—having a uniform structure without variations—or that traditional patterns were stable, harmonious, and without problems. Rather the increasing acceptance of nontraditional patterns offers the opportunity to contrast these emerging "variations" or "alternative" patterns with the accepted notions of traditional patterns; hence the comparison between traditional and nontraditional family norms, values, and behaviors.

Issues (that is, unresolved conflicts) exist because both traditional and nontraditional sets of norms and values exist simultaneously. In other words, certain groups and individuals resist the nontraditional norms and cling vehemently to the more traditional patterns; other individuals and groups find the traditional patterns unacceptable and adhere to a different set of norms and values. The result is that major issues (conflicts) occur primarily because of social change. If no change occurs and everyone accepts the traditional patterns of behavior, no issue or conflict results; similarly, if everyone adopts a nontraditional set of norms, no conflict exists.

Several ideal-type constructs are developed here to illustrate the conflicts that result when nontraditional sets of marital and family values coexist with traditional social values inherited from the past. It is in pluralistic societies that both the traditional and a multiple number of nontraditional patterns exist simultaneously. This results in conflict, confusion, and an unsettled state in the family system.

The issues that follow are not listed in any order of importance with the exception of the first. It is my belief that all other issues relate to or basically stem from the meaning given to marriage and the family itself.

## The meaning of marriage and the family issue

The most basic issue presented here centers around the meaning and the purpose of marriage and the family. It questions the sources of authority in marital and family decisions. It questions whether marriage is itself necessary.

The most traditional social norm, which represents one polar extreme of our ideal-type construct, views marriage as a *sacred* phenomenon. That is to say, the family and marriage are divine and holy institutions. They are created and maintained by God, Yahweh, or some supreme being greater than men and women. The phrase "marriages are made in heaven" is in many ways consistent with this perspective. This traditional social norm was perhaps

Table 1–1

**Traditional family norms and nontraditional alternatives**

| Traditional family norms | Nontraditional alternatives |
| --- | --- |
| Legally married | Singlehood—never married<br>Nonmarital cohabitation |
| Married once | Remarriage<br>Multiple marriages |
| Heterosexual marriage | Same-sex marriage |
| Endogamous marriage | Interfaith marriage<br>Interracial marriage<br>Interclass marriage |
| Two-adult households | Multi-adult households<br>Communal living<br>Affiliated families |
| Children | Voluntary childless |
| Two parents living together | Single parent<br>Joint custody<br>Stepfamilies (3 + parents) |
| Parent as key source of:<br>    education<br>    religion<br>    protection<br>    recreation | Tasks fulfilled by:<br>    schools<br>    churches<br>    government-police<br>    clubs, professional sports |
| Until death | Until divorce or separation |
| Male as provider | Female as provider<br>Dual careers<br>Commuter marriages |
| Male as "head" or authority | Female as "head"<br>Androgynous relationships |
| Self-supporting, independent | Welfare<br>Social security |
| Premarital chastity | Pre- or Nonmarital intercourse |
| Marital sexual exclusivity | Extramarital relationships<br>Sexually open marriages<br>Intimate friendships |

most widely prevalent prior to the turn of the century. In its extreme form, marriage is not only sacred but it is also in itself a sacrament. The Catholic church today views marriage as one of the seven sacraments. This implies that human beings and their personal wishes or wants are of secondary importance to that which is God-created and God-given. Basic to this view is the idea that the source of authority on all family and religious matters stems from God or connecting links (prophets, popes, cardinals, bishops, or priests) in the hierarchy of human-God positions.

    A second traditional norm, one in widespread existence at the turn of the

## Beliefs and practices of priests differ from church teachings

Differences exist between what the church teaches officially and what priests believe privately. Differences exist as well in what priests say publicly and privately about the teachings of the church. These findings come from a survey conducted by the Association of Chicago Priests of 140 priests in the Chicago Archdiocese.

The official teachings of the church place a ban on artificial birth control. Yet, 73 percent of the priests said they do not publicly support this ban. Even more, 87 percent, did not support the ban in their private counseling.

The official teaching of the church opposes masturbation, premarital sex, and homosexuality. Yet, in regard to masturbation, 60 percent of the priests

did not back the stand publicly and 78 percent did not support it in private counseling. On premarital sex, nearly one-fourth didn't back the stand publicly and nearly two in five didn't do so privately. And on homosexuality, 39 percent of the priests didn't publicly support the stand of the Vatican and 44 percent didn't support it privately.

Other areas of considerable difference between the stand of the church and the views or practices of the priests centered on divorce and remarriage and on giving communion to those whose previous marriages had not been judged invalid. Surprisingly, only one priest in ten claimed he was bothered by the gap between the position of the church and his public or private stance.

century and the first several decades thereafter, views the meaning of marriage and the family as centering primarily around *social* obligations. The social meaning of marriage, like the sacred meaning, represents traditional norms. But rather than the source of authority being God, authority becomes centered in human beings as represented by the kin group, community, church as a social institution, and society in general. Primary values within this meaning of marriage are to maintain social respectability, conform to kin and community wishes, and maintain a "proper image" within society. Thus, within this meaning of marriage, what other people think is very important. Divorce, premarital pregnancy, black-white intermarriage, and so forth are not undesirable per se but because "society" (friends, community, kin group, and others), in word and in action, disapproves.

A third meaning of marriage suggests that families and the marital relationship exist for the *individual*. Thus, the concern is not with God or with society but with "me." If I choose to marry outside of my race, religion, ethnic group, social class, and educational level, that is "my business." And if I choose a "marriage-like" relationship by cohabiting, either heterosexually or homosexually, that too is "my business." After all, I am not marrying my family, my church, my community, or American society. If I am happy in my marriage or intimate relationship, then it is a successful one. If I am unhappy, neither God nor society can dictate my behavior, nor can they force the endurance of an unsuccessful marriage. Within this meaning, the source of authority is the person alone; each individual is responsible for his or her own success or failure without regard to the community structure or the social conditions in which he or she operates.

Thus, there are at least three basic meanings of marriage, all of which exist today. To some persons and groups, marriage is sacred or sacramental;

with others, marriage is a social contract and success is viewed in terms of conformity to societal demands; to a third group, marriage is a highly personal, highly individualistic concern. The lack of uniformity in the source of authority on the meaning of marriage is basic to most issues and conflicts that exist in the marital and family system today in our society.

### Family organization issue

Closely related to the basic meaning of marriage is the "proper" form of marital and family organization. Traditionally, in the United States and in much of the world, the extended-family form was most common and most highly desired. Power resided in the elders, and they in turn were responsible for caring for other members of the kin group. Kin-group members were located in geographical proximity to one another. They followed and married those with a similar set of norms and rules, maintained intimate emotional ties to one another, and were isolated from outside contacts. This type of family organization resulted in behavior patterns and values that remained constant from one generation to the next, in children being socialized to be basically duplicates of their parents in thought and in action, and, in Bernard Farber's terms, in having an **orderly replacement**[5] among successive generations.

In contrast to the orderly-replacement concept is the idea of pluralism: many and varied forms of marital and family organization. The family organization that is preferred will vary both over time and from one individual to another. Some individuals may prefer to eliminate the marriage contract and simply live together. Others may desire some form of communal family where, at least economically, labor and goods are shared equally among all members. Certain members may choose not to marry at all. Some of those who choose not to marry may choose to be parents. The point is that the multiple forms of family organization will not be uniform among families nor necessarily within the same family over time. Again in Farber's terms, the result would be **universal permanent availability.**[6]

The universal-permanent-availability concept suggests that individuals are available for marriage with anyone at any time. Homogamous social characteristics decline in importance, and marriage becomes a personal rather than a kinship problem. Thus, love marriages rather than arranged marriages become prevalent, the rates of divorce and remarriage increase, the number of children declines, less emphasis is placed on premarital chastity and marital fidelity, emphasis is placed on competence and interpersonal relations, more married women enter the work force, and youth and glamour are emphasized. Thus polygyny, polyandry, homosexual marriages, nonlegal voluntary associ-

---

5. Bernard Farber, *Family Organization and Interaction* (San Francisco: Chandler, 1964), Chapter 4.

6. Ibid, p. 105.

ations, progressive monogamy, trial marriages, group marriages, communal families, single-parent families, or no marriage at all have a place within nontraditional forms of family organization.

A basic issue exists today over the "proper" form of family organization. Those who view marriage as sacred, those who view marriage as a monogamous lifelong relationship, and those who insist on two-parent permanent relationships will find difficulty in accepting and adjusting to the multiple (mostly nontraditional) forms of family organization that are becoming increasingly public. It is not that these forms are totally new; rather, it is that these forms are occurring with an increasing frequency, are being given an increasing amount of publicity, or are resulting in meaningful and realistic alternatives in the form of marital and family organization of thousands of persons in the United States today. A multiple number of acceptable forms of marriage and family life are part of the pluralistic scene of our society.

### Family functions issue

Many critics of the American family have included in their argument for the "breakdown" of the family the loss of functions which has taken place. Throughout written history, the family has been the major social institution. With changes that have occurred, particularly within the functions that a family has performed, the increasing specialization and complexity of modern society has led to a dehumanizing and fragmentizing process.

This issue is by no means a recent one. In the 1930s, William Ogburn argued that the dilemma of the modern family was due to its loss of functions.[7] It was his belief that prior to modern times the power and prestige of the family was due to the seven functions it performed.

1. Foremost was the *economic* function. The family was a self-sufficient unit in which the members of the family consumed primarily that which they produced. Thus banks, stores, and factories were not needed.
2. The family served the basic function of giving *prestige* and *status* to its members. The family name was important, and a member of the family was less an individual and more a member of the family.
3. The family performed the basic function of *education*, not only of infants and children but also of youths for their vocational education, physical education, domestic science, and so on.
4. The family provided the function of *protecting its members*. Not only did the father provide physical protection for his family but also children provided social and economic protection against economic and psychological needs in old age.
5. The family exercised a *religious* function, as was evidenced by grace at meals, family prayers, and reading together passages in the Bible.

---

7. William F. Ogburn, "The Changing Family," *The Family* (1938): 139–143.

6. The *recreation* function was performed at the homestead of some family or within the family rather than at recreation centers outside the home provided by the school, community, or industry.
7. The final function was that of providing *affection* between mates and the procreation of children.

Many people in our society today are committed to the idea that these traditional functions of the family should be maintained. That is, families should be relatively self-sufficient, familism should have priority over individualism, education should be centered in the home, children should care for their aging parents, prayer and religious rituals should be a basic part of the daily life of the family, recreation should be engaged in by the family as a unit, and affection should be received relatively exclusively within the family unit.

Emergent norms suggest that many of these traditional family functions are being performed by other agencies. The economic function has gone to the factory, store, and office. The prestige and status function is increasingly centering around a family member rather than the family name. Teachers have become substitute parents and are basically responsible for the education of the child. Police, reform schools, social security, medicare and medicaid, unemployment compensation, and other types of social legislation provided by the state have replaced the traditional protective function. The professional priest, rabbi, or clergyman has assumed the responsibility for fulfilling the religious function. Little league baseball, industrial bowling teams, TV-watching, or women's tennis groups have replaced the family as a source of recreation. And, although many would argue that the family still remains the center of the affectional life and is the only recognized place for producing children, one does not have to engage in an intensive investigation to discover the extent to which these two are sought and found outside the boundaries of the family and its members.

It is not only losses that have taken place in family functions; gains have occurred as well. The family and peer group, for example, have gained in importance as sources of emotional support. Within these primary group boundaries, its members may increasingly find a therapeutic milieu for personal and physical health problems. Also, families may increasingly be responsible for the development of family members' competence in the use of community and nonfamily resources. Existence in complex, highly specialized societies requires a knowledge of the range of options, an ability to make sound choices, and a flexibility toward new technologies and ideologies. Thus a major "new" family function is one of socialization for competence in a changing complex society and world. A further discussion of the concept and use of "function" as well as family functions is presented in Chapter 2.

### Marital- and gender-role differentiation issue

Marital and gender roles need to include masculine-feminine and man-woman roles as well. The confusion and uncertainty over "proper" role

*Some women are able to escape traditional gender, marital, and occupational roles. They work in both white-collar and blue-collar occupations that tend to fall near the bottom of the prestige hierarchy.*

definitions for the sexes became very evident to me when a group of students was asked to define and list characteristics of masculinity. Extreme difficulty existed, first, in listing characteristics, and second, in securing agreement. Traditionally, no such difficulty was likely to exist. The male, husband, and father was the head of the family, its main economic support, and its representative in the community. The father was the boss, the breadwinner, and the aggressive partner.

The apostle Paul in his letters to the Ephesians and the Colossians made his views clearly known on husband-wife roles. To the Ephesians he said:

> Wives submit yourselves unto your husbands . . . for the husband is the head of the wife . . . therefore as the church is subject unto Christ so let the wives be to their own husbands in everything.[8]

To the Colossians, Paul was very clear on the "proper" hierarchy of power and authority within the family. To them he wrote:

> Wives submit yourselves unto your own husbands, as it is fit in the Lord. Husbands, love your wives and be not bitter against them. Children, obey your parents in all things: for this is well pleasing unto the Lord. Fathers, provoke not your children to anger, lest they be discouraged.[9]

---

8. Ephesians 5: 22–24.
9. Colossians 3:18–21.

This traditional role pattern is consistent with the sacred meaning of marriage. The source of authority is not human beings, and the obligations are not fulfilled for men and women but for a supreme being.

The traditional expectations of appropriate marital and gender roles are clear and unmistakable. Women are expected to have marriage, home, and children as their primary concerns. The wife takes the husband's name, shares his income, and relies on him for status and identity. Women should be sympathetic, caring, loving, compassionate, gentle, and submissive, which in turn makes them excellent wives, mothers, nurses, and teachers of young children. To be feminine, the skin must be smooth and soft and the body slim and erotic.

In contrast, men earn livings to support their wives and children. To be masculine is to be self-reliant, strong, verbally and physically aggressive, dominant, tall, and muscular. Men are risk takers, decision makers, and protectors of those around them. The "ideal male" is thus hard working, responsible, achieving, and reliable. In addition, heterosexuality is greatly stressed in interests and activities, and departures from this, particularly as related to sexual desires and conduct, are strongly condemned.

This type of gender-role differentiation has benefits for both sexes, but it has great costs as well. For females, satisfaction may be derived from the stress on beauty, the lack of pressure to achieve, the wide range of emotional expression and intimacy, and the right to claim support. For males, satisfaction may be derived from the access to power, the ideology of male supremacy, the opportunities to develop skills and talents, the exercise of autonomy and independence, and the ability to be self-supporting. On the other hand, it is often at great cost to females that restrictions are placed on self-development, on training to cope with an increasingly complicated world, and on ability to obtain a loan, open a business, and be economically equal or superior to men. It is often at great cost to men that they are pressured to achieve, to assume responsibility for family members, to be in constant competition to excel, and to be unable to shed tears and express themselves emotionally.

The traditional differentiation of male-female roles has come into serious question. While *androgyny*, or a society with no gender-role differentiation, has not been achieved in full, pressures exist in this direction. Nonfamilial roles available to women, an increasing egalitarian emphasis in intimate family and nonfamily relationships, changing beliefs in both work and play, and changes in patterns of socialization and education are leading to increased alternatives for males and females as to appropriate attitudes and behavior. While the labels may vary—*androgyny, unisex, desegregation, new neuter*—the message is similar: men and women are increasingly pursuing their similarities, experiencing the thrill of escaping from traditional gender-role stereotypes, and choosing to behave as persons rather than as males or females. Both sexes are increasingly behaving in ways that are instrumental as well as expressive, assertive as well as yielding, and masculine as well as feminine.

It has been suggested that contemporary American marriages are shifting from the *complementary* type to the *parallel* type based on the kinds of work

The book of Genesis says:
"Man and Woman Created He Them"
The book of Genesis also says:
"God Created Man in His own Image"
Taken literally, this means:
"God is a ManWoman God"

husbands and wives do every day.[10] In complementary marriages, the husband and the wife perform interdependent but different tasks. He is employed outside the home and she does the domestic work. In parallel marriages the husband and the wife perform the same tasks on an equitable or at least negotiable and mutually acceptable basis. Both spouses are employed and both are responsible for child care and housework.

The transition from gender-role differentiation to androgyny or from complementary to parallel type marriage is far from complete. But women's participation in the world of paid employment is increasing, household responsibilities increasingly are shared by husbands and wives, and both sexes increasingly are thinking and behaving in ways traditionally linked to the opposite sex.[11] These changes are more fully described, particularly in Chapters 4, 5, 9, 12, 14, 15, and 17.

### Social class and social mobility issue

The issue of social class and social mobility centers around the extent to which it is desirable to have tremendous variations in wealth, status, and power, and the extent to which it is possible to move from one social status to another. Should some families accumulate vast amounts of wealth in a society where millions of people live at a level of poverty? This issue includes the distribution of resources (such as jobs, education, health care, and housing) as well as the ability to move from one status to another. It also includes the American Dream of going from the log cabin to the White House, from rags to riches, from being a nobody to a Supreme Court judge.

The polar extremes of an ideal-type construct would include an open class society, where anyone could move up or down in the social structure strictly on the basis of personal effort and ability, versus a closed class society, where everyone remains in the position to which they were born with no change in position possible through individual achievement or any other

10. Catherine E. Ross, John Mirowsky, and Joan Huber, "Dividing Work, Sharing Work, and In-Between: Marriage Patterns and Depression," *American Sociological Review* 48 (December 1983): 809–823.

11. See for example: Constance L. Shehan and John N. Scanzoni, "Gender Patterns in The United States: Demographic Trends and Policy Prospects," *Family Relations* 37(October 1988): 444–450.

means. The classic representation of the closed system is that of the caste system of ancient India. There, position was based on ancestry and was sustained by strict rules of same-caste marriage (endogamy), by religious beliefs, and by rigidly enforced legal and normative expectations.

No society has an absolutely open or a completely closed class system. In our own society, family position exerts a major influence on one's chances for getting an education; for exposure to literature, travel, and the arts; for inheritance; for marriage choices; and the like. On the other hand, factors such as educational achievement, marriage possibilities, or business successes do provide opportunities for upward social mobility.

Traditionally, factors such as the extended family system, the predominantly rural farming economy, the authority held by elders, and religious and ethnic ties appeared to make personal upward mobility extremely difficult. Likewise today, the lack of opportunity and resources of the poor makes planning for the future and social climbing exceedingly difficult if not impossible. Yet the dream of upward social mobility, of "doing better than my parents," of economic success, and of obtaining a new and superior life-style remains widespread. A further discussion of this issue and of the meaning and consequence of social class position is presented in Chapter 7.

## Mate selection issue

The issue of mate selection centers around two questions: who chooses and who is chosen. The polar extremes of an ideal-type construct would include arranged marriages with no voice given to the mates involved versus absolute free choice where decisions are made solely by the mates involved. Around the world and traditionally in the United States the most prevalent position falls toward the former (arranged) rather than the latter (free choice).

In our society, the traditional norms suggest that parents in particular, if not doing the choosing, should give their approval to the mate chosen. It is not uncommon today to find men in the fifty-and-older age group who formally and directly requested the girl's parents' permission for her hand in marriage. Although mates are not chosen by the parents, as in much of the Eastern world, they are chosen with a clear consciousness of the extent to which the spouse would meet the approval of the parents. And to marry without the future spouse having been known, not only by the parents but also within the kin group and community, is unthinkable. Thus who did the choosing? The most nontraditional norm, in the polar extreme, is to have "absolute free choice" of mate with a total absence of approval by parents, friends, or others.

Closely related to who chooses is a question of who is chosen. Traditionally, in-group (endogamous) selection was extremely important. The ideal spouse was a person from one's own ethnic, social-class, religious, racial, or neighborhood group. Outsiders were viewed with much suspicion, and marriage to an outsider was a sure sign of future marital problems. That the traditional norm still exists today is very obvious when one looks at the type of

"Marry women of your choice,
Two, or three, or four;
But if ye fear that ye shall not
Be able to deal justly (with them),
Then only one . . ."

*Source: The Holy Koran, Sura IV, Verse 3.*

material taught in marriage preparation classes within our education system, the position taken by most religious groups, or the advice of parents or columnists.

An emergent norm suggests that mate selection is increasingly coming under the control of youths themselves and that out-group selection (exogamous marriages) is increasingly common. Ask yourself if you would be willing to have your spouse chosen for you by your parents, relatives, or friends. Would you marry someone of a different religious background, of a different ethnic affiliation, or of a higher or lower social class? If you want to have the ultimate say in whom you choose to marry or if you are willing to marry outside of your religious, ethnic, or class grouping, you fail to conform to the most traditional mate selection norms. You might find it interesting to inquire of your married friends whether the husband asked the wife's parents for permission to marry or, perhaps today, a more realistic question is whether either set of parents knew about their unmarried cohabitation instead of, or prior to, their marriage. Consistent with the individualistic meaning of marriage is the idea that since it is "my spouse," I should choose any person with whom I am "in love" or with whom I choose to live. That the mate comes from a different community, social class, religion, or race is not the concern of relatives or church groups. These issues focusing on mate selection are discussed in detail in Chapters 8 and 9.

### Love issue

The issue of love as related to marriage centers around questions such as whether it is even necessary, to what degree of intensity, and to what extent of exclusiveness? On an ideal-type continuum, the polar extremes would be represented by: (1) love as not even a factor for consideration in marriage versus love as the sole and prime factor for marriage, (2) zero percent or no feelings of love versus 100 percent feelings of love (whatever that is), and (3) love with one other person only versus many loves.

You can quickly note the linkage between this issue and both the previous one of mate selection and the next one of sexual relationships. Traditionally in North America and today in much of the world, kin, economic, and status considerations are still the key determinants for marriage. After marriage, not before, love is expected to develop. In contrast is the nontraditional idea that marriage without love is unthinkable. After all, does not "love make the world go round" and cannot "love conquer all"?

Closely related to whether or not love is necessary is the problem of the intensity of love feelings. Clearly feelings are subjective and the question is how intense must these subjective feelings be before they are "real"? Thus reference is made to "puppy love" or "infatuation" as feelings that are superficial and not the type upon which lasting relationships are built. Other descriptions such as romantic love, conjugal love, spiritual love (agape), or sexual love (eros) have been used to clarify different types of love or love conditions. In any case, attempts at understanding what love is, measuring how genuine or "real" it is, and analyzing its intensity have been basic problems for centuries and still engender debate and conflict today.

Finally, the issue of love—particularly as it relates to marriage—centers on the exclusiveness or nonexclusiveness of love relationships. Can two people be loved at once? Does love with one's spouse eliminate the possibility of loving someone else's spouse? The traditional view of conjugal love demands a devotion exclusively to one person—in sickness and in health, for richer, for poorer, and so forth. This traditional relationship is all-absorbing and all-encompassing.

A conflicting view is that a spouse and/or lover neither can nor need meet all of a person's intimacy needs.[12] That is, individuals who are personally growing, developing, and changing find differing needs fulfilled by different individuals. Thus, the fulfillment of various intimacy needs can be met outside of marriage without diminishing the love for a spouse. From this nontraditional perspective, if an individual is to grow and develop, one other person cannot fulfill all intimacy needs of that individual. This type of relationship allows both self and other the right to new experiences and growth possibilities, both sexual and nonsexual. The result is a more enriched relationship with the spouse, with a drastic reduction in feelings of possessiveness, rigidity of role expectations, or feelings of confinement.

As with the other issues, traditional and nontraditional views of love are in conflict. A person cannot be both exclusive in love relationships and at the same time open to other relationships.

### Sexual relationships issue

The central question surrounding the issue of sexual relationships is whether sexual relations (coitus) should be limited to marriage. Are there conditions or circumstances under which premarital, extramarital, or postmarital inter-

---

12. A treatment of this idea can be found in Carolynne Kieffer, "New Depths in Intimacy," in *Marriage and Alternatives: Exploring Intimate Relationships*, by Roger W. Libby and Robert N. Whitehurst (Glenview, Ill.: Scott, Foresman, 1977): 267–293.

course is legitimate? In addition, are there rational arguments for a double standard, differentiating the sexual norms for men and women?

The traditional sacred norm is quite clear. Prior to the turn of the century, premarital, extramarital, postmarital, and even sexual relations for the purposes of pleasure within marriage were considered taboo. Officially, the mores allowed little deviation from this norm. Unofficially, a double standard existed whereby sexual deviation by men, although not sanctioned, was understandable. On the other hand, women were socialized to believe that the husband was the one to whom sex was important, that sex should remain solely within the marital relationship, and that a good wife "submits" because she "owes this duty" to her husband.

Various changes took place when the social meaning of marriage began to emerge. As with the sacred meaning, sexual relationships outside of marriage were basically taboo except among unmarried couples who were marriage-oriented or were "in love." The second traditional view of sex primarily limited intercourse to marriage, but it increasingly separated sex from reproduction and allowed it to become a source of pleasure for both sexes. Anything occurring within the marital relationship was perfectly normal and satisfactory as long as it was agreeable and unharmful to the couple involved. Although a double standard remains in effect, this latter view is likely the predominant position today.

The trend has been away from these traditional norms to sets of sexual norms that question the double standard and the necessity of limiting sexual relationships to marriage. If sex is fun (to which many agree), why should it be limited to a spouse, someone whom you intend to marry, or even someone with whom you are in love? If maturity and adulthood imply independence and the capacity to make one's own decisions, then two individuals, whether married or single, male or female, should have the choice as to when, where, and with whom sexual relationships will take place. The publicity given to premarital cohabitation and same-sex liaisons presents some documentation of the increasing prevalence of these sexual norms. As women seek equality with men, as increasingly it is possible to separate sex from parenthood, and as primary informal means of control lessen, sexual independence and permissiveness are likely to result.

The implications of this issue are far-reaching. It has affected and will continue to affect the family, the educational system, other social institutions, and legislative processes, as well as personal behavior. The conflict is again obvious. One cannot adhere to both polar extremes of sexual relationships—within marriage primarily for reproductive purposes or "sex as fun" in or out of marriage. These issues involving sexual relationships are discussed in premarital contexts in Chapter 10 and in marital contexts in Chapter 11.

### Family size and family planning issue

Closely related and directly limited to the issues of sexual relationships and marital and gender roles is the threefold issue of (1) limiting the number of children, (2) determining when and if to have them, and (3) selecting the appropriate means to accomplish these ends. In the 1960s and 1970s extensive publicity on zero population growth and on the population explosion focused attention on family size. More recently, controversies over abortion and whether public funds (tax money) should be used to pay for them, test-tube babies, surrogate parenting, and the long-term effects of various contraceptives such as the pill or IUD have raised new questions about how to have or prevent having children.

The most traditional norm—one highly consistent with the sacred meaning of marriage—suggests that the primary purpose of sex is reproduction and the only approved context for reproduction is within marriage. (One biblical admonition is that families should be fruitful and multiply.) One-child family situations were not viewed as the ideal, and a mother who only had one or two children was an issue of community concern. Even more problematic was pregnancy apart from a marital relationship. Premarital pregnancies forced hasty marriages. Nonmarital pregnancies and births brought shame to the family unit.

Since, traditionally, large families were an economic asset and contributed to security in old age, children within marriage were highly valued. Few were the families that consciously and successfully controlled family size. Many mothers took pride in proclaiming that they had produced and raised ten or fifteen healthy children. The spacing of children may have raised concern if pregnancy occurred very soon after a previous childbirth, but the concern centered more on the health of the mother than on the additional "blessing."

As the social norms changed, so did the view of large families. As population shifts removed families from farms, children became less of an economic asset. Increasingly, sex came to be viewed as being for pleasure as well as for reproduction. Children became a matter of choice rather than chance. And the emerging norm pertaining to family size now suggests that the maximum number of children should be two. For couples to have only one child or no children is granted social acceptability, to have four or six is to have too many, and to have ten or fourteen is disastrous.

The means of controlling the number of children has shifted as well. Again, the most traditional norm suggests that anything nonartificial or "God given" is appropriate. Since God has provided within each female a period of time each month when conception cannot occur, rhythm as a method of limiting family size is appropriate and consistent with the "will of God." The traditional sex-role norm maintains that women are responsible for the prevention of pregnancy. The timing of sexual relationships around the menstrual cycle is consistent with the sacred meaning attached to marriage.

The social meaning of marriage, and perhaps the one most widely adhered to by couples in our society today, suggests that any means of fertility control that works, is nonharmful, and is agreeable to both spouses is legitimate. As a result, the majority of both Catholics and non-Catholics in the United States today are using some form of "artificial" contraceptive or

### Beliefs prohibit student from attending school and professor from teaching

Only days apart in August of 1986, two events made headlines. In Toledo, eleven-year-old Sarabeth Eason was told by the pastor of St. Agnes parish that she could not re-enroll in the church school unless she disavowed her public support for abortion. Her mother operates a clinic in Toledo, The Center for Choice, where Sarabeth did some volunteer work. On two occasions Sarabeth spoke out publicly, once at a television rally and another time in a signed newspaper advertisement supporting abortion. The diocese spokesman who appeared on several network shows with Sarabeth said it's a cut-and-dried issue of a child and her family defying the stated precepts of their church.

The second event centered around a priest, the Rev. Charles E. Curran, a popular lecturer and theologian at Catholic University in Washington, D.C. The Vatican, in a letter to Father Curran, notified him that "you will no longer be considered suitable nor eligible to exercise the function of a Professor of Catholic Theology." The reason for this action was a result of his publishing and teaching that the church's opposition to divorce, birth control, homosexual acts, and abortion should not be absolute. Father Curran endorsed the morality of contraception, said that divorce should sometimes be permitted, and that abortion, masturbation, premarital sex, and homosexual acts are not always immoral.

birth-control method, and wide-spread use of abortion has occurred in the last decade. The social norm in regard to family planning agrees with the sacred meaning in that the planning should be limited to the marital relationship, but it differs in the reliance on means that relate to the menstrual cycle.

The most nontraditional norms pertaining to family size, family planning, and childbirth in or out of the marital context suggest that family limitation is an individual choice and the methods used (condoms, pills, diaphragm, jellies, abortion, sterilization) should not be limited by laws or measures that prevent couples from preventing pregnancy or childbirth. This social norm places the responsibility for preventing conception on men as well as women, single as well as married. These issues of parenthood, family size, and unwed parenthood are presented in Chapter 13. Less attention is focused on methods of birth control and means of family planning.

### Old age issue

The traditional norms concerning the role of the aged strongly suggest that these persons should be given deference, respect, and recognition. Traditionally, it was the eldest person who had the most prestige, the widest experience in living, and thus the greatest amount of wisdom. The aging family member had various important roles to fulfill, particularly in consulting and managerial positions in addition to those centering around the enjoyment and care of children and grandchildren.

The changing social scene has also changed the role of the aged person in the American family. The number of persons over the age of sixty-five in our population has increased steadily through the twentieth century. Most men and women of this age are no longer employed at their full-time jobs. For many, retirement means a lowered income, and for the husband it means the destruction of his major role as a productive worker. The ascribed status of age per se no longer brings prestige. The emergent norm suggests that play must be substituted for work. This means a drastic shift in activities, in self-definitions, and in role performance. The basic issue and conflict of the aged centers around providing a meaningful way of life, which includes being able to make a contribution to life and to the society in which the aged live. The role of older people, their marital patterns, retirement, and postmarital family styles are discussed in Chapter 15.

## Violence and abuse among intimates issue

The issue of violence and abuse among marriage and family members, while relatively new in terms of being a legitimate area of research, is not new to the American or world scene. The traditional norms and values are well understood. Family members should care for one another, provide emotional support, be understanding, and show kindness. Of all institutions, the family should be the haven where love, serenity, and security prevail in the midst of an impersonal, uncaring, crime-filled, and violent world.

The nontraditional reality of violence and abuse in family life is increasingly recognized. Reports of one family member killing another, husband or wife beatings, marital rape, parent-child incestuous relationships, elderly and sibling abuse, and other variations of violence among intimates are common. Most attention tends to focus on physical violence (shooting, hitting, slapping, biting, kicking, or throwing objects), although the family may be the number one source of verbal, psychological, and emotional abuse. Chapter 11 examines rape in marriage and incestuous relationships, and Chapter 16 examines other issues of family violence among intimates.

## Family permanence issue

The issue of family permanence raises the question as to whether marriages and families are permanent, life-long, until death commitments or are temporary, until divorce or separation arrangements. If they are viewed as temporary, what structural arrangements should be made to end one relationship and begin another, and what criteria should be used to determine when one relationship should end and another begin? Thus our ideal-type constructs might consist of models that include divorce/limited divorce/no divorce, total separation/partial separation/no separation, or any reason/no reason.

A sacred view of marriage suggests that marriage is for keeps. This most traditional view of dealing with marital conflict does not include the option of reorganizing the marital/family structure by means of divorce. Marriage is accepted as a lifelong permanent contract and exists until "death do us part" (unless one happens to be a Mormon who marries in the temple where the celestial marriage is for time and eternity). Marriage exists and remains legally intact irrespective of conflict in the relationship or personal unhappiness. This traditional norm was especially prevalent prior to 1920 or 1930. Even today this is the model used when divorce is viewed as marital or family "disorganization" rather than as a reorganization of structure to new forms such as single-parent or the reconstituted family involving at least one spouse who was previously married and divorced.[13]

Less extreme than the idea of marriage as a permanent relationship irrespective of persons or circumstances is a second traditional norm that suggests certain conditions or reasons are legitimate for ending marital and family commitments. Adultery has long been a socially acceptable reason for ending a legal marital contract. Even the Catholic church, which takes a sacramental view of marriage relationships, accepts the ending of the marriage if it is due to conditions that existed prior to the start of that marriage. This structural form of ending a relationship (annulment) is a legally recognized type of marital dissolution.

The most common means for ending a marital relationship (other than death) is divorce. The legal grounds for divorce are determined by individual states; thus the reasons for permitting divorce vary. Traditionally, there was general agreement that one party had to be guilty. With time, several states made legal changes and most states interpreted the existing laws more leniently. While many people believe that a major reason for the increasing divorce rates has been a change in the law, it is likely that the greater change has been in the increased tolerance toward divorce. Thus the changing social norm has been toward a greater acceptance of divorce, although a widely held social norm maintains that divorce should come only as a last resort after all other options have been considered. In any case, the 1970s witnessed a major increase in divorce rates, reaching levels in the 1980s unexceeded in U.S. history.

An emergent norm concerning family reorganization suggests that marital success stems less from existence and permanence and more from a meaningful dynamic interaction of persons even if the partners may change. Immorality stems not from getting a divorce but from maintaining a relationship that is for all practical purposes broken. Thus divorce, rather than being a social problem, may be viewed as a solution for other types of problems. The end result is the argument that marriages have become more "vital and successful" than ever before in our history. Marriages exist out of personal desire rather than out of social or sacred obligations. Norval Glenn, for one, takes exception to this argument. He claims that when the option exists or persons are encouraged to end an unsatisfactory relationship,

---

13. Margrit Eichler and others make this point in their argument of the inappropriateness of a monolithic model of the family. *See* Margrit Eichler, "The Inadequacy of the Monolithic Model of the Family," *Canadian Journal of Sociology* 6 (1981): 367–388; and Barrie Thorne with Marilyn Yalom, *Rethinking the Family: Some Feminist Questions* (New York: Longman, 1982): 2–6.

existing marriages may become so insecure that no rational person will invest a great deal of time, energy, or money into it. Individuals will not make more than tentative limited commitments in marriage or in intimate pairings to provide enough security and emotional support for its members to attain maximum happiness and satisfaction.[14]

The same traditional/nontraditional issue exists in regard to remarriage. Prior to the Civil War remarriage was a right only of the innocent party. Many clergy would refuse to marry divorced persons. In certain fundamentalist denominations this is still the situation today. Within the Catholic church as well, canon law prohibits the remarriage of divorced persons previously married in the church. In actual practice some priests do perform marriage ceremonies for divorced persons. And remarriage among the majority of divorced persons is high. Divorcees have a higher rate of marriage, age for age, than have single persons entering their first marriage or the widowed.

The basic nature of this issue of marital and family reorganization should be quite evident. Conflicts exist between those who adhere to a sacred meaning of marriage, accepting no reasons for ending a marriage, and those who grant social approval to a temporary marital relationship.

## Other contemporary family-related and policy issues

The list of issues that are not likely to be classified as marriage or family issues per se but that have a direct bearing on family life is extensive. At the most general level, every social policy and social problem is family related: pollution, international trade, taxation, immigration, affirmative action, student loans, school prayer, burning the flag, or whatever. Families are instrumental in the socialization process (*see* Chapter 14) that influences what issues are important to us as well as how we view or approach them. Likewise, social events, social circumstances, and social policy tend to influence our own behaviors and life-styles. Three significant social issues of this type will be addressed briefly.

### AIDS

One prominent social issue is **AIDS** (acquired immune deficiency syndrome). This disease was designated the number one health priority of the U.S. Public Health Service in the late 1980s. Since to date no cure has been found, it presents the world with a crisis with profound implications for mate selection, sexual relationships, parent-child interactions, and so forth. Although AIDS was originally perceived as a disease confined to homosexuals, current research indicates that its numbers are increasing in the heterosexual population. Traditionally, AIDS was nonexistent but there were other sexually transmitted diseases like syphilis, gonorrhea and, more recently, herpes.

14. Norval D. Glenn, "Continuity Versus Change, Sanguineness Versus Concern," *Journal of Family Issues* 8 (December 1987): 351.

The traditional *sacred* norm in regard to sexually transmitted diseases was one of avoidance through sexual abstinence apart from marriage. The traditional *social* norm toward sexually transmitted diseases, and more specifically toward AIDS suggests heterosexuality and, if one is sexually active, the use of condoms and the exclusive confinement of sexual relations to a love or marriage-oriented partner. The contemporary reality with nontraditional norms includes gay communities, homosexual partners (including some who define themselves as married), sexually active adolescents, and adults who are not married and have no intent to marry and who do not use condoms. The AIDS issue is very real and has profound implications for marriage and family life.

## Abortion

**Abortion** is a second highly visible social issue that has a direct impact on family formation, size, and career. It is related to the issues of sexual relationships and family size and family planning presented previously. But the abortion issue involves a pregnancy and focuses on the meaning and timing of "life" and the value of "choice" rather than on sexual behavior or family planning per se. Thus the abortion issue, while caused by a sexual act and influenced by the desire or lack of desire for a child or an additional one, focuses on a different set of values.

The *traditional sacred* norm sees a pregnancy as life, as God given, and not to be destroyed by social or personal concerns. This anti-abortion (pro-life) stance advocates restrictive policies toward abortion. The *traditional social* norm may or may not define a conception as a human life; it views the viability of that life as depending on the length of time since conception; and it supports the abortion decision based on social factors such as a defective fetus, age or health of the mother, and rape or incest. This stance toward abortion advocates restrictive policies under certain conditions and permissive policies under others. The *nontraditional* norm toward abortion focuses on individual and personal decisions. This pro-abortion (pro-choice) stance advocates a permissive policy allowing a woman to choose. Questions now focus on factors such as: was the pregnancy planned and desired, can the child be properly supported and cared for, and will the pregnancy and future birth disrupt college, marriage, and career plans? But most importantly, should a court, a group of legislators (both usually male dominated), or someone else be it a relative, a member of the clergy, or a physician, dictate what a woman does with her body or her life? Again, the abortion issue is one that impacts marriage and family life in a significant way.[15]

---

15. Interested readers may want to examine Barbara Ryan and Eric Plutzer, "When Married Women Have Abortions: Spousal Notification and Marital Interaction," *Journal of Marriage and the Family* 51 (February 1989): 41–50; and Jacqueline Scott and Howard Schuman, "Attitude Strength and Social Action in the Abortion Dispute," *American Sociological Review* 53 (October 1988): 785–793.

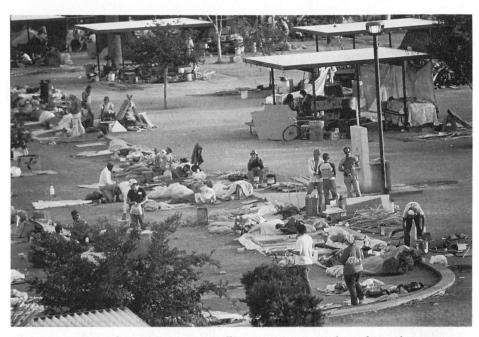

*Estimates suggest that as many as 3 million Americans are homeless. About one-third of these are families that have been hit with economic setbacks and policy decisions that adversely affect the poor.*

## Homelessness

The third and final issue to be addressed at this point is that of housing and the **homeless.** A house provides physical shelter. A home anchors a family in a community and provides couples and children with stability and a place with which each member identifies. Both could be argued to be essential basic human needs. The homeless issue is, however, not merely one involving isolated individuals, but is increasingly recognized as a family issue. One source claims that families represent over one-third of all homeless people and are the fastest growing group.[16] What these families share is an inability to afford a roof over their heads. Some lose a home they owned or rented because of a crisis in family finances. Others are forced to move because their home is sold from under them, is destroyed by fire, or is allowed by landlords to become uninhabitable. Some women and children subjected to

---

16. Marian Wright Edelman and Lisa Mihaly, "Homeless Families and the Housing Crisis in the United States," *Children and Youth Services Review* 11 (1989): 91–108. *See also:* Leland J. Axelson and Paula W. Dail, "The Changing Character of Homelessness in the United States," *Family Relations* 37 (October 1988): 463–469; Linda S. Dakin, "Homelessness: The Role of The Legal Profession in Finding Solutions Through Litigation," *Family Law Quarterly* 21 (Spring 1987): 93–126; and James D. Wright, "Address Unknown: Homelessness in Contemporary America," *Society* 26 (September/October 1989): 45–53.

### Homeless children and school performance

A private report prepared by Advocates for Children of New York said that students from homeless families suffer illnesses more often, have greater emotional problems, and fail classes at twice the rate of other public school students. It said that Board of Education statistics show 43 percent of homeless students read at or above grade level (compared to 68 percent of all students) and only 28 percent scored at grade level in mathematics (compared to 57 percent of all students). The poor student performance was attributed mainly to their families being moved from shelter to shelter.

The barrier to learning was not reported to be poor education but rather a lack of permanent housing and irregular and insufficient food. Dr. Edward Zigler, director of the Bush Center for Child Development at Yale, says that homelessness leaves children ''psychologically bombed out.'' A child cannot learn if there are much more pressing problems than doing arithmetic.

family violence flee their homes. Most families stay with friends or relatives and exhaust all other options before they turn to a shelter or to the streets.

It is not difficult to perceive the devastation to both parents and children of being without a home. The toll on health, education, emotional development, or self-identity from being poor or in poverty is in itself major (*see* Chapter 7), but being homeless magnifies all issues—heat, diet, sleeping arrangements, washing and bathing facilities, privacy, permanency, illness, insurance, education, and so forth.

The traditional norm and value is that all persons and families deserve and need housing and a home. But this norm also includes a basic belief that anyone who tries hard enough can prosper and that rugged individualism is more important than commitment to community. The result is the nontraditional alternative of many families being poor, unable to afford even low-income housing, and forced, quite literally, into the street. Climbing rents, lack of affordable housing, waiting lists for existing housing, and the retreat of the federal government from providing housing or legal assistance to the poor have magnified this issue throughout the 1980s. The long-term underlying effects of the crisis of homelessness are only beginning to be understood. Some issues surrounding family policy that can be applied to this or other issues can be seen in the final chapter. We will now turn to selected characteristics of families in the United States.

## CHARACTERISTICS OF FAMILIES IN THE UNITED STATES

The United States Bureau of the Census is the primary source of national numerical data about families in this country. To provide an introduction to the American family, a summary of various characteristics as portrayed by census material is presented. More specific characteristics, statements of relationships, and research findings are presented throughout the book in the chapters appropriate to their discussion.

In 1987 the total resident population of the United States was estimated at 243 million.[17] This included approximately 118 million males and 125 million females.

The United States population by race included 205.8 million classified as white (84.7 percent), 29.7 million classified as black (12.2 percent), and 7.8 million classified as other races (3.0 percent).[18] "Other races" as used by the Census Bureau does not denote any scientific definition of biological stock. It is based on the self-identification of respondents into one of fifteen groups that, in addition to white and black, includes American Indians, Eskimos, Aleuts, Japanese, Chinese, Filipinos, Hawaiians, Samoans, Asian Indians, Koreans, Vietnamese, Guamanians, and other individuals. Persons of Hispanic origin (who may be of any race) comprised 18.8 million persons or 7.7 percent of all households.

The United States population in 1987 had a median age of 32.1; whites had a median age of 33.0; and blacks had a median age of 27.2.[19] Approximately one-fifth of our population (21.6 percent) was under fifteen years of age; one-fourth was fifteen to twenty-nine (24.7 percent); close to one-fourth was thirty to forty-four (22.9 percent); one-fifth was forty-five to sixty-four (18.7 percent); and roughly one-eighth of all persons (12.3 percent) was sixty-five years or over.[20] Our changing age distribution shows a decrease since 1970 of about 8 percent in the proportion of the population under age twenty, an increase of 62 percent in the twenty-five to forty-four age group (the baby boomers), an increase of 7 percent in the age group of forty-five to sixty-four, and a 50 percent increase in the proportion of those age sixty-five or over. In other words, the United States experienced a decrease in the proportion of children and adolescents and a huge increase in the proportion of persons we might term young adults and the senior citizens or the aged. Some of the implications of these demographic shifts will become evident in later chapters.

## The number of families and households

The term **family,** as used in census reporting, refers to a group of two or more persons related by birth or "blood," marriage, or adoption, and who reside together in a household.

In 1988, there were 65.1 million families in the United States. Of these, 51.8 million were considered to be married couples, that is, husband-wife families,

---

17. U.S. Bureau of the Census, *Statistical Abstract of the United States: 1989*, 109th ed. (Washington, D.C.: U.S. Government Printing Office, 1989), Table 21, p. 17.

18. Ibid., Table 18, p. 16.

19. Ibid., Table 21, p. 17.

20. Ibid., Table 21, p. 17.

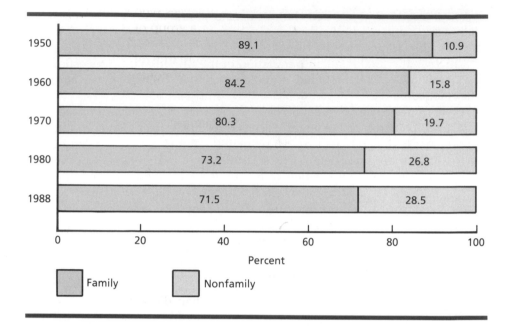

*Figure 1–1*
*Family and nonfamily households as a percent of all households: 1950 to 1988.*
(*Source:* U.S. Bureau of the Census, *General Population Characteristics: United States Summary* [Washington, D.C.: U.S. Government Printing Office, 1983], Figure 18, p. 15; *Statistical Abstract of the United States: 1989*, Table 58, p. 45.)

2.7 million were families with a male householder, no wife present, and 10.6 million were families with a female householder, no husband present.[21] Beginning with the 1980 Current Population Survey, the Bureau of the Census discontinued the use of the term "head" of the family or household, substituting the terms "householder" and "family householder." This change resulted from a recognition that household or family responsibilities are frequently shared among the adult members of either sex. This significant classification shift discontinues a longtime practice of always classifying the husband as the reference person (head) when he and his wife are living together. Today's "head of family," that is "family householder," is legitimately recognized as either female or male.

A family is different from a **household.** A household consists of all persons who occupy a housing unit. A house, an apartment or other group of rooms, or a single room are regarded as a housing unit when they are occupied or intended for occupancy as separate living quarters. A household includes the related family members and all other unrelated persons, if any,

---

21. Ibid., Table 58, p. 45.

such as lodgers, foster children, wards, or employees who share the housing unit. A person living alone in a housing unit, or a group of unrelated persons sharing a housing unit as partners, are also counted as a household. Thus not all households contain a family. In 1988, there were 91.0 million households,[22] and as can be seen in Figure 1–1 the proportion of nonfamily households is increasing. In 1950 only about one in ten households was of the nonfamily type but by 1988 more than one in four were nonfamily units. In other words, more people are living alone or with a nonfamily member.

## The size of families and households

**Family size** refers to the number of persons who are living together and are related to each other by birth, marriage, or adoption. The average size of all families was 3.17 persons in 1988. The average size of husband-wife families was 3.24 persons, compared to 2.68 for families with a male householder and 2.97 for families with a female householder. The average size of white families was 3.12 persons, compared to an average black family size of 3.49 and an average of 3.79 for Hispanic-origin families.[23]

Households had fewer persons per unit than did families in 1988. The average number of persons per household was 2.64 compared to the 3.17 average size of all families.[24] The number of persons per household has decreased considerably since the earliest census reports were taken (see Figure 1–2). The average size of a household was 5.4 in 1790, 4.2 in 1900, 3.3 in 1940, and, as shown, 2.64 in 1988. Thus, the average household has 2.8 fewer persons today than at the end of the eighteenth century. This decrease in the average size may have some positive influence on the interaction of its members and the social connectedness with others outside the household. While many households can adjust to a higher density, others report increased instances of aggression, disagreements, frustration, and general dissatisfaction.

One national study found that a shortage of household space affected parental attitudes negatively regarding their ability to control their children's actions, in the number of health complaints, and in their satisfaction with leisure time.[25] Another national survey concluded that persons living alone don't feel they are isolated and living alone against their will, but prefer this arrangement, provided that they have attachments outside the household; they frequently have higher levels of social contact and integration than those

22. Ibid., Table 58, p. 45.

23. U.S. Bureau of the Census, *Current Population Reports* Series P–20, No. 437, "Household and Family Characteristics: March 1988" (Washington D.C.: U.S. Government Printing Office, 1989), Table 1, pp. 3–6.

24. *Statistical Abstract: 1989*, Table 58, p. 45.

25. Mark Baldassare, "The Effects of Household Density on Subgroups," *American Sociological Review* 46 (February 1981): 110–118.

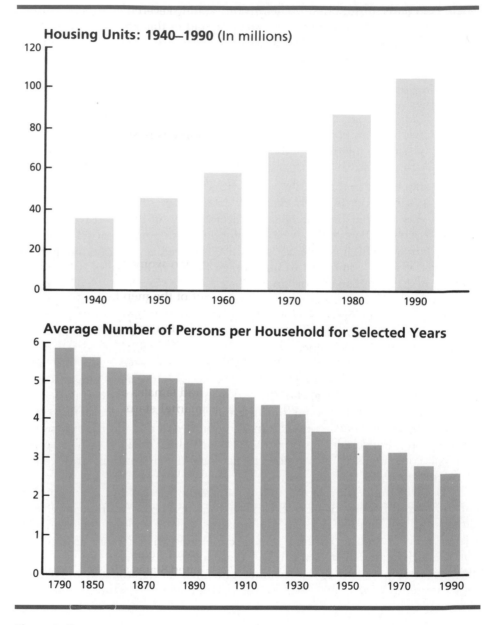

*Figure 1–2*
**Changes in number of housing units (1940 – 1990) and number of persons per house-hold (1790 – 1990)** (*Source*: U.S. Bureau of the Census, *Statistical Abstract of the United States: 1988; Historical Statistics of the United States: Colonial Times to 1970; 1980 Census of Population, Vol. 1, Chapter A: U.S. Summary; 1980 Census of Housing, Vol. 1, Chapter A: U.S. Summary; Current Population Reports, P–25 1017.*)
Note: All 1990 figures presented are projections; not census enumeration totals.

living with others.[26] The smaller household size and even the large increase in persons living alone (mentioned toward the end of this chapter) suggests an active preference made possible by rising affluence and the greater desire for autonomy among all age groups in society.

## Marital status

Census marital-status classification identifies four major categories: single, married, widowed, and divorced. A married couple is husband and wife who are enumerated as members of the same household and who may or may not have children living with them.

As can be seen in Table 1–2, approximately 83.7 million men and 91.9 million women were age eighteen or over in 1987. For men, 65.5 percent were married, 25.3 percent were single, 2.5 percent were widowed and 6.7 percent were divorced. For women, 60.5 percent were married, 18.6 percent were single, 12.1 percent were widowed, and 8.7 percent were divorced. Thus, ignoring age differences, men are more likely than women to be married or single, and women are more likely than men to be widowed or divorced.

Marriage is popular. More than 80 percent of the men between the ages of forty and seventy-four and more than 73 percent of the women between the ages of thirty and fifty-four are currently married. That only about 5 percent of both men and women are listed as single at a specific age would suggest that at least 95 percent (19 out of 20 persons) of both sexes marry at some point in their lives.

The large numbers of nonmarried males and females at the younger and older ends of the age spectrum reflect a premarital status for young single persons and a postmarital status (widowed or divorced) for older persons. Note the vast differences between widowed men and women between ages sixty-five and seventy-four (36.7 percent women versus 9.0 percent men) and after age seventy-five (67.0 percent women versus 23.6 percent men). The percentage of men and women who are divorced in a given year holds fairly constant for persons between the ages of thirty and sixty-four (7.3 percent to 10.9 percent for men; 9.0 to 14.5 percent for women). Even at the maximum age category, only 14 percent of women and about 11 percent of men are divorced. Thus, in spite of all the talk and concern about "easy divorce," "marital breakdown," and "family decay," most of the United States adult population at any given time is married, and when divorced, most remarry.

## Family income

**Family income** refers to the total amount reported by related persons who were members of the family at the time of enumeration. In the census, each

---

26. Duane F. Alwin, Philip E. Converse, and Steven S. Martin, "Living Arrangements and Social Integration," *Journal of Marriage and the Family* 47 (May 1985): 319–334.

Table 1–2
*Marital status of the population, by sex and age, 1987 (persons 18 years old and over)*

| Sex and Age | Number of Persons (1,000) | | | | | Percent Distribution | | | | |
|---|---|---|---|---|---|---|---|---|---|---|
| | Total | Single | Married | Widowed | Divorced | Total | Single | Married | Widowed | Divorced |
| **Male** | **83,706** | **21,145** | **54,854** | **2,120** | **5,586** | **100.0** | **25.3** | **65.5** | **2.5** | **6.7** |
| 18–19 years old | 3,530 | 3,418 | 111 | – | 1 | 100.0 | 96.8 | 3.1 | – | – |
| 20–24 years old | 9,499 | 7,380 | 1,965 | 11 | 144 | 100.0 | 77.7 | 20.7 | .1 | 1.5 |
| 25–29 years old | 10,694 | 4,513 | 5,597 | 3 | 581 | 100.0 | 42.2 | 52.3 | – | 5.4 |
| 30–34 years old | 10,448 | 2,414 | 7,186 | 13 | 835 | 100.0 | 23.1 | 68.8 | .1 | 8.0 |
| 35–39 years old | 9,163 | 1,137 | 7,018 | 14 | 995 | 100.0 | 12.4 | 76.6 | .2 | 10.9 |
| 40–44 years old | 7,365 | 509 | 6,025 | 35 | 797 | 100.0 | 6.9 | 81.8 | .5 | 10.8 |
| 45–54 years old | 11,151 | 658 | 9,379 | 129 | 985 | 100.0 | 5.9 | 84.1 | 1.2 | 8.8 |
| 55–64 years old | 10,277 | 591 | 8,641 | 293 | 752 | 100.0 | 5.8 | 84.1 | 2.9 | 7.3 |
| 65–74 years old | 7,608 | 354 | 6,200 | 685 | 368 | 100.0 | 4.7 | 81.5 | 9.0 | 4.8 |
| 75 years old and over | 3,970 | 172 | 2,731 | 937 | 129 | 100.0 | 4.3 | 68.8 | 23.6 | 3.2 |
| **Female** | **91,901** | **17,097** | **55,639** | **11,123** | **8,041** | **100.0** | **18.6** | **60.5** | **12.1** | **8.7** |
| 18–19 years old | 3,574 | 3,208 | 355 | – | 12 | 100.0 | 89.8 | 9.9 | – | .3 |
| 20–24 years old | 9,859 | 5,990 | 3,546 | 8 | 315 | 100.0 | 60.8 | 36.0 | .1 | 3.2 |
| 25–29 years old | 10,942 | 3,152 | 6,926 | 35 | 830 | 100.0 | 28.8 | 63.3 | .3 | 7.6 |
| 30–34 years old | 10,552 | 1,545 | 7,744 | 84 | 1,178 | 100.0 | 14.6 | 73.4 | .8 | 11.2 |
| 35–39 years old | 9,423 | 796 | 7,229 | 118 | 1,280 | 100.0 | 8.4 | 76.7 | 1.3 | 13.6 |
| 40–44 years old | 7,680 | 493 | 5,892 | 184 | 1,111 | 100.0 | 6.4 | 76.7 | 2.4 | 14.5 |
| 45–54 years old | 11,866 | 528 | 9,095 | 689 | 1,554 | 100.0 | 4.5 | 76.6 | 5.8 | 13.1 |
| 55–64 years old | 11,606 | 485 | 8,138 | 1,935 | 1,048 | 100.0 | 4.2 | 70.1 | 16.7 | 9.0 |
| 65–74 years old | 9,624 | 463 | 5,100 | 3,529 | 531 | 100.0 | 4.8 | 53.0 | 36.7 | 5.5 |
| 75 years old and over | 6,773 | 435 | 1,615 | 4,541 | 182 | 100.0 | 6.4 | 23.8 | 67.0 | 2.7 |

– Represents zero or rounds to zero.

*Source:* U.S. Bureau of the Census, *Statistical Abstract of the United States: 1989*, 109th ed. (Washington, D.C.: U.S. Government Printing Office, 1989), no. 49, p. 41.

family member fifteen years of age and over was asked the amount of income received in the preceding calendar year from sources such as wages or salaries, self-employment, social security, dividends, interest, rental income, public assistance or welfare payments, or other periodic income. It did not include amounts from sources such as the sale of property (stocks, bonds, a house, or a car), nor did it include borrowed money, tax refunds, gifts, or lump-sum inheritance or insurance payments. The total income of a family is the algebraic sum of the amounts received by all income recipients in the family.

Family income appears to have increased considerably since 1970. The median family income in 1987 was $30,853 compared to $9,867 in 1970. This 312 percent increase appears impressive until the figures are adjusted for the change in consumer prices and inflation. The median family income of $30,853, in constant 1987 dollars compared to a 1970 value of $28,880, is an increase of less than $2,000 in actual purchasing power.

As might be expected, rates of growth as well as median income for families varied widely by social categories. For example, in 1987 the median income of white families was $32,274, compared to $18,098 for black families and $20,306 for Hispanic families. Families with a male householder with no wife present had a median income much higher than those with a female householder with no husband present ($24,804 versus $14,620). Married couples with a wife in the paid labor force had a median family income of $40,422, while couples where the wife was not in the paid labor force had an income of $26,652. Families with householders who had a college education of four years or more had a median income of $50,908 compared to $30,958 for high school graduates and $15,264 for householders with less than an eighth-grade education.[27] Many other examples could be given to illustrate the wide range of median incomes that exists for families in the United States. In any case it should be clear that family incomes differ dramatically by sex, race, marital status, employment of one or both spouses, educational attainment, and other factors.

## TODAY'S FAMILIES: SIGNIFICANT CHANGES

Dramatic changes over time and diversity at any given point are illustrated by various demographic characteristics. Consider the following factors, which are supported by data from the Bureau of the Census.

The United States throughout the 1980s had one of the highest marriage and divorce rates among the world's industrialized countries.

27. All figures in this paragraph and the section that follows were taken from U.S. Bureau of the Census, *Current Population Reports*, Series P-60, No. 163, "Poverty in the United States: 1987" (Washington, D.C.: U.S. Government Printing Office, 1987); *Statistical Abstract of the United States: 1989*; and *Current Population Reports*, Series P-20, Nos. 433 and 437.

About 2.6 million unmarried couples lived together in 1988, about five times the 523,000 who lived together unmarried in 1970.

By 1988, the median age of first marriage had advanced more than two and one-half years since 1970, from 23.2 to 25.9 for men and 20.8 to 23.6 for women. More than one year of this advance occurred since 1980.

By 1988, 61.1 percent of the women aged twenty to twenty-four were single (never married), compared to 50.2 percent in 1980 and 35.8 percent in 1970. For men of similar age, 77.7 percent were single, compared to 68.8 percent in 1980 and 54.7 percent in 1970.

The number of divorced persons per thousand married persons in 1988 had increased nearly three times since 1970 (from 47 in 1970 to 133 in 1988).

Less than one-half (47.5 percent) of the nation's 51.8 million married couples in 1988 had children under age eighteen in the home. In 1970, 56 percent of married couples had them.

One-parent families accounted for 24.3 percent of all families with children under age eighteen in 1988, up from 11.9 percent in 1970.

In 1988, the most common household size was two persons (32.2 percent), but the next most common size was the one-person household (24.0 percent). The average size had decreased to 2.64 from 3.14 in 1970.

The number of persons living alone had increased from 10.8 million in 1970 to nearly 22 million in 1988.

The number of interracial married couples among the fifteen groups listed in the race item on the census questionnaire had increased more than two and one-half times (from 310,000 to 799,000) between 1970 and 1987, but still comprised only about 1.5 percent of all married couples. Black-white interracial married couples increased from 65,000 to 177,000, but comprised only 0.3 percent of the total.

Only about 5 percent of the people over age forty had never married. Statistics showed that most men and women marry at some time in their lives.

Approximately 18.6 percent of ever-married women aged fifteen to forty-four were childless in 1987, up from 16.4 percent in 1970.

Approximately 15.3 million single women in 1987 had given birth to children, 7.3 million more than in 1970.

Children born in 1987 had a life expectancy of about 75 years (78.3 for females; 71.5 for males). This is up from 73.7 in 1980, 68.2 in 1950, and 54 in 1920.

The number of persons below the poverty level was 31.9 million in 1988, comprising 13.1 percent of the population. This is up from 25.4 million in 1970 or 12.6 percent of the population that year.

The number of families below the poverty level in 1988 was 6.9 million or 10.4 percent of the total. This includes 7.9 percent of white families, 28.2 percent of black families, and 23.7 percent of Hispanic-origin families. Among female households with no husband present this includes 29 percent of white women, 52 percent of black women, and 55 percent of Hispanic women.

Need more illustrations be given? Census data alone, apart from the countless number of completed research studies, illustrate quite clearly the pluralistic, diversified, and changing nature of U.S. families. More detailed breakdowns of characteristics such as these are presented at appropriate places in the text.

## SUMMARY

1. This first chapter is intended to introduce some basic issues and characteristics of U.S. families. While all family systems adhere to similar basic general norms and values, great diversity exists in family structure, attitudes, and behavior.

2. Ideal-type constructs were introduced as a way to provide a range of perspectives between two polar extremes. It was the tool used to examine major issues in the U.S. family. Each issue was brought about by or was a result of social change; that is, traditional patterns coexist with nontraditional patterns. Were there no change or were there total change, no conflicts or issues would exist.

3. In my view, the most important issue to which all other issues are related centers on the meaning given to marriage and the family. The most traditional social norm holds that marriage and the family are sacred phenomena created and maintained by factors that are beyond human beings. Less traditional is the norm that suggests that marriage is created and maintained by society or by kin, by community, or by social institutions. The emergent norm suggests that marriage is created and maintained by the individual for the individual. Thus at least three meanings that are basically incompatible exist simultaneously. Only when individual meanings are identical to social meanings that are identical to sacred meanings, can there be no conflict.

4. Related issues include the "proper" form of marital and family organization; the functions of the family, marital, and gender role differentiation; social class and social mobility; the choice of a mate and the authority to choose; the degree of or need for love; the limiting of sexual relationships to marriage; the choice of the number and spacing of children and the means to fulfill that choice; the role of the aged in society; violence and abuse among intimates; the permanent or temporary nature of marriage; and other contemporary issues such as AIDS, abortion, and homelessness.

5. It is impossible to state that one issue is more important than another. For young single people, primary issues may focus on mate selection and sexual relationships. For married couples, the primary issues may focus on children, birth control, and marital roles. For elderly persons, the primary issues may focus on the functions of the family and their place in society. The meaning given to marriage, if maintained consistently from one issue to another, will influence whether one is for divorce or against it, for abortion or opposed to it, for extramarital coitus or opposed to it, or for accepting parental authority in selecting a mate or in personal choice irrespective of parental wishes.

6. This chapter, while highly descriptive, presents an overview of issues and changes in the family within the United States. The next chapter focuses on disciplinary and theoretical approaches to family study.

# KEY TERMS AND TOPICS

Ideal-type constructs   4
The meaning of marriage   6
Family organization   9
Orderly replacement   9
Universal permanent availability   9
Family functions   10
Marital and gender roles   11
Social class and social mobility   14
Mate selection   15
Love   16
Sexual relationships   17

Family size and planning   18
Old age   20
Violence and abuse   21
Family permanence   21
AIDS, abortion, homelessness   23
Family   27
Household   28
Family size   29
Marital status   31
Family income   31
Today's families   33

# DISCUSSION QUESTIONS

1. How many "ideal types" of polar constructs can you list that describe issues in families?
2. Check with five married adults as to their perceptions of the most important issues in the U.S. family today. Do the same with five single students. Compare results.
3. Which issue (of those listed or others) do you perceive as the most significant or serious today? Why? How can the conflict or issue be resolved?
4. Why do marriages exist today? What is their purpose? What or who should be the ultimate authority?
5. If conflicts exist between traditional and non-traditional marital and family norms, do the adherents of either position have a right to impose their position on the other? Take for example the couple that wants an abortion versus those who argue that abortion is wrong.
6. Can a person "love" more than one person simultaneously? Can intimate relationships with someone other than a person's spouse enrich a relationship with the spouse?

7. Has there been a greater change in sexual norms for men or for women? Why is this so? Is this issue or conflict primarily a thing of the past or will it be an issue ten years from now?
8. Is an increase in divorce rates indicative of a breakdown of the marital system in the United States or any other country? How about an increase in nonmarital and extramarital sexual relations, out of wedlock births, or interracial marriages? Why?
9. AIDS, abortion, and homelessness were listed as contemporary family-related issues. What ethical or moral issues are involved in each? What type of social policies need to be implemented and by whom?
10. This chapter ended with a section titled "Today's families: significant changes." Select several of the changes given and add the question "why?" For example: Why does the U.S. have one of the highest marriage and divorce rates among the world's industrialized countries? Why is there an increase in median age at marriage? Why is there an increase in persons living alone?

# FURTHER READINGS

Adams, Bert N., and Campbell, John L., eds. *Framing the Family: Contemporary Portraits*. Prospect Heights, Ill.: Waveland Press, Inc., 1984. A collection of twenty-eight readings covering numerous issues raised in this first chapter.

Adams, John S. *Housing America in the 1980s*. New

York: Russell Sage Foundation, 1987. Census data and other housing surveys are used to describe the housing supply and demand, patterns of use, and selected policy questions.

Caplow, Theodore; Bahr, Howard M.; Chadwick, Bruce A.; Hill, Reuben; and Williamson, Margaret Holmes. *Middletown Families: Fifty Years of Change and Continuity.* New York: Bantam Books, 1982. Middletown, a fictitious name given to Muncie, Indiana, was immortalized in two classic studies by Robert and Helen Lynd in 1929 and 1937. In the late 1970s a team of sociologists returned to Middletown for an extensive look at families in this community.

Chilman, Catherine; Nunnally, Elam W.; and Cox, Fred M. *Variant Family Forms.* Newbury Park: Sage Publications, 1988. An examination of issues resulting from families finding themselves in nontraditional life-styles.

Crosby, John F. *Reply to Myth: Perspectives in Intimacy.* New York: John Wiley, 1985. A listing of ten myths about sex, love, marriage, and the family with selected readings that address each myth.

Farber, J. Bernard. *Family Organization and Interaction.* San Francisco: Chandler, 1964. A book that concentrates on the explanation of stability and change in the family. Chapter 4 presents the orderly replacement and universal permanent availability models of change.

Feldman, Harold, and Feldman, Margaret. *Current Controversies in Marriage and the Family.* Beverly Hills: Sage Publications, 1985. Fourteen chapters brought together to illumine current controversies revolving around marriage and the family by using sets of paired comparisons.

Levitan, Sar A.; Belous, Richard S.; and Gallo, Frank. *What's Happening to the American Family?* Rev. ed. Baltimore: The Johns Hopkins University Press, 1988. An examination of factors that have led to the erosion of the traditional family structure, with a policy agenda to help secure family ties.

Macklin, Eleanor. "Nontraditional Family Forms" in *Handbook of Marriage and the Family* by Marvin B. Sussman and Suzanne K. Steinmetz (eds.). New York: Plenum Press, 1987, Chapter 12, pp. 317–367. A review of a wide range of nontraditional family forms including singlehood, cohabitation, childlessness, single parents, dual-careers, and extramarital relationships, among others.

Skolnick, Arlene S., and Skolnick, Jerome H., eds. *Families in Transition.* 6th ed. Glenview, Il.: Scott Foresman and Co., 1988. A book of readings, with major sections on the changing family, gender and sex, couples, parents and children, and a wider perspective that includes varieties of family experience and debating the future of the family.

Sussman, Marvin B., and Steinmetz, Suzanne K., eds. *Handbook of Marriage and the Family.* New York: Plenum Publishing Company, 1987. A primary sourcebook covering family perspectives and analysis, diversity in family life, life cycle processes, and family dynamics and transformation.

Sweet, James A., and Bumpass, Larry L. *American Families and Households.* New York: Russell Sage Foundation, 1987. Decennial census samples are used to document major transformations in family and household composition.

Teachman, Jay D.; Polonko, Karen A.; and Scanzoni, John. "Demography of the Family" in *Handbook of Marriage and the Family* by Marvin B. Sussman and Suzanne K. Steinmetz (eds.). New York: Plenum Press, 1987, Chapter 1, pp. 3–36. An overview of demographic factors in age at marriage, female labor force participation, fertility, marital disruption, remarriage, and household size and composition.

Wells, J. Gipson, ed. *Current Issues in Marriage and the Family.* 4th ed. New York: Macmillan, 1988. An examination of eight issues of central importance to the U.S. family system. Many of the thirty articles covering these issues provide excellent supplements to the issues discussed in Chapter 1.

# CHAPTER TWO

# DISCIPLINARY AND THEORETICAL APPROACHES TO FAMILY STUDY

From the collections of the Minnesota Historical Society.

Chapter 1 was devoted to a general introduction to the family, particularly the family in the United States. It provided some descriptive material on families, and then examined selected major issues in the American family by use of ideal-type constructs. This general overview was intended to set the general stage and introduce various issues, topics, and themes that follow throughout the book. There are many disciplines, approaches, and frames of reference used to study these family-related issues. These are examined in this chapter, with an emphasis given to the basic approaches and orientations emphasized in this book.

## DISCIPLINES INVOLVED IN FAMILY STUDY

The area of marriage and the family touches upon a wide range of topics, lends itself to many types of research, and uses the results of the research in various ways.[1] The orientation used in dealing with families will, in large part, determine the areas to investigate, the questions to ask about those areas, the research and theoretical approaches to apply, and the results that are derived. Since no single discipline is asking all the questions, obviously none has all the answers. Note in Table 2–1, for example, the wide range of disciplines that are concerned with families or family-related topics, and the examples of illustrative studies within each discipline.

No one discipline or occupation has a corner on the marriage and family market. The subject itself is highly interdisciplinary. The problem of disciplinary isolation is strikingly persistent. Anthropologists, who focus on families and family structures, often overlook emotional dynamics of family life. Psychologists, who focus on child development and personal adjustment, often overlook cultural variation and social organizational aspects. Sociologists, who focus on the social order, often overlook historical and personal developmental factors.

New interdisciplinary approaches may lead toward closing some of the gaps that separate disciplines and may bring forth new concepts and thus new meanings; yet each discipline will continue to focus attention in specific directions. The anthropologist will focus on family patterns in a cross-cultural and national context. The counsellor, usually in an applied context, will attempt to assist individuals, couples, or groups in resolving conflicts or modifying attitude or behavioral problems. The educator will attempt to convey ideas and elicit thought on child development, preparation for marriage, sexual concerns, or parental functioning. The historian will examine

---

1. For two reviews of family research over the past half century, *see:* Bert N. Adams, "Fifty Years of Family Research: What Does it Mean?" *Journal of Marriage and the Family* 50 (February 1988): 5–17; and F. Ivan Nye, "Fifty Years of Family Research," *Journal of Marriage and the Family* 50 (May 1988): 305–316.

*Table 2–1*
*Selected disciplines involved in areas of family study*

| Disciplines | Illustrative topics |
| --- | --- |
| Anthropology | Families in developing societies: cross-cultural studies; evolution; kinship |
| Biology | Human growth: genetics; conception and reproduction |
| Child Development | Infant growth; learning; personality formation |
| Counseling | Family therapy; interpersonal relationships; vocational guidance |
| Demography | Marriage; birth; divorce rates; mobility patterns |
| Economics | Family finance; consumer behavior; standards of living |
| Education | Family life; marriage preparation; child development; sex education |
| English | The family through literature, poetry, novels, and mass media |
| Gerontology | Family life of the elderly; intergenerational links; kin support systems |
| History | Family origins, trends, and patterns over time |
| Home Economics | Housing; nutrition; ecology; child development |
| Law | Marriage; divorce; abuse; adoption; welfare; child custody |
| Psychology | Interpersonal relationships; learning; human development |
| Public Health | Venereal disease; maternal and infant care; preventive medicine |
| Religion | Morality; marriage vows; love; sex; religious training |
| Social Work | Family, child, maternal, and aging assistance |
| Sociology | Family systems; interpersonal relationships; social change |

family patterns, events, and change in the past and over time. The politician will formulate policy and enact laws to deal with child care, marriage age, parental duties and responsibilities, or divorce. The social worker will direct knowledge and skills toward assisting families and family members in coping with problems of income, health, or behavior.

Neither the disciplines described nor the illustrative studies in Table 2–1 present an exhaustive listing of approaches to family study. Feminist scholarship is alerting the teacher, researcher, and family practitioner to be conscious of existing values and assumptions in their professions that ignore the perspectives of women.[2] This literature is critical of mainstream family

---

2. *See*, for example: Mirra Komarovsky, "The New Feminist Scholarship: Some Precursors and Polemics," *Journal of Marriage and the Family* 50 (August 1988): 585–593; Alexis J. Walker, Sally S. Kees Martin, and Linda Thompson, "Feminist Programs for Families," *Family Relations* 37 (January 1988): 17–22; and Katherine R. Allen, "Integrating a Feminist Perspective into Family Studies Courses," 37 (January 1988): 29–35.

studies which reflect the vision of the dominant male sex and tend to overlook the implications of a gender-stratified society.

Humanists have long been interested in the family. Poets have been writing about love, marriage, and family matters for centuries. Theologists, philosophers, artists, musicians, and linguists have not been immune from dealing with areas pertinent to the family. Biology, genetics, anatomy, and other biological sciences are interested in many facts that affect families. In fact, it may well be the biosocial science area that is providing the next major revolution, replacing the industrial one and having an impact on families far greater than anything experienced or known at this time.

The point is that a student could take a large number of family courses and encounter different ideas, approaches, and interests. Some courses would include theories and findings from other disciplines; others would have no interdisciplinary focus. The question becomes less "Which is better or correct?" than "Which fulfills the objectives or purposes desired?" The student interested in the portrayal of mothers in the mass media may not find much satisfaction in a course on child growth and development. Neither may the student interested in sex education care much about insurance plans or marketing behavior of nineteenth century English households.

Textbooks, like disciplines or courses, approach the family with a particular focus and orientation. That this book gives minimal attention to human anatomy, childhood diseases, and family nutrition is not meant to indicate a lack of importance of these areas. Rather, the orientation and frame of reference of this book basically follows that of the social sciences and more specifically that of sociology.

## A SOCIAL SCIENCE APPROACH TO THE FAMILY

As with the other areas mentioned, and perhaps to a greater extent, the social sciences have a primary interest in the family. Generally, the social sciences include sociology, anthropology, psychology, economics, and political science. Sometimes history, geography, and linguistics are added to this list. Each examines the same subject matter—the behavior of human beings—employs the same body of general explanatory principles, and shares similar aims and methods. Science is determined by its aims and methods, not by its results.

Regardless of the topic that is studied, be it the family or the economy, the social scientist is obligated to follow certain standards of inquiry. These include:

1. Objectivity. The personal biases and values of the people doing the research must never influence the data reported or the interpretation of results.
2. Replication. Research should be conducted and reported in such a way that someone else can duplicate it.

3. Precision of measurement. The phenomenon being studied should be measured in precise, reliable, and valid ways.[3]

All phenomena, including social phenomena, have certain regularities and uniformities that operate independently of the researcher or observer. These patterns or regularities can be discovered through objective observation. Science is predicated upon the assumption that there is a "real world," that something exists "out there"—something that is divorced from the individuals themselves and is empirically knowable.

The aims and goals of a social science approach to the family are to establish more-or-less general relationships, to require that they be based on empirical observation, and to view findings as tentative and open to multiple interpretations. Within the social science framework, let us examine the sociological approach to the family.

### The sociology of the family

Sociology per se is devoted to the study of how society is organized, its social structure, and its social processes. The primary units of investigation include human groups, social systems, and institutions.

A sociology of the family seeks to explain the nature of the social order and disorder of the family. The attempt is to discover, describe, and explain the order of family systems and family groups. A sociology of the family is interested in the organization of the family: its structures, functions, and changes. It is interested in how the family as a social system is sustained and modified. It is interested in how family relationships are formed and changed, how the components within the family are interrelated, and how the family as a unit is interdependent with other groups or systems.

A sociology of the family differs from either psychological or social-psychological approaches to the family. While both of these are primarily concerned with the behavior of individuals, sociology is interested in the social forms and structures within which this behavior takes place. Sociology has no primary interest in the individual, his or her personality, or his or her behavior, but rather with the nature of the groups to which the individual belongs and the society in which he or she lives. The separation of psychology, social psychology, and sociology is not always distinct, but each of the three branches of social science has different emphases. According to Eshleman, Cashion, and Basirico:

> Psychology is concerned with individuals. Social psychology is the study of how an individual influences his or her social interactions with other individuals or with groups, and of how social behavior influences the individual. Sociology deals primarily with groups and social systems.[4]

---

3. J. Ross Eshleman, Barbara G. Cashion, and Laurence Basirico, *Sociology: An Introduction* 3rd ed. (Boston: Little, Brown and Co., 1988): 63–66.
    4. Ibid., p. 15.

A sociology of the family will not focus on the motivation, drives, or perceptions of individuals. Technically speaking, a major segment of this book is a social psychology of marriage and the family. The sections that deal with interpersonal relationships (mate-selection processes, sexual behavior, parental interaction) focus on explaining how the structure and function of the family group influence the behavior of the members within that group and, reciprocally, how the behavior of each member modifies or shapes the family organization and its functioning.

A sociology of the family, operating within the social science framework, does not have as its major intent the direct application or utilization of the knowledge gained by the "pure," "concrete," or "basic" disciplines. On a pure-applied ideal-type continuum, and operating within an ideal-type construct (*see* Chapter 1), persons involved in the acquisition of knowledge do not devote their time and attention to the direct, day-to-day application of the knowledge. Thus the "basic" psychologist does not counsel family members, the sociologist does not work in adoption agencies, nor does the economist assist a family member in obtaining a loan. The psychologist, sociologist, or economist might, however, provide theoretical orientations, evaluation skills, research findings, data interpretations, policy suggestions, and the like to counsellors, teachers, social workers, politicians, or others. In this sense they too, as social scientists, become applied sociologists, psychologists, or economists.

Hopefully, this book will increase your knowledge about existing situations, present frameworks for analysis and/or action, and suggest alternate life-styles and directives. Based on the available knowledge and various interpretations of that knowledge, based on various theoretical explanations and methodological approaches, based on the presentation of multiple structures and various alternatives, I hope you, the reader, will be in a better position to make your own choices of action and make sound judgments on social policy and social action.

## *H*ISTORICAL *APPROACHES TO FAMILY STUDIES*

It was only after the middle of the nineteenth century that a systematic study of the family began. Prior to that time, thinking about the family had been based on emotion and superstition and was expressed by means of folklore, proverbs, and moralisms. Bert N. Adams says that the beginning of the movement toward systematic understanding rather than reliance on folklore can be traced roughly to the time of the appearance of Charles Darwin's *The Origin of Species* in 1859.[5] Adams subdivides the years from 1860 to the present into four thirty-year periods: social Darwinism (1860–1890), social reform

---

5. Bert N. Adams, *The Family: A Sociological Interpretation*, 4th ed. (Chicago: Harcourt Brace Jovanovich, 1986): 7–9.

(1890–1920), scientific study (1920–1950), and attention to family theory (1950–present).

Prior to the mid-1980s, family guidelines took the form of philosophical speculations, religious pronouncements, and often contradictory generalizations (such as today's "out of sight, out of mind" and "absence makes the heart grow fonder"). Although these types of speculation continue today, and many untested assumptions regarding the family are rigidly defended, various shifts have taken place in the development of the study of the family. In the middle of the nineteenth century, several writers began to apply Darwin's biological evolutionary scheme to changes within the family. Based on "primitive" peoples, these macroanthropological schemes traced the evolution of the family through a series of "natural" and "progressive" stages. For example, one series of stages might suggest the earliest relationship between men and women to be promiscuous, followed by a maternal (mother-child) family, and then by an original pair marriage. These schemes, which are often intuitive, raised questions such as how monogamy came to be and whether wife-capture or group marriage were earlier forms in a patterned sequence of stages.

Toward the end of the nineteenth century and the beginning of the twentieth, especially in the United States, social problems led to a concern for social reform. Many of these problems were closely related to the family: poverty, child labor, prostitution, illegitimacy, divorce, and the like. These problems were intensified by industrialization and urbanization, both of which disrupted kin ties.

The first half of the twentieth century emphasized large-scale comparative studies, aimed at attacking some of the social problems but emphasizing more of a value-free position and a more rigorous methodology. Various statistical techniques were developed and certain social psychologists and sociologists began to focus on individual personality adjustment, the family as a major factor in this adjustment, and the relationship between certain family problems and social problems in general.

A social-psychological orientation replaced the macroanthropological approaches of the earlier periods. Characteristic of this period of family study was an emphasis upon the internal relationship of family members. Charles Cooley, Robert Park, George Mead, W. I. Thomas, and others contributed to this emphasis, but it was Ernest W. Burgess who did most to both conceptualize and assist in the development of family studies. In 1926 he referred to the family as "the unity of interacting personalities," a definition that is still in wide use today. This was basically the beginning of the scientific orientation to family study, and by 1950 it was perhaps accurate to speak of the scientific study of marriage and the family.

Adams prefers to describe the 1950–1970 decades as a period of summarization of findings, of conceptual frameworks, of complaint about the lack of comprehensive theory, and of tentative theoretical attempts. He argues that it is instructive to view the 1960s as dominated by conceptual frameworks and

### Filipino marriage folk beliefs

If you awaken at 12:00 midnight and look at the mirror, you will see your future partner or sweetheart.

A person with dimples will marry someone from a place far away from his place.

It is not good for a girl or woman to sit at the head of the table because she won't get married and will eventually end up as an old maid.

A layman who goes through life without being married will not be admitted in heaven. He lacks the sacrament of matrimony and fails to comply with the commandment of God.

If a man marries a woman who is one year older than him their whole married life always meets problems and difficulties.

A girl who is always fainting should get married and she will be cured.

Marriage should be held at a date when the moon is getting big —half moon or full moon —for abundance of children.

If a husband can cut a banana plant with just one stroke of the blade (bolo), he is the master of the house. If he cannot, he is a henpecked husband.

*Source:* Francisco Demetrio y Radaza, S. J., ed., *Dictionary of Philippine Folk Beliefs and Customs*, Book III (Cagayan de Oro City, The Philippines: Xavier University, 1970): 619–622, 624–625.

the 1970s as oriented toward codification and theory building.[6] Research does appear to increasingly turn to cross-cultural and comparative studies, not purely for descriptive purposes but to discover relationships that are generalizable beyond a given societal context. Much evidence of this can be found in a two-volume work dealing with contemporary theories about the family that brought the 1970s to a close.[7]

What about the 1980s and 1990s? Thomas Holman and Wesley Burr[8] suggest that we seem no closer to the general theory of the family many have called for, but argue that such a theory may be not only an impossible dream, but also unnecessary. Instead they urge theorists to continue to improve existing theory, to develop metatheory (new and different forms of theory) and methodologies of building theory, to refine and validate theory with cross-cultural research, and to develop a reciprocal interaction with practitioners.

Jetse Sprey, in presenting an appraisal of current theorizing about the institutions of marriage and the family, raises (sees as unfinished business) three concerns.[9] First is the integration of existing conceptual schemes into broader, more flexible vocabularies. He would suggest, for example, that the five frames of reference listed in this chapter be viewed not as competitive or unique in their own right, but rather as attempts to incorporate ideas from one

---

6. Adams, *The Family*, p. 9.

7. Wesley R. Burr, Reuben Hill, F. Ivan Nye, and Ira L. Reiss, *Contemporary Theories About the Family*, vols. 1 and 2 (New York: The Free Press, 1979).

8. Thomas B. Holman and Wesley R. Burr, "Beyond the Beyond: The Growth of Family Theories in the 1970's," *Journal of Marriage and the Family* 42 (November 1980): 729–741.

9. Jetse Sprey, "Current Theorizing on the Family: An Appraisal," *Journal of Marriage and the Family* 50 (November 1988): 881–882.

into the other—a conceptual and theoretical integration. The second concern is about modes of explanation. Basically, this involves linking and integrating conceptual vocabularies with appropriate questioning and levels of explanation. The third concern is the ongoing ambiguous relationship between conceptualization and theory building. Theoretical models, while abstract, can be constructed with "ordinary language or mathematics," either of which may provide a way to think about reality.

Sprey emphasizes that theorizing cannot be considered static or unchanging, and he proposes three alternatives to current mainstream family theorizing. These include what he terms hermeneutics, critical, and feminist orientations.[10] **Hermeneutics** refers to the art or theory of interpretation. It takes us beyond the methods of science to any mode of experience in which truth is communicated. Subjectivity becomes not the opposite of objectivity, but an essential human way of interpretative understanding and of managing one's social life. **Critical social science** approaches societies and families both in terms of what exists and in terms of its possible future. It questions what types of social change are feasible and desirable as well as how they can be achieved. It links the actual with the possible. **Feminist theorizing** is aimed at recognizing the absence of women in the history of social and political thought. It challenges patriarchal and sexist notions about the family such as that it is natural or biological or that it is monolithic—having a single structure.

Each of these orientations—hermeneutics, critical, and feminist theorizing—presents serious challenges to mainstream family theorizing. As we approach the twenty-first century, these orientations will challenge traditional family scholarship and thinking. Keep them in mind throughout this chapter as we first step back a bit and examine the nature of theories and frames of reference and then present five major theories and attempt to illustrate throughout the text how they are relevant to everyday life. Since most of you will be or are family practitioners—as children, spouses, parents, or family-related professionals—the relevance of theory is of central importance.

## THE NATURE OF THEORIES AND FRAMES OF REFERENCE

Like the theoreticians in most other fields, family scholars are increasingly attempting to organize their accumulated knowledge in the form of concepts, generalizations, and theories. Specialists in the family area have been conscious of the need to organize concepts, develop hypotheses and propositions, and interrelate these propositions in a meaningful fashion in order to explain a particular aspect of marital or family organization and behavior. Concepts, conceptual frameworks, frames of reference, and theories are important in that they tell scholars where to focus their attention.

---

10. Ibid., pp. 882–886.

Family theories are neither right nor wrong but are basically ways of looking at and rationally explaining phenomena related to the family. An understanding of the most widely used frames of reference can enable the student to study and analyze family behavior in a way that is organized and logical. Rather than behavior within the family context being idiosyncratic and inconsistent, it becomes patterned, consistent, and predictable under certain given conditions.

## Concepts and variables

Basic to all theory and to all sociological research tools are **concepts**. A family concept, as in any area, is a miniature "system of meaning" — that is, a symbol, such as a word or phrase that enables a phenomenon to be perceived in a certain way. Concepts are tools by which one can share meanings. They are unitary and thus do not explain, predict, or state relationships. They are abstractions that are used as building blocks for the development of hypotheses, propositions, and theories. In family analysis, the segments of reality that are identified by concepts are typically qualities, attributes, or properties of social behavior. Examples of concepts within the family area would include the nuclear family, monogamy, roles, norms, values, legitimacy, sex ratio, and so on.

When these concepts take on two or more degrees or values they are referred to as **variables**. "Husband" is a concept; "years married" is a variable. The variable may be classified as *independent* (the presumed cause) or *dependent* (the presumed effect). The independent variable is antecedent, or simultaneous, to the dependent variable. Family income (a variable) may be dependent (the presumed effect) upon the number of years of education (the presumed cause).

Concepts and variables are undergoing continuous revision and refinement. Frequently, new concepts must be invented to symbolize some new idea or to identify some social property that had not previously been seen. Thus, *family* may in itself serve as an adequate term for lay people, but the professional differentiates between *families of orientation or procreation, nuclear, conjugal, extended, consanguine, stem,* and *joint.* New concepts like *sexually bonded relationships* and *family realm* were introduced in the first chapter. Because the particular concept used will affect what is seen, it must be constructed in a way that will not distort "reality." An extremely difficult task for the family scholar is to label phenomena in ways that will avoid undesired connotations. Could you imagine a family book bearing titles such as the honky, WASP, palefaced, or uncolored family in American society? Or notice the obviously different connotations of labels or concepts such as nigger, colored, Negro, black, Afro- or African-American. Halford Fairchild testifies to this argument that the differences are crucial.[11]

---

11. Halford H. Fairchild, "Black, Negro, or Afro-American? The Differences are Crucial," *Journal of Black Studies* 16 (September 1985): 47–55.

### Do concepts make a difference?

I used to think I was POOR. Then they told me I wasn't poor, I was NEEDY. Then they told me it was self-defeating to think of myself as needy, I was DEPRIVED. Then they told me deprived was a bad image, I was UNDERPRIVILEGED. Then they told me underprivileged was overused, I was DISADVANTAGED. I still don't have a dime, but I have a great vocabulary.

*Source:* Anonymous.

## Conceptual frameworks

When a set of concepts is interrelated to describe and classify phenomena, in this case phenomena relative to the family, the concepts are generally defined as a **conceptual framework**. In a strict sense of the term, a conceptual framework is not a theory; it is more frequently descriptive rather than explanatory and is generally employed as a classification scheme or taxonomy.

Considerable changes have occurred in the identification of current conceptual frameworks. In 1957, seven basic frameworks or approaches were defined by Hill and others; institutional-historical, interactional-role analysis, structural-functional, situational-psychological habitat, learning theory-maturational, household economics-home management, and the family development or family life cycle approach.[12]

In 1960, in what has become a classic article by Hill and Hansen, the chief conceptual properties and basic underlying assumptions of five frameworks were provided in taxonomic tables.[13] The frameworks delineated included these approaches: interactional, structural-functional, situational, institutional, and developmental.

These two initial works have stimulated a large number of articles and chapters on conceptual frameworks, frames of reference, and theories that are particularly applicable to the family area but seldom unique to it. These include conflict, legal, economic, institutional, exchange, evolutionary, biological, psychoanalytic, behavioristic, balance, game, ecological, and general systems frameworks, among others. The five frameworks covered in this chapter tend to appear regularly in the family literature, namely: structural-functional, symbolic interactional, social conflict, social exchange, and developmental. These conceptual classification schemes, models, or frames of reference are not to be substituted for nor are they to replace an interest in the creation of hypotheses, propositions, and theory.

---

12. Reuben Hill, Alvin M. Katz, and Richard L. Simpson, "An Inventory of Research in Marriage and Family Behavior: A Statement of Objectives and Progress," *Marriage and Family Living* 19 (February 1957): 89–92.

13. Reuben Hill and Donald A. Hansen, "The Identification of Conceptual Frameworks Utilized in Family Study," *Marriage and Family Living* 22 (November 1960): 299–311.

## Propositions and hypotheses

Conceptual frameworks can be used to generate or establish propositions, hypotheses, and theories. A **proposition** is a statement about the nature of some phenomenon. It generally involves a statement of the relationship between two or more concepts. For example, "young marriage is related to marital conflict" would be a proposition. If this, or other propositions, is formulated for empirical testing it is then considered a **hypothesis**. Thus a testable hypothesis would be "the younger the age at marriage, the higher the rate of divorce." Hypotheses and propositions are identical, with the exception that hypotheses carry clear implications for testing or measuring the stated relations. Hypotheses serve as the important branch between theory and empirical inquiry. Hypotheses and propositions are formed by combining concepts into statements that set forth some meaningful relationship.

Frequently, a proposition states that if one variable changes in some regular fashion, predictable change will take place in the other. For example, it has been suggested that "as industrialization increases, extended family ties decrease." Thus the two variables (industrialization and extended family) are stated as inversely related: as one increases the other decreases.

Wesley Burr and thirty-eight other experts in family study have presented a comprehensive work on establishing hypotheses and propositions in the area of family.[14] Covering areas such as family networks, change, fertility, work, mate selection, power, recreation, violence, social class, and many others, each author summarized and evaluated previous empirical and theoretical models. This work and others that followed represent yet another step toward systematic theory building in the area of family study.

## Theory

When it is possible to interrelate logically and systematically a series of propositions that explain some particular process, the result is a **theory**. A "good" theory should be testable, should be abstract, should have wide application, should be cumulative, and should give grounds for prediction. Thus, a theory is far more than mere speculation or a random collection of concepts and variables. It is a set of logically interrelated propositions that explains some process or set of phenomena in a testable fashion.

Like propositions, theories not only provide explanations of observed reality but also serve as important sources of new hypotheses. Examples of such efforts can be seen in most chapters of the *Contemporary Theory* books by Burr and others. For example, Lewis and Spanier (Chapter 12) identify

---

14. Wesley R. Burr, Reuben Hill, F. Ivan Nye, and Ira L. Reiss, eds., *Contemporary Theories About the Family*, vols. 1 and 2 (New York: The Free Press, 1979).

ninety propositions about factors relating to marital quality and marital stability and show the potential for a social exchange theory in explaining marital relationships.[15]

The use and application of theory, or perhaps more accurately *theoretical frames of reference*, are used extensively throughout this book. While no independent chapters exist on theory per se, you will note subsections that use a particular frame of reference. For example, the **structural-functional** frame of reference is applied extensively in Chapters 5, 6, and 7 to an analysis of family life-styles. The **social conflict** frame of reference is applied in Chapters 7, 12, 16 and 17 in dealing with social class, the marital system, violence, and divorce. The **symbolic interaction** frame of reference is applied throughout the book to an analysis of mate selection, sexual relationships, marital interaction, and child rearing (socialization). The **developmental** framework is applied from Chapters 12 through 15 in viewing marriage over the life cycle. **Social exchange theory** is applied to mate selection and the marital system. Other theories—frames of reference—not specifically summarized in detail in this chapter are presented where appropriate to offer a specific explanation of a particular aspect of the family: an orderly replacement theory of change, a complementary-need theory of mate selection, a learning-behaviorist and psychoanalytic theory of socialization, an ABCX model of crisis, and the like. From this list alone, it becomes obvious that many sets of logically interrelated propositions exist that explain some process or set of phenomena. Those more directly pertinent and widely used in a sociology of the family are summarized in the section that follows.

## FAMILY THEORIES AND FRAMES OF REFERENCE

### A structural-functional frame of reference

The structural-functional frame of reference, sometimes called *functional analysis*, is a major and dominant theoretical orientation in sociology. Within the family area, the scope of the approach is very broad; it provides a framework for dealing with the relationships within the family (husband, wife, sibling, and so on), as well as with the reciprocal influences on the family from other systems within the wider society (such as educational, religious, or occupational influences).

The structural-functional frame of reference has its origin in the functionalist branch of psychology, especially the gestalt position; in social anthropology, and in sociology, especially as seen by social-systems theorists such as Talcott Parsons.[16] The gestalt position focuses on the relation between

---

15. Burr et al., *Contemporary Theories*, Chapter 12, pp. 268–294.
16. Talcott Parsons, *The Social System* (Glencoe, Ill.: The Free Press, 1951).

a whole and its parts. A gestalt is an organized entity or whole in which the parts, although distinguishable, are interdependent. Numerous social anthropologists as well have stressed the impossibility of studying any particular aspect of life detached from its general setting. Functionalism is identified with the study of the interrelationships between the structures of any system.

To talk about social structures is to talk about social organizations, social systems, norms, values, and the like. Cultural structures, social structures, structural interrelations, or any other "structural" terminology refers to the interdependence of parts in a definite pattern of organization. Within this framework, societies (and families) are composed of interdependent parts that are linked together into a boundary-maintaining whole and are basically in harmony with each other. Since the parts of a system "need each other," there is a social bond and a high degree of order, cohesion, stability, and persistence. The implication is that groups, systems, or behavior are not purely random, individualistic, or unpredictable. Family groups and systems and the individuals that comprise them, like the other components of a society, are orderly and predictable units that must be viewed in a social context.

The social structure of a family refers to the way in which the social units are arranged, to the interrelationship of the parts, and to the patterns of organization. These patterns differ greatly around the world but, given a particular type of organization, definite recurrent consequences occur. Linda Bryan and others,[17] for example, found that a family structure consisting of stepparents and stepchildren appeared to lend itself to negative stereotypes. They hypothesized that family structure will be a cue by which stereotypes are formed and that stepparents and stepchildren will be seen more negatively than married or widowed parents or their children, but less negatively than divorced or never-married parents or their children. All hypotheses were supported.

To extend this argument of structure producing or resulting in patterned, recurrent consequences suggests that to have one wife or several, for newlyweds to establish a residence separate from parents, for both husband and wife to share in making the basic decisions, for inheritance to be given to the oldest child, or for there to be premarital sexual freedom is to suggest that recurrent, predictable consequences will occur within that given society and/or family system. *Nuclear, polyandry, partriarchy, avunculocal, bilineal, primogeniture, exogamy, arranged marriage,* or *consanguine* are words that define specific structural arrangements of a given family system. Most of these terms are described and illustrated in the next chapter.

The concepts "structure" and "function" can be discussed separately, although they are interrelated and one implies the other. Speaking in circular

---

17. Linda R. Bryan, Marilyn Coleman, Lawrence H. Ganong, and S. Hugh Bryan, "Person Perception: Family Structure as a Cue for Stereotyping," *Journal of Marriage and the Family* 48 (February 1986): 169–174.

## Apes provide humans with many models of family structure

According to the book, *Sociobiology: The New Synthesis*, the great apes, our closest relatives, exhibit a wide variety of family structures. Author Edward O. Wilson says the social organization varies greatly between species of higher primates, from solitary adults and mother-offspring groups in the orangutans, to monogamous pairs and offspring in the gibbon apes, to large social groups in the baboons, gorillas, and chimpanzees. Baboons, he states, are organized in male-dominated harems that are zealously guarded, while gorillas live in very gentle but male-dominated societies where overt sexual behavior is very rare, and chimpanzees live in large, loosely organized groups characterized by amiable, cooperative activities and sexual promiscuity. Thus nature provides us with many different models for family structure.

*Source:* Edward O. Wilson, *Sociobiology: The New Synthesis* (Cambridge: Harvard University Press, 1975).

terms, social structures are units of society that carry out or result in one or more basic functions. On the other hand, functions can be defined as results or consequences of given social structures. What specifically is meant by function?

Function is generally used in one of two related ways. One is to ask, "What does it do?" That is, in describing functions of the family in the United States or any given society, it is asked what the family does. Why does it exist? What functions does it perform? These functions may be *manifest*, that is, intended and recognized, or *latent*, that is, neither intended nor recognized. These functions may be performed for the individual personality, a particular social system or social institution, or the wider society.

It has been suggested that for individual members, some manifest functions of the family are to provide the basic personality formation, the basic status ascriptions, nurturant socialization, and tension management. For the larger society, some manifest functions are to replace members, to socialize the members to the norms and values of the society, and to act as an agent of social control. Talcott Parsons and Robert Bales suggest that the basic and irreducible family functions are two: (1) the primary socialization of children so that they can truly become members of the society into which they have been born, and (2) the stabilization of the adult personalities of the society.[18]

Families perform latent functions for persons and society as well. These latent functions, while real in the sense that they take place, are neither intended nor recognized. They may include socializing children to be abusive adults or instilling within them negative definitions of self-worth. For the larger society, some latent functions may be to keep women in inferior positions to men or to perpetuate inequality from one generation to the next. Generally, we

---

18. Talcott Parsons and Robert F. Bales, *Family Socialization and Interaction Process* (New York: The Free Press, 1955): 16–17.

do not intend families to fulfill such functions; nevertheless, such latent functions exist.

A second way in which function is used is related to the first usage. It is used in terms of consequences or results of activities that take place. Thus, given a certain type of structural pattern—for example, working mothers —one could ask, "What are some of the consequences (results) of the employment of mothers?" Note that the question is not "What do working mothers do?" but rather "What are some of the results or consequences of this type of behavior pattern?" Are smaller family size, higher levels of mental health, delinquent children, or marital instability consequences of mothers working? Do families in societies that permit mothers to join the labor force have a higher level of living, a "closer" parent-child relationship, or more egalitarian decision-making patterns? Are the consequences similar irrespective of cultural context, time, or location? How does this structure interrelate with other structures? Does it lead to the maintenance or to the breakdown of a particular system?

One example of noting manifest and latent consequences can be seen in an analysis of the functions of social conflict among children.[19] Douglas Maynard videotaped reading groups of first-grade children. He found that social conflict among children in these groups had the manifest function of creating their small-group society and its structure. Results of their disputes and arguments produced social organization and created political alignments. Studying these manifest functions served as a prelude to tracing latent functions of the reproduction of authority, friendship, and other social patterns that went beyond any single episode of interaction among children.

To repeat, these terms, *structure* and *function*, are complementary concepts. Although they can be discussed separately, they cannot be understood independently. The structure (parts) to which a social analyst imputes functions (consequences) includes norms, values, roles, rank, power, and sanctions, as well as factors such as emotions, beliefs, and goals.

Today, a major thrust of the structural-functional approach centers around explaining the parts or components (structure) of a society and the manner in which these parts interrelate with one another, both within and outside the particular system under study. Each component of society must be seen in relationship to the whole, since each component acts and reacts upon other components. Thus the task of functional analysis is to explain the parts, the relationship between the parts, the relationship between the parts and the whole, and the functions (both manifest and latent) that are performed by, or result from, the relationship formed by the parts.

On an ideal-type continuum, the level of analysis ranges from macroanalysis to microanalysis. The distinction between these is made purely in terms of the size of the unit chosen for analysis. The macrofunctionalists are

---

19. Douglas W. Maynard, "On the Functions of Social Conflict Among Children," *American Sociological Review* 50 (April 1985): 207–223.

concerned with the analysis of relatively large-scale systems and institutions. The microfunctionalists are concerned with the analysis of individual families or of relatively small-scale systems (often designated as *group dynamics*). Both positions conceive of their units of analysis as important to, and interrelated with, the other parts of the larger system.[20]

## A social conflict frame of reference

Conflict theory may be viewed as a special case of functional theory, as by Lewis Coser,[21] or as an entirely separate theory, as done by Rolf Dahrendorf.[22] Perhaps the most basic assumption of a conflict frame of reference is that conflict is natural and inevitable in all human interaction. Thus, rather than stressing order, equilibrium, consensus, or system maintenance as in functionalism, the focus is on conflict management. Rather than viewing conflict as "bad" and disruptive of social systems and human interaction, conflict is viewed as an assumed and expected part of all systems and interactions, including family systems and marital interactions. If family-employment, husband-wife, or parent-child norms or goals are in frequent conflict (as is to be expected), the issue is not how to avoid it but how to manage, deal with, and/or resolve it. In so doing, the conflict, rather than being disruptive or negative, may strengthen relationships, may force change and as a consequence make them more meaningful and rewarding than they were before.

The classical case for conflict theory stems from Karl Marx who assumed that economic organization, especially the ownership of property, generates revolutionary class conflict.[23] He believed that as the exploited and oppressed proletariats become aware of their oppression and their true "interests," they would revolt and form a revolutionary political organization aimed at overthrowing the dominant, property-holding bourgeoisie. Basic to Marx and influential in the contemporary thinking of conflict theorists are ideas such as:

---

20. Key concepts in structural-functional theory in sociology are social system, social structure, social function, dysfunctions, manifest and latent functions, functional requisites and prerequisites, equilibrium and order, status and norms.

Some of the leading advocates of this perspective include Talcott Parsons, Robert Merton, Kingsley Davis, Wilbert Moore, Robin Williams, Charles Loomis, Harry Johnson, Emile Durkheim, George Homans, Marion Levy, William Goode, and Robert Winch.

From the perspective of the family, you may wish to examine Rose Laub Coser, *The Family: Its Structures and Functions*, 2d ed. (New York: St. Martin's Press, 1974); Norman W. Bell and Ezra F. Vogel, *A Modern Introduction to the Family*, rev. ed. (New York: The Free Press, 1968); and William J. Goode, *The Family*, 2d ed. (Englewood Cliffs, N.J.: Prentice-Hall, 1982).

21. Lewis A. Coser, *Continuities in the Study of Social Conflict* (New York: The Free Press, 1967).

22. Rolf Dahrendorf, *Essays in the Theory of Society* (Stanford: Stanford University Press, 1968); and Rolf Dahrendorf, "Out of Utopia: Toward a Reorientation of Sociological Analysis," *American Journal of Sociology* 74 (September 1958): 115–127.

23. Karl Marx, *The Communist Manifesto*, trans. Samuel Moore (Baltimore: Penguin, 1967), originally published in 1849 with Friedrich Engels; C. Wright Mills, *The Marxists* (New York: Harcourt, Brace, 1948); and Rolf Dahrendorf, *Class and Class Conflict in Industrial Society* (Stanford: Stanford University Press, 1959).

*Few names evoke as strong a response as that of Karl Marx (1818–1883). He and his colleague Fredrick Engels claimed that capitalism favors patriarchy. Women and wives are exploited by receiving lower pay when employed and no pay or benefits for serving as housewives and mothers.*

(1) social systems systematically generate conflict, which (2) is an inevitable and pervasive feature of all social systems and (3) is manifest in the bipolar opposition of interests that (4) is brought about by the distribution of scarce resources, most notably power, which (5) results in change in social systems.[24]

Hypotheses stemming from these assumptions suggest that: the more unequal the distribution of scarce resources, the greater the conflict between the dominant and the subordinate; as the subordinate become aware of their collective interests, they increasingly question the legitimacy of existing patterns; the greater the questioning of inequities, the more likely they are to join in overt conflict against the dominant group; and the more overt or violent the conflict, the greater the change and the redistribution of these resources.

The family, from this Marxian economic-conflict perspective, serves to support the capitalistic system that exploits working-class workers by paying them lower wages. Similarly, it exploits women, not merely by paying lower wages to those who are employed, but by encouraging them to perform unpaid housework and child care so the husband can devote full time to his capitalist employer.

---

24. *See* Jonathan H. Turner, *The Structure of Sociological Theory* (Homewood, Ill.: Dorsey, 1974); 79–83.

Feminist conflict theorists, while not denying the economic inequalities argued by the Marxian theorists, do not place the source of all male-female inequalities in economic systems. Some feminists have substituted the word "patriarchy" for "bourgeois" and even for "sex roles." "Sex roles," with its theme of different but equal tasks and power, downplays the structured inequality, that is, male dominance, that is pervasive. This male dominance exists in its own right and cuts across all economic and class lines. In addition, male domination implies female oppression and sexism. The root source of this oppression and sexism is in the home, where for women, employed or not, housework and home are part of the same system. Until women increase their independence from men and gain resources (power, money, education, job opportunities, and the like) that decrease their oppressed status as women, the family will never become an egalitarian institution.

In brief, from either a Marxian or feminist conflict-model or perspective, the family is not the haven posited by an order model such as functionalism (*see* Table 2–2). Functionalists who see the family as the primary socialization agent of youth are seen by conflict theorists as promoting a false consciousness by teaching youth to accept the inequalities between the sexes and classes as "natural." Functionalists who see the family as perpetuating the same "life-chances" from one generation to another (that is, the rich stay rich and the poor stay poor) are seen by conflict theorists as maintaining and

*Table 2–2*
*Duality of social life: Assumptions of the order and conflict models of society*

|  | *Order model* | *Conflict model* |
|---|---|---|
| *Question:* | What is the fundamental relationship among the parts of society? | |
| *Answer:* | Harmony and cooperation. | Competition, conflict, domination, and subordination. |
| *Why:* | The parts have complementary interests. Basic consensus on societal norms and values. | The things people want are always in short supply. Basic dissensus on societal norms and values. |
| *Degree of integration:* | Highly integrated. | Loosely integrated. Whatever integration is achieved is the result of force and fraud. |
| *Type of societal change:* | Gradual, adjustive, and reforming. | Abrupt and revolutionary. |
| *Degree of stability:* | Stable. | Unstable. |

*Source:* D. Stanley Eitzen, *In Conflict and Order: Understanding Society*, 2d ed. (Boston: Allyn and Bacon, 1982): 45.

promoting inequality based on ascription rather than achievement. Functionalists who see the isolated nuclear family as consistent with the mobility needs of a capitalist society are seen by conflict theorists as being disruptive to individual members and their emotional needs. Functionalists who see the modern family as tranquil, passive, and in a state of equilibrium with other units of society are seen by conflict theorists as promoting a system fraught with potential and actual conflict. Conflict, as inevitable in society, in the family, and in interpersonal relationships, leads to change.

Issues related to conflict theory, such as power, decision making, marital adjustment, economic factors, and the like, are discussed elsewhere, particularly in Chapters 7 and 12.[25]

## A symbolic interaction frame of reference

*Symbolic interactionism* has come into use as a label that indicates a particular and distinctive approach to the study of the group life and personal behavior of human beings. As a social-psychological frame of reference, it addresses itself to two major questions, both of which are of central concern to the family: socialization and personality. The first—socialization—focuses on how the human being obtains and internalizes the behavior patterns and ways of thinking and feeling of the society. The second—personality—focuses on the way in which these attitudes, values, and behaviors are organized.

Within social psychology, symbolic interactionism constitutes both a theoretical perspective and a methodological orientation. Its theoretical uniqueness lies in the extent to which covert activity is a crucial dimension in the understanding of behavior and society. That is, *like* Pavlovian and Skinnerian radical behaviorism,[26] symbolic interactionism includes the observable actions of individuals; *unlike* radical behaviorism, it stresses the importance of "meanings," definitions of situations, symbols, interpretations, and other internalized processes.

Interaction among socialized human beings is mediated by the use of symbols, by interpretation, or by ascertaining meanings for the actions of

---

25. Key concepts in conflict theory are conflict, competition, negotiation, patriarchy, resources, scarcity, interests, change, power, and class.

Some of the leading advocates of the perspective include Karl Marx, Georg Simmel, Rolf Dahrendorf, Lewis A. Coser, and Pierre van den Berghe.

From the perspective of the family you may wish to examine Marie Withers Osmond, "Radical-Critical Theories" in Marvin B. Sussman and Suzanne K. Steinmetz, *Handbook of Marriage and the Family*, (New York: Plenum Press, 1987), Chapter 5, pp. 103–125; Randall Collins, *Sociology of Marriage and the Family: Gender, Love, and Property*, (Chicago: Nelson-Hall, 1985); Richard F. Curtis, "Household and Family in Theory on Inequality," *American Sociological Review* 51 (April 1986): 168–183; Jetse Sprey, "Conflict Theory and the Study of Marriage and the Family," in *Contemporary Theories About the Family*, vol. 2, by Burr et al., pp. 130–159.

26. Pavlovian and Skinnerian radical behaviorism, parallel to classical and operant conditioning, are described in Chapter 14 under the heading, "A Learning-Behaviorist Frame of Reference."

*George Herbert Mead (1863–1931) is widely regarded within sociology as having made the greatest contribution to explaining the process of socialization. Families are an important group of reference and source of interaction in the development of the self.*

others. Methodologically, the "world of reality" is known by any means or set of techniques that offers a likely possibility of obtaining what is going on: making direct observation, conducting interviews, listening to the conversations of people, securing life history accounts, using letters and diaries, consulting public records, arranging for group discussions, or any allowable procedure that ascertains the subjective meanings. Basically, it involves a phenomenological approach with participant observation, the use of personal documents, and ethnomethodological accounts as the preferred techniques. The use of the quotations from personal interviews is consistent with this particular frame of reference.

The interactionist approach makes the following assumptions:

Marriages and families must be studied at their own level; that is, we cannot infer the behavior of humans, of human interactions, or of social systems from the study of nonhumans or infrahuman forms.

Marriage and family and their components can only be understood in the context of the social setting and society in which they exist. The language spoken, the definitions given to situations, or the appropriateness of any activity only makes sense within a social context.

The human infant at birth is neither social nor antisocial but asocial and learns in interaction with others what is good or bad, accepted or unaccepted behavior.

A social human being is an actor as well as a reactor; that is, he or she can communicate symbolically and share meanings. Thus, individuals do not merely respond to objective stimuli but select and interpret them. Individuals can interact with themselves, can take the roles of others, and can respond to symbolic stimuli.

These assumptions, spelled out in more detail in Chapter 14, are basic to an understanding of the significance of this framework as applied to both marital and parental interaction and to human behavior in general.

Concepts from this framework are used extensively throughout the book. For example, the concept "role" is used both within a structural-functional framework and within an interactionist framework. However, its use varies significantly. An institutional or structural concept of role attaches societal expectations to statuses that we occupy. Certain statuses, such as sex, age, and race, are generally ascribed, whereas our marital, occupational, and parental statuses are likely to be achieved. Each of these statuses or status sets carries with it expected, appropriate behaviors. These expectations of what is appropriate for men or women, married or single, homosexual or heterosexual, are termed roles. These are culturally defined expectations, and exist independently of any given person.

Role, as it is used within an interactionist framework, does not deny the institutional usage but, rather than dealing with a package of behavioral expectations wrapped up in a set of rules, it deals with a relationship between what we do and what others do. The expectations (roles) are developed in interaction. The emphasis here is on process. The interactionist concept of role describes the processes of cooperative behavior and of communication. It involves the idea of "role taking," which is not a set of rules associated with a position but involves actions supplied in part by relationships to others whose actions reflect roles that are inferred. Role as a process involves each actor adjusting his or her behavior and reactions to what he or she thinks the other person is going to do. Perhaps a simple example may clarify the difference in the use of these two bodies of thought.

Suppose we have two students, one male and one female. The fact that they occupy student and sexual statuses implies that certain expectations or roles are associated with these statuses. But for the moment let's concentrate on the students as male and female. Some of the rules or expectations traditionally associated with the status "male" in relationship to "female" are that he walk on the outside, open doors, permit her to proceed first, assist her with a chair, and pay the bill. Thus the institutional concept of role emphasizes the society's prescribed expectations for behavior. Whether these rules are actually followed is secondary. The roles (expectations) exist independently of a given individual's fulfillment of them. Failure to conform to the expectations appropriate to status does not eliminate the normative expectations.

In contrast to the institutionalized concept of role, the interactionist concept involves the *process* of determining appropriate behavior in interaction with others. Now, the actor is not the occupant of a position for which there is a standardized set of rules; he or she is a person whose expectations for behavior are supplied in part by his or her relationship to another person or persons. Since the expectations of the other person can only be inferred rather than directly known, there is a continuous process of testing. The clues given by the other person in part determine the expected behaviors (roles) appropriate to that situation. Getting back to our male and female, as they interact the expectations (roles) for appropriate and approved behavior may vary widely from the socially ascribed expectations. The female may quite appropriately pay the bills, open the doors, be the aggressive sexual partner, drive the automobile, and the like. But these too become patterned and recurrent. This is what makes behavior predictable and interaction possible with either strangers or intimate lifelong friends.

These two conceptions of role are not totally independent and separate, for one never escapes the norms or roles provided by a given society. At best, however, the expectations associated with a given status offer only generalized guidelines; they do not determine specific behavior patterns for every situation. Thus, the norm prescribing that a male does not have intercourse with a female on a first date nevertheless may, as the couple interacts, result in coitus. The gestures, the clues, the symbols, the verbal communications, and the clarity of shared meanings may lead to intercourse as a highly appropriate role expectation for the dating partners—within the interactionist concept of role. The behavior of intercourse on a first date, within the institutional concept of role, however, is inconsistent with the culturally prescribed rules for unmarried couples in the United States.

Other concepts that are key to the understanding of this frame of reference include the social self, significant other, reference group, and generalized other. These are clarified and illustrated in various chapters throughout the text, with a more extensive presentation of the symbolic interactionist frame of reference in Chapter 14. At this point, let's be satisfied with recognizing the family as a "unit of interacting personalities"[27] involved in a never-ending, completed, or fixed process.[28]

---

27. Ernest W. Burgess, "The Family as a Unit of Interacting Personalities," *Family* 7 (1926): 3–9.

28. Key concepts in symbolic interaction theory are symbols, interaction, process, status, role, role playing, role taking, role conflict, meaning, reference group, significant other, generalized other, social self, "I," "me," socialization, actor, and identity.

Some of the leading advocates of this perspective include George Herbert Mead, Charles Cooley, William James, Herbert Blumer, Tomatsu Shibutani, Alfred Lindesmith, Anselm L. Strauss, Erving Goffman, and Sheldon Stryker.

From the perspective of the family, you may wish to examine Ralph H. Turner, *Family Interaction* (New York: Wiley, 1970); Sheldon Stryker, "Symbolic Interaction Theory: A Review and Some Suggestions for Comparative Family Research," *Journal of Comparative Family Studies* 3 (Spring 1972): 17–32; and Wesley R. Burr, Geoffrey K. Leigh, Randall D. Day, and John Constantine, "Symbolic Interaction and the Family," in *Contemporary Theories About the Family*, vol. 2, by Burr et al., pp. 42–111.

## A social exchange frame of reference

Seldom does a day pass in which certain exchanges do not take place. Work, gifts, cards, affection, or ideas are given in hopes of getting something in return. Certain exchanges, such as many economic ones, are institutionalized and predetermined—clarified in precise terms prior to the exchange. Thus I know that I can exchange 50 cents for a newspaper or $100 for a membership in the National Council on Family Relations. Other exchanges, including the type found in the social exchange frame of reference, leave unspecified the exact nature of the return, although a return—an expectation of reciprocity —does exist. For example, neighbors who borrow tools or food, friends who invite you to dinner, politicians who promise lower taxes, all expect something in return. That exact something is often unspecified.

Social exchange or social choice theory rests on the belief that human beings attempt to make choices that they expect will maximize their rewards and/or minimize their costs. Social exchange theory seeks to explain why certain behavioral outcomes occur (marriage, sex, employment), given a set of structural conditions (age, race, gender, class) and interactional potentialities. These assumptions are made:

Most gratifications of humans have their source in the actions of other humans (spouse, children, friends, colleagues, fellow workers).

New associations are entered into because they are expected to be rewarding and old associations continue because they are rewarding.

As we receive rewards or benefits from others, we're under obligation to reciprocate by supplying benefits to them in return.

Having social credit through giving is preferable to being socially indebted through receiving.

While it may be true that persons (saints) exist who selflessly work for others with no thought of reward, saints are rare, and even they seek social (or spiritual) approval. In brief, social exchange refers to voluntary social actions that are contingent on rewarding reactions from others. These actions cease when the actual or expected reactions are not forthcoming.

Social exchange theory has followed two differing schools of thought best represented by George Homans[29] and Peter Blau.[30] Homans, the recognized initiator of exchange theory, represents a perspective consistent with that of behavioral psychologists who believe in psychological reductionism and reinforcement theory, where the focus is on actual behavior that is rewarded or punished by the behavior of other persons. Humans, like animals, react to

---

29. George C. Homans, *Social Behavior: Its Elementary Forms* (New York: Harcourt, Brace and World, 1961); George C. Homans, "Social Behavior as Exchange," *American Journal of Sociology* 63 (May 1958): 597–606.

30. Peter M. Blau, *Exchange and Power in Social Life* (New York: Wiley, 1964); Peter Blau, "Justice in Social Exchange," *Sociological Inquiry* 34 (Spring 1964): 193–206.

stimuli based on need, reward, and reinforcement. It is expected that in exchange relationships the rewards will be proportional to the cost (a notion of distributive justice).

Blau differs considerably from Homans and represents a perspective consistent with that of the symbolic interactionist.[31] That is, not all exchange is explained in terms of actual behavior of individuals. The exchange is more subjective and interpretative. The exchange, like interaction, is a creative process between actors and not within individuals or in external factors. While humans want rewards, the choices and decisions are limited by social influences such as friends or kin. The human mind responds subjectively to stimuli through conceptualizing, defining, valuing, reflecting, and symbolizing. As a result, the explaining of behavioral outcomes (the goal of social exchange theory) is a function of the actors who interact symbolically, have social selves, and can take roles.

Both Homans and Blau agree that what is important is that each party receive in the exchange something perceived as equivalent to that which is given (to Homans—*distributive justice*, to Blau—*fair exchange*). All social exchange involves a mutually held expectation that reciprocation will occur.[32] If resources or exchange criteria are unequal or imbalanced, one person is at a distinct disadvantage and the other has power over, or controls, the relationship. Specific resources (money, position, physical assets, personality) may be more applicable in one exchange than in another and may have differing values in one exchange than in another. Their worth can only be accurately assessed through participation in actual social markets. Therefore, socialization in exchange and bargaining skills becomes vital to maximize the use of available resources.

The family literature is filled with many examples of social exchange. As you will note in the chapters on mate selection, Willard Waller suggests in his "principle of least interest" that interest is exchanged for control of the relationship in that the person who is least interested in continuing the dating relationship is in a position to dominate. In arranged marriages, labor, gifts, or a bride price are often exchanged for the right to marry. Robert Winch talks of complementary needs involving an exchange of needs that provide maximum gratification. The higher incidence of premarital sexual behavior of engaged females has been explained by an exchange of sex on the part of the female in return for a commitment on the part of the male. Throughout the text, note the value of different types of resources and the exchange processes

---

31. *See* Peter Singelmann, "Exchange as Symbolic Interaction: Convergence between Two Theoretical Perspectives," *American Sociological Review* 37 (August 1972): 414–424; Robert B. Schafer, "Exchange and Symbolic Interaction," *Pacific Sociological Review* 17 (October 1974): 417–434; and Richard M. Emerson, "Social Exchange Theory," *Annual Review of Sociology* 2 (1976): 335–362.

32. Alvin W. Gouldner, "The Norm of Reciprocity," *American Sociological Review* 25 (April 1960): 161–178.

at work in understanding authority and power, husband-wife interaction, mate selection, kin relationships, sexual patterns, parent-child conflict, and the like.[33]

## A developmental frame of reference

Having its beginning in the 1930s, the family development approach to family study attempts to join together various parts of previously delineated theoretical efforts. Hill and Hansen, discussing the characteristics of the developmental-conceptual framework, have indicated that this approach was not a precisely unique framework but was an attempt to transcend the boundaries of several approaches through incorporation of their compatible sections into one unified theme.[34]

> From rural sociologists it borrowed the concept of stages of the family life cycle. From child psychologists and human development specialists came the concepts of developmental needs and tasks. From the sociologists engaged in work in the professions it incorporated the concept of the family as a convergence of intercontingent careers. From the structure-function and interactional approaches were borrowed the concepts of age and sex roles, plurality patterns, functional prerequisites, and the many concepts associated with the family as a system of interacting actors.[35]

The developmental approach covers a very broad area tending to be both macro- and microanalytic in nature. The peculiar character of this approach lies in its attempt to account for change in the family system over time as well as to account for changes in patterns of interaction over time. Traditionally, the major conceptual tool among family scholars for this time analysis has been

---

33. Key concepts in social exchange theory are exchange, reciprocity, negotiation, transaction, resources, cost, distributive justice, fair exchange, and power.

Some of the leading advocates of this perspective include George C. Homans, Peter M. Blau, Kingsley Davis, Alvin W. Gouldner, John W. Thibaut, Harold H. Kelley, John N. Edwards, and John Scanzoni.

From the perspective of the family, you may wish to examine John N. Edwards, "Familial Behavior as Social Exchange," *Journal of Marriage and the Family* 31 (August 1969): 518–526; Marie Withers Osmond, "Reciprocity: A Dynamic Model and a Method to Study Family Power," *Journal of Marriage and the Family* 40 (February 1978): 49–61; Gerald W. McDonald, "Structural Exchange and Marital Interaction," *Journal of Marriage and the Family* 43 (November 1981): 825–839; F. Ivan Nye, "Choice, Exchange, and the Family," in *Contemporary Theories About the Family*, vol. 2, by Burr et al., pp. 1–41; F. Ivan Nye, ed., *Family Relationships: Rewards and Costs* (Beverly Hills: Sage Publications, 1982); and John Scanzoni, *Sexual Bargaining: Power Politics in the American Marriage*, 2d ed. (Chicago: University of Chicago Press, 1982).

34. Hill and Hansen, "The Identification of Conceptual Frameworks Utilized in Family Study," pp. 299–311.

35. Ibid., p. 307.

## Sans teeth, sans eyes, sans taste, sans everything

All the world's a stage,
And all the men and women merely players,
They have their exits and their entrances,
And one man in his time plays many parts,
His acts being seven ages. At first the infant,
Mewling and puking in the nurse's arms.
And then the whining school-boy, with his satchel
And shining morning face, creeping like snail
Unwillingly to school. And then the lover,
Sighing like furnace, with a woeful ballad
Made to his mistress' eyebrow. Then a soldier,
Full of strange oaths, and bearded like the pard,
Jealous in honour, sudden and quick in quarrel,
Seeking the bubble reputation
Even in the cannon's mouth. And then the justice,

In fair round belly with good capon lin'd,
With eyes severe and beard of formal cut,
Full of wise saws and modern instances;
And so he plays his part. The sixth age shifts
Into the lean and slipper'd pantaloon,
With spectacles on nose and pouch on side,
His youthful hose, well sav'd, a world too wide
For his shrunk shank; and his big manly voice
Turning again toward childish treble, pipes
And whistles in his sound. Last scene of all,
That ends this strange eventful history,
Is second childishness and mere oblivion,
Sans teeth, sans eyes, sans taste, sans everything.

*Source:* William Shakespeare, *As You Like It.* Act II, Scene vii.

termed the *family life cycle.*[36] Today, frequent reference is made to the *life course* in dealing with changes and differences over time.[37]

The most systematic, widespread, and long-term use of the family life cycle idea is provided by Evelyn Duvall, who has attempted to provide a link between life cycle stages with the developmental-task concept.[38] A *developmental task* is one that arises at or about a certain period in the life of an individual. Successful achievement of the task leads to happiness and success with later tasks, while failure leads to unhappiness in the individual, disapproval by society, and difficulty with later tasks. These tasks have two primary origins: (1) physical maturation, and (2) cultural pressures and privileges.[39] The number of developmental tasks an individual faces are innumerable. Many of them are delineated in human development textbooks.

This theory contends that, like the individual, families have tasks that arise at a given stage in the family life cycle. A family's developmental task is "a

---

36. For a discussion and empirical evaluation of this concept, *see* Paul C. Glick, "The Family Life Cycle and Social Change," *Family Relations* 38 (April 1989): 123–129; Graham B. Spanier and Paul C. Glick, "The Life Cycle of American Families: An Expanded Analysis," *Journal of Family History* 5 (Spring 1980): 97–111; and Elizabeth Menaghan, "Marital Stress and Family Transitions: A Panel Analysis," *Journal of Marriage and the Family* 45 (May 1983): 371–386.

37. *See* for example: Gunhild O. Hagestad, "Demographic Change and the Life Course: Some Emerging Trends in the Family Realm," *Family Relations* 37 (October 1988): 405–410; and Tamara K. Hareven and Kanji Masaoka, "Turning Points and Transitions: Perceptions of the Life Course," *Journal of Family History* 13 (1988): 271–289.

38. Evelyn M. Duvall and Brent C. Miller, *Marriage and Family Development,* 6th ed. (New York: Harper and Row, 1985): Chapter 3.

39. Ibid., p. 47.

growth responsibility that arises at a certain stage in the life of a family, the successful achievement of which leads to present satisfaction, approval and success with later tasks whereas failure leads to unhappiness in the family, disapproval by society, and difficulty with later family developmental tasks."[40] For families to continue to grow as a unit, they need to satisfy at a given stage: (1) biological requirements, (2) cultural imperatives, and (3) personal aspirations and values.

Duvall recognizes and depicts the family life cycle as consisting of eight stages:

*Stage 1.* Married couples (without children)
*Stage 2.* Childbearing families (oldest child birth–30 months)
*Stage 3.* Families with preschool children (oldest child $2\frac{1}{2}$–6 years)
*Stage 4.* Families with school children (oldest child 6–13)
*Stage 5.* Families with teenagers (oldest child 13–20 years)
*Stage 6.* Families as launching centers (first child gone to last child's leaving home)
*Stage 7.* Middle-aged parents (empty nest to retirement)
*Stage 8.* Aging family members (retirement to death of both spouses)[41]

These stages are determined by the age and school placement of the oldest child up to the launching stage, after which the situation facing those remaining in the original family is used. This type of scheme explicitly fails to recognize multiple-child families, overlapping stages, death of a spouse, and many other variations in families. But this scheme, as any, serves as a division for study and analysis, though in reality the family life cycle and each stage within it has no beginning and no end.

While Duvall used the oldest child as the basic determinant of stage divisions, Rodgers[42] believes that this usage does not account adequately for group initiates, thus giving a false impression of a smooth progression from one life-cycle stage to the next. He also rejected using the oldest child on the grounds that there was no way to account for families in which the death of a spouse or child occurred prior to the launching of all children, nor was there a way to handle families in which divorce, disability, or other events might interrupt the smooth progress from one stage to the next.

Rodgers also prefers to use the term *category* in preference to *stage* on the grounds that categories are analytical devices constructed by the researcher, rather than any "real" condition of families. It is Rodgers's belief that "a conceptual framework for family development investigations should lead to a better understanding of the phenomenon being described in the

40. Ibid., p. 61.
41. Ibid., p. 26.
42. Roy H. Rodgers, "Toward a Theory of Family Development," *Journal of Marriage and the Family* 26 (August 1964): 262–270.

various life-cycle category schemes and, ultimately, should lead to some theory of family development."[43] One example of an empirical study using family life-cycle categories can be seen in Chapter 12, which includes a section on marital satisfaction over the family life cycle. Chapters 12 through 15 in general follow a family life-cycle model.[44]

## SUMMARY

1. This chapter noted the range of disciplines, approaches, and selected frames of reference widely used in the study of the family. The marriage and family area is highly interdisciplinary with no single discipline either asking all the questions or knowing all the answers. This book uses a social science orientation with a major concentration focused on a sociology of the family.

2. Only in the last one hundred years has there been any systematic study of the family. In the mid-1800s, family interests focused on grand evolutionary schemes of change and philosophical speculation. By the turn of the century, social problems relating to the family led to a concern for social reform and with it to some systematic data gathering. This was followed by refinements in research methodology and a concern over social theory. It has only been since the middle of this century that the findings of earlier studies were summarized, conceptual frameworks were systematically presented, and theory building was of central concern.

3. As the foundation upon which the entire book is based, this chapter summarizes the nature of conceptual frameworks, frames of reference, and theory in general and provides an overview of five basic approaches: structural-functional, social conflict, symbolic interaction, social exchange, and developmental.

4. In this chapter and several that follow, considerable attention is given to concepts and their definitions. Although definitions of concepts are seldom the most interesting reading, they are miniature "systems of meaning" that permit the viewing of a phenomenon in a certain way and the sharing of that view with others. In addition, concepts are basic to the development of hypotheses, propositions, and theories. When concepts are interrelated to describe and classify phenomena,

---

43. Rodgers, "Toward a Theory," p. 263. His attempt to produce and apply this theory can be seen in Roy H. Rodgers, *Family Interaction and Transaction: The Developmental Approach* (Englewood Cliffs, N. J.: Prentice-Hall, 1973).

44. Key concepts in the developmental approach are life cycle, developmental tasks, norms, roles, role sequence, role cluster, role complex, position, positional career, and sanction.

Some of the leading advocates of this perspective include Reuben Hill, Roy H. Rodgers, Joan Aldous, Evelyn Duvall, and Robert J. Havighurst.

From the perspective of the family, you may wish to examine Joan Aldous, *Family Careers: Developmental Change in Families* (New York: Wiley, 1978); Evelyn M. Duvall and Brent C. Miller, *Marriage and Family Development*, 6th ed. (New York: Harper and Row, 1985); Roy H. Rodgers, *Family Interaction and Transaction: The Developmental Approach* (Englewood Cliffs, N. J.: Prentice-Hall, 1973); and Arthur J. Norton, "Family Life Cycle: 1980," *Journal of Marriage and the Family* 45 (May 1983); 267–275.

the result is a conceptual framework. Conceptual frameworks, generally descriptive classification schemes, provide a basis for the establishment of hypotheses and propositions — statements interrelating concepts. When propositions are logically and systematically interrelated to explain some particular process, the result is theory.

5. One of the most dominant "theories" or frames of reference in sociology is the structural-functional theory. This frame of reference has the social system as the basic autonomous unit of which the family is a subsystem. All systems have interdependent parts (structures) that do certain things for the individual or society and have various social consequences (functions). The basic task of functional analysis is to explain the parts, the relationship between the parts and the whole, and the functions that are performed by or result from the relationship formed by the parts.

6. A second frame of reference receiving increasing attention is that of social conflict. Two basic factors of significance in this perspective are the view of conflict (1) as natural and inevitable, and (2) as a major factor that can lead to social change. Marxian conflict-theorists focus on economic inequalities, while feminist conflict-theorists focus on gender inequalities and male dominance. Conflict theory is particularly applicable to a further understanding of the marital relationship, power, the division of labor, and conflict at both a macro (societal) and a micro (interpersonal) level.

7. The symbolic interaction frame of reference addresses itself to two major questions, both of central concern to the family: socialization and personality. The basic premises of this approach are that human beings act toward things on the basis of the meanings things have for them; these meanings are derived from interaction with others; and these meanings are modified through an interpretive process. The human being is unique unto himself or herself, understood only in his or her social context, is neither inherently good nor bad, and responds to self-stimulating or symbolically interpreted stimuli.

8. The social exchange framework helps us to understand why certain behavioral outcomes occur given a set of structural conditions and interactional potentialities. Two different approaches to exchange were examined. One was consistent with a behavioral frame of reference and the other more consistent with an interactionist frame of reference. At various points throughout the book, you will note the use of this framework in dealing with mate selection, marriage, power, and other topics.

9. The developmental frame of reference attempts to join together various parts of other delineated theoretical efforts but has the peculiar characteristic of attempting to simultaneously account for change in the family system and change in patterns of interaction over time. Thus, the central concepts include many used in the other frameworks with the additional basic concepts of the family life cycle and family life course. An outgrowth of these concepts has been numerous attempts to establish, describe, and analyze stages of development.

10. In this text, the general outline from Chapters 10 through 15 follows broad stages of the life cycle, moving from premarital processes to marital, parental, middle years, and aging. Our attention next turns to the family as a social institution, establishing the boundaries of marital, family, and kin groups and systems and examining selected structural features of this basic institution.

# KEY TERMS AND TOPICS

# DISCUSSION QUESTIONS

1. Examine the family and marriage books suggested for reading. What disciplines are represented? How do they differ in their content and approach to the family?

2. Since no one discipline has "all the answers" to any family problem, why isn't all research of an interdisciplinary nature? What problems exist in interdisciplinary research?

3. Of what value is a social science approach to the family? Within the social sciences, can you differentiate how psychology, social psychology, social anthropology, and sociology would approach the family as an area of study?

4. Identify folklore that relates to mate selection, weddings, sexual behavior, childbirth, "successful" marriages, and so on. Which tales are likely to be changed by "science"?

5. The period of 1890–1920 was characterized as an era of social reform. It was followed by empirical studies (1920–1950) and, more recently, theory building. Is it likely that these patterns are cyclical? That is, are we likely to get away from theory and return to reform, which will later be followed by a stress on science, followed by theory, etc.? Why or why not?

6. Differentiate between concepts and variables, hypotheses and propositions, and conceptual frameworks and theories.

7. Discuss what you perceive to be the major functions of the family in the United States. How are these different from the functions of families thirty years ago? What functions do you expect the family to perform thirty years from now?

8. Do you believe that conflict is natural and inevitable in all marriages and families? Is conflict essential for change?

9. What types of assumptions, questions, and concerns are basic to a symbolic interaction frame of reference? How is it similar to or different from other psychological or social-psychological theories? What difference does it make to assume that humans must be studied on their own level, the human infant is asocial, and the like? Relate these ideas to marriage or the family.

10. Write a paragraph on "Who I am." How often do you identify yourself by listing statuses you occupy? Lengthen this list of statuses and write one or two social expectations appropriate to each status. Which role expectations do you personally find displeasing? Are there conflicts between different expectations or between your personal preference and the social expectation? How do you handle them?

11. What exchanges can you identify in explaining male-female sexual behavior, husband-wife spending patterns, or parent-child disciplinary behavior? What is given by each and received in return? Can you think of examples where no reciprocity is expected or given in return for a favor or gift?

12. Identify the stage of the family life cycle for yourself and for your parents. Identify the central problems, concerns, and tasks of families at these particular stages.

# FURTHER READINGS

Adams, Bert N. *The Family: A Sociological Interpretation.* New York: Harcourt Brace Jovanovich, 1986. A sociological, cross-cultural, interpretative look at the family.

Aldous, Joan. *Family Careers: Developmental Change in Families.* New York: Wiley, 1978. A developmental analysis of families covering the framework, the important concepts, and their application from the time families are formed until they are dissolved.

Burr, Wesley R.; Hill, Reuben; Nye, F. Ivan; and Reiss, Ira L. *Contemporary Theories About the Family.* Vol. 2. New York: The Free Press, 1979. This second volume has five chapters dealing with exchange, symbolic interaction, general systems, conflict, and phenomenological approaches to the family.

Collins, Randall. *Sociology of Marriage and the Family: Gender, Love, and Property.* Chicago: Nelson-Hall, 1985. A sociology text that incorporates conflict and feminist perspectives into family issues and studies.

Filsinger, Eric E. *Biosocial Perspectives on the Family.* Newbury Park, CA: Sage Publications, Inc., 1988. A variety of disciplines examine the complex issue of biological influences on family behavior.

Goode, William J. *The Family.* 2d ed. Englewood Cliffs, N. J.: Prentice-Hall, 1982. A brief but intense look at the complex relationships between family systems and the larger social structure.

Hareven, Tamara K. "Historical Analysis of the Family" in *Handbook of Marriage and the Family* by Marvin B. Sussman and Suzanne K. Steinmetz (eds.). New York: Plenum Press, 1987, Chapter 2, pp. 37–58. An historical investigation of origins of the family field; family, household, and kinship structure; family development; and an understanding of social change.

LaRossa, Ralph, ed. *Family Case Studies.* New York: The Free Press, 1984. A presentation and analysis of fourteen case studies that attempts to get students involved in the discovery of how families work.

Larzelere, Robert L., and Klein, David M. "Methodology" in *Handbook of Marriage and the Family* by Marvin B. Sussman and Suzanne K. Steinmetz (eds.). New York: Plenum Press, 1987, Chapter 6, pp. 125–156. A discussion of the implications for conceptualization, research design, data collection, and data analysis of the family as a small group; the time-ordered and value-laden nature of the family; and other general methodological issues.

Miller, Brent C. *Family Research Methods.* Newbury Park, Calif.: Sage Publications, 1986. A concise synthesis of the methodological techniques used in studying families.

Mintz, Steven, and Kellogg, Susan. *Domestic Revolutions: A Social History of American Family Life.* New York: The Free Press, 1988. An historical overview of U.S. families starting with New England and including families during periods of slavery, industrialization, the Great Depression, and the radical departures in family life since 1960.

Nye, F. Ivan, ed. *Family Relationships: Rewards and Costs.* Beverly Hills, Cal.: Sage Publications, 1982. An application of choice theory—that is, exchange theory—to various aspects of family relationships.

Osmond, Marie Withers. "Radical-Critical Theories" in *Handbook of Marriage and the Family* by Marvin B. Sussman and Suzanne K. Steinmetz (eds.). New York: Plenum Press, 1987, Chapter 5, pp. 103–124. A discussion of the emergence of radical-critical sociology, critical views of other theories, and substantive applications.

Thomas, Darwin L., and Wilcox, Jean Edmondson. "The Rise of Family Theory: A Historical and Critical Analysis" in *Handbook of Marriage and the Family* by Marvin B. Sussman and Suzanne K. Steinmetz (eds.). New York: Plenum Press, 1987, Chapter 4, pp. 81–102. A review of family theory at three time periods: in the 1800s, from 1900–1950, and since 1950.

# CHAPTER THREE

# MARITAL, FAMILY, AND KINSHIP ORGANIZATION

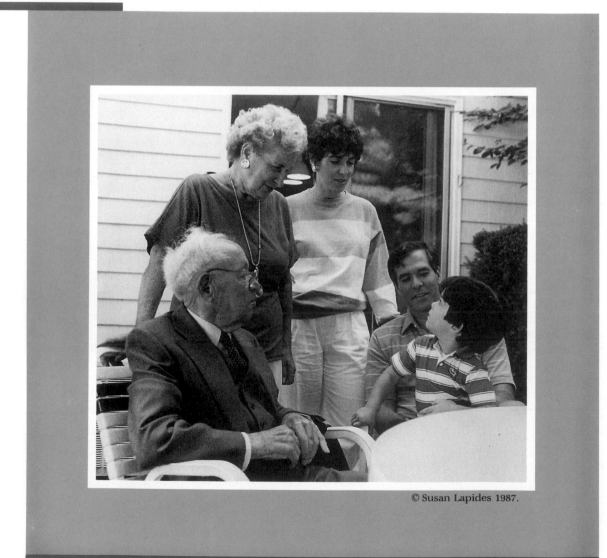

© Susan Lapides 1987.

Chapter 2 noted a variety of interdisciplinary, social science, and theoretical approaches to family study. Basic to any approach are selected concepts and distinctions that provide "systems of meaning" to an aspect of the world in which we live. You have already noted various ways in which "function" is used by family scholars, dual perceptions of "role"—depending upon its use in a structural or interactional frame of reference—and the different schools of thought evident in the social exchange framework. Likewise, families take on new and varied perspectives when viewed in institutional terms; when seen as a social group or social system; or when differentiated from marriages and kin, orientation and procreation, nuclear and extended, and the like. This chapter makes note of these and other conceptual distinctions in study and understanding of the family.

## THE FAMILY AS A SOCIAL INSTITUTION

Frequent reference is made to the family as the most basic of all institutions. It is most closely linked to the supporting institution of marriage. What is meant by this? The concept "institution" refers to certain specific areas of human social life that have become broadly organized into discernible patterns. It refers to the organized means whereby the essential tasks of a society are organized, directed, and carried out. In short, it denotes the system of norms that organize human behavior into stable patterns of activity.

*Institution* is a noun, *institutionalize* is a verb. The noun *institution* refers to "a system of norms, values, statuses, and roles that develop around a basic social goal."[1] All societies must deal with sexual activity, the care of dependent children, the social relations established by sexual unions, and the birth of children. The institutional norms concerned with these matters constitute the familial or kinship institutions.

The verb *institutionalize* means the establishment of expected, patterned, regular, and predictable behavior; thus, noninstitutionalized behavior is spontaneous and irregular. Typically, a husband-wife fight is noninstitutionalized behavior; a professional boxing match is institutionalized. When something such as dating, premarital sexual behavior, or child rearing becomes institutionalized, this means that it becomes accepted by the society as a necessary, proper, and predictable activity. At this time, although extramarital intercourse is a common activity in American society, it has not been institutionalized; that is, it has not become a part of our standardized, approved, and culturally safeguarded expected behavior.

---

1. J. Ross Eshleman, Barbara G. Cashion, and Laurence Basirico, *Sociology: An Introduction*, 3rd ed. (Boston: Little, Brown and Co., 1988): 133.

Several basic social institutions can be identified in all societies: the familial and kinship, educational, economic, political, and religious institutions appear to have existed in some form in all societies throughout every period of history. Each of these five institutions performs certain functions that are basic for the existence of a given society. However, these are not the only areas that have become institutionalized. In American society, marriage, war, business, communications, medicine, law, science, and recreation have become institutionalized, standardized, and basic to our way of life.

Few institutions have received more recognition, criticism, and critiques than the family system. It has been claimed to be the solution of most problems, on the one hand, and to be the basic cause of problems, on the other. It has been looked upon with hope and dismay. Scientists, clergy, newspaper columnists, parents, and even stockbrokers speak out with authority on this institution. This book is intended to examine the nature of, to describe and interpret, and, hopefully, to get you, the student, to examine and redefine your understanding of this particular social institution: the family.

## FAMILIES AS GROUPS OR SYSTEMS

Family and marital **groups and systems** are basic to a sociology of the family and to the family as a social institution. Family *systems* are used in sociology much as physicists and biologists speak of solar or biological systems. In each instance, a reference is made to a configuration of parts that are related interdependently. All systems, whether living or nonliving, have a characteristic organization and pattern of functioning. All major systems have subsystems that are part of the larger system.

To treat the family as a social system is to note the forms of social organization and its modes of functioning. The family system is one example of interrelated statuses that fulfill certain basic functions. It is a subsystem of the larger society that is related to and interdependent with other subsystems in the society. It fulfills selected tasks for the society that are highly patterned, recurrent, and organized. Within the family system are subsystems (marital systems, mate-selection systems, sexual systems, child-rearing systems) which are also highly patterned, recurrent, and organized in order to fulfill selected tasks. Although persons are a part of the system, it is the statuses, roles, norms, ways of ranking, means of social controls, and the values of those persons (the abstractions) that are of significance in dealing with social systems.

The basic units, therefore, of a marital or family system are not persons but the interrelated statuses (positions) and the expectations (roles) that accompany the interrelated statuses. These interrelated statuses in the family system would include, among others, parent-child, husband-wife, uncle-aunt, grandparent-grandchild, father-mother, or brother-sister. The norms (folkways and mores) and roles, the expectations and values, that accompany these positions are of primary concern to the sociologist. Thus, married males occupy the status of husband. They interact with married females who occupy the status of wife. These interrelated statuses (husband and wife) comprise the marital system. This system too, like the family system or any other system, has sets of norms and expectations that prescribe appropriate and inappropriate behaviors for the specific persons involved. Thus systems are abstractions, forms of social organization composed of interrelated statuses.

Family and marital *groups*, in contrast to systems, are composed of people. These people are concrete realities, rather than abstractions, who are physically present and who interact with one another in terms of their ascribed or achieved statuses. If married, we would belong to a two-person marital group. Our family group would consist of the married partners, the children, plus any other relatives included in the extended family context. Marital or family groups can have a specific address, a specific number of members, a specific income, and specific shared rituals. Marital and family groups are temporary, disbanding when their members depart. The system of which they are a part may continue for centuries—long after the departure or death of any specific member or specific family group.

It is the task of a sociology of the family to examine the nature of marital and family groups within societies and to understand the patterns of organization—the marital and family systems that provide order within and between the groups involved.

## Marriages and families as primary groups

Sociologists view groups as the core of their attention. They speak of in- and out-groups, primary and secondary groups, formal and informal groups, large and small groups, minority and majority groups, open and closed groups, organized and unorganized groups, independent and dependent groups, voluntary and involuntary groups, and others. Some of these ideal-type constructs are more useful to our understanding of family groups than others. One that appears to be particularly important is that of primary group relationships.

A **primary group** consists of a small number of people who interact in personal, direct, and intimate ways. Primary group relationships are facilitated by: (1) face-to-face contact, (2) smallness of size, and (3) frequent and intense contact. Most families in the Western world operate under these conditions. Unlike most primary groups, the family is of a special nature in that it is so essential both to individuals and to society that its formation is usually legitimized by the community through religious and legal rituals. While most other primary groups can disband voluntarily if the members wish it, the dissolution of the family can only be accomplished through institutionalized means.

Much of the importance of marital, family, and kin groups centers around their function as a primary group. First, for most individuals it is this

## The Amish family and community organization

The Amish have a family organization that is monogamous and patriarchal. From the time of marriage until death of one spouse, marriages remain intact. Divorce is extremely rare, desertion is nonexistent, and legal separations are not a matter of awareness—much less of occurrence—among the Amish. These people are highly endogamous in their selection of mates. The birth rate is extremely high when compared with that of the non-Amish American family. Illegitimacy is unknown, due to the fact that a premarital pregnancy necessitates marriage. In short, it would appear that the Amish have one of the most stable and cohesive family systems in the United States.

The Amish family cannot be understood apart from the recognition that it is entirely rural-oriented.

Strong religious convictions and the use of a distinctive language and dress have helped to preserve the Amish way of life. Their subculture would be referred to by sociologists as a *Gemeinschaft*. The Gemeinschaft, like the "folk" society, is conceptualized as a small, isolated, traditional, simple, homogeneous society. The folkways and mores are internalized from birth, and face-to-face oral communication retains a strong sense of togetherness. Customs, goals, and styles of life are not questioned as custom becomes sacred. The smallness, the homogeneous character, the self-sufficiency in economic life, and the distinctiveness of the Amish people and community are the key features of this rural subculture in an urbanized American society.

primary group that serves as the basic socializing agent for the acquisition or internalization of beliefs and attitudes. Second, the family as a primary group constitutes the chief focus for the realization of personal satisfaction. Perhaps more than any other source it is the family that provides each of us with a general sense of well-being, companionship, ego worth, security, and affection. Most of us, when away from home for the first time, experience "homesickness" or a nostalgia for the primary group from which our immediate ties have been severed. Third, the family as a primary group also serves as a basic instrument of social control. The family has an extraordinary capacity to punish deviation and reward conformity, since most of us are dependent upon other group members for meeting psychological needs and for realizing meaningful social experiences.

The polar extreme to the primary group is the **secondary group**. Many, if not most, of our involvements in school, work, or the community are not characterized by the intimate, informal, and personal nature of primary groups but rather are characterized by impersonal, segmental, and utilitarian contacts. Secondary groups are basically goal-oriented rather than person-oriented. The personal life of the bus driver, classmate in a lecture, or insurance salesperson is not of major significance in the fulfillment of the goals established for those situations.

In a society dominated by secondary group relationships, the family, time and again, provides the primary relationships that are vital to our health and happiness. It has been argued that the loss or absence of familial networks of social support has been linked to coronary disease, pregnancy disorders, accidents, suicides, mental hospital commitment, school truancy, ulcers, and lack of recovery from certain types of cancer.[2] Without primary group relationships or the presence of intimate family bonds, it is doubtful that even survival itself is possible. This idea has been fairly well substantiated with infants and adults who have "no" family or close friends. One possible conclusion to all of this is that rather than being in a state of decay, losing its significant function, and being "on its way out," the U.S. family may be fulfilling a primary group function that has seldom been more crucial and important to the stability of the person or the society.

## CHARACTERISTICS OF MARRIAGE, FAMILY, AND KINSHIP GROUPS

Marriage, family, and kinship groups are institutionalized social arrangements in all known societies. However, the nature of the arrangements differs greatly across societies, over time, and even within a given society at a specific time. Frequently, the legal and social norms themselves lack clarity as to what does or does not constitute a marriage, family, or kinship group. For example, is it a marriage if two males live together and recognize each other as spouse, if a male and female live together but have no marriage contract or ever experience a wedding ceremony, or if a man and woman go through a marriage ceremony and then almost immediately separate permanently? Can *any* group of persons be considered a marriage, a family, or a kinship group? Let's examine the boundaries of each.

### The boundaries of marriage

Throughout the world, marriage is an institutional arrangement between males and females who recognize self and other as husband and wife. Marriage is a social institution that is strictly human and assumes some permanence and conformity to societal norms.

William Stephens, the anthropologist, says that marriage is (1) a socially legitimate sexual union, begun with (2) a public announcement, undertaken with (3) some idea of performance, and assumed with a more or less explicit (4) marriage contract, which spells out reciprocal obligations between spouses and between spouses and their children.[3]

---

2. Marc Pilisuk and Charles Froland, "Kinship, Social Networks, Social Support and Health," *Social Science and Medicine* 12 (October 1978): 273–280.

3. William N. Stephens, *The Family in Cross Cultural Perspective* (New York: Holt, Rinehart and Winston, 1963): 7.

### Suicide and the family

In 1986, according to information supplied by the U.S. Bureau of the Census, approximately 30,900 persons in the United States committed suicide. This number was equal to 12.8 suicides per 100,000 persons, up from 11.0 in 1980 and 11.6 in 1970. Since 1970, the increase in suicide rates was most dramatic among persons under age 35.

Is it possible that the increase in the number and rate of suicide, particularly in the 15–35 year age group, is a result of less familial support, that is, a decrease in the family as a primary group? If we follow the lead of Emile Durkheim and his classic study of suicide first published in 1897, we would be aware that explanations focusing on the psychology of the individual are inadequate. Second, we would be aware that suicide, most likely the most individual act that anyone is capable of, can only be fully understood in a social and societal context. Third, we would be aware of his notion that the rate of suicide varies inversely with the degree of social integration that a society (or a family?) provides.

Steven Stack attempted to determine the effects of marital dissolution on suicide (*Journal of Marriage and the Family* February 1980). His argument was that a society marked by a high incidence of divorce is low in social integration with respect to the institution of the family. Given a higher incidence of divorce, one indicator of a broken marital and family tie, one would expect more suicidal behavior among those (divorced) persons. His results indicate that the incidence of divorce is closely associated with the rate of suicide even after controlling for the influence of the effects of age composition, percentage black, the rate of interstate migration, and income. While he suggests caution in accepting these results, they do lend some indirect support to the linkage between a lack of social integration in the family and the incidence of suicide and the importance of the family as a primary group.

Ira Reiss and Gary Lee, who are interested in providing a universal definition of marriage, say that marriage is "a socially acceptable union of individuals in husband and wife roles with the key function of legitimation of parenthood."[4]

Any definition of marriage or family is, in a certain sense, arbitrary. Most definitions of marriage exclude persons in same-sex relationships, persons such as children, or persons who do not meet the social or cultural norms that specify what marriage is and who the legitimate partners are. In fact, many phenomenological, conflict, and feminist theorists call into question the very use of labels such as marriage, family, or kin. The suggestion is that the very use of a label reifies, that is, makes real or concrete, a certain reality that ignores the historical origins and the range of meanings that persons in their day-to-day lives give to marriage or family.

Recognizing the danger of reifying the concept, marriage does appear to involve several criteria that are common both historically and cross-culturally. The criteria include:

---

4. Ira L. Reiss and Gary R. Lee, *Family Systems in America*, 4th ed. (New York: Holt, Rinehart and Winston, 1988): 39.

### Can lesbians and gays marry, divorce, and be a family?

In March 1989, an article in the *New York Times* was entitled "Gay Marriages: Make Them Legal." It cited the case of two women who exchanged vows and rings, pledged their love and lifelong devotion to one another, and were spouses for several years in every respect except the legal. However, one of the women was severely injured when her car was struck by a truck. She lost the capacity to walk or to speak more than several words at a time. She needed constant care. The partner sought a court ruling granting her guardianship. But the parents of the injured woman opposed the petition and obtained sole guardianship, moved their daughter 300 miles away from her partner, and forbade all visits between the two women. Were they allowed to be legally married, which at present all fifty states deny to millions of gay and lesbian Americans, this type of forced separation would not have been allowed. Should it have?

Several years earlier, two men in Pennsylvania sought a divorce. But the Pennsylvania State Superior Court ruled that people of the same sex could not contract a common law marriage, and thus were not eligible to divorce. The judges ruled that marriage as a heterosexual activity dated to the nation's beginnings when statutes spoke, as they do now, of husband and wife and bride and groom, which are interpreted to mean male and female. This ruling dismissed an appeal by John DeSanto who had sought for three years to file a divorce action against William Barnsley. Mr. DeSanto claimed that they were married in a common law ceremony on June 14, 1970, before friends and witnesses and now were seeking a divorce.

In July 1989, the New York Court of Appeals, the highest court in the state, ruled that a gay couple who had lived together for a decade could be considered a family under New York City's rent-control regulations. The court said the protection from eviction, previously granted only to people related by blood, marriage, or adoption, should not rest on fictitious legal distinctions or genetic history, but instead should find its foundation in the reality of family life.

In May 1989, the San Francisco Board of Supervisors approved a law that would allow unmarried partners to register their relationships with the city. San Francisco thus joins other cities and governments that are considering domestic partnership laws in a legal recognition of diverse family structures. What is your response to these four rulings?

A heterosexual union, including at least one male and one female

The legitimizing or granting of approval to the sexual relationship and the bearing of children without any loss of standing in the community or society

A public affair rather than a private, personal matter

A highly institutionalized and patterned mating arrangement

An assuming of mutual and reciprocal rights and obligations between the spouses

A binding relationship that assumes some permanence.

## MARRIAGE AND NUMBER OF SPOUSES

Marital status (single, married, separated, widowed, divorced) and number of spouses (none, one, more than one) are two major components of the boundaries of marriage. With a change in marital status and the number of spouses come variations in marital interaction patterns; living and sleeping arrangements, exclusive or nonexclusive sexual interactions; the likelihood of and number of children; patterns of support, decision making, and authority; and male-female roles, to mention a few. Obviously, never to have had a spouse is to have a nonmarital status. The never-married single can be expected to share certain characteristics of other single statuses, yet in many ways differs from that of the widowed or divorced single. The latter two single statuses are discussed in Chapters 15 and 17, respectively.

### Singlehood

In 1988 there were more than 27.0 million males and 22.5 million females in the United States age fifteen and over who were never-married singles.[5] These numbers comprise 29.9 percent of all males and 22.9 percent of all females. White males and white females (28.1 and 20.9 percent, respectively) were less likely to be single than black males (42.5 percent), males of Hispanic origin (36.9 percent), black females (36.9 percent), and females of Hispanic origin (27.3 percent). As expected, the number and percent never-married drops sharply with increasing age. About 97 percent of the men and 90 percent of the women age nineteen and under are single. By age forty-five, only 5.9 percent of the men and 4.5 percent of the women are not and have never been married (*see* Table 1–2).

Since 1970, the percentage of those remaining single has risen sharply. The increase in percentage that are single is particularly apparent in the age groups where most men and women have traditionally married. At ages twenty to twenty-four years, for example, there has been a 70.7 percent increase in the number of single women (from 35.8 in 1970 to 61.1 in 1988) and a 42.0 percent increase in the number of single men (from 54.7 in 1970 to 77.7 in 1988).[6] The increase in the twenty-five to twenty-nine age group is even more dramatic—181 percent for women and 127 percent for men.

Whether the tendency among the younger groups to refrain from marrying represents merely a postponement of first marriage or a development of a trend toward lifelong singleness is not known. However, Paul Glick states that just as cohorts of young women who have postponed childbearing for an unusually long time seldom make up for the child deficit as they grow older, so also young people who are delaying marriage may never make up for the marriage deficit later on.[7] They may try alternatives and like them.

---

5. U.S. Bureau of the Census, *Current Population Reports*, Series P-20, no. 433, "Marital Status and Living Arrangements, March 1988" (Washington, D.C.: U.S. Government Printing Office, 1989), Table 1, pp. 3–5.

6. Ibid., Table A-1, p. 59.

7. Paul C. Glick, "A Demographer Looks at American Families," *Journal of Marriage and the Family* 37 (February 1975): 18.

*Many definitions of marriages and families exclude persons in same sex relationships. While barred from legal marriage, many lesbians and gay men form long-term, committed, primary, intimate relationships which they honor as marriages and view as the basis of families.*

The legitimacy of singleness as a life-style is increasingly recognized by young people. The 1980 Study of American Families at the Institute for Social Research at the University of Michigan included data from 916 families composed of a mother and her eighteen-year-old child. Most of these respondents no longer regarded getting married as necessarily better than remaining single. This was in spite of the finding that more than 90 percent of the eighteen-year-olds expected to marry. To evaluate the strength of their commitment to marry, they were asked how much it would bother them if they did not marry. Only one-fourth indicated it would bother them a great deal, half said it would bother them a little or some, and the remaining quarter indicated it would not bother them at all if they did not marry.[8]

Apparently a new style of singlehood is emerging that represents one of choice and a status that has positive outcomes for happiness, career, and social mobility. Take happiness for example. Studies in the United States have consistently reported considerably higher levels of personal happiness for married persons than for persons in any unmarried category (never-married, divorced, or widowed). But these married/nonmarried differences in happiness appear to have lessened over the past two decades.[9] The change occurred primarily through an increase in the reported happiness of never-married males and a decrease in the reported happiness of married females. Findings

---

8. Arland Thornton and Deborah Freedman, "Changing Attitudes Toward Marriage and Single Life," *Family Planning Perspectives* 14 (November/December 1982): 297–303.

9. Norval D. Glenn and Charles N. Weaver, "The Changing Relationship of Marital Status to Reported Happiness," *Journal of Marriage and the Family* 50 (May 1988): 317–324.

## Consumer habits of singles are different

Staying single longer is reshaping the way persons in the United States live and spend their money. For instance, unmarried persons typically spend 50 percent of their food dollars dining out, compared with 37 percent for two-person households. In addition, specialized industries are emerging, such as singles travel agencies and dating services, for people of age-specific categories (such as under thirty). In Michigan, one grocery chain has a singles shopping night where the search extends beyond finding the dairy goods section.

It appears that the buying habits and social attitudes of still-single adults are increasingly mimicking those of married couples. Many singles are fashioning a satisfying independent way of life with the purchases of condominiums, china place settings, and items for the home that once were more likely the province of married couples.

such as these led the authors to question the strong statements about the continued importance of marriage and the widely held belief that the institution of marriage is as strong and viable as ever.

For singles of both sexes, friends are important to their happiness and life satisfaction, but there are some interesting gender differences. A study in Tennessee showed that single men's life satisfaction was related to self-esteem and the availability of a network of individuals with whom interests and values were shared. For women, life satisfaction was based on the presence of affectional close relationships that provided a sense of security and peace.[10] High levels of self-disclosure and emotional involvement with a few intimate friends were important.

The relationship for females between a single status and a higher educational level, higher median income, higher occupational status, and in general a higher level of achievement is a significant one.[11] As you will note in the discussion of the dual-career marriage in Chapter 4, marriage seems to impede career advancement for females. What is unclear is the extent to which the single status results from educational and economic success or the extent to which success results from the single status.

What is clear is that as the median age at marriage increases so does a longer period of singlehood. With later marriage comes the potential for an increased period of independent living away from the parental home. Some consequences of this pattern, particularly for women, were that they were more likely to plan for employment, they lowered their expected family size,

---

10. Janet Cockrum and Priscilla White, "Inferences on the Life Satisfaction of Never-Married Men and Women" *Family Relations* 34 (October 1985): 551–556.

11. Charles W. Mueller and Blair G. Campbell, "Female Occupational Achievement and Marital Status: A Research Note," *Journal of Marriage and the Family* 39 (August 1977): 587–593; and Stephen Mergford and Dorothy B. Darroch, "Marital Status and Female Achievement in Australia: A Research Note," *Journal of Marriage and the Family* 42 (August 1980): 653–656.

## The name of the bride

When a woman in the United States marries, the chances are very high that she will take the surname of the husband. Is this a matter of law or social tradition? Apparently social custom and tradition prevail.

According to a comment in *Parade*, in forty-nine of our states, the bride has a right to use any name she wishes and to maintain her own identity. Only in Hawaii does a law exist that requires the wife to assume the husband's name.

they became more accepting of the employment of mothers, and they were more nontraditional on sex roles than those who lived with parents.[12]

Even among women who never marry, evidence supports the notion that family ties and contacts remain important. One study of lifelong single women illustrated that throughout the life course, they maintained their ties to the family of orientation and emphasized extended kin relationships.[13] Although they did not establish their own families of procreation, the family remained central in the lives of single women.

### *Monogamy*

To most U.S. citizens, the most traditional as well as the "most proper" form of marriage is **monogamy**; one man to one woman (at a time). Throughout the world, this form of marriage is the only one universally recognized and is the predominant form even within societies where other forms exist. Where other forms do exist, most men are too poor to have more than one wife. However, it should be noted that on a societal basis, only about 20 percent of the societies are designated as *strictly* monogamous, that is, monogamy is the required form.[14]

Although the United States is designated as strictly monogamous, it is possible to have more than one husband or one wife. Since monogamy has never achieved perfect stability, certain married persons end their relationship and most of these remarry. Thus, the second spouse, although not existing simultaneously with the first, is sometimes referred to as fitting into a pattern of *sequential monogamy, serial monogamy,* or *remarriage* (*see* Chapter 17). Thus, in U.S. society it is both legally and socially approved to have more than one wife or more than one husband as long as they occur sequentially and not

12. Linda J. Waite, Frances Kobrin Goldscheider, and Christina Witsberger, "Nonfamily Living and the Erosion of Traditional Family Orientation Among Young Adults," *American Sociological Review* 51 (August 1986): 541–554.

13. Katherine R. Allen and Robert S. Pickett, "Forgotten Streams in the Family Life Course: Utilization of Qualitative Retrospective Interviews in the Analysis of Lifelong Single Women's Family Careers," *Journal of Marriage and the Family* 49 (August 1987): 517–526.

14. George P. Murdock, "World Ethnographic Sample," *American Anthropologist* 59 (August 1957): 686.

simultaneously. To a sizable proportion of our population, replacing marriage partners in a sequentially monogamous fashion is a variation on the lifelong, same-spouse, monogamous pattern. In addition, most nontraditional marital life-styles occur within the context of monogamy. Childless marriage, sexual equality, dual careers, androgynous role patterns, and the like are more likely to occur in a one-male–one-female marriage than in any other type. These marital life-styles are discussed elsewhere throughout this book, usually as found within a monogamous situation.

## Polygamy

Distinguished from monogamy is **polygamy**. The suffix -*gamy* refers to marriage or a union for propagation and reproduction. Thus *monogamy* (single), *bigamy* (two), *polygamy* (several or many), *allogamy* (closely related), *endogamy* (within) or *exogamy* (outside or external) describe the nature of marriage. Polygamy refers to the marriage of several or many. Theoretically, there could exist several or many wives (*polygyny*), several or many husbands (*polyandry*), or several or many husbands and wives (*group marriage*), all of which are polygamous marriages, as distinguished from monogamous (one) or bigamous (two) marriages.

The frequency with which the marriage of a plural number of spouses occurs normatively (i.e., as an expected or desired type of marriage) was investigated by George Murdock. In a world sample of 554 societies, polygyny was culturally favored in 415 (77 percent), whereas polyandry was culturally favored in only 4 (less than 1 percent): Toda, Marquesas, Nayar, and Tibet.[15] There is no known society in which group marriage is clearly the dominant, or most frequent, marriage form.[16]

Several words of caution need to be suggested concerning polygamy. First, it is necessary to maintain a clear distinction between ideology and actual occurrence. Occasionally in the United States, a group advocates the right to have as many or as few spouses as desired. Also, when multiple-spouse marriages or communes are located and/or studied, the results are exploited by the mass media and given considerable attention. Perhaps it is uniqueness or rarity that attracts the attention rather than commonality in numerical terms. Second, multiple spouses (except for group marriage) are only possible on a large scale where an unbalanced **sex ratio** (the number of males per 100 females) exists. Only if the sex ratio is either high or low will polygamy be possible without increasing the number of single persons of one sex. Third, polygamy, where it exists, like all forms of marriage, is highly regulated and normatively controlled. Rarely does it involve a strictly personal or psycholog-

---

15. Ibid.
16. Stephens, *The Family in Cross Cultural Perspective*, p. 33.

ical motive. Rather, it is likely to be supported by the attitudes and values of both sexes and linked closely to the sex ratio, economic conditions, and belief systems. Fourth, polygamy itself has many forms and variations of normative structure that determine who the spouse should be. Examples would be where all the multiple husbands are brothers *(fraternal polyandry)*, where all the multiple wives are sisters *(sororal polygyny)*, or in a levirate and sororate arrangement as existed in the ancient Hebrew family. The *levirate* was a situation (technically, sequential monogamy) in which the wife married the brother of her deceased husband, whereas the *sororate* was a situation in which the preferred mate for a husband was the sister of his deceased wife. From the perspective of families in North America, each of the above represents a nontraditional family form. Polygyny and polyandry will be examined in greater detail.

*Polygyny*     **Polygyny** is the most frequent form of polygamy. Although not a rare phenomenon throughout the world, researchers and writers often ignore contemporary polygyny. Charles Welch and Paul Glick suggest that this is due in part to the fact that systematic study is hampered by the persistent absence of adequate amounts of readily accessible and reliable data. However, they selected fifteen African countries to illustrate its incidence (polygynists per hundred married men), intensity (number of wives per polygynist), and general index (number of wives per married man).[17] The incidence of polygyny per hundred men was typically between twenty and thirty-five, that is, from about one in five to one in three married men having more than one wife. The intensity ranged from 2.0 to 2.5. This indicates that most polygynists had two wives rather than three or more. And for the country as a whole, the general index (number of wives per married man) ranged from 1.1 to 1.6. This indicates most men, even in highly polygynous countries, had one wife only.

Polygyny appears to be the privilege of the wealthy. Often, having several wives is a mark of prestige, distinction, and high status. Chiefs, the wealthy, the best hunters, and the leaders get the second or third wife. Even in Israel, throughout the Old Testament biblical period, polygyny was practiced but often restricted to men who were rich, occupied leading positions, or had some other claim to distinction. Even today in the Middle East, the "common man" has only one wife.

Why more than one wife? Many circumstances and motives contribute to polygyny. The prestige and status dimension has been mentioned. Sometimes there is a need or a desire to facilitate procreation, particularly that of male children; however, evidence also exists to show that polygyny tends to reduce

---

17. Charles E. Welch, III and Paul C. Glick, "The Incidence of Polygamy in Contemporary Africa: A Research Note," *Journal of Marriage and the Family* 43 (February 1981): 191–193.

fertility for women in these marriages.[18] This may be a consequence of age at marriage, of added wives having previous marital disruptions, of senior wives insisting on sexual abstinence later in life, or of husbands being considerably older at the time second and third wives are added. The husband's death results in widows with lower levels of completed fertility than among monogamous wives.[19]

Other reasons given for polygyny include wife capture (where the men from one village literally take, or capture, wives from another village), the economic value of wifely services, and in some instances religious revelation. The frequently cited example of Mormon polygyny originated in a religious revelation to Joseph Smith, the founder of the Mormon religion. Interestingly, some of the very factors that led to the occurrence of polygyny in this religion were the same factors that led to its being outlawed. It was begun and maintained by a devout conviction of carrying out God's will. It was ended by a revelation from God to the president of the church forbidding the continuation of polygyny.

One way in which Christianity stamped Western society was in this very manner—by outlawing polygyny. Polygyny was frequent among the pre-Christian tribes of Europe as well as in Old Testament Hebrew accounts:

> Gideon, the Israelite judge, had many wives who bore him seventy sons (Judges 8:30). King David had several wives (Samuel 25:39, 43: II Samuel 3:2 ff.: 5:13), and King Solomon, of course, had a huge number of them (I Kings 9:16; Song of Solomon 6:8).

Most readers of this text, socialized in the Western world and frequently in a Judeo-Christian tradition, are not likely to favor polygyny as a personal life-style. They suspect jealousy, competition, and conflict as disruptive factors among the multiple wives. In fact, data from Ibadan, Nigeria, where polygyny is a very common fact of life indicate that among all wives, when asked how they would feel if their husbands took another wife, some 60 percent said they would be pleased: to share the housework, husband care, and child minding and to have someone to gossip and "play" with.[20] Jealousy among plural wives, however, does seem to be considerably more frequent than jealousy among co-husbands. Several reasons may exist for this. The greater likelihood of jealousy among co-wives may stem from the fact that they are more frequently chosen, whereas men are more likely to do the choosing in determining

---

18. *See* Douglas L. Anderton and Rebecca Jean Emigh, "Polygynous Fertility: Sexual Competition versus Progeny," *American Journal of Sociology* 4 (January 1989): 832–855; Nan E. Johnson and A. M. Elmi, "Polygamy and Fertility in Somalia," *Journal of Biosocial Science* 21 (1989): 127–134; and Alfred A. Adewuyi, "Marital Fertility in Polygynous Unions in Nigeria," *Journal of Biosocial Science* 20 (1988): 393–400.

19. L. L. Bean and G. P. Mineau, "The Polygyny-Fertility Hypothesis: A Re-evaluation." *Population Studies* 40 (1986): 67–81.

20. Helen Ware, "Polygyny: Women's Views in a Traditional Society, Nigeria 1975," *Journal of Marriage and the Family* (February 1979): 188.

whether to be a co-spouse. Having less choice in the matter of being married may contribute to a much greater potential for jealousy. In addition, it has been suggested that multiple husbands are more likely to be brothers than are co-wives. If this is the case, it is possible that jealousy would be less among siblings than among nonsiblings. However, this factor needs additional clarification.

Viewing polygyny cross-culturally, polygynous families evidence specific organizational features:

1. In certain matters, sex particularly, co-wives have clearly defined equal rights;
2. each wife is set up in a separate establishment; and
3. the senior wife is given special powers and privileges.[21]

It has always been suggested that if co-wives are sisters, they usually live in the same house; if co-wives are not sisters, they usually live in separate houses. The deduction follows: for some reason, siblings can better tolerate, suppress, and live with a situation of sexual rivalry than can nonsiblings.

What about polygyny in the United States today? The most frequently cited sources of polygyny are those of certain Mormon fundamentalists living in underground polygynous family units in Utah and neighboring states. The number of these marriages is unknown.

*Polyandry*  This appears to be quite rare. Stephens makes several generalizations about polyandry.[22] First, he notes that polyandry and group marriage tend to go together; where you find one you are likely to find the other.

Second, co-husbanding is fraternal. In the few cases in which the husbands are not brothers, they are clan-brothers, that is, they belong to the same clan and are of the same generation. As stated, this factor of being brothers may reduce the likelihood of jealousy. Among the Todas, a non-Hindu tribe in India, it is understood that when a woman marries a man she becomes the wife of his brothers at the same time. In that tribe, jealousy does not seem to present difficulty and disputes among the brothers rarely arise.

Third, an economic inducement is often mentioned. A man tries to recruit co-husbands so they will work for him. In other instances, co-husbandry is practiced for economic security or as an answer to the land shortage. When several men marry one woman, the fragmentation of holdings, especially in land, is avoided. Cassidy and Lee argue that economic factors are

---

21. Note Joyce Sween and Remi Clignet, "Type of Marriage and Residential Choices in an African City," *Journal of Marriage and the Family* 36 (November 1974): 780–793; and Remi Clignet and Joyce A. Sween, "For A Revisionist Theory of Human Polygyny," *Signs: Journal of Women in Culture and Society* 6 (1981): 445–468.

22. Stephens, *The Family in Cross Cultural Perspective*, pp. 39–49.

the key to understanding the very existence of polyandry.[23] That is, the two most important antecedents to polyandry appear to be (1) extreme societal poverty with harsh environmental conditions, and (2) limited roles for women in the productive economy.

Where polyandry does exist, there is frequent mention of female infanticide. It is a curious anomaly that male infanticide is rarely, if ever, mentioned in the literature. Female infanticide eliminates the wife surplus among polyandrous families; however, male infanticide does not seem to be used to eliminate the husband surplus in polygynous societies.

Two studies of polyandry among a tribal group in Brazil tended to support some of the ideas just presented.[24] Polyandry was more prevalent in the tribe in earlier years when the sex ratio was very unbalanced (149 males per 100 females), female infanticide had been known to exist, and fraternal polyandry appeared to minimize family conflict. Unlike other reports, the Brazilian tribe had no marriage ceremonies for primary or secondary husbands, and property and inheritance rights were not considerations for marriage. In revisiting the Brazilian tribe in 1980, there was no polyandry but female infanticide was still practiced. There was no apparent cultural consciousness of the linkage between this practice and the shortage of female spouses of marital age. Males were wanted because they served as a protection against enemy raids. While polyandry is rarely found throughout the world, it is another variation of the traditional monogamous marital life-style.

*Group marriage*   This exists when several males and several females are married simultaneously to each other. Except on an experimental basis it is an extremely rare occurrence and may never have existed as a viable form of marriage for any society in the world. The Oneida community of New York State has been frequently cited as an example of a group marriage experiment (*see* "Oneida Today" insert). It involved economic and sexual sharing based on spiritual and religious principles. The Oneida group was an experimental religious community and not representative of the society. In addition, like most group marriages on record, its time span was limited. Rarely do they endure beyond one or two generations.

Where group marriage does exist, the strong negative reactions of persons who are aware of it force anonymity and secrecy. Thus, it seems reasonable to assume that group marriage will never become very popular. It has various difficulties and shortcomings that include, among others, getting all members to accept each other as "spouse"; avoiding jealousy over status,

---

23. Margaret L. Cassidy and Gary R. Lee, "The Study of Polyandry: A Critique and Synthesis," *Journal of Comparative Family Studies* 20 (Spring 1989): 1–11.

24. John F. Peters and Chester L. Hunt, "Polyandry Among the Yanomama Shirishana," *Journal of Comparative Family Studies* 6 (Autumn 1975): 197–207; and John F. Peters, "Polyandry Among the Yanomama Shirishana Revisited," *Journal of Comparative Family Studies* 13 (Spring 1982): 89–95.

### Oneida today: Group marriage out—profits in

The Oneida Community began in New York in 1848 with approximately twenty-five members. The leader, John Humphrey Noyes, gave up law to enter the ministry. He preached that human beings were capable of living sinless lives based on a spiritual equality of all persons: materially, socially, and sexually. Monogamy was a sign of selfish possessiveness.

Under the charismatic leadership of this man, the group grew and prospered. The emphasis was on "we" rather than on "I." Economically, there was self-sufficiency and equal ownership of property. They made traps, marketed crops in cans and glass jars, did silk spinning, and manufactured silverware. To eliminate feelings of discrimination and sexual inequality, jobs were rotated.

The group differed from most other communal groups in their "group marriage" or pantogamous (marriage for all) relationships. It was felt that romantic love made spiritual love impossible to attain and gave rise to jealousy, hate, and the like; therefore, everyone should literally "love" everyone else. Requests for sexual relationships were made to a central committee. A go-between, usually an older woman, would get the consent of the requested female (women rarely made requests), and, if agreed upon, the couple would go to the woman's bedroom.

Any discord or problems among the members was handled daily in a practice known as "mutual criticism" where the followers would subject themselves to criticism by the rest of the group. The criticized member would sit quietly while the others listed good and bad points. The result was said to be a catharsis, a spiritual cleansing, with remarkably successful outcomes.

When Noyes left the group for Canada in 1879, for whatever reason (outside pressures, age, health, intra-commune strife), the group marriage practice came to an end but the economically successful venture continued.

On November 20, 1880, the group incorporated as Oneida Community, Ltd., to succeed Oneida Community. The present title, *Oneida Ltd.,* was adopted in 1935. Today, you can find Oneida Ltd. listed on the New York Stock Exchange. A recent chairman of the board was Peter T. Noyes, a grandson of John Humphrey Noyes, the founder of the Oneida Community. The company makes flatware, silverplated and pewter holloware, jewelry, and gift items. The company also markets tableware products and makes cookware and industrial wire products. This international corporation has plants in Arkansas, New York (three), Massachusetts, Kansas, England (three), Canada, and Northern Ireland. In January 1990, the stock was selling at $15 per share and in the past year it paid a 48-cent dividend per share. Yes, Mr. Noyes, your children and grandchildren have prospered well. While group marriage is out, profits are in.

privileges, affection, or sex; and other problems related to housing, income, children, privacy, or division of labor in general.

## *The boundaries of the family*

The family signifies a set of statuses and roles acquired through marriage and through procreation, adoption, or both. Stephens defines a family as a social arrangement based on marriage and the marriage contract, including recognition of the rights and duties of parenthood; common residence for husband, wife, and children; and reciprocal economic obligations between husband and wife.[25]

25. Stephens, *The Family in Cross Cultural Perspective,* p. 8.

Reiss and Lee define the family institution as "a small, kinship-structured group with the key function of nurturant socialization of the newborn."[26] Again, recognizing the dangers of reifying the concept, the family also appears to include and share various criteria or elements:

It includes persons who are united by marriage, blood, or adoption.
Its primary members share a common residence.
Its members assume reciprocal rights and obligations to one another.
It provides the key function of socialization, particularly of the infant.

It could be said that all marriages are families but not all families are marriages. And certain functions expected in the marital relationship (such as sexual relationships) are taboo among certain family members (such as between brother and sister). As marriages differ structurally in the number of spouses, so do families differ structurally in their size and composition.

## A TYPOLOGY OF FAMILY STRUCTURES

One controversy in the family literature has focused on the extent to which families, particularly in the United States, are small, isolated, independent units as opposed to large, interdependent networks. The polar extremes are usually represented by a nuclear-versus-extended dichotomy with modified-nuclear and modified-extended as intermediate positions. The major characteristics of these types are outlined in Table 3–1.

### The nuclear and conjugal family

**Nuclear and conjugal families** refer to the family unit in its smallest form. Generally it includes the husband, wife, and their immediate children. The terms *nuclear* and *conjugal* are at times used interchangeably; however, the conjugal family must include a husband and wife. A nuclear family may or may not include the marriage partners but consists of any two or more persons related to one another by blood, marriage, or adoption, assuming they are of the same or adjoining generations. Thus a brother and sister or a single parent and child are nuclear families but would not, technically speaking, be conjugal families.

Since most persons marry, it is likely that during their lifetime they will be members of two different but overlapping nuclear families. The nuclear family in which they are born and reared (consisting of self, brothers and sisters, and parents) is termed the **family of orientation**. This is the family where the first and most basic socialization processes occur.

26. Reiss and Lee, *Family Systems in America*, p. 24.

*Table 3–1*
**A typology of family structures**

| Nuclear/Conjugal | Modified-nuclear/<br>Modified-extended | Extended |
|---|---|---|
| Small size | Intermediate size | Many kin |
| Geographic isolation | Kin within easy visiting distance | Geographic proximity |
| Minimal kin contact | Regular contact | Daily contact |
| Family autonomy | Family autonomy with kin influences in decision making | Intergenerational authority |
| Self-sufficient economically | Considerable exchange of goods and services | Economic interdependence |
| Non-kin models of socialization | Kin, friendship, non-kin models of socialization | Kinship network as model for socialization |
| Emotional support and protection from non-kin | Emotional support and protection from kin and non-kin | Kinship completed source of emotional support and protection |

When an individual marries, he or she forms a new nuclear (and conjugal) family: a **family of procreation**. This family is composed of self, spouse, and children.

The controversy over whether the family in the United States and Canada is nuclear centers on questions related to geographical isolation, economic independence, and social autonomy. Are there families living separately from kin? Do other relatives outside the nuclear unit provide financial assistance or aid in times of need? Are kin ties significant in relation to emotional support, visiting patterns, or social activities? And if the nuclear family is isolated, independent, and autonomous, would this not lead to high divorce, the need for more public assistance programs for the aged, single parents, or families in poverty, and an increase in personal instability (alcoholism, suicide, mental illness, and the like)? Whatever the actual state of the family, questions such as these seem to be highly relevant to the health of individuals as well as to the functioning of societies.

## The modified-nuclear and modified-extended family

A number of writers have suggested that the isolated nuclear family is largely fictitious. That is, families of procreation as well as never-married single, widowed, and divorced persons are actually functioning within a network of other nuclear families and social networks, offering services and gifts, and maintaining close contact with them.[27] Thus the idea of a modified form of nuclear or extended family has developed. In a *modified-nuclear* or *modified-extended* family structure, nuclear families retain considerable autonomy and yet maintain a coalition with other nuclear families where they exchange contacts, goods, and services. These modified-nuclear/modified-extended families take intermediate positions between the isolated, independent, small nuclear units and the interdependent kin networks of the extended family (*see* Table 3−1).

One indicator of the prevalence of the modified-extended family in the United States was provided by a fifteen-year study of extended households among middle-aged black and white women.[28] At some time over the fifteen-year period, nearly one-third of white, middle-aged women and two-thirds of black women of the same ages experienced this household form. This led the writers to conclude that contrary to popular perceptions, extended families are a relatively common form of living arrangement for adults in the United States, if only for short periods of time.

## The extended family

**Extended family** refers to family structures that extend beyond the nuclear family. As stated, there may be a multiple number of nuclear family groupings within the extended family. Sometimes the terms *consanguine families* and *joint families* are used interchangeably with *extended families.* The consanguine family refers to the joining of nuclear families on the basis of blood relationships or on the basis of descent from the same ancestors so that several generations of offspring are included within one family unit as in an extended family. The difference is that blood ties are emphasized—those between parents and children or between brothers and sisters—over marital ties.

The **joint family** is not used as frequently today as in times past. The term has most often been associated with large families in India where at least two brothers with their own wives and children lived together in the same household. The joint family was consanguine in that the brothers were related by blood and extended in that the wives of the brothers (sisters-in-law) and their children (nephews, nieces, and cousins) lived together. The family was joint in that there existed a common treasury, common kitchen and dining

---

27. Eugene Litwak and Stephen Kulis, "Technology, Proximity and Measures of Kin Support," *Journal of Marriage and the Family* 49 (August 1987): 649−661; and Naomi Gerstel, "Divorce and Kin Ties: The Importance of Gender," *Journal of Marriage and the Family* 50 (February 1988): 209−219. *See also* the classical article on this topic by Marvin B. Sussman, "The Isolated Nuclear Family: Fact or Fiction," *Social Problems* 6 (Spring 1959): 333−340.

28. Rubye W. Beck and Scott H. Beck, "The Incidence of Extended Households Among Middle-Aged Black and White Women," *Journal of Family Issues* 10(June 1989): 147−168.

*Most ethnic groups give high priority to extended kin relationship and, even when not sharing a common household, get together for special occasions, keep in touch with one another, and share goods and services.*

room, and common deities. This Indian form of joint family was usually patrilineal and patrilocal and emphasized filial and fraternal solidarity.

The smallest variety of extended family type is the **stem family**. Normally the stem family consists of two families in adjacent generations, based on economic blood ties. An example of this type of family would be the rural Irish where the family consists, for example, of a father and mother living in the same household with a married son, his wife, and children. This type of family is a common device for maintaining intact the family estate. In contrast to the joint family, the plural number of male members of the original family would not pool their resources. Rather, the estate would belong only to the son to whom it is given by the father. The father would continue to live in the place to contribute his labor and derive his living from it. The other sons are given a cash settlement in lieu of their share of the land, and they then leave the family place.

Irrespective of the specific structure of the extended family, kin have both instrumental and psychological value. Close emotional relationships, especially between grandparents and grandchildren, can be quite important. Close kin serve to relieve parents from being the sole sources of affection and care and can often diffuse overly intense relationships between parents and children. Kin can become important objects of identification and social learning. Older kin can provide experiences of historical continuity and awareness of important aspects of the life cycle. Extended kin are also important for stable transmission of an ideology and value system. Given the importance of these

## Mexican- or Spanish-Americans and compadrazgo

The Mexican- or Spanish-American family extends beyond the immediate family unit (la casa) to include two other similar but distinguishable systems—the extended family (la familia) and godparents (los compadres). The extended family is generally viewed as the primary and most important institution in the community and the key source of identity and support. The importance of this unit is reflected in familism, the idea that the family holds priority over the individual. In other words, individual values and wishes are secondary to the needs and interests of the family unit.

Ties between extended families are pro-moted by a social system involving godparenthood (compadrazgo). Its most common form is co-parenthood, linking two families through the baptismal ritual. The godparents are chosen with care from outside the immediate kinship network. It is preferred that the male *compadre* (the more important godparent) be a man of influence, status, and respect in the community. Compadres are expected to develop close relationships and in times of trouble have the right to call on one another for assistance. Compadrazgo is most common among rural families.

extended relationships, it may seem logical that as or if ties with extended kin weaken or decrease, people would increasingly suggest and experiment with new family forms that incorporate these extended kin features. These forms may include *communes* with a common ownership of goods and sharing of tasks, *family networks* where three or four nuclear families join together to share problems and exchange services, or *affiliated families* where a nuclear family accepts (socially adopts) one or more nonrelated older person who is recognized as part of the kin network. Let us look more closely at the boundaries of the kinship network and the major importance it holds for most of us today.

### The boundaries of kinship

The kinship system, like marital and family systems and groups, involves special ties, bonds, and linkages among its members. However, family groups and systems are units upon which the kinship system is built. A kinship system refers to a pattern of social norms regulating those relationships that are directly based on the facts of birth and the birth cycle. It is also a *set* of interpersonal social relationships involving strong interests and emotions, urgent problems of authority and order, and many reciprocal bonds of dependence and support.[29] These relationships, whether created biologically or socially, exist among people who are descended from one another (parents-children) or who have common descent (brother-sister).

---

29. Robin M. Williams, Jr., "Kinship and the Family in the United States," in *American Society*, 3rd ed. (New York: Alfred A. Knopf, 1970): 47 and 60.

Birth is the primary biological point of reference for kinship. But kinship relationships are also determined and defined by sex (male or female), birth order (older or younger children), time together (living together or casual visits), and seniority within the kin grouping. These characteristics combine to give each individual a different social position. As Robin Williams states:

> Children are not merely children; they are male or female, older or younger, with siblings or without. The sister of one's father is not in the same biological category as one's mother's sister, but both in our society are "aunt."[30]

As defined, these relationships based on the birth cycle (kinship system) are regulated by patterns of social norms. These norms vary widely from one society to another. Thus, it is impossible to categorize all of them. On the other hand, certain norms exist universally among kinship relationships. The most widely used example is that of a taboo on incest. All societies forbid sexual relations between persons in certain kinship positions. Violations of these norms arouse strong feelings among the kinship group as well as in the larger society. All societies also forbid intermarriage between certain kinship group members. The circle of prohibited relatives for marriage does, however, vary widely in different societies. One extreme, in ancient Egypt, permitted brother-sister and father-daughter marriages. The other extreme may be represented by the traditional clan system of China or certain extended families in India where the prohibition extended to a very wide group of relatives including cousins to the sixth degree.

The pattern of social norms tends to treat members of the kinship group differently. In most societies, women are accorded lower status than men. The eldest male or the eldest son may be accorded greater prestige, power, and responsibility than younger men. In general, status positions in the kinship network are differentiated by rights, privileges, and obligations; by inheritance; and by general social expectations.

In some societies, kinship is such an integral part of all aspects of the society that it is difficult to differentiate it from other (non-kinship) kinds of social institutions and relationships. Particularly in primitive and peasant societies, the political, educational, religious, economic, and property units are so interlinked and meshed with the kinship system or group that it becomes impossible to separate kinship networks from non-kinship networks. That is, other institutions are part of the kinship system itself. In contrast are the kinship systems known in most Western societies where kinship is separate and clearly distinguished from other institutions and relationships. The economic system, while not totally independent of kinship networks or influences, exists separate from and is distinguishable from the kinship

---

30. Ibid., p. 49.

network. This same differentiation is true for other institutionalized patterns of norms and activity.

Bert Adams suggests that kinship groups have tended to fulfill certain functions even when the kinship network is indistinguishable from other institutions.[31] These include: (1) property holding and inheritance; (2) housing and the maintenance of residential proximity; (3) obligation, or helping in time of need; and (4) affection, emotional ties, or primary relationships. It is difficult to do justice to these four basic characteristics of kinship groups in this chapter, but their importance merits some attention.[32]

*Property holding and inheritance*   The holding, ownership, and control of property and the transmission of this property from one owner to another is an issue of central concern to family sociologists and anthropologists in general and to conflict theorists and feminists more particularly. Property tends to indicate wealth and power. Inheritance tends to indicate how this wealth and power is transmitted. Within family systems, this transference is directly linked to inheritance and the rules of descent.

At birth, each of us inherits two separate bloodlines; thus a key issue in most societies (less so in the United States) is whose bloodline, the mother's or the father's, is more important. If the descent pattern is unilineal, as is true in most societies within Asia, India, and Africa, the name, property, authority, and marriage controls are traced through one line, usually that of the father and his bloodline—**patrilineal**. Much less frequently do anthropologists note a **matrilineal** pattern, a unilineal system that traces the lineage through the female line. The system of descent most prevalent in the United States is the **bilateral** system where power and property are transferred through both the mother's and father's line to both males and females. One key exception to this pattern is in name, where both sexes tend to assume the name of their father and females take their husband's family name upon marriage.

Patterns of descent take on a special significance to many feminists and conflict theorists because most family systems throughout the world tend to (1) perpetuate power and wealth through successive generations—that is, the rich stay rich and the poor stay poor; and (2) differentiate this power and wealth between the sexes with the males given preferential treatment. The result is that class and sexual inequality is built into most family systems in such a way that the inequalities come to be viewed as "natural" and "legitimate." In other words, some families have the "right" to be wealthier than others, males are expected to be dominant, and females are ordained to be housewives and mothers and submissive to their male counterparts.

---

31. Bert N. Adams, "Kinship Systems and Adaptation to Modernization," *Studies in Comparative International Development* 4 (1968–1969): 55.

32. Those interested in an extensive treatment of kinship should examine Bernard Farber, *Conceptions of Kinship* (New York: Elsevier-North Holland, 1981); and William J. Goode, *The Family*, 2d ed. (Englewood Cliffs, N. J.: Prentice-Hall, 1982), Chapter 7.

## The main structural features of the U.S. kinship system

The U.S. kinship system is marked by the following characteristics:

First, the incest taboo everywhere forbids a person to marry father, mother, child, grandparent, uncle, aunt, niece, or nephew. In twenty-nine states intermarriage of first cousins is forbidden; intermarriage of blood relatives is seldom otherwise limited.

Second, marriage is monogamous, and there is no prescriptive pattern for kinship marriages.

Third, no discrimination is made between paternal and maternal relatives for marriage purposes.

Fourth, although the family name descends through the male line, there is little other emphasis upon the male line of descent. The descent system tends to be bilineal or, more strictly, multilineal.

Fifth, there is an emphasis on the immediate conjugal family. In a highly developed consanguine kinship system, by contrast, the tightest unit is the descent group of siblings, a group of brothers and sisters whose spouses enter as strangers and remain always somewhat so. In the United States, the solidarity of spouses is stressed, to the exclusion of in-laws.

Sixth, the immediate family of father, mother, and children tends to be the effective residence, consumption, and social unit. No extended kin groupings are of more than secondary importance in these respects, except among a few relatively small population elements.

Seventh, in urban communities, which are increasingly representative of the country as a whole, the family group is typically a consuming rather than a producing unit. Kinship units as work groups and productive organizations have largely disappeared except in farming and certain types of small retail business.

Eighth, because the nuclear family is the unit and the kinship system is multilineal, U.S. society places relatively little emphasis on family tradition and family continuity.

Ninth, there is comparatively free choice of mates. In fact, U.S. mate selection is to a considerable extent an application of free competition in the institution of marriage. The choice of spouses is purely personal; the kin of the prospective mates have no right to interfere. Parents are usually asked to sanction the marriage choice, but this convention is residual. The individualistic system of mate choice is favored by the autonomous conjugal unit, the discontinuity of generations, the deemphasis of kinship, and the extensive geographic and social mobility found in U.S. society.

Tenth, linked to the father-mother-children unit and free marriage-choice is the tendency for adult children to disperse from the parental household.

*Source:* Selected sentences taken from Robin M. Williams, *American Society*, 3d ed. (New York: Alfred A. Knopf, 1970): 56–59.

*Housing and residential proximity*  All family systems have rules of residence that establish who lives where and with whom. Since husbands and wives come from different families and since most husbands and wives share the same residence,[33] one or both of them must move. The most common pattern is a **patrilocal** one, in which the bride changes residence and lives with the

---

33. Mitterauer reported on an historic family form in what is now Austria, where married persons did not live with their spouses. *See* Michael Mitterauer, "Marriage Without Co-Residence: A Special Type of Family Form in Rural Corinthia," *Journal of Family History* 6 (Summer 1981): 177–181.

## When adult children come home to live

A common, but underresearched event in the lives of many families in the United States is the return of adult children to the parental home. Factors such as a delay in the age at marriage, economic recessions, or divorce tend to increase the likelihood that launching of children from the home may be delayed or that children who left home for reasons such as college, marriage, or a job may return to live. This reuniting of parent-child networks, often including a son- or daughter-in-law, creates a modification in the typical pattern of residential and financial independence and an arena for increased potential conflict.

A report in the *New York Times* included interviews with a number of these families. A major reason for returning to the parental home focused on financial needs. Some couples and individuals couldn't afford the available housing while others felt it was the only way to save money for a home of their own.

Parents and children alike expressed great ambivalence about the housing arrangement. Some of the concerns focused on meal preparation, knowing what to expect and how to behave, adequate space, the loss of privacy which was most acutely felt by younger couples, and still being answerable to parental authority. On the other hand some of the benefits included an opportunity to better enjoy the grandchildren, a sense of continued familial closeness at a time of widespread personal alienation, and a feeling of being needed. Many couples insisted that the added strain on their marriage was more than offset by relief from other domestic tensions such as living "house poor" or being alone a great deal of the time.

parents of the groom. In the **matrilocal** pattern, much less frequently found than the former, the newlywed couple lives with the parents of the bride. In the United States, far more frequently found than either of the above is the **bilocal** system, in which the couple lives near the parents of either spouse, or the **neolocal** system, in which the couple lives in a home of their own that may be located apart from both sets of parents. The pattern of residence takes on a special significance as one looks at the third and fourth aspects of kinship, namely the obligation or helping aspect and the affection and emotional ties among kin. Helping patterns and showing affection to grandparents, parents, or siblings take on a different character if you share the same building, live in the same neighborhood or community, or reside hundreds of miles apart.

It appears that residence patterns in the United States show a surprising degree of local concentration. In the study of Middletown, for example, taking any resident of the city at random, the odds were one in five that a brother or sister lived in the city; one in three that one or both of his or her parents lived there; and two in five that a more distant relative such as a grandparent, aunt, uncle, or cousin lived there.[34] The respondents' immediate families were especially concentrated, with 54 percent of the grown children, 43 percent of the parents, and 31 percent of the brothers and sisters living right in

---

34. Theodore Caplow et al., *Middletown Families* (New York: Bantam Books, 1982): 206.

Middletown.[35] These percentages increased considerably when a fifty mile radius was used to establish residence. Thus while newlywed couples establish a residence separate from their parents, this residence tends to be in geographical proximity to parents and siblings. Other studies tend to indicate a similar finding.

*Obligation, or helping in time of need*    A range of kinship obligation patterns can be identified. One kin obligation is to *keep in touch*, particularly with parents, to a lesser extent with siblings, followed by other relatives such as aunts, uncles, or cousins. One study found that many extended families had a person who could be considered a "kinkeeper," usually a female, who worked at keeping family members in touch with one another.[36] Another kin obligation is to *share services* or *gifts* as gestures of good will and kindness.[37] A third obligation is to *help* or *assist* when in need. It is likely that all three obligation patterns are observed by most families throughout the world. What is likely to differ is the amount and type of contact, sharing, or helping pattern and the range of kin or relatives that are included.

In Middletown, almost everyone agreed that people ought to keep in touch with relatives and seemed to regard this as more a pleasure than a duty. Obligations to parents were more widely held than obligations to siblings. The authors summarize the norms that govern relations with kin in contemporary Middletown as follows:

1. People should enjoy contacts with their relations.
2. Children and parents and brothers and sisters are mutually obligated to remain in permanent contact.
3. Parents and their grown children are mutually obligated to provide needed help, if at all possible. There is much less obligation of this kind between siblings and practically none between cousins.[38]

The main determinants of the amount of interaction between relatives in Middletown were the distance between their homes and the closeness of their relationship. With increasing distance, visiting was replaced by telephone calls, which was replaced by letter writing. Almost no one corresponded regularly with cousins, although they might exchange Christmas cards. Consistently, women did more joint activities with parents and other kin

---

35. Ibid., p. 203.
36. Carolyn J. Rosenthal, "Kinkeeping in the Familial Division of Labor" *Journal of Marriage and the Family* 47 (November 1985): 965–974.
37. Theodore Caplow, "Christmas Gifts and Kin Network," *American Sociological Review* 47 (June 1982): 383–392; and David Cheal, "Showing Them You Love Them: Gift-Giving and the Dialectic of Intimacy," *The Sociological Review* 35 (1977): 150–169.
38. Caplow, *Middletown Families*, p. 206.

than did men. Again, while Middletown was cited, it appears that these patterns are highly representative of kin obligations elsewhere in the United States.[39]

*Affection and primary relationships*   Affection and primary relationships are the emotional and feeling dimension of visits, calls, and letters. Affection can be viewed as being emotionally close to kin. Women seem to be the "specialists" in affective kin relationships. In Middletown, as elsewhere, women expressed more affection than men did for every category of relative. The distribution of affection was highest for mothers, next highest for fathers and near siblings, and lowest for best-known cousins.

The affection dimension between children and parents seems to increase with age but seems to weaken with kin such as cousins. In Middletown, the increased closeness to parents was attributed to children's own maturity, their own parental experience, the belated recognition of the emotional debt they owe, the relaxation of parental authority, the increased needs of parents, and the expectation of bereavement. It can be said that in Middletown, as well as elsewhere, most people feel good about their parents, love them, and make sacrifices for them when necessary.[40] And surprising to many, there is little evidence of any weakening of kinship ties during the past fifty years.

This chapter first focused on the family as a social institution and as a group or system. It then explored the boundaries of marriage, family, and kin. The reader who desires to segment and isolate these three interrelated components for given family members is likely to face many difficulties, for the boundaries of each are seldom precise and distinct. This is true both conceptually and in real life experiences. Pauline Boss and Jan Greenberg, for example, write about family ambiguity as a new variable in understanding family stress.[41] They define boundary ambiguity as not knowing who is in and who is out of the family system. Remarriages, stepparents and stepchildren, in-laws, more distant relatives, and others may or may not be fully recognized as part of a particular family network. While families will differ from one cultural context to another in how they perceive their boundaries, the central notion suggests that a high degree of family boundary ambiguity over time will lead to a high level of stress in the family system. Who is in and who is out become major components in determining task performance, inheritance patterns, visiting, writing, or helping responsibilities, and the like.

---

39. *See* Goeffrey K. Leigh, "Kinship Interaction over the Family Life Span," *Journal of Marriage and the Family* 44 (February 1982): 197–208; Susan M. Essock-Vitale and Michael T. McGuire, "Women's Lives Viewed from an Evolutionary Perspective. II. Patterns of Helping," *Ethology and Sociobiology* 6 (1985): 155–173.

40. Caplow et al., *Middletown Families*, p. 220.

41. Pauline Boss and Jan Greenberg, "Family Boundary Ambiguity: A New Variable in Family Stress Theory," *Family Process* 23 (1984): 535–546.

Our attention turns in the next chapter to how the marital, family, and kin system are interrelated with other major systems, particularly the economic, employment, work related system. Note how the employment of none, one, or both spouses becomes a key ingredient in a better understanding of the functioning of marital, family, and kin networks. .

## SUMMARY

1. The family as a social institution refers to an organized, formal, and regular way of carrying out certain essential tasks in a society. It refers to the wide system of norms that organizes family units into stable and ongoing social systems. This chapter presented numerous ways in which marital, family, and kin groups and systems are organized to fulfill certain tasks.

2. The family system is an abstraction consisting of interrelated statuses and the social expectations that accompany them. The family group consists of a concrete reality of persons who are physically present and who interact with one another. The family as a primary group, with face-to-face contact, smallness of size, and frequent and intense contact, is distinguished from the secondary group of more formal, impersonal contacts that characterize much of an individual's life.

3. The boundaries of marriage are not always precise and clearly defined. Generally marriage includes a heterosexual union that includes at least one male and one female. It grants legitimacy to children and approval to sexual relationships. It is usually a public affair with reciprocal rights and obligations between the spouses. Finally, it is usually a binding relationship that assumes some permanence.

4. The variations in marriage and number of spouses cover singlehood, monogamy, polygyny, polyandry, and group marriage. The number of people choosing to remain single has risen dramatically over the past several decades. Available data indicate some extreme differences for the male and female who choose or who involuntarily occupy this particular nonmarital life-style.

5. Polygyny and polyandry, two forms of polygamy, occur in a wide range of contexts and take numerous forms. The plural spouses may be brothers or sisters, may marry simultaneously or sequentially, and may perform various functions. While polygyny is very common, polyandry is quite rare. Group marriage, as well, occurs extremely infrequently and may never have existed as a viable form of marriage for any society in the world.

6. Like marriage, the boundaries of the family vary considerably. Usually a family arises as a result of marriage and includes people united by marriage, blood, and adoption. The members, some of whom share a common residence, have reciprocal rights and obligations to one another. This institutionalized pattern fulfills certain basic functions for society, particularly as related to infants, socialization, and primary relationships.

7. One typology of family structures differentiates the nuclear/conjugal unit from a variety of types of extended units. Some of these include families of orientation and procreation, modified-nuclear or modified-extended families, and consanguine, joint, and stem families.

8. The boundaries of kinship serve as an extension of the marital and nuclear family unit. This system too involves special ties, bonds, and linkage among its members. It

tends to have key functions and characteristics that include property holding and inheritance, housing and the maintenance of residential proximity, obligation or helping in time of need, and affection and emotional ties.

# KEY TERMS AND TOPICS

# DISCUSSION QUESTIONS

1. What is meant by the family as a social institution? What does it mean for factors like homosexuality, illegitimacy, or child support to be institutionalized?

2. Differentiate family groups from family systems. Since systems are abstractional, of what relevance are they to an understanding of the family?

3. Describe what would be likely to happen to a person who is removed from all primary-group relationships. Why are they so crucial?

4. In your own words, define marriage and family in a way that would be comprehensive enough to include most societies in the world. How are the two similar or different? Is one necessary for the other? How do they differ from any other group or relationship?

5. What is the likelihood of an increasing percentage of people choosing to remain single? Why or why not? Will this be equally true for males and females?

6. Why is monogamy so strongly stressed in the United States as the appropriate form of marriage? What advantages or disadvantages do

you see in polygyny, polyandry, or group marriage for adults in the United States?

7. Around the world, when polygamy is culturally approved, polygyny appears to be far more common than polyandry. How is this explained? What factors explain the exceptions?

8. Thinking of your own kin group, how many persons do you know (uncles, cousins, and so on)? With how many do you interact on a regular basis? What differentiations do you make between kin on your mother's side and kin on your father's side?

9. What arguments are feminists and conflict theorists likely to make in opposition to traditional unilineal descent and inheritance systems?

10. Make a list of all your relatives that you personally know and can identify. Which ones do you visit, maintain contact with, and feel obligated toward? How is geographical proximity related to your visits, contacts, or feelings? How many commitments extend beyond parents and siblings?

# FURTHER READINGS

Adams, Bert N. *The Family: A Sociological Interpretation.* 4th ed. Orlando, Florida: Harcourt Brace Jovanovich, 1986. An introductory sociology of the family text that emphasizes current analytic frameworks and theoretical conceptions for organizing the wide body of information available on the U.S. family.

Farber, Bernard. *Conceptions of Kinship.* New York: Elsevier North Holland, Inc., 1981. An empirical study of kinship from the central perspective of collaterality, with considerable evidence of kinship as a significant element in maintaining social continuity.

Goode, William J. *World Revolution and Family Patterns.* Glencoe, Ill.: The Free Press, 1963. A description and interpretation of the main changes in family patterns that have occurred over the past half-century in the West, Arabic Islam, sub-Saharan Africa, India, China, and Japan.

Kephart, William M. *Extraordinary Groups: An Examination of Unconventional Life-Styles.* New York: St. Martin's Press, 3rd ed., 1987. A look at seven different cultural groups and life-styles that exist in the United States: the old order Amish, the Oneida Community, the Father Devine Movement, the gypsies, the Shakers, the Mormons, and the modern communes.

Lee, Gary L. "Comparative Perspectives" in *Handbook of Marriage and the Family* by Marvin B. Sussman and Suzanne K. Steinmetz (eds.). New York: Plenum Press, 1987, Chapter 3, pp. 59–80. A cross-national comparative look at the commonality and variations in family structure, marital power, and socialization.

Lee, Gary, R. "Kinship in the Seventies: A Decade Review of Research and Theory." *Journal of Marriage and the Family* 42 (November 1980): 923–934. The review article on kinship that appears in the special issue of family decade reviews covering the 1970s.

Milardo, Robert M. (ed.). *Families and Social Networks.* Newbury Park, CA.: Sage Publications, Inc. 1988. A systematic look at social relationships as they change during the transition to motherhood, in later stages of the life course, following separation and divorce, and so forth.

Simenauer, Jacqueline, and Carroll, David. *Singles: The New Americans.* New York: Simon and Schuster, 1982. A journalistic reporting of three thousand American men and women singles: how they meet others, their problems and pleasures, single parents, and other aspects of their private lives.

Simon, Barbara Levy. *Never Married Women.* Philadelphia: Temple University Press, 1987. A look at the lives of fifty women who had in common a never-married status.

Stein, Peter J. *Single Life: Unmarried Adults in Social Context.* New York: St. Martin's Press, 1981. A collection of articles concerning major life issues of the never-married, divorced, and widowed: friendship, intimacy, emotional and physical health, living arrangements, work, raising children, and aging.

# CHAPTER FOUR

# MARRIAGE, FAMILY, AND WORK

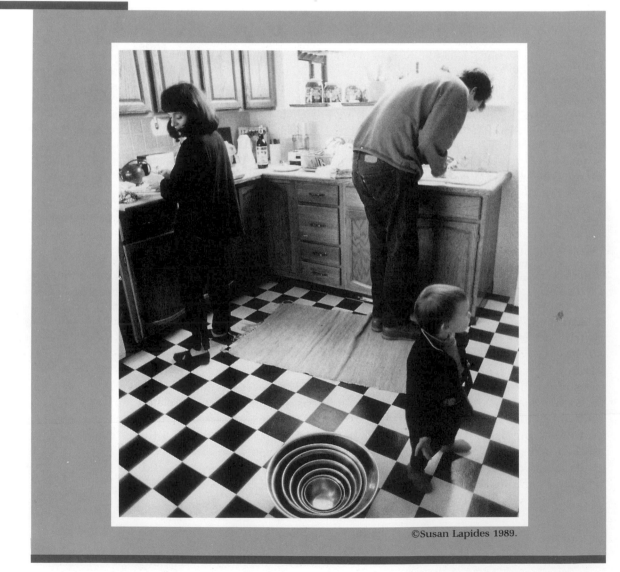

©Susan Lapides 1989.

T he last chapter provided an examination of how marriage, family, and kin groups and systems are organized, showing variation in the number of spouses, presenting a typology of family structures, and noting some of the basic functions of kinship networks. As noted in that chapter, in many societies family-kin networks are such an integral part of all aspects of the society it is difficult to separate and differentiate the family system from other major institutions. One example of these institutionalized linkages in the United States may be represented by the Amish subculture where the boundaries between family roles and responsibilities often are inseparable from their farming occupation; Anabaptist religious teachings; home-oriented educational training for appropriate adult male-female responsibilities; or their community-oriented political system where neighbors and friends provide protection, insurance, welfare, and justice functions. In the wider society—and in most of the western world— it is much easier to separate the family system from the work, school, church, politics, health, communication, military, recreation, and other systems.

While this chapter will focus primarily on linking marriages and families to the world of employment, work, and the economic system, first it will briefly note how religion, politics, and education affect and are affected by the family. Many of these institutionalized linkages are re-emphasized throughout the text, such as discussions of economic and social-class matters (Chapter 7), interfaith marriage (Chapter 8), the significance of a formal education (Chapters 6, 7, 13, and 17), and governmental policies (Chapter 18).

## LINKAGES BETWEEN THE FAMILY AND RELIGION, POLITICS, EDUCATION, AND THE ECONOMY

It appears obvious that linkages exist between family systems and other systems, yet at a more macro-level of analysis, it is frequently ignored in family studies. A structural-functional frame of reference reminds us of the interdependence of the parts of a system. As the economy changes so do employment rates and family spending patterns. As wars influence international relations, so do they affect divorce rates. As political decisions determine policies related to health and welfare, so do they affect attitudes toward one-parent families and child support responsibilities. And as education, employment, and the advancement of fertility control methods modify the opportunities and options available to women and men, so do these changes affect male-female, husband-wife, and parent-child interactions and expectations.

### Religion and the family

Cross-culturally as well as historically, the relationship between the religious system and the family system has been reciprocal.[1] Many family celebrations in most societies are religious ones. Religious norms influence speech patterns, nonmarital as well as marital sexuality, male and female roles, husband-wife and parent-child relations, and so forth. The marriage contract, the baptism of infants and children, and the death rituals frequently involve the clergy and religious organizations.

The pathbreaking study on the relationship between family and religion in the United States was carved out by Gerhard Lenski in the 1950s.[2] In comparing religious groups, he found, for example, that Protestants had higher divorce rates than Catholics, Catholics had more children than Protestants or Jews, Jews and Protestants were more likely than Catholics to see personal autonomy as the key value in preparing children for life, Catholics were less mobile than Protestants and Jews, and so forth. More recently, an increasing body of evidence suggests a general converging of values and behaviors among major religioethnic groups in the United States. Duane Alwin documents substantial changes in the social experiences of groups such as U.S. Catholics to the point that few, if any, differences exist among religioethnic groups in their orientation to the extended family. In dealing specifically with child rearing, he lends support to earlier predictions suggesting a decline in differences in values and orientations between these groups, possibly to the point of nonexistence.[3]

What has not changed is the linkage between the religious system and the family system, between religiosity and familism, and between religious beliefs and practices and family beliefs and practices. What has changed is the convergence of denominational differences. That is, differences between churchgoers and non-churchgoers are more pronounced than differences between particular religious groups such as Protestants or Catholics. Church-goers, for example, are more likely to be married; have more children; be more conservative on issues relating to sexuality, such as abortion, homosexuality, or premarital sexual relationships; stress more traditional gender roles; and so forth.

In spite of widely held assumptions about the weakening and decline of both religion and the family, evidence from "Middletown" (mentioned in the previous chapter) suggests that family ties in the late 1970s were at least as strong as in the 1920s, and citizens seemed to be at least as religious. Judging from statements today about what people believe, how much money they donate to churches, and how often they attend church meetings, they take

1. See, for example, Arland Thornton, "Reciprocal Influences of Family and Religion in a Changing World," *Journal of Marriage and the Family* 47 (May 1985): 381–394, and the entire special section on religion and the family in this issue of the journal, pp. 369–465.

2. Gerhard Lenski, *The Religious Factor* (Garden City, N.Y.: Doubleday, 1961).

3. Duane F. Alwin, "Religion and Parental Child-Rearing Orientations: Evidence of a Catholic-Protestant Convergence," *American Journal of Sociology* 92 (September 1986): 412–440.

their religion at least as seriously as did their grandfathers fifty years previously.[4] The message is clear. "Families that pray together, stay together" irrespective of religioethnic orientation. Differences are linked more closely to intensity of religious participation than to denominational differences.

Many contemporary examples of the linkage between the religious and family systems are provided throughout the text. Examples of recent interest include various social movements started and sustained by religious groups against abortion and the Equal Rights Amendment (ERA). The profamily movement included under its umbrella reestablishing prayer in the schools, outlawing busing for racial balance, and requiring parental notification about dispensing contraceptives and contraceptive information to minors. All these issues had the backing of certain fundamentalist and right-wing religious groups and were aimed at the general good of protecting, solidifying, and reestablishing the traditional family. While the degree of success of any of these movements is unclear, the reciprocal linkage between the religious and the family institutions is not.

## Politics and the family

A study of politics and the family examines the relationship between the family and the state (or government). The state refers to the civil laws, rules, and regulations created by legislators that we (families) elect or have selected, and that are enforced by agents of a local, state, or the federal government. The state or political system influences families through laws that regulate or support families.

Families are regulated through laws that govern who may marry whom, the number of spouses, the age at which marriage is permissible, the necessity of a blood test, the acceptance or non-acceptance of common-law marriages, the prohibition or acceptance of same-sex marriages, what family relatives are seen as incestuous, the "soundness" of the mental condition, and so forth. Families are regulated through laws that specify the rights and duties of parenthood, such as those that relate to contraception, pregnancy, and abortion; define legitimacy; regulate custody of children; or define abusive practices. Other regulations of families relate to factors such as divorce and legal separations or the distribution of property. Some of these laws are very general, and establish guidelines or boundaries of permissible behavior, while others are very precise and specific.

The state or government not only regulates families; it supports them as well. The extent to which the state has this responsibility is one of ongoing controversy. Homelessness, for example, was mentioned in the first chapter as

---

4. Howard M. Bahr and Bruce A. Chadwick, "Religion and Family in Middletown, USA," *Journal of Marriage and the Family* 47 (May 1985): 407–414.

an issue of concern. Should the government assume the responsibility of providing housing for the homeless and the poor? Is the government's responsibility that of guaranteeing adequate housing for everyone or simply serving as a "safety net," a last resort when all else fails? And welfare—is that a term that generates a positive response of government fulfilling its responsibility to the poor or does it generate feelings of anger that tax dollars are distributed to those who haven't contributed their fair share in work or money? AFDC (aid to families with dependent children), OASDI (old age, survivors, and disability insurance), social security, medicare (medical care for the elderly), medicaid (medical care for the poor), food stamp coupons, school lunch programs, subsidized student loans, energy allowances, and tax breaks for children and the elderly are support programs for families. These too have all sorts of regulations specifying conditions of eligibility, but here the focus is on the assistance (support) of families and family members in need. How this support is given, who gets it, and the extent of distribution are items of debate in every election. These are issues that separate the "liberals" from the "conservatives."

Most governmental programs and laws that affect families are not established for or directed specifically at them. Examples might include laws directed at drugs, discrimination, driving, unemployment, draft registration, health, and the environment. What should be clear at this point is the extent to which the family is related to and influenced by the state or government. The political system represents power, determining who gets what in society. Does the family have no recourse or power in return?

Many would argue that in most of the world, including the United States, the power of an individual or family is extremely limited. This may generally be the case. On the other hand, collective activity, kin networks, and the solidarity of family ties form vital forces in political activities and voting patterns. The stability of family systems takes on a symbolic importance to political figures. They too attempt to present themselves and their families as moral citizens and supportive of a strong family life. Thus, often in subtle and even deceptive ways, families take on an importance in the political arena. The polity issue is addressed more explicitly in the final chapter.

## Education and the family

Our lives, as persons or as members of families, are influenced by our schools and educational system. Our socialization, employment, and vacations are or were affected by them. The extent of social literacy and social competence are linked to our educational system. Schools group students according to their ages, and family life changes when our young children enter school, become active in school endeavors, and move through the K–12 system. Schools take our children through an established curriculum of academic subjects, yet they focus heavily on the "hidden curriculum" of teaching civic and moral responsibility, obedience to rules, respect for authority, punctuality, success through competition, conscientiousness, and other areas traditionally believed to be family functions.

The family and educational systems tend to supplement one another in teaching selected cultural values, norms, and skills. One intended function of education is to supplement family socialization. The schools use experts (teachers) to teach children knowledge, values, and selected skills that parents frequently are incapable of teaching and that are necessary to have in order to function in a changing world outside the family. The close relation between these two systems appears in many studies that show educational training in the home to be directly linked to the success of training in the school. Why then the school?

Participation in the educational system from early childhood is expected to increase the level of knowledge and mental and interpersonal skills. Ideally, these skills are expected to have positive consequences in marital and parental performance in addition to employment performance. Sometimes the training provided adolescents in the educational system is at variance with that of parents or at a level that exceeds the training that parents have had. Thus the authority of the family may be undermined or the parental skills may be less than that of the child. In such instances parental authoritarianism may give way to more egalitarian parent-child relations or may set the stage for emancipation from the household. Again the linkages between the educational and family systems become evident.

## Economy and the family

Perhaps as much as any other institution, the economy influences family organization and interaction. The economy is the component of society concerned with the creation, distribution, and consumption of goods and services. The family contributes labor and skills and in turn receives wages or other forms of compensation (prestige, insurance, services, and the like). The impact of the economic-family linkage is most evident when issues such as unemployment, families in poverty, one-parent families, wife-mother and dual-career employment, or the inequality of wealth and resources are examined.

At a macro-level of analysis, conflict theorists view the economic system as the key to understanding all inequality within or outside of the family system. More than one hundred years ago, Karl Marx's co-writer, Friedrich Engels,[5] argued that marriage represents a class antagonism in which the well-being and development of one group are attained by the misery and repression of the other. In marriage, as in the economy, the dominance of the

---

5. Friedrich Engels, *The Origin of the Family, Private Property, and the State* (New York: International Publishing, 1942). (Originally published in 1884.)

**Go on—ask me if I work**

Why is it when a man is a chef or chauffeur,
Or designs interior decoration,
Everybody understands he's working.
Ready for some startling information?
So am I.

Why is it when a husband is a teacher,
Or talented at making sick children well,
Everybody understands he's working.
Ready for less show and more tell?
So am I.

Why is it when a man repairs appliances,
Or practices guidance and counseling,

Everybody understands he's working.
Ready for an important announcement?
So am I.

No Social Security, no old-age pension,
No titles, not even honorable mention.
But if you wonder how much I'm earning,
Even though I'm not working for pay,
Figure out what it would cost to replace me
If I didn't show up just one eighteen-hour day.

*Source:* Rochelle Distelheim, *McCall's,* December 1976. Copyright ©
The McCall Publishing Company.

husbands and the suppression of the wives is evident, and the linkage between the two is unmistakable.

This dominance-suppression issue is at the heart of gender role discussions. Conflict theorists, be they Marxian, feminist, or other, link the male-female division of labor to economic specialization and domination. Traditional norms state that men are expected to "bring home the bacon," meaning "support the family," thus constituting the basic employed paid-labor force. Women's place is in the home, and domestic chores such as cooking, cleaning, and child care are women's work. This household labor, according to one branch of conflict theory, is intricately linked to a capitalistic type of economic system in that the "free and unpaid" labor of women makes it possible for a man to leave the home to work, earn wages, and support the family. His wages, in turn, contribute to his dominant position and make the wife-mother-female dependent on the male. The employed male can play the role of capitalist within his own household.

In light of this discussion, one can understand why "working wives" are those who are employed outside the home. Housework is not "real work," and—as will be shown later in the chapter—remains the task of women whether they are full-time housewives or paid employees outside the home. Let us examine more closely the housewife and employed wife and mother.

## *The housewife*

Traditionally, few roles of women held a higher priority than to be a wife and homemaker. The housewife has been relatively neglected by social scientists as a central problem for research, with the attention granted women in paid employment overshadowing the attention given to women who are *not* in the paid-labor force (in 1988, 44.1 percent of the female population age sixteen and over and 43.5 percent of married women with a husband present).[6]

The qualifications for the status of housewife are only two: marriage and female. Age, education, specific skills, time off, overtime, level of productivity, and other characteristics are basically ignored in job performance. The role of housewife is generally categorized as a low status position with both low prestige and a low economic value. "I'm only a housewife" is a phrase well familiar to most readers. This exists in spite of the performance of tasks that are economically valuable to society and costly for a family to purchase: cook, baker, waitress, teacher, sexual partner, seamstress, housekeeper, bookkeeper, secretary, chauffeur, nurse, therapist, tutor, counselor, hostess, and recreation director.

Joann Vanek states that there are several important misconceptions about housework.[7] People often think that housewives work fewer hours, at a slower pace, and less strenuously than other workers. Many believe that housework has little productive value. And some believe the present assignment of tasks between husband and wife is equitable.

First, do housewives work less than others? One could argue that household technology, such as canned and processed foods, automatic washers, electric refrigerators, and other "labor-saving" equipment, has reduced the burdens of housework significantly. Data from a national survey of two-parent families with at least one child under twelve reported that the median number of hours per week that wives who were *not employed* spent in housework and childcare was 49.8 for white women and 38.0 for black women.[8] *Employed* wives reported that they spent less time in housework and child care than those not employed. The pattern for husbands was reversed. While the number of hours that husbands spent in housework and child care increased slightly (about four hours per week) if the wife was employed, and the number of hours that wives spent in these tasks decreased if they were employed, husband-wife equity in housework and child care was and is nonexistent. Women, whether housewives or in paid employment, perform most of the domestic work.

Using a national sample to analyze change in men's housework and child care over a ten-year period, Shelley Coverman and Joseph F. Sheley conclude that there were no significant changes in men's mean housework and

6. U.S. Bureau of the Census, *Statistical Abstract of the United States: 1989*, 109th ed. (Washington, D.C.: U.S. Government Printing Office, 1989), Table 638, p. 385.

7. Joann Vanek, "Housewives as Workers," in *Women Working* by Ann H. Stromberg and Shirley Harkess (Palo Alto, Cal.: Mayfield Publishing, 1978): 392–414.

8. Joyce O. Beckett and Audrey D. Smith, "Work and Family Roles: Egalitarian Marriage in Black and White Families," *Social Service Review* 55 (June 1981): 314–326. For a study of how time in housework varies throughout the family life cycle *see* Cynthia Rexroat and Constance Shehan, "The Family Life Cycle and Spouses' Time in Housework," *Journal of Marriage and the Family* 49 (November 1987): 737–750.

child-care time through the mid-1970s.[9] Some changes did occur among certain categories of men, such as an increase in the amount of time men with younger children devoted to child care. But they conclude that men's involvement in the traditional "women's sphere" if occurring at all, is lagging considerably behind women's entry into the traditional "men's sphere." Clearly, their findings cast doubt on any significant convergence of sex roles.

Other research supports the ideas that the household division of labor has changed very slowly over the years and that little convergence has occurred in household roles of men and women.[10] Changes that do occur are related to the employment of wives who now face the double burden of paid and unpaid work. Typically, employed wives first adjust in ways that do not require the husband's participation: by cleaning house less often, entertaining less, or eating out more often. The education and attitudes of the wife do not significantly affect the division of labor.

Catherine Ross and others, found as well that the household division of labor is shaped by the husband's values and the relative power of husband and wife.[11] Well-educated husbands and husbands with less traditional sex-role beliefs are more likely to participate in the household tasks. Ross also found that the smaller the gap between the husband's earnings and his wife's, the greater his relative contribution. In other words, the more the husband's earnings exceed his wife's, the less housework he does.

An alternative argument to the idea that the husband's attitudes may be more influential than his wife's in predicting his household contribution comes from a study in Kentucky.[12] The findings suggest that it is only when wives hold liberal attitudes and demand a sharing of household tasks that men are encouraged to increase their participation in housework. Liberal husbands, it is suggested, probably will not offer to help with housework because they can hold egalitarian views of women's work roles while maintaining their privileged position in the home. The result is that the attitudes of women, not men, are transforming the distribution of home labor, small though the transformation may be.

Second, does housework have little productive value? Again, specific data are difficult to obtain since payroll checks and dollar expenditures seldom accompany this task. But, the work a woman does contributes to the family

9. Shelley Coverman and Joseph F. Sheley, "Change in Men's Housework and Child-Care Time, 1965–1975," *Journal of Marriage and the Family* 48 (May 1986): 413–422.

10. Frances Cogle Lawrence, Peggy S. Draughn, Grace E. Tasker, and Patricia H. Wozniak, "Sex Differences in Household Labor Time: A Comparison of Rural and Urban Couples," *Sex Roles* 17 (1987): 489–502.

11. Catherine E. Ross, "The Division of Labor at Home," *Social Forces* 65 (March 1987): 816–833; and Yoshinori Kamo, "Determinants of Household Division of Labor," *Journal of Family Issues* 9 (June 1988): 177–200.

12. Constance Hardesty and Janet Bokemeier, "Finding Time and Making Do: Distribution of Household Labor in Nonmetropolitan Marriages," *Journal of Marriage and the Family* 51 (February 1989): 253–267.

economy and to the society's total economic output. Without the services referred to earlier (cook, baker, waitress, etc.), the family's standard of living would be lowered drastically and the cost of purchasing them would be extremely expensive.

Third, is the present holding of power and the assignment of tasks between husband and wife equitable? Vanek argues that it is not.[13] Neither a wage nor a visible product results from her work. She is deprived of economic benefits such as insurance and medical care for her own efforts.

From a Marxist-feminist perspective, housework serves as a prime example of an unequal division of labor between men and women that generates tension, conflict, and change. Being a housewife augments the power of men. As stated earlier, the fact that housewives are excluded from paid employment and an opportunity to support themselves reinforces their dependence on their husbands. Heidi Hartmann pinpoints time spent on housework to support the proposition that the family remains a primary arena where men exercise their patriarchal power over women's labor. She says that

> men's control of women's labor power is the lever that allows them to benefit from women's provision of personal and household services, including relief from child rearing and many unpleasant tasks both within and beyond households, and the arrangement of the nuclear family, based on monogamous and heterosexual marriage, is one institutional form that seems to enhance this control.[14]

Another inequality in marriage occurs in the way in which the household tasks are divided. What husbands and wives do is not only different but may not have changed much over several decades. In *Middletown Families*, the way men and women, whether cohabiting or married, divided up household tasks is along traditional lines with the women bearing the brunt of the labor. In 90 percent of the families the wife does all or most of the housekeeping, and in 85 percent of the families with young children, the wife does all or most of the caring for them. About 84 percent of Middletown husbands earn all or most of the family income.[15] These figures parallel a Utah study that showed the wife doing the housekeeping among more than 90 percent of the families and caring for preschool children in about 80 percent of the families (77 percent for Catholics, 80 percent for Protestants, and 85 percent for Mormons). The husband earned all or most of the family income in about 88 percent of the families.[16]

13. Vanek, "Housewives as Workers," pp. 405–406.

14. Heidi I. Hartmann, "The Family as Locus of Gender, Class, and Political Struggle: The Example of Housework," *Signs: Journal of Women in Culture and Society* 6 (Spring 1981): 372.

15. Theodore Caplow et al., *Middletown Families: Fifty Years of Continuity and Change* (New York: Bantam Books, 1982): 69.

16. Howard M. Bahr, "Religious Contrasts in Family Role Definitions and Performance: Utah Mormons, Catholics, Protestants and Others," *Journal for the Scientific Study of Religion* 21 (September 1982): 209.

The literature in general suggests that when wives are compared with husbands, "his" marriage is considerably better than "her" marriage. Jessie Bernard[17] stated this most explicitly by reporting that more wives than husbands: reported marital frustration and dissatisfaction, negative feelings, and marital problems; considered their marriages unhappy; regretted their marriage; sought marital counseling; initiated divorce proceedings; felt they were going to have a nervous breakdown; had more feelings of inadequacy in their marriage; and blamed themselves for their own lack of general adjustment. She described housework as menial labor, isolating, and a dead-end job with no chance of promotion. Finally, she said, in truth, being a housewife makes women sick.

If being a housewife makes women sick, apparently employment outside the home is not the medication needed to make them any better. Evidence from six large national surveys consistently failed to support the hypothesis that women with jobs outside the home are generally happier and more satisfied with their lives than full-time housewives.[18] Both work outside the home and full-time housework were found to have benefits and costs attached to them: the net result is that there were found to be no consistent or significant differences in patterns of life satisfaction between the two groups. Constance Shehan, as well, in comparing employed wives and housewives, found no significant difference between the two groups in depression, health anxiety, or life satisfaction. The majority of respondents of both groups were "well-off" psychologically.[19]

While this discussion tended to present the housewife status as negative in terms of low prestige, no salary or fringe benefits, overwork, and the like, it should not be overlooked that many women find satisfaction in the performance of the role. The job is not competitive. The work schedule is highly flexible. The position may be one of choice. Some women prefer housekeeping to any other type of work. Some women define their highest contribution as service to their husband and children. And as reported by Shehan in her study cited above, the home and family are not the only source of gratification that housewives have. Pursuing hobbies, participating in voluntary organizations, and visiting with friends and relatives are important sources of social interaction and interesting activity.

A report from national surveys conducted by the Survey Research Center at the University of Michigan indicated that 50 percent of housewives had a positive opinion of housework and 44 percent had a neutral or ambivalent

---

17. Jessie Bernard, *The Future of Marriage* (New Haven: Yale University Press, 1982): 26–53.

18. James D. Wright, "Are Working Women Really More Satisfied? Evidence from Several National Surveys," *Journal of Marriage and the Family* 40 (May 1978): 301–313. *See also* Myra Marx Ferree, "Class, Housework, and Happiness: Women's Work and Life Satisfaction," *Sex Roles* 11 (1984): 1057–1074.

19. Constance L. Shehan, "Wives' Work and Psychological Well-Being: An Extension of Gove's Social Role Theory of Depression," *Sex Roles* 11 (1984): 881–899.

opinion.[20] Only 6 percent perceived housework as negative. Positive views were inversely related to level of education, that is, housewives with more formal education were less likely to respond positively to housework. They were also most likely to want a career. The least likely to favor housework were college-educated, younger wives. These findings parallel other results that show that women who had wanted a career outside the home were more dissatisfied with their own lives than homemakers who had never wanted a career. It was the career-oriented homemakers who showed the dissatisfaction previous research has suggested characterizes homemakers as opposed to employed women. The home-oriented homemakers, on the other hand, were slightly more satisfied with their lives than employed women.[21]

In observing household work, two sociologists found three overall, prevailing views.[22] Some women spoke with disdain about household work. These women could not deny household work as a full-time activity but addressed in detail their "worthless" activities. A second view was rather positive. Household work was justified through such values as "making a good home," "keeping the family happy," or exploring the creative dimensions of child care, cooking, and home decoration. The third view was one of ambivalence. On the one hand, "it was about time" someone noticed the complexity of household work, the amount of labor involved, and who, in fact, bore the brunt of "making a home," especially when they genuinely loved the people for whom household work was being undertaken. One obvious point that did emerge was that few women in their entire sample felt that household work was an entirely worthwhile, dignified activity.

## THE EMPLOYED WIFE AND MOTHER

In 1988, 55.9 percent of all females age sixteen and over (a total of 54 million) were employed in the labor force. This was up from 49.2 percent (or 42 million) just ten years earlier in 1978 and up from 42.6 percent since 1970 (*see* Table 4–1). Of these 54.0 million females, 25.2 percent were single, 59.2 percent were married, and 15.6 percent were widowed or divorced. While the total number of women in the labor force and the proportion of females in the labor force relative to the female populations have both increased dramatically over the past several decades, the marital distribution, particularly since 1960, has changed very little. Over the past thirty years, at any one time, about one-fourth

---

20. Alfreda P. Iglehart, "Wives, Work, and Social Change: What About the Housewives?" *Social Service Review* 54 (September 1980): 317–330.

21. Aloen Townsend and Patricia Gurin, "Re-Examining the Frustrated Homemaker Hypothesis," *Sociology of Work and Occupations* 8 (November 1981): 464–488.

22. Sarah Fenstermaker Berk and Catherine White Berheide, "Going Backstage: Gaining Access to Observe Household Work," *Sociology of Work and Occupations* 4 (February 1977): 41–42.

*Table 4–1*

*Marital status of women in the civilian labor force, 1960–1988. (Persons 14 years old and over through 1965; 16 years old and over thereafter.)*

|  | 1960 | 1970 | 1980 | 1988 |
|---|---|---|---|---|
| *Female labor force* | | | | |
| Total (thousands) | 22,516 | 31,233 | 44,934 | 53,987 |
| Single | 5,401 | 6,965 | 11,242 | 13,617 |
| Married | 13,485 | 19,799 | 26,828 | 31,946 |
| Widowed or divorced | 3,629 | 4,469 | 6,864 | 8,424 |
| *Percent distribution of female labor force* | | | | |
| Single | 24.0% | 22.3% | 25.0% | 25.2% |
| Married | 59.9 | 63.4 | 59.7 | 59.2 |
| Widowed or divorced | 16.1 | 14.3 | 15.3 | 15.6 |
| *Female labor force as percent of female population* | | | | |
| Total | 34.8% | 42.6% | 51.1% | 55.9% |
| Single | 44.1 | 53.0 | 61.5 | 65.2 |
| Married | 31.7 | 41.4 | 50.7 | 56.8 |
| Widowed or divorced | 37.1 | 36.2 | 41.0 | 43.4 |

*Source:* U.S. Bureau of the Census, *Statistical Abstract of the United States: 1989*, 109th ed. (Washington, D.C.: U.S. Government Printing Office, 1989), no. 638, p. 385.

of the female labor force has been single, three-fifths has been married, and about one in six or seven has been widowed or divorced.

What are some other characteristics of the female work force? Of the married women in 1988, 57.1 percent had at least one child under six years of age (*see* Figure 4–1.) This was also true for 70.1 percent of separated and divorced women.[23] These figures gain added relevance when viewed in the light of certain theoretical orientations that stress the importance of a "mother at-home" for young children (*see* Chapter 14) and the widespread public concern over the working mother. The extent of the legitimacy of these concerns in terms of consequences for the children is examined in the pages that follow.

The largest percentage of employed women in 1987 were in what the U.S. Census categorizes as technical, sales, and administrative support (about 45 percent). This includes occupations such as technicians, retail sales workers, secretaries, and typists. An additional 25 percent were in managerial and professional occupations such as teachers, writers, nurses, and managers; 18 percent were in service occupations such as child-care workers, waitresses, health aides, or hairdressers; 9 percent were operators and laborers, such as machine operators, inspectors, and non-construction laborers; and the remaining percent were in occupations such as mechanics, construction

23. U.S. Bureau of the Census, *Statistical Abstract of the United States: 1989*, 109th ed. (Washington, D.C.: U.S. Government Printing Office, 1989), no. 639, p. 386.

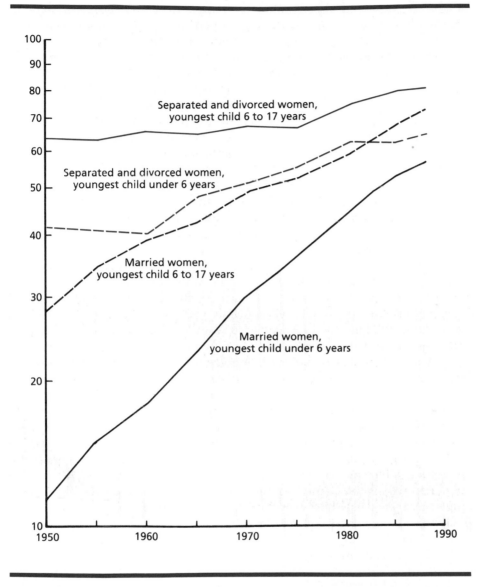

*Figure 4–1*
**Labor force participation rates of mothers with children under eighteen years old:
March 1950 – 1982.** (*Source:* U.S. Bureau of the Census, *Current Population Reports*,
Series P-23, no. 117, "Trends in Child Care Arrangements of Working Mothers"
[Washington, D.C.: U.S. Government Printing Office, 1982], Figure 1, p. 4; and U.S. Bu-
reau of the Census, *Statistical Abstract of the United States: 1989*, 109th ed.
[Washington, D.C.: U.S. Government Printing Office, 1989], no. 639, p. 386.)

trades, and agricultural occupations.[24] Many occupations are held predominantly by females: registered nurses, 95 percent; secretaries and typists, 98 percent; telephone operators, 92 percent; child-care workers, 96 percent; welfare service aides, 91 percent; and elementary teachers, 85 percent. In contrast, occupations with few females include engineers and dentists with about 8 percent, the construction trades with less than 2 percent, and fire fighters and vehicle equipment mechanics with less than 1 percent. This concentration or absence of women in particular occupations may help us understand differences by gender in income, benefits, power, and authority.

Of those women with incomes, the median income in 1987 was $8,101 (compared to $17,752 for men).[25] The sharpest income discrepancy between men and women appears in the $15,000 and over categories. Fifty-seven percent of all employed men fell within this category, as opposed to 28.5 percent of all employed women. Some of the income gap can be explained by the differences just shown in type of work and extent of employment. About two-thirds of employed women were in clerical, service, and blue-collar occupations. In addition, approximately one out of every four employed women (26 percent) was listed as *part time*. If the median income of only the women employed full time in 1987 is used, the median income of women becomes $17,504, a figure still well below the $26,722 of full-time male workers.[26] A simple mathematical computation of these figures indicates that, among full-time workers only, women earn $0.65 to every $1.00 earned by men.

This male-female difference in income is explained by Patricia Roos[27] as the result of women being adversely affected by the sex-segregated character of the labor market. Because of their concentration in selected occupations and industries, women operate in a very different employment context than men. Roos analyzes five measures of positional inequality, or characteristics of jobs, that improve our understanding of why women earn less than men. First, the few occupations in which women work are *low-paying*. Second, the occupations in which women work are *heavily female*—that is, rather than men and women on average doing similar work, women are highly concentrated in a few jobs. Third, working women relative to men are characteristically less likely to *control the means of production*. Women-owned businesses represent only about 5 percent of the U.S. firms. Fourth, women are less likely than men to *exercise authority* over others. Even when they hold authority

24. Ibid., no. 642, pp. 388–389.
25. Ibid., no. 728, p. 449.
26. Ibid., no. 727, p. 448
27. Patricia A. Roos, "Sex Stratification in the Workplace: Male-Female Differences in Economic Returns to Occupation," *Social Science Research* 10 (September 1981): 195–224. For variations in women's wages *see* Cynthia Rexcoat and Constance Shehan, "Differential Effects of Industrial and Worker Resources in Women's Wages," *Social Science Research* 15 (1986): 1–27. For household labor time as an explanation *see* Beth Anne Shelton and Juanita Firestone, "An Examination of Household Labor Time as a Factor in Composition and Treatment Effects on the Male-Female Wage Gap," *Sociological Focus* 21 (August 1988): 265–278.

positions, they are likely to be less important than those held by men. Finally, women are *segregated by industry*. These industries, such as service and retail trade rather than mining, manufacturing, or wholesale trade, both pay less and generate less return to investment.

## Reasons for wife-mother employment

Why do wives and mothers work? They work for the same mysterious reasons that husbands and fathers work, although men are much less likely to be asked. Women are asked because of the institutionalized bias that has traditionally existed against married women and mothers working for any reason other than economic remuneration. Since the place of a wife— particularly one who is also the mother of preschool-aged children— is widely believed to be in the home, the traditional bias will lead again to the question, "Why do wives and mothers work?"

Many individualistic reasons could be given, but all personal and seemingly idiosyncratic factors share much in common. The most frequently articulated reason for working is money or financial need. But clearly, many factors other than money influence the decision to seek paid employment. Results from Ireland have shown that three factors predict a significant amount of the variance in the married woman's employment status: (1) her perceived approval from four of her important others (husband, mother, father, and closest friend); (2) her own attitude toward maternal employment; and (3) her expected family size.[28] Results from North Carolina women suggest that the best predictor of a wife's employment was her husband's support.[29] That is, the relationship between the husband and wife seems to take precedence over financial considerations in determining the wife's employment.

In addition to these is a long list of factors that influence the employment likelihood for wives and mothers. Some of these factors include: the availability of jobs; the number and age of her children; her age and level of education, work experience, and work skills; the income level of her husband; status maintenance and status enhancement; and a range of attitudinal variables, including those of her husband.[30] It is easier to work, as in the middle years, when one does not have children. Generally, it is easier to find a job if one has training, skills, and experience. The absence of a husband, a part-time

28. Margret Fine-Davis, "Social-Psychological Predictors of Employment Status of Married Women in Ireland," *Journal of Marriage and the Family* 41 (February 1979): 145–158.

29. Becky L. Glass, "A Rational Choice Model of Wives' Employment Decisions," *Sociological Spectrum* 8 (1988): 35–48.

30. See, for example, Marianne A. Ferber, "Labor Market Participation of Young Married Women: Causes and Effects," *Journal of Marriage and the Family* 44 (May 1982): 457–468; David J. Eggebeen, "Determinants of Maternal Employment for White Preschool Children: 1960–1980," *Journal of Marriage and the Family* 50 (February 1988): 149–159; and Sandra Cotton, John K. Antill, and John D. Cunningham, "The Work Motivations of Mothers with Preschool Children," *Journal of Family Issues* 10 (June 1989): 189–210.

employed husband, or a husband with low income forces women into the work force. Generally, an *inverse* relationship exists between the husband's level of income and the percentage of wives employed.

Since opportunities to work are available, Kingsley Davis raises the question of not only why so many wives work, but also why so many of them do not.[31] The answer, he claims, is not that they have calculated the dollar costs and benefits and found that employment does not pay. Rather, it is that they have calculated the psychosocial costs and benefits, and found employment deficient.

Interestingly, a direct relationship exists between economic attainment and an unmarried status. Singleness may be less a "marriage reject" for many employed single women than one of "rejecting marriage." In brief, the lower the husband's income, the higher the percentage of wives employed; the higher the woman's income, the more likely she is to be or remain single.

## Employed women and children

Few sociocultural differentials have equaled the strength of the inverse relationship between female labor-force participation and fertility. Simply, working women have fewer children. Marital female employment before childbearing has been found to be associated with lower fertility levels later, longer first-birth intervals, and earlier use of birth control.[32] On the other hand, there has been a dramatic increase in labor-force participation among women with school- and preschool-aged children (*see* Figure 4–1). The presence of young children remains a deterrent to women's labor-force participation but only minimally so in contrast to thirty years ago (again note Figure 4–1).

A pregnancy and first birth clearly has a major impact on female employment. A national longitudinal survey of over 19,000 seniors beginning in 1972 with four follow-up surveys reported that the majority of ever-married women have jobs prior to pregnancy: most leave these jobs as the pregnancy progresses, so that only one woman in five remains employed in the month that the child is born.[33] Following the birth, some women return to work but employment rates only rise to about 60 percent of their previous levels. Had these women not become parents, the proportion employed would have steadily increased. Thus, parenthood does lead to an employment deficit. Even women who retained their jobs were found to show some decline in hours at work.

---

31. Kingsley Davis, "Wives and Work: The Sex Role Revolution and Its Consequences," *Population and Development Review* 10 (September 1984): 413.

32. H. Theodore Groat, Randy L. Workman, and Arthur G. Neal, "Labor Force Participation and Family Formation: A Study of Working Mothers," *Demography* 13 (February 1976): 115–125.

33. Linda J. Waite, Gus W. Haggstrom, and David E. Kanouse, "Changes in the Employment Activities of New Parents," *American Sociological Review* 50 (April 1985): 263–272.

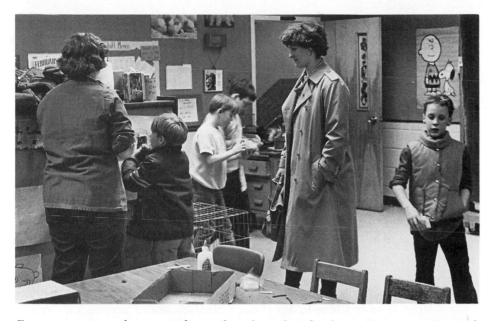

*Day care centers, when properly run, have been found to be positive, supportive, and enriching environments for children of employed parents.*

It is often assumed that maternal employment has many effects on a child—all bad. However, endorsement of this belief has declined, especially among women,[34] and research in the last several decades has seriously challenged this view. Few studies seem to exist that report meaningful differences between the children of working mothers in general and the children of nonworking mothers. When differences do exist, it is often explained less by the mother working than by other factors: social class, part- or full-time employment, age of the children, mother's attitude toward employment, or other social and psychological factors. For example, the occupational status of the position the mother held was found to be of greater consequence to the children than whether she worked or not.[35] Low-status mothers produced the most traditional children; mothers holding high-status positions produced the most nonconventional or liberal offspring; and housewives as well as women in medium-status positions produced children intermediate in their attitudes to the high- and low-status offspring.

34. Karen Oppenheim Mason and Yu-Hsia Lo, "Attitudes Towards Women's Familial Roles: Changes in the United States, 1977–1985," *Gender and Society* 2 (March 1988): 39–57.
35. Alan C. Acock, Deborah Barker, and Vern L. Bengtson, "Mother's Employment and Parent–Youth Similarity," *Journal of Marriage and the Family* 44 (May 1982): 441–455.

Lois Hoffman reviewed research organized around five general hypotheses related to maternal employment and its effect on children.[36] Hypothesis 1 suggested that maternal employment affects the child, particularly the daughter, because the role models provided by working and nonworking mothers differ. Considerable support was provided for this hypothesis. In general, daughters of working mothers had less traditional sex-role concepts, a higher level of female competence, and compared favorably with daughters of nonworking mothers with respect to independence and achievement-related variables.[37] Another source found the status of mothers' occupation to be an important influence on sons' and daughters' educational and occupational status with the somewhat surprising finding that mothers' occupational status had a more powerful effect than fathers' on sons' attainments.[38]

Hypothesis 2 suggested that a child would be affected by the mother's emotional state: morale or satisfactions from employment status, emotional stress because of dual-role demands, and guilt about the child. The data about the mother's emotional state suggest that the working mother who obtains satisfaction from her work, who has adequate arrangements so that her dual role does not involve undue strain, and who does not feel so guilty that she overcompensates is likely to do quite well and, under certain conditions, better than the nonworking mother.[39] This is quite consistent with data on child abuse that show working mothers are not more likely to be abusive. Richard Gelles and Eileen Hargreaves reported that women who worked full time had the lowest rate of overall violence toward their children, while mothers with part-time jobs and mothers who were not working reported higher rates.[40] The tendency for mothers at home and mothers employed part time to hit their children was increased if these mothers had preschool children. Rates of violence were very high where husbands were unemployed.

Hypothesis 3 suggested that maternal employment affects the child through its influence on child-rearing practices. In some studies, maternal employment increased the father's participation in child rearing while in others the active participation of the father had a positive effect on the child. Children of working mothers were found to have more household responsibilities and to experience a milder form of discipline.[41]

Hypothesis 4 suggested that the working mother provides less adequate

36. Lois Wladis Hoffman, "Effects on Child," in *Working Mothers* by Lois Wladis Hoffman and F. Ivan Nye (San Francisco: Jossey-Bass, 1974): 126–166.

37. Ibid., p. 136.

38. Mary Holland Baker, "Mother's Occupation and Children's Attainments," *Pacific Sociological Review* 24 (April 1981): 237–254.

39. Hoffman, "Effects on Child," p. 142.

40. Richard G. Gelles and Eileen F. Hargreaves, "Maternal Employment and Violence Toward Children," *Journal of Family Issues* 2 (December 1981): 509–530.

41. Hoffman, "Effects on Child," pp. 142–147.

supervision, resulting in more delinquency. Hoffman does suggest that particularly in the lower classes, children of working mothers may receive less adequate supervision, which may be linked to delinquency. But other research points out the complex nature of linking the family in general with delinquency. Clearly, peer and school variables are more powerful predictors of delinquent involvement than family variables, but family processes assume a major role in one of the most powerful models of delinquency—social control theory. Generally, variations in family structure, including the employment of mothers, do not show a direct linkage to delinquency.[42]

Hypothesis 5 suggested that the working mother's child is a victim of maternal deprivation. No solid evidence supports this hypothesis.[43]

In brief, maternal employment per se appears to be too broad a concept to produce major distinctions in effects on children. The numbers and percentages of women and working mothers do, however, focus attention on other areas such as an increasing interest in, and need for, day-care services. It also focuses attention on the husband-wife relationship and the balance of power between them, which will be discussed next.

## Employed women and marriage

The effect of female employment on a marriage, on the marital relationship, and on other family relations could be expected to vary considerably depending on whether the employment is full time or part time, on whether there are preschool children, on the age of the couple, on their stage in the life cycle, and on many other factors.[44]

A female employment factor that affects the marriage negatively is that of holding a job not traditionally occupied by women. Women holding nontraditional positions were about twice as likely to divorce as those with jobs traditionally held by women.[45] Another factor having a significant impact on marital dissolution is the amount of hours the wife works or spends away from the household.[46] The greater the number of hours worked, the greater the probability of marital instability, divorce, or both. In contrast, a female

42. *Note:* Stephen A Cernkovich and Peggy C. Giordano, "Family Relationships and Delinquency," *Criminology* 25 (1987): 295–321.

43. Hoffman, "Effects on Child," p. 157.

44. An excellent review of the effects of women's employment on families can be seen in Glenna Spitze, "Women's Employment and Family Relations: A Review," *Journal of Marriage and the Family* 50 (August 1988): 595–618.

45. William W. Philliber and Dana V. Hiller, "Relative Occupational Attainments of Spouses and Later Changes in Marriage and Wife's Work Experience," *Journal of Marriage and the Family* 45 (February 1983): 161–170.

46. Glenna Spitze and Scott J. South, "Women's Employment, Time Expenditure, and Divorce," *Journal of Family Issues* 6 (September 1985): 307–329; and Alan Booth, David R. Johnson, Lynn White, and John N. Edwards, "Women, Outside Employment, and Marital Instability," *American Journal of Sociology* 90 (November 1984): 567–583.

employment factor that affects the marriage positively is the extent to which the family experiences accommodate the wife's employment. Major factors seem to be having a supportive husband and freedom from childrearing responsibilities.[47] The most important conclusion from a review of twenty-seven studies spanning over thirty years and exploring the relationship between employment status and marital adjustment was that the wife's employment status alone appears to have little or no effect on marital adjustment.[48] This finding challenges the common belief that employment of wives per se places marital interaction and harmony in jeopardy.

Employment of the wife is certain to bring changes in the husband-wife relationship. Changes in the roles of companion, housewife, entertainer, lover, and the like are certain to require readjustments on the part of both spouses. The wife's job may reduce the amount of personal care the husband receives, increase his responsibilities for child care and household tasks, and require a modification in his career plans. While these and other changes may at times create stress and conflict, it appears that husbands of employed women evidence no more signs of marital discord and stress than the spouses of housewives.[49] They may, however, experience other consequences of female or dual employment.

Considerable shifts in power in the husband-wife relationship seem to occur when the wife is employed. In general, the wife's power tends to increase. In a later chapter, a resource theory is used to explain shifts in power. Thus, as the wife becomes employed, she gains income, independence, and new contacts (resources) that increase her contribution to the marriage. This increase in power among employed wives appears not only in the United States but cross-culturally as well.

Employment of mothers affects far more than their children and their marriage. It affects them as well. Mere presence in the paid labor force was found to have a substantial liberalizing effect on women's roles and responsibilities, but only small effects on their support of feminist positions (such as support for the Equal Rights Amendment, approval of legal abortion, approval of sexual behavior between consenting adults, and so forth).[50] Employed mothers were likely to enjoy their activities and relationships with children, reveal positive feelings about themselves, project an image of ability

47. Sharon K. Houseknecht and Anne S. Macke, "Combining Marriage and Career: The Marital Adjustment of Professional Women," *Journal of Marriage and the Family* 43 (August 1981): 651–661.

48. Drake S. Smith, "Wife Employment and Marital Adjustment: A Cumulation of Results," *Family Relations* 34 (October 1985): 483–490.

49. Alan Booth, "Does Wives' Employment Cause Stress for Husbands?" *The Family Coordinator* 28 (October 1979): 445–449; and Alan Booth, "Wife's Employment and Husband's Stress: A Replication and Refutation," *Journal of Marriage and the Family* 39 (November 1977): 645–650.

50. Eric Plutzer, "Work Life, Family Life, and Women's Support of Feminism," *American Sociological Review* 53 (August 1988): 640–649.

and confidence, and evaluate their communities as a satisfactory place to live.[51]

In the middle years, with the children gone from the home, the interests of the employed mother are no longer divided between her children and her job. Some women turn from part-time to full-time employment. Some begin work for the first time or at least the first time since the marriage or birth of children. Employment may take on a new meaning, presenting a perspective on the world and her own values considerably different from that known previously.

## The employed husband and father

In 1987, 76.2 percent of all males aged sixteen and over (a total of 66.2 million) were employed in the labor force. This was down slightly from the 77.4 percent (61.5 million) in 1980 and down from 80.0 percent (51.2 million) in 1970.[52] As can be seen, while the number of males in the employed labor force increased, the proportion of employed men relative to the total male population decreased. This is unlike the data presented for females which showed both a number and percentage increase.

Apart from number differences in the employment status of males and females, the significant differences center around social norms and expectations. Take note of some of the questions raised about women in the section on the employed wife and mother. Do we seriously raise questions as to why men work, the effect of paternal employment (versus nonemployment) on family size, the "negative" effect of employment on children—especially preschool-aged children—or the career-oriented males as "marriage rejects"? If we ask a boy what he wants to be when he grows up, a "correct" answer is not "married," or "a father," but rather some employment status, particularly one of a prestigious nature: doctor, lawyer, banker, or president. For men, work defines their worth, their success or failure, and their major source of identity.

If that last sentence is true and employment is so important to men, it could be assumed that unemployment is a crucial dimension in their lives. The evidence from depression studies shared the finding that the husband's unemployment had a negative effect on his self-esteem, personal functioning, and marital and family relationships. Similar results appear in more recent studies. Earlier in this chapter, it was stated that rates of violence were very high among unemployed husbands. In a look at blue-collar families, while finding unemployment of men not to have a negative effect on their self-esteem, Jeffry Larson did report that it corresponded to significantly lower

---

51. *See* Ronald C. Kessler and James A. McRae, Jr., "The Effect of Wives' Employment on the Mental Health of Married Men and Women," *American Sociological Review* 47 (April 1982): 216–227.

52. U.S. Bureau of the Census, *Statistical Abstract of the United States: 1987*, no. 621, p. 376.

## Husband roles among the Amish

Amish family organization and expected gender roles are centered around the father. This patriarchal structure can be seen by the extent to which his wife and children are subject to him. However, the line of authority is not rigid; the wife is consulted, particularly about child rearing, family problems, and decisions relating to home purchases. The children may also be consulted in planning farming matters. However, the husband's word is regarded as final.

The husband's way of life, as with most Amish behavior, stems from the scriptures. As stated in I Corinthians 11:3, "The head of the woman is the man." Thus, both husband and wife are well aware that the husband is the head of the house, although age too is a significant status factor. The oldest male, or grandfather, is respected as the patriarch and his social status increases at least until he reaches the age where he simply moves into the *Gross Dawdy* (grandfather) house and the younger generation takes over.

The husband's major activities center around farming. He will purchase the equipment and livestock without seeking the advice of his wife. He will perform the majority of the farming activities with the assistance of his wife and children. Only on occasion would the husband assist his wife in household tasks.

Personal relationships between husband and wife are quiet and sober, with no apparent demonstration of affection. Irritation between mates, expressed in a variety of ways, is conditioned by informally approved means of expression: the tone of voice, a gesture, or a direct statement. The husband may express disapproval by complete silence at the dinner table and the wife is left to guess what is wrong.

marital adjustment, poorer marital communication, and lower satisfaction and harmony in family relations.[53] The unemployed spent less on entertainment, food, gasoline, and home energy consumption, all of which might be expected to affect marital-family relationships.

Whether unemployed or employed, men's sense of worth and work satisfaction does not exist independently of the family. One paper[54] identified some ways that specific aspects of work-family structures relate to men's satisfaction at work. It was found that men in traditional one-career marriages felt more successful at work than did men in two-career marriages. This traditional family structure added to the man's feelings that he achieved success according to the traditional standards of the culture. Here he enters a career, starts a family in early adulthood, is upwardly mobile, and successfully provides for his family. The work satisfaction for men in two-career marriages was greatly influenced by the presence of children. This two-paycheck marriage appeared to allow the man greater flexibility in his attitudes toward his career and his identification with the "provider" role. Childless men in two-career marriages felt less successful and less self-actualized at work than did fathers in the same type of marriage.

53. Jeffry H. Larson, "The Effect of Husband's Unemployment on Marital and Family Relations in Blue-Collar Families," *Family Relations* 33 (October 1984): 503–511.

54. Samuel Osherson and Diana Dill, "Varying Work and Family Choices: Their Impact on Men's Work Satisfaction," *Journal of Marriage and the Family* 45 (May 1983): 339–346.

Men, like women, work for financial reasons. But the emphases on getting a job, getting ahead, and gaining prestige or achieving power are stressed in the sex-role socialization process to a far greater extent for men than for women. For men, their work often becomes their home away from home. Bosses or the corporate hierarchy tend to serve as a surrogate parent in holding authority, defining duties, and dispensing rewards or punishments. Workmates serve as siblings with their competition, rivalry, friendships, and relatively equal status. In brief, while women are likely to gain status and identity through their marriage, men are often married to their work and gain their status and identity accordingly.

## THE HOUSEHUSBAND

Work, to men and husbands, is generally defined and described in terms of labor-force employment, not in terms of housework and child care. In an article on men's family work, Joseph Pleck described three different perspectives concerning this work: the traditional, the exploitation, and the changing-roles perspectives.[55]

The *traditional perspective* holds that husbands are not responsible for any substantial amount of housework and child care in the family. The responsibility of the husband to the family is to provide economic support through paid employment. In terms of "role differentiation," the male holds primary responsibility for relationships and needs external to the family; the female holds responsibility for relationships and needs internal to the family. In terms of "exchange," the husband exchanges his work and economic services for the wife's companionship and household services. In terms of "resources" (*see* Chapter 12) relative to housework and child care, women have *time* for these activities which the full-time employed husband does not have.

The *exploitation perspective* identifies the unequal burden of housework and child care carried by women as an important aspect of their inferior status in society. As suggested previously, one argument suggests that male avoidance of housework and child care is a deliberate strategy to maintain power over women. Studies have revealed that (1) the husband's performance of housework is small in tasks or time relative to the wife's and, more significantly, that (2) husbands of employed wives do *not* spend much more time in housework than husbands of nonemployed wives. That is, employed wives do less than nonemployed wives, but husbands work about the same amount of time irrespective of the employment status of the wife. What these

---

55. Joseph H. Pleck, "Men's Family Work: Three Perspectives and Some New Data," *The Family Coordinator* 28 (October 1979): 481–488.

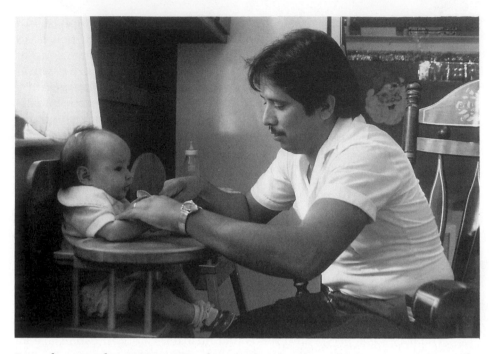

*Few role reversal marriages exist where husbands voluntarily give up employment to serve as full-time househusbands. However, with the trend toward female employment, men are assuming more reponsibility for the care of children.*

two findings reveal is a substantial work "overload" on the wives in a combined housewife-employed wife role compared to their husbands.

There appears to be a significant disjunction between the perceptions of husband and wife concerning the amount of husband's help with household tasks.[56] Husbands believe that they help more than wives think husbands help. If men hold greater family power and perceive themselves as offering a significant degree of assistance with household labor, it appears unlikely that they will volunteer more or accept the next perspective, that of changing roles.

The *changing-roles perspective*, while acknowledging the traditional and exploitation perspectives, interprets men's work responsibility in a different light. Basically the argument is that in the evolution of work and family roles, as women add a second and new role of paid employment to their traditional role of housewife, men too need to add a second and new role of work in the home and with children to their traditional role of paid employment. The

56. John G. Condran and Jerry G. Bode, "Rashomon, Working Wives, and Family Division of Labor: Middletown, 1980," *Journal of Marriage and the Family* 44 (May 1982): 421–426.

problem today is one of a psychosocial lag between the slower rate of change for men toward housework and the more rapid rate of change for women toward paid employment.

The first perspective (traditional) sees no reason for change. The second perspective (exploitation) sees little hope for change. The third perspective (changing roles) sees change as possible, likely, and emerging. Evidence for the third perspective is seen in subgroups such as single-parent fathers, fathers deliberately holding part-time jobs, single adoptive fathers, and househusbands; in these situations, men are assuming major household and child-care duties. What is not known is the extent to which contemporary househusbands relinquish traditional male roles. A small study of Hispanic househusbands, for example, revealed that their househusband role was brought about by external economic circumstances and was viewed as a temporary status. [57] They did, however, report a greater involvement in family life, increased insight into their spouses' experiences, and as a result, closer relations with their spouses and children.

While there is no question that wives continue to hold the primary responsibility for housework and child care, and while the pace of change may seem both slow and minimal, it seems important to recognize that men's behavior appears to be changing. While we are not witnessing a major trend toward full-time househusbands, an increased participation of men in household and child-care tasks does seem to be taking place in dual-employment and dual-career marriages.

## DUAL-CAREER MARRIAGES

While dual-employed marriages and the employment of women have been common, particularly increasing since the Second World War, the common occurrence of *dual-career* marriage is a newer life-style. *Career* is used in place of *work* or *paid employment* to designate a level of commitment and continuous developmental sequence that is intrinsically rewarding, conditions less likely to be found in a job taken primarily for additional income purposes. The dual-career argument rests upon assumptions of increasing female access to high-level professions and managerial positions, of norms of gender equality, and of employment motivations centering on personal self-development and interpersonal relationships rather than economics.

Harold Benenson argues that these assumptions about dual careers, while widely believed, are fundamentally flawed and run counter to certain

---

57. Sharon Kantorowski Davis and Virginia Chavez, "Hispanic Househusbands," *Hispanic Journal of Behavioral Sciences* 7 (1985): 317–332.

basic realities.[58] For example, in spite of recent gains, married women practicing the elite professions of law, medicine, and college teaching remain a numerically insignificant group among married women as a whole. In spite of high-education levels, most wives of high-income husbands maintain and enhance their families' class position by providing vital assistance to their husbands' and children's career advancement. In spite of the dual-career image, women in professions and management positions are far more likely than comparable men to be single, married with no children, or divorced as a consequence of their career involvement. And married women who are in professional and managerial categories are still basically in the traditional female, low-paid professions of school teaching and nursing. Thus, the dual-career pattern tends not to represent equality, access to high-level professions, or work motivations separate from income for the majority of married couples. Others have made related arguments about existing assumptions of dual careers and have even proposed that dual-career marriages be banished from the research literature.[59]

Irrespective of these assumptions, existing literature on dual-career marriages suggests a range of common problems. One of these problems relates to stress, role strain, or difficulties related to a work overload. This recurring topic of dual-career and dual-earner families concerns the role overloads and strains experienced as a result of time pressures in discharging simultaneous work and family obligations. One remedy for this time bind is a reduced work week for one or both parents, a preference found in one study for over half of mothers and two-thirds of fathers.[60] But the discrepancy between *actual* work hours and *desired* work hours combined with being locked into a job where hours are fixed only increased the role strain. And this role strain from difficulty in meeting work and family demands was found to be associated with more depression, pessimism, a lower level of togetherness in the marriage, and family conflict.[61]

This overload situation is what Karen Fox and Sharon Nikhols refer to as the "time crunch."[62] Time is limited to precisely twenty-four hours per day but, dual careers or not, there are multiple roles and tasks to be performed. The way many couples alleviated the time crunch was for the employed wife

---

58. Harold Benenson, "Women's Occupational and Family Achievement in the U.S. Class System: A Critique of the Dual-Career Family Analysis," *The British Journal of Sociology* 35 (March 1984): 19–41.

59. Dana Vannoy Hiller and Janice Dyehouse, "A Case for Banishing 'Dual-Career Marriages' from the Research Literature," *Journal of Marriage and the Family* 49 (November 1987): 787–795.

60. Phyllis Moen and Donna I. Dempster-McClain, "Employed Parents: Role Strain, Work Time, and Preference for Working Less," *Journal of Marriage and the Family* 49 (August 1987): 579–590.

61. Nancy L. Galambos and Rainer K. Silbereisen, "Role Strain in West German Dual-Earner Households," *Journal of Marriage and the Family* 51 (May 1989): 385–389; and Patricia M. Ulbrich, "The Determinants of Depression in Two-Income Marriages," *Journal of Marriage and the Family* 50 (February 1988): 121–131.

62. Karen D. Fox and Sharon Y. Nickols, "The Time Crunch: Wife's Employment and Family Work," *Journal of Family Issues* 4 (March 1983): 61–82.

to spend less time in housework. There is a consistency of data, some reported in this chapter, that shows husbands do not provide a corresponding increase in time allocation to housework to offset the wife's decrease.

Another related issue in dual-career or dual-earner marriages involves the relationship between parents and children. In these marriages, as with the employed single female parent, mother's place is not exclusively in the home. Thus concerns such as "latchkey children" and child care take on increased importance. Latchkey children are "self-care" children who come home after school to an empty house, let themselves in with a "latch key," and remain there alone until a working parent gets home. Virginia Cain and Sandra Hofferth suggest that there are fewer latchkey children than popularly believed (about 2.4 million); they are such for only a short period of time each day (most for two hours or less); and they are not the children of low-income, single parents who cannot afford stable child-care arrangements for them.[63] Thus while latchkey children may be an important concern for some dual-career parents, the more significant issue is child care.

How can dual-career couples participate jointly in nonfamilial work and also rear their children? An obvious answer is that they make alternative child-care arrangements for the hours they are employed. But many parents face major constraints, such as the unavailability or high cost of such arrangements. Harriet Presser documents a remarkably high prevalence of non-day shifts among dual-earner spouses with the result being high rates of parental child care, including father care.[64] For many dual-career families, however, shift work is not a possibility and the whole issue of day care or child care takes on an increased importance (as it does for single parents as well). Both day care and after-school care are currently in limbo. The need is extensive, group care is limited in availability, and costs are often high. Thus a major concern for many employed parents, single or dual-career, is adequate child care.

After reading about the dilemmas and the resultant strains produced by dual careers, one could ask, "Why dual careers?" Clearly, there are gains beyond economic ones in this type of life-style. These are satisfactions derived from creating something, achieving recognition, expanding energies beyond the home and children, or enriching marriage. Recent results suggest that men are responding less positively to the dual-earner arrangement than women.[65] There may be subtle forms of resistance among men (avoidance of housework, inadequate parenting, domestic violence, high divorce rates) who could potentially benefit most if they had a traditional, conventional wife. It would

---

63. Virginia S. Cain and Sandra L. Hofferth, "Parental Choice of Self-Care for School-Age Children," *Journal of Marriage and the Family* 51 (February 1989): 65–77.

64. Harriet B. Presser, "Shift Work and Child Care Among Young Dual-Earner American Parents," *Journal of Marriage and the Family* 50 (February 1988): 133–148.

65. Sandra C. Stanley, Janet G. Hunt, and Larry L. Hunt, "The Relative Deprivation of Husbands in Dual-Earner Households," *Journal of Family Issues* 7 (March 1986): 3–20.

appear that the husband of the employed wife loses part of his active support system when the wife fails to function as a servant, homemaker, and mother. Employed wives, on the other hand, expand into roles that have more positive value for them.

While the professional employment of women is gaining increasing respectability and acceptance, a state of sexual equality has not and perhaps will not be achieved. This is in spite of a WASP (Wives as Senior Partners) marital pattern that is being chosen by some couples where the wife's occupation is seen as more important than the husband's.[66] Wives are still generally expected to give up their own jobs for the sake of their husbands and to shoulder the primary responsibility for housework and child care. Janet and Larry Hunt argue that dual-career families have not represented a radical departure from conventional sex roles. They suggest that as careers become more legitimate for women, careers and families will become increasingly polarized rather than more effectively integrated.[67] They predict a growing institutional separation of careers and families. For the highly successful of both sexes, families will be less necessary, less helpful, and more of a liability than in the past.

Margaret Paloma and others would agree with the idea just presented. Data suggest that the structure of the U.S. family makes it virtually impossible for married career women to have career lines like those of their male counterparts.[68] The dual pressures of both family responsibilities and career obligations for the married career woman may mean the increased separation of career and family or, when integrated, may occur primarily later in life when child-care responsibilities are lessened. In brief, today's aspiring married professionals face difficult choices: lowering career aspirations, consciously rejecting parenthood, divorce, withdrawal of one spouse from the top-professional tier, or for some, commuter marriages.

### Commuter marriages

What about the dual career where the husband and wife live separately? The pattern of one spouse leaving home temporarily is nothing new and the amount of separation is known to vary both by occupation or profession as

66. Maxine P. Atkinson and Jacqueline Boles, "WASP (Wives as Senior Partners)," *Journal of Marriage and the Family* 46 (November 1984): 861–870.

67. Janet G. Hunt and Larry L. Hunt, "The Dualities of Careers and Families: New Integrations or New Polarization?" *Social Problems* 29 (June 1982): 499–510; and Janet G. Hunt and Larry L. Hunt, "Dual-Career Families: Vanguard of the Future or Residue of the Past?" in Joan Aldous, ed., *Two Paychecks: Life in Dual-Earner Families* (Beverly Hills: Sage Publications, 1982): 41–59.

68. Margaret M. Paloma, Brian F. Pendleton, and T. Neal Garland, "Reconsidering the Dual-Career Marriage: A Longitudinal Approach," in Joan Aldous, ed., *Two Paychecks: Life in Dual-Earner Families* (Beverly Hills: Sage Publications, 1982): 173–192; and Mary C. Regan and Helen E. Roland, "Rearranging Family and Career Priorities: Professional Women and Men of the Eighties," *Journal of Marriage and the Family* 47 (November 1985): 985–992.

well as by distance. Politicians, professional athletes, and various salespersons are known to routinely spend time apart from their spouse. In addition, military service, imprisonment, and seasonal work in selected occupations separate husbands and wives.

Today, the decision for family members to live apart and establish dual residences is increasingly a result of women's participation in the professions and an unwillingness to either divorce or relocate in the community of employment of the spouse. This pattern stands in sharp contrast to the traditional pattern of the married couple and their children living and moving where the husband has employment. Now, however, the wife's career may require her to spend the week days in New York or Chicago while the husband's career may require him to be in Detroit or Boston.

The traditional option would be for one spouse, usually the wife, to give up his or her job to live with the spouse. Newer options include marital separation or divorce, with each person pursuing career patterns independently, or remaining married but establishing separate residences with commuting between the residences possible. Both these options have few social or cultural supports. Marriage as defined by most people includes sharing a common residence. Friends or relatives are prone to question the satisfaction with or commitment to a marriage where the husband and wife reside in separate locations. Friends of the couple may exclude the "single" spouse from invitations to social events. And the couple themselves, as well as others, may tend to define aspects of their life-style more like that of single unmarrieds than of married people. The complexity of these living patterns increases for couples with dependent children.

Harriet Gross studied forty-three spouses representing twenty-eight dual-career marriages. Spouses were legally married and lived apart for at least four days at a time for at least several months.[69] For the most part, these couples were not newlyweds, were relatively affluent, and were executives or professionals. About half the husbands and wives saw each other weekly, about 10 percent from once a week to once a month, and about 40 percent less than once a month. Their decision to live apart rested upon advantages such as the freedom it granted to each spouse's work, and also the ability to work long and uninterrupted hours without building meals, sleep, or recreation around the other.

Wives tended to miss the emotional protection they expected from their husbands and sensed that this was a cost of their gain in independence. They also recognized that responsibilities for household and car repairs were theirs to manage singlehandedly. Husbands expressed loneliness and some guilt for being unable to provide the emotional protection they sensed their wives needed. What became evident to the couple was the difficulty of the transition

---

69. Harriet Engel Gross, "Dual Career Couples Who Live Apart: Two Types," *Journal of Marriage and the Family* 42 (August 1980): 567–576.

from the older, traditional role definitions to the newly emerging definitions of marital roles that accompanied two-resident living. A summary of Gross's findings suggested that older couples, those married longer, those among whom at least one spouse had an established career, and those who were freed from childrearing responsibilities found their life-style less stressful.

For many commuter couples, the telephone becomes a means of regular contact. Time together becomes well planned and not spent in meaningless socializing with uninterested others. The ease of the separation appears to be related to a high career commitment on the part of both parties, financial resources to meet the added expenses of maintaining two places of residence, phone calls, travel to see one another, shorter distances so they can get together more often, and long established patterns of interaction.

# *Summary*

1. This chapter began by briefly looking at selected linkages between the family and other institutions. Cross-culturally as well as historically, major interchanges and connections have existed at a macro-level between basic systems within all societies. Families are linked to religion, not only at weddings and funerals but also in terms of sex roles, sexual behaviors, and family size. Families are linked to politics in terms of social policy and legislation that ranges from taxation deductions for dependents to providing income for the elderly through social security. Families are linked to education in terms of learning social norms, skills, and mobility patterns.

2. The key focus of the chapter centers on economics, work, and the world of employment. Conflict theorists in particular view the economic system as the key to understanding inequality within or outside the family. Even household labor is intricately linked to a capitalist type of system that enables men to hold a dominant position over women.

3. A primary role for most married women is that of housewife. Often accorded low status, it appears that it involves long hours, is of high productive value, and produces an inequitable assignment of marital tasks. Yet it is a source of satisfaction and gratification for many women, particularly those adhering to more traditional marital-role expectations.

4. The number and proportion of wives and mothers in the paid labor force is increasing yearly. A majority are employed in the traditional female clerical and service occupations. They work for many of the same reasons men work, namely income, but derive many other rewards from their employment as well: status, prestige, recognition, and feelings of success and achievement. Very few negative effects on children are directly attributable to the employment of the mother. Similar results exist for marriage. While employment of wives affects husband-wife relationships, there are no more signs of marital discord and stress on such relationships than on those where the wife does not work.

5. The number of employed husbands and fathers is increasing, but the proportion of men working relative to the total male population is decreasing. There is wide-spread agreement on the expectation that men should be employed. Work appears to be the key source of identity, success or failure, and worth for men.

6. Househusbandry, unlike housewifery, is rarely a full-time job. Three perspectives on the role of husbands in relation to housework and child care were presented: the traditional, the exploitation, and the changing-roles perspectives. Each exists today, but there is evidence that some changes are occurring, although slowly, in the amount of time and frequency men are investing in these household tasks.

7. The increasing employment of women combined with the constant high employment of men is resulting in a large number of dual-employed and dual-career marriages. Numerous assumptions about these marriages run counter to certain basic realities. They involve various strains for both sexes and force difficult choices between family and career.

8. One issue resulting from the employment of both parents or of an existing parent focuses on the care of children in their absence. Latchkey children, or "self-care" children who come home from school to a parentless house, are of concern to many, but the more significant issue is child care in general. For some parents, shift work is a possibility, but for single parents and many two-parent households this is not a possibility. Day care for children is a major need, group care is limited in availability, and costs for any type of care are often high.

9. This chapter ends with a brief look at commuter marriages where the husband and wife live separately. For some, this type of living arrangement serves as the compromise between giving up the marriage or the career.

10. Chapters 1 through 4 have provided an introduction to family issues and changes; disciplinary and theoretical approaches to the family; marital, family, and kinship organization; and a look at institutional linkages with the family with a specific focus on work and employment. Next, we turn our attention to variations in family life-styles with chapters on Chinese and African-American families and a chapter on social class variations in family life-styles.

# KEY TERMS AND TOPICS

# DISCUSSION QUESTIONS

1. Show how the family engages in interchanges or is linked to other systems such as religion, politics, or education. What does each contribute to and receive from the other?

2. Discuss the statement that differences between churchgoers and non-churchgoers are more pronounced than differences between denominations or particular religious groups.

3. Why is the assumption made that housework is not work when wives and mothers are asked, "Do you work?" What arguments can be made in linking housework to male-female

roles, to the dominance-submission issue, or to a capitalistic type of society?

4. One writer stated that "being a housewife makes women sick." What was meant by this? What does research suggest in this regard?

5. What arguments, if any, exist against the employed wife and/or mother? What social factors are most influential in determining who will work? Explain reasons for the increase in female paid employment.

6. Discuss the consequences of the employed wife and mother on her marriage, on her children, and on the wife herself. Are there circumstances in which the negative consequences outweigh the positive?

7. Discuss the consequences of the employed husband and father on his marriage, on his children, and on the husband himself. Are there circumstances in which the negative consequences outweigh the positive?

8. Examine the various perspectives on male roles in relation to housework and child care. Do you feel significant changes are occurring on the part of men in the United States or around the world in this regard?

9. What strains may occur in dual-career marriages that are less likely to occur in one-career marriages? What rewards exist in each type?

10. Discuss the pros and cons of commuter marriages. What type of conditions add to or decrease the strain on the couple's relationship?

## *FURTHER READINGS*

Aldous, Joan. *Two Paychecks: Life in Dual-Career Families.* Beverly Hills: Sage Publications, 1982. A compilation of twelve articles on the dual-career family, covering such topics as work schedules, marital and family adjustment, conjugal roles, and housework by husbands.

Berk, Sarah Fenstermaker. *The Gender Factory: The Apportionment of Work in American Households.* New York: Plenum Publishing Corp., 1985. This book includes a vast amount of research information and looks at who is doing what, what gets produced, and why.

Dornbusch, Sanford M., and Strober, Myra H. *Feminism, Children and the New Families.* New York: The Guilford Press, 1988. From a feminist perspective, behavioral scientists analyze children and families, raising policy questions and dealing with issues surrounding employment, divorce, single parents, stepfamilies, and others.

Gerstel, Naomi, and Gross, Harriet Engel. *Families and Work.* Philadelphia: Temple University Press, 1987. A collection of twenty-seven articles covering work in historical perspective, in the home, as related to family life, and policy of the state and of employers.

Hertz, Rosanna. *More Equal Than Others: Women and Men in Dual-Career Marriages.* Berkeley: University of California Press, 1986. A study of a small number of men and women who are defined as economic equals: dual-career married couples in the corporate world.

Johnson, Miriam M. *Strong Mothers, Weak Wives: The Search for Gender Equality.* Berkeley: University of California Press, 1988. A look at issues addressed by feminists with a particular focus on women as wives versus women as mothers.

Lewis, Robert A., and Sussman, Marvin B., eds. *Men's Changing Roles in the Family.* New York: The Haworth Press, 1986. A look at men's roles as persons, husbands, and fathers in the context of work, friendship, and caring relationships. Excellent bibliography and filmography listing.

Pleck, Joseph H. *Working Wives, Working Husbands.* Beverly Hills: Sage Publications, 1985. Data from two national studies are used to examine the time working wives and husbands allocate to housework with a major focus on work overload and its consequences.

Reskin, Barbara F., and Hartmann, Heidi I., eds. *Women's Work, Men's Work: Sex Segregation on the Job.* Washington, D.C.: National Academic Press, 1986. A report by the Committee on Women's Employment and Related Social Issues that reviews evidence showing that employment segregation by sex has grave consequences for women (particularly women), men, families, and society.

Vannoy-Hiller, Dana, and Philliber, William W.

*Equal Partners: Successful Women in Marriage* Newbury Park: Sage Publications, Inc., 1989. An insightful treatment of the connection between high achieving women and family patterns and processes.

Voydanoff, Patricia. *Work and Family Life.* Beverly Hills: Sage Publications, 1987. An examination and review of the current knowledge on the relationship between work and family.

Voydanoff, Patricia, and Majka, Linda C., eds. *Families and Economic Distress: Coping Strategies and Social Policy.* Newbury Park: Sage Publications, Inc., 1988. The work of an interdisciplinary group of scholars who address the impact of structural economic changes on families.

Winfield, Fairlee E. *Commuter Marriage: Living Together, Apart.* New York: Columbia University Press, 1985. A brief, readable description of married couples who maintain separate residences.

# CHAPTER FIVE

# *L*IFE-STYLES AMONG CHINESE FAMILIES

The Picture Cube © Stan Riese.

This chapter examines three family systems of the Chinese of mainland China: the traditional system, the system brought about by the Marriage Law of 1950, and the contemporary Chinese family system. Each of these patterns of family organization and life-styles differs considerably from the others when viewed in either an historical or contemporary perspective. While major changes have occurred in the traditional Chinese family, none of the new forms is viewed as simply experimental or as a trial. Each includes ways of life that its members have learned to regard or have been instructed to regard as good and important.

Much is to be gained by examining the Chinese family or any family system other than our own. While a fascination may exist in examining the bizarre or sensational, perhaps more fruitful outcomes may be found in gaining a perspective on the possible variety and wide range of family patterns and practices. It is equally important to discover the threads of commonality among family systems: the prevalence of monogamy, the strong ties between mother and child particularly during the child's early years, the lack of unregulated promiscuity, the status affiliation afforded by the family, the significance of the kin networks as a system of support, and the like. An examination of families other than our own may decrease our own ethnocentrisms and provincial orientations; may enable us to consider alternatives to traditional practices; may help us to understand the close linkages between families and the larger social and cultural context within which those families operate; may alert us to question the obvious and destroy false stereotypes; may, in addition to *describing* life-styles and social patterns, help us in *explaining* human behavior and social organization; and may lead to a discovery of more general propositions and principles. The person who "knows it all" may be one who has had no exposure to life-styles other than his or her own. Thus, let's examine selected family systems beyond the North American boundaries with a particular focus on families in mainland China.

## *THE CHINESE OF MAINLAND CHINA*

Mainland China has a land area about equal to that of the United States but has a population more than four times as large. It opened its borders and allowed observers to enter the country in the early 1970s. It provides a remarkable case of a massive country with more than one billion inhabitants, accounting for about 22 percent of the world's population, making a transition from a patriarchal family system using ancient techniques of agricultural labor to a more egalitarian system under a developing and modernizing economy.

Until the early part of this century, the Chinese family is said to have withstood extensive change for nearly two thousand years. With the end of the Ch'ing Dynasty in 1911, the culmination of the Chinese Revolution in 1949 and the Marriage Law of 1950, dramatic changes were brought about in the lives of Chinese families of all classes and in the lives of women in particular.

While this brief presentation tends to describe the traditional and emerging Chinese family as a relatively uniform entity, there are many exceptions to the generalized patterns presented. In addition to class and gender differences described in some detail, differences also existed in the traditional family between clans, villages, and regions of the country. For example, women were not expected to work in the fields in the north, but the practice was acceptable in the south. Women are described as severely oppressed, yet some women were highly educated and became known for their music, art, or poetry. Suicide is described as a socially acceptable solution to a variety of problems, yet its practice was not considered widespread. Recognizing such limitations, our attention is first directed to the traditional Chinese family.

## THE TRADITIONAL CHINESE FAMILY

In a broad sense, the **traditional Chinese family** refers to the type of general system that existed up to approximately 1900 or even 1950. Two important status distinctions that need to be understood in this traditional system centered around class differentiations as witnessed particularly within the clan and the sex differentiation as witnessed in the father-son relationship and the oppression of women.

### The clan in traditional China

The clan system of traditional China was extremely important to the maintenance of ancestral linkages and group solidarity. A **clan,** sometimes referred to as the **tsu,** included all persons with a common surname who traced descent from a common ancestor. The *tsu,* operated through a council of elders, often involved several thousand persons, sometimes included entire villages, and was composed of everyone from the gentry to peasants. The **gentry** were intellectuals who did no manual labor but who received income as landlords or from holding government offices or academic positions. The **peasants** comprised the bulk of the population. They cultivated the land, were generally very poor, and often aspired for the attainment of gentry status. In a country greatly "overpopulated" in the sense that the cultivated land was not sufficient to give the average peasant an adequate livelihood, infant and general mortality rates were high. Widespread conditions of poverty contributed to undernourishment and lack of medical care. Indirect consequences of poverty, particularly for females, included infanticide, abandonment, selling and out-adoption (giving up of children for adoption), nonmarriage, and late marriage.

The significance of this large clan group to the family can be seen in the functions it performed: lending money to its members; helping individual families to pay for extravagant weddings and funerals; establishing schools; exercising judicial authority within the clan; acting as a government agent in collecting taxes; and maintaining ancestral graves and *tsu* property.[1] This "family" network performed most of the functions we generally associate with government: taxes, law enforcement, schools, welfare, etc. As you might guess, the *tsu* came under serious attack when the revolutionary government came into power.

The clan network was maintained in a variety of ways. One widely described practice included **ancestor worship.** An individual existed by virtue of his (not her) ancestors, and they in turn continued to exist through their descendants. In life, parents cared for children and the children, in turn, took on care and shelter of their parents in old age. After death, while the form of care changed, the duty did not. In life, parents were served and respected. In death they were served and worshipped. If in life parents needed food, clothing, shelter, and money, then when dead, the children supplied them with these essentials. The transfer of goods from this world to the next was achieved primarily by burning. Food, however, could be offered directly. In return, the ancestors gave blessings and assistance through their supernatural powers. They, like Greek gods, could bless warfare, hunting, or agriculture or punish with famine, defeat, sickness, or death. Thus, there was a continuing reciprocal relationship between the living and the dead clan members.[2]

Closely related to ancestor worship was the principle of **filial piety,** the duty and subordination of a son to his father. Giving proper deference to parents and other ancestors tended to perpetuate and maintain property within the family, grant universal authority to the male elders, serve as a major source of both formal and informal social control, and perhaps above all, maintain stability and continuity, that is, prevent drastic change.

### Gender roles in traditional China

As the principle of filial piety alone would suggest, an extremely favorable position of males relative to females existed in the traditional Chinese system. In traditional Chinese cosmology, the world was composed of two complementary elements: the **yin,** the female, stood for all things dark, weak, and passive; the **yang,** the male, stood for all things bright, strong, and active.[3] Paul Chao says that a wife had to obey three persons: her father before marriage, her husband after marriage, and her son after her husband died.[4]

---

1. Paul Chao, *Women Under Communism: Family in Russia and China* (Bayside, N.Y.: General Hall, 1977): 123.

2. An excellent treatment of ancestor worship as well as Chinese Kinship can be found in Hugh D. R. Baker, *Chinese Family and Kinship* (New York: Columbia University Press, 1979).

3. Katie Curtin, *Women in China* (New York: Pathfinder Press, 1975): 10.

4. Chao, *Women Under Communism*, p. 124.

At all stages of life, recognition of women never approached that of men. Female infanticide was common, especially among the poorer peasants, for girls were both an expense to raise and later would need a dowry to marry. Marriages were not based on love and "free choice" but were arranged by parents through matchmakers. Since persons with the same surname or from the same clan could not marry, marriage usually meant the female would be completely removed from her family, friends, and community. In addition, many women only met their husbands for the first time on their wedding day and then entered a husband-wife relationship that was considered subordinate and supplementary to the parent-son, particularly father-son, relationship.

The wife's chief responsibilities were to bear male children and to aid in the work. Failure of a wife to bear male children could lead to repudiation and the obligation of a husband, among the gentry at least, to take a concubine or additional wives. A woman could have only one husband and if he died, she was not allowed to remarry. A wife or mother had few legal or property rights but could wield some power over other women, particularly her daughters-in-law. The latter peacefully endured harsh treatment until they, in turn, became mothers-in-law.

Not all women tolerated the harsh treatment. Margaret Wolf[5] says that for peasant women, suicide was a socially acceptable solution to a variety of problems that offered no other solution. A young widow, particularly a childless one, could expect little from the future. Even among the gentry women, suicide was considered a proper response for a woman "whose honor" had been tampered with or who in any way brought dishonor or disgrace to her husband's family.

Another indication of the oppression of women is seen in the traditional practice of binding women's feet. The feet, bound from early childhood, were reduced to three inches in length from toe to heel with the result of permanent crippling. **Footbinding,** extending back to the tenth century, was prevalent among the upper classes not so much as a sign of beauty but to restrain women's movement. Peasant women, heavily involved in agriculture and production, were exempted from this practice. Footbinding, as well as other oppressive practices, came under heavy attack in the Chinese Revolution.

## CHANGES IN THE CHINESE FAMILY

It is difficult to distinguish any major single influence behind the dramatic changes that occurred in the Chinese family. Events in Russia, in the Western

---

5. Margaret Wolf, "Women and Suicide in China," in Margaret Wolf and Roxanne Witke, *Women in Chinese Society* (Stanford: Stanford University Press, 1975): 111–141.

*Radical changes have taken place in Chinese family structure and gender roles. Women still assume greater household and child care responsibilities than men but the state has had remarkable success in limiting family size and achieving gender equality.*

world, and within China itself combined to force new patterns of existence in all social areas, including the family.

Major changes in the Chinese family were greatly influenced by the Russian Revolution and the Bolshevik party. Between 1917 and 1927, the Soviet government passed laws aimed at revamping marriage and divorce laws, granting free abortions on demand, and giving women legal equality with men. The ideas of Friedrich Engels[6] clearly provided a basis for the formulation of official family policy in both the Soviet Union and mainland China. Of prime significance was his principle that as private property emerges, man's status prevails over that of women. Some of his claims included: family property elevates man's position; monogamy was instituted for women only; the married woman sells her body once and for all into slavery; a woman becomes the slave of a man's lust and a mere instrument for the production of children.[7]

---

6. Friedrich Engels, *The Origin of the Family, Private Property and the State* (New York: International Publishers, 1942). Originally published by Charles H. Kerr, Chicago, 1902.

7. Ibid., pp. 49–51, 56, 65.

While the Bolshevik Revolution and the teachings of Karl Marx, Engels, and Vladimir Lenin influenced events in China, Judith Stacey notes that the course of the family revolution in China digressed in noteworthy ways from the Russian case.[8] First, the Chinese Communist party's (CCP) attack on traditional family life was never as radical as that of the Bolsheviks. The CCP was involved in significant efforts to conform the Confucian family, but it never advocated or promoted the "withering away" of the family. On the contrary, the Maoists in China saw family reform as the means to more successful and harmonious marriage and family life. Second, because reform goals were comparatively temperate, they were also implemented with greater effort and effectiveness. Third, the consequences of these different approaches to family transformation were significantly different. For example, in rural China, the Communist Revolution appears to have strengthened a reformed version of traditional peasant family structure, eradicating the worst abuses of Confucian patriarchy yet making it possible to realize traditional values of extended three-generational households and more geographic stability.

Since the system of family property and the concept of traditional family solidarity were incompatible with communist ideals, it became mandatory to make a major effort to change the traditional system. A Chinese Communist party conference in 1922 called for voting rights for all regardless of sex and the abolishment of all legislation restricting women. The low status of women and the traditional maltreatment of wives, daughters-in-law, and domestic maids were branded as vestiges of the evils of the traditional family system. As Chao states, the attempt of the communist government to bring about a fundamental, drastic revolution in the family system was implemented by means of the Marriage Law of 1950, whose effect was to implant in the minds of people, especially youths, new ideas regarding marriage and the family and to dismiss the Confucian virtue and ethics of the family.[9]

The following quotations from Chairman Mao Tse-tung provide a clear picture of his goal, which was the elimination of sexual differences in work and family life.

> Protect interests of the youth, women and children, provide assistance to young student refugees, help the youth and women to organize in order to participate on an equal footing in all work useful to the war effort and to social progress, ensure freedom of marriage and equality as between men and women, and give young people and children a useful education. . . .
>
> Enable every woman who can work to take her place on the labor front, under the principle of equal pay for equal work.[10]

---

8. Judith Stacey, "Toward a Theory of Family and Revolution: Reflections on the Chinese Case," *Social Problems* 26 (June 1979): 500.

9. Chao, *Women Under Communism*, p. 126.

10. Ibid., p. 127.

## The Marriage Law of 1950

Ideals such as those of Mao just cited were the basis for the new Marriage Law officially promulgated by the Chinese Communist Central Government at Peking on May 1, 1950. The two major principles of this law are:[11]

1. The abolishment of the feudal marriage system which was based on arbitrary and compulsory arrangements and the supremacy of men over women and which was in disregard of the interests of children. Enacted instead was a new, democratic marriage system based on free choice of partners, monogamy, equal rights for both sexes, and the protection of the lawful interests of women and children.
2. The prohibition of bigamy, concubinage, child betrothal, interference in the remarriage of widows, and the extraction of money or gifts in connection with marriage.

The law, in defining the rights and duties of husband and wife, gives them equal status in the home. The marital pair are in duty bound to love, respect, assist, and look after each other, live in harmony, and engage in productive work. Both have the right to a free choice of occupation and free participation in social activities. They have equal rights to possess or manage property. Each has the right to use his or her own family name.

The law, in defining the relations between parents and children, prohibits infanticide and provides a duty of parents to rear and educate their children and a duty of children to support and assist their parents. Children born out of wedlock enjoy the same rights as children born in lawful wedlock. With the consent of the mother, the natural father may have custody of the child.

Divorce is granted when husband and wife both desire it. When only one party insists on divorce, the district People's Government may try to effect a reconciliation. If this fails, the county or People's Court makes a decision without delay after assurance that appropriate measures have been taken for the care of children and property. Interestingly, the law prohibits a husband from applying for a divorce when his wife is pregnant, and he may only apply one year after the birth of a child.

No matter which parent gets custody of the children, they remain the children of both parties. Both parents have the duty to support and educate their children. If a divorced woman remarries and her husband is willing to pay the cost of maintaining and educating the children, the father is entitled to have his cost reduced or eliminated.

---

11. These principles are derived from Chao, ibid., Appendix II, pp. 221–226.

After divorce, the wife keeps property that belonged to her prior to her marriage. The disposal of other family property is subject to agreement between the husband and wife or, if agreement cannot be reached, it is based on a decision by the People's Court. Debts incurred jointly are paid out of property jointly, but debts incurred separately are paid off by the person responsible.

### Changes resulting from the Marriage Law

It may be difficult to imagine a greater contrast in family systems than between the traditional Chinese family system and that prescribed by the Marriage Law of 1950. In the traditional system marriage was arranged by parents. The communist government took the view that arranged marriage is a bourgeois form that makes the woman a slave to her husband and his family. The traditional system emphasized the subjugation of women and the lack of freedom in love or marital choice. The communist government encouraged marriage for love and free choice of spouse. To those whose marriages were typed as "feudalistic," old-fashioned, compulsory, arranged, business matches, polygamous marriages, loveless marriages, or marriages in which the in-laws or the husband held supreme authority, the government was ready to give "easy" divorces.

Drastic changes such as these, in China or elsewhere, are likely to be threatening to the stability and authority patterns of families and households. Elisabeth Croll, drawing on case studies from the early 1960s, found that parents felt their controls to be threatened. They frequently perceived the operation of free-choice marriages to be a direct attack on their authority. The initiative of young people in the marriage negotiations was commonly interpreted as a direct expression of disobedience or rebellion against parental authority. She quotes a poem taken from a July 1962 Beijing publication:

> With freedom of marriage,
> Gone is the father's prestige;
> Now comes the Marriage Law,
> Mothers are no longer held in awe.[12]

Lucy Jen Huang, writing in this same time period, remarked on the new freedom of mate selection suggesting that, due to the increasing number of women participating in the labor force, most young people now met through working together under various circumstances: in offices, in factories, or on

---

12. Elisabeth Croll, *The Politics of Marriage in Contemporary China* (Cambridge: Cambridge University Press, 1981): 33.

farm cooperatives.[13] Other changes in mate selection patterns included: (1) a shorter dating and courtship period, (2) the exploitation of males by females capitalizing on their new freedom to negotiate, (3) a simple wedding ceremony in contrast to the traditional elaborate and expensive weddings, and (4) early marriage, meaning as soon as the legal age of eighteen for women and twenty for men was reached.

Certain practices of the traditional Chinese family came under sharp attack as incompatible with the newer communist ideology. Thus, the confiscation of lineage property, the subsequent collectivization of family landholdings, the mobilization of women for regular agricultural work, and the expansion of education and other nonfamilial activities for youth in particular clearly had an important impact.[14] Filial piety, footbinding, and the oppression of women common in the traditional family were defined as serving neither the revolution nor the economic goals of the state. The existence of the *tsu* or clan was supplanted by urban and rural people's communes.

In spite of changes such as those described, a strong stable family system has emerged. Paul Chao says:

> There is no doubt that China has succeeded remarkably in removing the traditional family system to help industrialization and make women participate in production in rural and urban areas. Weakening a good deal the traditional family, the Chinese Communists have not destroyed the family as an economic unit as well as a social unit, but established nurseries and kindergartens where old women are called for taking care of babies while their mothers are free to work outside the home. All Chinese families have joined communes in productive units, they have had a stable base of agriculture and small-scale industry that is self-reliant. The family continues to be an economic unit, though the state has brought home to people the greater importance of the state.[15]

## THE CONTEMPORARY CHINESE FAMILY

Whether viewing the family in traditional China, China under the revolution, or contemporary China, mention must again be made to use caution in perceiving the family as a uniform entity, either by region, clan, or class. Drastic changes have taken place in family systems throughout the nation. But the changes have been neither uniform nor complete.

---

13. Lucy Jen Huang, "Some Changing Patterns in the Communist Chinese Family," *Marriage and Family Living* 23 (May 1961): 137–139.
14. You may be interested in Part III, pp. 131–297 of William J. Parish and Martin King Whyte, *Village and Family in Contemporary China* (Chicago: The University of Chicago Press, 1978).
15. Chao, *Women Under Communism*, p. 155.

In noting family patterns in rural versus urban areas, Martin King Whyte[16] says that trends since 1949 have not reduced the gap between rural and urban family patterns, but have widened it still further. In Chinese cities, clan organizations were never as important as in villages. The patterns of family to be found in contemporary cities also seem somewhat more varied than is the case in the countryside. Patrilocal residence (in the man's father's house) after marriage is less the general rule in cities than it is in the villages. Urban youths marry later than rural youths. Urban parents play a less central role in choice of mate. Marriage finance is negotiated less between the two families in urban areas. In husband-wife relations, it appears that while women do more of the domestic chores than do men this factor is more pronounced in rural areas. Urban divorce is said to be more evenhanded or even-biased in favor of women.

The continuation of and changes in rural-urban differences are documented in terms of the average number of children ever born per family. As recently as 1955, the average number of children was 6.39 in rural areas compared to 5.67 in urban areas. Twenty years later, by 1975, these figures were 3.95 (rural) and 1.78 (urban). In 1987, the comparable figures were 2.45 (rural) and 1.38 (urban).[17] These figures reveal both the long-standing discrepancy in number of children between the cities and country, as well as the powerful impact of the one-child policy (discussed later).

Like rural-urban differences, age, sex, and educational differences exist as well. But, recent information clearly illustrates that irrespective of age, sex, or education, the traditional family no longer holds attraction to Chinese rulers. This is particularly evident in the national **Marriage Law of 1980** that went into effect in January 1981. The People's Republic of China promulgated a marriage law that replaced the marriage law of 1950 described earlier. This later law reflects the massive changes that have taken place in the intervening thirty-year period since the end of the Chinese Revolution and the earlier marriage law. As described, the 1950 law was aimed at correcting many of the practices of the previous feudal society: arrangement of marriages by parents, the inequality of husbands and wives, bigamy and concubinage, the extraction of gifts in connection with marriage, and the like. The new law provided a model for the responsibilities of family members to each other and a guide for their relationships.

---

16. Martin King Whyte, "Family Change in China," *Issues and Studies* 16 (July 1979): 48–62.

17. Xiangming Chen, "The One-Child Population Policy, Modernization, and the Extended Chinese Family," *Journal of Marriage and the Family* 47 (February 1985): 193–202; and Griffith Feeney, Feng Wang, Mingkun Zhou, and Baoyu Xiao, "Recent Fertility Dynamics in China: Results from the 1987 One Percent Population Survey," *Population and Development Review* 15 (June 1989): 297–322.

*Posters that focus on birth planning are prevalent throughout China today. Couples who have only one child receive financial rewards and can expect their child to be given priority in school enrollment and, later, in employment and housing.*

In presenting China's marriage law of 1980, Rachel Hare-Mustin[18] indicates the concern for the lawful rights and interests of women, children, and the aged, a change in the minimum age for marriage, the encouragement of family planning, and the emphasis on personal independence and equality among family members. Under the new law, a man may choose to become a member of the woman's family and the children may adopt the mother's name. Provisions are made for adoption and the rights of stepchildren. Although still not common, divorce is easier to obtain and granted when mutual affection no longer exists and mediation has failed.

While a new law has been passed, many traditional family patterns continue. For example, a patrilineal and patrilocal pattern still exists in taking the father's surname and in the bride moving to her husband's village. Both sons and daughters are eligible to inherit under the law but married-out daughters are not likely to inherit from either her blood family or her family by marriage.

Ceremonies for the dead, like those for the living, are much curtailed today. In cities, cremation appears to have become the norm. But in the

---

18. Rachel T. Hare-Mustin, "China's Marriage Law: A Model for Family Responsibilities and Relationships," *Family Process* 21 (December 1982): 477–481. *See also* John W. Engel, "Marriage in the People's Republic of China: Analysis of a New Law," *Journal of Marriage and the Family* 46 (November 1984): 955–961.

countryside burial remains common, although the place of burial is often viewed as a waste of land. And since the land no longer belongs to the family, increased difficulty exists in maintaining kin loyalty, totally irrespective of any religious significance. Religious beliefs in general have been labeled as superstitious, and religious practices have been discouraged.

It would appear that while the family in mainland China today is different from the traditional one, many parallels exist. Filial piety is seen in the relationships between parents and children and to the extent to which sons and daughters-in-law care for their parents. John Dixon reports that the problems of urban youth, especially juvenile delinquency, have always been and continue to be a source of concern for the Chinese Communist party. He claims that this problem has been compounded by a weakening of family discipline, by the inevitable delays in job assignments for young people, by a youth policy dominated by the permanent deportation of young people to distant places, and by a continuing confusion as to youth's proper role in Chinese society.[19] As evidenced by the protests of youth in 1989 and the subsequent killing and arrest of many students in Tienamen Square in Beijing, youth remain a source of concern for government officials.

While women in China have made significant progress toward emancipation, aspects of traditional sex-role differentiation still persist.[20] In work outside the home, women still experience discrimination in pay and important jobs. In the political area, only a small proportion of the persons elected to the Central Committee of the Chinese Communist party are women. In household tasks, most responsibilities have remained the woman's. In mate selection, accounts exist of women who retain bourgeois ideas in selecting a husband who will support them. After years of communist rule, sons are valued over daughters, the traditional protective attitude toward girls seems to survive, and most of the important jobs in politics, the educational system, agriculture, factories, and hospitals are held by men.

Marriage in urban areas is no longer an arrangement between families based upon economic and social alliances that take little account of the personal preferences of the young people. Yet, more than three decades after the Marriage Law made free choice legal, the role of the matchmaker is still crucial. To some extent, the continuing activity of matchmakers bespeaks a

19. John Dixon, "The Welfare of Urban Youth in China 1949–79," *Journal of Adolescence* 4 (March 1981): 1–12. *See also* Thomas B. Gold, "China's Youth: Problems and Programs," *Issues and Studies: A Journal of China Studies and International Affairs* 18 (August 1982): 39–62; and Wei Zhangling, "Chinese Family Problems: Research and Trends," *Journal of Marriage and the Family* 45 (November 1983): 943–948.

20. Rachel T. Hare-Mustin and Sharon E. Hare, "Family Change and the Concept of Motherhood in China," *Journal of Family Issues* 7 (March 1986): 67–82. For an excellent review of the women's movement in China and the role of women in the family and economy *see* Joan M. McCrea, "The Socio-Economic Role of Women in the People's Republic of China," *Women's Studies International Forum* 6 (1983): 57–72.

## Can only children be good communists?

Why did China's students revolt in 1989? As reported in the *Charlotte Observer* (July 23, 1989), Steve Palay, a freelance writer, claims that his Dad's sure he's tumbled onto something the TV networks and the State Department all missed. He figures that when the Chinese government started programs to keep population growth in line, the leaders never considered what it would mean if the average Chinese child were an only child.

You just can't make a good communist revolutionary out of a kid who already thinks the world revolves around him, Dad said. What China's got now is a generation that never had to give up a favorite toy or share a bedroom, that never worried about older siblings cracking down on them or lived in fear that a younger brat would suddenly squeal on them. In short, it's a generation that never learned the basic rules of communism at home. Your basic only child is just not going to make a good communist.

society in which members of the opposite sex still find it extremely difficult to meet or interact casually. Powerful cultural restraints, such as the fear of gossip at one's school or workplace, constrain male-female interaction. As stated by Hershatter:

> The restraint required of schoolgirls is particularly pronounced. They are expected to deny any interest in affairs of the heart, and to react with appropriate embarrassment or even disgust when the subject is broached. Some groups of young people, like university students, are discouraged by the school authorities from courting and are forbidden to marry while they are in school.[21]

Margery Wolf interviewed three hundred women in both cities and rural communes about various aspects of their lives, including courtship and marriage. Even in cities, love was an ideal for the women, but few could define it and few had an opportunity to develop it or other intimate feelings before marriage. She claims that the sad thing about many of the new marriages is that couples often seem as mismatched as they were in the old days when marriages were arbitrarily arranged by parents. In her words

> The young person who is taught that his or her spouse will be a friend and lifelong companion often finds "after the rice is cooked," that they have very little in common. Even though marriage is delayed until both parties are in their mid or late twenties, both are usually sexually inex-

---

21. Gail Hershatter, "Making a Friend: Changing Patterns of Courtship in Urban China," *Pacific Affairs* 57 (Summer 1984): 239.

perienced, and, from all reports, many women wish they had stayed that way.[22]

Husband-and-wife relationships are greatly influenced by the very tight housing situation in many urban areas. Wolf cited one woman as saying that if you want to have an argument, you either take a walk or resign yourself to involving the whole family. Still, the control of the family is far greater in rural areas than in urban areas. Rural couples are less influenced and controlled by the state and are more controlled by their families and extended kin. In short, the new marriage decree, while granting couples increased freedom of choice and male-female equity in relationships, has in large part fallen on deaf ears in the countryside.[23]

### One-child family policy

One area of significant change in the 1970s and 1980s has been the decrease in the birthrate and the increase in one-child families. The magnitude of the fertility declines in certain provinces has been so great across educational levels for a short period and for such a large population that some writers claim it is probably unprecedented in history, apart from periods of famine, epidemics, wars, or other overwhelming disasters.[24]

As a result of an intensive Chinese family planning program (called *birth planning* by the Chinese), the birthrate was reduced from 34 per 1,000 in 1970, to 20.9 in 1981, to 17.5 in 1984. In 1986, however, the birthrate rose to about the 1981 level.[25] While some of this increase was due to a shift in the age structure (more women in the peak childbearing ages of 21–30), much of the rise was due to an increase in fertility. Chinese leaders became concerned about rumors that the policy had changed to allow couples to have two children and about evidence that family planning work had not been stringently implemented in many areas of China in the mid-1980s. By 1987 and 1988 Chinese leaders had issued commentaries that stated that party committees on all levels must never lower their guard and become negligent—the population

---

22. Margery Wolf, "Marriage, Family, and the State in Contemporary China," in Norval D. Glenn and Marion Tolbert Coleman (eds.), *Family Relations: A Reader* (Chicago: The Dorsey Press, 1988): 106.

23. For an extensive analysis of marriage and domestic relations including rural and urban differences, *see* Margery Wolf, *Revolution Postponed: Women in Contemporary China* (Stanford: Stanford University Press, 1985): Chapters 6–9; Emily Honig and Gail Hershatter, *Personal Choices: Chinese Women in the 1980s* (Stanford: Stanford University Press, 1988): Chapters 4–6; and Ming Tsui, "Changes in Chinese Urban Family Structure," *Journal of Marriage and the Family* 51 (August 1989): 737–747.

24. Ronald Freedman, Xiao Zhenyu, Li Bohua, and William Lavely, "Local Area Variations in Reproductive Behaviour in the People's Republic of China, 1973–1982." *Population Studies* 42 (1988): 57.

25. Karen Hardee-Cleveland and Judith Banister, "Fertility Policy and Implementation in China, 1986–88," *Population and Development Review* 14 (June 1988): 247, Table 1.

## The United States and China's family planning

In November 1986, James Scheuer (Democrat, N.Y.), a member of the House Science and Technology Committee, led a congressional delegation to China. Their intent was to study China's family planning program and to discuss charges that the government was using coercion and forced abortion to reduce the population growth. Charges of this type, made by conservatives in the Reagan administration, prompted Washington to withdraw financial support from the United Nations Fund for Population Activities.

As reported in the *New York Times* (January 24, 1987), the delegation during their ten days in China found that the much publicized one-child policy was not what it seemed. The national average is actually 2.2 children per family, with the strongest adherence to the one-child policy occurring in urban areas where housing is in short supply. The policy is far less rigid in the rural areas where 80 percent of the Chinese reside.

Last year nearly 50 percent of the births in China were in families that already had one child. Flexibility is given to the local officials who run the family planning program in the field. "Practical difficulties" such as when a first child is mentally or physically handicapped, is female, has a father who is a disabled serviceman, or when both parents are single children, provide justification for sanctioning second children. Indications are that the policy may be relaxed even further. If the current birth rate of 2.2 children per family can be maintained, China can meet its goal of not exceeding 1.2 billion people by the year 2000.

The United Nations Fund for Population Activities spends $10 million a year in China. This is an amount equal to less than 1 percent of China's own $1 billion annual commitment to birth planning. Their program involves expert assistance in training and introduction of the full array of contraceptive technology. Even so, anti-abortion zealots in the U.S. government have successfully blocked U.S. contributions to the fund and have irritated relations with China by misapplication of a federal law that prohibits contributions to any agency involved in the management of a coercive abortion or involuntary sterilization program. The fund's role in China's birth-planning program is not a "management" role and as Scheuer suggests, "The administration should set aside its ideological interpretation of the law, administer the law objectively, and follow Congress's legislative intent in an intelligent manner."

must be strictly controlled. The population target of 1.2 billion by the end of the century was still in effect.[26]

The one-child policy, introduced in 1979, included the innovation of a one-child pledge. By 1983, 24.8 million couples had reportedly signed this pledge (72 percent of all couples with one child) and received **single-child certificates.** This certificate entitles a couple to increased income, lower-cost health care, better nursing, larger pensions, and eventually preferential treatment in schooling and employment for their only child. In some areas, a slightly larger monetary bonus is allowed if the couple's first child is a girl than if it is a boy. In rural areas of many provinces, couples today can have two

---

26. Ibid., p. 249.

children if their first child is a girl, giving recognition to the preference for a son and providing a practical way of dealing with its implications.[27] Otherwise, couples who have more than two children have penalties imposed on them.

The Chinese government not only tells couples that they must practice birth control, but it also often tells them what type of contraceptive they must use. In 1982, for example, the government announced that women with one child must use an IUD, couples with two children must have one partner sterilized, and those with unauthorized pregnancies must undergo abortions. This practice of forcing abortions, by the way, led the U.S. government in 1985 to withhold all contributions from the United Nations Population Fund (*see* the insert on the U.S. and China's family planning).

To overcome the traditional desires for a son to provide support in old age, the government has designed additional incentives for the one-daughter family. Today, property can be distributed to daughters as well as sons, daughters are legally responsible for the parents' welfare in the same way as sons, and a daughter as well as a son may take over the father's job when he retires. These practices may not, however, eliminate fear, especially in rural areas, about security in old age. In rural areas the welfare of the aged is closely tied to the economic well-being of the communes and, increasingly, also to the ability of individual households to realize higher incomes. It has been suggested that as the rural population as a whole ages, the changing balance between labor force participants in their prime productive ages and the aged may have a serious negative impact on productivity and, by extension, on the well-being of the aged.[28]

One evaluation of future problems resulting from the one-child family policy includes, among other things, (1) experiencing an aged population which (2) will place increasing pressure on social welfare and (3) present a labor shortage in the twenty-first century. An unexpected result of this one-child-per-couple policy is (4) the revival of female infanticide across mainland China.

The practice of female infanticide seems to be particularly true in rural areas which for several years had a consistently higher sex ratio than the urban areas.[29] The strong preference for sons, of which female infanticide was one consequence, led to a relaxation of the strict one-child policy in certain areas of the country. New regulations were adopted in certain provinces that permitted families in certain hardship circumstances (e.g., handicaps, hazard-

---

27. Fred Arnold and Liu Zhaoxiang, "Sex Preference, Fertility, and Family Planning in China," *Population and Development Review* 12 (June 1986): 221–246.

28. Alice Goldstein and Sidney Goldstein, "The Challenge of an Aging Population," *Research on Aging* 8 (June 1986): 179–199.

29. Tin-yu Ting and Hsin-mu Chen, "Involuntary Family Size: An Evaluation of Mainland China's One-Child Family Policy," *Issues and Studies: A Journal of China Studies and International Affairs* 22 (February 1986): 45–63.

ous occupations, or residence in poor, remote areas) to have a second child. But, as stated by one writer, the unwritten hardship is the birth of a daughter; it is improbable that any economic circumstances would permit the birth of a second son.[30]

The one-child family policy has both direct and latent effects in the physical formation of the extended family, the manner in which family members relate to one another, and the content and features of intergenerational ties. Xiangming Chen states that first, the thrust of the one-child policy's impact has begun to weaken the extended family network by greatly trimming the average family size. The absence of siblings; the subsequent loss of in-laws, uncles, and aunts; and the thinning out of extended consanguineous relationships remove a large number of branches from the previously complex family tree.[31]

Second, Chen goes on to state that the immediate and long-term effect of reduced family size is reflected in expected changes in the power relationships among the generations. Taking care of one child usually requires less time and effort than two or more and this further lessens married women's traditional role of child rearing and related household chores. It reinforces the fact that the great majority of married Chinese women work and, thus, may facilitate the formulation of an equal marital relationship between the husband and the wife by giving the latter more leisure time and bargaining power.

Lawrence Kong makes some related points which illustrate latent ramifications of the one-child program in China.[32] He argues that it could drastically reduce the size and significance of the patrilineal lineage, promote the popularity of uxorilocal marriages (the husband resides in the wife's household), and encourage women to make nontraditional career choices. Taken together, the result could be a major advance in reducing gender-based inequality.

## Divorce

Prior to the Marriage Law in 1980, divorce could be granted after mediation by the courts if "legitimate" reasons existed. What appeared to be most legitimate were reasons of political differences. Following the law of 1980, the absence of love became a primary criterion in the consideration of divorce cases. Cases were of two types: those where both husband and wife desired it and those

---

30. William R. Lively, "China's One-Child Policy and Gender Equality," *Gender and Society* 21 (June 1988): 242.

31. Xiangming Chen. "The One-Child Population Policy, Modernization, and the Extended Chinese Family," *Journal of Marriage and the Family* 47 (February 1985): 193–202.

32. Lawrence K. Kong, "Potential Effects of the One-Child Policy on Gender Equality in the People's Republic of China," *Gender and Society* 1 (September 1987): 317–326.

where only one partner desired it. Procedures for divorce in the first category, referred to as *divorce by agreement*, were simple and without cost to the applicants. The couple simply went to the local marriage registration office and completed an application. If no coercion was involved and the couple was able to reach agreement on custody of the children and the division of family property, a divorce certificate was issued. When only one partner wanted a divorce, that person could go to the marriage registration office and apply. This was followed by a mediation attempting reconciliation. If that failed, the case went to the People's Court, which would decide for or against the divorce and, if there were children, who should get custody.

Have the marriage law changes and changes in family size and gender roles led to an upsurge in divorce? In percentage terms, yes, but the numbers involved appear to be very small. For example, an increase from 207,000 divorce court cases in 1979 to 450,000 in 1986 is an increase of nearly 120 percent. But in a country of over 1 billion people this is equal to 0.43 cases per 1,000 population.[33] Viewed in a global perspective this figure is very low, particularly when compared with that of most countries in the industrialized West. Without a doubt, today most marriages in China are stable, most individuals expect to stay married for life, and both the local kinship structure and government policy favor such stability.

It appears that the statements of Marx and Engels regarding family property, monogamy, marital love, married women selling their bodies into slavery, and the like are not reaching fruition in mainland China. The communist government is making major efforts to renovate housing, maintain stability in monogamous marital relationships, and provide for the care and protection of children by responsible parents. For all intents and purposes, important roles are assigned to the family system, and it is not heading toward decay or abolishment. There seems to be a melting of the traditional and the revolutionary in many aspects of Chinese family life. As Mao himself said, "Let the past serve the present."

# SUMMARY

1. This chapter on family life-styles in mainland China examines, in one sense, at least three family systems. The traditional Chinese family that existed for several thousand years stands in sharp contrast to the family proposed in the Marriage Law of 1950 which, in turn, seems to contrast with the contemporary Chinese family.
2. The traditional Chinese family withstood extensive change for a period covering two thousand years. It was characterized by sharp class and gender distinctions. The gentry, who were well educated and owned the land, stood in contrast to the

---

33. Erila Platte, "Divorce Trends and Patterns in China: Past and Present," *Pacific Affairs* 61(Fall 1988): 431.

peasants who cultivated it. Similarly, the male, highly valued from birth onward, stood in contrast to the female whose purpose was to serve, honor, and bear male children for the men.

3. The Marriage Law of 1950 was the official promulgation by the Chinese Communist party (CCP) to abolish the supremacy of men over women, the arrangement of marriages, female infanticide, footbinding, and the like. In turn, it created a family system that gave men and women equality in jobs or in the home, permitted widows to remarry, allowed women to own and hold property, legitimized illegitimacy, and sanctioned divorce. The general goal of Mao was to protect the interests of women, youths, and children, who under the traditional system had had few legal rights or privileges.

4. The Chinese family system today appears to be a blend of the traditional and that proposed by the law. The clan has been replaced by the rural and urban commune; the oppression of women, youths, and children has been vastly decreased; the worship of ancestors has declined; women have entered the labor force in great numbers; daughters-in-law are no longer estranged newcomers to the family unit; and suicide and divorce are infrequent.

5. Some recent changes in policy and practice are noted in the Marriage Law of 1980 that went into effect in 1981. The old Marriage Law of 1950 was aimed at correcting many of the practices of the previous feudal society. The new marriage law provides a model for the responsibilities of family members to each other and a guide for their relationships.

6. A specific area of dramatic change in the contemporary Chinese family is evident in the one-child family program. Nearly half of all births in China are first births and the majority of these couples received a one-child certificate indicating a pledge to have no more. Incentives are given to the one-child family, with some additional incentives if that child is a female.

7. The one-child family policy, enforced by birth control measures, sterilization, and abortion, is not without serious future problems including an aging population, pressure on social welfare, a labor shortage in the next century, and the revival of female infanticide. The policy has already changed the power relations among the generations and sex-role differentiation in the home.

8. While changes in Chinese family size and gender roles have been quite dramatic, the increase in numbers getting divorced is quite small. The contemporary Chinese family is alive and well, vastly different from the traditional family in structure and function, yet not in a state of decay or withering.

9. The next chapter brings us to the United States, where African-American families are examined. This family system stands in sharp contrast to any of the Chinese families examined.

## KEY TERMS AND TOPICS

# DISCUSSION QUESTIONS

1. What value exists in studying family life-styles other than one's own?

2. How is it possible that the traditional Chinese family system withstood extensive change for several thousand years? Is it possible for any family system to resist change in the twentieth century? How?

3. Describe the significance of the clan or the *tsu* to the individual member of a Chinese family. How did it influence marriage, children, employment, and the like?

4. Why were women so oppressed in the traditional Chinese family? Include in your response some justification for practices such as female infanticide, footbinding, arranged marriage, and the prohibition against widows remarrying.

5. Contrast the efforts to transform the family by the Bolsheviks in Russia and the Maoists in China.

6. Attempt to evaluate the degree of success of the Marriage Law of 1950 based on what we know about the contemporary Chinese family.

7. Discuss some of the implications of a one-child policy in terms of population control, family interaction, preference for a male child, and effect on the only child.

8. How is the decrease in age at marriage likely to affect Chinese families, population control, or gender and work roles?

9. What similarities exist between the contemporary Chinese family and that of other systems such as the contemporary kibbutz family? Include a discussion of communes, sex roles, child rearing, divorce, and religion in your response.

10. Based on urban-industrial changes, population growth, trends in mainland China, or general family trends in a world-wide perspective, what thirty-year projections can you make in regard to kinship or clan networks, sex or gender roles, frequency of marriage and/or divorce, and family size in mainland China?

# FURTHER READINGS

Chen, Pi Chao, and Kols, Adrienne. "Population and Birth Planning in the People's Republic of China." *Population Reports* Series J, 25 (January/February 1982): J-578-618. A comprehensive overview of population in China: its distribution, changes, methods of birth planning, current policies, program results, and demographic projections.

Coale, Ansley J. *Rapid Population Change in China, 1952–1982.* Washington, D.C.: National Academy Press, 1984. A report on China over a thirty-year period by the Committee on Population and Demography, with Chapter 3 on marriage and Chapter 4 on childbearing in China since 1950.

Croll, Elisabeth. *Chinese Women Since Mao.* Armonk, New York: M. E. Sharpe, Inc., 1983. An examination of the role and status of Chinese women since the 1950s, with one chapter devoted to domestic labor and child care and another to love, marriage, and divorce.

Goode, William J. *World Revolution and Family Patterns.* New York: The Free Press, 1963. This book deals with world changes in family patterns and has chapters on the West, Arabic Islam, sub-Saharan Africa, India, China, and Japan.

Hanley, Susan B., and Wolf, Arthur P., eds. *Family and Population in East Asian History.* Stanford: Stanford University Press, 1985. A collection of thirteen papers on various aspects of family and fertility in East Asia, including five from China.

Ho, David Y. F. "Continuity and Variation in Chinese Patterns of Socialization," *Journal of Marriage and the Family* 51 (February 1989): 149–163. A discussion of two central issues on Chinese patterns of socialization: continuity versus change through time and variation across geographical locations.

Honig, Emily, and Hershatter, Gail. *Personal Voices: Chinese Women in the 1980s.* Stanford: Stanford University Press, 1988. Each of the nine chapters in this book is devoted to an aspect of women's lives that has become a subject of controversy or change in the 1980s.

Osmond, Marie Withers. "Cross-Societal Family Research: A Macrosociological Overview of the Seventies," *Journal of Marriage and the Family* 42 (November 1980): 995–1016. A decade review article that examines methodological and substantive issues in cross-societal family research.

Parish, William L., and Whyte, Martin King. *Village and Family in Contemporary China.* Chicago: University of Chicago Press, 1978. A study describing the economic and political structures of contemporary rural Kwangtung as they effect change in village and family life.

Song, Jian; Tuan, Chi-Hsien; and Yu, Jing-Yuan. *Population Control in China: Theory and Application.* New York: Praeger Publishers, 1985. Written primarily for demographers, the authors focus on population growth trends and apply population control theories to China's planned birth program.

Tsai, Wen-hui. "Mainland Chinese Marriage and Family Under the Impact of the Four Modernizations," *Issues and Studies: A Journal of China Studies and International Affairs* 24 (March 1988): 100–119. A readable overview of changes in Chinese marriages and families from the "traditional" family, to the family under Mao, to the current one.

Wolf, Margery. *Revolution Postponed: Women in Contemporary China.* Stanford: Stanford University Press, 1980. A research study of several hundred women as workers and wives with extensive rural-urban contrasts in their lives.

# CHAPTER SIX

# *L*IFE-STYLES AMONG AFRICAN-AMERICAN FAMILIES

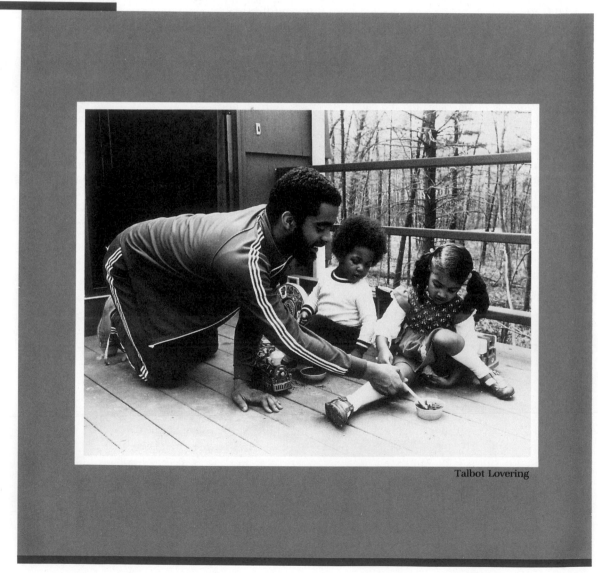

Talbot Lovering

Anyone who has any interest in the area of race relations or, more specifically, in the black-white issue in U.S. society, cannot afford to overlook the role of the family in this total, complex situation. In our society it is the family, and more specifically the conjugal family, that serves as the focal point for the accumulation of material resources by individuals; for the purchase, distribution, and consumption of those resources; for the development and formulation of personality; and for the formation of identity.

African-American families are basically more similar than dissimilar to the dominant family forms that exist in the larger society. For blacks or whites, social status is positively related to marital stability, children receive their basic identity and status subscription within the family context, and parents ascribe to the basic achievement and mobility values that exist within the larger society. On the other hand, there are, of course, clear variations by social class, ethnicity, and religion. In addition, unique historical experiences, such as slavery, legal and social segregation, and economic discrimination, have resulted in differences in life-styles and value patterns for African-Americans. These factors will be discussed in the sections that follow.

## MAJOR TRANSITIONS OF THE AFRICAN-AMERICAN FAMILY

There are various ways in which African-American families are unique and different from white-American families. Many of these differences can be traced to selected historical factors unique to African-American families, and then various changes that have taken place or are taking place can be noted. These changes are identified as major social transitions that include:

1. from Africa to the United States,
2. from slavery to emancipation,
3. from rural and southern areas to urban and northern ones,
4. from negative to positive social status,
5. from negative to positive self-image.

### From Africa to the United States

Three factors in the transition from Africa to the United States have profound relevance. First is color. It is this factor that is the most influential characteristic of African-American people in society, and it is color that identifies them as such. African-Americans who can "pass" as white-Americans are confronted with a different set of interaction patterns than are African-Americans who cannot "pass." In this chapter, the terms *black, black American*, and *African-American* are used interchangeably.

Second is cultural discontinuity. The system of behavior that was socially learned and shared by members of the African society was not applicable to the social conditions to be faced in the United States. It is perhaps difficult, if not impossible, to find any other group who came or was brought to the United States who faced such a disruption of cultural patterns. Yet many African cultural patterns were maintained. Thus arose the concept of *African-American*.

Third is slavery. Again, unlike almost any others in the United States, the African did not choose to come. With few exceptions, Africans came here only as slaves. The impact of slavery on family patterns and norms at the time of slavery, as well as its significance for understanding African-American families today, has become an issue of controversy. For decades, most sociologists accepted almost uncritically the interpretations of African-American family history given by E. Franklin Frazier, Stanley M. Elkins, and W. E. B. DuBois. They emphasized the instability of marriages and family ties, the disruption of husband-wife and kin networks, the extent of matrifocality, and the lack of authority of fathers.[1]

A number of studies have raised serious questions about the conclusions of these earlier writers. Herbert Gutman vigorously attacks the "misdirected emphasis" on marital and family disruption by showing that most households (70 to 90 percent) have had a husband or father present and have had two or more members of a nuclear family unit.[2] The matrifocal family has been infrequent; unmarried African-American women under thirty have lived with their parents, middle-aged African-American women have lived with their husbands and children, elderly African-American women have lived with their husbands or their married children, and subfamilies headed by single, widowed, or abandoned mothers have been incorporated into large households. Frank Furstenberg and others caution as well against presenting a monolithic interpretation of slavery as having only a destructive impact on the African-American family.[3] They argue that the slave family was considerably stronger than has been believed. It was not patterned by instability, chaos, and disorder but rather by two-parent households. While a somewhat higher proportion of African-American families have been headed by a female than has been true for other ethnic groups, reasons other than slavery conditions explain it.

---

1. E. Franklin Frazier, *The Negro Family in the United States*, rev. ed. (New York: Macmillan, 1957); Stanley M. Elkins, *Slavery: A Problem in American Institutional and Intellectual Life* (Chicago: University of Chicago Press, 1959); and W. E. B. DuBois, *The Philadelphia Negro* (Philadelphia: University of Pennsylvania Press, 1899).

2. Herbert G. Gutman, *The Black Family in Slavery and Freedom, 1750–1925* (New York: Pantheon, 1976), Chapters 1 and 10 in particular. *See also:* "The Shaping of the African-American Family" in Steven Mintz and Susan Kellogg, *Domestic Revolutions: A Social History of American Family Life* (New York: The Free Press, 1988): Chapter IV, pp. 67–80.

3. Frank F. Furstenberg, Jr., Theodore Hershberg, and John Modell, "The Origins of the Female-headed Black Family: The Impact of the Urban Experience," *Journal of Interdisciplinary History* 6 (Autumn 1975): 211–233; Herman R. Lantz, "Family and Kin as Revealed in the Narratives of Ex-slaves," *Social Science Quarterly* 60 (March 1980): 667–675; and Mike Meacham, "The Myth of the Black Family Matriarchy Under Slavery," *Mid-American Review of Sociology* 8 (1983): 23–41.

In the first place, the great majority of black families were couple-headed. Second, ex-slaves were more likely to reside in couple-headed households. Third, when property holding among the different ethnic groups was held constant, variations in family composition largely disappeared. Finally, we were able to show that economic status had a powerful effect on the structure of the black family because blacks suffered extremely high mortality and females with children faced difficulties in remarrying.[4]

Perhaps there is some accuracy to both the traditional view that emphasized instability and family disruption and the more contemporary view that emphasizes high degrees of stability and couple-headed households. Data on family residential patterns for African-Americans in a southern farming county in 1870 and 1885 reveal some interesting differences.[5] The 1870 data, drawn from the first census after the Civil War, show high percentages of African-American families in nonfamily or nonnuclear family households. This lends support to traditional beliefs. In 1885, following fifteen years of accommodation to the reconstruction period, data indicate that the two-parent family was the norm. The major changes in the two-parent African-American family structure over this time may have been brought about by an ability to carry out what had long been an ideal norm as well as a need for an economic partnership and a community defense against hostility.

Supporters on both sides of this controversy are likely to agree that slavery in the United States had a major impact. In the United States, slavery assumed inferiority. The slave had no legal rights, marriages were not licensed, many female slaves were sexually used and abused, and miscegenation,[6] which violated the social norms of the times, was frequent.

## From slavery to emancipation

In 1863, a proclamation issued by Abraham Lincoln freed the slaves in all territories still at war with the Union. At last the slave was free from servitude, bondage, and restraint—at least in theory. For thousands of African-Americans, however, emancipation brought with it a freedom to die of starvation and illness. In many ways this transition presented a crisis for many black families.

At least three patterns of family life emerged from this crisis. First, the majority of African-Americans remained on the plantations as tenants of their former owners with little or no wages for their labor. Second, families that had been allowed to establish common residence worked common plots of ground for extra food for the family. Families where the man was an artisan, preacher,

---

4. Furstenberg et al., "The Origins of the Female-headed Black Family," p. 232.

5. Barbara Finlay Agresti, "The First Decades of Freedom: Black Families in a Southern County, 1870 and 1885," *Journal of Marriage and the Family* 40 (November 1978): 697–706.

6. *Miscegenation* refers to marriage and interbreeding between members of different races, especially in the United States between whites and blacks.

or house servant made the transition with the least difficulty. Third, and perhaps most disruptive of family life, in situations where only loose and informal ties held a man and woman together, those ties were severed during the crisis of emancipation. This occurred despite the presence of children. In search of work, many men joined bands of other homeless men who wandered around the countryside. This factor entrenched some females as the major productive and dependable family element.

Emancipation did offer some advantages for the African-American family. As stated by Andrew Billingsley:

> Although family members could be whipped, run out of town, or mur-
> dered, they could not be sold away from their families. Marriages were
> legalized and recorded. The hard work of farming, even sharecropping,
> required all possible hands—husband, wife, and children. . . . Some
> "screens of opportunity" did enable large numbers of families to survive,
> some to achieve amazingly stable and viable forms of family life, and a
> few to achieve a high degree of social distinction.[7]

### From rural and southern areas to urban and northern ones

In 1988 there were 30.1 million African-Americans (referred to in U.S. Census material as blacks), comprising 12.3 percent of the 245.1 million total population. Geographically, blacks were overrepresented in the South (where they comprise 18.8 percent of the total population) and underrepresented in the other three regions (11.3 percent in the Northeast; 10.0 percent in the Midwest; and 5.6 percent in the West). The movement of African-Americans from rural areas and from the South has in general followed that of the rest of the population; however, very few African-Americans have migrated to western states, with the exception of California. In 1930 about four-fifths of all African-Americans lived in the South compared to slightly more than half (53 percent) in 1988. Likewise, a change has occurred in the transition to metro-politan areas. In 1960, 64.8 percent of all black families lived in MSAs (metropolitan statistical areas). By 1970 this figure increased dramatically to 79.1 percent and by 1988 it had increased slightly more to 82.7 percent. Fifty-eight percent of all African-American families lived in central cities, 25 percent lived in the ring around central cities, and 17 percent were rural, that is, not living in a metropolitan statistical area.[8]

The significance of these migration patterns largely evolves around their selectivity: not all ages or complete families were caught up in the movement

---

7. Andrew Billingsley, *Black Families in White America* (Englewood Cliffs, N.J.: Prentice-Hall, 1968): 71.

8. U.S. Bureau of the Census, *Statistical Abstract of the United States, 1989,* 109th ed. and *Current Population Reports,* Series P-20, No. 437, "Household and Family Characteristics: March 1988" (Washington, D.C.: U.S. Government Printing Office, 1989). Figured from Table no. 5, p. 9 and Table 2, p. 10 respectively.

to urban areas or to the North, since the industrial pool preferred young men. This had a tremendous impact both on the community left behind and on the community into which African-Americans migrated. It affected family life by disrupting the nuclear family and by geographically separating extended-family ties; it affected the educational-occupational structure of both communities; and it had an effect on other factors such as housing, ghetto life, and patterns of discriminatory behavior. African-American males, in particular, brought with them aspirations for economic improvement that they expected to have fulfilled but which, for many, were not. Unlike the middle-class mobility patterns due to a job offer involving relocation, the lower-class male was more likely to migrate because of current unemployment or an irregular work schedule.

On the other hand, the consequences of the shift from rural to urban and northern areas that has occurred and is taking place today are not all negative. Many stabilizing factors and positive aspects have resulted. Although the city is often portrayed as a center of evil in our society, in a very real sense it has been the center of hope. As stated by E. E. LeMasters and John DeFrain:

> With all of its problems for parents, the urban community actually offers many advantages: better school systems, with special classes for the handicapped child; better social welfare services, both private and public; better medical and public health facilities; more tolerance for racial and religious minorities; and greater chance for vertical social mobility.[9]

Occupational and earnings gains as well appear to result from residence in the North. While men who migrate to the North as adults have lower returns than northern natives, the occupational and earnings achievements of African-American men who migrated to the North as children closely resemble those of men who are natives of the North.[10]

The geographical transitions have been occurring for the last sixty years or more. In some ways these transitions produce a generation gap among African-Americans. On the one hand we have a sizable number of transplanted parents who were reared in rural Mississippi or Alabama in a highly segregated society, and who would be considered blue-collar class or else are living below the poverty level. On the other hand we find an increasing number of children of these parents living in large urban centers; they are integrated into the school system, have aspirations and hopes for a college education, and have occupational and earnings achievements considerably higher than exist in southern states and equivalent to persons born in the North.

---

9. E. E. LeMasters and John DeFrain, *Parents in Contemporary America: A Sympathetic View* (Homewood, Ill.: The Dorsey Press, 4th ed., 1983): 224.

10. Dennis P. Hogan and Michele Pazui, "The Occupational and Earnings Returns to Education Among Black Men in the North," *American Journal of Sociology* 87 (January 1982): 905–920.

### From negative to positive social status

Some would argue that the single most important variable to understanding the African-American family today is social class. Many family forms are more likely to be the consequence of class rather than either skin color or race. Major differences seem to exist within the African-American family if a distinction is made between those living below the poverty level and the "middle class" of the subculture. It is the African-American middle class that is seldom publicized. This is a stratum in which most of the marriages are stable, two-parent units where husbands have a high school education or better and occupy positions in business, government, or in the educational system. These families are basically more similar than dissimilar to the dominant white-family form that exists in our society.

This shift from a negative to a positive social status includes a shift in the approach to and the interpretation of African-American families. The traditional and old model of the African-American family projected a negative stereotype, viewing the family as being a monolithic lower-class entity—as a social problem in itself, as a pathology of illegitimacy and broken homes, as centering around the female as a dominating matriarch, and as including males with low self-esteem. The emerging or new model challenges these negative views, stressing the African-American family as a variety of types at different social-class levels; rejecting the social problem and pathology orientation as an expression of middle-class ethnocentrism; viewing the family as having strengths such as egalitarianism, self-reliant males, strong family ties, and high achievement orientations; and, finally, being worthy of study as forms of social organization in their own right.

The old model of the African-American family was vividly portrayed twenty-five years ago by Daniel Patrick Moynihan in his now classic **Moynihan Report.**[11] It was his contention that there had been a serious weakening in the African-American social structure and that there was a trend away from family stability in lower socioeconomic levels. He concluded in his report that the structure of family life in the African-American community constitutes a "tangle of pathology" and that at the heart of the deterioration of the fabric of African-American society is the deterioration of the family. The major block to equality centers around the matrifocal family. The implication is that young African-American children grow and are reared in a mother-centered family without the helpful influence of both parents. This, in turn, Moynihan argued, was a major reason why African-Americans were making only limited gains during the prosperous 1960s.

Billingsley and others disagreed directly and strongly with Moynihan's central tenet.[12] They contended that the African-American family is not a

---

11. Daniel P. Moynihan, *The Negro Family: The Case for National Action* (Washington, D.C.: U.S. Government Printing Office, U.S. Department of Labor, 1965).

12. Billingsley, *Black Families in White America*, p. 33.

cause of the "tangle of pathology," but rather that it is an absorbing, adaptive, and amazingly resilient mechanism for the socialization of its children and the civilization of its society.

Data indicate that in terms of delinquency, aspirations, educational expectations, perceptions of the education desired by the parents, self-conceptions, and notions of appropriate gender-role behavior of adults, the empirical evidence does not provide adequate support for the conclusions of the Moynihan Report.[13] In fact, Alan Berger and William Simon suggest that even in the lower-class broken family, there is no indication that the African-American family is dramatically different from the white family in the way it treats its children and the results it produces. Billingsley further supports this opinion in a point made later in this chapter: the majority of African-Americans live in two-parent nuclear families with the man gainfully employed and working every day but who is often unable to earn enough to pull his family out of poverty.

Let's examine if specific shifts have occurred from a negative to a positive social status as portrayed primarily by census data in regard to employment, income, and education. Note particularly (1) the tremendous gains made in recent years in the United States for both black males and females and (2) the major disparities that still exist between blacks and whites.

*Employment* An increasing number of African-Americans are entering positions of leadership in the professions, in business, and in government. This is overshadowed, however, by the number and rate of African-Americans who are not employed. For many years the unemployment rate among blacks was double the rate of the nation as a whole. That is, if the national unemployment rate was 5 percent, one could assume a 10 percent rate for blacks. In 1987, the annual average unemployment rate was 5.4 for white males and 12.7 for black males. The unemployment rate for black females was slightly higher than that for black males (*see* Table 6–1), but they joined black males in having unemployment rates more than twice that of white males or females. For the population as a whole, evidence does not support the widespread belief that a double-negative status (i.e., being both black and female) provides an occupational advantage. And most black females who are employed are overrepresented in service, clerical, and blue-collar jobs that generally are low status and pay low wages.

The 1987 unemployment rate for black teenagers was most dramatic: 34.7 percent. Employment opportunities for less educated, unskilled, young blacks are not sufficient to meet the employment and income needs of this segment

---

13. Alan S. Berger and William Simon, "Black Families and the Moynihan Report: A Research Evaluation," *Social Problems* 22 (December 1974): 145–161; and Roberta H. Jackson, "Some Aspirations of Lower Class Black Mothers," *Journal of Comparative Family Studies* 6 (Autumn 1975): 171–181.

*Table 6–1*
*Unemployment rates by sex and age: 1970, 1980, and 1987 (annual averages)*

|  | Black | | | White | | |
|---|---|---|---|---|---|---|
|  | *1970* | *1980* | *1987* | *1970* | *1980* | *1987* |
| Adult males | 5.6 | 13.3 | 12.7 | 3.2 | 6.1 | 5.4 |
| Adult females | 6.9 | 13.1 | 13.2 | 4.4 | 6.5 | 5.2 |
| Teenagers* | 29.1 | 35.8 | 34.7 | 13.5 | 15.5 | 14.4 |

*Teenagers include persons sixteen to nineteen years old.
   *Source:* U.S. Bureau of the Census, *Statistical Abstract of the United States, 1989*, 109th ed. (Washington, D.C.: U.S. Government Printing Office, 1989), no. 625, p. 379.

of our population during times of economic prosperity, and this group also suffers disproportionately during times of economic recession.

*Income*   There is no doubt that the African-American population made substantial social status gains over the past thirty years. These gains seem to exist whether one looks at occupation, education, or income. Yet, irrespective of absolute gains, the paradox is that blacks remain significantly deprived when compared to whites at the same status level. The economic gap that separates the whites and blacks in the United States is growing, despite all the efforts of recent years.

   According to census data (*see* Table 6–2), the dollar gap between blacks and whites actually grew in the last quarter century. In 1960, the median white family income was $5,835; the median black family income was $3,230—a dollar gap of $2,605. By 1975, after widely heralded social reforms, white income soared to $14,268 and black income rose to $8,779, with a constantly increasing dollar difference reaching $5,489. As of 1988, the median income for white families was $33,915, and for black families it was $19,329, with a dollar difference of over $14,500.

   The ratio of black to white income was 57 in 1988. However, ratios mean very little when dollar amounts are insufficient to maintain families. In 1988, the poverty threshold for a nonfarm family of four was $12,092 (*see* Table 7–1 in the next chapter). This figure is only about $7,000 less than the median family income for blacks in 1988 and includes 33.1 percent of the total black population. The seriousness of the implications to family life is illuminated by at least one study, which found the husband's income to be the most important predictor of marital disruption in black families.[14] In general, an established sociological finding positively relates socioeconomic status to marital stability.

---

   14. Robert L. Hampton, "Husband's Characteristics and Marital Disruption in Black Families," *The Sociological Quarterly* 20 (Spring 1979): 255–266.

Table 6–2
*Median income in current dollars of white and black families,*
*1960–1987*

| Year | White ($) | Black ($) | Difference | Ratio: black to white |
|------|-----------|-----------|------------|------------------------|
| 1988 | 33,915 | 19,329 | 14,586 | 57 |
| 1987 | 32,274 | 18,098 | 14,176 | 56 |
| 1986 | 30,809 | 17,604 | 13,205 | 57 |
| 1985 | 29,152 | 16,786 | 12,366 | 58 |
| 1980 | 21,904 | 12,674 | 9,230 | 58 |
| 1975 | 14,268 | 8,779 | 5,489 | 62 |
| 1970 | 10,236 | 6,279 | 3,957 | 61 |
| 1965 | 7,251 | 3,993 | 3,258 | 55 |
| 1960 | 5,835 | 3,230 | 2,605 | 55 |

*Source:* Adapted from U.S. Bureau of the Census, *Statistical Abstract of
the United States: 1989*, 109th ed. (Washington, D.C.: U.S. Government
Printing Office, 1989), no. 721, p. 445; and *Current Population Reports*
Series P-60, no. 166, "Money Income and Poverty Status in the United
States: 1988" (Washington, D.C.: U.S. Government Printing Office, 1989),
Table A, p. 3.

*Education*    Transition from a negative to a more positive social status can also
be seen by examining the percentages of the African-American population age
twenty-five years and over who have obtained at least a high school education.
In 1987, 63.0 percent of black males and 63.7 percent of black females had
completed four years of high school or more. These figures are about double
the comparable 1970 percentages of 30.2 and 32.6 for black males and females,
respectively, and show greater percentage increases than for either whites or
Hispanics (*see* Table 6–3).

These changes appear quite dramatic for the time span involved. The
figures may be equally dramatic in understanding mate selection and marriage
for African-American men and women. If an equal or greater number of black

Table 6–3
*Percent of persons 25 years and over completing four years of high school or more by sex, race, and
Hispanic origin: 1970–1987*

|  | White | | Black | | Hispanic | |
|------|-------|--------|-------|--------|----------|--------|
|  | *Male* | *Female* | *Male* | *Female* | *Male* | *Female* |
| 1987 | 77.3 | 76.8 | 63.0 | 63.7 | 51.9 | 50.0 |
| 1980 | 69.5 | 68.0 | 50.7 | 51.5 | 44.0 | 42.6 |
| 1970 | 54.0 | 55.0 | 30.2 | 32.6 | 33.4 | 30.9 |

*Source:* U.S. Bureau of the Census, *Statistical Abstract of the United States*, 1989, 109th ed. (Washington, D.C.: U.S.
Government Printing Office, 1989), no. 212, p. 131.

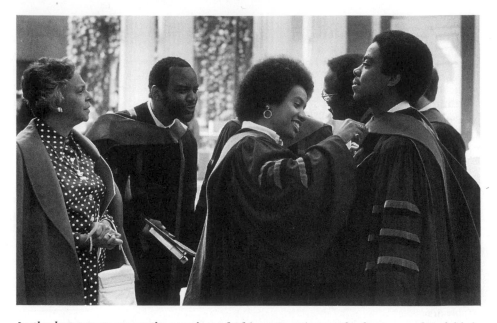

*In the last twenty years, the number of African-Americans who have completed high school has about doubled. But access to colleges and graduate schools has become more difficult and the number of African-Americans getting a PhD appears to be decreasing rather than increasing.*

females than males is completing high school, note the implications this has for black women finding a mate with an education or income equal to or better than their own. Note the potential for increased strain and conflict for marriages that exists in a society that stresses a male provider role. Addressing these issues directly, Paul Secord and Kenneth Ghee suggest that strains in black marriages would be somewhat relieved if black men had better employment prospects, more occupational mobility, and higher educational attainment relative to black women.[15] The educated black woman who still expects her husband to be the primary provider is likely to be dissatisfied with his performance. The educated black woman who is more likely than the less educated to expect her husband to be more sensitive, emotionally nurturant, and companionable may have difficulty in finding the black husband who can fulfill her expectations. Factors such as these may help us understand the high incidence of divorce and separation among black couples.

One study of blacks in the United States suggests that the difficulties many black men have in providing adequately for their families often lead to

---

15. Paul F. Secord and Kenneth Ghee, "Implications of the Black Marriage Market for Marital Conflict," *Journal of Family Issues* 7 (March 1986): 21–30.

difficulties in spousal relationships and satisfaction with their own lives. They also attribute marital difficulties to the disparities in education—with women marrying less-educated men—and the sex-ratio issue—where black women have a more restricted field of eligible partners than do white women.[16]

Frazier, writing in 1957, seemed convinced that conformity to more traditional family norms and stable marriage patterns would result as the educational and economic position of blacks improved.[17] It was his conviction that a black middle class would arise made up of salaried professionals and white-collar workers, and family stability would evolve in relation to economic improvement. Generally, as economic conditions improve, the incidence of family disorganization decreases, family life becomes increasingly stable, there are higher aspirations for children, and there is a greater conformity to the sexual mores of society. For African-American families, however, there is the added dimension of male-female disparities in education and in eligible marital partners.

## From negative to positive self-image

A basic tenet of social psychology states that we develop our selves, our identities, and our perceptions of our worth in interaction with others. As the black is the last to be hired and the first to be fired, as he or she interacts in a white world, and as the black child interacts in a society that encourages feelings of inferiority and degrades self-worth, it might be expected that a self-fulfilling prophecy would be operative: the growing black child believing and acting out the societal messages bestowed upon her or him. The prevailing view of African-Americans over the years has been that they suffer from negative self-esteem manifested in feelings of self-hate and a lack of self-actualizing behavior.

Numerous studies call into question that prevailing view. Although it cannot be denied that racism and discrimination abound and take their toll on African-Americans, empirical evidence does not support the view of negative self-evaluation.[18] From studies he received comparing blacks and whites on measures of self-esteem, Guterman[19] concluded that the level of self-esteem among blacks does not differ significantly from that of whites or else is actually

---

16. Richard E. Ball and Lynn Robbins, "Marital Status and Life Satisfaction Among Black Americans," *Journal of Marriage and the Family* 48 (May 1986): 389–394.

17. Frazier, *The Negro Family in the United States*, p. 333.

18. *See* for example Janet G. Hunt and Larry L. Hunt, "Racial Inequality and Self-image: Identity Maintenance as Identity Confusion," *Sociology and Social Research* 61 (July 1977): 539–559; Anthony R. Harris and Randall Stokes, "Race, Self-evaluation and the Protestant Ethic," *Social Problems* 26 (October 1978): 71–85; and Castellano B. Turner and Barbara F. Turner, "Gender, Race, Social Class, and Self-Evaluations Among College Students," *The Sociological Quarterly* 23 (Autumn 1982): 491–507.

19. Stanley S. Guterman, ed., *Black Psyche: Modal Personality Patterns of Black Americans* (Berkeley, Calif.: Glendessary Press, 1972): 87.

### Does slavery live today?

In the *Journal of Black Studies* (December 1986) Joe Feagin's article titled "Slavery Unwilling to Die: The Background of Black Oppression in the 1980s" appeared. In this article, Feagin argues that the semi-slave system remains firmly in place in regard to employment, housing, and educational segregation as well as in terms of violence, ideological racism, color coding, and resistance to intermarriage. And, he proclaims, the likelihood of future change without militant black action is close to zero.

Why is this so? Basically, it resides in the ideological position of white U.S. citizens who vigorously oppose any significant government program, whether it be affirmative action in jobs or prosecution of homeowners and realtors who discriminate. Whites tolerate a few black employees at work, a few black employees at school, and a few black families in the larger residential neighborhood but most whites do not accept more substantial desegregation. Survey after survey shows whites do not favor federal government intervention to see that blacks get fair treatment in jobs or housing or in getting rid of segregation in schools.

In brief, most white U.S. citizens believe that the tremendous imbalance of power, reflected in a system of semislavery, should not be eradicated by race-conscious action. And Feagin (p. 199) concludes that "this does not bode well for the future of blacks in the United States."

*Source:* Joe Feagin, "Slavery Unwilling to Die: The Background of Black Oppression in the 1980s," *Journal of Black Studies* (December 1986): 199.

higher than that of whites. A Detroit study [20] on the quality of life reported higher levels of self-evaluation among blacks than among whites. Specifically, 75 percent of blacks, compared to 61 percent of the whites, were completely or highly satisfied with themselves.

A follow-up on that study was done to see whether levels of self-evaluation vary among blacks based on demographic characteristics or satisfaction with internal and external factors in their lives.[21] It was found that older blacks tended to appraise themselves more positively than did younger blacks. Those with higher evaluations of themselves felt they had more control over life plans and were more satisfied with their job, income, and life as a whole. High self-evaluation was strongly associated with satisfaction with family life, particularly for women. This finding further strengthened the notion that the family plays an important role in shaping blacks' attitudes about themselves. The family for African-Americans has been one of the primary sources of support and a major reference group for boosting self-pride.

How is it possible that African-Americans have positive concepts of themselves in spite of oppressive social and economic conditions? Foster and Perry [22] provide several explanations. One is that over the past few decades,

20. *A Study of the Quality of Life: Metropolitan Detroit* (Ann Arbor: Institute for Social Research, University of Michigan, 1975).

21. Madison Foster and Lorraine R. Perry, "Self-valuation Among Blacks," *Social Work* 27 (January 1982): 60–66.

22. Ibid., p. 65.

## What does it feel like to be white?

I wonder what it feels like to be white. I have no idea, but I am, on occasion, curious.

I've never, on the other hand, found myself wondering what it feels like to be male, although I have wanted in times of stress to have bulging biceps so I could knock an adversary flat on his back.

But white is something else again. I wonder if the collective white experience, if indeed there is such a thing, can be probed, explored, and subjected to the same kinds of generalizations that routinely are applied to the collective black experience?

I doubt it. Still, I can't resist the temptation to ask, in a general way, some questions that come from my experience.

I wonder if little white girls played with little black dolls whose hair had to be oiled and straightened into submission? Of course, that's an unfair question. Little black girls didn't play with those dolls either. We played with pink or brown cloth-bodied babies whose hair could be brushed and teased into big fat curls.

Kinky hair, mahogany skin, thick lips, and a wide nose were not things you paid money for. No. You paid money to straighten your hair, to lighten your skin, to buy a lip liner to make your lips look smaller. I started thinking about all of this after I was given a new face by an extremely nice makeup artist who brushed dark powder down the sides of my nose to narrow it and then outlined my lips in brown to give them less substance and more form.

Somehow I never thought my lips would become a metaphor for life.

### The usual questions

In any event, I wonder what it would feel like to walk into the Free Press one day and be a member of the majority population?

I wonder what it would feel like to walk into a General Motors management meeting or to go into a restaurant in Traverse City and see your skin tone repeated over and over again throughout the room?

I wonder what it feels like to walk into an office or store filled with white shoppers and not feel out of step, if only for a second?

I wonder what it feels like never to have been told: "I never think of you as black."

I wonder what it feels like to go through an entire week at work without being asked:

My opinion on a black political or social situation.

The name of a black expert on a particular subject.

If a story is racially significant.

I wonder what it feels like to go on vacation, get a deep tan, walk up to a black person and put your tanned arm next to that black arm and say: "See how dark I am? We're almost the same color."

I wonder what it feels like to have someone ask what nationality your parents are?

### Are there answers?

I wonder what it feels like to be able to go to almost any movie at any time and see people who look like you up on the screen — to see loving, laughing, fighting, heroic, or cowardly people, each one reflecting an aspect of humanity. I've often thought that the controversy over "The Color Purple" really stemmed from the fact that blacks are woefully underrepresented in movies. Thus, every "black" movie becomes a statement about black life and is given greater significance than it deserves.

I wonder what it feels like to set up a lunch date with a stranger at a fancy restaurant in some upscale suburb and have to give a detailed description about what you'll be wearing and the color of your hair?

Perhaps there are no answers to these questions. Perhaps the inherent generalizations make them meaningless.

Still, I do wonder . . . about the questions and about the responses I'll get from those folks, black and white, who think they know the answers.

*Source:* Susan Watson, *Detroit Free Press*, June 18, 1986, p. 3A.

*Table 6—4*
*Suicide rates per 100,000 population by race and sex, 1970, 1980,*
*and 1986*

|  | Black | | White | |
| --- | --- | --- | --- | --- |
|  | *Male* | *Female* | *Male* | *Female* |
| 1986 | 11.1 | 2.3 | 22.3 | 5.9 |
| 1980 | 10.3 | 2.2 | 19.9 | 5.9 |
| 1970 | 8.0 | 2.6 | 18.0 | 7.1 |

*Source:* U.S. Bureau of the Census, *Statistical Abstract of the United States,* 1989, 109th ed. (Washington, D.C.: U.S. Government Printing Office, 1989), no. 125, p. 84.

black organizations and social interactions have served to bolster self-pride, identification with blackness, and appreciation of black culture and life. Second, historical black writing and poetry "damn as a falsehood" the concept of inferiority. Third, the family, church, fraternal groups, friendships, and general social relationships provide positive support systems that influence blacks' self-evaluation. Hoelter[23] supports these views by suggesting that blacks get more than whites out of interpersonal rewards because those significant others perceived to give the most positive evaluations have a greater impact on the self-esteem of blacks compared to the impact of similar evaluations on whites. His study concludes that the black community, or at least the segment that "counts," serves to enhance rather than destroy its members' self-images.

All of these factors suggest that the African-American community and family teach their children to act, feel, and think positively and to be proud. These are factors that may explain the finding, surprising to many, that suicide rates in the United States (certainly an extreme index of depression and low self-esteem) are consistently lower for blacks than for whites. For example, in 1986, the suicide rate per 100,000 population was 11.1 for black males and 22.3 for white males. The rate was 2.3 for black females and 5.9 for white females (*see* Table 6—4). For many years, suicide rates have been higher for males than for females. When controlled for race, the rates are much higher for white males than for black males and for white females than for black females. Clearly, not all blacks have high self-concepts and self-esteem, but evidence suggests a highly positive self-image among black Americans.

23. John W. Hoelter, "Race Differences in Selective Credulity and Self-Esteem," *The Sociological Quarterly* 23 (Autumn 1982): 527–537.

# PATTERNS OF AFRICAN-AMERICAN FAMILY LIFE

At least three distinct patterns of African-American family life have emerged from the social transitions described. These can be referred to as the **matricentric female-headed pattern,** the **middle-class two-parent pattern,** and the **patriarchal affluent pattern.** Although these refer primarily to the nuclear family unit, they do not exclude other relatives. Not uncommon among African-American nuclear families is the presence of nephews, aunts, grandparents, cousins, and other adult relatives. These extended kin, plus unrelated kin living in as roomers, boarders, or guests, exert a major influence on the life-style of African-American families. At this point, you, the reader, need to recognize (1) the wide range of family structures beyond the matriarchal, egalitarian, and patriarchal family patterns and (2) the extreme resiliency of the African-American family institution. Neither the mother-centered nor any other type of family is necessarily "falling apart" but is capable of major adaptations to the historical and contemporary social conditions confronting it.

## The matricentric female-headed family pattern

The matricentric female-headed family pattern, the least stable of the three patterns, is one in which the female is the dominant member. The female may be a mother or grandmother who resides with children, usually without the continuous presence of a husband or father. These one-parent family units raise one-half of all African-American children. Early motherhood, lack of education, and insufficient income lead to the characterization of this family pattern as "multiproblemed." Here is where we are most likely to find families below the level of poverty.

There were 9.7 million blacks and 21.4 million whites below the poverty level in 1987.[24] Low-income blacks comprise 33.1 percent of the black population; this figure is more than three times the comparable proportion of low-income whites (10.5 percent), and greater than the 28.2 percent of those of Hispanic origin. Families which are headed by females without a husband comprise a sizable proportion of low-income families. In 1987, 54.8 percent of all black families, 55.0 percent of Hispanic-origin families, and 29.5 percent of all white families below the census-defined poverty level were female households with no husbands present.[25] It is a debated issue whether the

---

24. Families are classified as being above or below the poverty level by using a poverty index based on a sliding scale of money income that is adjusted for such factors as family size, composition, and farm-nonfarm residence. The poverty threshold for a family of four was $12,092 in 1988 (see Chapter 7 and Table 7–1).

25. U.S. Bureau of the Census, *Current Population Reports* Series P-60, no. 163, "Poverty in the United States: 1987" (Washington D.C.: U.S. Government Printing Office, 1989), Table 1, pp. 7–8.

family structure of the female householder with no husband present explains the family's poverty or whether the poverty explains the family's structure. It is likely that each contributes to the other and that governmental policies contribute to both.

The matricentric pattern may take several forms. One is the family in which there is no father. In this situation, the child is given the surname of the mother who lives in her own house or the house of her parents with her own children. Second is the family that has a temporary father or a series of temporary fathers. The father may appear when he has a job and live with his wife and then leave when the income ceases. A third subtype of the matricentric pattern is one in which the father may be present but the mother is the dominant authority figure. These families include those with fathers who cannot support a family and who cannot exercise the authority of parenthood.

Robert Staples indicates that the proliferative growth of female-headed households is probably the most significant change in the black family in the last thirty years.[26] One of the most visible reasons for the dramatic increase in households headed by women has been a corresponding increase in out-of-wedlock births. While the nonmarital sexual activity rate of black and white women is converging, the black female initiates intercourse at earlier ages, is more likely to be engaged in unprotected intercourse, and is less likely to marry or have an abortion if she becomes pregnant.

The likelihood of becoming pregnant is greatest among black teenagers who are from high-risk environments. A study conducted by the research division of the Chicago Urban League showed that considered in combination, teenagers who are from high-risk environments (lower class, resident in a ghetto neighborhood, non-intact family, five or more siblings, a sister who became a teenage mother, and lax parental control of dating) have rates of pregnancy 8.3 times higher than girls from low-risk environments (upper class, resident in a good neighborhood, intact family, four or fewer siblings, no sister who became a teenage mother, and strict parental control of dating).[27]

A less visible reason than out-of-wedlock births for the increase in female-headed households is related to the shortage of men relative to the number of women during the marriageable years. The deterioration in the marriage market, is, according to William Julius Wilson, a fundamental cause for the increased percentage of black families that are headed by females.[28] In

---

26. Robert Staples, "Changes in Black Family Structure: The Conflict Between Family Ideology and Structure Conditions," *Journal of Marriage and the Family* 47 (November 1985): 1005–1013. Note also: Ann M. Nichols-Casebolt, "Black Families Headed by Single Mothers: Growing Numbers and Increasing Poverty," *Social Problems* 33 (July/August 1988): 306–313.

27. Dennis P. Hogan and Evelyn N. Kitagawa, "The Impact of Social Status, Family Structure, and Neighborhood on the Fertility of Black Adolescence," *American Journal of Sociology* 90 (January 1985): 825–855.

28. William Julius Wilson, *The Truly Disadvantaged: The Inner City, the Underclass, and Public Policy* (Chicago: University of Chicago Press, 1987): 179.

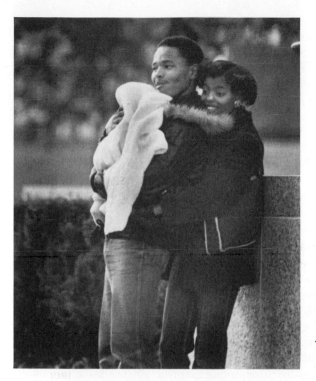

*Contrary to the stereotype of African-American families, more than fifty percent of these families have two parents present with more than three-fourths of black men working and supporting their household.*

addition to the decreasing number of available black men, Wilson argues that the erosion of the industrial bases and lack of jobs for many less-educated blacks have severely damaged the ability of black men to provide for their families and to maintain traditional male roles. It is this decrease in the population of black males as well as the decline in the number of black males able to adequately provide for their families, rather than factors such as an economic motivation brought on by welfare dependency,[29] that appear to be key driving forces behind the increase in black female-headed families.

According to the U.S. Bureau of the Census, in 1987 there were 1.65 million more black women than black men over the age of fourteen. Since there is an excess number of black males at birth, the shortage of males over age fourteen is attributed both to their higher infant mortality rate and a considerably greater mortality rate of young black males through homicide, accidents, suicide, drug overdose, and war casualty. To these numbers can be added black males who are divorced or separated due to military service, unemployment, or institutional confinement—such as prison or mental

29. William A. Darity, Jr. and Samuel L. Myers, Jr., "Does Welfare Dependency Cause Female Headship? The Case of the Black Family," *Journal of Marriage and the Family* 46 (November 1984): 765–779.

hospitals—and those with serious alcohol or drug problems. Factors such as these magnify the serious disadvantages of black women in choosing from the eligible and desirable males in the marriage pool or in staying married.

A third and generally unrecognized reason for the increase in female-headed households is referred to by Andrew Billingsley as the impact of technology.[30] He cites three levels of technological development since World War II that have had particular relevance to African-American families in general and to female-headed families in particular. The *first* level is *domestic technology* associated with the home. The most dramatic impact comes from television, which he claims robs parents of their capacity to think critically and inundates children with a glorification of violence, irresponsible sexual behavior, and unbridled materialism. The *second* level is *construction technology* associated with community development. The automobile, the super highway, and the construction industry combined to produce suburbia. Suburbs provided an escape from the problems of the city, drained resources from the cities, and became synonymous with middle-class white flight. Social forces such as these were responsible for the expansion of black underclass neighborhoods, poverty, and fear in the central cities of the nation. The *third* level is *industrial technology* associated with the production of goods and services in the wider society. The launching of spacecraft, the decline in manufacturing jobs and explosion of service jobs, the accompanying high unemployment rates for blacks (again note Table 6–1), and the acceleration of the civil rights revolution were four major events driven by changes in industrial technology. All of these factors, from unemployment to the exploitation of African-American women by means of low paying jobs, to poor housing and homelessness, to policies that fail to retrain workers or provide job skills for the school drop-out, had major impacts on the African-American family and particularly on increasing the one-parent, mother only, family.

Robert Hill extends these ideas of Billingsley considerably by contending that institutional racism, whether intended or not, has contributed significantly to the erosion of the social and economic well-being of black families over the past two decades.[31] The rise of single-parent families, out-of-wedlock births, adolescent pregnancies, and the like were affected by economic trends such as back-to-back recessions, double-digit inflation, and industrial and population shifts. Economic policies that undermined black family stability included anti-inflation fiscal and monetary policies, trade policies, plant closings, block grants, and federal per capita formulas for allocating funds to state and local areas that were not corrected for the census undercount.

---

30. Andrew Billingsley, "The Impact of Technology on Afro-American Families," *Family Relations* 37 (October 1988): 420–425.

31. Robert B. Hill, "Economic Forces, Structural Discrimination and Black Family Instability," *The Review of Black Political Economy* 17 (Winter 1989): 5–23.

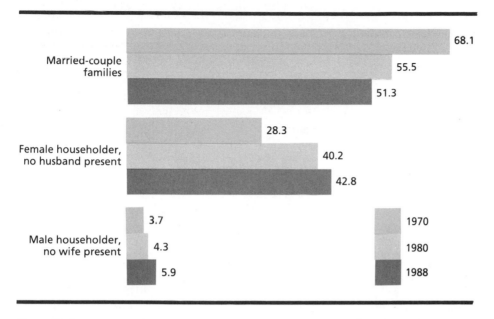

*Figure 6–1*
**Black families, by type: 1970 to 1988 (In percent)** (*Source:* U.S. Bureau of the Census, *Current Population Reports* Series P-23, no. 159, "Population Profile of the United States, 1989" [Washington D.C.: U.S. Government Printing Office, 1989], p. 36.)

Female-headed households are not the predominant family pattern among African-American families but the proportion of families of this type is increasing (*see* Figure 6–1). Neither are female-headed families exclusive to black families. In 1988, of the 7.2 million black families in the United States, 3.07 million or 42.8 percent were female-headed households with no husband present (*see* Table 6–5 and Figure 6–2). In comparison, 12.9 percent of white families and 23.4 percent of Spanish-origin families were female headed with no husband present. Of those female-headed households among black families which had children under the age of eighteen, about one-fourth of the women were married with the husband absent, only 7 percent were widowed, one-fifth were divorced, and nearly half (47.6 percent) were single.

An examination of Table 6–5 will show how these figures compare with white and Spanish-origin families for the same year. In 1988, white females heading households that included children under the age of eighteen were considerably more likely to be widowed or divorced and much less likely to be single. Women heading Spanish-origin families were most likely to be married but separated from their husbands. Note from the same table that the average number of children under the age of eighteen per family is greater for female-headed household families with no husband present than for all other

*Table 6–5*

*Selected characteristics of white, black, and Spanish-origin family households, 1988*

| Characteristic | White | Black | Spanish-origin |
|---|---|---|---|
| Total number of family households in the United States | 56,044,000 | 7,177,000 | 4,588,000 |
| Female householder, no husband present | 7,235,000 | 3,074,000 | 1,072,000 |
| Percentage of total | 12.9% | 42.8% | 23.4% |
| Average number of children under age eighteen per family, total | 0.90 | 1.32 | 1.51 |
| Female householder | 1.06 | 1.59 | 1.70 |
| Male householder | 0.71 | 0.86 | 0.81 |
| Marital status of female householder families with children under age eighteen, by percent | | | |
| Married, husband absent | 22.4% | 24.1% | 30.3% |
| Separated | (18.8) | (21.7) | (25.7) |
| Other | (3.6) | (2.4) | (4.6) |
| Widowed | 7.9 | 7.0 | 6.9 |
| Divorced | 53.4 | 21.3 | 31.3 |
| Single (never married) | 16.3 | 47.6 | 31.5 |
| Total | 100.0% | 100.0% | 100.0% |

*Source:* U.S. Bureau of the Census, *Current Population Reports,* Series P-20, no. 437, "Household and Family Characteristics: March 1988" (Washington, D.C.: U.S. Government Printing Office, 1989), Tables 1 and 12, pp. 4–6 and 75–78.

families irrespective of race. Male-headed householders, however, have fewer children per household than either female-headed householders or all other households irrespective of race.

In our society it has been assumed that adults cannot maintain family stability unless they are married and living with their spouse. And the assumption is that children cannot be adequately socialized unless they are reared in a two-parent family. Yet black families have managed to survive and have demonstrated many positive outcomes irrespective of family structure, in this case, number of parents.[32] Perhaps stability and positive outcomes include far more than the presence of two parents. An increase in income, a

---

32. *See* for example, Essie Manuel Rutledge, "Afro-American Socialization Experiences by Family Structure," *Journal of Black Studies* 19 (December 1988): 204–215.

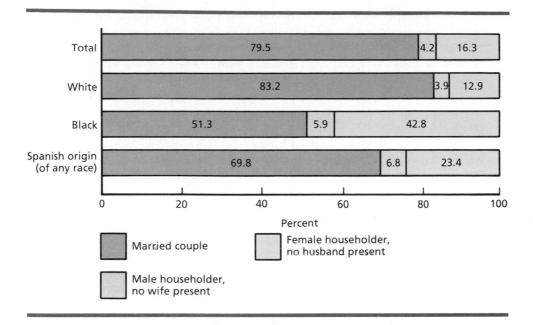

*Figure 6–2*
**Family type as a percent of all family households by race and Spanish origin: 1988.**
(*Source:* U.S. Bureau of the Census, *Current Population Reports*, Series P-20, No. 437, "Household and Family Characteristics: March 1988" [Washington D.C.: U.S. Government Printing Office, 1989]. Figured from Table 1, pp. 3–6.)

greater availability of housing, and the maintaining of kin ties with persons other than a spouse may permit more families to maintain a degree of stability equal to that of families with both parents present.

## The middle-class two-parent family pattern

Family stability, life satisfaction, and personal happiness are not dependent on a two-parent family pattern, but marriage itself appears to contribute to the life satisfaction of black adults. Generally, married black persons tend to be happier and more satisfied with life than unmarried black persons. National survey data from several studies found this relationship to hold regardless of gender, age, education, or structure of the respondents' family of orientation (reared by both parents, one, or neither).[33]

---

33. Ann Creighton Zollar and J. Sherwood Williams, "The Contribution of Marriage to the Life Satisfaction of Black Adults," *Journal of Marriage and the Family* 49 (February 1987): 87–92; and Clifford L. Broman, "Satisfaction Among Blacks: The Significance of Marriage and Parenthood," *Journal of Marriage and the Family* 50 (February 1988): 45–51.

The two-parent family is the type of family structure most commonly found among African-Americans in our society. This is one in which the husband and wife are living together in their first marriage. Here we have two parents in distinctive but complementary and flexible roles. The husband is more likely to have stable employment and at least an operational level of education. Families of this type are more likely to be middle-class or higher-income working-class families but are not limited to these classes. For example, one study of black families in a predominantly lower-class urban area focused on intact—that is, husband-wife—families and found little, if any, evidence that husband-fathers renounced their positions in the family or of reversed husband-wife roles where the female assumed the traditional male responsibilities. The results overwhelmingly indicated that in these intact lower-class families, the husbands were the main providers for their families, were positive role models for their children, participated actively in child rearing, and were active participants with their spouses in the decision-making process.[34]

As of March 1988, 68.1 percent of all ever-married black men (age fifteen and over) were living with their wives. The other 31.9 percent included 10.9 percent who were married without a wife present, 6.2 percent who were widowed, and 14.8 percent who were divorced. Of all ever-married black women (age fifteen and over), 50.1 percent were living with their husbands. The other 49.9 percent included 19.3 percent who were widowed, 15.1 percent who were married with the husband absent, and 15.5 percent who were divorced. Comparable data on the marital status of ever-married white persons and those of Spanish origin can be seen in Table 6–6.

This majority pattern destroys the myth that the majority of black men are separated or divorced from their wives. That nearly one-fifth of ever-married black women are widowed adds significantly to the percentage of black women with no husband present. Clearly the majority of adults are currently married and live in husband-wife families with their spouses.[35]

Despite being a dominant pattern, the two-parent intact family has been relatively neglected by most social scientists. Perhaps the two-parent family

34. Bernice McNair Barnett, Ira E. Robinson, Wilfred C. Bailey, and John M. Smith, Jr., "The Status of Husband/Father as Perceived by the Wife/Mother in the Intact Lower Class Urban Black Family," *Sociological Spectrum* 4 (1984): 421–441; and Ira E. Robinson, Wilfred C. Bailey, and John M. Smith, Jr., "Self-Perception of the Husband/Father in the Intact Lower Class Black Family," *Phylon* 46 (1985): 136–147.

35. In 1988, while most black adults were married, a very high percentage of both black males (42.5 percent) and females (36.9 percent) age fifteen and over were never-married singles. The comparable figure for white males was 28.1 percent, for white females 20.9 percent, for Spanish-origin males 36.9 percent, and Spanish-origin females 27.3 percent. U.S. Bureau of the Census, *Current Population Reports* Series P-20, no. 433, "Marital Status and Living Arrangements, March 1988 (Washington, D.C.: U.S. Government Printing Office, 1989), Table 1: 4–5.

*Table 6–6*
*Marital status of ever-married persons 15 years old and over by race and sex, March 1988*

| Marital status | White | | Black | | Spanish-origin | |
|---|---|---|---|---|---|---|
| | Male | Female | Male | Female | Male | Female |
| Married, spouse present | 84.5% | 71.5% | 68.1% | 50.1% | 78.2% | 70.1% |
| Married, spouse absent | 3.4 | 3.6 | 10.9 | 15.1 | 10.9 | 9.7 |
| Separated | (2.1) | (2.5) | (9.7) | (12.7) | (4.8) | (7.2) |
| Other | (1.3) | (1.1) | (1.2) | (2.4) | (6.1) | (2.5) |
| Widowed | 3.4 | 14.5 | 6.2 | 19.3 | 2.1 | 8.5 |
| Divorced | 8.7 | 10.4 | 14.8 | 15.5 | 8.3 | 11.7 |
| Total | 100.0% | 100.0% | 100.0% | 100.0% | 100.0% | 100.0% |

*Source:* Percentages figured from data presented in U.S. Bureau of the Census, *Current Population Reports*, Series P-20, no. 433 "Marital Status and Living Arrangements: March 1988" (Washington, D.C.: U.S. Government Printing Office, 1989), Table 1, pp. 4–5.

pattern has been ignored because these families are relatively stable, conforming, achieving, and cause few problems to anyone.

One study of stable black families in Indianapolis was done by Scanzoni. These families included husbands and wives who had lived together for five years or more.[36] Using black interviewers, data were gathered from four hundred households in an attempt to describe and analyze the urban black family system above the under class or lower class. A central hypothesis of Scanzoni's study was that an inextricable link exists between economic resources and black family structure.

The inescapable conclusion of Scanzoni is that:

> The black family in America, as much as the white family, is shaped by its relationship to the economic-opportunity structure. This relationship is mediated primarily via the occupation of the male head-of-household. Where he is not present, as is often the case in the lower class, this has certain negative consequences for the family. And where he is present, the degree of his integration with the opportunity system influences most, if not all, aspects of husband-wife and parent-child interaction.
>
> That there is a "black community" and a "white community" reflects in part differential access to the economic rewards of the total society.

---

36. John H. Scanzoni, *The Black Family in Modern Society* (Boston: Allyn and Bacon, 1971).

That there are certain "black family patterns" which may differ
somewhat from "white family patterns" reflects this same differential economic access.[37]

More recent support for the influence of economic resources on both
family structure and satisfaction with family life comes from a study of
southern black husbands. Husbands in families with greater per capita
financial resources tended to be more satisfied with life in their families.[38] The
authors suggest that reciprocity is involved, with higher incomes leading to
greater satisfaction, but also greater satisfaction lending itself to cohesion and
stability, and thence, higher incomes.

It appears that families in which both husband and wife are present are
those from which black leaders emerge. A three-generation analysis of the
social origin of contemporary blacks from the United States revealed that most
of these eminent blacks were reared in stable families, with 67.8 percent living
with both parents (15.3 percent lived with mother, 4.1 percent with father, 5.6
percent with a relative, and 4.9 percent with someone else).[39] Interestingly,
these eminent blacks were also predominantly the descendants of families
characterized by antebellum (before the Civil War) freedom, lighter skin, urban
residence, and higher educational and occupational attainment. It is in the
two-parent family pattern that the father plays a more dominant role and the
children develop a greater identification with him. The role of the father as
playmate, teacher, and disciplinarian to his children is less likely to take place
in the matricentric form of family organization when he is present and
impossible when he is not.

Once again we return to the point made at the beginning of this chapter.
Families are not isolated groups existing independently from the society of
which they are a part. The success or failure of a two-parent pattern or a
matricentric pattern relates very closely to the opportunity structure which is
provided to them.

## The patriarchal affluent family pattern

The patriarchal affluent family pattern can perhaps more accurately be
illustrated by using Willie's concept of "affluent conformists."[40] These are

37. Ibid., pp. 309–310.

38. Richard E. Ball and Lynn Robbins, "Black Husbands' Satisfaction with Their Family
Life," *Journal of Marriage and the Family* 48 (November 1986): 849–855.

39. Elizabeth I. Mullins and Paul Sites, "The Origins of Contemporary Eminent Black
Americans: A Three-Generation Analysis of Social Origin," *American Sociological Review* 49
(October 1984): 672–685.

40. Charles V. Willie, *A New Look at Black Families*, 2nd ed. (Bayside, New York: General Hall,
1981): 58.

two-parent families heavily represented among professional and higher income African-Americans. Both spouses are likely to have college or graduate degrees and the husband-father is likely to take the primary responsibility for most of the major decisions. Among these families, the problems so often associated with blue-collar or poverty-level families are almost nonexistent. Endogenous marriages are highly encouraged. Much of a given generation's wealth is inherited from a previous generation. These wealthier African-Americans in large part tend to isolate themselves from the majority of black families and many college graduates from this background do not engage actively in black organizations.

A patriarchal family pattern exists among many middle- and lower-class families as well. In interviews with both the husbands and wives of forty-three black working-class families in Ohio, it was found that both sexes perceived the power structure of the family to reside with the husband.[41] Specifically, only 2 percent saw the wife as dominant, 25 percent saw equality, and 73 percent saw the husband as dominant. These results differ profoundly from the popular stereotype of the matriarchal black family. Another study of black married couples from an urban North Carolina area demonstrated that the husband-led power pattern was associated, in general, with the highest level of marital quality.[42] Egalitarian and wife-led couples reported similar, lower levels of marital quality. In this research report of black couples, the husband-dominant family was suggested as the goal to be obtained rather than egalitarianism. Husband-wife equality in power, it was suggested, could be construed to be the effect of the financial and social discrimination that prevented black husbands from clearly surpassing their wives in income and education and thus assuming undisputed leadership of their families.

For our purposes, perhaps the most noteworthy features of this particular pattern of family life are its stability and strict patterns of socialization and social control defined according to the values shared by the dominant group in our society. As suggested previously, if economic factors are held constant, African-American families, particularly at the higher socioeconomic levels, differ little from white-American families. One difficulty with this economically based perspective, however, is that it ignores the influence of social-cultural forces and transitions, such as those described earlier in the chapter, in the lives of U.S. blacks. And African-American families in the United States cannot be understood without acknowledging the importance of race and culture.

---

41. Jerry M. Lewis and Paul Sites, "Decision Making in Black Working Class Families," unpublished paper sent to the author.

42. Bernadette Gray-Little, "Marital Quality and Power Processes Among Black Couples," *Journal of Marriage and the Family* 44 (August 1982): 633–646.

# Summary

1. The African-American family in U.S. society, like any family system, is not a uniform entity, nor is it isolated and separate from other social systems within the community and society. The basic structural patterns, the interpersonal processes, and the personal value positions can only be understood within the context in which they exist.

2. African-American families have been and still are affected by numerous major social transitions. The transition from Africa to the United States is relevant to understanding factors such as the influences of skin, color, slavery, and cultural discontinuity. The transition from slavery to emancipation had a major influence on the emergence of multiple family forms, occupational patterns, kin relationships, and the forms of families. The transition from rural and southern to urban and northern areas, while presenting the opportunities for better wages, schools, and health services, also tended to disrupt kin ties and community linkages.

3. The transition from negative to positive social status refers to changes in employment, income, and education. The controversial Moynihan report placed the blame for changes in the black community on the deterioration of the family. Other writers strongly disagreed and argued that the family is a key force in stability and socialization. What is clear is the direct linkage between socioeconomic status and family life. For African-Americans, the unemployment rate is consistently much higher than for white Americans, while income is consistently lower. Significant gains, however, have been made in levels of income and education and these gains are likely to be reflected in styles of family life.

4. The transition to a positive self-concept and self-evaluation appears to be one area where African-Americans excel. Numerous studies suggest a higher level of self-esteem and self-valuation among African-Americans than among white-Americans. Suicide rates as one extreme index of self-esteem show much lower rates for African-American males and females than for white-American males and females. The family and other primary and secondary groups provide positive support systems that influence blacks' evaluation.

5. From these major social transitions, distinct patterns of African-American family life have emerged. The *matricentric* female-household family, while not the most prevalent, is the family type where multi-problems are most frequently found. In these families a father may not exist, may be present only temporarily, or may be present but unable to exercise authority. Those families with a female householder and no husband present are most likely to be low-income, have a greater number of children than white families or other black families, and appear to face the greatest difficulties in meeting the daily demands of existence.

6. The *middle-class* two-parent family, the most prevalent type, is one in which both husband and wife are living together and the spouses have distinctive and complementary roles. These families, often ignored in the social science literature, are relatively stable, conforming, and achieving. They desire to participate in the economic and social benefits of the larger society and tend to share the general values and goals of the larger society.

7. The *patriarchal* affluent family pattern, although less common than the other forms, is heavily represented among African-Americans in the higher socioeconomic levels

of society. Here the father is present, makes most of the major decisions, and is dominant in most respects. Noteworthy features of this pattern are its stability and strict patterns of socialization and social control.

8. This chapter and the one preceding it focused on the family patterns and life-styles of two major groups: the Chinese of mainland China and African-Americans. Significant differences in structure and interaction patterns seem apparent in historical and contemporary settings. A further continuity of thought exists as we turn our attention to the next chapter to variations in family life-styles among families that are identified with particular social classes.

## KEY TERMS AND TOPICS

African-American families   159
Africa to America   159
Slavery to emancipation   161
Rural and southern areas to urban and
    northern ones   162
Negative to positive social status   164

Moynihan Report   164
Negative to positive self-image   169
Matricentric female-headed family pattern   173
Middle-class two-parent family pattern   179
Patriarchal affluent family pattern   182

## DISCUSSION QUESTIONS

1. Is there a unique African-American family to-day?

2. What family characteristics of today can be traced directly to an African heritage? How does an understanding of slavery contribute to an understanding of patterns of African-American family life today?

3. Compare black and white families on dimensions such as family size, educational level, rural-urban residence, and marriage rates. How can differences be explained? What differences exist if one controls for social class?

4. From the use of state census data, contrast the demographic characteristics by race of your county or state with national data. Explain similarities or differences that may exist.

5. Examine the "Moynihan Report." What data are presented that are subject to interpretations other than those given? Why did this report become an object of alarm and controversy?

6. What significance for families is attached to movements from south to north or from rural to urban residences? Are these factors any different for blacks than for whites?

7. How do you explain the level of self-evaluation among African-Americans? What place does the family hold in your explanation?

8. What dangers lie in dealing with the African-American family as a homogeneous grouping? Describe variations in life-styles and marital patterns within the African-American family.

9. It has been claimed by several scholars that life for African-American families in the inner city appears to be getting worse. Explain.

10. Discuss the unique role and status of the woman in the African-American family. How is it explained? Why or why isn't it likely to change?

# FURTHER READINGS

Billingsley, Andrew. *Black Families in White America*. Englewood Cliffs, N.J.: Prentice-Hall, 1968. A look at the black family as a complex institution within the black community, which is in turn highly interdependent with other institutions in the wider white society.

Edelman, Marian Wright. *Families in Peril: an Agenda for Social Change*. Cambridge, MA: Harvard University Press, 1987. A brief and highly readable look at the black family in America, poverty and teen pregnancy, welfare-reform strategies, and effective leadership essential for change.

Hampton, Robert L. (ed.). *Violence in the Black Family: Correlates and Consequences*. Lexington, MA: Lexington Books, 1987. A collection of fourteen articles and writings that examine child maltreatment, interspousal violence, homicides, and other issues of black families victimized by the violence process.

Hill, Robert B. *The Strengths of Black Families*. New York: Emerson Hall, 1971. The director of the research department of the National Urban League strips away many myths and stereotypes surrounding the black family.

Landry, Bart. *The New Black Middle Class*. Berkeley: University of California Press, 1987. While dealing very little with black families per se, this book examines shifts in social mobility over time among blacks in America.

Liebow, Elliott. *Tally's Corner*. Boston: Little, Brown, 1967. A sensitive analysis of the life-styles of black men who hang out on a particular street corner in Washington, D.C.

McAdoo, Harriette Pipes. (ed) *Black Families* 2nd ed. Newbury Park, Cal.: Sage Publications, 1988. A collection of twenty-one articles addressing a variety of issues, both historically and contemporarily, in black families.

McAdoo, Harriette P., and McAdoo, John L., eds. *Black Children: Social, Educational, and Parental Environments*. Beverly Hills, Cal.: Sage Publications, 1985. A collection of empirical research focusing on the experiences of black children and their parents as they develop skills to be functional in both black and non-black cultures.

Moynihan, Daniel Patrick. *The Negro Family: The Case for National Action*. Washington, D.C.: U.S. Government Printing Office, 1965. This, the "Moynihan Report," created a major controversy by arguing that the structure of family life in the black community was increasingly unstable and was the fundamental source of weakness in the community.

Peters, Marie F., and McAdoo, Harriette P. "The Present and Future of Alternative Life-styles in Ethnic American Cultures." In Eleanor D. Macklin and Roger H. Rubin, eds., *Contemporary Families and Alternative Lifestyles*. Beverly Hills: Sage Publications, 1983, Chapter 14, pp. 288–307. The vast diversity of black family life-styles is examined in this chapter: singlehood, cohabitation, single-parents, extended and augmented, dual-income, and polygamous formation, and the effects of the sex ratio and of social class.

Stack, Carol B. *All Our Kin: Strategies for Survival in a Black Community*. New York: Harper, 1974. An anthropologist who lived in the Flats, the poorest section of a black community in a midwestern city, reports on men, women, kin, and domestic networks.

Staples, Robert. *Black Masculinity: The Black Male's Role in American Society*. San Francisco: The Black Scholar Press, 1982. An examination of the black male in the United States, including sections on crime and violence, sex and sexuality, and male-female relationships.

Wilkinson, Doris. "Ethnicity," in *Handbook of Marriage and the Family* by Marvin B. Sussman and Suzanne K. Steinmetz (eds.). New York: Plenum Press, 1987, Chapter 8, pp. 183–210. An overview of demographic patterns, regional variations, and marital and kinship relationships of ethnic groups with major sections on African-Americans, Hispanics, Asian-Americans, and American Indians.

Willie, Charles V. *Black and White Families: A Study in Complementarity*. Bayside, N.Y.: General Hall, 1985. A presentation of forty-eight case studies including twenty-four white and twenty-four black, middle-class, working-class, and poor families.

Wilson, William J. *The Truly Disadvantaged: The Inner City, the Underclass and Public Policy*. Chicago: The University of Chicago Press, 1987. A description of inner city neighborhoods, causes of the deterioration of the ghetto underclass, and the recommendation of a comprehensive public policy agenda to address these groups. Chapter three on poverty and family structure is particularly pertinent.

# CHAPTER SEVEN

# SOCIAL CLASS VARIATIONS IN FAMILY LIFE-STYLES

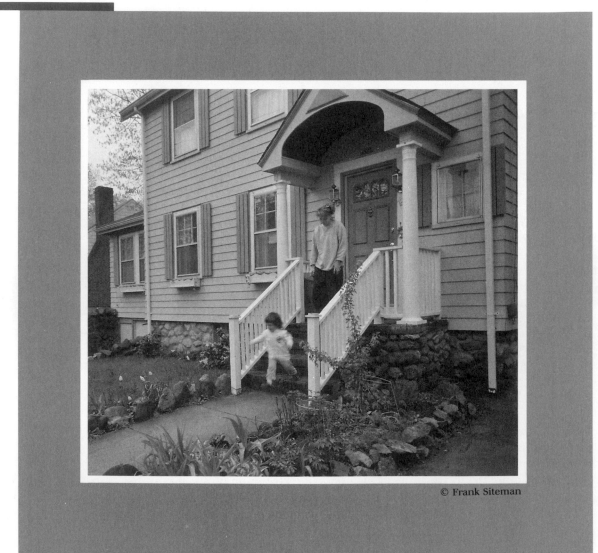

© Frank Siteman

The discussions in the two previous chapters on Chinese and African-American families included aspects of social class. In the traditional Chinese family, the life-styles of the gentry were radically different from those of the peasants. In contemporary Chinese families, while class extremes have been diminished, class and power distinctions were shown to still exist. Among African-American families, specific attention was given to the life-styles of families from different social classes. In this chapter the class dimension is examined: what it means, how it is determined, and how families who comprise a general class category experience and express differing life-styles. The chapter ends with a discussion of family mobility—changing life-styles by moving from one class category to another.

## THE MEANING OF SOCIAL CLASS

The concept of "social class" refers to an aggregate of individuals who occupy broadly similar positions on scales of wealth, prestige, and power. As even the most untrained observer can note, some kinds of work, some styles of life, and some types of homes, automobiles, or dress are viewed as more prestigious than others. All persons, families, and societies differentiate some roles and positions as more important, more powerful, more privileged, more prestigious, and more highly rewarded than others. This differential in power, prestige, money, and the like results in inequality between persons and families. The grouping or ranking of persons in a hierarchy of unequal positions is referred to in sociology as **social stratification.** This term, borrowed from geology, refers to a differential ranking of people into horizontal layers (strata) of equality and inequality.

Two of the theories described in Chapter 2, the **functionalist** and the **conflict theories,** are particularly relevant to our understanding of social class and the stratification system. A functionalist perspective views stratification as both an inevitable and a necessary feature of society. The assumption is that all societies have a wide range of tasks that need to be performed in a society. These tasks are essential for the stability and maintenance of that society but they carry with them differential levels of prestige and rewards. Someone must collect the garbage, repair faulty plumbing, and perform the labor to assemble automobiles, while others must teach students, plan defense strategies, research the activity of molecules and atoms, and engage in heart surgery. Some tasks require greater levels of skill and training and these are likely to be more highly rewarded. This unequal distribution of social rewards is functional for society because it enables all roles and tasks to be completed, with those that demand the most scarce talents being performed by the most able and skilled persons.

For many years, this functionalist perspective was the predominant one among sociologists and for many, it remains so today. However a number of people began to question why some families are highly rewarded with family fortunes for generations when they perform little of value to society; why people such as film stars or boxers earn millions overnight for doing tasks that are viewed as less important than those of social workers, scientists, or even the president, who may not earn as much in a lifetime; and why poor people need to stay poor from one generation to the next. Sociologists also began to raise value questions about the justice of unequal rewards and the fairness of assignment by birth of certain groups to positions of low prestige, wealth, and power. An awareness of these and other inequities among persons and families led conflict theorists to reject a functionalist view of a stratified society.

Conflict theorists saw a stratified society, not as leading toward stability and order, but as leading to dissatisfaction, alienation, and exploitation. The differentiation of economic rewards led one of the classical theorists of nineteenth-century sociology, Karl Marx, to believe that conflict in capitalist countries would result between those who have and those who have not; between those who control the means of production and those whose labor is the instrument of production; between management and labor; between the bourgeoisie who use capital, natural resources, and labor for profit, and the proletariat who sell their labor to buy the products produced by their labor. Translated into family terms, this means conflict between the families that own and control the wealth and means of production and the families who are forced to work for wages and produce the products or provide the services. Translated into gender terms, this means conflict between the males (husbands) who are employed, who receive higher wages, and who are the order givers, and the females who are less likely to be employed, who receive lower wages, and who are the order takers.

Rayna Rapp[1] uses this Marxian dichotomy in analyzing family and class in the contemporary United States. While granting recognition to class variations in households and families, she argues that social class is a shorthand for a process, not a thing. That process is one by which different social relations to the means of production are inherited and reproduced. Categories of people get swept up at different times and places and deposited into different relations to the means of production and to one another. People then get labeled "blue collar" or "white collar." While people carry these class category labels, Rapp stresses that it is important to recognize class not as a static place that individuals inhabit but as a process determined by the relationships set up in capital accumulation.

Erik Wright and others[2] make similar arguments in their explicitly Marxian relational perspective of the U.S. class structure. They define classes

---

1. Rayna Rapp, "Family and Class in Contemporary America: Notes Toward an Understanding of Ideology," *Science and Society* 42 (Fall 1978): 278–300; also in Barrie Thorne with Marilyn Yalom, *Rethinking the Family: Some Feminist Questions* (New York: Longman, 1982): 168–187.
2. Erik Olin Wright, David Hachen, Cynthia Costello, and Joey Sprague, "The American Class Structure," *American Sociological Review* 47 (December 1982): 709–726.

not in terms of categories of occupations, but in terms of social relations of control over investments, decision making, other people's work, and one's own work. National survey data using these dimensions of social relations of production yielded four general results the authors see as particularly important: (1) the working class is by far the largest class in the U.S. class structure; (2) close to half of all locations within the class structure have a "contradictory character," meaning that their class content is determined by more than one basic class and implying that no simple scheme of class polarization represents the U.S. class structure; (3) lower status white-collar occupations are as polarized as manual occupations, and thus it makes little sense to consider these white-collar occupations as part of the middle class; and (4) women and blacks are considerably more polarized than white males, with the result that a sizable majority of the United States working class is composed of women and minorities.

## THE DETERMINATION OF SOCIAL CLASS

The discussion presented thus far would suggest that class is determined by examining who owns, manages, oppresses, and controls. This group is distinguished from those who are managed, oppressed, and controlled. However, only relatively recently has class been analyzed in terms of ownership and authority relations. Traditionally, class determination and categorization was based on an examination of the husband's or head-of-household's occupation. These occupations were ranked on a scale of prestige, and all other family members were granted the same ranking. More recently, while occupational prestige has remained the key determinant of social class, the employment and occupational prestige of the wife and other family members has been considered as well.[3]

Given the increasing number of women and wives in the paid labor force, research evidence today makes it clear that the class-identification process differs for men and women; thus it needs to be gender specific.[4] Conclusions from research on the effects of workplace and occupational variables concluded that: (1) Working wives do not simply borrow their class identification from their husbands. Work experiences are a core part of the class-identification process of employed wives, just as is true for husbands. (2)

3. Marc L. Berk and Paul W. Kingston, "Working Couples and Class Identification," *Sociological Spectrum* 2 (January/March 1982): 31–39; Judith Treas, "U.S. Income Stratification: Bringing Families Back In," *Sociology and Social Research* 66 (April 1982): 231–251; and Joan Huber, "A Theory of Family, Economy and Gender," *Journal of Family Issues* 9(March 1988): 9–26.

4. Randall Collins, "Women and Men in the Class Structure," *Journal of Family Issues* 9(March 1988): 27–50; Ida Harper Simpson, David Stark, and Robert A. Jackson, "Class Identification Processes of Married, Working Men and Women," *American Sociological Review* 53(April 1988): 284–293; and Leonard Beeghley and John Cochran, "Class Identification and Gender Role Norms Among Employed Married Women," *Journal of Marriage and the Family* 50(August 1988): 719–729.

The workplace and occupational variables related to class identification differ for men and women, without any overlap. For men, the identification variables are whether they do manual or nonmanual work and whether they are subordinated in a chain of command. For women, the identification variables are work in a female occupation, self-employment, and membership in unions. The result is that a middle- or working-class identification differs for men and women. (3) The class work of men is much more crystalized around the workplace than women's work, which is more occupationally based. That is, as stated before, manual work or place in the chain of command shapes men's classifications, while a female occupation, self-employment, or union membership shapes women's.[5]

These gender-specific variables were not used in earlier studies. What they did to determine strata, rankings, or class identification was to take one or several prestige indicators (e.g., occupation, income, education, wealth, self-rankings, etc.), place them on a continuum from high to low, and divide them into any number of categories or strata. The studies of "Middletown" (Muncie, Indiana), among the most famous community studies in sociology, used two classes: the business class and the working class.[6] Most students may think in terms of three classes: upper, middle, and lower. The classical work by August Hollingshead, entitled *Elmtown's Youth*, subdivided the community into five classes: upper, upper-middle, lower-middle, upper-lower, and lower-lower.[7]

If social class or a stratification system represent systems of inequality, who is to determine that objectively there are two, five, or seventeen classes of strata? Perhaps few distinct and separate strata exist at all, but rather they represent a continuum of inequalities of wealth, income, prestige, power, age, sex, or race. What is clear is that differences do exist between men and women; they exist among families in their income and spending power, in their owning or serving production processes, in their recognition of wealth and power differentials, and in the consequences these differences have for families and their members.

## CONSEQUENCES OF SOCIAL CLASS TO FAMILY MEMBERS

The real significance of the class structure stems from some of its consequences. In addition to influencing our chances to live (which determine the likelihood of being born in the first place), of living through the first year, or of

5. Simpson, et. al., op. cit., pp. 284–293.

6. Robert S. Lynd and Helen Merrell Lynd, *Middletown* (New York: Harcourt, Brace and World, 1939); Robert S. Lynd and Helen Merrell Lynd, *Middletown in Transition* (New York: Harcourt, Brace and World, 1937); and Theodore Caplow et al., *Middletown Families* (New York: Bantam Books, 1982).

7. August B. Hollingshead, *Elmtown's Youth* (New York: Wiley, 1949).

reaching retirement, social class influences our early socialization, the organization of society, the role expectations and role projections that we hold, the values that we stress, the types of behavior defined as deviant, and the likelihood of mental illness. In addition, class affects the likelihood of an education, its type, the motivation to get it, and the ends for which education is meant. It affects dropout rates, scores on intelligence tests, grades, occupational-vocational aspirations, and almost any other factor related to education.

Most significantly, social class both determines and results in important differences in influence, power, and opportunities. The ascribed status of birth into a certain social stratum has important consequences for the ability to make decisions and wield power. The links of differing classes to political organizations, financial institutions, and corporate boards affect the available opportunities and rewards. To be bourgeoisie or proletariat, management or labor, represents a determinant of one's class position as well as being an influential factor in determining the consequences that result from the position.

Similar consequences of class hold true for marriages and families. Social class affects the age at which one is likely to marry, the success of that marriage, the meanings attached to sexual behavior, the size of family, the recreation engaged in, the type of food eaten, the discipline and care given to children, sleeping arrangements, and contraceptive usage. On this last point for example, a survey of sexually active black adolescents from Chicago showed that 41 percent of the young women from the highest social class used contraceptives at first intercourse, but only 17 percent of those from the lowest class did so. For males, 32 percent of adolescents from the highest class compared to 11 percent from the lowest practiced contraception at first intercourse.[8] Irrespective of race, ethnicity, or gender, differences in behaviors are evident at varying class levels.

Although it is true that there are no sharply defined boundaries from one class to another, a great many of the normal life experiences of certain people are highly similar to those of other people who share a similar class subculture. For example, where polygyny is practiced, it is the men of higher social or economic position who are most likely to have a number of wives. Divorce rates go up as class level goes down. Birth rates increase as social class levels drop. Upper-social-strata young persons are granted less freedom of choice of a mate than are lower-social-strata persons. In the Western world particularly, the age of men at marriage rises with class position. If class lines are crossed in marriage, the woman is more likely to be upwardly mobile (hypergamy). The upper social stratum has more extended kinship networks

8. Dennis P. Hogan, Nan Marie Astone, and Evelyn M. Kitagawa, "Social and Environmental Factors Influencing Contraceptive Use Among Black Adolescents," *Family Planning Perspective* 17 (July/August 1985): 165–169.

than does the lower stratum. Higher-social-strata couples are more likely to use contraceptives than are lower-social-strata couples. One could continue indefinitely with a list of family variables that are highly related to class position. This list is not meant to be complete nor has each relationship been established to hold true cross-culturally. A key point is, however, that within a culture as well as between cultures, significant regularities occur between a family's attitude and behavior patterns and the class position that that family occupies.[9]

## WEALTHY FAMILIES

Wealthy families have been identified as the "very rich," the "upper class," and the "ruling class." Compared to other categories of families, relatively little recent data are available on them. Rayna Rapp observed that one sociologist (either quite naive or quite sardonic) commented, "We know so little about the wealthy because they don't answer our questionnaires."[10] Indeed! They fund them rather than answer them.

This grouping of families, while small in number relative to other groupings, is large in power and influence. They possess enormous resources of wealth and social standing. They have a network of affiliations on important boards in banking, insurance, and manufacturing. These are the elite who own and control the means of production and make the rules for the workers to follow.

When we turn to the family structure of the very rich, some interesting bits and pieces emerge. Families are described by researchers as extremely lineal and concerned with who they are, rather than what they do. They are quite ancestor-oriented and conscious of the boundaries that separate the "best" families from the others. Families are obviously the units within which wealth is accumulated and transmitted.

Women in this class are said to serve as gatekeepers of many of the institutions of the very rich. They launch children, serve as board members at the private schools, run social and service clubs, and facilitate the marriage pools through events like debuts and charity functions. Susan Ostrander conducted interviews with thirty-six upper-class women and indicated that they held a clear preference for being with people like themselves (such as through private and exclusive clubs by invitation only), felt a sense of being better than other people (materially, morally, and in terms of volunteer work and contributions to the community), and conveyed an awareness that people

---

9. Note for example, Russell W. Rumberger, "The Influence of Family Background on Education, Earnings and Wealth," *Social Forces* 61 (March 1983): 755–773; and Anne Locksley, "Social Class and Marital Attitudes and Behavior," *Journal of Marriage and the Family* 44 (May 1982): 427–440.

10. Rapp, "Family and Class in Contemporary America," p. 297.

## Richest get richer and poor get poorer in the 1980s

The *New York Times* reported (March 23, 1989) that judging from congressional data, the gap between the nation's rich and poor widened from 1979 to 1987. Taking inflation into account, the average family income of the poorest fifth of the population declined by 6.1 percent from 1979 to 1987, while the highest paid Americans saw family income rise 11.1 percent. The study, done for the House Ways and Means Committee, found that the average family income of the poorest one-fifth of the population dropped from $5,439 in 1979 to $5,107 in 1987. In that same period the family income of the top fifth increased to $68,775 from $61,917. To make the figures comparable despite inflation, they are all expressed in constant 1987 dollars.

Mr. Thomas J. Downey, a congressman from New York, said this growing gap between rich and poor could lead to increased crime and drug abuse. In his words, "You're not going to have enough locks on the doors or police in the street to protect you from a generation of people who are not part of the mainstream of American economic life."

define and judge them by who they are rather than by what they do.[11] As wives, like traditional wives in other social classes, they held a subordinate position to their husbands, had an unequal voice in family decisions, and maintained sole responsibility for home and family. But at this class level, women did not perform the nitty-gritty tasks of housework and child care. Women of other races and classes did such work for them. At this class level, women did not need—economically, personally, or socially—to seek paid work outside the home. At this class level, their accommodative and supportive function to their husbands enabled the men to manage the economic and political affairs of the society and to perpetuate the dominance of the upper class. Without doubt, the upper class is very gender segregated. Interestingly, this gender segregation is an accepted fact, virtually unchallenged by upper-class women. Why? Ostrander suggests that perhaps the gains of *gender* equality are not enough to balance the losses of *class* equality.

By any measure, this category of persons is the smallest numerically of all social classes but has the highest prestige and influence. Since they are at the very top of the class hierarchy, the members maintain their positions by preserving symbols of status such as genealogies, autobiographies of ancestors, heirlooms, and records of ancestral achievement. They also maintain their position by carefully controlling the marriage choices of their children.

It seems reasonable to assume that many changes are taking place among families of wealth which are parallel to changes in the society in general. For example, since mid-century the continuing push of egalitarian and democratic forces, the push for racial and class integration of private and

---

11. Susan A. Ostrander, *Women of the Upper Class* (Philadelphia: Temple University Press, 1984).

"Ivy-League" schools, the assumption by the middle classes of status symbols once associated only with the rich, and so on would lead one to assume the death of "high society." Yet, in an interesting study of upper-class marriages, Paul Blumberg and P. W. Paul found a major theme of continuity in these marriages over thirty years.[12] They stated:

> Although tremendous forces have shaken American society in the past generation, the upper class has maintained itself remarkably intact, and having done so, is perhaps the most untouched group in American life. . . . It is the upper-class territory of school, neighborhood, club, and bluebook which remains the most racially segregated turf in America.[13]

## MIDDLE-CLASS FAMILIES

Ask most Americans to what class they belong and you will likely be told "middle." Relatively few people could honestly respond "wealthy" and few people take pride in responding "poor" even if it's true. Furthermore, a response of *middle class* generally carries positive connotations, implying that while some people occupy a higher occupational status and prestige position, others obviously occupy a lower position. The middle-class families form the linkage between the powerful wealthy families and the working-class and powerless, financially poor families. Residing in a middle position, the possibility exists of moving upward as well as the threat of moving downward. One consequence of this appears to be that the middle classes are very conscious of social values, involved in the major issues brought on by social change, and relatively rigid in moral standards. Some middle-class families closely resemble the wealthy families in their economic status and degree of influence. Other middle-class families vary little from blue-collar workers in terms of their family patterns. This suggests that a precise analysis of the middle class as a distinct family type or life-style is highly ambiguous in its results and extremely difficult.

From a Marxian perspective, the middle class is composed of the **bourgeoisie:** those people who own small amounts of productive resources and have control over their working conditions in ways not found among the **proletariat:** those working-class people who work for wages. Today, middle class is more likely to refer to people employed as professionals or corporate and government bureaucrats. In Middletown[14] this group was categorized as the business class: those who made their living by selling or promoting ideas

---

12. Paul M. Blumberg and P. W. Paul, "Continuities and Discontinuities in Upper-Class Marriages," *Journal of Marriage and the Family* 37 (February 1975): 63–77.

13. Ibid., p. 75.

14. Caplow et al., *Middletown Families*, p. 86.

and by arranging the goods and services produced by the working class. They wore suits to their jobs in offices, banks, and businesses.

Middle-class families are likely to receive salaries rather than the hourly wage prevalent among blue-collar or working-class families. This more stable income resource base appears to be one key factor in differentiating this class grouping from those below it. The higher levels of income and greater "job security" allow for some discretionary spending and leisure activities. With this stable resource base is likely to come a range of amenities that lessen the shock of unanticipated crisis events: medical coverage, pension and retirement plans, bank credit, investment income, and the like. Rayna Rapp suggests that middle-class households probably are able to rely on commodity forms rather than kinship processes to ease both economic and geographic transitions.[15]

In the same article, Rayna Rapp goes on to suggest two hunches she has about middle-class kinship patterns. One is that kinship probably shifts from the lateral to the lineal. By this she means that material and economic resources are invested lineally among parents, children, and grandchildren rather than being dispersed into larger kin networks, as is more likely to be found in blue-collar and poor families. Some evidence of this is seen in the emphasis given to children's education, wedding gifts, music and art lessons, and so forth. Her second hunch is that friendship rather than kinship is the nexus within which the middle class invests its psychic and familial energies. Friendship allows for a great deal of affective support and exchange but usually does not include major resource pooling.

These hunches appear to be consistent with findings from a study in England of middle-class couples, suggesting that the experience of higher education and a professional career promoted value systems emphasizing personal autonomy and the ability to develop and carry out rational plans.[16] The women commenced their married lives with high expectations of being able to realize their family building plans by preventing unwanted conceptions, by conceiving when they chose to do so, and by controlling events rather than being subject to forces over which they have little influence. Wives who exercised initiative and responsibility at work were likewise effective in their other social roles. This ability to control and logically plan one's own life seems to be highly characteristic of this class and may partially explain the belief of many members that people of all classes should be able to do likewise.

The nuclear family of the middle class tends toward the ideal of equality of status between husband and wife. For example, in Middletown,[17] the overwhelming majority regarded family roles as joint activities. More specifi-

---

15. Rapp, "Family and Class in Contemporary America," p. 181.

16. Diana Woodward, Ann Heath, and Lynne Chisholm, "Patterns of Family Building and Contraceptive Use of Middle-Class Couples," *Journal of Biosocial Science* 10 (January 1978): 39–58.

17. Caplow et al., *Middletown Families*, pp. 67–70.

cally, business-class women were more than twice as likely as working-class women to say that housekeeping should be equally shared between spouses (31 percent versus 14 percent), while working-class women were more likely to say that housekeeping is mainly a wife's responsibility (85 percent versus 69 percent). The tendency toward the *ideal* of equality was evident in the extent of role enactment: the actual behavior of Middletown families showed more division of roles by sex than their opinions called for. In about 84 percent of Middletown families, the husband earned all or most of the family income. In 85 percent of the families with young children, the wife did all or most of the caring for them. Role flexibility was supported in principle at the same time that families faithfully practiced quite traditional roles.

Another widely studied area showing differences between the middle-class grouping and those below them is in parent-child relations and in childrearing practices. More than twenty-five years ago Melvin Kohn[18] suggested that, in terms of discipline, middle-class parents were more likely to use reason, verbal threats, or withdrawal of rewards to punish a child or solicit the child's compliance. In contrast, blue-collar parents were more likely to rely on physical punishment. Kohn's reasoning was that by virtue of experiencing different conditions of life, members of different social classes come to see the world differently and to develop different conceptions of social reality, different aspirations, and different conceptions of desirable personality characteristics. The middle class (white-collar occupations), in contrast with the lower class (blue-collar occupations), requires the individual to: (1) deal more with the manipulation of ideas, symbols, and interpersonal relations, (2) be involved in work that is more complex and requires great flexibility, thought, and judgment, and (3) be less closely supervised. From these occupational differences come different values that are reflected in patterns of discipline. Middle-class values are likely to deal with self-direction, freedom, individualism, initiative, creativity, and self-actualization. Thus parents encourage in their children *internal* standards such as consideration, curiosity, and self-control. Discipline is based on the parents' interpretation of a child's motives for a particular act.[19]

Kohn's ideas in regard to parent-child interaction by social class have received widespread attention and attempts at extension and replication. Most studies have found that since Kohn's original survey, clear trends have

---

18. Melvin Kohn, "Social Class and Parent-Child Relationships: An Interpretation," *American Journal of Sociology* 68 (January 1963): 471–480; and Melvin Kohn, *Class and Conformity* (Homewood, Ill.: Dorsey, 1969).

19. In contrast, lower-class or blue-collar workers deal more with the manipulation of physical objects, require less interpersonal skill, have more standardization of work, and are more closely supervised. This leads to values of conformity to *external* standards such as orderliness, neatness, and obedience. Discipline is based on the consequences of the child's behavior rather than on the interpretation of motive for the behavior. *See,* for example, Gary W. Peterson and David F. Peters, "The Socialization Values of Low-Income Appalachian White and Rural Black Mothers: A Comparative Study," *Journal of Comparative Studies* 16 (Spring 1985): 75–91.

existed in self-direction values among middle-class parents and that social class is a primary differentiation in childrearing values. One more recent study extended the value differences to varying parental behavior as well.[20] Even studies outside the United States tend to confirm the effect of social class on childhood socialization with the middle-class tendency to use psychological rather than physical approaches to discipline.[21] This class effect appears to be largely due to the higher level of educational attainment of middle-class parents.

## BLUE-COLLAR FAMILIES

Blue-collar or "working-class" families are made up of workers classified by the U.S. Bureau of the Census as employed in (1) precision production, craft, and repair, (2) machine operating, assembling, and inspecting, (3) transportation and material moving, and (4) handling, equipment cleaning, helping, and laboring. Service works are generally also classified as blue-collar occupations. Most women would fit into this categorization.

Randall Collins argues that most women are either white-collar working class or blue-collar working class because in terms of a power position women are order takers, not order givers.[22] Even women married to middle-class men, who are assumed to take their husband's class position, still provide the services of cooking, cleaning, and emotional support for men and children. Women in paid employment as secretaries, clerks, retail sales personnel, operators of machines, and most other jobs in which women are found are order takers. Even nurses, he claims, in spite of a professional classification, tend to be assistants (order takers) who perform manual work for physicians.

The job of a blue-collar worker generally requires some sort of manual skill.[23] The "elite" of the blue-collar workers—usually male electricians, plumbers, and highly skilled operators—frequently earn more than members of the middle classes. For example, public school teachers, generally assigned to a middle-class position, are likely to average $3,000 to $6,000 a year less than do certain blue-collar workers. However, formal education beyond a trade or high school is not generally required for the manual skills necessary for the members of this class. Physical health is quite crucial to blue-collar workers,

---

20. Tom Luster, Kelly Rhoades, and Bruce Haas, "The Relation between Parental Values and Parenting Behavior: A Test of the Kohn Hypothesis," *Journal of Marriage and the Family* 51(February 1989): 139–147.

21. Robert C. Williamson, "A Partial Replication of the Kohn-Gecas-Nye Thesis in a German Sample," *Journal of Marriage and the Family* 46 (November 1984): 971–979.

22. Randall Collins, "Women and Men in the Class Structure," *Journal of Family Issues* 9(March 1988): 27–50.

23. For a perceptive view of the meaning of work in the working class, *see* Lillian Breslow Rubin, *Worlds of Pain: Life in the Working-Class Family* (New York: Basic Books, 1976), Chapter 9, pp. 155–184.

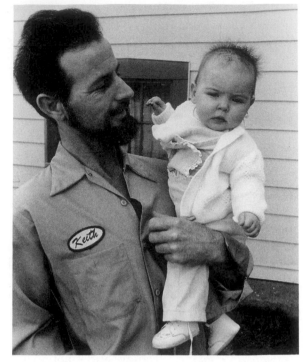

*Jobs of blue-collar workers generally require some sort of manual skill. Compared to other social classes, these families tend to conform more closely to traditional images of husband and wife roles with the husband as the provider and final authority.*

since many jobs are dependent upon an ability to perform physical labor. These groups are generally represented by trade unions. A great amount of faith is placed in the unions to protect persons from those above them in the work hierarchy, to provide help with family medical expenses, and to prevent a dismissal from work.

Since members of this class are almost completely dependent on the swings of the business cycle in our wage-price-profits system, the economic stability described among middle-class families is less prevalent. Most income is received from wages earned by the hour, the piece, the day, or the week. To supplement the income of the husband, a considerable proportion of wives are employed outside the home. Unlike a sizable proportion of female workers from the middle class, the blue-collar wife is more likely to take a job out of economic necessity than the desire for a career. She is also likely to be the target of frequent and severe sexual harassment. James Gruber and Lars Bjorn, in an article titled "Blue-Collar Blues," predicted that women with lower status—namely black, young, or "unattached" (single or divorced) women, as well as those who have low seniority or job status—will experience sexual harassment. Over a third of the blue-collar women autoworkers reported harassment in the form of sexual propositioning, abusive language,

## Japan is starting to confront sexual harassment

A few years ago, virtually no one in Japan had heard of sexual harassment. But today, Japanese lawyers and feminists have brought sexual harassment to the forefront with a flurry of surveys, studies, articles, legal actions, conferences, and organizing.

As reported in *The New York Times* (November 13, 1989), their activity is another sign of awakening feminist consciousness in a male-dominated society, particularly the office, where women are slowly growing restive over their low pay, status, and promotion prospects. Among the symbols of such discrimination is the standard requirement that women, no matter what their sta-

tus, serve tea to men. In 1987, the Tokyo Office of Labor Problem Consultation recorded one sex-related complaint from a woman charging she had been sexually assaulted while on a business trip with the company president. By 1989 the office received ten such cases a month.

The concept of sexual harassment is so new in Japan that beyond rape or assault, no consensus exists on what constitutes a grievance. Japanese magazines are filled with arguments, for instance, about whether it is proper for a man to put a nude pin-up at his desk, to inquire about someone's sex life, to pat a woman on the rear, or to make a suggestive comment.

physical attacks, and other behavior such as body language, whistling, and stares.[24]

The strains associated with the uncertainties of many facets of life for members of this class present a high degree of family instability. Divorce occurs with greater frequency among this grouping than among any of the higher income, education, or occupational groupings.

It is the blue-collar family, more than any other, whose members conform to the traditional image of husband and wife roles.[25] The husband's role is to be a good provider, and the wife's role, although she is often employed, is to do housework and care for the children. As the primary wage earner, the husband is the final authority and disciplinarian.

The wife and mother rears the children. If the family is broken by divorce or separation, the children will remain with her. It is expected that she will remain faithful to her husband as long as he remains faithful to her. If these obligations are broken, the offended party is likely to seek separation or divorce.

The role of children is definitely one of subordination to the parents. Unlike middle-class parents who stress that children stay in school and who make major sacrifices to keep them there, the working-class blue-collar

---

24. James E. Gruber and Lars Bjorn, "Blue-Collar Blues: The Sexual Harassment of Women Autoworkers," *Work and Occupations* 9 (August 1982): 271–298. Note also: James E. Gruber and Lars Bjorn, "Women's Responses to Sexual Harassment: An Analysis of Sociocultural, Organizational, and Personal Resource Models," *Social Science Quarterly* 67 (December 1986): 814–826.

25. Note in particular Rubin, *Worlds of Pain*, Chapters 5–7, pp. 69–133.

families are more likely to expect that children will leave school after fulfilling the minimum legal requirements or at most after completion of high school. Boys and girls are taught to be self-sufficient, to be tough-minded, and to be able to compete for personal rights and privileges. Working-class boys begin their heterosexual intercourse experiences earlier and have them more frequently than do boys from middle- and white-collar families. Working-class girls marry early, with a high proportion of pregnancies conceived premaritally. Many teen-aged girls interviewed by Rubin reported that when they grow up they will marry for love and that it will be better than their parents' marriage. While love may be desirable, what they get is babies. Forty to 60 percent of teen-aged pregnancies are conceived premaritally and approximately 50 percent of working-class women married in their teen years.[26]

Although it is now more than twenty-five years old, a vivid glimpse into the lives of these families can be found in Mirra Komarovsky's book *Blue Collar Marriage.*[27] Using a case-study approach, fifty-eight "stable" families with children were interviewed. The respondents were chosen from a community the author termed Glenton that had a total population of about 50,000.

Husbands and wives in Glenton knew what was expected of them and generally agreed about marital ideals. However, the role consensus or the clarity of role definition was not necessarily suited to the conditions of life under which Glenton's families had to live. A transition to new roles was often hindered by certain circumstances such as the poverty of some young couples, the poor occupational adjustment of the young unskilled workers, and the need to reside in the parental home after marriage. The following illustration of a thirty-two-year-old husband, taken from Komarovsky's book, illustrates how unfavorable these circumstances can be. This quote might well have come from a blue-collar worker who experienced the recession of the early 1980s.

> You keep thinking you can do almost anything and get away with anything when you're still young. There had been a couple of big layoffs when we got married, but work was still pretty good and I thought I could do anything and that I was going places and I was going to be somebody. Nothing was good enough for my wife, and we didn't think nothing of charge accounts and buying things. We hadn't been married long and I got my first layoff. They said I was young. They laid off others and they said they was old. We couldn't keep up our payments on the furniture, and we lost every stick of it, and she was pregnant. And I mean to tell you. We went and stayed at her ma's for a few days, and then up to my ma's for a while. There wasn't no room for us at her ma's and my ma had a spare room, and we must have stayed there about a month while I was looking for work and then I got it, and then we moved out again. And then this time, we got one thing by paying the

26. Ibid., Chapter 4.
27. Mirra Komarovsky, *Blue Collar Marriage* (New York: Random House, 1962).

whole money on it that we borrowed the money for. We borrowed it from people, and not the bank. And we bought a bed. We figured we could sit on that, and we had our cooking pots and could eat out of them. But we didn't want to think of sleeping on the floor anymore. It would have been all right if it was summer and she wasn't pregnant.[28]

The majority of men and women interviewed saw the principal marital ties as sexual union, complementary tasks, and mutual devotion. Within this class, if one of the functions of modern marriage is to be friends, to share one's hurts, worries, and dreams with another person, a large number of couples fail to find such fulfillment.

## FAMILIES AND THE FEMINIZATION OF POVERTY

According to data supplied by the U.S. Bureau of the Census, in 1988 more than 31.9 million persons in the United States were below the poverty level.[29] This included 6.9 million families (*see* Figure 7–1). This figure equals 10.4 percent of all families; more than one in every ten families in the United States is classified as having an income below the poverty level (*see* Figure 7–2). For white families the poverty rate was 7.9 percent compared to 23.7 percent for Hispanic-origin families and 28.2 percent for black families. Among families with a female householder with no husband present the percentages increase to 29.3 for white families, 52.1 for black families, and 55.1 for Hispanic-origin families. The single-parent family is discussed later in this chapter. The female-headed single-parent family is one important aspect of the feminization of poverty.

A look at sex differences in poverty over a thirty-year period provides additional evidence that the feminization of poverty is not a myth.[30] Between 1950 and 1980, women's poverty rates increased relative to men's across all age groups and among blacks as well as whites. Much of this increase was due to changes in parental obligations. Women were much more likely to live with children than men and to have greater parental responsibilities both in terms of finances and domestic labor. The situation does not seem to be improving. Many women today must rely on their own work or on welfare to support themselves and their children. Yet the jobs that are available are low-paying and the public benefits to single mothers have declined.

---

28. Ibid., p. 47. Reprinted by permission.

29. U.S. Bureau of the Census, *Current Population Reports*, Series P-60, no. 166, "Money Income and Poverty Status in the United States: 1988" (Washington, D.C.: U.S. Government Printing Office, 1989), Tables 17 and 18, pp. 57–59.

30. Sara S. McLanahan, Annemette Sorensen, and Dorothy Watson, "Sex Differences is Poverty, 1950–1980," *Signs: Journal of Women in Culture and Society* 15(Autumn 1989): 102–122. Note also: Maxine Baca Zinn, "Families, Race, and Poverty in the Eighties," *Signs: Journal of Women in Culture and Society* 14 (Summer 1989): 856–874.

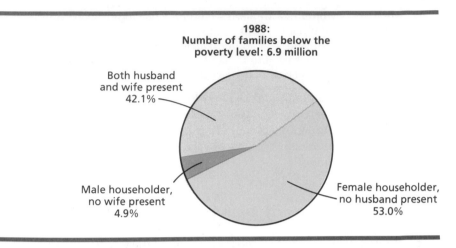

*Figure 7–1*
**Families below the poverty level by type of family, 1988.** (*Source:* U.S. Bureau of the Census, *Current Population Reports* Series P-60, no. 166, "Money Income and Poverty Status in the United States: 1988"
[Washington, D.C.: U.S. Government Printing Office, 1989], Table 20, p. 62.)

A variety of interwoven demographic and socioeconomic trends are evident in the feminization of poverty. First is the one just mentioned: the female-headed family where women are living independently with custody and primary responsibility for their dependent children. Second is the rise in teen and young parenting where economic self-sufficiency is difficult. Third is the income inequality where women earn much less than their male counterparts in the labor market. Fourth is the inadequate level of personal and child support from absent husbands, social assistance, and other programs.

For example, one study showed that child support varies greatly by race and marital status, with non-blacks twice as likely as blacks and ever-married six times as likely as never-married to receive child support.[31] Seldom is the amount received adjusted for inflation, further contributing to the increasing feminization of poverty. In combination, factors such as these place a disproportionate number of women below the level of poverty. This is true not only in the United States, but in Canada and most other industrialized countries as well.[32]

31. Andrea H. Beller and John W. Graham, "Child Support Awards: Differentials and Trends by Race and Marital Status," *Demography* 23 (May 1986): 231–245.
32. Deborah A. Abowitz, "Data Indicate the Feminization of Poverty in Canada, Too," *Sociology and Social Research* 70 (April 1986): 209–213; and Sheila B. Kamerman, "Women, Children and Poverty: Public Policies and Female-Headed Families in Industrialized Countries," *Signs: Journal of Women in Culture and Society* 10 (1984): 249–271.

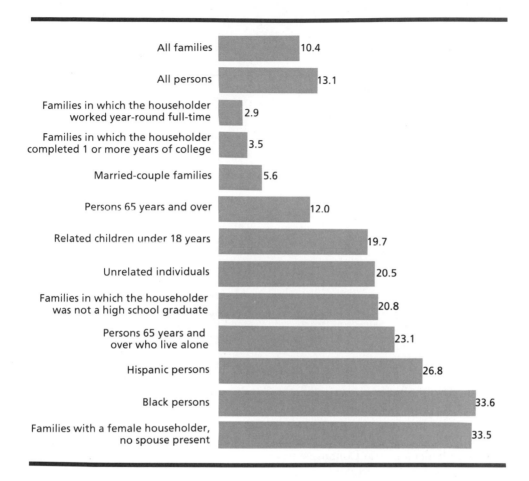

*Figure 7–2*
**Poverty rate for persons and families with selected characteristics: 1988 (in percent)**
(*Source:* U.S. Bureau of the Census, *Current Population Reports* Series P-60, no. 166,
"Money Income and Poverty Status in the United States: 1988" [Washington, D.C.:
U.S. Government Printing Office, 1989], Figures 1 and 2, pp. 6 and 8.)

A logical question is, How are figures on poverty derived? How is it
determined that a family be considered at the poverty level or not? Cannot a
three-person family live on much less than a seven-person family? Obviously,
the small family can live on less than the large one and family size is a key
factor in determining the poverty threshold. The poverty index, developed by
the Social Security Administration, is based solely on money income and does
not reflect noncash assistance or governmental benefits such as food stamps,
medicaid, or public housing. The poverty index is based on the Department of
Agriculture's 1961 Economy Food Plan and reflects the different consumption

*Table 7–1*
*Weighted average poverty thresholds in 1988*

| Size of family unit | Threshold |
|---|---|
| 1 person (unrelated individual) | $ 6,024 |
|     Under 65 years | 6,155 |
|     65 years and over | 5,674 |
| 2 persons | 7,704 |
|     Householder under 65 years | 7,598 |
|     Householder 65 years and over | 7,158 |
| 3 persons | 9,435 |
| 4 persons | 12,092 |
| 5 persons | 14,305 |
| 6 persons | 16,149 |
| 7 persons | 18,248 |
| 8 persons | 20,279 |
| 9 persons | 24,133 |

*Source:* U.S. Bureau of the Census, *Current Population Reports* Series P-60, no. 166, "Money Income and Poverty Status in the United States: 1988" (Washington, D.C.: U.S. Government Printing Office, 1989), Table A-2, p. 88.

requirements based on family size and composition. Operating on the assumption that families of three or more persons spend approximately one-third of their income on food, the poverty level is set at three times the cost of the Economy Food Plan. Poverty thresholds are updated every year to reflect changes in the Consumer Price Index. Thus, as can be seen in Table 7–1, the average poverty threshold for a family of four in 1988 was $12,092. For one person it was $6,024, and for a family of eight it was $20,279.

The poverty rate in 1988 dropped slightly from the level in 1983, the highest level since 1966. Among the factors contributing to the increase in poverty in the early 1980s was a recession, an associated rise in unemployment, and tightening of eligibility standards for certain government aid programs. Hit the hardest and receiving the largest increase in rates of poverty were metropolitan areas, in particular the central cities; persons under age forty-five, and more specifically young people; and blacks and persons of Hispanic origin. These data are consistent with an earlier study that indicated the factors most highly associated with poverty to be: female-headed families, large family size, minority group status, age (children, youths, the aged), unemployment and underemployment, and lack of income from sources other than wages.[33]

---

33. Catherine S. Chilman, "Families in Poverty in the Early 1970s: Rates, Associated Factors, Some Implications," *Journal of Marriage and the Family* 37 (February 1975): 49–60.

The greatest amount of public assistance goes to households below the poverty level. This is true of nearly three-fourths of all households receiving food stamps, half of those receiving free or reduced-price school lunches, 55 percent of those in publicly owned or other subsidized housing, and 59 percent of those with one or more members covered by medicare.[34] Clearly, cuts in governmental food, housing, and health benefits hit those living at a poverty level the hardest.

Even if cuts in governmental programs hit those living in poverty the hardest, is there reason for concern? In other words, is it not true that welfare and other governmental "handouts" simply increase dependency and breed additional poverty? This perspective goes beyond "blaming to victim," the poor, to "blaming the program." This argument suggests that welfare benefits and governmental programs simply make living in poverty a meaningful option for the poor, thus increasing poverty, maintaining dependency, and decreasing the need for self-support or employment. Using data over a twenty-four-year period, Sanford Schram and Paul Wilken examined the relationship between welfare spending and poverty; they present evidence that casts doubt on the validity of the welfare-breeding-poverty hypothesis. Their analysis indicates that welfare spending and benefits cannot be singled out as primary factors in creating more welfare dependency and therefore more poverty.[35]

What about women on welfare having more children to receive more benefits? The idea that women receiving governmental assistance have a high fertility rate is often implicitly accepted by social and policy analysts. Such beliefs are simply not supported. In fact, Mark Rank found that women on welfare have a rate of fertility considerably below that of women in the general population. Furthermore, the longer a woman remains on welfare, the less likely she is to give birth.[36] Why do both of these findings exist? The women themselves suggested that the financial and social situation they find themselves in is not conducive to having more children. The economic, social, and psychological costs of becoming pregnant and having a child are perceived as clearly outweighing the benefits. Given these findings, one could ponder the economic, social, and psychological implications of formulating policy, as many states have done, that eliminates public finding for pregnant women, particularly those in poverty, to obtain an abortion.

34. U.S. Bureau of the Census, *Current Population Reports*, Series P-60, no. 155, "Receipt of Selected Noncash Benefits: 1985" (U.S. Government Printing Office, Washington, D.C., 1987), Table A, p. 2.

35. Sanford F. Schram and Paul H. Wilken, "Its No 'Laffer' Matter: Claim that Increasing Welfare Aid Breeds Poverty and Dependence Fails Statistical Test," *American Journal of Economics and Sociology* 48(April 1989): 203–218. *See also:* Sanford F. Schram, J. Patrick Turbett, and Paul H. Wilken, "Child Poverty and Welfare Benefits: A Reassessment with State Data of the Claim that American Welfare Breeds Dependence," *American Journal of Economics and Sociology* 47 (October 1988): 409–422.

36. Mark P. Rank, "Fertility among Women on Welfare: Incidence and Determinants," *American Sociological Review* 54(April 1989): 296–304.

## The survival of families in poverty

Given the nature of welfare legislation, the state of the job market, and segregated slum housing, households and family life are unstable. In human terms, not only do the poor pay more, but they also share more as well. One national study of black Americans found both family and friends to be important sources of assistance.[37] Stack's monograph dealing with strategies of survival in a black community provides vivid descriptions of the way "what goes round comes round."[38] That is, clothing, furniture, food, appliances, money, and kids make the rounds among individuals and households. People give what they can and take what they need. These exchange patterns result in a **fictive kinship** by which friends are turned into family. The swapping of goods and services results not merely in the norms of reciprocity that seem prevalent in most social exchanges, but also in stable friendships that pattern those of kin. As Stack says:

> Non-kin who live up to one another's expectations express elaborate
> vows of friendship and conduct their social relations within the idiom of
> kinship. Exchange behavior between those friends "going for kin" is
> identical to exchange behavior between close kin.[39]

Poverty in black, white, Hispanic, or other families is directly linked to unemployment or underemployment and since employment is irregular, income is irregular. Because income is irregular, a considerable amount of insecurity exists in regard to food, clothing, shelter, transportation, and other essential items. Children may be forced or encouraged to contribute to the financial needs of the family, and few remain in school beyond the minimum legal age. These conditions contribute to and are highly related to other concerns. For example, families in poverty have the highest rates of divorce, psychoses, and physical disabilities; the least amount of dental and health care; the largest proportion of people on public welfare; the greatest rejection rate from the armed services; the highest crime rate; the largest number of children; the highest rate of venereal disease; the most unemployment; and, as perceived by many middle-class persons, "the most of the worst."

The majority of persons and families below the level of poverty typically live within this level for intermittent periods of time. Researchers at the Survey Research Center at the University of Michigan found that over a fifteen year period, children had frequent transitions into and out of poverty.[40] While

---

37. Robert Joseph Taylor, Linda M. Chatters, and Vickie M. Mays, "Parents, Children, Siblings, In-laws, and Non-kin as Sources of Emergency Assistance to Black Americans," *Family Relations* 37 (July 1988): 298–304; and Linda M. Chatters, Robert Joseph Taylor, and Harold W. Neighbors, "Size of Informal Helper Network Mobilized during a Serious Personal Problem among Black Americans," *Journal of Marriage and the Family* 51 (August 1989): 667–676.

38. Carol B. Stack, *All Our Kin: Strategies for Survival in a Black Community* (New York: Harper & Row, 1974), Chapter 3, pp. 32–44.

39. Ibid., p. 40.

40. Greg J. Duncan and Willard L. Rodgers, "Longitudinal Aspects of Childhood Poverty," *Journal of Marriage and the Family* 50(November 1988): 1007–1021.

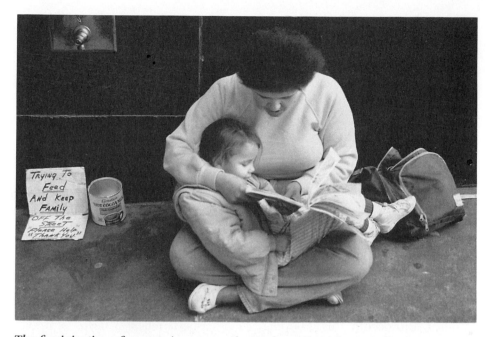

*The feminization of poverty is not a myth. Single mothers in particular must rely on their own work or welfare to support themselves and their children.*

about one-third of the children in the United States actually fell below the official poverty line, nearly half of the children found themselves in a vulnerable economic position at least once during their childhood. The researchers claimed that the average black child could expect to spend more than five years in poverty before reaching the age of fifteen (the comparable average for white children was about nine months). A surprising result of the research was that the single most important event associated with the transition into and out of poverty for both black and white children was substantial changes in the labor supply of secondary earners in the family other than the head.

## An entrenched underclass

While poverty for many families is not a persistent condition—that is, they move in and out of it—this is not the case for millions of children and adults. Within the poverty population is a U.S. **underclass** characterized by persistent poverty and a variety of associated problems, such as welfare dependency, joblessness, crime, and substance addiction. The underclass is geographically concentrated in ghettos of cities, and its members have high participation in the underground economies that flourish in the neighborhood.

While the underclass cuts across racial lines, it is particularly evident and prevalent among blacks or African-Americans. As indicated in Chapter 6, the scarcity of employed black men increases the prevalence of families headed by females in black communities. In turn, Robert Sampson found that black family disruption substantially increased the rates of black murder and robbery, especially by juveniles.[41] While there is nothing inherent in the black culture that is conducive to crime, persistently high rates of black crime appear to stem from the structural linkages among unemployment, economic deprivation, and family disruption. The black underclass has a high incidence of all the above.

Robert Kelly argues that underclass crime and welfare dependency, while overdetermined by objective economic circumstances, is also influenced by stress mediated at the social, psychological, and social network levels. The primary locus of this mediation exists in family, kinship, and informal social networks.[42] A key point is that extended and fictive kin networks are critical intervening variables in the analysis of economic and stress-related behaviors among the underclass.

It is difficult for most students and teachers to describe the life-styles of families in poverty without imposing middle-class evaluations upon them. To even use terms such as "poor," "poverty," "lower class," or "underclass" may be imposing negative connotations and interpretations on persons and families who occupy this grouping. To describe families in terms of unemployment, welfare, illegitimacy, venereal disease, crime, and disabilities is to repeatedly apply negative labels and convey an impression of fault and blame.

Rayna Rapp notes that it is particularly ironic that the ideology of family, so important to poor people, is used by ruling-class ideologies to blame the poor for their own condition. She notes that the very poor have used their families to cement and patch tenuous relations to survival; out of their belief in "family" they have invented networks capable of making next-to-nothing go a long way.[43] A middle- or ruling-class response is that their notion of family is inadequate, deviant, or even pathological. Perhaps the family is less inadequate or pathological than the relationship between the family or household and the productive resources available to them. Few people rationally and consciously choose or desire the styles of life that accompany poverty. The single-parent situation is no exception.

## THE SINGLE PARENT AND POVERTY

The fact that the section on the single parent follows the section on poverty should not lead readers to assume all one-parent families are poor. They are not. But Norton and Glick, in presenting a social and economic profile of

---

41. Robert J. Sampson, "Urban Black Violence: The Effect of Male Joblessness and Family Disruption," *American Journal of Sociology* 93(September 1987): 348–382.

42. Robert F. Kelly, "The Family and the Urban Underclass," *Journal of Family Issues* 6(June 1985): 159–184.

43. Rayna Rapp, "Family and Class in Contemporary America," pp. 179–180.

one-parent families, state that by most objective measures, the vast majority of these families hold a disadvantageous position in society relative to other family groups.[44] They are characterized by a high rate of poverty, a high percentage of minority representation, relatively low education, and a high rate of mobility. Survey studies have consistently revealed that psychologically, single parents are more depressed, are more anxious, have lower self-images, and are less satisfied with their lives. In short, single parents generally have little equity or stature in U.S. society and constitute a group with pressing social and economic needs.

These pressing social and economic needs become most acute among black and Spanish-origin female-headed families, over half of whom fall below the poverty level. Census data indicate that in 1988 the median income of female-householder families with the husband absent was $15,346. This is about 57 percent of the $26,827 median income of male-householder families with the wife absent and about 42 percent of the $36,389 median income of married male-householder families with the wife present (married couple family).[45] That same year, using the poverty index developed by the Social Security Administration described in a previous section of this chapter, one-third (33.5 percent) of all families with a female householder and no husband present were below the poverty level. As indicated previously, this included 29.3 percent of white, 52.1 percent of black, and 55.1 percent of Spanish-origin female-householder families without a husband present. The social concern about female-householder families increases when it is noted that, in addition to the proportion at a poverty level, a large proportion of these families are on welfare, and women with unstable sources of income feel less able to plan for their lives (fate control).[46]

Who are these single parents? How many children in the United States reside in this type of family structure? Drawing from 1988 census data, more than 17 million children under the age of eighteen, or about one in four, were not living with both parents. As can be seen in Table 7–2, this included 21 percent of the white, 61 percent of the black, and 34 percent of Spanish-origin children. Most of these were living with mother only (16 percent white, 51 percent black, and 27 percent Spanish-origin), but about 3 percent were living with the father only, and the remaining 3 percent were not living with either parent.

The number of children in a single-parent context is quite dramatic when children's actual living arrangements are examined over a period of time

44. Arthur J. Norton and Paul C. Glick, "One Parent Families: A Social and Economic Profile," *Family Relations* 35 (January 1986): 9–17.

45. U.S. Bureau of the Census, *Current Population Reports*, Series P-60, no. 166, "Money Income and Poverty Status in the United States: 1988" (Washington, D.C.: U.S. Government Printing Office, 1989), Table 6, p. 32.

46. Sally Bould, "Female-headed Families: Personal Fate Control and the Provider Role," *Journal of Marriage and the Family* 39 (May 1977): 339–349.

*Table 7–2*

*Living arrangements of children under 18 years: 1988 (excludes persons under 18 years old who were maintaining households or family groups)*

| Living arrangements of children and marital status of percent | 1988 | | | |
|---|---|---|---|---|
| | All races | White | Black | Spanish origin* |
| All children under age 18 | 63,179 | 51,030 | 9,699 | 6,786 |
|   Living with both parents | 45,942 | 40,287 | 3,739 | 4,497 |
|   Living with one parent | 15,329 | 9,624 | 5,247 | 2,047 |
|   Living with neither parent | 1,908 | 1,119 | 714 | 242 |
|   (Numbers in thousands) | | | | |
| Living with two parents | 72.7% | 78.9% | 38.6% | 66.3% |
|   Mother only | 21.4 | 16.0 | 51.1 | 27.2 |
|   Father only | 2.9 | 2.9 | 2.9 | 3.0 |
|   Other; relatives only | 2.3 | 1.6 | 6.4 | 2.7 |
|   None; relatives only | 0.7 | 0.6 | 1.0 | 0.8 |
|   Percent | 100.0% | 100.0% | 100.0% | 100.0% |
| Marital status of single parents | | | | |
|   Never married | 30.5% | 18.0% | 54.2% | 32.8% |
|   Married, spouse absent | 24.9 | 24.9 | 23.9 | 31.3 |
|   Widowed | 6.3 | 6.8 | 4.8 | 5.9 |
|   Divorced | 38.3 | 50.3 | 17.1 | 30.0 |
|   Percent | 100.0% | 100.0% | 100.0% | 100.0% |

*Persons of Spanish origin may be any race.

*Source:* U.S. Bureau of Census, *Current Population Reports*, Series P-20, No. 433, "Marital Status and Living Arrangements March: 1988," (Washington, D.C.: U.S. Government Printing Office, 1989), Table A-4 and A-5, pp. 61 and 62.

rather than considered for a given year or at a single point in time. Sandra Hofferth, drawing data from the Panel Study of Income Dynamics (interviews with a national probability sample of about 5,000 families that have been followed longitudinally since 1968), projects that 70 percent of white children born in 1980 will spend at least some time with only one parent before they reach age eighteen.[47] For black children born in 1980 the projection is 94 percent. These figures stand in sharp contrast to the 19 percent of white children and 48 percent of black children born between 1950 and 1954 who have lived with one parent.

Why the dramatic increase? How is it possible that 70 percent of white and 94 percent of black children will probably experience a single-parent living arrangement before they reach age eighteen? An overly simplified but partial

---

47. Sandra L. Hofferth, "Updating Children's Life Course," *Journal of Marriage and the Family* 47 (February 1985): 93–115.

answer to this question can be obtained by examining the marital status (never married, married but spouse absent, widowed, or divorced) of single parents by race and ethnicity (black, white, Spanish-origin) as presented in the lower third of Table 7 – 2. Of all white single parents, more than one-half are divorced (50.3 percent) and another one-fourth are married but with a spouse absent (24.9 percent). Thus, most of these children under age eighteen came from a two-parent household but as a result of divorce or an absent parent now find themselves in a one-parent context. Black children, in contrast, are highly likely to have been born into a single-parent situation because the mother never married (54.2 percent). Less than one-fifth of black children entered a one-parent situation because of divorce. Thus, while white one-parent families typically result from divorce and black one-parent families typically result from a never-married parent, Spanish-origin one-parent families balance between divorce (30.0 percent), a married but absent parent (31.3 percent), and a never-married parent (32.8 percent). Relatively few one-parent situations of any of the three groups result from widowhood, as might be expected since most widowhood occurs at older ages when the children are no longer teenagers or younger. But given the increase in births to unmarried women, the frequency of divorce, and the number of married couples with a spouse absent, it can be projected that the vast majority of children born in the 1980s will experience a one-parent living arrangement.

Over the past several decades, the major increase in single-parent families has occurred among children living with mother only. Similar increases have not taken place in the percentage of persons living with the father only; however it is of interest that these father-child families have only recently come to the attention of researchers at all. The mother was always the focus of attention, since she gave birth to the child, was primarily responsible for the nurturant socialization responsibilities, was more likely to be a widow than was the husband likely to be widower, and was generally given legal custody of the children by the courts in cases of divorce and separation. Thus, as could be expected, most literature on this topic deals with the mother-child unit. Even this literature, rather than dealing with the mother who is present, deals with the father who is absent: the fatherless family.

Let's turn our attention briefly to these two single-parent situations: the mother-child family (the father-absent family) and the father-child family (the mother-absent family).[48]

## Mothers as single parents (the father-absent family)

In 1988 more than thirteen and one-half million children under the age of eighteen were in homes with a mother-only–father-absent situation, and the

---

48. Readers interested in this topic should consult the special issue of *Family Relations* on "The Single Parent Family" 35 (January 1986) as well as the annotated bibliography compiled by Benjamin Schlesinger in that issue, pp. 199–204.

number increases yearly. Concurrent with this factor is the widely held view that every child needs a father or his social equivalent.

The trend toward an increasing percentage of children in homes without a father present represents an issue of national concern. Heather Ross and Isabel Sawhill[49] state that these concerns focus on: (1) the precarious financial status of female-headed families, almost half of whom are poor, spend some time on welfare, and run a high risk of living under conditions of poverty; (2) the possible effect on children of not having an adult male influence in the home; and (3) the lack of clarity about how public policy has contributed to these changes and the role it could play with respect to this type of family structure.

Sara McLanahan and Karen Booth address issues such as these in an essay focusing on problems, prospects, and politics in mother-only families.[50] When compared with two-parent families, mother-only families are much more likely to be poor, to have higher levels of stress, and to have lower levels of social integration. Economic insecurity, they suggest, is high in mother-only families because of the low earning capacity of single mothers, the lack of child support from nonresidential parents, and meager public benefits. They also found evidence of negative intergenerational consequences. Children in mother-only families were more likely to be poor in adulthood than children who lived with both parents. They were also more likely to become single parents themselves.

Previous research led McLanahan to conclude that single-female heads of households with children experienced more stress than their married two-parent counterparts in chronic life strains (being poor, black, and less educated), the occurrence of major life events (changes in income, household composition, and residence), and the lack of social and psychological supports (known neighbors, living within walking distance of relatives, or participation in clubs and organizations). It was suggested that the higher incidence of major life events experienced by female heads of households is primarily a function of the marital disruption process rather than a characteristic of the state of single parenthood.

Apart from the fact that the children of these households are themselves more likely to be poor and to be single parents, what are the consequences for children who are raised in mother-only households? What happens to children in female-headed families? Barbara Cashion reviewed the social psychological research pertaining to female-headed families published between 1970 and 1980, and concludes that children in these families are likely to have good emotional adjustment, good self-esteem except when they are

49. Heather L. Ross and Isabel V. Sawhill, *Time of Transition: The Growth of Families Headed by Women* (Washington, D.C.: Urban Institute, 1975), pp. 3–4.

50. Sara McLanahan and Karen Booth, "Mother-Only Families: Problems, Prospects, and Politics," *Journal of Marriage and the Family* 51 (August 1989): 557–580.

stigmatized, intellectual development comparable to others in the same socioeconomic status, and rates of juvenile delinquency comparable to others in the same socioeconomic status.[51] Major problems in these families stem from *poverty* and *stigma*. Poverty as a general social problem is associated with problems in school, juvenile delinquency, the mother's poor attitudes about her own situation and, as noted earlier, in her sense of not being in control. The negative stigma is associated with a lowered self-esteem in children and in the labeling or defining of father-absent children as problematic even in situations where problems are minimal or nonexistent. Cashion's general conclusion is that the majority of female-headed families, when not plagued by poverty, have children as successful as those from two-parent families.

While most research reported was carried out in the United States, similar findings come from cross-cultural studies on female-headed families and households. Bilgé and Kaufman contend that such families are found to be neither pathological nor inferior. To condemn female-headed or one-parent families as abnormal or "pathological," they claim, is "a coverup for the economic inequalities of our society."[52] Around the world, one-parent, female-headed families function to bring up children and provide emotional support. When combined with an extended network of concerned kin, it can often tender more emotional support and offer more options to family members than an isolated nuclear family. This suggests that no single family form produces an optimal milieu for a growing child and that mother-child forms, like others, can provide the support systems and methods of socialization that are positive to a child's emotional, intellectual, and social development.

## Fathers as single parents (the mother-absent family)

The father-child family, like the mother-child family, is a result of widowhood, divorce, separation, nonmarriage, and, more recently, single-parent adoption. While only about 3 percent of all children under age eighteen are living with their fathers only, Thompson and Gongla[53] suggest that the number of single-parent families maintained by fathers may very well begin to increase as a by-product of the following:

1. men's changing life-styles,
2. normative shifts favoring single fatherhood,
3. noncustodial fathers' desire to continue their parenting role,

---

51. Barbara G. Cashion, "Female-Headed Families: Effects on Children and Clinical Implications," *Journal of Marital and Family Therapy* (April 1982): 77–85.

52. Barbara Bilgé and Gladis Kaufman, "Children of Divorce and One-Parent Families: Cross-cultural Perspectives," *Family Relations* 32 (January 1983): 59–71.

53. Edward H. Thompson, Jr. and Patricia A. Gongla, "Single-Parent Families: In the Mainstream of American Society," in Eleanor D. Macklin and Roger H. Rubin, *Contemporary Families and Alternative Lifestyles* (Beverly Hills: Sage Publications, 1983): 97–124.

4. single fathers' greater access to economic resources and better economic well-being than single mothers,

5. research findings that suggest single fathers and single mothers can effectively function as custodial parents, and

6. research that suggests that the positive and negative experiences of being a single parent are similar for both fathers and mothers.

Research on fathers as single parents has been relatively infrequent and generally limited to small nonprobability samples. Yet they may prove to be more insightful than mother-child studies in light of the extreme importance placed upon mothers as key agent of socialization. Can men "mother"?

This is a question posed by Barbara Risman who surveyed fathers about their experiences as homemakers, the nature of the father-child relationship, and overall role satisfaction.[54] Her major finding was that most men felt comfortable and competent as single parents, regardless of the reason for custody or their financial status. This was true even though four out of five single fathers had no outside housekeeping help, either paid or volunteer. These men felt very close to and very affectionate toward their children, were glad to be fathers, and had little trouble fulfilling either the instrumental or expressive functions of single parenthood. Clearly successful mothering is not an exclusively female skill. Men *can* "mother."

Similar support for men as single parents comes from a study that examined whether significant differences existed between children reared in single-mother and single-father families. Examined were factors such as self-perceptions, self-esteem, social competencies, and the frequency and severity of reported behavioral problems. Support did *not* exist for the historical assumption that single mothers are more effective parents than single fathers.[55]

In a number of ways, fathers who maintain a family alone are better situated than their female counterparts. Fathers as single parents are known to have higher levels of education, are more likely to be in the labor force, and as shown earlier, are much better situated economically. One study suggested that the greatest strain single-parent fathers experienced in their transition to single parenthood was in becoming single rather than in becoming single parents. Many fathers experienced loneliness and missed a wife's companionship. The presence of children helped them adjust to being single.[56]

---

54. Barbara J. Risman, "Can Men 'Mother'? Life as a Single Father," *Family Relations* 35(January 1986): 95–102. Note also: Barbara J. Risman and Kyung Park, "Just the Two of Us: Parent-Child Relationships in Single-Parent Homes," *Journal of Marriage and the Family* 50(November 1988): 1049–1062.

55. A. Reuben Schnayer and R. Robert Orr, "A Comparison of Children Living in Single-Mother and Single-Father Families," *Journal of Divorce* 12(1989): 171–184.

56. Richard M. Smith and Craig W. Smith, "Child Rearing and Single-Parent Fathers," *Family Relations* 30 (July 1981): 411–417.

Can any conclusions be drawn from the data available? It does seem clear that, just as a two-parent family does not guarantee happiness, adjustment, and well-behaved children, neither does a one-parent family signify the opposite. Nor are the findings meant to imply that the absence of a father or mother has no effect whatsoever. There are definite limitations on time and energy for the fulfillment of various tasks. Children in single-parent families are assumed to have more responsibility than children in two-parent families. Gender-role patterns tend to remain traditional, with children doing sex-stereotyped chores and engaging in sex-stereotyped activities. But Marie Richmond-Abbott contends that since single parents exhibit behavior typically stereotyped as both masculine and feminine, this context may serve as a model and be the vanguard of more nontraditional and flexible sex-role values and behavior by the children.[57]

Many other effects of single parenthood can be cited. In regard to the power structure, with one parent it is impossible for the child to play one adult against the other. This situation may also create certain problems in adjusting to the parent of the opposite sex. In terms of affectional support, the danger of the one-parent family is that the demands of one to fulfill the needs ordinarily met in marriage by two may prove intolerable to the solitary parent, with the result being physical and emotional exhaustion.

What about the parent-absent family, those 7.4 percent of black children, 3.5 percent of Spanish-origin children, and 2.2 percent of white children who in 1988 were living with neither parent (Table 7–2)? Apparently most of these children, while not living with a parent, are living with relatives, especially grandparents. As they get older they become more likely to live in families with brothers or sisters, or with other relatives. White children are more likely than black children to be placed in public agencies and institutions.[58] The conditions that result in children living separately from their parents, the effect of parent absence on the children, and the existing support services for these children are questions in need of research.

## *FAMILY MOBILITY: CHANGING CLASS LIFE-STYLES*

One fundamental characteristic of families and class is the extent to which there is opportunity to move from one class to another. Although mobility is often thought to mean improvement, it can be upward, downward, or lateral. The first two types are referred to as *vertical social mobility* (upward or downward) and the latter is referred to as *horizontal social mobility*.

---

57. Marie Richmond-Abbott, "Sex-Role Attitudes of Mothers and Children in Divorced, Single-Parent Families," *Journal of Divorce* 8 (Fall 1984): 61–81.

58. Raymond Montemayor and Goeffrey K. Leigh, "Parent-Absent Children: A Demographic Analysis of Children and Adolescents Living Apart from Their Parents," *Family Relations* 31 (October 1982): 567–573.

## The likelihood of social mobility

The likelihood of vertical social mobility may be regarded as a function of three separate phenomena. First is the *opportunity structure* to which the individual has access. This is the organizational structure of a society that defines the ultimate achievement possibilities for the individual as well as the channels available to realize the achievements. Different opportunity structures apply to different individuals, groups, or subcultures within the same society. However, the structure of the society, including the presence or absence of jobs, the availability of educational and training programs, and other social characteristics, will in large part determine the extent to which mobility occurs.

The second component of the likelihood of vertical social mobility may be said to be the *individual* him- or herself. In this regard, personality characteristics determine the individual's capacity for exploiting the opportunity structure and will influence the likelihood of mobility. These characteristics may include factors such as intelligence, motivation, motor skills, and value systems.

The third component may be termed the *frictional factor.* That is, two identically equipped individuals confronting the same opportunity structure may nevertheless attain disparate levels of mobility. These factors, inherent neither in the individual nor in the opportunity structure, may be referred to as chance, luck, or fortune.[59]

Bradley Schiller postulates that the family's economic circumstance is the key accessibility condition for the various opportunity strata available to sons.[60] Thus each economic class confronts a separate and distinctive set of achievement opportunities. In comparing the pattern of socioeconomic achievement of children from welfare families with that of the general population, sharp differences are found. Schiller suggests that the lack of achievements of poor children is largely due to the inequality of opportunity that exists along class lines. That is, a substantial portion of the underachievement of sons who grew up in families receiving Aid to Families with Dependent Children (AFDC) cannot be explained by differential abilities or by the sons' motivations or aspirations. The argument that the poor remain poor because they lack the motivation to rise above their origin receives little empirical support.

## The extent of social mobility

The American dream suggests that in this land of opportunity anyone can go from "rags to riches." The widespread belief is that with hard work and

---

59. Bradley R. Schiller, "Stratified Opportunities: The Essence of the "Vicious Circle,'" *American Journal of Sociology* 76 (November 1970): 427.

60. Ibid., pp. 426–439.

endurance, any motivation to get ahead will enable anyone who so desires to move upward on the social-class ladder. Data do seem to suggest that social mobility in our society probably is increasing. However, social mobility and equality of opportunity probably never have been as widespread as U.S. citizens believe.

It has been estimated that one of every four or five persons moves upward at least one social-class level during his or her lifetime. It is among blue-collar workers that the greatest amount of upward mobility occurs. What is less frequently recognized and studied is downward mobility. Kathleen Newman, in her book on the experience of downward mobility in the American middle class, claims it is widespread, serious, and a problem for families at all levels of the class structure.[61] Downward mobility is more than a loss of job and a drop in income. It includes a drop in occupational prestige and one's place in society as well. Getting married, having children, divorce, widowhood, and the employed status of wives all affect families. As will be shown in Chapter 17, divorce in particular is a traumatic event leading to the downward mobility of women. Most victims of downward mobility, male or female, express feelings of anger, dismay, and a sense of injustice.

Empirical studies of social mobility suggest several general conclusions. One is that more children will find themselves at the same level as their parents than at any other level. Secondly, a substantial proportion of sons and daughters have experienced some mobility. Third, upward mobility is more prevalent than downward mobility. Fourth, when mobility does occur, it is likely to mean a shift to class levels adjacent to those of the individual's parents, that is, short-distance mobility is more frequent than long-distance mobility.

## Consequences of social mobility

Few of us are immune to the possibility of downward social mobility and it is unlikely that many of us would reject the opportunity for upward social mobility. With this opportunity we envision a better job, higher income, a more luxurious home, a more prestigious neighborhood, opportunities to travel, better clothes, a new car, freedom from debt, and generally a more luxurious as well as refined life-style. And many, if not most, who are reading this believe that education is one means to obtain these rewards. Within our society, with its fairly open class system and its increasing requirements for specialized and highly trained technicians and experts, brain power frequently means higher status. But a closer investigation of the open class system shows that not all consequences of mobility, even upward social mobility, are positive. In various

---

61. Katherine S. Newman, *Falling from Grace: The Experience of Downward Mobility in the American Middle Class* (New York: The Free Press, 1988).

ways, the costs of upward social mobility may be great and its penalties quite severe.

Many students will discover, or may have already discovered, some disruptive effects of their increased education (a potential contribution to upward social mobility). The most obvious is likely to be an increasingly estranged relationship with parents. Particularly if parents are working-class people of limited formal education, many students will find that they are modifying their beliefs and value systems in ways that may conflict with those of their parents. The paradox of this situation is that these are frequently parents who make major sacrifices to provide a college education for their children, with the painful consequence of having their children become socially distant from them.

There are instances in which marriage itself may be threatened by upward social mobility. The wife who works to assist her husband in completing his education may find that his value system and life-style changes while hers remains more static. Success in business may encourage certain husbands to seek the friendship of more "sophisticated" females. Career-oriented wives may discover the existence of many men whose values and behavior patterns are more to their liking than those of their husbands. Two existing spouses may differ in their ability to readjust to the new requirements of a higher social status. These and many other examples of upward social mobility illustrate how this supposedly desirable phenomenon may disrupt husband-wife relationships.

Obviously, not all social mobility has negative consequences. In a relatively open class system, a high rate of social mobility may tend to stabilize the social order by providing outlets to persons with particular skills or talents who are dissatisfied with their present social status. The possibility for upward social mobility may prevent the rebellious and revolutionary tactics that result from persons who are frustrated in their social position and have little opportunity for advancement. Families may receive new recognition and social prestige by their social climbing. Thus the question is not so much whether social mobility is good or bad, but rather what types of consequences to individuals and families result within societies that have closed or open class systems?

## Summary

1. The term *social classes* refers to aggregates of individuals who occupy differential positions on scales of wealth, prestige, and power. This differential ranking results in inequalities between persons and families.
2. Two theories particularly relevant to an understanding of social class are those of functionalism and conflict. The former sees a stratified system as inevitable and necessary for the fulfillment of tasks needed to maintain a society. The latter sees a stratified system as leading to dissatisfaction and conflict between the laborers

who are the instrument of production and the owners and managers who control the means of production.

3. The determination of social-class position varies widely from examining who owns, manages, and controls production to noting differential rankings of occupational prestige, income, or education. This chapter makes no effort to establish a set number of strata or classes but notes some of the consequences of differential ranking of persons and families, and then provides a description of four general social categories of families: the wealthy, the middle class, blue-collar families, and families in poverty.

4. Wealthy families are identified as the very rich, the upper class, and the ruling class. This elite group owns and controls the means of production. Families are concerned with who they are and serve to protect their names and wealth.

5. Middle-class families serve as the linkage between the small group of wealthy families and the group of working-class, blue-collar families. They are the bourgeoisie who own small amounts of productive resources. They are the professionals and corporate white-collar bureaucrats. Family resources are directed lineally to the children and grandchildren. Married couples tend toward the ideal of equality between the spouses but in reality perform highly segregated roles. In child rearing they were found to use reason, verbal threats, or withdrawal of rewards to punish their children.

6. Blue-collar or working-class families comprise nearly half of all U.S. workers. They do not have the economic stability found in middle-class families since they are more highly dependent on the swings of the business cycle in our wage-price-profits system. Marriages are more unstable than among the higher social groupings, husband-wife roles are highly traditional, and children are subordinate to the parents. Early marriage and parenthood are frequent.

7. Families in poverty include about one in ten U.S. families altogether, but include about one-fourth of Spanish-origin families and close to one-third of black families. Evident in the feminization of poverty is the growth in female-headed families and the rise in teen and young parenting, income inequality, and inadequate personal and child support. The greatest amount of public assistance goes to these households but many rely on the swapping of goods and services. This results in a *fictive kinship* where friends become like family. Most serious poverty is characterized by an underclass of persistent poverty and a variety of associated families.

8. A disproportionate number of single-parent families are families in poverty. This is particularly true of female-headed households where no husband or father is present. Increasing rates of unmarried motherhood and high rates of divorce and spouse-absent families make it probable that the majority of children born in the 1980s will experience a one-parent living arrangement before they are eighteen. Clear differences exist between mothers as single parents and fathers as single parents, with the fathers faring much better. Studies suggest children from this type of family structure compared well with those from a two-parent structure when socioeconomic status is controlled.

9. What are the chances for and consequences of family social mobility? Social mobility does seem to be increasing, but was probably never as widespread as has been widely believed. While seen as desirable by most persons, upward mobility can result in new recognition and social prestige or may bring rejection and social isolation. Clearly, extended-family cohesion is likely to decrease and lower levels of family participation are likely to result.

10. Chapters 5–7 have examined structural and subcultural variations in family life-styles. Chapters 8 and 9 will examine premarital structures and processes and deal primarily with mate selection. In a general sense, the next eight chapters follow the marital and family life cycle, from the point of selecting a mate and premarital factors through marriage, parenthood, middle years, and, finally, the later years. As you will note, a variety of frames of reference or theoretical approaches (structural-functional, exchange, conflict, psychoanalytic, behaviorist, symbolic-interactional) are used in the examination of these organizational and processual patterns at various stages of the life cycle.

# KEY TERMS AND TOPICS

# DISCUSSION QUESTIONS

1. What is meant by social class? How many classes exist? How is that determined?
2. Compare and contrast a functionalist perspective of class with that of the conflict perspective.
3. Discuss "all men (women, families) are created equal."
4. How valid are the ideas of Marx on class conflict between the bourgeoisie and the proletariat? Where does the middle class fit into his scheme?
5. Make a stratification study of the families in your home community. Where do they live, work, and worship? Where do or will their children attend college (if at all)? What kind of cars do they drive? What hobbies do they pursue? What are their family sizes, attitudes toward child rearing, and the like? Outline their style of living.
6. Describe the family and work life of the very rich. Summarize the life-styles of the husband, wife, sons, and daughters.
7. Discuss: "When a college student from a mid-

dle-class family takes a job in a factory, he or she becomes a member of the working class." Or: "When the same student becomes unemployed, he or she enters into the poverty level."
8. What is meant by "fictive kin" and the "feminization of poverty"? Explain reasons for their existence.
9. What kind of programs or policy may be effective in getting families above a level of poverty? Should food stamps, subsidized housing, welfare programs, etc. be cut or eliminated? Why or why not?
10. How do you explain the increases in one-parent families? Why is this increase of concern to policy makers or to the general public? What differences exist in one- or two-parent situations? Does it make a difference if the single parent is a father or a mother? Why?
11. What types of factors foster upward mobility? Downward mobility?
12. Why are many consequences of upward social mobility disruptive to kin and community ties?

# FURTHER READINGS

Garfinkel, Irwin, and McLanahan, Sara S. *Single Mothers and Their Children: A New American Dilemma*. Washington, D.C.: Urban Institute Press, 1986. A look at families headed by single women with children, their economic and social problems, and the public policies that affect their lives.

Gongla, Patricia A., and Thompson, Edward H. Jr. "Single-Parent Families" in *Handbook of Marriage and the Family* by Marvin B. Sussman and Suzanne K. Steinmetz (eds.), New York: Plenum Press, 1987, Chapter 15, pp. 397–418. A comparison of single- and two-parent families and a review of single mothers, single fathers, and family relations.

Greif, Goeffrey L. *Single Fathers*. Lexington, Mass.: Lexington Books, 1985. Questionnaire returns from over 1,100 single fathers who had custody of their children were used to describe how they handle various aspects of parenting, including housework, child care, going to work, the legal system, and interpersonal relationships.

Komarovsky, Mirra. *Blue Collar Marriage*. New York: Random House, 1962. A case study of fifty-eight working-class families that provides a wealth of material on most aspects of blue-collar married life.

Langman, Lauren. "Social Stratification" in *Handbook of Marriage and the Family* by Marvin B. Sussman and Suzanne K. Steinmetz (eds.), New York: Plenum Press, 1987, Chapter 9, pp. 211–249. A discussion of various theories of stratification and an examination of families at six class levels.

Lynch, Katherine A. *Family, Class and Ideology in Early Industrial France: Social Policy and the Working-Class Family, 1825–1848*. Madison, Wisconsin: University of Wisconsin Press, 1988. A look at middle- and working-class family life and values in nineteenth-century France and its influence on social action.

Newman, Katherine S. *Falling From Grace: The Experience of Downward Mobility in the American Middle Class*. New York: The Free Press, 1988. An analysis of the downward mobility experience of 150 "focused life histories" with specific chapters on the family and on women.

Ostrander, Susan A. *Women of the Upper Class*. Philadelphia: Temple University Press, 1984. Interviews with thirty-six upper-class women and a look at their lives as wives, mothers, club members, and volunteers.

Rapp, Rayna. "Family and Class in Contemporary America: Notes Toward an Understanding of Ideology." *Science and Society* 42 (Fall 1978): 278–300; also in Barrie Thorne with Marilyn Yalom, *Rethinking the Family: Some Feminist Questions*. New York: Longman, 1982: 168–187. An examination from a conflict perspective of class differences between those who own and control the means of production versus those who provide the labor and work for wages.

Rubin, Lillian Breslow. *World of Pain: Life in the Working-Class Family*. New York: Basic Books, 1976. A subjective analysis of fifty working-class families and a comparison group of twenty-five professional middle-class families.

Vanneman, Reeve, and Cannon, Lynn Weber. *The American Perception of Class*. Philadelphia: Temple University Press, 1987. An examination of class consciousness in America with specific chapters on blaming the victim, women, and blacks.

Williams, Terry M., and Kornblum, William. *Growing up Poor*. Lexington, Mass.: D. C. Heath and Co., 1985. An investigation of U.S. teenagers who are growing up under extremely difficult economic and social conditions.

Wilson, William Julius. *The Truly Disadvantaged: The Inner City, the Underclass, and Public Policy*. Chicago: The University of Chicago Press, 1987. An examination of black urban poverty in the U.S., its consequences for continued racial inequality, and Wilson's response to the appropriate public policy responses to the problem.

Yorburg, Betty. *Families and Societies: Survival or Extinction*. New York: Columbia University Press, 1983. A brief portrait of changes in family life. Chapter 6 examines class differences in U.S. families.

# CHAPTER EIGHT

# HOMOGAMY AND ENDOGAMY IN THE SELECTION OF MATES

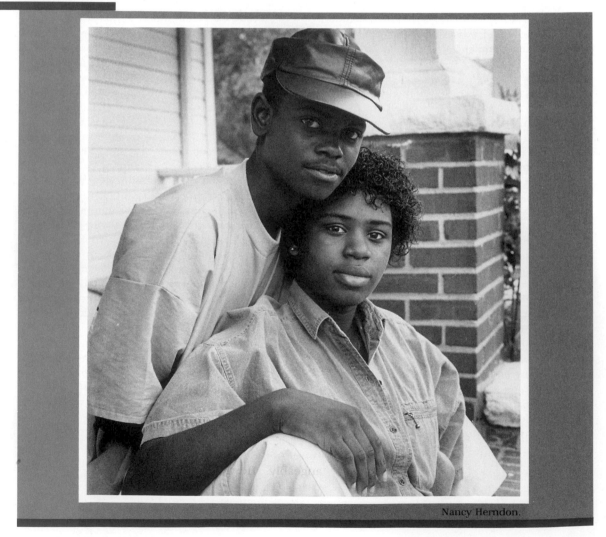

Nancy Herndon.

With this chapter we shift our discussion from family institutions and variations in family life-styles to premarital structures and processes in the creation of the marital status. This chapter examines five normative structures surrounding mate selection in the United States: age, residence, class, religion, and race. The terms generally employed to describe mate selection among those who share similar characteristics are **homogamy** and **endogamy**: homogamy denotes something about the likeness or similarity of married couples; endogamy refers to in-group marriages of almost any kind. That people marry those like themselves more often than could be due to chance is known as *assortive mating*. The "assorted" mates are matched on specific structural dimensions.

Homogamy and endogamy are critical factors in the continuity of the U.S. family system (as well as of other social institutions). Homogamy functions to maintain the status quo and conserve traditional values and beliefs. These functions can be dysfunctional in that they reduce or eliminate contact with other people and cultures and restrict the free choice of a mate. But as long as marriage is perceived to be an important and significant institution in the United States or in any society, it is not very difficult to understand why the same characteristics that are viewed as important in a society (age, race, religion, class) are also important in the selection of a mate.

It is common for students to operate on the idea that they are free to marry anyone they please. In reality, there is probably no society in which people actually choose their marriage partners on a completely individual basis. Only when persons consciously consider the socialization processes that lead them to prefer certain types of persons for marriage, consider the social pressures to marry certain types of persons, and investigate the extent of homogamy and endogamy within a given society, do they become aware of the limited freedom of choice that does exist.

Studies throughout the world report high rates of racial, religious, class, educational, and age homogamy. No society in the world leaves the selection of a marriage partner unregulated and indiscriminate. Whether the choice is by the persons getting married, by parents, relatives, delegated persons or groups, or by specific social agencies, it is always subject to regulation by social and cultural controls.

One should not be led into believing that endogamy and homogamy are the preferred or required norms in all respects. The most universal of all norms regarding marriage—the incest taboo—is an exogamous norm. Exogamy rules that members of a society marry outside their kin group. Thus, all marriages are exogamous in that they are forbidden between members of the same nuclear-family unit. Generally, the same could be said for sex. **Exogamy** and **heterogamy** are often used interchangeably. However, technically speaking, exogamy *requires* differences whereas heterogamy *denotes* differences. If both heterogamy and exogamy are used to indicate marriage between persons of a different group, then no "purely" endogamous marriage exists.

Our discussion of homogamy, exogamy, or both in the selection of mates will be confined to specific characteristics or groups that are culturally conceived as relevant to the choice of a spouse. A marriage could conceivably be considered endogamous in regard to race, exogamous in regard to kin, heterogamous in regard to religion, and homogamous in regard to values and personality traits.

## FACTORS INFLUENCING RATES OF INTERMARRIAGE

Prior to discussing specific dimensions of mate selection such as age or race, several general questions need to be addressed. For example: Who is included or excluded in determining whether a marriage is, in actuality, mixed? How are rates influenced by the reporting of them, particularly in using figures of marriages as opposed to individuals? What social and cultural factors are likely to foster or affect the likelihood of intermarriage? These three questions appear to be applicable to any intermarriage whether based on age, class, race, religion, height, weight, or eye color.

### Who is included in a mixed marriage?

How much age difference must exist before a marriage becomes age-exogamous? Is a marriage between a Methodist and a Lutheran (both Protestant) an interfaith marriage? At what point does any difference or characteristic determine homogamy or heterogamy, endogamy or exogamy? Obviously, in any study or in any reporting of rates some definition must be used to determine whom to include or whom to exclude. In research, *operational definitions* are used; in other words, variables are defined according to the way they are measured. As a result, an age difference of more than four years may be arbitrarily defined as age exogamous. Or an interracial marriage may be defined as any marriage in which the couple defines themselves accordingly irrespective of color or lineage. This problem of what is or is not an intermarriage is a serious one in determining rates or in comparing studies. Greater attention is devoted to this issue in dealing with specific social dimensions.

### Can intermarriage rates be influenced?

Specifically, can intermarriage rates be influenced by the reporting of marriages as opposed to individuals? Most published rates of mixed marriage (or intermarriage) are based on the total number of a group's *marriages*. But sometimes they are interpreted as if they were based on the number of *individuals* who marry. A **marriage rate** refers to the percentage of marriages that are mixed of all marriages involving individuals in a specific category. A

**marriage rate for individuals** refers to the percentage of married individuals in a specific category who enter a mixed marriage.

Suppose we have ten marriages, four that are black-white, or interracial, and six that are white-white, or intraracial. Is the mixed (interracial) marriage rate 40 percent or 25 percent? Four of the ten marriages (40 percent) are interracial, but four of the sixteen white persons (25 percent) married interracially.

Unless none of the marriages or all of the marriages are mixed, the mixed-marriage rate for marriages is always greater than the mixed-marriage rate for individuals. Thus, if your objective is to prove that mixed marriages are occurring in greater frequency, you could use the mixed-marriage rate for marriages. If you wish to prove that the incidence of mixed marriage is not as great, you could use the mixed-marriage rate for individuals. Statistically, both figures would be accurate. Thus, one way to lie with statistics "honestly" is to use the rate that best fits your purpose or interest.

In addition to distinguishing rates between marriages and individuals, it is also possible to distinguish a group's **actual rate** of intermarriage from its **expected rate.** The ratio between the two is important in determining if intermarriage is greater than could be expected to occur by chance or if marriage partners had been chosen randomly. The *expected intermarriage rate* is the percentage of people who would have selected a mate outside their own group if they had chosen their marriage partners randomly, knowing the frequency distribution of the particular groups in the population. The *actual rate* refers to those marriages that do take place. Glenn, for example, illustrates that based on the relative size of religious categories, 68 percent of Protestants, 26 percent of Catholics, and only 2.3 percent of Jews could be expected to be endogamous with random mating. In actuality, as will be shown later, an overwhelming majority of Protestant, Catholic, and Jewish members marry endogamously.[1] Clearly, assortive mating processes are operative for religious as well as most social groupings: people marry endogamously in frequencies far greater than could be expected simply by chance or at random.

## What factors foster intermarriage?

Actual rates of intermarriage are influenced by various factors, many of which center around the normative eligibility rules for mate selection, such as role compatibility, value consensus, and similarity in age, class, religion, or race. However, apart from the normative rules there are nonnormative factors that favor endogamous marriages. Consider, for example, factors such as group size, community heterogeneity, sex ratio, controls over marriage, the develop-

---

1. Norval D. Glenn, "A Note on Estimating the Strength of Influences for Religious Endogamy," *Journal of Marriage and the Family* 46 (August 1984): 725–727.

ment of cultural similarities, the romantic love complex, and the influence of certain psychological factors.

*Size of a group*    The size of a group relative to the larger population is likely to influence the extent to which the actual intermarriage rate is larger or smaller than would be expected by chance. Generally the larger the group, the lower its intermarriage rate. Or the smaller the group relative to the total population, the faster its rate goes up with each intermarriage. For example, in Utah, the heart of the Mormon population in the United States, marriages are highly endogamous. But in Florida, where Mormons constitute less than 1 percent of the population, it was ascertained that about two-thirds of the Mormons living there had married a non-Mormon.[2] That such a difference exists in the proportion of Utah and Florida Mormons who marry interfaith stems far less from the difference in degree of religious intensity of members in Florida than from the probability that Florida Mormons will meet and interact with persons from a non-Mormon background.

Similarly, a study of intermarriages in Hawaii over more than a thirty-year period supported the effect of group size on intermarriage. The larger the group, the smaller the rate of intermarriage in Hawaii, whether the groups were age cohorts, ethnic groups, residential communities, occupational groups, or people with the same marital status.[3]

*Heterogeneity*    Blau and others propose that in addition to size, the degree of heterogeneity in the community will influence the rate of intermarriage.[4] That is, intermarriage is more likely to occur when people reside in communities with many persons who are different from them. On the other hand, evidence supports the idea that inequality is antagonistic to homogamy.[5] Thus, a paradox exists. People in heterogeneous communities are more likely to meet, interact with, and marry persons different from themselves. Yet inequality in education and socioeconomic status exerts constraints on intermarriage and increases the desire for status homogamy.

*Sex ratio and group controls*    The sex ratio (number of males per 100 females) is likely to influence the rate of intermarriage (*see* Figure 8–1). In a community or setting where one sex outnumbers the other, traditional barriers are crossed with increased frequency as the sex with greater numbers selects from the

2. Brent A. Barlow, "Notes on Mormon Interfaith Marriages," *The Family Coordinator* 26 (April 1977): 148.
3. Teresa Labov and Jerry A. Jacobs, "Intermarriages in Hawaii, 1950–1983," *Journal of Marriage and the Family* 48 (February 1986): 79–88.
4. Peter M. Blau, Terry C. Blum, and Joseph E. Schwartz, "Heterogeneity and Intermarriage," *American Sociological Review* (February 1982): 45–62.
5. Steven Rytina, Peter M. Blau, Terry Blum, and Joseph Schwartz, "Inequality and Intermarriage: A Paradox of Motive and Constraint," *Social Forces* 66(March 1988): 645–675.

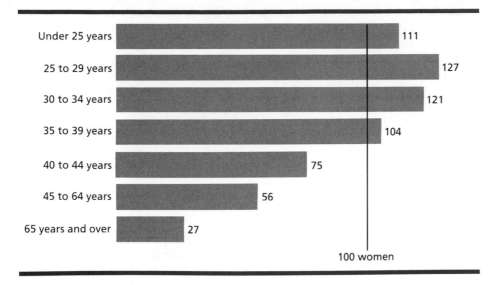

*Figure 8–1*
**Ratio of unmarried men per 100 unmarried women: 1988** (*Source:* U.S. Bureau of the Census, *Current Population Reports*, Series P-23, No. 162, "Studies in Marriage and the Family,"[Washington, D.C.: U.S. Government Printing Office, 1989], Figure 2, p. 5.)

smaller pool of available partners. Intermarriage rates are likely to be influenced as well by the extent of social or *group controls* over the individuals involved. The Amish and Jews, both religious minorities in the United States, maintain group sanctions through teachings and religious practices that discourage marriage with "outsiders."

*Cultural similarities*    Another factor that influences intermarriage rates is the development of cultural similarities and the elimination of differences. As ethnic minorities attend public schools, work in diverse social environments, and identify with the new or larger society, the differences in language, dress, or traditional practices decrease and the likelihood of intermarriage increases.

*Romantic love complex*    An increase also occurs as a result of what might be called the *romantic love complex*, the idea that love is more important than group controls, cultural differences, or homogamous characteristics. Related to this complex is a personal choice ideal that suggests each person has the right to choose whom to marry with minimal interference from others.

*Psychological factors*    Finally, intermarriage rates are likely to be influenced by certain psychological factors: rebellion against one's own group, feelings of alienation, emotional immaturity, or other psychological characteristics. As is the case with all factors mentioned, no given individual influenced by any of these factors will necessarily intermarry. But probabilities of intermarriage increase under conditions or circumstances such as those described.

The discussion that follows examines the role of selected social-structural dimensions as they affect interpersonal relations in the selection of a marriage partner. These include age, residence, social class, religion, and race. Obviously, this list is not, nor is it intended to be, inclusive of all social structures relating to the selection of a mate. However, it should give a clear indication of the extent to which endogamous marriages are predominant in the United States.

## AGE AT MARRIAGE

### Age homogamy

Most couples in the United States are relatively homogamous in terms of the age at which they marry. Although a person is "free" to marry someone considerably older or younger (within legal limits), most single persons select a member of the opposite sex from a closely related age group. In 1988, the median age at first marriage was 25.9 for males and 23.6 for females, an age difference of 2.3 years (*see* Table 8–1).

An examination of Table 8–1 shows that the median age at first marriage as well as the age difference between males and females has changed con-

*Table 8–1*
**Median age at first marriage, by sex, for the United States: 1890–1988**

| Year | Male | Female | Difference | Year | Male | Female | Difference |
|------|------|--------|------------|------|------|--------|------------|
| 1988 | 25.9 | 23.6 | 2.3 | 1977 | 24.0 | 21.6 | 2.4 |
| 1987 | 25.8 | 23.6 | 2.2 | 1976 | 23.8 | 21.3 | 2.5 |
| 1986 | 25.7 | 23.1 | 2.6 | 1975 | 23.5 | 21.1 | 2.4 |
| 1985 | 25.5 | 23.3 | 2.2 | 1970 | 23.2 | 20.8 | 2.4 |
| 1984 | 25.4 | 23.0 | 2.4 | 1960 | 22.8 | 20.3 | 2.5 |
| 1983 | 25.4 | 22.8 | 2.6 | 1950 | 22.8 | 20.3 | 2.5 |
| 1982 | 25.2 | 22.5 | 2.7 | 1940 | 24.3 | 21.5 | 2.8 |
| 1981 | 24.8 | 22.3 | 2.5 | 1930 | 24.3 | 21.3 | 3.0 |
| 1980 | 24.7 | 22.0 | 2.7 | 1920 | 24.6 | 21.2 | 3.4 |
| 1979 | 24.4 | 22.1 | 2.3 | 1910 | 25.1 | 21.6 | 3.5 |
| 1978 | 24.2 | 21.8 | 2.4 | 1900 | 25.9 | 21.9 | 4.0 |
| | | | | 1890 | 26.1 | 22.0 | 4.1 |

*Source:* Adapted from U.S. Bureau of the Census, *Current Population Reports*, Series P-20, no. 433, "Marital Status and Living Arrangements: March 1988" and Series P-23, no. 159, "Population Profile of the United States: 1989" (Washington, D.C.: U.S. Government Printing Office, 1989), Table A-2, p. 60, and Table A-1, pp. 46–47.

siderably since the turn of the century. From 1890 until the mid-1950s, the trend in the United States was toward an earlier age at marriage and a narrowing of the age difference between bride and groom at first marriage. Data for 1890 show the median ages at first marriage to be 26.1 years for males and 22 for females, an age difference of 4.1 years. In 1956, the median age at first marriage reached an all-time low (22.5 for men and 20.1 for women). Since that time there has been a gradual, though not continuous, increase in, the median age at first marriage for both men and women. In the last twelve years there has been more than a two-year increase in the median age at first marriage for both males and females.

How would you explain this incredible two-year increase in just a twelve-year period? Are people delaying marriage because they are spending more time in school? Is it due to increased job opportunities or the lack of them? Does an absence of a satisfactory level of income lead people to delay marriage? Are delays in marriage, as suggested by one writer, influenced by highly segregated gender roles and work structures that facilitate or impede assortive mating?[6] Can it be attributed to an increase in cohabitation that delays or replaces marriage? Or might the "marriage squeeze," relating to a shortage of marital partners, be a contributing factor? The marriage squeeze is described in the next section.

Age homogamy is in itself a function of the age at marriage. Without exception, the median age at marriage for grooms is always higher than that for brides. It is estimated that in six out of seven marriages in the United States, the male is as old or older than his bride. And an empirical study of marital-age heterogamy showed that in 1980, 27 percent of these males were five or more years older. In contrast, only 3.1 percent of the males were five or more years younger.[7] In both types of age heterogamy (husband older as well as husband younger), when compared with homogamous-age marriages (operationally defined as plus or minus four years), a tendency existed for the heterogamous marriages to be characterized by lower-educational level, multiple marriages, lower-family income, and lower-occupational status of the husband.

Why the overwhelming likelihood that males will be older than females? Several explanations include the husband's slower physiological maturity than that of his wife, the traditional responsibility of the husband to be the major breadwinner (which requires more preparation time), the slight excess of males through the early twenties, the mating gradient (described later in this chapter), or the continued subjugation of women. This last gender argument

6. Valarie Kincade Oppenheimer, "A Theory of Marital Timing," *American Journal of Sociology* 3(November 1988): 563–591. For a look at the determinants of marital timing for males and females separately by race, *see:* Jay D. Teachman, Karen A. Polonko, and Jeoffrey K. Leigh, "Marital Timing: Race and Sex Comparisons," *Social Forces* 66(September 1987): 239–268.

7. Maxine P. Atkinson and Becky L. Glass, "Marital Age Heterogamy and Homogamy, 1900–1980," *Journal of Marriage and the Family* 47 (August 1985): 685–691.

*On the average, men tend to marry about two and one-half years later than women. But these differences increase as age increases. As men get older, they increasingly marry younger women, further adding to the proportion of widows and older unmarried women in U.S. society.*

is consistent with the proposition that suggests female-male marital age differences decrease or narrow as societies become more egalitarian.

Age differences in marriage are the smallest at the younger ages and increase as age goes up. Although it is the usual pattern for men to choose women younger than themselves, the difference in their ages increases as the age at first marriage for the male increases. This indicates that as men get older they increasingly marry younger women. A different pattern exists for women. As women get older they marry men who are more nearly their own age.

The reason for these seemingly contradictory data is that in the first case the median age of the bride is based on the actual age of the groom. In the latter case the median age of the groom is based on the actual age of the bride. That is, men of actual age (such as fifty-five, sixty-three, or sixty-eight) tend to marry brides who, taken together, constitute a computed median age that is considerably younger. For women, their actual age (such as fifty-five, sixty-three, or sixty-eight) is very close to the computed median age of the men they marry. There are considerable differences in average ages at marriage between previously married persons such as widows and divorcees, but the generalizations of differences in age at marriage seem to hold true regardless of age, sex, or previous marital status.

Would you believe that age differences in marriage affect how long women live? One analysis of this issue showed that women married to younger men tended to live longer than expected, while women married to older men

## Child marriages in India

At midnight, the priest lit a sacred fire and called for the bride and groom. The bride was nursing at her mother's breast. The groom, burdened with a huge turban, a sword, and marigold garlands, was yawning. The bride you see, was two years old and the groom was eight years old. This child couple was among an estimated 40,000–50,000 children married across India's state on this single weekend in violation of a law banning child marriage.

As reported by the Associated Press (*Detroit Free Press*, May 9, 1989) these marriages in rural Vorawas, India, take place on the first and second days of the full moon cycle in May. The village elders, in keeping with a centuries-old tradition, study the stars and predict rain, the source of life in a state where 80 percent of the land is desert. These weddings are normally kept secret from outsiders, lest the parents be persecuted for marrying their children so young. If convicted, an offender can be jailed for three months, fined about $330, or both. But convictions are extremely rare. These Hindu traditions are deeply rooted and parents believe they are doing the right thing.

At the marriage ceremony itself, the child groom is required to take an oath in front of a fire that personifies the fire god, Agni Devta. Then the bride and the groom walk seven times around the flames. If either of them budges from the vow of being man and wife, he or she will face the anger of the fire god. The elders hold their rite as well. The eldest man makes a watery paste of opium, which is offered to all. The adults are required to drink it from his hand and then to bless the newly wedded couple.

tended to die sooner than expected.[8] These results were explained in two ways. One explanation suggested a mate selection factor. That is, healthier or more active women select, or are selected by, younger men and would live longer whomever they married. The second explanation based women's longevity on the biology, psychology, or sociology of marital interaction. Combinations of genetic factors, interpersonal interactions, and social norms lead partners to develop similar activities, interests, appearances, emotional states, and so forth. The causal factor of age difference in marriage and longevity may be related to the "literal" chemistry that people create in close relationships.

A final question dealing with age homogamy is whether age differences make a difference in the quality of marriage. Are May-December marriages, as referred to in the popular literature, more problem-ridden and less stable? Evidence tends to suggest they are not. An analysis of two public-use data sets yielded no significant differences in marital quality among couples from various age-dissimilar categories.[9] This finding, a dramatic contradiction to

8. Laurel Klinger-Vartabedian and Lauren Wispe, "Age Differences in Marriage and Female Longevity," *Journal of Marriage and the Family* 51(February 1989): 195–202.

9. Herman Vera, Donna H. Berardo, and Felix M. Berardo, "Age Heterogamy in Marriage," *Journal of Marriage and the Family* 49 (August 1985): 553–566.

conventional wisdom, might suggest that age is becoming a less compelling determinant of adult attitudes and behavior in U.S. society.

### The marriage squeeze

The "marriage squeeze" is used to describe the effects of an imbalance between the number of males and females in the prime marriage ages. Consider the hypothetical population where males age twenty-six typically marry females age twenty-three. If the annual number of births is decreasing each year, the twenty-six-year-old males will be looking for brides among the smaller cohort (an age-specific group) of females born three years later. The males would be caught in a marriage squeeze because they are encountering a shortage of females. Conversely, if a population experiences a substantial increase in the annual number of births, the same process would operate but it would be the females who would be caught in the marriage squeeze. That is, the male population born three years earlier would be smaller in number than the larger number of females born three years later.

The marriage squeeze phenomenon is a significant factor in marriage behavior. In the 1950s it was men who faced a shortage of women. The situation reversed in the 1980s to women facing a shortage of men and will reverse again in the 1990s and the turn of the century to a shortage of women. How are these imbalances and shifts explained? Basically, the 1950s marriage squeeze was the result of a decline in the absolute number of births each year during the late 1920s and early 1930s, combined with the fact that men tended to marry women two or three years younger than themselves. Because there were more men born in 1930 than women born in 1932 or 1933, the pool of women two or three years younger from whom to choose was smaller. Thus a male marriage squeeze. A reverse female marriage squeeze resulted in the 1970s and early 1980s due to the increased number of births during the post-World War II "baby boom" of the 1950s. And finally, given the sharp decline in the birth rate in the 1960s and 1970s, we can predict a return to the male marriage squeeze in the 1990s. Assuming a two- or three-year difference in marriage age, the smaller female population born several years later than the larger male population born earlier will have a larger pool from which to select.

Spanier and Glick[10] demonstrate how the marriage squeeze affected black females far more than white females in the mid-1970s. While the ratio of white males to females remained fairly close to 100 in the marriage age group, the ratio for black males to females was lower. In the 20–24-year age group there were 11 percent more black females than black males. This increased to 16 percent in the 25–29-year age group and to more than 19 percent among

---

10.  Graham B. Spanier and Paul C. Glick, "Mate Selection Differentials Between Whites and Blacks in the United States," *Social Forces* 58 (March 1980): 707–725.

## With increasing age, a "real" marriage squeeze of too few men: potential consequences.

Jean Veevers writes in *Sociological Perspectives* (April 1988, pp. 169–189) that the "real" marriage squeeze occurs among persons in midlife. And although changes in fertility and mortality are contributing factors, the real squeeze is due largely to the norm that husbands should be older than their wives. The result is a markedly unbalanced sex ratio with increasing age. What does it mean for women to have less and less access to potential grooms as they get older?

Veevers suggests that among the many scenarios that might result from too few men and too many women are:

1. Single subcultures—More persons who delay marriage, never marry, or never remarry
2. Antinuptialism—Ideologies that support remaining single

3. Innovations in mate selection—Trends toward unorthodox strategies of mate selection including classified advertisements and marriage bureaus
4. Heterogamy—Broadening the field of eligibles to persons of different religious, racial, or marital characteristics
5. Illegitimacy—More out-of-wedlock births
6. Divorce—Higher marital dissatisfaction for wives and lower marital commitment among husbands resulting in an increase in separation and divorce
7. Female independence—less need to depend on marriage for social and economic status
8. Female-headed households—A result of several of the above: illegitimacy, never marrying, or remarrying
9. Man-sharing—A greater tolerance and occurrence of multiple partners.

---

those 30–34. This marriage squeeze resulted in a restricted field of eligibles for black women, causing an unusually large proportion of black women to remain unmarried or to marry men who tend to be older, who have lower educational attainment, and who have previously been married.

Heer and Grossbard-Shechtman[11] argued that the marriage squeeze against females in the 1970s was instrumental in reducing both the proportion of females who could marry and the compensation which men were obliged to give women for traditional wifely and maternal duties. Combined with a contraceptive revolution, it became increasingly possible for women to have sexual relationships without procreative or marital intent. These factors in turn served to increase divorce and illegitimacy and fostered the women's liberation movement. Schoen and Baj, however, caution us against giving the marriage squeeze a mystique that credits it with an importance beyond its due.[12] Testing its impact in five western countries, they conclude that its

---

11. David M. Heer and Amyra Grossbard-Shechtman, "The Impact of the Female Marriage Squeeze and the Contraceptive Revolution on Sex Roles and the Women's Liberation Movement in the United States, 1960 to 1975," *Journal of Marriage and the Family* 43 (February 1981): 49–65; *see also* Robert Schoen, "Measuring the Tightness of a Marriage Squeeze," *Demography* 20 (February 1983): 61–78.

12. Robert Schoen and John Baj, "The Impact of the Marriage Squeeze in Five Western Countries," *Sociology and Social Research* 70 (October 1985): 8–19.

influence on recent marriage behavior seems less than that of other forces: the changing structure of industrial labor markets, increased female labor-force participation, low fertility, and changing sex roles. In contemporary third world countries, however, they suggest that its importance is probably much greater than has been appreciated to date.

## The law and the age at marriage

The legal control of age, marriage, and divorce in the United States lies with the states rather than with the federal government. Most state laws have two provisions regarding age at marriage: one is the age at which young people may marry *without* the consent of their parents; the other is the age at which young people may marry *with* parental consent. To be married *without* parental consent, all states require that the groom be eighteen (in Georgia the age is sixteen and in Utah counties are authorized to provide for premarital counseling as a requisite to the issuance of a license to persons under nineteen). To be married *with* parental consent, the minimum age is typically sixteen for both sexes. The minimum age is fourteen in states such as Alabama, New Hampshire, New York, Texas, and Utah. As of 1988, some states such as California had no age limit for marriage if parental consent was given, and many states gave exceptions to parental consent with permission of the court, for a pregnancy or birth, or with a physician's approval if parents were ill. No state has a legal age at marriage for females that is older than that for males; however, at least eight states permit females to marry younger than males with parental consent.[13] Over the past decade, a majority of states lowered the legal minimum age for marriage. Interestingly, this came at a time when the median age at marriage was increasing sharply, lessening the need for concern over young marriages.

## The concern over young marriages

Data presented about the median age at marriage show that half of all males and females marry for the first time below the ages of twenty-six and twenty-four respectively. Some of these marriages occur among adolescents or teenagers, an age category that most people view as too young for marriage. The consequences of these teenage marriages are fairly well known, and most are defined as serious, unfortunate, and with negative long-range consequences.[14] The consequences include a high incidence of dropping out of

---

13. These figures came from *The World Almanac and Book of Facts: 1989* (New York: Newspaper Enterprise Association, 1989): 800.

14. Douglas M. Teti, Michael E. Lamb, and Arthur B. Elster, "Long-Range Socioeconomic and Marital Consequences of Adolescent Marriage in Three Cohorts of Adult Males," *Journal of Marriage and the Family* 49(August 1987): 499–506; and Douglas M. Teti and Michael Lamb, "Socioeconomic and Marital Outcomes of Adolescent Marriage, Adolescent Childbirth, and Their Co-occurrence," *Journal of Marriage and the Family* 51(February 1989): 203–212.

school,[15] high unemployment rates among teenagers (refer back to Table 6–1), higher than average fertility rates[16] (the consequences of young parenthood are discussed in Chapter 13), lower than average lifetime earnings, and a high divorce rate[17] (estimated for teenage marriages to be from two to four times that for marriages begun by persons after age twenty).

Some support was found for the idea that people who marry young are unprepared for the mate selection process and marital role performance, experience relatively low marital satisfaction as a result, and therefore appear disproportionately in divorce statistics.[18]

Apart from these young marriages, by itself, age at marriage does not appear to be a major point of difficulty in family life. Considering the upturn in the divorce rate in the latter half of the 1960s and in the 1970s and considering the stabilization or increase in ages at marriage, it is not likely that any rise in the divorce rate can be accounted for by age at marriage.

# RESIDENTIAL PROPINQUITY

Well established in the sociology-of-the-family literature is the idea that mate selection involves a "propinquity factor." A lengthy list of studies over the last thirty years seems to have established the general conclusion that in the United States, urban persons tend to marry someone who lives within a fairly limited distance of their home. Evidence to support this idea usually takes the form of a frequency distribution or cumulative percentage of marriages in some community, classified by the distance separating the bride's residence from the groom's residence just prior to marriage.

## Studies of propinquity

Most studies take the lead of James Bossard who, in the early 1930s, checked five thousand consecutive marriage licenses in which one or both applicants were residents of Philadelphia.[19] A tabulation was made of the distance

15. George D. Lowe, D. Lin Hughes, and David D. Witt, "Changes in the Influence of Early Marriage on the Educational Attainment of Men and Women," *Sociological Spectrum* 9 (1989): 163–173; and Gus W. Haggstrom, David E. Kanouse, and Peter A. Morrison, "Accounting for the Educational Shortfalls of Mothers," *Journal of Marriage and the Family* 48 (February 1986): 175–186.

16. Margaret Mooney Marini, "Effects of the Timing of Marriage and First Birth on Fertility," *Journal of Marriage and the Family* 43 (February 1981): 27–46.

17. Kristin A. Moore and Linda J. Waite, "Marital Dissolution, Early Motherhood and Early Marriage," *Social Forces* 60 (September 1981): 20–40; and Stephen J. Bahr and Richard J. Galligan, "Teenage Marriage and Marital Stability," *Youth and Society* 15 (June 1984): 387–400.

18. Alan Booth and John N. Edwards, "Age at Marriage and Marital Stability," *Journal of Marriage and the Family* 47 (February 1985): 67–75.

19. James H. S. Bossard, "Residential Propinquity as a Factor in Marriage Selection," *The American Journal of Sociology* 38 (September 1932): 219–224.

between the residences of the couple. Of the total number of applicants, one in eight gave the same address, one in six lived less than a block from one another, one in four lived within two blocks or less, one in three lived within five blocks or less, and one in two lived within twenty blocks or less. The obvious point is that the percentage of marriages decreased steadily and markedly as the distance between residences of the contracting parties increased.

Since the work of Bossard, at least a dozen studies have been conducted that support an inverse relationship between mate selection and distance between contracting parties. Most have been concerned exclusively with proximity of addresses just before marriage, and their findings have been based on the records of marriage license applications.

Since most propinquity studies were completed two or three decades ago, it is difficult to determine whether place of residence is as significant a factor in mate selection today. One might also expect considerable variations among different groups such as rural residence, marriage among college students, or age. However, it is expected that people would tend to marry those who live near them.

### Explanations of propinquity

How can one account for the propinquity factor in mate selection? One obvious explanation is that we meet and interact with people who live near us and attend the same schools, churches, and social events. While the pool of potential mates increases dramatically with increasing distance, proximity facilitates contact. We are less likely to meet and get to know intimately those who don't live near us. We are not likely to "fall in love with" or marry those we don't meet.

Another explanation has been called the **norm-segregation theory**. This theory suggests that we marry people who adhere to similar cultural norms and that these people reside in segregated clusters. People of similar normative categories related to race, class, religion, ethnic affiliation, or educational level tend to cluster together residentially. Neighborhoods and communities often tend to be characterized by norm-homogamous groupings. Thus the combinations of norm-similarity and geographical proximity provide an additional explanation of residential propinquity in mate selection.

In a highly mobile society one might expect nearness of residence to become a less relevant factor in mate selection. For certain groups and persons this will likely be true. Higher-status groups may be less propinquitous than lower-status groups because factors such as cost and time may be more readily accessible. Higher-status groups may be willing to travel farther and at greater cost than lower-status groups. Propinquity differences of class and occupational groups could then be ascribed to differential perception of the time-cost function.

One final point is that propinquity does not mean nonmobility. As individuals move about for college, jobs, military service, or whatever, they

### Looking for a mate? Go west women and go east men

The nation has a supply of never-married men and women. As of 1987, there were 21 million single males aged 18 and over compared to 17 million single females of the same ages. But where does one go to meet them? The husband-hunter should go to Alaska, Hawaii, Wyoming, Nevada, or the Pacific Coast states. The wife-hunter has his best chances in Massachusetts, Minnesota, New York, Pennsylvania, New Jersey, or any of the New England States.

In addition, females should avoid cities and search out rural areas: the opposite is true for males. Urban areas have about 115 single males per 100 females, compared to about 139 in rural areas. The nation's capital, Washington, D.C., may be the best place of all for males, as the number of never-married single women actually exceeds the number of never-married single men.

become increasingly more likely, as time passes, to marry someone currently close by than someone formerly propinquitous. Again the time and cost factors become operative. The individual who spent her childhood and adolescent years in Pennsylvania but goes to school and takes a job in Los Angeles may well marry someone from the southern California area. Most people do not become intimately acquainted with many eligible persons of the opposite sex but those they do know are likely to be residentially propinquitous.

## SOCIAL STATUS

Class endogamy, in our own society and around the world, is a desirable social norm, particularly for higher-status parents in regard to their children. Whether mates are selected by the individuals themselves, parents, or by someone else, conditions supporting class endogamy are essential to preserve family lineage and status. On the other hand, persons from lower statuses have much to gain by marriage to persons of a higher standing. Irrespective of the desired or preferred circumstances, most marriages are class endogamous.

### Class endogamy

Numerous studies in the past fifty years have found that both men and women marry persons from within their own class with a greater consistency than could be expected simply by chance. As early as 1918, an analysis of marriages in Philadelphia showed that intermarriage between men and women in the same industry was distinctly more common than chance expectancy, revealing something of an endogamous trend.[20]

---

20. D. M. Marvin, "Occupational Propinquity as a Factor in Mate Selection," *Publications of the American Statistical Association* 16 (1918–19): 131–150.

In a study by the author at a state university, endogamous norms were found to exist among married college students. In personal interviews it was found that men from high-status homes, where the father was a professional or a marginal professional, were most likely to marry women who had fathers in the same occupational strata. The same was true of the middle grouping of business, secretarial, and minor government occupations, as well as for the lowest grouping of skilled, unskilled, or farming occupations. The same pattern existed for married women.

Like occupational endogamy, educationally endogamous or homogamous marriages occur at levels higher than expected by chance. Richard Rockwell, in examining marriage cohorts from census data, found that for virtually every marriage cohort, at least half of all marriages that *could* have been homogamous *were* homogamous.[21] Nevertheless, both education and occupation remain major factors in mate selection.

This intraclass pattern is often viewed by exchange theorists as a process in which individuals attempt to achieve the best possible bargain for themselves and their children by weighing marital resources and alternatives. If this is true, it would be highly surprising if the endogamy pattern were not the most prevalent. It is at similar class levels where the marital resources would most likely be similar. If this is the case, what does a person of lower social class have to trade with persons of a higher social status? Let us examine some of these patterns of marriage across class lines.

### Mésalliance

Marriage with a person of an inferior position has been termed **mésalliance.** Special cases of mésalliance are **hypergamy,** denoting the pattern wherein the female marries upward into a high social stratum, and **hypogamy,** where the female marries downward into a lower social stratum.

With particular reference to the United States, a number of writers have concluded that hypergamy is more prevalent than hypogamy—women marry men of higher status more frequently than men marry women of higher rank. On the basis of an exchange-theory argument, the social advantages of hypergamy seem to exist primarily for the low-status woman. For equity to occur, this type of exchange would require that the woman be exceptional in those qualities the culture defines as desirable. Depending on the society, qualities in women that determine status might include factors such as shade of skin color, facial and morphological features, and relative age.

---

21. Richard C. Rockwell, "Historical Trends and Variations in Educational Homogamy," *Journal of Marriage and the Family* 38 (February 1976): 83–95. An interesting examination of how educational status influences linguistic homogamy can be seen in Gillian Stevens and Robert Schoen, "Linguistic Intermarriage in the United States," *Journal of Marriage and the Family* 50(February 1988): 267–279.

Men in the United States rank physical attractiveness at or near the top among the qualities they desire in women, and this seems to be especially true of the upwardly mobile or strongly ambitious. Thus it would be expected that a male who achieves status through his occupation exchanges his social rank for the beauty and personal qualities of the female. The idea that physical attractiveness is of great exchange value, particularly among women of working-class origin, was one factor that Elder attempted to determine.[22]

Elder's research confirmed his basic hypothesis. Women who became upwardly mobile through marriage were characterized by physical attractiveness, a desire to impress and control others, high aspirations for the future, and an avoidance of steady dating. Among women from the working class, physical attractiveness was more predictive of marriage to a high-status man than was educational attainment, while the relative effects of these factors were reversed among women of middle-class origins.

Certain ideas related to mésalliance seem to be confirmed. One is that when males marry outside of their class, they will more frequently marry down than up. And the higher the occupational stratum of the male, the more commonly he is found to have married down. Conversely, when females marry outside of their class, they will more frequently marry up than down. In brief, hypergamy is more prevalent than hypogamy. This notion extends to dating as well and is referred to as the mating gradient.

## The mating gradient

If, as stated, when persons marry outside their social class men tend to marry down and women tend to marry up, then we can assume the same processes occur prior to marriage. When men and women date or engage in intimate types of personal interaction, it can be expected that women will seek out similar or higher status men and men will seek out similar or lower status women. This tendency has been called the **mating gradient**. It results from the suggestion that men at the top have a wider range of mate choice than do men at the bottom, with the reverse being true for women: those at the top have a more narrow range than those at the bottom.

As stated by Gerald Leslie and Sheila Korman:

> An interesting implication of the . . . mating gradient is that it works to keep some of the highest-status women and the lowest-status men from marrying. Women at the highest levels have a smaller pool of potential mates to begin with because it is not generally acceptable for them to marry downward. In addition, these high-status women must compete both against one another and against women from other status levels for high-status men. To the extent that high-status men marry downward,

---

22. Glen H. Elder, Jr., "Appearance and Education in Marriage Mobility," *American Sociological Review* 34 (August 1969): 519–533.

they leave high-status women without partners. Among men, the reverse obtains. The lowest-status men generally are not eligible to marry higher-status women; yet higher-status men may select lower-status spouses. Thus, unmarried women may be, disproportionately, high-status women, and unmarried men may be, disproportionately, low-status men.[23]

The mating gradient also seems to operate in dating on college campuses. It is the freshman male and the senior female that have the smallest choice of probable dating partners. The freshman girl is the choice of college males at any class ranking, whereas the freshman male must, to a greater extent, limit his choices to the freshman females. At the other extreme, the situation is reversed. By the time the male and female are seniors, the male can select from any of the class rankings of females, whereas the female is more limited to senior or junior men.

### Class heterogamy and marital conflict

What about the consequences of social-class heterogamy (hypergamy or hypogamy) in terms of marital conflict or divorce? One literature search of social-class heterogamy and marital success revealed highly inconsistent findings regarding the hypothesis that marrying someone of a higher or lower social class background leads to marital incompatibility and divorce.[24] Leonard Pearlin attempted to explain the inconsistency of findings relating class intermarriage to marital success by suggesting that status heterogamy by itself is a trivial element of marriage. Status inequalities became an important force in marital relations only when combined with certain status values: marrying down while striving to move up. This brings disruption because it involves the sacrifice of something valued, namely status.[25] From an exchange perspective, when status consciousness invades marriage, exchange equivalence is difficult to maintain.

In an attempt to test the Pearlin hypothesis, Stephen Jorgensen found the conflict to be true for wives but not for husbands.[26] That is, a positive relationship existed between social-class hypogamy (wife marrying down) and the wife's perception of marital conflict frequency given that she values status advancement at the same time. The explanation for this finding was that

23. Gerald R. Leslie and Sheila K. Korman, *The Family in Social Context*, 6th ed. (New York: Oxford University Press, 1985): 376.

24. Norval D. Glenn, Sue Keir Hoppe, and David Weiner, "Social Class Heterogamy and Marital Success: A Study of the Empirical Adequacy of a Textbook Generalization," *Social Problems* 21 (April 1974): 539–550.

25. Leonard I. Pearlin, "Status Inequality and Stress in Marriage," *American Sociological Review* 40 (June 1975): 334–357.

26. Stephen R. Jorgensen, "Social Class Heterogamy, Status Striving, and Perceptions of Marital Conflict: A Partial Replication and Revision of Pearlin's Contingency Hypothesis," *Journal of Marriage and the Family* 39 (November 1977): 653–661.

although a high percentage of wives are entering the labor force, the social status of married women still depends to a large extent on the career aspirations and accomplishments of their husbands. On a normative basis, males are not as dependent on their wives for social placement as the role of primary breadwinner remains their major responsibility.

# RELIGION

All studies have found that the number of people who marry within their own religion is far greater than chance occurrence can explain. Carter and Glick, using census data, inferred in 1976 that if all persons had completely disregarded religion as a factor in mate selection, 56 percent of married couples would have spouses of like religion and 44 percent would have spouses of a different religion.[27] This inference is based on the assumption that 70.4 percent of the Protestants in the United States would have married Protestants, that 26 percent of Catholics would have married Catholics, and that 3.6 percent of Jews would have married Jews. The sum of the squares of these three values equals 56.49 percent: the *expected* percentage of endogamous marriages. The *actual* percentage of all married couples with a spouse of the same religion was 91.4 for Protestants, 78.5 for Catholics, and 92.8 for Jewish. These figures substantiate the major influences that religion, or at least religious affiliation, plays in the selection of a marital partner.

## Determining if a marriage is interfaith

Determining what is within one's religion can be an extremely complex research problem. To even define, much less measure, a mixed religious or interfaith marriage involves problems that few persons have satisfactorily resolved. For example, if you were engaged in a research study to determine the frequency of interfaith marriage at your school or in your community, would you, as suggested at the beginning of this chapter, place a Methodist– Lutheran marriage in the intra- or interfaith category? Would a devout Catholic married to a person reared in the Catholic tradition but presently indifferent to religion make a mixed marriage? If an atheist marries an agnostic would they be marrying endogamously or exogamously? If a Protestant marries a Catholic and then the Protestant converts to Catholicism, is this an inter- or intrafaith marriage?

Most studies of interreligious marriage are limited to three broad categories—Catholic, Protestant, and Jewish—with only an occasional break-through to account for finer classifications. Rarely are any divisions made in

27. Hugh Carter and Paul C. Glick, *Marriage and Divorce: A Social and Economic Study,* rev. ed. (Cambridge, Mass.: Harvard University Press, 1976): 358.

Catholicism. In Judaism, even though definite differences regarding interfaith and intra-Jewish marriages have been found to exist within the three major branches—Orthodox, Conservative, and Reform—it is relatively infrequently that studies distinguish among them. The same is true among some of the major denominations of Protestantism: Methodist, Presbyterian, Lutheran, Baptist, and the like. This lack of differentiation is very unfortunate, for even the most untrained persons in religious thought recognize differences in beliefs and practices *among* Protestant denominations to say nothing of those *within* denominations.

To deal with interfaith marriage solely on the basis of Catholic–Protestant, Catholic–Jewish, or Protestant–Jewish sets up an artificial distinction. However, it does provide general data that make possible the testing of hypotheses concerning the significance of religious endogamy within the major religious categories in the United States.

### The frequency of interfaith marriage

The frequency of interfaith marriage is determined in most research studies by checking religious affiliation on public records or by asking people directly. From these studies, indications seldom exist as to the frequency of conversion or anticipated conversion of a spouse or interdenominational mixtures with religious groups. They do indicate that among Protestants, Catholics, and Jews in the United States, intermarriages are most common among Catholics and least common among Protestants and Jews.[28] In addition, interfaith marriages are most frequent among those persons who are religiously less devout than among the religiously more devout.

Irrespective of religious affiliation, most marriages are endogamous. Using combined data from six United States national surveys conducted from 1973 to 1978, Glenn reported a rate of 92.6 of Protestants married to Protestants, 88.2 of Jews married to Jews, and 82.0 of Catholics married to Catholics. Overall, 89.7 percent of all Protestants, Catholics, and Jews were married to persons of the same religion.[29]

While these figures may appear to be quite high, Glenn reported a substantial decrease in religious homogamy. He concludes that in the recent past in the United States, norms of religious endogamy have not been as strong as most writers addressing the topic have thought them to be. The apparent

---

28. Norval D. Glenn, "Interreligious Marriage in the United States: Patterns and Recent Trends," *Journal of Marriage and the Family* 44(August 1982): 555–566. For selected denominational trends over this century *see:* Allan L. McCutcheon, "Denominations and Religious Intermarriages: Trends Among White Americans in the Twentieth Century," *Review of Religious Research* 29(March 1988): 213–227.

29. Glenn, "Interreligious Marriage in the United States," Table 1, p. 557. These percentages differ slightly from the Carter and Glick figures reported earlier due to different time periods as well as different data bases.

fact that many persons are now willing to marry a person of a different religion and to change their own religion to that of the spouse led Glenn to state that "marriage in the United States has become very largely a secular institution, with religious institutions exerting only weak influences on marital choice."[30]

It is interesting to note that endogamy is not merely the predominant pattern when the broad Protestant–Catholic–Jewish classification is used but is also the predominant pattern among Protestant denominations as well. Not only are Protestants married to other Protestants, as previous studies have shown, but they are also married to Protestants who share the same denominational affiliation. The ratio of mixed marriages does not vary much across denominational lines.

## Some consequences of interfaith marriages

The general opposition to interfaith marriages stems from the widespread belief that they are highly unstable and create a multitude of problems that intrafaith marriages do not experience. Some empirical evidence supports this belief. Heaton suggests that interreligious marriages are less satisfying than religiously homogamous marriages.[31] Other evidence includes higher aggregate levels of marital happiness reported by persons in religiously homogamous marriages. For example, a study of a representative sample of more than 1,000 Protestants and Catholics living in Nebraska found that Protestants who married homogamously within each of five doctrinally different categories (Baptist, Calvinist, fundamentalist, Lutheran, Methodist) were found to be happier with their marriages than were those married across doctrines. On the other hand no statistically significant differences were found in the marital happiness scores of Catholics married to Catholics, Catholics married to Protestants, or Protestants married to Protestants.[32]

Caution must be given in the interpretation of findings from these cross-sectional, homogamous-heterogamous comparisons even if their reports are accurate. Marriages that were unhappy and have already ended in divorce do not contribute to unhappiness in the currently married population. Nevertheless, even taking this factor into account, it is likely that lower levels of happiness and slightly higher rates of divorce occur among interreligious marriages than among intrareligious homogamous marriages.

What about the children of interfaith marriages? It has been argued that these children, compared to children of homogamous marriages, are subjected to less intense and less consistent religious socialization with the

---

30. Ibid., p. 564.

31. Tim B. Heaton, "Religious Homogamy and Marital Satisfaction Reconsidered," *Journal of Marriage and the Family* 46 (August 1984): 729–733.

32. Suzanne T. Ortega, Hugh P. Whitt, and J. Allen William, Jr., "Religious Homogamy and Marital Happiness," *Journal of Family Issues* 9(June 1988): 224–239.

## Black blood law repealed

In July of 1983, the governor of Louisiana signed into law legislation repealing a state statute that established a mathematical formula to determine if a person was black. The law stated that anyone having one thirty-second or less of "Negro blood" should not be designated as black.

The change in the law came about as a result of national attention focused on a court case of Susie Guillory Phipps who wanted to change her birth certificate description to "white" from the existing description of "col.," an abbreviation for "colored." Mrs. Phipps, whose skin was white and who was married to a successful white businessman, failed in numerous cases against the state to have this change made. The failures came because most of the older records attesting her racial background and other evidence indicating race had corroborated the

information on her birth certificate, placed there by a midwife.

Mr. Lee Frazier, the legislator who wrote the law repealing the formula, said that the new legislature will allow a person to change birth records by presenting "a preponderance of evidence" to prove that the record was wrong. The old state law required evidence that "left no room for doubt." Now the preponderance of evidence could include sworn statements from family members, doctors, and others. Mr. Ronald Davis, the assistant attorney general of the state at the time, said that the new legislation will make it easier for people to change their racial designation and that it is meaningful from a symbolic point of view because Louisiana had appeared to be in the Dark Ages.

---

consequence of being weakly religious themselves. In other words, the assertion is that interfaith marriages have a secularizing effect on the children. For the most part, this assertion was not found to be true. Larry Peterson, in studying over 1,000 adult Catholics, claimed that contrary to the secularization hypothesis, interfaith marriages have relatively inconsequential effects on religious commitment.[33] Offspring from interfaith marriages did not consistently score lower on the general religiosity measures than offspring of homogamous marriages. Catholics who are the offspring of interfaith marriages and Catholics who form them were as firmly committed to Christianity in general and Catholicism in particular as Catholics in homogamous families. In sum, the negative consequences often assumed of interfaith marriages on the success of the marriage or the secularization of the children do not appear to find much empirical support.

## RACE

Of all the norms involving intermarriage, few are more widely held or rigorously enforced than in the area of race. Despite scientific findings and the removal of legal barriers, the restrictions concerning interracial marriage still remain the most inflexible of all the mate-selection boundaries.

---

33. Larry R. Peterson, "Interfaith Marriage and Religious Commitment among Catholics," *Journal of Marriage and the Family* 48 (November 1986): 725–735.

Among most people of the world, interracial marriage is accepted both legally and socially. With the possible exception of the Republic of South Africa, few countries are as race conscious as the United States. The intermingling of people of different races is nothing new in world affairs. Based on historical and biological evidence, the idea of a "pure race" is totally inaccurate—race mixture has been going on throughout all of recorded history, and some evidence suggests that even in prehistory racial intermingling occurred. As there is no evidence to support a pure race, neither is there evidence to support the idea that racial mixtures result in biologically inferior offspring. Biologically, there is nothing to prevent marriage of persons of different races.

Removal of the legal prohibition against interracial marriage in the United States came in 1967 when the United States Supreme Court struck down as unconstitutional a 1924 Virginia law forbidding marriage between persons of different races. According to the Court, a law of this type violates rights guaranteed to all persons under the Fourteenth Amendment to the Constitution. Irrespective of the Supreme Court's decision declaring such laws unconstitutional, the social mores and the disfavor placed on interracial marriage by all major racial, religious, and ethnic groups are so strong in most areas that relatively few marriages of this type take place.

The strength of the prohibition against interracial marriage, particularly black-white marriage, in itself increased the difficulty of obtaining the type of research evidence necessary to substantiate factors such as frequency, male-female differences, or the stability of marriages of this type. It must be noted and made clear that a discussion of race in relation to marriage is not independent of, or isolated from, age, residence, social class, religion, educational level, region of the country, whether the marriage is black-white or Oriental-Caucasian, whether it involves a marriage or a remarriage, or any other dimension. To deal with racial endogamy alone is impossible.

## The frequency of black-white intermarriage

Determining the frequency of black-white marriage is exceedingly difficult. As with religion, there is the matter of classification. If a black passes for white and marries a white, is this an intermarriage or an endogamous marriage? If, as is on the law books of various states, a person is one-eighth or one-sixteenth black (an empirical impossibility), would it not be an intermarriage irrespective of which race one marries? Even if a categorization could be agreed upon and precisely determined, it could be argued that social sanctions against such marriages are so severe in most parts of the United States that the reported number of such marriages would be less than the actual number.

In 1960, for the first time, the United States census was tabulated to show the number of husbands and wives who had the same or different racial backgrounds. This information, like all census information involving race, does not denote any clear-cut scientific definition of biological stock. Rather, it is

*Table 8–2*

*Interracial married couples: 1970, 1980, and 1987*

|  | 1970 | 1980 | 1987 | Percent Increase 1970–1980 | 1980–1987 |
|---|---|---|---|---|---|
| Total married couples | 44,597,000 | 49,714,000 | 52,286,000 | 11.5 | 5.2 |
| Interracial married couples | 310,000 | 651,000 | 799,000 | 110.0 | 22.7 |
|    Percentage of total | 0.70% | 1.31% | 1.53% |  |  |
| Black-white married couples | 65,000 | 167,000 | 177,000 | 156.9 | 6.0 |
|    Percentage of total | 0.15% | 0.34% | 0.34% |  |  |
|    Husband black, wife white | 41,000 | 122,000 | 121,000 | 197.6 | -0.8 |
|    Wife black, husband white | 24,000 | 45,000 | 56,000 | 87.5 | 24.4 |
| Other interracial married couples | 245,000 | 484,000 | 622,000 | 97.6 | 28.5 |

*Source:* Adapted from U.S. Bureau of the Census, *Statistical Abstract of the United States: 1989,* 109th ed. (Washington, D.C.: U. S. Government Printing Office, 1989), Table 55, p. 44.

based on self-identification by respondents. The data represent self-classification by people into one of fifteen groups listed on the Census questionnaire.[34]

As can be seen in Table 8–2, of the 52.3 million married couples in the United States, in 1987, 799,000, or 1.5 percent of the total, were classified as interracially married. Only 177,000, or 0.34 percent of the total number of married couples, were classified as black-white married couples. While caution must be advised on the accuracy of these census-assembled figures because they are based on self-reports and devoid of reliability or validity checks, it does provide one valuable source of information on frequency, the increase over time, and the black husband/white wife or white husband/black wife differential.

Several findings appear of interest in Table 8–2. For example, while the number of married couples increased by 11.5 percent between 1970 and 1980 and by 5.2 percent between 1980 and 1987, the number of interracial couples increased by 110 percent between 1970 and 1980 and by 23 percent between 1980 and 1987. Thus the number of reported interracial marriages increased at a much higher rate than did the number of all marriages. Yet the number of interracial marriages relative to the total number of marriages is small: 1.5 percent of all interracial marriages and only 0.34 or one-third of one percent of black-white marriages. This figure, although small, more than doubled in the decade of the 1970s (a 157 percent increase), while it only increased by 6.0

34. These fifteen groups listed in the race item on the census questionnaire included: white, black, American Indian, Eskimo, Aleut, Chinese, Filipino, Japanese, Asian Indian, Korean, Vietnamese, Hawaiian, Samoan, Guamanian, and "other."

*Interracial marriages in the United States have increased considerably over the past twenty years, but the social norms opposing these marriages have kept the number and proportion very low.*

percent between 1980 and 1987. The percent of the total did not change at all (0.34 percent in both 1980 and 1987). This suggests (1) that the occurrence of interracial marriages of any type and particularly of black-white marriage is infrequent, and (2) that the political and social conservatism of the 1980s was manifest in the number of interracial marriages as well. If, as suggested later in this section, the frequency of interracial marriage and the percent of increase or decrease is one indicator of racial integration and equality, the decade of the 1980s showed little improvement.

Interracial marriage rates vary widely from one state to another. For example, the percentage of black-white marriage reported for 1967–1970 by Thomas Monahan was 1.94 in the District of Columbia, .73 in Massachusetts, and .45 or higher in Alaska, Hawaii, Maryland, New Hampshire, Rhode Island, Connecticut, and New Jersey. In contrast, North Carolina, Georgia, Tennessee, Alabama, Mississippi, and Louisiana had a percentage of black-white marriage under .09. The rates are much higher when all racially mixed marriages are considered. For example combining white-other or black-other rates with the black-white rates, the percentages vary from 32.54 in Hawaii, 10.79 in Alaska, and 2.11 in Montana to .03 in Alabama and .07 in Mississippi.[35]

Heer suggests that although marriages between blacks and whites are relatively infrequent in number, they are sociologically important because they serve as an indicator of the relationship between the two races. He hypothesizes that a low frequency of black-white marriage serves to reinforce the pattern of inequality between the two races. He advances several reasons for this:

> First of all, on a per-capita basis white persons hold a far higher share of the nation's wealth than do blacks and a low frequency of racial inter-marriage makes it unlikely for a black to inherit wealth from a white. Secondly, blacks are by and large excluded from the many unionized manual jobs to which entrance is strongly determined by kin connections because existing jobs of this type are usually held by whites and black persons rarely have white kin. Thirdly, the lack of close relatives among whites affects the socialization of black youth. In particular, they cannot obtain an easy familiarity with the social world of whites and hence are inhibited from applying for jobs demanding such familiarity even when their technical qualifications are completely satisfactory. Finally, over the long run it may be surmised that prejudice against blacks on the part of white persons would be diminished if the proportion of whites with black relatives were substantial rather than negligible, as at present.[36]

## Male-female intermarital racial differences

Most articles and books dealing with black-white marriage indicate that black males marry white females more frequently than white males marry black females. This black husband-white wife contention is strongly supported by census data (see Table 8–2). Of the 177,000 reported black-white marriages in 1987, 121,000 or 68.4 percent of them included a black husband and a white wife. Fifty-six thousand or 31.6 percent of the total had a black wife and a white husband.

There is a lack of consensus on the reasons for a different incidence of interracial marriage by sex. Research attempts aimed at racial-class or racial-sexual exchanges failed to provide empirical support. Educational factors fail to provide consistent results in that higher educated black men are more likely to marry interracially but this tendency is less true for highly educated black females or white males. Availability provides little help in

---

35. Thomas P. Monahan, "An Overview of Statistics on Interracial Marriage in the United States, with Data on Its Extent from 1963–1970," *Journal of Marriage and the Family* 38 (May 1976), Table 5, p. 227.

36. David M. Heer, "The Prevalence of Black-White Marriage in the United States, 1960 and 1970," *Journal of Marriage and the Family* 36 (May 1974): 246.

finding an answer for the greater number of black females than black males would lead us to expect more intermarriage among black females.

Randall Collins suggests that one possible explanation may be that there is a particularly strong distinction between male and female cultures in the black community.[37] He suggests that black women have a tradition of independence (not being very subservient to men) which may account both for their own lower rate of intermarriage and for the tendency of black males to seek wives elsewhere.

I would hypothesize as well, that differential norms operate for white and black males in relation to females. For example, for both races, males are more likely to be the mate selection-marriage initiators. In addition, given historical and socioeconomic differences, it may be a more prestigious factor for a black male to initiate interaction with a white female than for a white male to initiate interaction with a black female. Other factors or explanations as well may be operative.

## The success of interracial marriages

Do black-white marriages succeed?

A generally accepted view is that those who enter a racially mixed marriage are more likely to get divorced. Analyzing a set of data in the state of Iowa covering almost thirty years, Monahan inferred that blacks, both males and females, have contributed almost twice as many divorces to the picture as one would expect from their proportion of marriages. But when the divorce rate of mixed marriages of blacks with whites was examined, Monahan found that in Iowa the mixed marriages were more enduring (i.e., less likely to divorce) than were black-black marriages. As a whole, in Iowa black-white marriages would appear to have a greater stability than do marriages where both parties are black, and intermarriages of black males with white wives are more enduring than marriages of whites with white.[38]

Monahan found a somewhat similar pattern in Hawaii by examining the rates of divorce.[39] He concluded that, whatever the explanation, interracial marriage does not necessarily lead to a weakening of family ties. Despite the considerable increase in interracial marriage in Hawaii, the divorce rate had stabilized at a level lower than in previous decades, and, as a whole, the mixed-race marriages were only moderately less successful than the same-race marriages.

Recognizing that Iowa and Hawaii may be unique cases, recognizing that interracial marital success depends upon which races are intermarrying and

37. Randall Collins, *Sociology of Marriage and the Family: Gender, Love, and Property,* 2nd ed. (Chicago: Nelson-Hall, 1988): 220.

38. Thomas P. Monahan, "Are Interracial Marriages Really Less Stable?" *Social Forces* 48 (June 1970): 464–469.

39. Monahan, "An Overview of Statistics on Interracial Marriage," pp. 40–47.

the circumstances surrounding the marriage, and recognizing different methodological and research problems, the findings of Monahan should certainly lead to a serious questioning of the negative aspects of interracial marriage to the couple themselves. The question then follows, What about the children? Are they at risk for developing personality and adjustment problems?

Popular literature, often based on speculation or on unrepresentative case histories, is strongly biased toward the notion that offspring of cross-racial-ethnic marriages are likely to suffer from adjustment problems. Data from Hawaii, at least, suggest that this literature is incorrect.[40] There, children of cross-ethnic-racial marriages are not much different from children of endogamous marriages. And male offspring of exogamous marriages, for example, scored higher in social desirability and lower in interpersonal abrasiveness measures than did offspring of endogamous marriages. Daughters of exogamous marriages were found to be more extroverted with no other differences approaching significance. Results such as these may be due to the low level of community-wide stigma associated with mixed marriages in Hawaii. If that is true, then pressures outside the marriage and the parent-child relationship are the key dimensions in producing negative effects of such marriages on offspring.

Whether dealing with husband-wife, parent-child, or employer-employee relationships, the success of the relationship depends upon the total situation and not merely upon the fact that one partner is black and the other is white. Interpersonal relationships of any sort are affected by external forces as well. Thus parents, kin, neighbors, local politicians, or society in general lend support or opposition with varying degrees of pressure and influence on the marriage, family, or job situation. Success is relative, extending far beyond the boundaries of any two persons—with skin color alike or different.

## The trend in intermarriage

As was evident in Table 8–2, the trend in interracial marriages is upward. Yet the total incidence (799,000) is still so low that these marriages relative to all marriages (52.3 million) are not likely to have any major effect in the achievement of assimilation, racial integration, decreasing social distance, or even in affecting black-white relationships in general.[41]

---

40. Ronald C. Johnson and Craig T. Nagoshi, "The Adjustment of Offspring of Within-Group and Interracial/Intercultural Marriages: A Comparison of Personality Factor Scores," *Journal of Marriage and the Family* 48 (May 1986): 279–284.

41. Gurak and Fitzpatrick describe the intermarriage patterns of five Hispanic groups in New York City arguing that intermarriage provides an excellent indicator of assimilation and of the social distance separating ethnic groups. *See* Douglas T. Gurak and Joseph P. Fitzpatrick, "Intermarriage Among Hispanic Ethnic Groups in New York City," *American Journal of Sociology* 87 (January 1982): 921–934.

It is hard to imagine a set of conditions under which black-white marriage rates would increase so rapidly as to achieve any large intermingling within the foreseeable future. It is likely that interacting forces are at work. For example, if schools become integrated, if educational opportunities become available to blacks, if job opportunities increase, then it is likely that the incidence of interracial marriage will increase. And if black-white marriages continue to increase, this may play some role, albeit small, in improving relationships between African- and white-Americans.

## SUMMARY

1. *Homogamy* and *endogamy* refer to the extent of intermarriage among people who share similar characteristics or are of like groups. This chapter examined the nature of intermarriage and five normative structures surrounding mate selection in the United States: age, proximity of residence, class, religion, and race. The choice of a mate along these and other structural dimensions has significant consequences for the society, the marriage, or the persons involved.

2. The reporting and interpreting of any type of intermarriage has its difficulties. The boundaries of race, class, or religion are rarely clear-cut and precise. Rates for individuals are often confused with rates for marriages. Actual rates of intermarriage vary according to numerous social factors such as group size, heterogeneity, sex ratio, controls over marriage, the development of cultural similarities, the romantic love complex, and the influence of certain psychological factors.

3. Most couples in the United States are relatively homogamous in the age at which they marry. Since the turn of the century, the tendency has been for the male-female age difference at the time of marriage to narrow. Age at marriage as well decreased for both sexes between 1890 and the mid-1950s. Since then there has been an increase, which has accelerated in the last decade.

4. The marriage squeeze is used to describe the effects of imbalance between the number of males and females in the prime marriage ages. This squeeze resulted in a shortage of women in the 1950s, a shortage of men in the 1980s, and predictably will result in a shortage of women at the turn of the century. The marriage squeeze is particularly acute among black women.

5. The age at marriage is of major concern when it involves teenagers. These concerns relate to higher rates of high school drop-outs, unemployment, fertility, and divorce.

6. Mate selection involves a "propinquity factor." Studies seem to conclude that people choose mates who live within a fairly limited distance of their own homes. Explanations for propinquity center around the opportunity to meet, a norm segregation theory, and a time-cost factor.

7. Mate selection studies conclude that marriages are highly endogamous by social class far greater than could be expected to occur simply by chance. When marriage occurs with someone from a lower position (mésalliance) it may denote hypergamy or hypogamy. The general tendency for men to date and marry downward more frequently than upward has been termed the *mating gradient*. The literature on social class heterogamy and marital success reveals highly inconsistent findings.

8. Religious endogamy, although less rigid than racial endogamy, remains an important factor in mate selection. Precise data on the frequency of intermarriage are difficult to determine. There seems to be consensus that the religiously devout marry endogamously in greater frequency than the religiously less devout and that endogamous marriages have higher levels of happiness and slightly lower rates of divorce than the interfaith marriages. Those with no religion have lower rates of marital happiness or success.

9. In the United States, racial endogamous norms are more rigorously enforced than any others described in this chapter. Findings suggest that black males marry white females more frequently than white males marry black females. The success of these marriages tends to contradict public opinion. While the trend in interracial marriage is upward, the incidence is low and the number will, in all probability, have little effect on an integration of the races.

10. In general, intermarriage of all types appears to be on the increase, but endogamous marriages continue to occur in frequencies far greater than one could expect to occur by chance alone. The next chapter continues to concentrate on mate selection, but the frame of reference shifts from a structural orientation to more of a processual and interactional orientation. What are the explanations of choosing one mate over another? What are the processes followed in moving from meeting to marriage? These and related issues follow.

# Key Terms and Topics

# Discussion Questions

1. Differentiate between endogamy and exogamy, homogamy and heterogamy. What is meant by assortive mating? What constitutes intermarriage or a mixed marriage?

2. Discuss factors that are likely to increase the incidences of intermarriage. What factors operate most strongly to discourage or prohibit them?

3. What trends do you predict in regard to age at marriage, place of residence, social class, religion, and race?

4. What are the laws in your state regarding age at marriage? Do differentiations exist for male and female as to the age at marriage? Why is this? What legal changes do you think would be advisable?

5. Describe the marriage squeeze. What factors account for a shift from a shortage of women to a shortage of men and a return to a shortage of women? Why is the marriage squeeze so significant for black women?

6. Discuss hypergamy and hypogamy—their likelihood, their explanation, and some consequences of their occurrence.
7. Does the mating gradient occur in your school? Why or why not? Is the basic pattern likely to change in ten years?
8. Take a brief survey among your friends as to the importance of religious endogamy in dating or marriage. What additional problems, consequences, or both may be more likely in interfaith than intrafaith marriages?

9. To what extent is an exchange theory adequate in explaining interclass or interracial marriages? What are factors offered in exchange? How are exceptions handled?
10. In regard to black-white interracial marriages: Why are they so infrequent? How do you explain the predominance of black husband–white wife marriages rather than the reverse? What objections to interracial marriages are likely to lack empirical support?

## *F*URTHER *READINGS*

Heer, David M., and Grossband-Schechtman, Amyra. "The Impact of the Female Marriage Squeeze and the Contraceptive Revolution on Sex Roles and the Women's Liberation Movement in the United States, 1960 and 1975." *Journal of Marriage and the Family* 43 (February 1981): 49–65. A fascinating empirical account arguing that the advent of the Women's Liberation Movement was directly linked to a female marriage squeeze and the revolution in contraceptive technology.

Lenski, Gerhard. *The Religious Factor: A Sociological Study of Religion's Impact on Politics, Economics and Family Life.* Garden City, N.Y.: Doubleday, 1961. A study completed in Detroit attempting to discover the impact of religion on secular institutions including the family.

Mayer, Egon. *Love and Tradition: Marriages between Jews and Christians.* New York: Plenum Press, 1985. A look at Jewish–Christian marriages within a historical and cultural context based on survey data and personal interviews over a ten-year period.

Murstein, Bernard I. "Mate Selection in the 1970s." *Journal of Marriage and the Family* 92 (November 1980): 777–792. One of the decade review articles dealing with major trends in mate selection issues and research.

# CHAPTER NINE

# MATE SELECTION: EXPLANATIONS AND PROCESSES

The Christian Science Monitor/R. Norman Matheny.

$A$s should have become very clear from reading the last chapter, mate selection is not simply a matter of preference or free choice. Despite the increases in freedom and opportunities that young or old people have to select "anyone they please," many factors that are well beyond the control of the individual severely limit the number of eligible persons from whom to choose. The taboo on incest and the restrictions placed on age, sex, marital status, class, religion, ethnicity, race, and others in most societies narrow considerably the "fields of eligibles."

## ARRANGED MARRIAGE VERSUS FREE CHOICE OF MATE

A sizable volume of research suggests that all societies have systems of norms and sometimes specific rules about who may marry whom and how marriage partners are selected. These norms are likely to vary from one culture to another and to differ for a first marriage or a remarriage, males or females, wealthy or poor, and so forth. However, norms, rules, and controls appear in all societies.

On an ideal-type continuum, these norms may vary from totally arranged marriages at one extreme to total free choice of mate at the other. Where marriages are arranged, the couple has nothing to say about the matter. The selection is usually, but not always, made by parents or kin. The other extreme, total free choice, is so rare that to discuss it would simply be conjecture. The United States is, however, one of the few societies of the world that approaches this end of the continuum. In its extreme form, parents and kin are not consulted and in some instances not even informed of the impending marriage. Between these two extremes are various combinations of arranged–free choice possibilities. Parents may arrange a marriage and give their son or daughter a veto power. The son or daughter may make his or her own selection and give the parents the veto power. One of the persons to be married, usually the son, may select the bride with his parents. Regardless of the method of mate selection, every society has a set of norms to prescribe the appropriate procedure.

Where mate selection is arranged, the family is generally the chief and only source of employment; rather than establishing a new family, marriage is a means of providing for the continuity and stability of the existing family. Arranged marriage has the effect (functions) of providing the elders with control over the younger family members and control over who from the outside enters and becomes part of the family unit. In addition, it preserves family property, furthers political linkages, protects economic and status concerns, and keeps the family intact from one generation to another. As a result, almost without exception, the chosen partners must share similar group identities. Racial, religious, and particularly economic statuses must be similar. Arranged marriage, rather than being based on criteria such as romantic love, desire for children, loneliness or sexual desire, will likely include factors such as the size of the bride's price, the reputation of the potential spouse's kin group, levirate and sororate obligations, and traditions of prescribed marriage arrangements.

An example of an arranged marriage between the groom and the bride's parents is provided by John Peters, who spent eight years in the jungles of northern Brazil. He described mate selection among the Shirishana as follows:

> The female has no choice in the selection of her spouse. Any person who is in the *Wanima* kinship relationship to the potential bride and who is acceptable to her family could be her mate. The selection is generally made when the female is three years of age and the male 14 to 20 years of age. (In several instances the male has been an estimated 34 years.) The selection may be initiated by the mother of the male, but more commonly is done by the male himself. On occasion a male has asked the family of a pregnant woman that the unborn child become his wife, should it be a girl.[1]

Arranged marriages result in a commitment among the selected partners that is, in many instances, as binding as the marriage itself. Since the marriage exists primarily to fulfill social and economic needs, concerns such as incompatibility, love, or personal need fulfillment are not at issue. As a result, divorce is practically unknown or occurs only infrequently. Instances where marriages must be terminated frequently bring a great sense of shame and stigma to the entire family and kin group.

Evidence suggests that as traditional cultures are exposed to "Western" models of modernization and as they industrialize and adopt new technology from the outside world, those segments of cultures with the greatest exposure to these influences tend to increasingly depart from an arranged marriage pattern to one of increasing "free" or "love" matched marriages. Gary Lee and Lorene Stone[2] extend this proposition slightly by suggesting that autonomous mate selection based on romantic attraction is more likely to be institutionalized in societies with nuclear family systems than in those in which families are typically extended. In other words, extended families tend to exert greater control over the mate selection process than do nuclear families.

As suggested, total free choice is practically nonexistent anywhere in the world. This would imply freedom to choose a person for marriage without regard to the wishes of anyone else, and certainly not the wishes of parents or kin groups. Also, it would imply that instrumental considerations such as money, power, social rank, occupation, education, age, incest, family ties, or even sex would not be major considerations in the choice. Limited free choice

1. John Fred Peters, "Mate Selection Among the Shirishana," *Practical Anthropology* 18 (January/February 1971): 20–21.

2. Gary R. Lee and Lorene Hemphill Stone, "Mate Selection Systems and Criteria: Variation According to Family Structure," *Journal of Marriage and the Family* 42 (May 1980): 319–326.

## Mail-order brides give men an empty dream come true

Mail-order brides are back in the news. I say back because of the previous boom in the mail-order bride business that took place in this country roughly 150 years ago. News is cyclical. One learns that in the newspaper business.

When the West was being won (or lost, from the perspective of native Americans), lots of hearty men who went alone into the wilderness found they had little to do after their fortunes were found. There were very few discos in which to meet members of the opposite sex. What good is money without someone to share it? Finding a wife in the wilderness, however, was impossible.

The mail-order bride business evolved to fill this need. Through it, women with few marriage prospects at home, impoverished women, adventuresome women, all kinds of women offered themselves to brokers as potential brides. Love might come, but partnership was the bargain. Thus was the story line provided for "Paint Your Wagon" and "Seven Brides for Seven Brothers."

### Young, beautiful, and obedient

The phenomenon of contemporary mail-order brides is similar, with one unwholesome difference. The old-time bridegrooms were attempting to coax a little reality into their unreality. The new-time bridegrooms are trying to replace reality with unreality. They are surrounded by genuine women, but want fantasy creatures.

The modern mail-order brides are primarily young Oriental women, many from the Philippines. They are willing to marry lonely American men in return for the opportunity to live in relative comfort as U.S. citizens. Their opportunities for a comfortable life-style at home are limited. They have that in common with some of our pioneer mothers.

Men who have availed themselves of this contemporary service are happy to explain its appeal. They complain that American women are too outspoken, too demanding, too self-interested. These men say they yearn for an "old-fashioned" wife, one who is docile, domestic, and subservient.

One recent mail-order bridegroom explained himself on TV recently: "Look at me. How else is a man my age with my looks going to get a beautiful, talented, 25-year-old woman who will love him, live with him and be faithful to him?"

How indeed? This man was grossly overweight and well over 50, with a face to stop a truck. He exhibited little wit, charm, or grace. Maybe he's a great guy, but there was no evidence.

His bride sat expressionless at his side. She had long black hair and almond eyes. She was pleasant appearing, but not beautiful. I know nothing of her talent. I'll accept that she is 25.

### Till death parts them

I wonder if this man and others like him understand how ridiculous they are. They reach for a dream. They convince themselves it can be ordered from a catalog and bought for the price of an airline ticket and a marriage license.

The fantasy each cherishes is that he will find a young, beautiful woman who will fall in love with him on sight, or after a brief exchange of letters. That's pretty silly, especially since these men generally admit they've had trouble in past romantic pursuits.

Then this exotic child-woman is supposed gladly to abandon her past life and culture, marry the dreamer, be happy, faithful, and obedient, devoting all her energies to serving her master for the rest of his or her life, whichever comes first.

One wonders if these men also believe in Santa Claus and the Tooth Fairy.

The lonely men in the Wild West weren't so silly. But they weren't looking for ego props. The catalog women pay a high price for their trip to the U.S. Living with a loonie tune and playing to his fantasies can't be any fun at all.

*Source:* Nickie McWhirter, *Detroit Free Press,* March 7, 1984, p. 1-B. Reprinted with the permission of the Detroit Free Press.

## Mate selection and marriage in Swaziland

Swaziland, an independent country in Africa, is located between the Republic of South Africa and Mozambique. Mate selection and marriage in Swazi society differs from western marriage in various ways.

First, rather than marriage being a union of two individuals, it is essentially a union of two groups of kinsmen. The opinion of senior members of the lineage is often as important as that of the prospective bride and groom. Second, there is a clearly stated rule that children born to the union belong to the kin group of the father. Third, the residence pattern is patrilocal. Fourth, marriages are legitimized only after the payment of *bridewealth*. This is a form of compensation to the kin of the bride for their loss of the woman and her procreative capacities. The amount of bridewealth ranges from ten to twelve head of cattle for a commoner's daughter to as many as fifty or sixty for an important royal princess.

Fifth, marriage is closely related to the continuance of society, therefore childlessness is viewed as a serious problem. Sixth, the production of as many children as possible is a primary aim of marriage. Thus, polygyny is not only permissible, it is considered the ideal form of marriage. Finally, divorce is kept to a minimum as the termination of a marriage is an extremely complex process.

*Source:* Gary P. Ferraro, "The Persistence of Bridewealth in Swaziland," *International Journal of Sociology of the Family* 13 (Spring 1983): 1–16.

takes these factors into consideration and permits a choice of a mate by the spouses themselves within the limits of the permitted social groupings. Given this choice, then, love and prestige ratings become significant as do the processes of getting to know one another and of moving the relationship toward increasing commitment. Personal needs and values also become significant. Thus our attention is turned to the premarital dyad and to various theories and processes that explain mate selection.

## INDIVIDUALISTIC EXPLANATIONS OF MATE SELECTION

With a decrease in kinship control over mate selection, particularly in Western societies, has come a freedom that has brought about an enormously complex system. It would seem obvious that this process occurs long before the first "date." Since in the United States it is possible to have more than one mate (although legally only one at a time), for many the mate-selection process never ends. Most psychological and other "individualistic" theories explaining this choice are based on a wide range of experience, along with a variety of subconscious drives and needs.

### Instinctive, innate, or biological

One of the oldest, and perhaps most radical, explanations of mate selection suggests that what guides a man to a woman (rarely was it thought to be the other way around) is instinct. Instinct is established by heredity and deals with unlearned behavior. In my opinion, there is no such thing as a human instinct, but to many biologists and psychologists instincts are basic to human behavior.

Related to the instinct theory is the genetic-similarity argument.[3] The idea is that genetically similar others, be they strangers or kin, have a tendency to seek each other out and provide supportive environments. In contrast, genetically dissimilar others have a tendency to form natural antipathies and provide mutually hostile environments. As assortive mating in animals is based on genetic similarity, so too is assortive mating in humans.

As far as is known, no one has ever discovered any instinctive, unconscious, or purely biological determinants for mate selection. Of course, the fact that they are unconscious or innate make them difficult, if not impossible, to discover. However, to attribute explanations of selecting a mate to the unconscious adds little more to our understanding of basic processes involved in mate choice than does explaining it by spirits, fairies, or supernatural powers.

## Parental image

Closely related to the instinct theory is the psychoanalytic idea of Sigmund Freud and his followers suggesting that a person tends to fall in love with and marry a person similar to his or her opposite-sex parent. This, too, is generally unconscious and centers around the **Oedipus complex.** Early in a male child's life, his mother becomes his first love object. But the presence of his father prohibits him from fulfilling his incestuous desire, and, as a result, the male infant develops an antagonism toward his father for taking his love object from him. This, in turn, results in an unconscious desire to kill his father and marry his mother. The male infant's desire for his mother and fear of his father is so great that he develops a fear of castration or, as Freud called it, **castration anxiety**—a fear that his father wants to emasculate him by removing the penis and testes. But since the father is also protective, helpful, and respected by the mother, a great amount of ambivalence exists, which is resolved only by a primary type of identification with the father. The Oedipus complex is thus temporarily resolved for the male, but the repressed love for his mother remains. By adolescence, when the male is free to fall in love, he selects a love object that possesses the qualities of his mother.

The opposite, but parallel, result occurs for the female. She at an early age becomes aware of lacking a male sexual organ and develops *penis envy.* Feeling castrated, her feelings are transformed into the desire to possess a penis, especially the father's. These feelings for the forbidden object remain repressed throughout childhood, but her love for her father, known as the

---

3. J. Philippe Rushton, Robin J. H. Russell, and Pamela A. Wells "Genetic Similarity Theory: Beyond Kin Selection," *Behavior Genetics*, 14 (1984): 179–193.

**Electra complex,** culminates in marriage when she selects a mate with the qualities of her father. Both the Oedipus complex and the Electra complex are discussed more fully in Chapter 14.

Although it seems very reasonable to believe that young people, in selecting a mate, would be keenly aware of the qualities of their parents and the nature of their marriage, no clear evidence has been produced to support the hypothesis that the boy seeks someone like his mother and that the girl seeks someone like her father. There are times when very close resemblances seem to exist between a man's wife and his mother and between a woman's husband and her father. Jedlicka[4] argues that this occurrence is more frequent than could be expected by chance; however, whether the explanation is rooted in Oedipus or Electra complexes is subject to question.

### Complementary needs

The theory of complementary needs in mate selection was developed and enhanced by Robert F. Winch. It was his belief that although mate selection is homogamous with respect to numerous social characteristics such as age, race, religion, ethnic origin, residential propinquity, socioeconomic status, education, or previous marital status, when it comes to the psychic level and individual motivation, mate selection tends to be complementary rather than homogamous. The idea grew out of a modified and simplified version of a need-scheme theory of motivation; but rather than the needs being similar, they tend to complement one another.

To test his hypothesis of mate selection, Winch subjected to intensive study twenty-five husbands and their wives. In each of three early papers, Winch claimed that the bulk of the evidence from these couples supports the hypothesis that mates tend to select each other on the basis of complementary needs.[5] Conversely, in each of these three papers, he claimed that support is not available for the conflicting hypothesis that spouses tend to be motivationally similar.

Several years later, Winch published his book on mate selection.[6] For mate selection to take place on the basis of love, that is, due to complementary needs, it is understood that both man and woman must have some choice in the matter. The theory would not be operative in settings where marriages are arranged (as by parents, marriage brokers, or others). Thus love will likely only

---

4. Davor Jedlicka, "Indirect Parental Influence on Mate Choice: A Test of the Psychoanalytic Theory," *Journal of Marriage and the Family* 46 (February 1984): 65–70.

5. Robert F. Winch, Thomas Ktsanes, and Virginia Ktsanes, "The Theory of Complementary Needs in Mate Selection: An Analytic and Descriptive Study," *American Sociological Review* 19 (June 1954): 241–249: Robert F. Winch, "The Theory of Complementary Needs in Mate Selection: A Test of One Kind of Complementariness," *American Sociological Review* 20 (February 1955): 52–56; and Robert F. Winch, "The Theory of Complementary Needs in Mate Selection: Final Results on the Test of the General Hypothesis," *American Sociological Review* 20 (October 1955): 552–555.

6. Robert F. Winch, *Mate Selection* (New York: Harper, 1958).

be an important criterion under cultural conditions where: (1) the choice of mates is voluntary, (2) the culture encourages premarital interaction between men and women and (3) where the marital friendship is culturally defined as a rich potential source of gratification. Since love is defined in terms of needs, the general hypothesis is that where people marry for love, their needs will be complementary.

Reports by Winch and his colleagues led to a constant flow of articles attempting to retest the complementary needs hypothesis. The results were basically negative, failing to provide empirical support to the idea that people tend to choose mates whose needs complement their own.

Various interpretations have been presented to explain why the complementary needs theory refutes popular opinion and fails to gain research support. Perhaps there are problems in the measurement of needs. Perhaps the basic theoretical considerations of the complementary needs theory are incorrect. Perhaps, like findings of endogamous factors presented in the previous chapter, needs also are more homogamous than heterogamous, more similar than different, and "likes do marry likes" rather than "opposites attract."

Any or all of these reasons may be correct. What is clear is that relatively little empirical support exists for the theory of complementary needs as originally formulated. In fact, most research attempting to explain mate selection on the basis of personality traits, whether similar, different, complementary, or some combination thereof, seems to have bogged down into a morass of conflicting results. Most findings suggest the probable futility of further pursuits of personality matching. Perhaps instincts, drives, needs, complexes (including Oedipus ones), or personality traits all fail to find empirical support because they are based within persons rather than resulting from interactions. All fail to consider the cultural contexts and social situations in which the needs, drives, or traits are expressed. In spite of the research, unsupported theories—whether instinctive, mother-images, complementary needs, or personality traits—die hard and further research on these ideas is sure to follow.

## SOCIOCULTURAL EXPLANATIONS OF MATE SELECTION

Age, residential propinquity, class, religion, and race are sociocultural factors that influence mate selection. Any factor in which social norms and endogamous factors play a part in who marries whom falls into this category. Roles and values, although basic to norms of endogamy, can also be viewed as interaction processes that explain the choice of a mate.

### Role theory

Role theory, at least to this author, appears to be conceptually more justifiable as an overall explanation of marital choice than any of the previous explanations of theories. All social humans or, more specifically all marriage-able persons, have expectations regarding the behavior desired by themselves and by their prospective mates. One perception of role, as described in Chapter 2, refers to a set of social expectations appropriate to a given status: husband, wife, male, female, single, and the like. These expectations, implicit or explicit, have been internalized and serve to direct and influence personal behavior as well as the behavior desired in a prospective marriage partner. Basically, we tend to desire (internalize) the roles defined by our society, subculture, and family.

Roles and personality needs differ in a very important respect. With role, the focus of attention is on behavior and attitudes appropriate to a situation irrespective of the individual, whereas with personality needs, the focus is on behavior and attitudes that are characteristic of the person or individual irrespective of the situation. The difference is crucial. Role focuses on definitions, meanings, and social expectations. In regard to mate selection, individuals select one another on the basis of role consensus, role compatibility, or on the basis of courtship, marital, and family-role agreement.

Role consensus or agreement, widely used as an indicator of marital success or adjustment and found to have a strong, positive association with marital satisfaction,[7] has been applied relatively infrequently to mate selection. However, similar processes could be expected to be as operative prior to marriage in the selection process as after marriage. Where role discrepancies exist, marriage is less likely to occur in the first place. Would Joe, who expects a wife to care for children, cook meals, and clean the house, marry Mary, who despises these activities? Or reciprocally, would Mary want to marry Joe if that is what he expects of her?

Disparity in role agreement can be obtained by listing series of expectations associated with various statuses and comparing the responses of the couple. The expectations of the couple on any given dimension can be used: decision making, recreation, sex, church attendance, care of children, employment, and the like. A given role expectation is less crucial than the agreement of the persons involved. For example, if Joe expects that sleeping on the Sabbath is more important than church attendance, no conflict exists if Joe's spouse holds a similar expectation or attaches little importance to the expectation. The role itself is not as important as the consensus of the partners in regard to the role. Also the role expectation itself may change as the situation changes. Maybe Joe's spouse thinks Joe should attend church on the Sabbath but does not expect him to do so when out of town or on vacation.

In brief, the couple likely to marry is the male and female who share similar role definitions and expectations. This assumes, of course, that forces

---

7. Stephen J. Bahr, C. Bradford Chappell, and Geoffrey K. Leigh, "Age at Marriage, Role Enactment, Role Consensus, and Marital Satisfaction," *Journal of Marriage and the Family* 45 (November 1983): 795–803.

*People tend to choose partners of similar age, race, religion, and class. In addition, similarities of values (what is important and of worth) and roles (social expectations) seem to be key factors in explaining who marries whom.*

such as an existing marriage, age, parents, money, schooling, or other sociocultural factors do not hinder or prevent it.

## Value theory

A value theory of mate selection suggests that interpersonal attraction is facilitated when persons share or perceive themselves as sharing similar value orientations. Values define what is good, beautiful, moral, or worthwhile. They are the criteria or conceptions used in evaluating things (including objects, ideas, acts, feelings, and events) as to their goodness, desirability, or merit. Values are not concrete goals of action but are criteria by which goals are chosen.

A value theory of mate selection suggests that when persons share similar values, this in effect validates each person, thus promoting emotional satisfaction and enhancing the means of communication. When a value is directly attacked or is ignored under circumstances that normally call it to attention, those who hold the value are resentful. Because of this emotional aspect it seems reasonable to expect that persons will seek their informal social relations with those who uncritically accept their basic values and, thus, provide emotional security. Such compatible companions are most likely to be those who feel the same way about "important" things, i.e., those who possess similar values. This accounts for the tendency to marry homogamously and explains why friendships (homophily) and marriages involve people with similar social backgrounds.

In brief, the theory posits that: (1) persons with similar backgrounds learn similar values; (2) the interaction of persons with similar values is rewarding, resulting in effective communication and a minimum of tension; and (3) rewards leave each person with a feeling of satisfaction with his or her partner and thus a desire to continue the relationship.

The inverse is equally true. Persons from different backgrounds learn different values; interactions among such persons are less rewarding—they result in feelings of tension and dissatisfaction and little desire to continue the relationship. Suppose, for example, you place a high value on heterosexual dating, marriage, and sexual activity. Holding this value, would you accept as a dating or marriage partner someone who is known to have engaged in homosexual activities? This theory suggests (predicts) that you would not, and research tends to strongly support this very example.[8]

The theory of value consensus helps explain the findings that exist which deal with homogamy, endogamy, propinquity, parental image, or ideal-mate conception. Sharing values brings people together, both spatially and psychologically. Thus a person may want to marry a member of the same religious denomination, for example, because this might be a very important value in and of itself, or because persons who share similar social backgrounds will likely be socialized under similar conditions and consequently develop similar value systems. The same would hold true for other explanations, such as parental image. Since it is parents who are the major socializing agents for most children, it could be expected that a relationship would exist between personal values and values of parents as well as between values desired in a mate and values of parents. Thus it is perhaps not parent image that influences marital choice but rather parent-image influence via the internalization of a set of values.

### Exchange theory

Exchange theory was described briefly in Chapter 2. Also, as mentioned in several instances in the previous and current chapters, the idea of some type of exchange is basic to the mate selection process. Whether it is an exchange of athletic prowess for beauty, or an exchange of sex for money, the central idea is that some type of transaction and bargaining is involved in the mate

---

8. John D. Williams and Arthur P. Jacoby, "The Effects of Premarital Heterosexual and Homosexual Experience on Dating and Marriage Desirability," *Journal of Marriage and the Family* 51 (May 1989): 489–497.

selection process. Prior to 1940, a major contribution of Willard Waller's treatise on the family was his analysis of courtship conduct as bargaining and/or exploiting behavior. In his words: "When one marries he makes a number of different bargains. Everyone knows this and this knowledge affects the sentiment of love and the process of falling in love."[9]

Today it is doubtful that "everyone knows this." The criteria Waller used for exchange have since come under attack but the fact that bargaining takes place in the mate selection process has received further investigation and support.

Articles lend support to mate selection as a process of social exchange.[10] They suggest that few people get something for nothing. And although bargaining may not always take place, some type of social exchange will. The difference between bargaining and exchange is that bargaining implies a certain purposive awareness of the exchange of awards. Bargaining entails the knowledge of what one has to offer and what the other person can get, whereas under a simple exchange this awareness is not always readily apparent.

Exchange theorists argue that the behavior of socialized persons is purposive or goal-oriented and not random. Implicitly this indicates that behavior is rewarded and intended to avoid nonrewarding situations. It also indicates that each party in a transaction will attempt to maximize gains and minimize costs. Over the long run, however, in view of the principle of reciprocity, actual exchanges tend to become equalized. If reciprocity does not exist—that is, nothing is given in return—the relationship will likely terminate. A key factor in exchange theory that may deter or delay a termination of an inequitable exchange is the lack of an alternative to the current relationship. But if an alternative to the current relationship is perceived as superior to the present relationship, one of the partners will terminate the present relationship in favor of the more attractive alternative.

There are perhaps few areas where social exchange appears more evident than in the research dealing with dating and mate selection. In dating, for example, the male may consider sexual intercourse as a desired goal and highly valued reward. To achieve this reward he may have to offer in exchange flattery (my, how beautiful you look tonight), commitment (you are the only one I love), goods (I thought you might enjoy these flowers), and services (let me get you a drink).

The social exchange approach to the explanation of mate selection neither explains how interaction arises nor describes the larger social

9. Willard Waller, *The Family: A Dynamic Interpretation* (New York: Cordon, 1938): 239.

10. James W. Michaels, Alan C. Acock, and John N. Edwards, "Social Exchange and Equity Determinants of Relationship Commitment," *Journal of Social and Personal Relationships* 3 (1986): 161–175; and Rodney M. Cate, Sally A. Lloyd, and Edgar Long, "The Role of Rewards and Fairness in Developing Premarital Relationships," *Journal of Marriage and the Family* 50 (May 1988): 443–452.

environment, rather, it seeks to explain why certain behavioral outcomes take place.

### Sequential theories

Up to this point it should be evident that, although single factors were stressed as significant in the process of mate selection, most explanations take into account factors implied in other explanations. Several writers consciously and intentionally combine or place in sequence selected single factors: role, values, needs, exchanges, and the like. Three of these ideas will be considered briefly: the "filtering" idea of Alan Kerckhoff and Keith Davis,[11] the process or development idea of Charles Bolton[12] and the SVR idea of Bernard Murstein.[13]

*Kerckhoff and Davis*   Kerckhoff and Davis introduce a longitudinal perspective during the mate selection period. They hypothesize that (1) the degree of value consensus is positively related to progress toward a permanent union, and (2) the degree of need complementarity is positively related to progress toward a permanent union.[14]

To test these hypotheses, the authors conducted a longitudinal study of college students who were engaged, pinned, or "seriously attached." The authors considered the degree of consensus in family values, the degree of need complementarity, and the movement of the couple toward a permanent union. They found that value consensus was significantly related to progress in the relationship for only the short-term couples, whereas complementarity was significant for only the long-term couples. They interpreted the finding to indicate a series of "filtering factors" operating in mate selection. Early in the relationship social attributes such as religion, education, and the occupation of the father are in operation. As the relationship continues, a consensus of values becomes significant. Still later in the relationship, complementary needs play an important part. They suggest that the complementary factor is seen later in the relationship due to the unrealistic idealization of the loved ones in the early states of the relationship.

*Bolton*   Bolton sees mate selection as a development of a relationship. Rather than basing mate selection on the personal or social attributes of the specific

11. Alan Kerckhoff and Keith Davis, "Value Consensus and Need Complementarity in Mate Selection," *American Sociological Review* 27 (June 1962): 295–303.

12. Charles Bolton, "Mate Selection as the Development of a Relationship," *Marriage and Family Living* (August 1961): 234–240.

13. Bernard I. Murstein, "Stimulus-Value-Role: A Theory of Marital Choice," *Journal of Marriage and the Family* 32 (August 1970): 465–481; and Bernard I. Murstein, "A Clarification and Extension of the SVR Theory of Dyadic Pairing," *Journal of Marriage and the Family* 49 (November 1987): 929–933.

14. Kerckhoff and Davis, "Value Consensus and Need Complementarity in Mate Selection," p. 366.

individuals involved, mate selection is viewed from the perspective of the development process itself. Like many other explanations of mate selection, endogamous or homogamous factors are included, but unlike many other explanations, mate selection is viewed as a developmental process wherein the interpersonal transactions have their own course of events and one interaction tends to shape another.

This perspective parallels very closely the symbolic interactionist frame of reference described in Chapter 2. At that point, role was viewed in two ways: (1) as a package of behavioral expectations attached to a status, and (2) as the relationship between what we do and what others do with the role or expectations developed in the interaction process. Mate selection is seen to occur in much the same manner as in the second view. That is, the outcome of the interaction of the individuals involved is not mechanically predetermined, but rather, it is the end product of a sequence of interactions characterized by advances and retreats along the paths of available alternatives. In short, the development of love relations is problematic because the product bears the stamp of what goes on between the couple as well as what they are as individuals.[15]

*Murstein*  A third sequential explanation of mate selection is provided by Murstein who sees mate selection as a three-stage sequence involving stimulus-value-role (SVR). These three stages refer to the chronological sequence in the development of the relationship. Social exchange theory is used within each to explain the dynamics of interaction and attraction.

SVR theory holds that in a relatively "free choice" situation, as exists in the United States, most couples pass through three stages before deciding to marry. In the stimulus stage, an individual may be drawn to another based on the perception of his or her own qualities that might be attractive to the other person (e.g., physical attributes, voice, dress, reputation, social standing, etc.). Because initial movement is due primarily to non-interactional cues not dependent on interpersonal interaction, these are categorized as "stimulus" values.

If mutual "stimulus" attraction has occurred between a man and a woman and they are both satisfied, they enter the second stage of "value comparison." This stage involves the appraisal of value compatibility through verbal interaction. They may compare their attitudes toward life, politics, religion, abortion, nuclear energy, or the role of men and women in society and

---

15. Ibid., p. 236. In many ways the dyadic formation theory of Lewis follows the process or developmental idea of Bolton. Lewis posited six pairing processes experienced by dating couples: the achievement by pairs of (1) perceiving similarities, (2) rapport, (3) openness, (4) role-taking accuracy, (5) interpersonal role fit, and (6) dyadic crystallization. *See* Robert A. Lewis, "A Developmental Framework for the Analysis of Premarital Dyadic Formation," *Family Process* 11 (1972): 17–48; and Robert A. Lewis, "A Longitudinal Test of a Developmental Framework for Premarital Dyadic Formation," *Journal of Marriage and the Family* 35 (February 1973): 16–25.

"We met and fell in love at first sight."
"Then why didn't you get married?"
"Oh, we met again and the second sight was different."

in marriage. If, as they discuss these and other areas, they find that they have very similar value orientations, their feelings for one another are likely to develop. Murstein suggests that couples may decide to marry on the basis of stimulus attraction and verbalized value similarity. But for most persons it is important to be able to function in compatible roles, an ability that is not as readily observable as verbalized expressions of views on religion, politics, and the like. For this reason Murstein places the role stage last in his three-stage time sequence leading to marital choice.

The role stage requires the fulfillment of many tasks before the couple is ready to move into marriage. It is not enough to have similar values if each partner is dissatisfied with how the other is perceived in such roles as lover, companion, parent, and housekeeper. The partners must increasingly confide in each other and become more aware of each other's behavior. They must measure their own personal inadequacies and those of their partner. If the couple navigates the three stages successfully, the partners are likely to become a permanent pair (they marry or cohabit), subject to such influences as parents, friends, a job transfer, the entrance of a more attractive partner, and so forth.

While agreement may exist on the importance of a stimulus attraction, value similarity, and role consensus, do these exist in sequence and is there a progression of stages? One test of Murstein's theory provided little support for a sequence of value and role stages; difficulties were encountered in identifying when couples were in a particular stage or when they moved from one to another.[16]

Other sequential ideas exist. For example, Bert N. Adams establishes a series of propositions in summarizing mate selection that include (1) conditions or barriers such as proximity; (2) early attractions such as physical attractiveness, similar interests, disclosure or rapport; (3) deeper attractions such as the development of consensus, personality similarity, lack of unfavorable parental intrusion, empathy, or role compatibility; and (4) a final series of escalators or perpetuators that move the persons toward marriage: defining the other as "right" or "the best I can get."[17]

---

16. Geoffrey K. Leigh, Thomas B. Holman, and Wesley R. Burr, "An Empirical Test of Sequence in Murstein's SVR Theory of Mate Selection," *Family Relations* 33 (April 1984): 225–231.

17. Bert N. Adams, "Mate Selection in the United States: A Theoretical Summarization," in *Contemporary Theories About the Family*, vol. 1, ed. by Wesley R. Burr et al. (New York: The Free Press, 1979): 259–267.

Without exception, each of the sequential theories of mate selection sees the movement toward marriage in terms of a series of changing criteria, stages, or patterned regularities. However, the progression to marriage may not be as orderly as postulated by the proponents of the sequential models. Rodney Cate and co-authors,[18] for example, identify alternative pathways to marriage and suggest that existing models represent an overly simplistic view of the mate-selection or heterosexual-relationship development process. As the course toward marriage was earlier claimed *not* to reside in personality traits or needs, perhaps it does not reside totally on interactional sequential factors either. Factors external to the person or couple (family-kin influence, socioeconomic conditions, community heterogeneity, technological changes, etc.) are likely, from a sociological perspective at least, to be important factors or dimensions in an understanding of the process of changing status from single to married.

## PROCESSES OF STATUS CHANGE: SINGLE TO MARRIED

The mate selection process is the manner in which an individual changes status from single to married or from divorced or widowed to remarried. All human societies have some socially approved and structured procedures to follow in getting married, particularly for the first marriage. Remarriage, an increasingly common event in industrialized societies, appears to have less established norms and procedures for mate selection that may or may not parallel those of the first marriage.[19] A mate selection process that involves the individuals themselves only exists where there is some degree of personal choice in marital partners. As described, where marriages are "arranged" the process generally occurs between kin groups. In any case, it is rare for mate selection processes to exist independently of other institutions such as schools, churches, or business.

In the United States, the mate selection process, particularly for first marriages, is highly youth-centered and competitive. It encompasses a wide range of social relationships prior to marriage that involves an increasing degree of commitment. Writers use different terminology to describe this process but generally it entails a series of stages that may include group activities, casual dating, going steady, being pinned, cohabiting, being engaged,

---

18. Rodney M. Cate, Ted L. Huston, and John R. Nesselroade, "Premarital Relationships: Toward the Identification of Alternative Pathways to Marriage," *Journal of Social and Clinical Psychology* 4 (1986): 3–22; and Rodney M. Cate and James E. Koval, "Heterosexual Relationship Development: Is It Really a Sequential Process?" *Adolescence* 18 (Fall 1983): 507–514.

19. *See:* Roy H. Rodgers and Linda M. Conrad, "Courtship for Remarriages Influences on Family Reorganization after Divorce," *Journal of Marriage and the Family* 48 (August 1986): 767–775; and Kathleen M. O'Flaherty and Laura Workman Eells, "Courtship Behavior of the Remarried," *Journal of Marriage and the Family* 50 (May 1988): 499–506.

or some other type of classification indicating a more binding relationship or a marriage commitment. The flexibility of the system permits this process to be followed once or many times prior to marriage, covering a time span of days to years, and including or omitting one or several of those stages.

Perhaps the mate selection process in the United States can be compared to a male-female game, which has rules, goals, strategies, and counter-strategies.[20] In one sense, playing the game is voluntary since it is not mandatory that everyone play, but it is probably more difficult to avoid than to achieve. In elementary school (or before) parents inquire about boyfriends or girlfriends. As children mature, the pressure from parents, peers, and, usually by now, an internalized self-concept, all encourage getting involved. The goals of the game may simply involve enjoyment, affection, group approval, learning to play better, or getting a mate. Since a double standard exists, females have a different set of rules, norms, and goals than do males.

The social norm for the male in the United States implies that his basic goal in this game is to move the relationship toward sexual intimacy. Even before the first "date" or meeting, a key question is "Will she or won't she?" The extent to which direct or "rapid" approaches are used to answer the question will depend on a wide range of social and interpersonal factors: previous marriage, age, social class, income, religion, beauty, friends, as well as on factors of social exchange: what you have to offer relative to what you want.

The social norm for the female in the United States implies that her basic goal in this game is to move the relationship toward commitment. Even before the first date, key questions might be "Will he ask me out again?" or "Is he a potential husband?" To get the commitment, the female has the responsibility to regulate the progression of the intimacy goal of the male. To get intimacy (sex is a more accurate term at this point), the male must convince the female that she is not like all other girls but is different, unique, and special.

These two norms work reciprocally. Progress toward one calls for progress toward the other. They work together. As commitment increases, intimacy increases and vice versa. Most communication in this game is likely to be in the form of nonverbal cues, signs, gestures, and other symbolic movements.

Suppose the rules are not followed—the male makes no moves toward intimacy or the female makes no moves to halt the intimacy or to get a commitment. The female, after one date, may say to herself or others, "What a nice guy, he really is a gentleman," or the like. Suppose after two, four, or eight dates, he still makes *no* move toward intimacy. Now the female is likely to ask questions such as "What's wrong with him?" or "What's wrong with me?" Suppose the female makes no moves to stop or slow down the intimacy moves

---

20. This idea is an expansion of Waller and Hill's "courtship bargains" and "courtship barter." *See* Willard Waller (revised by Reuben Hill), *The Family: A Dynamic Interpretation* (New York: Holt, Rinehart and Winston, 1951): 160–164.

of the male, or, she makes the initial moves. The game may continue to be played but now under a new set of less traditional rules and conditions.

More extensive analysis of stages for mate selection such as dating, going steady, and getting pinned or engaged can be found in most more "functionally oriented" marriage textbooks. Thus they will be touched upon only briefly at this point.

## Dating

One form of behavior experienced by most persons in the United States, be they young or old, seeking intimate or close relationships, marriage, or remarriage, is dating. Of all the stages of the mate or partner selection process, dating is the one that carries the least commitment in continuing the relationship. Dating has been defined as a U.S. invention that emerged after World War I among college students and other young adults. In most of the world where parents have an extensive involvement in the selection of marriage partners, dating is not a relevant factor to be considered. However, as shifts occur away from family control over the selection of a marriage partner, an increasing amount of emphasis is placed on establishing social structures that permit the persons themselves to interact and get to know one another. In the United States, dating is one of these structural patterns, although certainly not the only one established for purposes of male-female interaction.

The traditional "date"—where the male called a female several days or a week ahead and verbally contracted a time and activity, picked her up at her house, wined and dined her at his expense, took in a movie or social activity, and returned her to her residence prior to the time established by her parents—may be a dying or dead event. Today it seems more likely that dating involves students or youth congregating in groups, evolving into pairs while retaining allegiance to the group, sharing food or entertainment expenses, and engaging in less highly structured and predetermined behaviors. Apart from the student scene, one consequence of the later age at marriage has been the emergence of new forms of partner selection for dating. These include computer matchups, videotape selections, singles clubs, newspaper advertisements, singles bars, and other less formal opportunities for meeting.[21]

The fact that dating is not what it once was does not mean it doesn't exist or is unimportant. It has, however, changed its structure. Sheila Korman,[22] in looking at nontraditional dating behavior, found that while feminists tended to

---

21. Note, for example: Stanley B. Woll and Peter Young, "Looking for Mr. or Ms. Right: Self-presentation in Videodating," *Journal of Marriage and the Family* 51 (May 1989) 483–488; Stanley Woll, "So Many to Choose From: Decision Strategies in Videodating," *Journal of Social and Personal Relationships* 3 (1986): 43–52; and Rosemary Bolig, Peter J. Stein, and Patrick C. McKenry, "The Self-Advertisement Approach to Dating: Male-Female Differences," *Family Relations* 33 (October 1984): 587–592.
22. Sheila K. Korman, "Nontraditional Dating Behavior: Date-Initiation and Date Expense-Sharing Among Feminists and Nonfeminists," *Family Relations* 32 (October 1983): 575–581.

*Functions of heterosexual interaction in dating may range from recreation, friendship, or social recognition with various individuals to a focus on intimacy and a potential cohabitation or marriage agreement with a particular person.*

initiate dates and share dating expenses more than nonfeminists, even the nonfeminists who held traditional beliefs were venturing into these nontraditional forms of heterosexual dating interactions.

Among feminists or nonfeminists, males or females, writers agree that dating fulfills various functions for the individual. Dating may be:

1. *A form of recreation.* It provides entertainment for the individuals and is a source of immediate enjoyment. Since it's something that's fun to do as an end in itself, it carries no future obligations or commitments.
2. *A form of socialization.* It provides an opportunity for individuals of the opposite sex to get to know each other, to learn to adjust to each other, and to develop appropriate techniques of interaction.
3. *A means of status grading and status achievement.* By dating and being seen with persons who are rated "highly desirable" by one's peer group, an individual may raise his or her status and prestige within his or her group.
4. *A form of courtship.* It provides an opportunity for unmarried individuals to associate with each other for the purpose of selecting a mate whom they may eventually marry.

## Bundling as a mate selection process

Bundling is frequently associated with the Amish courtship system. A practice that was started in Northern Europe, brought to America, and practiced in the New England colonial family, bundling has been known to take several forms. The most common was using a bed with a "bundling board." (The bed was divided by a board down the middle.) Under this arrangement a boy and a girl would lie on the bed without undressing. Second was the use of "bundling bags." Under this system, the female got into a large sack with a wax seal at the neck. Obviously, this seal was supposed to remain unbroken. Third, there were also instances recorded where the female's ankles were tied together.

To understand bundling, it must be seen in the context in which it occurred. Among New England families and among the Amish, wood and candles were commodities that required much time and labor. To use these commodities throughout the evening hours would be a waste of materials. Also, where winters are cold and distances of travel are sometimes great, bundling provided an opportunity for the male and female to visit alone without disturbing the rest of the family or using the heat and light commodities. One should also recognize that within the household were likely to be parents, six to fourteen children, and often grandparents and other relatives. Thus the sexual connotations that many people associate with it today were perhaps minimal. Add to this the rigid sexual codes that existed and one should get a relatively accurate picture of bundling in its social context. This subject has been widely exploited by the popular press; however, it is not known that bundling exists today among the Amish.

The primary reasons for dating and the functions the date fulfills influence the dating role.[23] In other words, it could be expected that persons who date for recreation will behave differently from those who date for socialization, status achievement, or mate selection. For example, emotional involvement, sexual intimacy, exclusivity of the relationship, who pays the bills, or discussions of future plans could be expected to differ depending on if the motive for dating is to have something to do, to be "seen with" a prestigious person, or to find a husband or wife. It could be expected that the person who is more emotionally involved and more committed to the relationship will be hurt most if the relationship ends. It could be expected that the person with the lower status or prestige will have less say (power) in what interactions and activities occur.

This idea parallels that of Waller more than fifty years ago, in what he termed **the principle of least interest**.[24] He observed that seldom are both persons in a dating relationship equally interested in continuing the relationship. Since both parties are not equally emotionally involved, if the dating were terminated, it would be more traumatic for one than for the other. Thus, essentially, the principle of least interest says that the person who is less

---

23. Note, for example: Bruce Roscoe, Mark S. Diana, and Richard H. Brooks, II, "Early, Middle, and Late Adolescents' Views on Dating and Factors Influencing Partner Selection," *Adolescence* 22 (Spring 1987): 59–68.

24. Waller, "The Family: A Dynamic Interpretation," p. 275.

interested in continuing the dating relationship is in a position to dominate, and possibly exploit, the other party.

This principle may also suggest a factor involved in the continuation or breakup of a relationship. If an imbalance or unequal interest exists, it would suggest difficulty in continuation and further development of a relationship. Consistent with exchange theory, when a perception of equity does not exist in what one is receiving relative to what one is giving, the relationship is more likely to end or result in a power imbalance where one can dominate the other. This principle, by the way, may not only apply to dating interactions but to friendships or marriages as well.

### Steady dating, going with someone, or being pinned

In the mate selection process, it is highly typical that most adolescents make the move from an uncommitted relationship to a premarital relationship that involves some commitment to one another and an exclusion of others. Irrespective of the term used, whether *going steady, steady dating, going with someone, being pinned,* or any other, societies that permit the individuals themselves to choose their spouses need some device for individuals to lessen the open competition with others and at the same time provide anticipatory socialization for the marital role. Opportunities are needed to focus in on the "field of eligibles," to get to know what is expected of self and others, and to get to know someone better without a major commitment or norm of permanence attached to the relationship. Steady dating or "going with someone" fills the gap between recreational or dalliance dating and engagement or marriage.

The functions filled by this form of interaction are highly similar to those described under dating. They may provide recreation, socializing experiences, status achievement, or selection of a mate. The specific patterns of activity or meanings attached to the relationship may vary considerably from one context to another.

On college campuses, over the past few decades, a series of terms (*pinned, pearled, lavaliered,* etc.) and a variation of meanings were available to categorize relationships as perhaps more serious than steady dating but with less commitment than engagement. Perhaps the best known of these arrangements was that of pinning. The custom involved a gift of the male's fraternity or dormitory pin to the female. The pin was considered a temporary gift and was returned to the male in case the pair broke up. Pinning was one means of publicly announcing to the campus community that the couple had a commitment to one another. In many instances, the commitment may have been little more serious than steady dating, whereas others may have defined it as similar to engagement.

### Engagement

Engagement in some form has existed in almost every society in the world. Since marriage is seldom taken lightly, most societies have provided some

## Planning a wedding? Check out the folkways.

Somewhere I've read or heard that more marriages occur in December than in June; nevertheless, given their druthers, few prospective brides would turn down the sixth month if opportunity beckoned.

Why? Possibly because June is conceived as a sunny month, and, indeed, "happy the bride the sun shines on today." Further, if the wedding day be Wednesday or if the dates of June 1, 3, 11, 19, or 21 be feasible, the chances for a happy marriage are very good.

And why not a rainy day? No bride, of course, would wish to have her wedding dress ruined, but there's more to it than that. After all, raindrops are a symbol for tears: so many raindrops, so many tears in a marriage.

In addition, there is the matter of the blue sky on a sunny day—the color of the heavens and thus a divine assurance of good luck. Thus also the in-clusion of "something blue" in the couplet, "Some-thing old, something new/Something borrowed, something blue."

The idea of blue for good luck also carries over into possible early conception: it may also bring the fortune of a male child to the couple. Can this be the basic reason the young male is first dressed in blue?

Many other superstitions surround the custom of marriage, the why of each often forgotten with time.

Generally the bride should effect no color other than a touch of blue, since white (representing inno-cence and purity) is the traditional garb.

Neither should the bride wear pearls, for these, like raindrops symbolize tears.

Silk should be the bride's first choice of mate-rial for her gown, for satin and velvet are deemed unlucky. Bridesmaids, on the other hand, have much more freedom of choice as to color and material, though the luckiest colors are supposed to be blue, pink and gold.

Red and green are frowned on, the first being associated with blood and the second with jealousy (unless, of course, one is Irish).

A veil is absolutely necessary for the bride to protect her from the evil eye or from evil spirits, who, finding her attractive, might try to carry her away. As a matter of fact some say the reason the bridesmaids were originally included in the wedding ceremony was to help protect the bride.

Incidentally, when after the ceremony the groom raises the veil in order to kiss the bride, she is supposed to muster up a few tears—of joy or triumph. Otherwise she is reserving tears to be spread throughout her married life.

The throwing of rice on the married couple as they leave the church is a time-honored fertility exercise, and occasionally one also sees an old shoe tossed after the couple as a guarantee of both fertil-ity and happiness.

More often than not, however, shoes are tied to the wedding car, along with pots, pans and other symbols of the married state.

As for the cutting of the wedding cake, the custom of the bride and groom cutting the first slice together results from its symbolizing the sharing of all things in their marriage.

In fact, should the groom attempt the cutting by himself, he may be facing the possibility of a childless marriage.

The best part of the wedding cake ceremony, however, is reserved for the young, unmarried female attendants. Rather than eat their cake, they must sleep with it under their pillows.

An absolute guarantee of sweet dreams and a vision of their own future mates!

*Source:* Rogers Whitener, "Folkways" *Watauga Democrat* (May 29, 1989): 14A.

social structure to instill an awareness in the couple and the community that the relationship is a serious one and that marriage will likely occur. In many societies engagement is considered extremely important and much more binding than it is in the Western world today. Since it implies the final transition in the process of changing status from single to married, and since it involves a transfer from dating availability to dating exclusiveness, various rituals, gifts, and interactions occur to implant in the minds of the couple and the public the importance of the relationship.

Engagement serves a variety of functions for both the couple and society. For the couple, it provides a clear indication that marriage is about to occur. Due to the exclusive nature of the relationship, personal and interpersonal testing can continue with less threat from competitive forces. A more thorough awareness of marital-role expectations, value consensus or dissensus, and future aspirations can be examined. It provides the final opportunity prior to the legal union for each person to understand himself or herself in relation to the partner. It is likely that many couples view an engagement as a kind of trial marriage, including total sexual intimacy, the sharing of certain financial obligations, and in some instances living together (note the nonmarital cohabitation section that follows).

Engagement also provides the function of making public the plans of the couple. This can best be seen by the placement of the female's or couple's picture in community newspapers. In colonial days the announcement was accomplished by the posting of *banns*. A number of days or weeks prior to the marriage, a public notice of intent to marry would be published, posted at key locations in the community, and announced in the churches. In the smaller folk- or gemeinschaft-like communities characterized by a sense of solidarity and a common identity, the word traveled quickly and the community served as a key force in the binding of the relationship. Today, in our urbanized societies, it could be questioned how significant the formal newspaper announcement is in making public the plans and applying community pressures upon the couple.

An engagement ring, like a public announcement, serves the purpose of enabling the female to publicly and continuously display her symbol of commitment. The ring, which involves a financial commitment on the part of the male (and sometimes on the part of the female), symbolizes the seriousness of the relationship and the intent of a forthcoming marriage. In a time of calling for equality between the sexes, perhaps the time is near when the male will expect an engagement ring as well. At least one article has suggested that the emergence of a groomal shower, a male variation of the traditional female bridal shower, is a reflection of our changing attitudes toward marriage and an indication of some movement toward greater egalitarianism.[25]

## NONMARITAL HETEROSEXUAL COHABITATION

Is it possible that mate selection in the 1990s is not marriage-oriented, is not oriented toward a single partner, and does not stress permanence? Is it

---

25. Felix M. Berardo and Herman Vera, "The Groomal Shower: A Variation of the American Bridal Shower," *Family Relations* 30 (July 1981): 395–401.

possible that a decrease in a double sexual standard will totally eliminate the male-female sex game described earlier? Is it possible that dating, pinning, and engagement are premarital structural arrangements only significant as historical phenomena? Or are we simply witnessing major modifications in, and additional alternatives to, traditional mate selection and marriage process?

An alternative to marriage and an increasingly prevalent nonmarital arrangement is nonmarital cohabitation, unmarried couple households, living together, or consensual unions. These involve a situation where a man and a woman who are not married to each other, neither by ceremony nor by common law, occupy the same dwelling. The arrangement, among the young or the old, may or may not be marriage-oriented; may be the beginning of a long-range life-style or be for short-term convenience; may or may not involve an intimate, unrestricted sexual union; and may or may not include the knowledge of parents among youths or perhaps the knowledge of the children among older people.

The extent to which, for all practical purposes, nonmarital cohabitors are married couples minus a legal marital document could be questioned. One way to answer this is to note if these relationships, like dating, serve functions such as recreation, socialization, status grading, or selecting a marriage partner or if they serve functions of marriage such as procreation, exclusive sexual intimacy, extension of a kin network, economic partnership, tension management, or socialization of children. Maybe what exists today is a large number of nonmarried marrieds. Let's examine these couples: their prevalence, how they differ from noncohabitants, some consequences of their cohabitation, living together if they are elderly, and legal factors related to their cohabitation.

## The prevalence of nonmarital cohabitation

How prevalent is the living together of persons who are not married to one another? Recent U.S. census reports show some interesting data. The United States has witnessed a dramatic increase in the number of unmarried couples who live together. In 1988 there were about 2.6 million unmarried couple households, a 63 percent increase since 1980 when there were an estimated 1.6 million and about a 500 percent increase since 1970 when there were an estimated 523,000 households of this type.[26] More than two-thirds (69 percent) of the unmarried households in 1988 consisted solely of the two partners, and nearly one-third (31 percent) of the couples had one or more children living with them.

More than one-fourth of the men (28 percent) and one-fifth of the women (20 percent) of all unmarried couple households were under age twenty-five,

---

26. U.S. Bureau of the Census, *Current Population Reports*, Series P-20, no. 433, "Marital Status and Living Arrangements, March 1988" (Washington, D.C.: U.S. Government Printing Office, 1989), Table A-7, p. 63.

43 percent of both sexes were ages twenty-five to forty-three, about one-fourth (25 percent) were ages thirty-five to sixty-four, and about 5 percent of the men and 4 percent of the women were age sixty-five and over. More than half of the adults in unmarried couple households had never been married, more than one-third were divorced, and the others were married but separated (about 7 percent), currently married to someone else (about 1 percent), or widowed (about 7 percent of the women and 3 percent of the men.[27]

Another way to examine the prevalence of nonmarital cohabitation is to look at married couples who have cohabited with each other prior to their marriage. This approach, rather than counting the unmarried couple households, counts the marriages in which the unmarried couple established a household prior to the marriage. This perspective places cohabitation in the sequence of a couple's relationship from dating to marriage. This was done in Oregon by checking all marriage licenses in one county for 1970 and 1980.[28] Couples were coded as cohabiting if they supplied identical home addresses on their application. In 1973, 13 percent gave identical home addresses. By 1980, the percentage cohabiting increased to 53 percent. The author, Patricia Gwartney-Gibbs, suggests that when over half of a marrying population cohabits premaritally, as was the case in her study, it signals that a new normative pattern in courtship and marriage rituals may be emerging. Cohabitation prior to marriage may indeed become institutionalized as a new step between dating and marriage for many couples.

This idea finds support in a study investigating transitions from single life into cohabitation and marriage.[29] Arland Thornton shows that although cohabitation without marriage is experienced by many people, it is also a transitional state toward marriage for a large proportion of people. Many cohabiting unions were dissolved and many others were transformed into marital unions. Koray Tanfer as well,[30] in studying single women in their twenties, suggests that cohabitation does not appear to be a permanent replacement for marriage or a long-range life-style. It seems to be a new dimension and a part of the courtship process.

As the data indicate, unmarried couple households are not an exclusive domain of youth and college students. In fact, 118,000 men and 96,000 women in the United States over age sixty-five were living in a two-person household with an unrelated adult of the opposite sex. But the large increases exist primarily among the young and much of the available information comes from college student populations.

---

27. Ibid., Table A-8, p. 64.

28. Patricia A. Gwartney-Gibbs, "The Institutionalization of Premarital Cohabitation: Estimates from Marriage License Applications, 1970 and 1980," *Journal of Marriage and the Family* 48 (May 1986): 423–434.

29. Arland Thornton, "Cohabitation and Marriage in the 1980s," *Demography* 25 (November 1988): 497–508.

30. Koray Tanfer, "Patterns of Premarital Cohabitation among Never-Married Women in the United States," *Journal of Marriage and the Family* 49 (August 1987): 483–497.

## Josie recommends nonmarital cohabitation

Josie is a 30-year-old undergraduate student at Wayne State University. She was raised in a devout Catholic family, got married at age 20, divorced at age 27, moved back to her parents' home for two years, then, over a year ago moved in with Joe. Was that a good idea for her, and would she recommend it to others? In her words:

"Cohabitation is definitely a good idea before you get married. You get a clearer idea about someone when you see them morning, noon, and night rather than on an occasional evening and weekend. In many ways I'm very traditional. I do all the housework and cooking but I want to work full time when I finish school. Joe accepts that but he'd be just as happy with me in the traditional housewife role.

"I guess I'm very traditional in my commitment to Joe. I wouldn't even consider going out with or sleeping with anyone else, although I did go to bed with several men after my divorce. But now I'm really committed to Joe and would be badly hurt if he went out with someone else. I know he feels the same. I love him and know he loves me.

"We have thought about marriage but I don't believe that would change much. The only reason I can think of for marrying is that it might be a statement on the part of each of us of the trust we really have for each other. Sometimes I feel that my life is secondary to his, less important, since he's earning all the money. But I saved quite a bit from when I worked full time before I went back to school. Since I have a merit scholarship and he pays all the groceries, I don't see anything changing with marriage. I don't ask him for money now and don't think I could any easier if we were married.

"Joe's really a great guy. Unlike my ex-husband, we can talk openly about anything. For example, my ex-husband would never talk about sex—what I liked or how I felt—and he never seemed to hear me or give any expression of hearing. Now it's so different. For me, physical pleasure isn't enough. I must feel strongly about someone and be able to communicate and share openly with them.

"I really believe God led me to Joe. He's all I ever could want in a guy—warm, affectionate, expressive, willing to talk, caring. We might marry someday but he brings it up more than I do. I like living with him and don't see how marriage would improve anything. So for now, I'm happy with things as they are."

Unmarried cohabitation is not unique to the United States. Jan Trost reports that in Sweden all those persons married and younger than thirty had cohabited prior to marriage and more than half of all cohabitants age twenty to twenty-four were unmarried.[31] He estimated that in Iceland, two-thirds of all persons marrying had lived together before marriage. In Norway, Finland, Denmark, and the Netherlands from 5 to 10 percent of all cohabiting couples were unmarried.

### Comparing cohabiting and noncohabiting couples

Eleanor Macklin, in an overview of the literature, compared cohabiting couples with married couples and noncohabiting engaged or going steady couples.[32]

---

31. Jan Trost, "Cohabitation in the Nordic Countries: From Deviant Phenomenon to Social Institution," *Alternative Lifestyles* 4 (November 1981): 401–427.

32. Eleanor D. Macklin, "Nonmarital Heterosexual Cohabitation: An Overview," in Eleanor D. Macklin and Roger H. Rubin, eds., *Contemporary Families and Alternative Lifestyles* (Beverly Hills: Sage Publications, 1983): 49–74.

She found that nonmarried cohabitants indicate significantly less commitment than do married couples. When compared with engaged couples, the unmarried cohabitants tended to be as committed to their partners and to the relationship but less committed to the idea of marrying their partner.

In regard to a division of labor, it was noted that cohabiting couples tended to mirror the society around them and engage in sex-role behavior characteristic of other couples their age. The same was true for exclusivity. While most believed in sexual freedom within the relationship, most voluntarily restricted their sexual activity as evidence of their commitment to the relationship. In regard to communication, satisfaction, and problems experienced, few differences have been noted between married and unmarried cohabiting couples.

Cohabiting couples were found to have intercourse significantly more frequently than either married women or noncohabitants.[33] In a study of nearly 8,000 women conducted by the National Center for Health Statistics, slightly over 60 percent of all unmarried cohabitants had intercourse either daily or several times a week, compared with 47 percent of married women and about 23 percent of unmarried noncohabitants. However, cohabitants were considerably more likely than noncohabitants to practice contraception, particularly if they had never been married.

In providing a profile of social and economic characteristics of unmarried cohabiting individuals, Spanier notes several items of interest.[34] One, it was more likely for a previously married man to be living with a never-married woman than vice versa. Two, unmarried couples were more likely than married couples to live in metropolitan areas. Three, cohabitation rates among blacks were three times that of whites. Four, unmarried cohabiting men were less likely to be employed and unmarried cohabiting women were more likely to be employed than married men and women respectively. And, five, low income was found to be especially characteristic of unmarried couples.

### Consequences of unmarried cohabitation

Is unmarried cohabitation a cure-all for traditional sex- or gender-role inequality, for creating successful long-term relationships, for lowering divorce or marriage rates, and the like? Apparently not exactly. Rebecca Stafford et al. studied the division of labor in household tasks using matched samples of married and cohabiting college men and women.[35] Both cohabiting groups still divided housework along traditional lines with the women bearing the

33. Christine A. Bachrach, "Cohabitation and Reproductive Behavior in the U.S.," *Demography* 24 (November 1987): 623–637.

34. Graham B. Spanier, "Married and Unmarried Cohabitation in the United States: 1980," *Journal of Marriage and the Family* 45 (May 1983): 277–288.

35. Rebecca Stafford, Elaine Barkman, and Pamela Dibona, "The Division of Labor Among Cohabiting and Married Couples," *Journal of Marriage and the Family* 39 (February 1977): 43–57.

## Trauma for unmarried couples who break up

A psychologist in Colorado studied unmarried couples who were living together and found that breaking up can be as traumatic for them as getting a divorce. The researcher, Kitty Mika, said that unmarried couples often say they are living together because they're not ready for marriage but may be kidding themselves about how easily they can withdraw from such a relationship.

Fifty persons were interviewed who had been involved in live-in relationships that didn't work. All the respondents were over twenty-one and had recently broken up with their live-in lovers.

The men and women reacted differently to the end of a live-in relationship. Women seemed to fall apart initially and look better later. Men were still suffering two years later. After the separation, the women showed emotional turmoil, while the men seemed happy until you talked with them.

Ms. Mika suggests that it's a good idea to look at what you're doing before you do it. You can get pretty attached to people, even when you don't expect to.

*Source:* Based on data supplied in an Associated Press article.

---

brunt of the labor. Compared to their parental generation, the young men were sharing the dishes and laundry more and the young women were sharing the lawn mowing and home repairs more. But women in both the married and unmarried groups still took most of the responsibility for and performed most of the household tasks. Apparently unmarried cohabitation is not a cure for gender inequality.

Does establishing an unmarried couple household provide a basis for a successful long-term relationship or make for a better marriage? One study examining the relationship between cohabitation and subsequent marital quality found that having cohabited premaritally was associated with significantly lower perceived quality of communication for wives and significantly lower marital satisfaction for both spouses.[36] Part of this effect was accounted for by differences between cohabitors and noncohabitors on sex-role traditionalism, church attendance, and other sociocultural variables but even after controlling for such differences the cohabitors still exhibited lower marital satisfaction for both husbands and wives. These types of data do not lend support to the contentions that cohabitation serves as an effective training period for marriage or that it results in improved mate selection.

Similar results come from other studies of national samples in both the U.S. and Sweden. Alan Booth and David Johnson, in a national sample of over 2,000 married persons in the United States, reject the idea that cohabitation improves mate selection and marital training.[37] They state that cohabitation is

---

36. Alfred DeMaris and Gerald R. Leslie, "Cohabitation with the Future Spouse: Its Influence upon Marital Satisfaction and Communication," *Journal of Marriage and the Family* 46 (February 1984): 77–84.

37. Alan Booth and David Johnson, "Premarital Cohabitation and Marital Success," *Journal of Family Issues* 9 (June 1988): 255–272.

negatively related to marital interaction and positively related to marital disagreement and proneness to divorce. Some support was found for the explanation that some of those who cohabit are poor risks before they marry. While the authors claim they found no support for the idea that cohabitation itself causes a decline in marital quality, they cannot reject this argument with confidence based on their data.

In Sweden as well, a national sample of nearly 5,000 women produced results indicating that women who cohabited premaritally had almost 80 percent higher marital dissolution rates than those who did not.[38] Those who cohabited for over three years had over 50 percent higher dissolution rates than women who cohabited for shorter periods. With increased marital duration the difference in dissolution rates between cohabitors and noncohabitors decreased with no differences found among those whose marriages remained intact for eight years. The conclusion strongly suggests a weaker commitment to the institution of marriage on the part of those who cohabit premaritally.

Why is cohabitation related to less marital stability and higher rates of marital dissolution? Cohabitors as a poorer risk for marriage in the first place was already mentioned. In addition, perhaps cohabiting couples are more committed to personal independence than are married couples. This commitment is reflected in data that show a lower likelihood of pooling income, jointly owning property, and sharing activities. Cohabiting couples are less likely to expect the male to assume the role of provider and to think monogamy is important.

Given the extremely high frequency of unmarried cohabitation in Sweden and the tremendous increases taking place in the United States, it obviously provides functions that are viewed as being positive and of value. Among other factors, for many couples it provides a financially practical condition, a warm, homelike atmosphere, more privacy than a dormitory or co-operative housing arrangement, easy access to a sexual partner, an intimate interpersonal relationship, a nonlegal, nonpermanent, nonbinding union, and a form of trial marriage. At this point it appears to be an institutionalized life-style for a temporary time period. The great majority of both cohabitants and noncohabitants desire to marry at some point in the future.

### Cohabitation among the elderly

It was stated earlier that more than 200,000 persons (1988 figures) over the age of sixty-five are living in unmarried couple households. Since 1970, the proportion of unmarried couples involving persons age sixty-five and over has

---

38.  Neal G. Bennett, Ann Klimas Blanc, and David E. Bloom, "Commitment and the Modern Union: Assessing the Link between Premarital Cohabitation and Subsequent Marital Stability," *American Sociological Review* 53 (February 1988): 127–138.

declined significantly, while the number has remained relatively constant. In 1970, they numbered about 115,000 couples representing 22 percent of the total. By the late 1980s they numbered about the same, but represented less than 5 percent of all unmarried couple households. The negligible change in number and the significant change in proportion of cohabiting older persons is noteworthy given the significant increase in the elderly population. This may be explained by changes in Social Security regulations which make remarriage more practical for the elderly unmarried, or by the large increase in young or unmarried couples who choose to live together.

The advantages of nonmarital cohabitation for older persons are likely to be similar to those for college-aged and younger persons: companionship, financial savings, sexual gratification, and the like. Two areas in which older persons may differ from younger ones might include: (1) greater disapproval from their age cohort in general and their friends and associates in particular, and (2) interference in their relationships with their children and grandchildren. This may be a fruitful area for research.

## Cohabitation and the law

It has been suggested that family law is undergoing a more rapid rate of change in substance and procedure than any other area of the law. Note for example the legal concerns surrounding male alimony, test-tube babies, surrogate motherhood, embryo transplants, abortion, contraceptives for minors, rights of illegitimate children, joint custody, spousal immunity, or divorce kits for the "do-it-yourselfer." Beyond these are the issues related to unmarried cohabitation.[39] The legal controversy becomes acute when one partner dies or the couple separates. At this point problems tend to arise in the areas of real and personal property, insurance, wills, estates, and child custody. The legal rights, particularly for women and children, are unclear. Traditionally, an unmarried woman who intentionally lived with an unmarried man acquired no property rights. If she contributed any service, she was not entitled to recover an interest in resulting property. Similar situations existed for children. They were considered illegitimate and on the death of the father received no financial or property benefits.

Within the past decade there appears to be a trend toward increasingly granting legal protection for the "spouse" and the children of cohabitants.[40] In 1973, a California appellate court held that a meretricious spouse (one

---

39. Charles F. Crutchfield, "Nonmarital Relationships and Their Impact on the Institution of Marriage and the Traditional Family Structure," *Journal of Family Law* 19 (1980–81): 247–261; and F. Patrick Hubbard and Mary Johnson Larsen, "Contract Cohabitation: A Jurisprudential Perspective on Common Law Judging," *Journal of Family Law* 19 (1980–81): 655–706.

40. Lenore J. Weitzman et al., "Contracts for Intimate Relationships: A Study of Contracts, Within, and in Lieu of Legal Marriage," *Alternate Lifestyles* 1 (August 1978): 303–378; and Lenore J. Weitzman, *The Marriage Contract: Spouses, Lovers, and the Law* (New York: The Free Press, 1981).

who is intentionally living with a person of the opposite sex and is unmarried) had the same property rights as a married person. Three years later, in the much publicized case of Michelle and Lee Marvin who had an alleged oral contract at the beginning of their seven-year nonmarital relationship, the California Supreme Court set a precedent by defining the value of the woman's services for the purpose of property settlement. This decision also recognized the validity of an oral contract between cohabitants by making it legally binding upon both parties. A similar trend seems to be occurring for children born of cohabiting nonmarried parents. In 1972 a Supreme Court decision found the Social Security Act to be discriminatory against illegitimate children in the payment of death benefits. Another court held a father responsible for child support. Decisions such as these have reduced but not eliminated the negative legal consequences of cohabitation for adults or children. Wide variation exists in state laws and most states have not defined the rights of cohabitants or their children.

## SUMMARY

1. The processes followed in mate selection vary widely from one society to another, ranging from totally arranged marriages to limited "freedom of choice." The difference is centered in who is making the choice.

2. A range of explanations exists as to who selects whom and why. At one extreme are individualistic explanations with the answers rooted in instincts, genetic similarity, needs, drives, parental images, and complementary needs. In contrast are sociocultural explanations with the answers rooted in norms, roles, values, and social exchanges.

3. Sociocultural explanations operate at a more conscious level, are more readily testable, and have greater research support than individualistic explanations. These, too, are not fully adequate to explain mate selection, but they do appear to be more fruitful. One sociocultural theory involves roles—the internalized, learned, social expectations as to what attitudes and behavior are appropriate or inappropriate in the selection of a mate. In brief, the couple likely to marry is the male and female who share similar role definitions and expectations.

4. Closely related to role theory is the idea that interpersonal attraction is facilitated when persons share or perceive themselves as sharing similar value orientations. This sharing of values, in effect, validates one's self and thus promotes emotional satisfaction and enhances the means of communication.

5. Exchange theorists view mate selection as a bargaining or social-exchange process. While not explaining how interaction arises, the theory does explain the behavioral outcomes. The mate selection choice is based on the selection of persons who share equivalent resources, each having something to offer that is desired by the other. Relationships may continue in unequal exchanges if no better alternative to that relationship is perceived.

6. Some writers see mate selection as the result of several of these processes operating simultaneously or sequentially. One explanation involves a series of "filtering factors." Another sequential explanation sees mate selection as a developmental

process of interactions between individuals, the outcome of which is not mechanically predetermined but is the end product of a sequence of events along the paths of available alternatives. A third sequential explanation involves a three-stage chronological sequence involving stimulus, value, and role (SVR).

7. The mate selection process is the manner in which an individual changes status from single to married. The process involves all sorts of rules and roles applicable to male-female interaction. Generally, it involves a series of types of dating that fulfills a variety of functions and leads to increasing degrees of intimacy and commitment such as steady dating and engagement.

8. Finally, consideration was given in this chapter to unmarried heterosexual cohabitation, unmarried couple households, living together, or consensual unions. Descriptive data were provided to indicate prevalence; a comparison was made between cohabiting and noncohabiting couples; and some of the consequences of unmarried cohabitation were examined. Brief attention was devoted to cohabitation among the elderly and cohabitation and the law. While certain legal and social difficulties may result, the rapid increase in unmarried heterosexual cohabitation represents an attractive life-style, even if temporary, for couples of all ages.

9. This chapter and the previous one provided an overview of selected structural characteristics, functions of and processes involved in the selection of mates. Examined were selected types of endogamous and exogamous marriages as well as various explanations as to why certain mate choices occur. Although the male-female sexual relationship is generally an important dimension to consider in understanding mate selection, only minimal attention was given to it.

10. Sexual relationships, of significance to marriage and the family throughout the world, are more fully analyzed and described in Chapters 10 and 11. Chapter 10, on nonmarital sexual standards and relationships, further enhances an understanding of this and the previous chapter on mate selection. Attention is now directed to sexual norms and relationships.

## KEY TERMS AND TOPICS

## DISCUSSION QUESTIONS

1. Would there be any advantages for young people to have their marriage arranged for them? Would the consequences in marriage be different? How?

2. To what extent was or is your mate likely to be a result of instincts, innate drives, parental image, or complementary needs?

3. In spite of the logical and rational basis of the

theory of complementary needs, why is there so little empirical support for it?

4. In what ways is role theory consistent or inconsistent with homogamy and value and sequential theories?

5. List a number of role expectations that you hold for yourself and your spouse. Have a dating partner do the same. Then on a rating scale of one to five indicate whether you agree or disagree with the expectations. Compare and discuss the results. Examples: "I expect the male should do the laundry." "I expect the female to see that the children get religious training." "Both the husband and wife should be employed full-time."

6. What do you value most? Could you marry anyone who did not share these values? Why?

7. To what extent is the portrayal of the male-female game in the mate selection process an accurate one?

8. Recall your own past love affairs or those of your friends. Is the "principle of least interest" applicable? How was it manifested?

9. How do you explain the increase in cohabitation as well as its seemingly negative relationship to future marital satisfaction?

10. What advantages or disadvantages of cohabitation exist for males in contrast to females, for youth in contrast to the elderly, or in verbal contracts in contrast to legal, written ones? Review some of the legal implications of cohabitation. Should it be viewed and treated as a marital relationship?

## FURTHER READINGS

Adams, Bert N. "Mate Selection in the United States: A Theoretical Summarization." Vol. 1. *Contemporary Theories About the Family.* Edited by Wesley R. Burr et al. New York: The Free Press, 1979: 259–267. An attempt to develop propositions and a theoretical model on who married whom.

Cancian, Francesca M. *Love in America: Gender and Self-development.* New York: Cambridge University Press, 1987. An investigation of the history of love and the emergence in the twentieth century of an androgynous love that combines love and self-development and gives both partners responsibility for the relationship.

Douglas, Jack D., and Atwell, Freda Cruse. *Love, Intimacy and Sex.* Newbury Park, Ca.: Sage Publications, Inc., 1988. An effort at establishing a systematic scientific model of love including its major dimensions and their interdependencies.

Eekelar, John M., and Katz, Sanford N., eds. *Marriage and Cohabitation in Contemporary Societies.* Toronto: Butterworth and Company, 1980. An international and interdisciplinary overview of areas of legal, social, and ethical issues surrounding cohabitation and marriage.

Eshleman, J. Ross, and Clarke, Juanne N. *Intimacy, Commitments and Marriage: Development of Re-lationships.* Boston: Allyn and Bacon, 1978. A look at the process of becoming a human being, the development of relationships, and variations in commitments throughout the life cycle.

Lasky, Judith F., and Silverman, Helen W., eds. *Love: Psychoanalytic Perspectives.* New York: New York University Press, 1988. A collection of sixteen papers presented at a conference on love, covering topics such as what love is, falling and being in love, sibling relationships, fantasies, and the self.

Macklin, Eleanor D. "Nonmarital Heterosexual Cohabitation: An Overview." In Eleanor D. Macklin and Roger H. Rubin, eds., *Contemporary Families and Alternative Lifestyles.* Beverly Hills: Sage Publications, 1983: 49–74. A comprehensive overview of cohabitation among the unmarried covering its prevalence, the nature of relationships, their characteristics, a comparison with noncohabiting couples, and the effects of cohabitation.

Mullan, Bob. *The Mating Trade.* London: Routledge and Kegan Paul, 1984. A cross-national look at topics ranging from choosing partners from arranged marriages in Jewish and Japanese cultures to contemporary mating industries, such as computer and videodating.

Murstein, Bernard I. *Paths to Marriage.* Newbury

Park, Cal.: Sage Publications, 1986. A concise theoretical and research-oriented work on marital choice, including historical, sociocultural, developmental and tactical determinants.

Rubin, Lillian B. *Just Friends: The Role of Friendship in Our Lives*. New York: Harper and Row, 1985. While not a book on mate selection, it is a clear expression of friendship relationships between women, men, women and men, couples, families, and kin.

Spanier, Graham B. "Married and Unmarried Cohabitation in the United States: 1980." *Journal of Marriage and the Family* 45 (May 1983): 277–288.

Data from the March 1980 Current Population Survey are used to contrast married couples living together with unmarried heterosexual cohabitors. Provides an excellent look at trends as well as a profile of the social and economic characteristics of cohabitors.

Waller, Willard. *The Family: A Dynamic Interpretation*. New York: Holt, Rinehart and Winston, 1951. (Revised by Reuben Hill. Originally published by Cordon in 1938.) One of the classical early textbooks on the family, taking a look at the personal interactive aspects of marriage and the family.

# CHAPTER TEN

# *S*EXUAL RELATIONSHIPS IN PREMARITAL AND NONMARITAL CONTEXTS

© Frank Siteman MCMLXXXI.

Few topics occupy as much widespread attention and thought as do matters relating to sex, both as a social and as a personal phenomenon. The significance of sex in modern life is evidenced by the recent controversies centering around abortion, gay liberation, sex education in the public schools, pornographic literature, X-rated movies, the availability of contraceptives to adolescents, and the general concern over sexual identity and male-female roles, to mention a few.

Ira Reiss, in a sociological analysis of human sexuality, defines sexuality as erotic and genital responses produced by the cultural scripts of a society.[1] He suggests that sexuality is universal in that everywhere it is viewed as important and in need of societal regulation of some sort. The basic reason for this importance is that it encompasses the elements of physical pleasure and self-disclosure. These are crucial elements in forming relationships in a society, sexual or otherwise.

All societies have social norms that grant approval to certain sexual behaviors and disapproval to others. Perhaps the most universal taboo on sexual behavior relates to incest; the most universal approval is granted to sexual behavior in marriage (both are discussed in Chapter 11). Clearly, no society grants unrestricted sexual liberties: all societies control sexuality. John DeLamater[2] and Christie Davies[3] both argue that social institutions, primarily family and religion, are the source of both general perspectives and specific norms that govern sexual expression. In the United States, for example, the Judeo-Christian doctrine embodies a procreational orientation toward sex. Acts that have no reproductive value such as masturbation, sodomy (anal, oral, bestiality), or homosexuality are taboo and sinful, as are activities that threaten the family unit such as incest and adultery. The family plays a primary role in the regulation and control of sexual conduct through the socialization process, controlling who marries whom and providing negative sanctions when sexual norms are violated.

Processes of controlling sexuality take many forms. Some societies attempt to enforce norms of chastity by secluding single girls. Some provide escorts or duennas when girls are with the opposite sex in public. Ethnic and subcultural differences regulate sexual matters by a lifelong process of instilling sexual norms into the consciousness of the members within that ethnic group.

The stratification system also serves to regulate sexual expression. Class and caste systems operate both to separate groups geographically as well as to

1. Ira L. Reiss, *Journey into Sexuality: An Exploratory Voyage* (Englewood Cliffs, N.J.: Prentice-Hall, 1986), p. 37.

2. John DeLamater, "The Social Control of Sexuality," *Annual Review of Sociology* 7 (1981): 263–290.

3. Christie Davies, "Sexual Taboos and Social Boundaries," *American Journal of Sociology* 87 (March 1982): 1032–1063.

define appropriate or inappropriate sexual partners. Sex is also highly regulated by the statuses we occupy. Males may behave differently from females in many situations, priests behave differently from school teachers, divorcees behave differently from married persons, and grandparents behave differently from grandchildren.

Most societies use the reproductive cycle to regulate sex. Taboos may be placed against sexual intercourse during pregnancy, during the menstrual period, immediately following childbirth, or through the period of lactation. Special events also serve to regulate sex. Intercourse may be required or forbidden during times of certain festivities, religious ceremonies, weddings, harvest time, or the like. Quite clearly, there are no societies which do not use various means to regulate and control the sexual behavior of their members.

Sexual control may be indicated by the forms of sexual outlet granted social approval, availability or both to members of a given society. Certain societies display pornography openly, whereas others prosecute those who sell or display this type of literature. Some societies have burlesque movie houses; others forbid them. While the most approved sexual outlet occurs in marriage, the norms of most societies discourage practices such as rape, child molesting, bestiality, voyeurism, prostitution, homosexuality, group sex, and the like.

In our own society, as well as in virtually all others, the primary and most pervasive sexual interest is with heterosexual behavior and relationships, both marital and nonmarital. These relationships generally refer to far more than simply coitus or sexual intercourse. They may include overt acts such as kissing, petting, and the like but also are likely to include attitudes, social values, and norms appropriate to the acts.

Many distinctions can be made in classifying heterosexual relationships. Most often they involve one male and one female, but multiple partners are at times involved. They may involve persons who are not married but whose relationship is marriage-oriented (premarital). They may involve persons who are not married and to whom marriage is not a factor (nonmarital). They may involve a husband and wife (marital). They may involve a married person with a partner other than his or her spouse (extramarital). They may involve a sexual exchange of married partners (swinging or wife/husband swapping). They may involve divorced or widowed persons who were once married but are currently socially and legally single (post-marital). This chapter will examine selected sexual standards and relationships that exist in premarital and nonmarital contexts.

## BIOLOGICAL PREDISPOSITIONS AND PREMARITAL SEXUAL BEHAVIORS

The arguments usually given to explain differing premarital sexual attitudes and behaviors between men and women have, among most sociologists, been credited to socialization and social control factors. Socialization theories explain how sexual attitudes and values are learned. The argument that men and women develop differing sexual scripts explains in large part the different standards for and behaviors of males and females (note the section on sexualization in this chapter). Social control theories assume "everyone wants to do it" and without societal restraints or controls, everyone would engage in socially undesirable (deviant) sexual activity. The fact that social controls exist to regulate sexual activity has already been described at the beginning of this chapter.

But how much of sexual behavior in general and male-female differences more specifically can be credited to biological factors? Considerable data exists to show that men and women appear to be very similar in their needs, drives, and responses. Research findings of Masters and Johnson more than twenty years ago indicated that women have as definite an orgasm as do men and that, in general, women have a greater potential for sexual responsiveness than do men, since they tend to respond faster, more intensely, and longer to sexual stimulation. Aside from obvious anatomical variants, men and women are homogeneous in their physiologic responses to sexual stimuli.[4] Kinsey came to the same conclusion almost fifteen years earlier when he reported:

> The anatomic structures which are most essential to sexual response and orgasm are nearly identical in the human male and female. The differences are relatively few. They are associated with the different functions of the sexes in reproductive processes but they are of no great significance in the origins and development of sexual response and orgasm. If females and males differ sexually in any basic way, those differences must originate in some other aspect of the biology or psychology of the two sexes. They do not originate in any of the anatomic structures which have been considered here.[5]

Ideas such as these led most social scientists to ignore or overlook any biological predispositions to sexual behavior. Biological components, while necessary, were not sufficient to explain or predict values and behaviors. And besides, are not biological factors believed to be the business of biologists, whose theories will not affect the sociologist? J. Richard Udry, a sociologist at the University of North Carolina, does not believe so. With colleagues, he has explored the interplay between biological predispositions and sociological models of adolescent sexuality and he argues that biological components cannot be ignored.[6]

---

4. William H. Masters and Virginia E. Johnson, *Human Sexual Response* (Boston: Little, Brown, 1966), Chapter 17 and p. 285.

5. Alfred C. Kinsey, Wardell B. Pomeroy, Clyde E. Martin, and Paul H. Gebhard, *Sexual Behavior in the Human Female* (Philadelphia: W. B. Saunders, 1953): 593.

6. J. Richard Udry, "Biological Predispositions and Social Control in Adolescent Sexual Behavior," *American Sociological Review* 53 (October 1988): 709–722. *See also:* J. Richard Udry and John O. G. Billy, "Initiation of Coitus in Early Adolescence," *American Sociological Review* 52 (December 1987): 841–855; and J. Richard Udry, Luther M. Talbert, and Naomi M. Morris, "Biosocial Foundations for Adolescent Female Sexuality," *Demography* 23 (1986): 217–230.

## If you can't talk of rock, how can you discuss sex?

This column is about sex. Parental discretion is advised.

[Politicians seem] to be going ahead with a rule requiring that any organization receiving federal funds for dispensing contraceptives to a minor must notify the parents within 10 days of the request.

[Their] heart is in the right place. But trying to put such a rule into effect presents problems. Many parents can't talk with their teenagers about rock music, much less discuss with them the subject of sex.

Let's assume that the Wallingfords have just received a letter from Planned Parenthood, noting that their daughter Sue Anne has requested a prescription for the Pill.

Both are waiting for her when she comes home from school.

"And what were you doing in school?"

"I don't know. I just went to class, and stuff."

"What kind of stuff?" Wallingford yells.

"You know, just stuff. What are you guys all excited about?"

"Are you sure you didn't sneak off in a clothes closet and do it with some boy?"

"Do what? And with what boy?"

"Any boy. We know everything," she says, waving the letter from Planned Parenthood. "So what do you have to say for yourself?"

"I knew if I asked you for permission to buy the Pill you wouldn't give it to me."

"You're damn right we wouldn't give it to you. What kind of parents do you think we are?" Wallingford says.

"I know what kind of parents you are. That's why I went somewhere else to protect myself."

"To protect yourself from what?"

"Having a baby."

"What do you know about having babies?" Mrs. Wallingford says.

"Well, when the male's sperm fertilizes the woman's ovum . . ."

"That's enough of that kind of dirty talk," Wallingford shouts.

"Relax, Daddy-O. I haven't done it. But if I ever decide to, I want to be protected. They told us at the clinic, it's the woman and not the man who has to take precautions. Men couldn't care less about the consequences."

"You seem to know a lot about sex, young lady," Wallingford says. "You certainly didn't learn any of this at home."

"I know. That's why I went to the clinic. Every time I brought up the subject you said it was none of my business."

"It isn't any of your business," Mrs. Wallingford says. "You're 17 years old and nice girls don't discuss such things with their parents."

"Where are you going?"

"To the basketball game with Jack."

"So that's where you're going to do it," Wallingford cries.

"How am I going to do it at a basketball game?"

"In the parking lot," Wallingford says. "That's where I used to do it."

"I can't take any more of this. Goodby."

After Sue Anne leaves, Mrs. Wallingford wipes the tears from her eyes. "You know, George, I think we both would be happier today if Planned Parenthood had never let us know."

*Source:* Art Buchwald, *Detroit Free Press*, February 10, 1983, p. 13-B. By permission of the author.

Udry examined hormonal changes of puberty, commonly regarded as the foundation to sexual behavior, for evidence of their role in adolescent sexual behavior. His arguments state that since adolescents mature at different rates and at different ages, some adolescents will be more predisposed to sexual activity than others. The inclusion of a hormone measure with the social control measures would not make the sociological models wrong, but would make them more complete. Thus he tested a biosocial theory that combines elements of social science with a biological model of hormonal dispositions.

The biological component is based on the proposition that androgenic (male) hormones, which increase at puberty for both sexes, increase the predisposition to engage in sexual behavior. This androgenic hormone reaches a ceiling level for males beyond which there are no additional androgen effects. For females, however, the testosterone levels (the most potent androgen) double at puberty, whereas males' levels increase by a factor of 10 to 20. This makes adolescent females an appropriate group for studying hormone-behavior relationships.

What Udry found for boys were strong biological and weak sociological effects on coitus with more balanced effects on subjective (thoughts and feelings) sexual variables. For girls, the subjective sexual variables showed balanced biological and sociological effects as well, but for the most strongly sanctioned behavior (coitus), hormonal effects disappear and only sociological variables control. Social controls act as suppressors of the effects of hormones on behavior. What Udry concludes is that a biosocial model of sexual behavior produces results that are more convincing than either a sociological or biological model alone. He urges caution however, in applying his results only to early adolescence and not to coital transitions occurring earlier or later.

Male and female sexual behaviors in adulthood go beyond hormonal and biological factors to include social and technological ones. Male-female differences are thought to have been weakened by the feminist movement (with its platform of equality), the development of contraception (with its removal of much of the fear of pregnancy), and the Industrial Revolution (which gave women greater economic opportunities). But behavior differences are still very much a part of U.S. society. And few would dispute the notion that gender differences are relevant to far more than sexual behavior and standards. It is applicable to business, politics, religion, education, and any other sphere of social life. Let us turn our attention to how we are sexually socialized.

## SEXUALIZATION AND SEXUAL SCRIPTS

*Sexualization*, that is, sexual socialization, is the process by which persons learn and internalize their sexual self-concepts, values, attitudes, and behaviors. It is a process that begins at birth and continues into adulthood and old age. Details of the socialization process, with regard to sexuality, gender, violence, or other factors, are described in Chapter 14. Our attention at this point will focus specifically on the learning and development of sexual knowledge, attitudes, and values. These aspects of sexualization appear to be the key to understanding sexual behavior.

Symbolic interaction theory would posit that we become sexual beings through the process of social interaction. As suggested previously, while there

## Sexual standards in Sweden

Scandinavian countries, particularly Sweden, are often viewed by U.S. citizens as "sexually liberated" and without a double standard. While not true in absolute terms, in comparison with the United States this would appear to be accurate. Swedish norms about premarital intercourse, sex education, availability of abortion and contraception, free clinical treatment of venereal disease, and the open discussion of human sexuality are more permissive and sexually equal than those in the United States.

Swedish policy on sexual matters has been adopted explicitly to reduce sexual inequality. Young Swedes, both men and women, are permitted to responsibly and freely express their sexuality. Most young people live together and have intercourse before marriage. But most relationships, rather than being indiscriminate or promiscuous, are cultivated in a context of intimacy with particular persons. Couples are not as likely to be forced into marriage by pregnancy as occurs among couples in the United States. What this means is that women are not penalized if they become pregnant before marriage. The adverse effects of pregnancy are reduced by government assistance in the forms of child care centers, abortion clinics, sex education classes, and the like. Government policy, while protecting the rights of women, also aims at guaranteeing equal opportunity to every child in Sweden, irrespective of the circumstances of birth.

is an important biological and hormonal basis to sexual development, simply having genitals associated with the female or male does not guarantee that our gender identity or preferences follow anatomical components. This is evidenced in transvestism (dressing in the clothing of the opposite sex), transsexualism (trapped in the body of the wrong sex), or homosexuality (sexual activity or preference for same sex relationships). It is evidenced as well in the wide range of acceptable or nonacceptable attitudes and behaviors that exists among persons in general: sexual abstinence, cunnilingus, fellatio, masturbation, sadism, sodomy, voyeurism, or sexual positions in heterosexual coitus. Research on hermaphrodites (persons with both male and female sex glands) seems to provide strong evidence that conventional patterns of masculine and feminine behavior can be altered.

Symbolic interaction theory would posit as well that sexual behavior can only be understood in terms of internalized symbolic meanings. This suggests that the definitions of the situation, and the meanings or interpretations given to various behaviors, are basic to understanding that behavior or lack of behavior. If premarital coitus is defined as sinful, if masturbation is believed to cause insanity, and if homosexuality is perceived as perverted, these meanings and definitions will have a major, but not absolute, influence on behavior or the absence of it. That is, definitions, attitudes, meanings, values, and other internalized mental processes predispose behavior.

These ideas, basic to a symbolic interaction frame of reference, parallel the ideas of John Gagnon and William Simon. They conceptualize the outcome

*Sexual socialization is a lifelong process, but adolescent peer group interaction appears to be particularly important in the development of sexual attitudes and in influencing sexual behavior.*

or product of what is here termed sexualization in terms of *sexual scripts*.[7] The sexual script designates the who, what, where, when, and why of sexuality. Like a script for a play or movie, it provides an overall blueprint of what sexuality is and how it is practiced.

Scripts are the plans that people have in their heads. The sexual script defines *who* one does sex with. Sex is not allowed with certain categories of people, but others are fantasized about and on the "approved list." The script defines *what* sexual behaviors are right or wrong, appropriate or inappropriate. While kissing or masturbation may be on the approved list, intercourse or oral sex may not. The script includes the *whens* and *wheres* of sex. Is it appropriate only at night in the dark in a bedroom? Is it appropriate at noon in an automobile? And finally, it includes the *why* issue. Is sex for fun, intimacy,

---

7. John H. Gagnon, *Human Sexualities* (Glenview, Ill.: Scott Foresman 1977), pp. 5–9; and William Simon and John H. Gagnon, "Sexual Scripts: Permanence and Change," *Archives of Sexual Behavior* 15 (1986): 97–120. For a more detailed discussion of sexual scripts *see:* William Simon and John H. Gagnon, "A Sexual Script Approach," in James H. Geer and William T. O'Donohue, *Theories of Human Sexuality* (New York: Plenum Press, 1987), Chapter 13, pp. 363–383.

reducing tension, procreation, or some other reason? One's sexual script is the internalized notions of these who, what, when, where, and why questions. It is learned in interaction with others and contains notions of the society, subculture, reference groups, and significant others in which we are members and with whom we interact. In interaction with others we build our scripts, those cognitive schemes that we carry in our heads and that affect our actual conduct.

The process by which these sexual scripts are formulated tends to illustrate the importance of adult socialization in contrast to the Freudian emphasis on the early years (*see* Chapter 14). At puberty, a young person may be largely ignorant of adult sexuality. Adolescence is a period when adult sexual scripts become formulated, experienced, and modified. Scripts are devices for organizing, guiding, and understanding our behavior. They justify action that is in accord with them and cause us to question those that are not. Simon and Gagnon[8] argue that for behavior to occur, something resembling scripting must occur on three distinct levels: cultural scenarios, interpersonal scripts, and intrapsychic scripts.

*Cultural scenarios* are the instructional guides that exist at the level of collective life. The enactment of virtually all roles reflects the institutions, groups, and social context in which we were born, raised, and function. *Interpersonal scripts* transform the person trained in cultural scenarios and general social roles to context-specific behavior. What we do is influenced by the response of others. These cultural scenarios and interpersonal scripts result in *intrapsychic scripting*, an internal dialogue, a world of fantasy, or—in interaction terms—a personal self that is in reality a social self. The private world of individual wishes and desires is bound to social life. All sexual behavior involves and includes all three levels of scripting.

Sexual scripting, like the general process of sexual socialization, follows the life cycle. Until recently, infancy, childhood, and old age were periods where the appearance of sex-seeking behavior was viewed as pathological in that these people were either too young or too old to be capable of comprehending or experiencing the full meaning of the behavior. In the context of this and most family texts, sexual life cycles tend to be subsumed under headings of premarital, marital, extramarital, or postmarital experiences. Any of these ideas suggest profound changes in the requirements and meanings attached to sexual scripts. Thus, a traditional premarital sexual script that suggests "nice girls don't" changes to "nice girls do" after they are married. According to Simon and Gagnon, the power of sexual scripts—perhaps the power of the sexual—is tied to the extrasexual significances of confirming identities and making them congruent with appropriate relationships.[9]

---

8. Ibid., pp. 98–104.
9. Ibid., p. 117.

This section on sexualization and sexual scripts focuses on the processes by which sexual definitions and meanings become internalized; they are part of the basic process of socialization in general and may become more clearly understood after reading Chapter 14. At this point let us examine briefly the consistency between the attitudinal and behavioral aspects of sexual scripts.

## Sexual attitudes and behavior: how consistent are they?

Sexual scripts include both attitudinal and behavioral components. How consistent are sexual beliefs, values, and attitudes with what is done? One could assume that, for the most part, attitudes and behavior are highly related. In earlier editions of this text, I hypothesized that when they differ, beliefs about what is appropriate or proper sexual behavior tend to be more conservative than actual behaviors. The contention was that socialization practices in Judeo-Christian cultures lead to the internalization of sexual attitudes and beliefs that are highly restrictive (don't masturbate, engage in oral-genital sex, have premarital intercourse, and the like). During adolescence, as young people get involved in the courtship process, as going steady and a commitment type of relationship take place, behaviors will probably go beyond the boundaries of what is believed to be proper. After engaging in the behavior, the belief toward that behavior is likely to change in the direction of greater permissiveness. An interaction process is at work. More permissive behavior modifies the belief.

There are several reasons for greater permissiveness of actual behavior than of belief about proper behavior. It is likely that traditional values continue to be applied even when the behavior is changed. Also, it is possible that premarital sexual behavior is subject to more rapid social change than are attitudes. When behavior exceeds the belief limits, this conflict may produce guilt. While guilt is likely to be a common component of the sexualization process, a tendency exists to continue the behavior until it is accepted. Once accepted, the feelings of guilt are reduced or totally eliminated.

Considerable support appears to exist for the ideas just presented. One example comes from a study of about 3,500 high school students.[10] Selected results indicated that 83 percent of sexually experienced adolescents cited a best age for first intercourse that was older than the age at which they themselves experienced that event, and 43 percent of them reported a best age for first coitus older than their current age. Among the sexually active who agreed with the statement that they would only have sex if using birth control, about one-fourth used no contraceptive at last intercourse. A much higher proportion of virgins believed premarital sex is wrong than did non-virgins,

---

10. Laurie S. Zabin, Marilyn B. Hirsch, Edward A. Smith, and Janet B. Hardy, "Adolescent Sexual Attitudes and Behavior: Are They Consistent?" *Family Planning Perspectives* 16 (July/August 1984): 181–185.

and even among the non-virgins about one-fourth of both sexes said they believe sex before marriage is wrong. In other words, findings such as these tend to suggest that attitudes or beliefs are more restrictive or conservative than behavior, whether the adolescents were sexually active or virgins. And as could be expected, those who engaged in various sexual behaviors had more permissive sexual scripts than those who did not. The authors of this study conclude that the majority of young people have values and attitudes consistent with responsible sexual conduct, but not all of them are able to translate these attitudes into personal behavior.

## ANTECEDENTS OF SEXUAL BEHAVIOR

*Antecedents of sexual behavior* are factors that preceded or took place prior to a given sexual activity. Many antecedents are family centered because this institution is central in the formation of sexual attitudes and behaviors; the family provides role models, a social and economic environment, and standards of sexual conduct. Many social structural dimensions such as ethnicity, age or education of the parents, the employment of one or both parents, the presence or absence of siblings and the number of them, religious affiliation and commitment, and a never-married/divorced/remarried parental status may all influence the likelihood of the incidence or prevalence of intercourse prior to or separate from marriage.[11] One study suggests that the family may influence adolescent attitudes more than behavior—a relationship just examined in the previous section.[12]

Simple logic would seem to indicate that a major antecedent or preceding factor in explaining or understanding premarital sexual behavior would be parental influence in the sexual socialization process. For example, is it not logical to assume that individuals brought up in sexually conservative homes will have less premarital heterosexual involvement than those from more liberal home environments? In other words, homes in which parents do not openly display affection, have a rigid and concerned attitude toward nudity, never discuss sex openly, and never have books or pamphlets available on sexual subjects would be expected to produce or lead to more conservative behavior or less sexual involvement by their children. This hypothesis was put to a test in a national probability sample of nearly 1,200 college students.

---

11. *See* for example: Renata T. Forste and Tim B. Heaton, "Initiation of Sexual Activity Among Female Adolescents," *Youth and Society* 19 (March 1988): 250–268; Judith A. Howard, "A Structural Approach to Sexual Attitudes," *Sociological Perspectives* 31 (January 1988): 88–121; and Arland Thornton and Donald Camburn, "Religious Participation and Adolescent Sexual Behavior and Attitudes," *Journal of Marriage and the Family* 51 (August 1989): 641–653.

12. Arland Thornton and Donald Camburn, "The Influence of the Family on Premarital Sexual Attitudes and Behavior," *Demography* 24 (August 1987): 323–340.

Interestingly, the findings showed no significant relationship for males or females between parental sexual conservatism and premarital socio-sexual involvement.[13] This seems to indicate that perceived sexual conservatism leads neither to increased nor decreased sexual activity.

In fact, data from two independent studies that include teenagers and their mothers indicate that neither parental attitudes toward premarital sex nor parent-child communication about sex and contraception appear to affect teenagers' subsequent sexual and contraception behavior.[14] Teens who communicated little with their mothers were as likely to use effective birth control as were those who communicated well. Authors of both studies suggest that the findings do not indicate that family communication counts for very much in terms of either sexual behavior or contraceptive usage. One reason may be that parental communication about sex and contraception is generally so vague or so limited as to have no impact.

How about the related issue of parental discipline? Would we not expect adolescents from homes with very strict discipline and rules about dating to be more sexually conservative and those from homes with few rules and lenient discipline to be sexually permissive? Survey data from several thousand adolescents (ages 15–18) and their parents were analyzed to determine how parental discipline was related to the sexual permissiveness of their children.[15] As just hypothesized, sexual permissiveness was highest among adolescents who viewed their parents as not being strict or not having rules about dating. But interestingly, adolescents who experienced very strict parental discipline and many dating rules were more permissive than those with moderate parental strictness and rules. In other words, a curvilinear relationship was found in that both strict and lenient disciplinary patterns resulted in higher levels of sexual permissiveness with the lowest permissiveness among adolescents with moderately strict parents.

How might the preceding findings be explained? First, perhaps children do not interpret the presence or absence of sexual behavior on the part of parents as being particularly relevant to their own sexual needs and experiences. Second, perhaps parental disciplinary behaviors are a consequence of adolescent permissiveness. That is, if parents suspect their teenager

---

13. Graham B. Spanier, "Perceived Parental Sexual Conservatism, Religiosity, and Premarital Sexual Behavior," *Sociological Focus* 9 (August 1976): 285–298.

14. Susan F. Newcomer and J. Richard Udry, "Parent-Child Communication and Adolescent Sexual Behavior," *Family Planning Perspectives* 17 (July/August 1985): 169–174; and Frank F. Furstenberg, Jr., Roberta Herceg-Baron, Judy Shea, and David Webb, "Family Communication and Teenagers' Contraceptive Use," *Family Planning Perspectives* 16 (July/August 1984): 163–170. *See also* Kristin A. Moore, James L. Peterson, and Frank F. Furstenberg, "Parental Attitudes and the Occurrence of Early Sexual Activity," *Journal of Marriage and the Family* 48 (November 1986): 777–782.

15. Brent C. Miller, J. Kelly McCoy, Terrance D. Olson, and Christopher M. Wallace, "Parental Discipline and Control Attempts in Relation to Adolescent Sexual Attitudes and Behavior," *Journal of Marriage and the Family* 48 (August 1986): 503–512.

## Sex and the single Russian—"your place or mom's?"

MOSCOW—"It's our No. 1 national problem," a young carpenter complained recently. He wasn't referring to the faltering economy, the frequent food shortages, or some foreign policy setback. He was talking about how tough it is for young singles here to find a place for romancing.

"I'm 24, and I live in a two-room flat with my mother, grandmother, and younger sister," he said. "Figure out for yourself how many times in a month the apartment is empty and I can have a girl over. Weeks go by without an opportunity, and I really don't have any other place available."

For Soviet singles, finding a bedmate is a lot easier than finding a bed. Housing here is in such short supply that even young marrieds must move in with their parents, and it's practically unheard of for single people to have their own pads.

The younger generation may be liberal about lovemaking, but most of their parents disapprove of premarital sex and would rather not have it taking place in their apartments.

"My mother knows I have girls over when she's away," said a 26-year-old medical technician from Minsk who is lucky enough to have his own bedroom. "But it's something we never talk about because she definitely doesn't like the idea."

Occasionally, he confessed, he sneaks a lover in late at night after his mother has been asleep for some time. "But if she ever woke up, oy-oy-oy!" he said with a grimace, holding his head in mock horror.

As for little love nests—even makeshift ones—away from home, they're very difficult to find here. In the summer many singles snuggle up in the parks, but in the winter it's too cold for cuddling outdoors, with temperatures frequently falling below zero.

"Forget about going to a hotel," said a Leningrad lass. "In the first place it's almost impossible to get a reservation, and in the second place you have to present your internal passports when you register. Two unmarried people would get chased away or worse, because strictly speaking that sort of thing is against the law."

Singles sometimes overcome these obstacles by making friends—or private arrangements—with a hotel employee. "I know a night clerk," said a student in Stavropol, "and for five rubles he finds me an empty room for a few hours. It's a service he provides for a lot of young people, and the money he makes this way is much more than his salary."

The Saturday night standby of so many

is engaging in sexual intercourse they may impose more dating rules. Third, while parents may be extremely influential in general socialization, they may be less influential than significant others outside the home, particularly peers, in sexual socialization.

Support for this latter idea comes from a national probability sample of fifteen- to nineteen-year-old women.[16] A majority of young women had views on socioeconomic status which were like their parents' views. But in regard to

---

16. Farida Shah and Melvin Zelnik, "Parent and Peer Influence on Sexual Behavior, Contraceptive Use, and Pregnancy Experience of Young Women," *Journal of Marriage and the Family* 43 (May 1981): 339–348. For an extensive overview of literature on this and related topics *see* W. M. Strahle, "A Model of Premarital Coitus and Contraceptive Behavior Among Female Adolescents," *Archives of Sexual Behavior* 12 (1983): 67–94.

young Americans—the back seat of a car—is not accessible to most singles here. An automobile can cost several years' salary, and special permission is needed to purchase one.

A young Yugoslav studying at Moscow State University—where unmarried students can be expelled for making love in their rooms—is constantly besieged by classmates who want to borrow his car. "Sometimes they offer me money and gifts," he said.

What makes the problem easier to put up with is the fact that this is still a puritanical society where mass media stimulation does not take place. Suggestive advertising, sexy songs, girlie magazines are strictly forbidden in the Soviet Union.

"Here, having sex is not a fixed idea," said 23-year-old Sergei, who is studying the management of mass demonstrations at an institute in the Ukraine. "We're not busy thinking about it all the time, which I think is the case with young men and women in the West."

Still, he said, when the opportunity presents itself, young people here feel no compunction to turn it down. "We're interested in having sex, but it's not the main thing on our minds," he said.

Another factor interfering with the sex lives of singles here is the absence of social activities oriented toward the unwed. Singles bars do not exist, and admission to the only discotheque in this city is limited to a few hundred people at a time. Long lines form outside every Saturday night.

A survey by two Leningrad sociologists showed that most Soviets meet their spouses at work, at school, or on vacations. The problem of meeting a potential mate is so serious among older women that lonely hearts clubs have recently been set up in several of the principal cities.

In the age brackets above 30, single women greatly outnumber single men, and the disparity increases with age.

A young Muscovite, an engineer, may have put it all in perspective when he said: Even if you meet someone, "finding a place where you can make love when you want to is even more difficult than finding a comfortable pair of shoes in the shops. And frankly, I haven't been able to find either yet."

*Source:* Jim Gallagher, *The Chicago Tribune,* February 1, 1979, Section 2, pp. 1–2. Copyrighted © 1979, *Chicago Tribune.* Used with permission. All rights reserved.

premarital sex, very little agreement existed between parents and peers and more young women were influenced by friends than by parents. The same study showed that sexually experienced young women influenced by their peers were more likely to use contraceptives than those influenced by their parents. Sexually experienced women whose views were like their parents' were more likely to "deny" their sexual behavior and either fail to use contraceptives or to use mainly nonmedical methods, such as withdrawal, thereby implying a lack of readiness on their part to engage in sex.

## The relevance of formal sex education

Formal sex education, that is, education dealing with the general area of sexuality in a structured context of classes, seminars, workshops, clinics, and the like, is generally supported by the public. Disagreement exists over such

## Ethical values in sex education in Sweden

All children in Sweden receive sex education. It is compulsory, and as a result Swedish children between the ages of five and fifteen are likely to have a better understanding and knowledge of sexual matters than children anywhere in the world. Sex education, or as it is termed today, "education about living together," is an indispensable component of the school curriculum at all grade levels. Contraception information is given to six- and seven-year-olds. Ideas about sexually transmitted diseases, nocturnal emissions, and homosexuality are taught to ten- and twelve-year-olds. By the junior-high-school level, masturbation, intercourse, abortion, sexual deviations, impotence, love, companionship, and so forth are common and acceptable topics for the classroom. What about values and ethics? Are these topics taught in a vacuum of appropriateness, morality, and responsibility?

The Swedish National Board of Education has issued a teachers' manual that stresses the broad ethical dimensions and foundations of human, and particularly, sexual relationships. As summarized from Carl Gustof Boethius (*Family Planning Perspectives,* November/December 1985, p. 277) these include, among others:

No human being is to be regarded and treated as a means of selfish gratification.

The use of psychological pressure and physical force in any context is a violation of the personal freedom of others.

Sexuality involves more than casual sex (not implying moral disapproval of sexual relationships but stressing the more sustained interpersonal relationships).

Schools should support the conviction that sexual fidelity in a permanent relationship is a duty (a conviction held by nearly all young people).

Frankness about sexual life in words and deeds is a goal but pornography that degrades humans is distinguished from nonpornographic illustrations and texts.

Men and women must be subject to identical standards of sexual morality (the old double standard is viewed as having an undesirable effect on sexual relationships).

Schools should not discourage sexual relationships among the mentally or physically handicapped, prisoners, or the aged.

Schools should try to promote an atmosphere of tolerance.

issues as appropriate content, who should teach it, the inclusion or exclusion of moral values, and so forth.

The need for formal sources of education stems from many sources, including the difficulty many parents and children face in communicating openly and freely about sexuality and birth control. Even when parents have accurate knowledge and make conscientious efforts to encourage sexual discussion and effective contraceptive behavior, emotional factors in the relationship may make such discussions difficult. Sexually active teenagers, who are likely to perceive their parents as wanting them to be sexually inactive, are not likely to discuss their oral-genital or intercourse experiences with them. Neither are they likely to seek out contraceptive information or devices from them. And numerous efforts to require clinics and agencies to inform parents of their adolescents' inquiries about contraception and abortion may have the unintended consequence of more unwanted pregnancies and sexually transmitted diseases rather than the intended consequence of improving parent-child communication.

*Information about sexual values, behavior patterns, or contraceptives may be derived from informal interaction patterns with peers, from books or the mass media, or from formal classes, workshops, or clinics.*

The difficulty in communication between parents and children; the inadequate factual information from parents or peers; the widespread discomfort and embarrassment in the area of sexuality and contraception; the need for privacy about sex and birth control; the spread of sexually transmitted diseases; the growth in teenage, unwanted, and out-of-wedlock pregnancies; and so forth are reasons supporting formal sex education programs and clinics. Do these formal programs and clinics, as some infer, lead the sexually inactive to become active, increase knowledge, decrease unwanted pregnancies, or in short, make any difference at all?

The results of formal programs are mixed at best. Few lead to the negative consequences feared or the positive consequences hoped for. In general, it appears that sex knowledge gained through school classes and programs has little, if any, influence on premarital sexual behavior or on the subsequent probability that a teenager will begin to have intercourse. Data provide overwhelming support for the claim that the decision to engage in sexual activity is *not* influenced by whether or not teenagers had sex education in school.[17] In fact, a large proportion of teenagers initiate coitus before they have taken a sex education course.

Sex education does, however, influence knowledge and behavior regarding contraceptives. Sexually active teenagers who have had formal instruction

17. Melvin Zelnik and Young J. Kim, "Sex Education and Its Association with Teenage Sexual Activity, Pregnancy and Contraceptive Use," *Family Planning Perspective* 14 (May/June 1982): 117–126.

report knowing how to use more methods of contraception and they use them more effectively than do adolescents who have had no instruction.[18] Also, sexually active women who had sex education were less likely to become pregnant than those who did not. The availability of contraceptives, like the taking of a sex education course, does not appear, however, to have much influence on premarital sexual behavior.

Further evidence of no direct relationship between the initiation of sexual activity and the availability of contraceptives resulted from a study of adolescent women seeking contraceptives from a family-planning clinic.[19] Ninety-six percent of the adolescents had already had sexual intercourse before coming to the clinic for the first time. Over half the adolescent women who had been sexually active before coming to the clinic had never used any kind of contraceptive protection at all, and many of those who had used it in an irregular fashion. Most adolescents came to the clinic after they had made a conscious decision to continue to be sexually active and did not want to become pregnant.

While most research shows that formal education programs fail to achieve their intended purposes, exposure to informal education, peer-group interaction, mass media publications, and the like explains the considerable variation in behavior. Even greater variation is explained by factors such as dating frequency and religiosity. All these factors do not discount the idea that courses and programs have merit beyond the prevention of intercourse or unplanned pregnancies. Many courses provide young people with a greater understanding of human physiology, interpersonal relationships, and social values.

## PREMARITAL HETEROSEXUAL INTERCOURSE

**Premarital sexual intercourse** indicates that at least one of the partners is single and has not been previously married. It is premarital in that the person has never been married, not in the sense that the relationship is confined to the person one will marry.

Cross-culturally, it appears that most societies permit or even encourage premarital relationships, particularly for the males. The taboo that falls primarily on females appears to be more a precaution against childbearing out of wedlock rather than a moral sanction. Using a global perspective, the crucial question, particularly for females, may not be whether premarital intercourse

---

18. Deborah Anne Dawson, "The Effects of Sex Education on Adolescent Behavior," *Family Planning Perspectives* 18 (July/August 1986): 162–170; and William Marsiglio and Frank L. Mott, "The Impact of Sex Education on Sexual Activity, Contraceptive Use and Premarital Pregnancy Among American Teenagers," *Family Planning Perspectives* 18 (July/August 1986): 151–162.

19. Ruth Kornfield, "Who's to Blame: Adolescent Sexual Activity," *Journal of Adolescence* 8 (1986): 17–31.

## Premarital sex as a societal characteristic, not an individual one

Leonard Beeghley and Christine Sellers assert that the rate of premarital sex is a characteristic of a society, not an individual. Their argument suggests that rates of behavior reflect how social organization influences people's range of options. Their article shows that the rising rate of premarital sex during this century can be accounted for by changes in the American social structure which was much different in 1900 than it is today.

In 1900:

1. The time between puberty and marriage was less.
2. There was little public reference to sexuality.
3. Youths were closely supervised by parents and community.
4. Likely results of sex were venereal disease and pregnancy.
5. Traditional roles meant that to secure a suitable mate, women had to withhold sex.
6. Social norms preached sexual abstinence.

These characteristics of society, without exception, existed independently of individuals and directed their behavior in one way rather than another, with the result that the rate of premarital sex was low.

Today, social organization has changed.

1. The gap between puberty and marriage allows more time for premarital sex.
2. Sexual pervasiveness conveys the idea that premarital sex is okay.
3. Social autonomy provides the opportunity for premarital sex.
4. Medical care and contraception reduce the risks of venereal disease and pregnancy.
5. Egalitarian sex role norms encourage more complete relationships rather than exploitive ones.
6. The norm of sexual abstinence has declined, meaning increased social acceptance.

These factors exist independently of individuals and direct their behavior in a different way. The result is a high rate of premarital sex. Individual morality has not declined but society has changed and these changes have led to changes in the rate of premarital sex.

*Source:* Leonard Beeghley and Christine Sellers, "Adolescents and Sex: A Structural Theory of Premarital Sex in the United States," *Deviant Behavior* 7 (1986): 313–336.

will be permitted, but whether unmarried motherhood will be allowed. It is likely that a commitment to norms of chastity lessens as a separation of premarital intercourse from pregnancy becomes possible. Thus, if contraceptives, sterilization, abortion, or other social arrangements exist to prevent or terminate a pregnancy, premarital sexual permissiveness will increase.

Premarital sexual permissiveness will also increase as a couple approaches marriage or a commitment to a relationship. As stated in Chapter 9, premarital sexual behaviors are related to the courtship process. The most conservative behaviors could be expected on a first meeting or date; behavior becomes increasingly permissive as the couple moves from casual dating to a more serious commitment both to the relationship and to each other, and toward marriage or a marriage-like relationship. Since marriage is the context of the greatest approval or legitimization of coitus, it could be expected that the closer the relationship is to a marriage type or to one of exclusivity, the more permissive the sexual behavior. This hypothesis has had research support for many decades.

A recent test of the permissiveness-commitment relationship came from an attempt to revise the Reiss Premarital Permissiveness scale published in the *Journal of Marriage and the Family* in 1964.[20] Whether the behavior was heavy petting, sexual intercourse, or oral-genital sex, the percentage that agreed each behavior was acceptable increased by relationship stage with the lowest level of acceptability on a first date and increasing for casual dating, serious dating, pre-engaged, and engaged. More than three-fourths of all respondents agreed to all three behaviors during engagement.

### The frequency of premarital intercourse prior to the 1980s

Changes in the frequency of premarital intercourse prior to the decade of the 1980s and since then can be viewed in a number of ways. One way is to look at the *incidence*, that is, the occurrence or nonoccurrence of an experience. Generally, one has or has not had intercourse, is or is not a virgin, has or has not experienced orgasm. Another way to view frequency is to deal with *prevalence*, that is, the frequency of the experience. Premarital intercourse may have occurred once or a thousand times. It may occur infrequently or on a regular basis. Thus, the incidence rate (number who have or have not) differs considerably from the prevalence rate (frequency). Both incidence and prevalence appear to have increased significantly over the past several decades.

Many social forces have appeared on the U.S. scene that have led to behavioral changes regarding premarital coitus; these forces also have the potential for producing further changes. In the 1960s a high proportion of college students was deeply involved in the civil rights movement and later in the protest over the Vietnam War. On most university campuses, the birth control pill became available and acceptable for personal use to a large number of unmarried college women. In addition, sexual candor became increasingly legitimized in the mass media, even by one of the most conservative media—television. The result of these social forces developing in the latter half of the 1960s led to an increase in the rejection of many traditional values.

The result of social forces such as these produced research results strongly suggesting that significant changes took place in the 1960s and 1970s in the sexual behavior of the never-married. An analysis of premarital sexual behavior and attitudes over an extensive period of time—1965, 1970, 1975, and 1980—reveals a continued but asymptotic increase in reported premarital

---

20. Susan Sprecher, Kathleen McKinney, Robert Walsh, and Carrie Anderson, "A Revision of the Reiss Premarital Sexual Permissiveness Scale," *Journal of Marriage and the Family* 50 (August 1988): 821–828.

sexual behavior among both men and women.[21] This indicates that the increase in rate of premarital coitus continued between 1975 and 1980 but at a slower rate of increase than occurred earlier. The reported change in the percentage of college males engaging in premarital sexual activity increased by 12 percent between 1965 and 1980. In 1965 and 1970, 65 percent of the males reported having had premarital intercourse, increasing to 74 percent in 1975 and to 77 percent in 1980. For females the increase was 35 percent between 1965 and 1980 with 29 percent reporting premarital intercourse in 1965, increasing to 37 percent in 1970, 57 percent in 1975 and 64 percent in 1980. Note that in addition to the increase for both sexes, the increase was far greater for females, resulting in a narrowing of the difference between men and women.

Apart from samples of college students, nearly all research reports indicate an increased permissiveness of premarital sexual behaviors in the 1970s. Melvin Zelnik and others showed by national probability samples of females aged fifteen to nineteen that in 1971, 28 percent were nonvirginal (23 percent of the white teenagers and 54 percent of the black teenagers). By 1976, just five years later, 55 percent had had sexual intercourse (incidence) and most of these, 85 percent, had had it more than once (prevalence).[22] The average age at which young women had their first sexual experience was 16.2 compared with 15.7 among the men. A majority of young women interviewed in 1979 first had intercourse in the context of a "commitment relationship" such as being engaged or going steady, but most young men indicated their first sexual partner was in a more casual relationship.[23] For both sexes the initiation of sex appears to have been a spur-of-the-moment decision. Only 17 percent of the men and 25 percent of the women planned their first act of intercourse. While most adolescents did not want to get pregnant or get their partners pregnant, a large proportion of them did not use a contraceptive method.

A review of thirty-five studies conducted over the past eighty years notes two major trends that are apparent.[24] One is a major increase in the proportion of young people reporting coital involvement. The second is a more rapid increase in the proportion of females reporting coital involvement than

21. Ira E. Robinson and Davor Jedlicka, "Change in Sexual Attitudes and Behavior of College Students from 1965 to 1980: A Research Note," *Journal of Marriage and the Family* 44 (February 1982): 237–240.

22. Melvin Zelnik, Young J. Kim, and John F. Kantner, "Probabilities of Intercourse and Conception Among U.S. Teenage Women, 1971 and 1976," *Family Planning Perspectives* 11 (May/June 1979): 177–183.

23. Melvin Zelnik and Farida K. Shah, "First Intercourse Among Young Americans," *Family Planning Perspectives* 15 (March/April 1983): 64–70.

24. Carol A. Darling, David J. Kallan, and Joyce E. VanDusen, "Sex in Transition, 1900–1980," *Journal of Youth and Adolescence* 13 (1984): 385–399. Note also: Sandra L. Hofferth, Joan R. Rahn, and Wendy Baldwin, "Premarital Sexual Activity Among U.S. Teenage Women over the Past Three Decades," *Family Planning Perspectives* 19 (March/April 1987): 46–53.

males, although the initial base for males was greater. By 1980, the proportion of men and women reporting coital involvement was nearly equal. Data suggest that the so-called "sexual revolution" in the United States was real but it has been restricted to premarital heterosexual relations. Attitudes toward extramarital and homosexual relations remained distinctly restrictive.

As shown, the changes prior to the 1980s were most pronounced for females and moved in the direction of greater permissiveness. One report explained this greater change among females by differentiating between *developing* and *established* or existing, sexual scripts.[25] The conditions found prior to the 1970s and proposed as causes of change in sexual behavior (freedom of youth from parental control, the development of a strong youth culture, the availability of the birth control pill) could not be expected to have automatically provided new sexual scripts. Men had an *established* traditional script pattern for premarital coitus that permitted permissiveness. Women, in contrast, had had no sexual script for premarital coitus, and time was needed to develop one in response to the changed conditions. Thus, a *developing* script pattern for women led to greater changes in their behavior than that for men. While the male-female differences decreased, a distinct double standard remained. What about the 1980s and 1990s?

### Frequency of premarital intercourse in the 1980s and 1990s

In contrast to the social forces supporting increased sexual permissiveness in the 1960s and 1970s, the 1980s saw the arrival of conservative political and religious movements. In addition, a new and serious epidemic that could be transmitted sexually, now widely known as AIDS, appeared on the world social scene. Forces such as these could be expected to place restrictive influences on the sexual activities of all ages. So have the major changes toward sexual permissiveness come to a halt in the United States? Has the AIDS phenomenon in particular had a restrictive impact on the incidence and frequency of heterosexual intercourse?

### The Impact of AIDS

AIDS (Acquired Immune Deficiency Syndrome), first reported in 1981, has since become a household term. Because of the deadliness of the AIDS virus and the increasingly broad spectrum of its victims, the National Center for Health Statistics reported that by November 1987, more than 99 percent of persons age eighteen and older had heard of AIDS.[26] Nearly three-fourths of adults said it is definitely or probably caused by a virus, and 90 percent knew

---

25. David Reed and Martin S. Weinberg, "Premarital Coitus: Developing and Established Sexual Scripts," *Social Psychology Quarterly* 47 (1984): 129–138.

26. "Digest" *Family Planning Perspectives* 20 (March/April 1988): 99.

## Ready for the female condom?

According to a report in *Contraceptive Technology Update* 10 (1989, p. 49), two variations on the female condom are ready for the U.S. market. One, dubbed "Barrier" by its developers, is made of latex, is about 50 percent larger than a male condom, and is held in place by straps that loop around the woman's thighs. The tube-like pouch contains a silicone lubricant.

The second female condom, now known only as WPC 333, purportedly resembles a child's sock in size and shape; it is made of polyurethane and is lubricated with nonoxynol-9. The developers of WPC 333 have submitted to the FDA their data on the experience of 450 couples in the United States who have used the device, but it remains unclear how long the FDA's approval process will take.

the three major ways the virus was transmitted: sharing needles for drug use with someone who has AIDS, having sex with someone who has AIDS, and birth by a woman with AIDS. Although AIDS was originally perceived as a disease confined to homosexuals, it is now recognized that its numbers are increasing in the heterosexual population.

AIDS education is reported to be taught in some form in more than 90 percent of public high schools. Almost all teachers in biology, health education, home economics, physical education, and school nursing believe education relating to the prevention of pregnancy, AIDS, and other sexually transmitted diseases (STDs) should be taught. Most felt these topics should be covered by grades seven or eight at the latest.[27] Given the seriousness of AIDS, the growing body of knowledge about it, and the awareness that it can be transmitted by heterosexual intercourse, it seems reasonable to expect that the disease would have an impact on sexual behavior in general as well as on the practice of behaviors (such as condom use) that reduce the chances of its transmission. Numerous studies in the 1980s, done primarily with student populations, have looked at this question and have produced mixed results.

One sample of college students at the University of Rhode Island reported that concern about AIDS was widespread and that over half of the sexually active students claim to have altered their behavior in some way as a result of this concern.[28] While many students claimed to have become more selective in their choice of partners, it did not appear that a significant number of them had entered exclusive dating relationships or had modified the frequency of their intercourse experiences.

A sample of sexually experienced students at the University of California, Riverside, revealed that students concerned about AIDS agreed they increased

---

27. Jacqueline Darroch Forrest and Jane Silverman, "What Public School Teachers Teach about Preventing Pregnancy, AIDS, and Sexually Transmitted Diseases," *Family Planning Perspectives* 21 (March/April 1989): 65–71.

28. Leo Carroll, "Concern with AIDS and the Sexual Behavior of College Students," *Journal of Marriage and the Family* 50 (May 1988): 405–411.

## He needs sex for intimacy; she needs intimacy for sex

This is about a marriage that is falling apart. Only the names and some of the identifying details are changed.

He complains to her, "If we just had better sex, everything would be all right again."

She complains to him, "If everything were just all right again, we would have better sex."

Then they glower at each other. A separation is in the works. That ought to take care of the sex part, and the all right part, too.

Maybe these people don't read magazines or books. Lots of shrinks and quasi-shrinks have written about this kind of standoff.

### An old problem

Part of what's been written is that many, if not most, women need to feel intimate with a man before they are comfortable having sex with him. A woman likes to feel she is privileged to share a man's dreams and secrets, because he thinks she's special. She likes to feel chosen, appreciated, cherished, loved . . . add whatever warm and wiggly qualities you like to the string.

Only after she has achieved this intimacy is she eager to engage in sex. Sex is an affirmation and culmination of the closeness the two of them share.

Lots of men, however, do it the other way around. Sex is the path to intimacy. A man is not ready to share his private world or thoughts with a woman until after they have had sex. Before that, he feels alienated and separated, somehow in jeopardy and at risk. The sex act is the green light that tells him he's safe with this particular woman. She won't hurt or damage him. It's OK to get close and closer. She gives him her body. She cares about him.

### The honeymoon never lasts

Evidently, marriage doesn't change these basics. The people I know who are splitting have been married nearly 20 years. He's still saying more and better sex would mend the marriage. She's still saying the marriage needs mending before better sex is possible. They're both sick of mouthing these lines, and they've pretty much quit. He's looking for an apartment. She's looking for a lawyer.

I don't know who's right. Maybe nobody's right. Probably they're both right, sort of.

I think it's funny how we court each other, bending and yielding, understanding and responding to each other's needs and whims when we are unmarried or newly married. Then, when it could be much easier to do all those things, because we know each other better and have more time to study each other, we give up on it.

We abandon what was formerly successful behavior and expect that will have no effect on our partner or the union. It always does. A marriage is a living organism, highly sensitive to even slight changes in its environment. When a significant change persists, the organism is sometimes permanently damaged.

### That special touch

The woman in the vignette above says she has no interest anymore in attempting a reconciliation. It's been too cold around the house for too long, she says. She has no feeling that her husband thinks she's special. He doesn't share. He doesn't hug. He doesn't tell her she's wonderful. She says it will be better to feel alone and be alone than to feel alone and unloved by a husband demanding his sexual privilege. Maybe.

I don't know what he feels. Frustrated. Confused, probably. Cheated, emasculated, that he's married to a crazy lady who doesn't understand his need to feel secure before he can feel intimate.

Maybe it's all the same thing. If sharing sex is security for a man, confirming to him that a woman thinks he's special, certainly being stroked and sweet-talked represents the same security for a woman. One is an act, one is a voice. Both say the same thing: I love you; you are special.

Why is that so difficult a lesson for us to learn? Vive la difference, of course, but la difference is not so much as we make it.

*Source:* Nickie McWhirter, *Detroit Free Press,* January 20, 1982, p. 1-D. Reprinted with the permission of the Detroit Free Press.

the length of time before intercourse, inquired about the sexual history of the partner, were more likely to use condoms, and were less likely to engage in oral or anal sex.[29] Knowledge about AIDS per se, without a concern about the disease, neither increased the likelihood of condom use nor decreased high-risk behavior such as oral or anal sex.

Data from a 1988 national survey of adolescent males indicated that 60 percent of never-married young men ages fifteen to nineteen were sexually active. More than half of the sexually active males reported they had used a condom the last time they had had intercourse. This was more than double the reported rate of condom use in a similar study conducted nine years earlier in 1979.[30] The authors suggest the substantial increase in condom use may be a direct result of both the increase in awareness of the risks of AIDS and the increase in knowledge about the capacity of condoms to prevent the transmission of the virus.

Another national study found that 47 percent of women aged fifteen to forty-four (or their partners) used any contraceptive at first intercourse. The leading method at first intercourse was the condom, followed by the pill and withdrawal. Use of a contraceptive at first intercourse increased sharply in the 1980s because of an increase in the use of the condom. The proportion who used a method at first intercourse varied from 22 percent among Hispanic women to 74 percent among Jewish women; it was higher among white than black women, higher in higher socioeconomic categories. A higher age at first intercourse increased the likelihood that intercourse was planned, that sex and contraception were discussed with the partner, and that the degree of commitment to the relationship was higher.[31]

Perhaps the full impact of social forces such as AIDS and the conservative religious and political orientation of the 1980s on sexual behavior is only beginning to be felt. A 1987 Gallup poll revealed that the percentage of Americans who think that premarital sex is wrong has increased since 1985 (from 39 percent to 46 percent).[32] Eighty-three percent who disapproved did so because of moral or religious reasons.

Numerous changes in sexually related behaviors seem to be taking place: more disapproval of premarital sex, greater selectivity of partners, increased condom use, more AIDS education, and so forth. Studies of three samples of college students at a small New England liberal arts college in 1974, 1979, and 1986 revealed that sexual behavior increased dramatically from 1974 to 1979

29. Masako Ishii-Kuntz, "Acquired Immune Deficiency Syndrome and Sexual Behavior Changes in a College Student Sample," *Sociology and Social Research* 73 (October 1988): 13–18.

30. Freya L. Sonenstein, Joseph H. Pleck, and Leighton C. Ku, "Sexual Activity, Condom Use and AIDS Awareness among Adolescent Males," *Family Planning Perspectives* 21 (July/August 1989): 152–158.

31. William D. Mosher and Christine A. Bachrach, "First Premarital Contraceptive Use: United States, 1960–1982," *Studies in Family Planning* 18 (March/April 1987): 83–95.

32. "Digest," *Family Planning Perspectives* 20 (July/August 1988): 180–181.

and then decreased by 1986 to approximately where it was in 1974.[33] It was suggested that newly prominent sexually transmitted diseases (STDs), such as herpes and the most dreaded disease of all, AIDS, have succeeded in pushing college youth toward more committed sexual relationships, though not to abstention. In the short term at least, these trends can be expected to continue.

# SUMMARY

1. Premarital sexual relationships are generally thought to include a wide variety of sexual activities performed by those who have never been married. "Nonmarital" may be a more encompassing concept, referring to any type of sexual activity occurring outside of marriage, but the intent of this chapter was not directed to nonmarital sexual activities involving married or previously married persons. Irrespective of marital status or gender, all sexual activities have controls or restrictions placed upon them. These activities include coitus but in a more general sense encompass a wide variety of touching, kissing, and caressing activities as well.

2. Male-female differences in premarital sexual attitudes and behaviors have generally been explained by sociologists as due primarily to socialization and social control factors. However, a number of researchers have explored the interplay between biological predispositions and sociological models of adolescent sexuality. The biological component tends to focus on hormones and to influence early adolescent sexuality.

3. Sexualization was described as the process by which people acquire their sexual self-concepts, values, attitudes, and behaviors. Attention was given to learning processes in social interaction and the need to consider meanings and definitions of the situation to more fully understand behavior. These meanings and definitions make up our sexual scripts, designating the who, what, when, where, and why of sexuality.

4. Sexual attitudes and behaviors are highly interrelated. When they differed, it was argued that attitudes and beliefs will be more conservative or restrictive than will actual behavior. During adolescence, more permissive behaviors in dating, love, and interpersonal relationships will tend to modify the belief-attitudinal script.

5. Selected antecedents to sexual behavior include parental influence; however, neither parental attitudes nor parent-child communication appear to affect teenagers' subsequent sexual and contraceptive behavior. Parental discipline appears to have a curvilinear effect with both the most restrictive and permissive disciplinary patterns resulting in greater permissiveness.

6. Formal sex education programs seldom result in the type of positive consequences desired or negative consequences feared. The decision to engage in sexual activity

---

33. Bernard I. Murstein, Michelle J. Chalpin, Kenneth V. Heard, and Stuart A. Vyse, "Sexual Behavior, Drugs, and Relationship Patterns over Thirteen Years," *Adolescence* 24 (Spring 1989): 125–139.

is not influenced by sex education classes but appears to have some effect on contraceptive knowledge and effective use.

7. Premarital heterosexual intercourse has attracted widespread attention, particularly for females. The greater interest in females focuses not merely on premarital sexual norms but on norms linked to unmarried parenthood, an issue traditionally of less concern for males.

8. Studies completed prior to the 1980s indicate major changes in the sexual behavior of the never-married. These changes were most pronounced for females and moved in the direction of increased permissiveness, lessening the male-female difference but not eliminating a double standard.

9. As social forces occurred in the 1960s and 1970s that tended to encourage increased sexual permissiveness, so did the 1980s witness events (particularly AIDS and conservative religious and political movements) that tended to dampen the permissive trend. The 1990s appear to be a decade of increased selectivity of sexual partners and greater condom use, but not of abstention from sexual activity.

10. The chapter that follows continues an examination of human sexuality, with attention focused on the marital relationship, married persons, or previously married ones. Most of the social and cultural factors of significance prior to marriage continue to influence sexuality within a marital context.

# KEY TERMS AND TOPICS

Biological predispositions   292
Sexualization   295
Sexual scripts   297
Sexual attitudes and behaviors   299
Antecedents of sexual behavior   300
Formal sex education   303

Premarital intercourse prior to
   the 1980s   308
Premarital intercourse in the 1980s
   and 1990s   310
The impact of AIDS   310

# DISCUSSION QUESTIONS

1. It was mentioned that all societies control sexual activities. How is this done? Why?

2. Compare the sexual norms portrayed by the Catholic church, selected Protestant groups, soap operas on TV, *Playboy* magazine, the law, nudists, or topless bar girls. Within the same society, how can such differences be explained? What impact do they have on attitudes and behavior?

3. In your opinion, which is more important to understanding sexual behavior: (1) biological needs, drives, hormones, and the like, or (2)

(2) norms, values, attitudes, and so on? Explain.

4. Are males and females inherently different in sexual socialization? If so, in what ways does society contribute to the difference?

5. Give some thought to your own sexual scripts. What factors do you define as most influential in your current attitudes relating to inappropriate or acceptable sexual behaviors in regard to physical intimacy—with whom, where, why, under what conditions, and so forth?

6. Examine the relationship between what you

believe and what you do or have done. For you, how accurate is the idea that behaviors often exceed the acceptable belief-value script which in turn modifies the belief or value?

7. How would you explain the finding that parental attitudes and parent-child communication seem to have little effect on adolescent sexual behavior and contraceptive usage?

8. Discuss the impact, if any, of sex education on sexual attitudes, sexual behavior, or contraceptive usage. Contrast the impact of formal sex education classes relative to the impact of peers and informal sources.

9. Contrast the degree of sexual permissiveness prior to the 1980s to that of today. How do you account for the changes that have occurred?

10. How might nonmarital sexual behavior influence relationships, sexual or nonsexual, in marriage?

## FURTHER READINGS

Byrne, Donn, and Fisher, William A., eds. *Adolescents, Sex, and Contraception.* Hillsdale, N.J.: Lawrence Erlbaum Assoc., 1983. A book of readings on the noncontraceptive sexual behavior of adolescents, the reasons for that behavior, and possible solutions to the problem.

Chilman, Catherine S. *Adolescent Sexuality in a Changing American Society.* New York: John Wiley and Sons, 1983. A combination of research-based knowledge and theory from the social sciences, oriented to human service professionals who work with adolescents.

D'Emilio, John, and Freedman, Estelle B. *Intimate Matters: A History of Sexuality in America.* New York: Harper and Row, 1988. An interpretation of American sexual history showing how over three centuries the meaning of sexuality has changed from a family-centered reproductive system to a romantic, intimate, but conflicted one to a commercialized and personalized one.

Feldman, Harold, and Parrot, Andrea, eds. *Human Sexuality: Contemporary Issues.* Beverly Hills, Cal.: Sage Publications, 1984. Representatives of opposing moral, religious, legal, and political positions debate questions of contemporary human sexuality.

Francoeur, Robert T. "Human Sexuality" in *Handbook of Marriage and the Family* by Marvin B. Sussman and Suzanne K. Steinmetz (eds.). New York: Plenum Press, 1987, Chapter 19, pp. 509–534. A focus on sexual development, social factors in scripting sexual values and roles, and trends and projections of sexual behaviors.

Gagnon, John H. *Human Sexualities.* Glenview, Ill.: Scott, Foresman, 1977. An examination of the range of human sexualities including gender roles, sexual response, masturbation, homosexuality, offenses and offenders, therapies, and other topics.

Geer, James H., and O'Donohue, William T. (eds.). *Theories of Human Sexuality.* New York: Plenum Press, 1987. Fourteen approaches to human sexuality are covered, including feminist, developmental, anthropological, and sociological approaches, and sexual scripts, among others.

Hayes, Cheryl D., ed. *Risking the Future: Adolescent Sexuality, Pregnancy and Childbearing.* Washington, D.C.: National Academy Press, 1987. An excellent report on adolescent sexuality and fertility including five chapters on trends, determinants, and consequences, and four chapters on preventive interventions and policies.

Kinsey, Alfred C.; Pomeroy, Wardell; and Martin, Clyde. *Sexual Behavior in the Human Male.* Philadelphia: W. B. Saunders, 1948. With the following book, these are the classic Kinsey studies presenting an intensive analysis of male and female sexual behaviors ranging from sexual activities to male-female comparisons of the anatomy, physiology, psychology, and neural mechanisms of sexual response.

Kinsey, Alfred C.; Pomeroy, Wardell; Martin, Clyde; and Gebhard, Paul. *Sexual Behavior in the Human Female.* Philadelphia: W. B. Saunders, 1953. With the preceding book, these are the classic Kinsey studies presenting an intensive analysis of male and female sexual behaviors ranging from sexual activities to male-female comparisons of the anatomy, physiology, psychology, and neural mechanisms of sexual response.

Reiss, Ira L. *Journey into Sexuality: An Exploratory Voyage.* Englewood Cliffs, N.J.: Prentice-Hall, 1986. An attempt to develop an overall explanation of human sexuality that will apply cross-culturally and explain how society organizes and shapes our sexual lives.

Scarf, Maggie. *Intimate Partners: Patterns in Love and Marriage.* New York: Random House, 1987. Based on extensive interviews with a small number of couples, the author looks at what happens in intimate relationships including becoming a couple, third parties, marital problems, sexuality, parenting, and postparenting.

Schur, Edwin M. *The Americanization of Sex.* Philadelphia: Temple University Press, 1988. An assessment of the current state of American sexuality including an exploration of the sexual system as a whole in the light of its sociological groundings.

# CHAPTER ELEVEN

# *SEXUAL RELATIONSHIPS IN MARITAL CONTEXTS*

© Frank Siteman MCMLXXX

Were it not for the legal and social norms pertaining to sex, there would be very little reason for differentiating marital sex from premarital, nonmarital, extramarital, postmarital, or any other type of sexual relationship. This is why, although both married and unmarried men and women were included in the research population of the Masters-Johnson studies, no controls were made for marital status. Early in their investigation, a nonmarried group provided the opportunity for comparison-controlled studies with established marital groups. However, in their words:

> The unrehearsed physiologic and anatomic response patterns of the unmarried were recorded and contrasted to the mutually conditioned and frequently stylized sexual response patterns of the marital units. This technique for experimental control was abandoned as soon as it was established unequivocally that there is no basic difference in the anatomy and physiology of human sexual response regardless of the marital status of responding units.[1]

The legal and social norms regarding sex in American society make coitus between husband and wife the one totally approved type of heterosexual activity. Cross-culturally as well, marital coitus is recognized as the most important of all sexual outlets because of the significant role it plays in the maintenance of the family system.

## SEX AND MARRIAGE

Few would deny the importance of sexual intercourse to marriage. It is the one factor that, normatively at least, differentiates the marital relationship from any other social relationship. The relative importance of the sexual aspects of a marriage as compared with nonsexual aspects of a marriage will differ by sex, social class, and other factors. Let's examine, first, some selected results of the Kinsey studies; then we'll turn our attention to recent changes in marital sexual activity and sexual adjustment; finally we'll turn to other factors that relate to married persons but involve a nonspouse: extramarital coitus, incest, and postmarital coitus.

### Selected results of the Kinsey studies

Sexuality was brought into the public arena with the publication of the **Kinsey studies** in 1948 and 1953. This landmark research revealed two major surprises: (1) that what people actually did was far more permissive than the publicly proclaimed legitimate sexual codes, norms, and values, and (2) that

---

1. William A. Masters and Virginia E. Johnson, *Human Sexual Response* (Boston: Little, Brown, 1966): 16–17.

most people, married and single, were extremely misinformed or uninformed about sexuality. This research set the stage to make sexuality a legitimate area of research and provided a wealth of information making sexuality a legitimate subject for discussion as well.

While this research may today be viewed as "old," you will quickly note that while the frequencies and statistics may be different, many of Kinsey's findings and interpretations hold true over time. Let's note several examples. Question whether the following findings would be equally valid today.

The frequency of marital coitus, according to Kinsey, decreased with age, dropping from an average of 3.7 times per week during the teens to about 2.7 at the age of thirty, 1.4 at the age of forty, and 0.8 at the age of sixty.[2] Male and female estimates were highly comparable although females tended to estimate the frequencies of their marital coitus higher than males estimated them. Females who desired less coitus than they had were likely to overestimate, whereas males who wished for more than they obtained were likely to underestimate. The incidence and frequency of marital coitus reached their maximum in the first year or two after marriage. From that point, they had steadily dropped into minimum frequencies in the oldest age groups. There was no other activity among females to show such a steady decline with advancing age.[3]

Kinsey stated that one tragic finding for a number of marriages was that many of the husbands reported that early in their marriages they had wanted coitus more often than their wives, and the younger married females reported that they would be satisfied with lower coital rates than their husbands wanted. On the other hand, in the later years of marriage, many of the females expressed the wish that they could have coitus more frequently than their husbands were then desiring it. Over the years, most females became less inhibited and developed an interest in sexual relations that they might then maintain until they were in their fifties or even sixties.[4]

There were surprisingly few differences between the frequencies of marital coitus among females of the several educational levels represented in Kinsey's sample. But the men provided an interesting contrast. In the lower educational groups, about 80 percent of the total outlet in the early years of marriage was provided by marital coitus, and the incidence for this group increased to 90 percent as the marriage continued. For the college-educated men, marital coitus provided 85 percent of the total outlet during the early part of marriage, but by the time they reached the age of 55, only 62 percent of their total sexual outlet was provided by marital coitus. At no time in their lives did college-bred males depend on marital intercourse to the extent that lower-level males did throughout most of their marriages.[5]

---

2. Alfred C. Kinsey, Wardell B. Pomeroy, Clyde E. Martin, and Paul H. Gebhard, *Sexual Behavior in the Human Female* (Philadelphia: W. B. Saunders, 1953): 77.

3. Ibid., p. 348.

4. Ibid., p. 353.

5. Alfred C. Kinsey, Wardell B. Pomeroy, and Clyde E. Martin, *Sexual Behavior in the Human Male* (Philadelphia: W. B. Saunders, 1948): 567.

## Secrets of a trim, attractive body

Do you want to achieve or maintain a good-looking, sleek body? In a report in *Sexology,* a New York doctor, Abraham I. Friedman, stated that "sex is the ideal substitute for the gratification of emotional overeating."

Dr. Friedman, who has worked exclusively on weight control problems, said that increased sexual activity can help overweight people lose as much as four to five pounds a month in addition to the loss from regular dieting. He said the cause of many of his patients' overeating was emotional and that most of them had sexual difficulties. "They were substituting food for sex and love."

Dr. Friedman reported that the center of sexual response is in the same area of the brain that contains the center of appetite control. So, aside from the calories burned up (about 200) in the physical activity of lovemaking, "it is very likely that the increased activity of one center—sex—may have a dampening effect on the other—appetite."

Psychologically, there is a close link between our basic needs for food and sex. "When people are deprived of love and sex," said Dr. Friedman, "they often turn to food and overeat." Conversely, pounds and inches can be lost by sensibly substituting one basic need for another. The doctor said that for every three times you substitute sex for a 700-calorie snack, you'll lose more than one pound."

Moral: Next time you feel the urge to reach for a peanut-butter-and-banana sandwich, now you know what you really should be reaching for.

---

Kinsey suggested that only upper-level males become increasingly interested in extramarital relations as they grow older.[6] Why is this so? It may be that increased frequency of extramarital intercourse is due to: (1) a conclusion that the early restraints on their sexual lives were not justified, (2) a conclusion that extramarital experience should be secured before old age has interfered with the capacity to do so, (3) an increasing dissatisfaction with the relations with restrained upper-level wives, or (4) a preoccupation of the educated male with the professional or business affairs of his life leading to a decrease in marital intercourse—and perhaps to increased nonmarital opportunities.

The precoital techniques used in marriage were quite the same as those found in premarital petting that may or may not have led to coitus. In Kinsey's sample:

> Simple lip kissing between the spouses had almost always (99.4 percent) been an accompaniment to the marital coitus. In order of descending incidences, the other techniques which were used at least on occasion had included the manual stimulation of the female breast by the male (in 98 percent); the manual stimulation of the female genitalia by the male (in 95 percent); the oral stimulation of the female breast (in 93 percent); the manual stimulation of the male genitalia by the female (in 91 percent); extended oral techniques in deep kissing (in 87 percent); and finally the oral stimulation of the female genitalia by the male (in 54 percent) and of the male genitalia by the female (in 49 percent).[7]

---

6. Ibid., p. 568.
7. Kinsey, *Sexual Behavior in the Human Female,* p. 361.

How do Kinsey's data compare with more recent research? Note selected similarities and differences in marital sexual activity reported by Kinsey at the middle of the century with reported activity today.

### Changes in marital sexual activity and related factors

Some of the changes in frequency of sexual activity mentioned in the last chapter on premarital sexual behavior appear to be paralleled in marriage. Charles Westoff, reporting on data from national probability samples of married women of reproductive age in 1965 and 1970, showed an increase in this five-year time period in the overall coital frequency.[8] The increase was slightly higher among women in their twenties than among older women, but the increase appeared among women at all ages studied. This rise in reported coital frequency was found to exist almost regardless of method of birth control used and even where no method was used. Thus, it is not accurate to attribute the increase in coital frequency entirely to the increase in the proportion of women using the pill. On the other hand, Westoff noted that it seems reasonable to infer that the greater use of more reliable methods decreased anxiety about unintentional pregnancy and, therefore, relaxed some of the constraints on sexual expression (or perhaps on the willingness to talk about it).

Since there remains an increase in coital frequency over and above that accounted for by types of exposure to risk, how can this increase be explained? In addition to the influence of modern contraceptive technology, the availability of legal abortion could be said to further reduce anxiety about unwanted pregnancy. Other factors likely include the increase in openness about sex since the mid-1960s, the exploitation of sexual themes by the mass media, the developing emphasis on women's rights to personal fulfillment, a shift from the traditional passive sexual role to more assertive behavior among women, and the viewing of sex itself as a more natural, less taboo topic.

Figure 11−1 supports what Kinsey and other studies suggest about the relationship between coital frequency and age, the length of time together, or years married. In each category the frequency of coitus decreases.

Philip Blumstein and Pepper Schwartz, in an intensive examination of couples in the United States (married, cohabitors, gay men, and lesbians), found that for all couples, the frequency of sex declined with the length of time together.[9] Their data for married couples can be seen in Figure 11−1. For those married up to two years, 45 percent reported sex three times a week or more.

---

8. Charles F. Westoff, "Coital Frequency and Contraception," *Family Planning Perspectives* 6 (Summer 1974): 136−141.

9. Philip Blumstein and Pepper Schwartz, *American Couples* (New York: Pocket Books, 1983): 195−201.

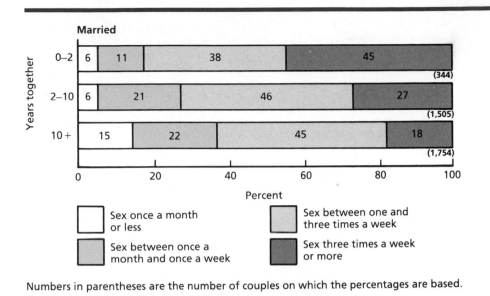

**Married**

Years together

| Years together | | | | | |
|---|---|---|---|---|---|
| 0–2 | 6 | 11 | 38 | 45 | (344) |
| 2–10 | 6 | 21 | 46 | 27 | (1,505) |
| 10+ | 15 | 22 | 45 | 18 | (1,754) |

Percent

☐ Sex once a month or less

☐ Sex between one and three times a week

☐ Sex between once a month and once a week

☐ Sex three times a week or more

Numbers in parentheses are the number of couples on which the percentages are based.

*Figure 11–1*
**Years married and sexual frequency.** *(Source:* Philip Blumstein and Pepper Schwartz, *American Couples.* [New York: Pocket Books, 1983], p. 196.)

This drops to 27 percent for those married two to ten years and to 18 percent for those married ten or more years. The opposite situation is equally true. While only 17 percent of those married two years or less had sex less than once a week, this increased to 27 percent for those married two to ten years, and to 37 percent for those married ten years or more. This last figure, assessed in reverse, would tell us that 63 percent of the married couples, even after ten years of marriage, have sex at least once a week. People who jest that marriage "ruins" sex by making it non-existent, find little support in these findings.

The first year of marriage is clearly the time of most frequent marital coitus. However, a striking finding of a study of persons married five years or less was the wide range of responses. Men reported monthly frequencies from 1 to 43, while the women's reports ranged from 2 to 45.[10] Male and female responses were fairly similar in that both had wide ranges, similar average frequencies (14.43 for men and 13.81 for women), and similar medians (12.0 for men and 12.5 for women). The best predictor of frequencies in the next few years proved to be frequency in the first year. After the first year, everything that happens to a couple—children, jobs, commuting, housework, financial

---

10. Cathy Stein Greenblat, "The Salience of Sexuality in the Early Years of Marriage," *Journal of Marriage and the Family* 45 (May 1983): 289–299.

*Sexual interaction and intimacy is a key aspect and function of marriage throughout the life course. Our sexual scripts, in or out of marriage, determine what is appropriate, with whom, when, why, and where.*

worries, fatigue, familiarity—combines to reduce intercourse frequency while nothing leads to increasing it. Despite the lower frequencies, sex was considered by the respondents as important or very important in marriage.

The discussion of declining coital frequency with age should not be interpreted to mean that sex becomes unimportant in marriage after age twenty-five, forty, or sixty. But it may call for a redefining of aging sexual behavior and the development of values that maximize the sexual relationship of aging couples. This may include the elimination of a stereotype that only links sex with youth and the early years of marriage. This may include viewing sexual activity as being more than "performance" oriented, more than genitally or intercourse oriented, and more than orgasm oriented. Other forms include nongenital sexual pleasuring and oral and digital manipulations that may or may not result in actual physiological orgasm and/or ejaculation.[11]

Many factors other than contraceptive usage and age have been found to be highly related to marital sexual activity. For example, intercourse is less frequent during menstruation. This was true even among a highly educated

11. Martha Cleveland, "Sex in Marriage: At 40 and Beyond," *The Family Coordinator* 25 (July 1976): 233–240; Ruth B. Weg, *Sexuality in the Later Years: Roles and Behavior* (New York: Academic Press, 1983); and Catherine G. Adams and Barbara F. Turner, "Reported Change in Sexuality From Young Adulthood to Old Age," *The Journal of Sex Research* 21 (May 1985): 126–141.

sample of married couples where one might anticipate less adherence to tradition.[12] Intercourse appears as well to be related to stress within the marriage. John Edwards and Alan Booth indicate that the more severe the marital strain, the lower the frequency of marital coitus.[13] They suggest that the sexual behavior of both males and females is largely contextual, determined to a greater extent by present circumstances (like marital strain) than past background.

Westoff reported that coital frequency increases with the amount of education of the wife, is higher among women who work in paid employment than those who do not work (highest among career-motivated women), and is positively associated with the effectiveness of contraception.[14] The highest frequencies are reported by women who are using the pill or the IUD or whose husbands have had vasectomies. The lowest frequencies are associated with the use of the rhythm method and the douche.

It is of interest to note that national survey data of married women under age forty-five show that, except for sterilization, Catholic and non-Catholic contraceptive practices are quite similar.[15] As of 1975, between 75 and 80 percent of both groups were using contraception. Very small percentage differences exist in the use of the pill (34 percent for both non-Catholic and Catholic), IUD (9.0 vs. 7.6), diaphragm (4.1 vs. 3.5), condom (9.6 vs. 14.9), or foam (3.9 vs. 2.6). Sterilization was more common for both non-Catholic wives (17.5 percent vs. 12.9) and husbands (15.6 vs. 13.1).

While certain female-male or Catholic–non-Catholic differences appear to be decreasing, marital sexual activities still vary considerably in numerous respects, such as by social class. Contrary to the notion that the lower classes are less sexually inhibited, the middle and upper classes are more likely to have intercourse in total nudity, use a variety of positions in intercourse, and engage in oral-genital contacts. While the stratification literature suggests that working-class people are increasingly adopting middle-class values and behaviors, Weinberg and Williams suggest that social class is still an important determinant of sexual behavior.[16] Compared to the lower and working classes, middle-class men and women started their sexual activities at a later age, were more likely to enjoy their first sexual experiences, and were more likely to react positively to masturbation.

One key reason for these differences may be related to gender roles. Generally, the lower the class, the greater the division between traditional

---

12. Naomi M. Morris and J. Richard Udry, "Menstruation and Marital Sex," *Journal of Biosocial Science* 15 (1983): 173–181.

13. John N. Edwards and Alan Booth, "Sexual Behavior In and Out of Marriage: An Assessment of Correlates," *Journal of Marriage and the Family* 38 (February 1976): 73–81.

14. Westoff, "Coital Frequency and Contraception," pp. 139–140.

15. Charles F. Westoff and Elise F. Jones, "The Secularization of U.S. Catholic Birth Control Practices," *Family Planning Perspectives* 9 (September/October 1977): 203–206.

16. Martin S. Weinberg and Colin J. Williams, "Sexual Embourgeoisment? Social Class and Sexual Activity: 1938–1970," *American Sociological Review* 45 (February 1980): 33–48.

male and female roles. Where there exists a high degree of role segregation between husbands and wives, the couple will tend not to develop as close or as gratifying an interpersonal sexual relationship. Where husbands and wives are likely to segregate work, recreational, or domestic activities into male or female roles, so too are they likely to clearly differentiate sexual roles. The result? Different sexual expectations and behaviors by social class.

## Autoeroticism in marriage

Masturbation, or autoeroticism, is widely recognized as a common sexual outlet. One would assume and expect that if masturbation is considered a substitute for intercourse, the frequency of masturbation would be low among the married who have daily access to a sexual partner. This hypothesis was not borne out by researchers. J. S. Greenberg and F. X. Archambault did not find significant differences between frequencies of masturbation and intercourse.[17] Hans Hessellund found that while there was a significant difference in intercourse frequency among married and unmarried subjects, there were no significant differences in frequency of masturbation between married and unmarried subjects.[18]

In or out of marriage, more men than women masturbate and do so more frequently. Hessellund tentatively concluded that for men masturbation functions more as a supplement to sexual life, while for women it is to a greater extent a substitute for intercourse.[19] Gagnon and Simon attribute the continued masturbation of men after marriage—and not only when their wives are absent—to continuation of the acting out of sexual fantasies that first developed in early adolescence.[20]

For women, it could be predicted that as gender role training includes the development of sexual imagery, an increase in masturbatory activity, for both married and single women, would follow. Masturbation permits independent and autonomous control of pleasure, producing an orgasm that females particularly find to be more intense physiologically than occurs from intercourse. This may result from the fact that the masturbator does not have to regulate his or her own sexual pleasure to the sequence or routines of another person and thus inhibit the power of self-gratification.[21]

## Rape in marriage

Until recently, marital rape has been ignored in the marital-family literature. It has been brought to light more recently as a feminist issue involving an act of

17. J. S. Greenberg and F. X. Archambault, "Masturbation, Self-Esteem and Other Variables," *Journal of Sex Research* 9 (February 1973): 41–51.

18. Hans Hessellund, "Masturbation and Sexual Fantasies in Married Couples," *Archives of Sexual Behavior* 5 (1976): 133–147.

19. Ibid., p. 139.

20. John H. Gagnon and William Simon, *Sexual Conduct* (Chicago: Aldine, 1973): 65.

21. Ibid., p. 65.

## A substitute for overeating and drinking

Dr. Sol Gordon, professor emeritus at Syracuse University and the author of many books on sexuality, suggests in *Psychology Today* (October 1986) that if you must have a compulsion, please choose masturbation rather than overeating or overdrinking. Nobody has ever died from overmasturbating.

While written somewhat in jest, he argues that the issue is more important than it appears. Masturbation is one of the biggest concerns of young people, and they need to know that masturbation is a normal expression of sexuality. While few take seriously the myths that masturbation causes acne, tired blood, mental illness, or blindness (Gordon questions if that's why he wears glasses), most parents don't give outright approval to their children to masturbate. Some people suggest it may be all right if done in private and if not done too much. But Gordon questions how much is too much? After every meal, twice a week, once a year?

Since teenagers and adults have strong sexual urges, Gordon questions why we create dumb solutions, such as taking cold showers. He questions the value of how we deal with anxieties—by eating when not hungry or drinking when not thirsty. Why not encourage people to masturbate, which is a much more effective solution to coping with high levels of anxiety, tension, or sexual needs. In his thirty years of clinical work, he has yet to hear about a rapist, child molester, or chronically sexually dysfunctional person who grew up feeling comfortable about masturbation. In response to researchers who suggest that masturbation itself provides a powerful stimulus for sexual abuse, Gordon says this is found to be true only if the molester despises masturbation, feels guilty about it, or both.

*Source:* Sol Gordon, "What Kids Need to Know," *Psychology Today* 20 (October 1986): 22–26.

physical violation against women. It is only in the past few decades that victims of rape, in or out of marriage, were recognized as people who needed assistance.

Rape, simply defined, is forced sex without consent. Legal definitions generally involve three separate factors: sexual intercourse involving vaginal, anal, or oral penetration; force or threat of force; and nonconsent of the victim. As recently as 1977, laws in twenty-nine states specifically stated that a man cannot be prosecuted for raping his wife.[22] Yet Russell reports that one out of every seven women interviewed who had ever been married reported at least one, and sometimes many, experiences of rape by her husband.[23]

Bowker, in reviewing studies of marital rape, makes several points.[24] First, marital rape may be more common than all other kinds of rape combined. Second, marital rape is commonly found among battered wives. Third, motivating factors for marital rape include anger, the need to dominate, and occasionally sexual obsession. Fourth, marital rape may be as psychologically disturbing as nonmarital rape and have long-term severe effects. Fifth, marital rape within violent marriages seems to affect women's self-esteem negatively

---

22. "The Marital Rape Exemption," *New York University Law Review* 52 (May 1977): 306–323.
23. Diana E. H. Russell, *Rape in Marriage* (New York: Macmillan, 1982).
24. Lee H. Bowker, "Marital Rape: A Distinct Syndrome?" *Social Casework* (June 1983): 347–348.

as well as their attitudes toward men and heterosexual behavior. And sixth, husbands who rape their wives are likely to have problems with alcohol, to have had serious dysfunctions in their families of orientation, and to dominate totally their marriages.

Frieze reported similar findings from interviews with women in attempting to investigate the determinants and consequences of marital rape.[25] Sexual pressuring or being forced to have sex was the most commonly reported form of marital rape. Most of the women felt the cause stemmed from their husbands' belief that such an action served to prove his manhood. They all saw the rape as the responsibility of the husband and brought on by factors in his personality rather than by the wife's provocation. Her study confirms that marital rape is a serious matter, that many women undergo severe emotional and behavioral reactions, that it is often associated with battering, and that the women need sources of help. What seemed clear was that the quality of the couple's sexual relationship was closely linked with the health of the marriage.

## SEXUAL ADJUSTMENT

Sexual adjustment has been highlighted by certain writers as the keystone to marital adjustment. However, it is highly unlikely that adjustment of any sort is a dichotomous either/or phenomenon. Within any marriage, there are certain times and situations in which sex is "better or worse" than other times or situations. Also, to assume that frequency of intercourse, attainment of female orgasm, or an uninhibited sex life is equal to sexual adjustment is both misleading and false. It is very difficult to separate sex from the total complex of interaction that constitutes married life. Sexual adjustment may be one indicator of general marital adjustment, but it is doubtful that sexual adjustment alone will maintain an otherwise poor relationship. Dissatisfaction in a marriage is likely to be reflected in the frequency and performance of marital coitus, and conflict in sexual coitus may be symptomatic of other tensions within the marital relationship.

The Blumstein and Schwartz study of couples in the United States cited earlier supports this linkage between sexual adjustment and the quality of the relationship.[26] Their findings led to the overwhelming conclusion that a good sex life is central to a good overall relationship. Their married couples felt so strongly about having sex often that those who said they have it with the partner infrequently tended to be less satisfied with the entire relationship. What is not known definitively is whether an unsatisfactory relationship leads to less frequent sexual activity or whether the problems begin in the bedroom

---

25. Irene Hanson Frieze, "Investigating the Causes and Consequences of Marital Rape," *Signs: Journal of Women in Culture and Society* 8 (1983): 533.

26. Blumstein and Schwartz, *American Couples*, pp. 201–206.

and eventually corrode the entire relationship. This author tends to lean more heavily toward the notion that when nonsexual parts of a marital relationship are going poorly, the quality and frequency of the sexual relationship will decline as well.

The last statement is not meant to deny the effect that sexual inadequacies have on the quality of a relationship. Masters and Johnson estimate that 50 percent of all marriages in the United States have some form of sexual inadequacy, such as primary or secondary impotence, vaginismus, premature ejaculation, orgasmic dysfunction, unequal level of response, or others.[27] This may be a partial explanation for the popularity of sex manuals.

### Marriage/sex manuals

An indirect indication of the desire for sexual adjustment in marriage may stem from the sale of marriage manuals. This assumes, perhaps falsely, that the purchases are made (1) primarily by married persons and (2) for purposes of improving sexual relations within marriage. Whether marriage manuals are read, the advice is followed, or the relationship is affected is another issue. Sales alone, however, indicate widespread interest and present great potential for influencing public opinion.

What kind of messages do sex manuals portray? One publication reporting on models of female sexuality in forty-nine United States sex manuals from 1950 to 1980 indicated that they generally reflect one of three distinct models.[28] The first model of female sexuality, and the one predominant in the 1950s and 1960s, portrays males and females as *different and unequal.* Female sexuality was naturally emotional and male sexuality was more animalistic or physical. This model assumed that female sexual response lies dormant until it is awakened by an experienced and skillful male partner, teacher, and leader. The second model most prevalent in the early 1970s was one of *humanistic sexuality.* These manuals portray sex as a basic human quality and remove it from the context of marriage. That is, partners are no longer referred to as husband and wife but as male, female, partner, or couple. Traditional sex roles in the bedroom are denounced and sex is portrayed as an experience to be explored, experimented with, and enjoyed without rules or roles. The third model, *sexual autonomy,* prevalent since 1975, portrays women as independent agents, self-sufficient and in control of their own sexuality. While the first two models view the sexual experience dyadically as primarily an interactive phenomenon, this model focuses on the private sexual experience of women, who are told to take responsibility for their own satisfaction. Orgasm, a

---

27. William H. Masters and Virginia E. Johnson, *Human Sexual Inadequacy* (Boston: Little, Brown, 1970): 351–369.

28. Martin S. Weinberg, Rochelle Ganz Swensson, and Sue Kiefer Hammersmith, "Sexual Autonomy and the Status of Women: Models of Female Sexuality in U.S. Sex Manuals from 1950 to 1980," *Social Problems* 30 (February 1980): 312–324.

product of learning, is viewed as every woman's right with or without a man, thus emphasizing both coital and noncoital techniques.

Brissett and Lewis, who described sex manuals in the 1960s as stressing work themes requiring a good deal of study, practice, and preparation, examined more recently published manuals to see if the old work ethic still prevails.[29] They found that basically it does. What a person can choose, however, is, to a certain degree, the style of work, and to a much greater degree, the life-style surrounding the work. Unlike the previous manuals analyzed, the recent manuals do not define good sexual relations as merely a product of proper techniques, diligent applications, and marital orgasm. The newer manuals seem obsessed with making sexual relations interesting through the stylization of time, place, equipment, and maneuvers. Instead of feeling guilty for having too much sexual pleasure, sexual partners now may very well experience anxiety for not having enough. Since almost everything is now permitted in the realm of sexuality, Brissett and Lewis suggest that it is just possible that "nothing any longer is good enough."[30]

Unfortunately, many popular manuals, magazines, and journals, in fulfilling a basic function of educating and informing men and women about sex, have also contributed to a fear of sexual performance. To be informed about the average number of coital experiences per week among married couples, multiple orgasms, or coital positions may be very interesting but may also lead to serious questioning and doubts about one's own performance. The male and female whose sexual practices do not conform to the social norms may seriously question their own adequacy or "normality." If other couples are having intercourse three or four times a week and we are engaging in coitus once a month, is something wrong? If other women during orgasm turn blue, feel the earth move, hear bells chime, or pant and scream ecstatically, am I less of a woman if I quietly experience a pleasant sensation? Masters and Johnson state that these grave self-doubts and usually groundless suspicions are translated into fears of performance.

> It should be restated that fear of inadequacy is the greatest known deterrent to effective sexual functioning, simply because it so completely distracts the fearful individual from his or her natural responsivity by blocking reception of sexual stimuli either created by or reflected from the sexual partner.[31]

### Dealing with sexual inadequacies

Probably no therapy program for dealing with sexual inadequacies has ever been undertaken with as solid a research base as that of the Reproductive

---

29. Dennis Brissett and Lionel S. Lewis, "The Big Toe, Armpits, and Natural Perfume: Notes on the Production of Sexual Ecstasy," *Society* 16 (January/February 1979): 63–73.
30. Ibid., p. 73.
31. Masters and Johnson, *Human Sexual Inadequacy*, pp. 12–13.

Research Foundation under the directorship of Masters and Johnson. The purpose of their treatment program is aimed at restoring sex to its natural context so it functions like breathing—that is, without conscious effort and with spontaneity. The types of dysfunctions they attempt to correct include primary (total) and secondary (partial) impotence, premature ejaculation, and ejaculatory incompetence on the part of the male; orgasmic dysfunction and vaginismus on the part of the female; dyspareunia (painful intercourse); and the aging process on the part of both sexes.[32]

Two concepts that appear particularly significant to behavioral scientists are what Masters and Johnson term the **spectator role** and the **sexual value**

---

32. Here, *dysfunction* refers to a sexual malfunction, usually social and psychological in origin. *Primary impotence* refers to the inability to ever achieve or maintain an erection sufficient for intercourse. *Secondary impotence* refers to failure at some times, success at others. *Premature ejaculation* refers to ejaculation before, immediately upon, or shortly after penetration. *Orgasmic dysfunction* refers to the inability and failure of the female to reach orgasm. *Vaginismus* refers to the psychosomatic illness that affects a woman's ability to respond sexually by virtually closing the vaginal opening to male entry. *Dyspareunia* refers to painful intercourse.

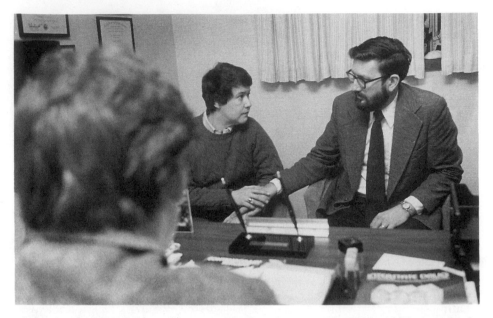

*That many couples fail to achieve sexual adjustment, satisfaction, and pleasure leads some to read self-help books or seek out sex counselors or therapists. A fear of inadequacy has been found to be a major deterrent to effective sexual functioning.*

**system.** The spectator role involves learning to eliminate the negative effect of self-consciously trying to produce certain sexual results. It attempts to eliminate the deliberate placing of the mind on what is desired rather than on a "natural response." In reference to the spectator role of the impotent husband, the authors note:

> As sex play is introduced and mutual attempts made by marital partners to force an erective response, the impotent husband finds himself a spectator to his own sexual exchange. He mentally is observing his and his partner's response (or lack of it) to sexual stimulation. Will there be an erection? If and when the penis begins to engorge, how full will the erection become? When erection is obtained, how long will it last? The involuntary spectator in the room demands immediate answers for these questions from the anxious man in the bed, so intensely concerned with his fears of sexual performance. Rather than allowing himself to relax, enjoy sensual stimulation, and permit his natural sexual responsivity to create and maintain the erective process, he as a spectator demands instant performance.[33]

The problem is compounded because the wife too is operating in the spectator role. In her attempt to provide her husband with an erection, she too

---

33. Masters and Johnson, *Human Sexual Inadequacy*, p. 65.

may be questioning what she is doing wrong in assisting him to perform adequately.

The sexual value system, termed *SVS* by Masters and Johnson, refers to those sensory experiences an individual has had under circumstances that he or she finds pleasurable on the one hand and, on the other, is not offensive to the values he or she has learned from society (e.g., family, church, school, peer group, or other). Physiologically, male and female sexual responses are very similar, but where the female differs radically is in her sexual value system—her psychosocial aspect of sexuality.

In many ways society prohibits the female in U.S. society from developing a positive sexual value system. While the male may often be praised or honored in his sexual performance, the reality of the female's sexual function still carries many implications of shame and misbehavior—neither of which contributes to high levels of marital sexual harmony. Many women are reared in our society to believe that "nice girls don't involve themselves," "sex is for reproductive purposes," or "sex is a man's privilege."

Treatment of sexual dysfunction, according to Gagnon and others, is viewed in the broad context of sexual scripts.[34] Rather than explaining and treating narrowly conceived terms such as vaginismus or premature ejaculation, one needs to look at the total script. Finding solutions to problems means focusing on both the performance and the cognitive script and modifying what one does and/or what one thinks. If, as Masters and Johnson claim, the greatest overall cause of malfunction is fear, this too is part of our sexual script. And problem solving thus revolves around modification of the behaviors and ideas that make up our performance and cognitive sexual scripts.

## EXTRAMARITAL COITUS

A chapter on sexual relationships in marital contexts may well be incomplete without a look at sexual relationships among married persons with persons (married or single) other than their spouse.

The terms *extramarital coitus* or *adultery* refer to nonmarital sexual intercourse between a man and a woman, at least one of whom is married at the time to someone else. Almost without exception in the United States, adultery is legally punishable. And although actual prosecution is rare, the moral condemnation that accompanies extramarital coitus is, in general, much stronger than that directed at premarital or postmarital coitus. It is widely held that adultery is condemned in practically all Western cultures because of the threat it poses to the family unit. Secondly, it is assumed (and

---

34. John H. Gagnon, Raymond C. Rosen, and Sandra R. Leiblem, "Cognitive and Social Aspects of Sexual Dysfunction: Sexual Scripts in Sex Therapy," *Journal of Sex and Marital Therapy* 8 (1982): 44–56.

sometimes falsely so) that marriage provides a socially approved legitimate sexual partner, and thus sexual deprivation is minimized.

Lynn Atwater argues that several myths contribute to an unrealistic faith in sexual exclusivity in the United States.[35] One is that one person can and will supply all of another's emotional, social, and sexual needs. A second is that people grow to love each other more as years go by. A third is that sexual exclusivity comes easily and naturally. These myths lead us to blindly believe that if only our partners are faithful, all of our emotional needs will be satisfied. Yet the extent of extramarital relations suggests otherwise.

Sexual relationships in general have traditionally held very different standards for men and women. While a double standard continues to exist, the previous chapter illustrated a trend toward a convergence of attitudes and behavior in the area of premarital sex. There does not seem to be evidence for such a trend regarding extramarital sex. Today, much greater concern centers around the extramarital behavior of the wife than that of the husband. Kinsey noted that most societies permit or condone extramarital coitus for the male if he is reasonably circumspect about it and if he does not carry it to extremes that would break up his home, lead to the neglect of his family, outrage his in-laws, stir up public scandal, or start difficulties with the husband or other relatives of the women with whom he has relationships.[36] On the other hand, such extramarital activity is much less frequently permitted or condoned for the female.

Even though a double standard exists in the United States, it is far less pronounced than in many countries that provide and permit considerable freedom for the male with harsh restrictions and taboos placed on the female. For example, Japan prior to World War II could be considered a "man's world." Shin'ichi Asayama, reporting on Japan, noted that all Japanese husbands enjoyed some form of sexual contact outside of marriage.[37] In contrast, infidelity by a wife was condemned as a crime from both a legal and moral point of view. Since World War II, the social and economic conditions for women have improved, changing the situation radically. However, sexual freedom for women does not approach the same level as for men. Even today, it is felt that Japanese men openly enjoy more sexual freedom than do U.S. and probably European men. Women in the United States enjoy more freedom than Japanese women, but U.S. women seem to be less tolerant than Japanese women about their husbands' extramarital sexual relations.[38]

A unique feature of extramarital sex involving Japanese women is their emotional involvement with their partner. While Japanese women may not

35. Lynn Atwater, *The Extramarital Connection* (New York: Irvington Publishers, 1982): 18.
36. Kinsey, *Sexual Behavior in the Human Female*, p. 414.
37. Shin'ichi Asayama, "Adolescent Sex Development and Adult Sex Behavior in Japan," *The Journal of Sex Research* 11 (May 1975): 107.
38. Minako K. Maykovich, "Attitudes Versus Behavior in Extramarital Sexual Relations," *Journal of Marriage and the Family* 38 (November 1976): 693.

## Can you afford both a querida and a wife?

Polygyny is not permissible for the Christian Filipino male, but those who can afford it have a querida. In the Philippines, the querida system involves a married man, usually of higher status, seeing, supporting, and possibly having children by a woman other than his wife. While a "mistress relationship" is frowned upon, the civil code provides for the maintenance of his illegitimate children. The double standard is seen in that equal privileges do not exist for the wife. He can separate from her for adultery on her part, but she cannot do likewise. Nor can the wife bring an action for legal separation against the husband unless he maintains his mistress in the same dwelling as his legitimate wife. The wife can, of course, simply leave him or refuse to cohabit, which would be a separation de facto. But the former would simply create additional problems of support and custody of the children.

The frequency of this keeping a "mistress," "second wife" (not legally), or querida, is unknown. But an informal survey of priests from twenty-two dioceses suggests that the percentage of men with queridas is about one or two, although in certain urban social strata it is probably much higher.

The querida often represents a serious threat to a wife and children in diminishing their man's affection and support. Thus while wives may know about their husband's querida, they may pretend they do not. As long as the man adopts some measure of self-control and fidelity, his morality is secure and his role adequately discharged. The wife, in turn, avidly participates in religious life and, in effect, prays for two, her piety making up for both her own and her husband's failings.

approve of extramarital sex, once exposed to the opportunity they are inclined to be emotionally involved. Women in the United States, in contrast, are less likely to be pushed into an extramarital relationship by an unhappy marriage but rather are pulled or drift into the relationship.[39] In the absence of restrictive cultural norms regarding sexual activity, U.S. women who engage in extramarital sex approve of it, but their commitment to it is weak. This is consistent with Ralph Johnson's findings that 60 percent of adulterous wives had high marital adjustment (compared to 30 percent of the husbands), showing a low association between extramarital sex and marital dissatisfaction for U.S. wives.[40]

Like any other sexual outlet, it is impossible to know with any high degree of accuracy how frequently adultery takes place. Kinsey's figures indicate that by age forty, 26 percent of the females and 50 percent of the males had experienced extramarital coitus.[41] Minako Maykovich found that 32 percent of middle-class U.S. women aged thirty-five to forty had experienced extramarital sex at least once.[42] Ralph Johnson noted that 69 percent of the

---

39. Ibid., pp. 696–698.
40. Ralph E. Johnson, "Some Correlates of Extramarital Coitus," *Journal of Marriage and the Family* 32 (August 1970): 454.
41. Kinsey, *Sexual Behavior in the Human Female*, p. 437.
42. Maykovich, "Attitudes Versus Behavior," p. 695.

husbands and 56 percent of the wives in his study indicated a positive inclination to interact with a person of the opposite sex when their spouse was out of town. This does not mean coitus would result from such interaction but it does indicate the potential, given the opportunity.[43]

What factors account for or are highly related to extramarital coital experience? Of all the factors that Kinsey examined, religious devoutness, more than any other, affected the active incidences of extramarital coitus, particularly for the females. The lowest incidences of extramarital coitus had occurred among those who were most devoutly religious, and the highest incidences had occurred among those who were least closely connected with any church activity. This was true of all the Protestant, Jewish, and Catholic groups in the sample.[44]

David Weeks and Joan Jurich employed five national surveys to investigate the relationship between attitudes toward extramarital sexual relations and a measure of size of community of present residence.[45] Size of community was strongly and directly related to extramarital attitudes. As persons from small communities are more likely to be politically conservative, to be less supportive of the Equal Rights Amendment, to express greater opposition to sex education, communism, or welfare, so are they more likely to disapprove of premarital and extramarital sexuality. Greatest approval of extramarital sexual relationships was found to exist among persons who reside in or near large metropolitan centers, as well as among those who hold permissive premarital sexual attitudes, who are either unmarried or unhappily married, and who have high levels of education.

Atwater, in studying fifty feminist-oriented women, suggests that extramarital coitus for these women is a direct response to the women's movement. They are breaking out of a traditional scene that demanded faithfulness for them but not for their husbands. And extramarital behavior for women is an arena where they are free to establish the kinds of sexual patterns they prefer with no social pressure to maintain less than satisfactory relationships, no deep investment of love and romance, and no long-term institutional pattern that defines sex as having purposes other than personal pleasure. For these women, participation in extramarital sex signals continued liberation from traditional sexuality and, in Atwater's words, is "the final assault on the double standard."[46]

Another partial assault on the double standard is a specific type of extramarital coitus referred to as "swinging," "consensual adultery," "mate swapping," "wife swapping," "co-marital sexual behavior," or "group sexual

43. Ralph Johnson, "Some Correlates of Extramarital Coitus," p. 452.

44. Kinsey, *Sexual Behavior in the Human Female*, p. 424.

45. David L. Weis and Joan Jurich, "Size of Community of Residence as a Predictor of Attitudes Toward Extramarital Sexual Relations," *Journal of Marriage and the Family* 47 (February 1985): 173–178.

46. Atwater, *The Extramarital Connection*, pp. 190–191.

**Please reply in confidence**

Chicago West Suburbs—Happily marrieds, 26 and 33, white, would like to hear from social minded married for fun evenings and good times. Phone and photo please.

Pontiac Area Marrieds—Attractive, would like to hear from other similar-minded adults for dining, nights out, and games. Not necessarily in that order.

Texas Marrieds—Late 30s, attractive, Latin, would like to hear from other Latin or Anglo marrieds for adult fun and friendship. Answer all. Phone and photo please.

Florida Marrieds—Liberal minded, affectionate, attractive, late 20s, would like to hear from other similar qualified marrieds. We can travel. Phone, photo, and address if possible.

Jersey Marrieds—White, 29 and 30, happily married, discreet and liberal-minded. Would like to hear from other liberal-minded marrieds who enjoy photography and correspondence. Age and race no barrier. Photo please with phone will bring prompt reply.

Northern Calif. Marrieds—Attractive, white, liberal-minded. Would like to hear from other marrieds for adult fun. Discretion assured. Will answer all who include phone and photo.

Southern N.Y. Area—Attractive and happily marrieds, 28 and 25, white, would like to hear from other liberal-minded marrieds. Phone and photo and must be discreet.

activities." While these involve a single standard of sexual permissiveness, it is doubtful they will find widespread acceptance or will ever approach the frequency of nonconsensual extramarital sexual relationships. They differ from adultery, however, in their nonsecrecy, openness, and greater degree of honesty between the marital partners.

# INCEST

**Incest** refers to sexual intercourse between certain family members, particularly those within and closest to the nuclear family: father-daughter, mother-son, brother-sister, stepfather-stepdaughter, and the like. A taboo on incest is believed to be universal in human culture although sexual relations between family members do occur.

George Murdock, in drawing data from 250 societies, set forth a number of empirical conclusions concerning incest taboos. Among others, these included: a universal application to all persons of the opposite sex within the nuclear family; a universal application to at least some relatives outside the nuclear family but variations as to which specific relatives are included or excluded (such as aunts or uncles, half-siblings, nieces or nephews, cousins); a universal principle of no instances where relatives outside the nuclear family are more stringently tabooed than ones within it; a lack of coincidence of the taboo with nearness of actual biological relationship outside the nuclear unit; a tendency of incest taboos to be associated with those relatives who are given terms such as *mother, sister,* or *daughter;* a failure of taboos against adultery or fornication to exceed in strength the taboo against incest; and an apparent

Here lies the child, here lies the father,
Here lies the sister, here lies the brother,
Here lies the wife and the husband
Yet there are but two bodies here.

Inscription on a grave at Ecouis in Europe, 1512

This late-medival inscription (riddle) is about
how a woman and man are, at one and the same

time, wife and husband, sister and brother, and
daughter and father. The tradition is that a son of
Madame d'Ecouis had by his mother, without
knowing her or being recognized by her, a daughter named Ceclia, whom he afterwards married.

*Source:* Marc Shell, *The End of Kinship* (Stanford, CA.: Stanford
University Press, 1988):65—66.

universal violation of the incest taboo in spite of the strength of this sexual
prohibition.[47]

Most concern over incestuous relationships has tended to focus on
father-daughter incest. But more recently a picture has emerged of substantial
numbers of boys who were victims of father-son incest and sexual interactions
among siblings and cousins.[48] If incest is defined in a broad sense to include
sexual stimulation and arousal rather than more narrowly as intercourse, then
these types of brother-sister, cousin-cousin, and even mother-child incestuous
relationships are universal and common.

Because of the secrecy which surrounds the violation of this most basic
sexual taboo, no accurate statistics exist on its prevalence. In the United States,
most data come from police or court records, and it is highly probable that
most cases of incest are not reported. It does, however, seem reasonable that
more incest than is reported occurs in intact families and escapes the
attention of social agencies and survey researchers. One report indicated that
approximately 10 percent of all women report a childhood sexual experience
(not necessarily intercourse) with a relative, and 1 percent are victims of
father-daughter incest.[49] Family sexual abuse occurs in all social classes and in
urban as well as rural environments. The most frequent victim is a daughter,
and the most frequent perpetrator is a biological father but often is a step- or
foster father or even a boyfriend or lover of the mother.

In interviews with a random sample of more than 900 adult women in
San Francisco, Diana Russell found that while the most frequent incest
perpetrators were biological fathers (since most women lived with and were
accessible to biological fathers), the next largest group was stepfathers.[50] The

47. George P. Murdock, *Social Structure* (New York: Macmillan, 1949): 284—289.

48. Mark Williams, "Father-son incest: A Review and Analysis of Reported Incidents,"
*Clinical Social Work Journal* 16 (Summer 1988): 165—179; and Allan R. DeJong, "Sexual Interactions
among Siblings and Cousins: Experimentation or Exploitation," *Child Abuse and Neglect* 3 (1989):
271—279.

49. Judith Herman, "Father-Daughter Incest," *Professional Psychology* 12 (February 1984):
76—80.

50. Diana E. H. Russell, "The Prevalence and Seriousness of Incestuous Abuse: Step-fathers
vs. Biological Fathers," *Child Abuse and Neglect* 8 (1984): 15—22.

likelihood of incestuous abuse was far greater if a stepfather was the principal figure in the woman's childhood years (17 percent or one out of approximately every six women) than if a father was the principal figure (2 percent or one out of approximately forty women). And perhaps more significantly, when stepfathers sexually abused their daughters, they were much more likely than any other relatives to abuse them at the most serious level (forced penile-vaginal penetration, oral–vaginal-penis sex, or anal intercourse) in contrast to experiences such as digital penetration of the vagina, touching of breasts, buttocks, thigh, leg, forced kissing, and so forth. She explains these differences by suggesting that stepfathers, not being biologically related to their daughters, may feel less bound by the normative taboo on incest. Another explanation was that the bonding that commonly occurs between biological fathers and daughters may often be absent between stepfathers and daughters. A third explanation suggested that the daughter, often feeling betrayed by the mother who remarried, may compete with the mother for the attention of the stepfather. Whatever the explanation, the far greater prevalence and serious-ness of stepfather-daughter incest over biological father-daughter incest suggests that daughters in remarriage face substantial risks of incestuous abuse.

### Explanation for the taboo against incest

How can the taboo against incest be explained? One theory attributes it to the recognition by primitive people of the dangers of close inbreeding.[51] However, it is doubtful that early societies were aware of the genetic effects or the principles of heredity. Even if they were, it seems logical that it would have been used to produce a higher quality human such as has since been widely adopted with animals. Furthermore, these variable taboos do not coincide with biological nearness, thus discounting the idea that incest rules have their basis in biological or genetic factors.

A second explanation attributes incest prohibition to instinct. But if it were instinctive, avoidance of incest would be automatic. How would one explain the diversity of the taboos and their lack of correlation with actual consanguinity?[52] It is a fallacy to attempt to explain social phenomena that vary widely from one society to another on the basis of a relatively stable biological factor, and thus instinctive interpretations of social phenomena are rarely seen in the social sciences.

Some writers regard the prohibition of incest as habits formed during childhood. Habits of avoidance result from the dulling of the sexual appetite through prolonged associations. This idea suggests that to grow up in the

---

51. Melvin Ember, "On the Origin and the Extension of the Incest Taboo," *Behavior Science Research* 10 (June 1975): 249–281.

52. Ibid., p. 290.

same household with a person of the opposite sex eliminates that person as a sexual or marital partner. However, as Murdock suggests, this theory does not harmonize with cases where marriage with a housemate is actually favored, is inconsistent with the widespread reference for levirate and sororate unions, is contradicted by the enduring attachments between husband and wife that occur in most societies and, above all, overlooks, and even inverts, the vast body of clinical evidence showing that incestuous desires are regularly engendered within the nuclear family and are kept in restraint only through persistent social pressure and individual repression.[53]

Murdock suggests that no unitary theory of incest taboos appears capable of accounting for all their aspects. For his explanation, he draws upon psychoanalysis, sociology, cultural anthropology, and behavioristic psychology. According to Murdock:

> It thus appears that a complete scientific explanation of incest taboos and exogamous roles emerges from a synthesis of the theories of four separate disciplines that deal with human behavior. *Psychoanalytic theory* accounts for the peculiar emotional quality of such taboos; for the occurrence of violations, which neither an instinct hypothesis nor Westermarck's theory of acquired aversion explains; for the diminished intensity of taboos outside of the nuclear family; and for the universal occurrence of incest avoidance tendencies which serve as a basis for cultural elaboration. *Sociological theory* demonstrates the social utility of both intra-family and extended incest taboos and thus accounts for the universality. *Psychological behavior theory* reveals a mechanism by which extension occurs and that by which social utility becomes translated into custom, thus supplying an essential part of the reasons for both the universality and the variety of extended taboos. *Cultural anthropology*, finally, contributes to our explanation of the varied conditions of social structure and usage which channelize generalization or produce discrimination, and thus accounts for the differential incidence of exogamous rules and extended incest taboos, for their correlation with conventional groupings of kinsmen, and for their lack of correspondence with actual biological relationship.[54]

It would be difficult to imagine the nature of the full system of rules within the family and between families if there were no prohibitions against sexual relations and marriage between members of the same nuclear family. Take simply the confusion of statuses that would result should inbreeding occur. "The incestuous male child of a father-daughter union . . . would be a brother of his own mother, that is, the son of his own sister; a step-son of his own grandmother; possibly a brother of his own uncle; and certainly a grandson of his own father."[55]

---

53. Murdock, *Social Structure*, p. 291.
54. Ibid., p. 300.
55. Kingsley Davis, "Legitimacy and the Incest Taboo," in *A Modern Introduction to the Family* ed. by Norman W. Bell and Ezra F. Vogel (Glencoe, Ill.: The Free Press, 1960): 401.

Some writers argue that the incest taboo is not universal and in certain instances is highly dysfunctional. The cases most frequently mentioned are those of brother-sister marriages among the Incas, the Hawaiians, and the ancient Egyptians. However, for our basic purposes, isolated instances such as these rarely pertain to a society as a whole but only to limited groups of high prestige where maintenance of status takes precedence over other factors. Exceptions to the taboo on incest are sanctioned primarily among royalty and rarely for commoners.

# POSTMARITAL COITUS

Compared to the subjects of premarital, nonmarital, marital, or extramarital coitus, relatively little attention has been given to the subject of coitus after the dissolution of marriage through death, separation, or divorce. An intense interest exists in the sexual activities of the young prior to marriage and the importance of coitus in marriage. But after marriage, the importance of coitus enters into a state of limbo between an activity that is vital and necessary to psychological and emotional health and an activity that contradicts the conventional morality of confining coitus to marriage. Paul Gebhard states that the escape from this dilemma is to ignore and minimize the problem as much as possible, but if forced to take a position to condemn publicly and condone privately.[56] This dilemma between the public and private norms as they relate to postmarital coitus indicates a social permissiveness insofar as publicity is kept minimal.

## The incidence of postmarital coitus

It is generally assumed that most if not all previously married men and women engage in coitus. Reporting on the incidence of postmarital coitus based upon interviews with 632 white females, the Institute for Sex Research, with which Kinsey was associated, found major differences between the postmarital sexual behavior of the widowed and the divorced. Eighty-two percent of the divorced had had such coitus compared to 43 percent of the widowed.[57] At all ages, substantially more divorced women had had coitus than had widowed women. The age-specific incidence of postmarital coitus indicated that during their twenties and thirties, roughly two-thirds to three-quarters of the divorced had coitus in contrast to one-third to one-half of the widowed. In their forties, the divorced widened their lead: about three-fifths to two-thirds of them experienced coitus, as opposed to roughly one-quarter to one-third of the

---

56. Paul Gebhard, "Postmarital Coitus Among Widows and Divorcees," in *Divorce and After* ed. by Paul Bohannan (Garden City, N.Y.: Doubleday, 1970): 81–96.
57. Ibid., p. 84.

### The new other woman: Could she be you?

Do the words "mistress," "other woman" and "paramour" conjure up visions of a potential home wrecker, a "kept woman" who sits around in a black lace teddy keeping martinis on ice for her lover?

Scratch that image, says author and Ohio State University sociology professor Laurel Richardson.

"The contemporary Other Woman is likely to be our neighbor, our sister, our daughter, our mother, ourselves: regular, normal, everyday single women," writes Richardson, author of "The New Other Woman" (Free Press).

Most often, they are career women, some of whom earn more than their lovers. They come from all social strata. Many are divorced and raising children alone. Often, she says, the last thing they want is for their lovers to become their husbands.

Changes have occurred, Richardson said during a recent Detroit visit, because there are many more single women today. "Women are delaying marriage, divorcing more often, and they are in daily contact with married men at work," she says.

"Between 40 and 50 percent of husbands report having at least one affair during their marriages, and almost 70 percent of married men under age 40 imagine they will have one," Richardson says. "Fifteen percent of married men are chronic womanizers and will have repeat affairs."

Single women don't set out to become the "other woman," but fall into these relationships because there are so few single men for them to date, she says. Today there are 33 million single women in America, Richardson says, and one in five does not have a potential mate.

Given the imbalance, "it is likely that the single woman over 25 who has never had a relationship with a married man will be in the minority," she says.

These women have to "learn to feel good about themselves and the lives they choose," Richardson says.

Problems arise, she says, when a woman's married lover—who started out as the object of a carefree fling—suddenly becomes the most important thing in the woman's life.

Although she thinks she's going into an affair with her eyes open, romantic mist may soon cloud her vision, Richardson says. The secret nature of the affair itself creates a situation in which it's easy for a woman to fall in love, changing the nature of her supposedly light-hearted dalliance.

"Mystical explanations for her falling in love are unnecessary," writes Richardson. "The conditions—secrecy, privacy and time constraints—under which her relationship with a married man is built are aphrodisiacal enough to afford ample explanation."

Soon, the woman is spending too much of her leisure time waiting for her married lover to call, waiting for him to get away from home, leaving her calendar free for spur-of-the-moment opportunities. And when the affair ends, many go through the same traumas a divorcing woman does, without the support system.

"I wrote the book because I saw how one of my best friends suffered when her relationship ended," says Richardson, who was in the midst of a divorce herself at the same time the friend was ending an affair. Friends and family rallied around Richardson, but her friend, who had kept her affair

---

widowed. After age fifty, the differences lessened as age exerted its leveling influence, but they were still very marked.

Gebhard found enormous differences between the widowed and the divorced deriving from several interrelated factors.[58] One of these was religion, with the critical matter proving to be the degree of devoutness rather than the denomination. From 30 to 40 percent of the widowed were labeled devout on

---

58. Ibid., p. 86.

secret, had no one with whom to share her pain.

Richardson does not condone or condemn such relationships, but points out the pitfalls. "I want the book to help these women handle their guilt and other feelings they never expected to have," she says.

Richardson says she tried to start an "other woman anonymous" group at Ohio State to help gather material for her book, but could find no one interested in revealing herself. Over eight years, she interviewed women at conferences and eventually conducted in-depth interviews with 55 women aged 24 to 65.

Their case histories are unique, but touch on common themes. Most of the couples met through work. Once they succumbed to a mutual sexual attraction and established relationships, the women faced similar problems, involving sex, emotional entanglements, guilt and fighting the logistics of the affair.

She says "other women" should keep these points in mind:

Do not withdraw from your regular life. Continue to see friends and family, and keep busy rather than saving all your free time for your lover.

Include someone in your life who knows about your relationship. This person, a sister, a best friend, is a source of realistic feedback: "They can say to you, 'Don't kid yourself.'"

Don't give away your independence. If your lover tries to control your activities and you comply because you're afraid to upset him or end the affair, you may be in for further emotional trouble.

It may be better to be involved with more than one married man, to cut down the strength of attachment to a single man. Also, Richardson says, it's not uncommon for a woman to discover she isn't the only "other woman" in a man's life.

Plan for the ending at the beginning. The women Richardson interviewed seldom married their lovers. One of the most successful endings, she says, involved a psychiatrist and his patient who remained friends after their affair ended and she married someone else.

What is her advice to the wife?

If she loves him and wants to maintain the marriage, Richardson says, "She should ignore (the affair) as long as possible." With luck, the affair might end before it becomes public knowledge and the wife feels pressured to take action.

Richardson suggests the wife talk to a counselor and not automatically feel she is at fault, or take rash action.

"Having the love of a man is the strongest cultural imperative women have been conditioned to seek to value themselves," says Richardson. When their husbands find love elsewhere, or if a single woman has no man in her life, they often feel a personal devaluation. Meanwhile a man's feeling of self-worth comes from his success in work, Richardson says, and does not depend as much on a woman's love.

*Source:* Marj Jackson Levin, *Detroit Free Press*, November 22, 1985, pp. 1B and 4B. Reprinted with the permission of the Detroit Free Press.

the basis of church attendance, as opposed to 15 to 29 percent of the divorced. There was a moderate tendency for both groups to become more devout with increasing age. A second factor was prior experience in coitus outside of marriage. If an individual had had premarital or extramarital coitus, he or she was more likely to engage in postmarital coitus. No great differences existed in premarital coitus (28 percent widowed, 37 percent divorced), but greater differences existed in extramarital coitus (8 percent widowed, 33 percent divorced). The divorced had a "head start" on the widows in that 31 percent were having extramarital coitus in their final year of marriage. A third factor centered around the type of relationship desired. Widows appear to be more interested in an emotional rather than a purely sexual relationship. Emotional relationships take longer to develop than do sexual ones. A fourth factor was the trauma of being widowed. Even after the initial phase of acute grief has ameliorated, the widow may find it difficult to find a mate who measures up to the image of her deceased husband, an image which tends to benefit from selective memory. A fifth factor related to remarriage. Divorcees were more likely to engage in coitus. That is, many women who would have ordinarily avoided coitus for moral (or other) reasons had it when marriage seemed impending.

It is perhaps surprising to note that when the coital-orgasm rate in the postmarital period is compared to that of the previous marriage, both the widowed and divorced have a greater orgasmic response in postmarital life. This may be attributable to the greater proportion of postmarital women who decide whether or not coitus will occur. It may also be attributable to the newness and the happier emotional relationships of the postmarital situation. Particularly for the divorced, one can generally assume unhappiness in the terminal years of the marriage. And it has been demonstrated that marital unhappiness is associated with a lower orgasm rate for wives. A third factor accounting for the higher postmarital orgasm rate may relate to the relaxation of inhibition that accompanies age, experience, and maturity. It could be assumed that different partners and new experiences would result in learning-educational benefits.

## SUMMARY

1. Marriage legitimizes the sexual relationship. The social norms that surround sex and marriage are the key factors in differentiating marital sex from premarital, extramarital, or any other circumstance outside the marital relationship. Coitus within marriage comprises a larger proportion of the total sexual outlet than any other type of heterosexual activity and is recognized cross-culturally as important in the maintenance of the family system.
2. Studies indicate that the incidence and frequence of marital coitus reach their maximum in the first year or two after marriage, with a steady decline from that time on. As in premarital coitus, marital coital rates showed an increase during the latter part of the 1960s. A variety of explanations account for this shift including a decrease in exposure to the risk of pregnancy and an increased societal openness about sexual matters.
3. Two issues within marriage that are typically ignored are autoeroticism and rape. While frequency of intercourse varies considerably in or out of marriage, the frequency of masturbation appears less likely to do so. Rape, on the other hand, may be more common in marriage than in any other context. It is often associated with physical brutality.
4. Sexual adjustment is one factor in marital adjustment, but it is doubtful that this factor alone would maintain an otherwise "poor" marital relationship. The interest

in this topic can be seen in the widespread sale of sexual manuals and books. These reflect a variety of models concerning relations between the sexes and the nature and meaning of sexuality.

5. One of the most extensive, research-based programs for dealing with sexual inadequacies is the Reproductive Biology Research Foundation under the director-ship of Masters and Johnson. Two concepts of significance to the social scientist include the spectator role and the sexual value system. Treatment of sexual dysfunctions was viewed in the broad context of sexual scripts.

6. As indicated, not all heterosexual coitus of married persons occurs with the spouse. Extramarital coitus, incest, and postmarital coitus appear to be widespread with major differences between males and females and across cultures. Extramarital coitus appears to be highly related to premarital permissiveness, to marital strain, to alienation and powerlessness, to community size, to higher levels of education, to autonomy of interaction, and other factors. Swinging, or co-marital sexual behavior, is a form of extramarital coitus involving both husband and wife.

7. Incest, while exhibiting a universal taboo, appears to be an occurrence that is neither unknown nor rare. Growing up with stepfathers, in contrast to biological fathers, greatly increases the likelihood of incestuous abuse as well as the seriousness of it. The chapter includes an examination of various explanations for this widespread taboo on sexual relationships between selected family members.

8. The chapter concludes with an examination of postmarital coitus. Among the formerly married, nearly all the men and the large majority of the women engage in coitus at some time. Major differences in the incidence of coitus exist between divorced and widowed women.

9. This chapter examined sexual relationships in marital contexts by reviewing key findings, discussing sexual adjustment and inadequacies in marriage, and conclud-ing with extramarital, incest, and postmarital coitus. All are significant to marital interaction. Continuing within a premarital and marital life-cycle sequence, attention is directed in the following chapter to marital structures and processes.

## KEY TERMS AND TOPICS

Sex and marriage   319
Kinsey studies   319
Changes in marital sexual activity   322
Autoeroticism in marriage   326
Rape in marriage   326
Sexual adjustment   328
Marriage/sex manuals   329

Dealing with sexual inadequacies   330
Spectator role   331
Sexual value system   331
Extramarital coitus   333
Incest   337
Postmarital coitus   341

## DISCUSSION QUESTIONS

1. Examine the two volumes of the Kinsey stud-ies. What do you perceive to be their most significant findings? To what extent are their findings influenced by their samples, their

methods of gathering data, and their interpre-tation of the data? How applicable are these findings today?

2. In what ways is marital coitus likely to be in-

fluenced by employment of husband and/or wife, income, religion, number and/or presence of children, age, and other factors? How do you explain changes that have taken place?

3. Discuss the implications and seriousness of marital rape. What types of control, punishments, laws, programs, and the like might be effective in dealing with this issue?

4. What, in your estimation, constitutes "good" sexual adjustment in marriage? Is it possible to have "good" sexual adjustment and "poor" marital adjustment? Is the opposite possible?

5. Describe husband-wife and male-female differences in sexual response through the life cycle. How are these differences explained?

6. Review five leading sex manuals. To what extent are social norms and values discussed? In what ways might they be helpful, harmful, or both to marital sexual relationships?

7. Make a list of sexual difficulties in marriage. Are some of them unsolvable? What factors are most likely to lead to these difficulties? What factors are significant in resolving them?

8. Examine the significance of concepts such as the spectator role or sexual value system.

9. What are the arguments for and against extramarital sex, swinging, or mate swapping? How can they be disruptive to or improve marriage?

10. Which explanations for the universality of the incest taboo can you accept? Are there possible explanations other than those given in the chapter? What are they?

11. In what ways is postmarital coitus different from marital or premarital coitus? In what ways would you expect similarities or differences between the sexual behavior and activity of the divorced versus the widowed?

12. Read the insert on "The New Other Woman." Why do these "other women" select married men? What are the pros and cons of such relationships?

# FURTHER READINGS

Atwater, Lynn. *The Extramarital Connection.* New York: Irvington Publishers. 1982. A sociological perspective of extramarital involvements based on intensive interviews with fifty women.

Cuber, John F., and Harroff, Peggy B. *The Significant Americans: A Study of Sexual Behavior Among the Affluent.* New York: Appleton-Century, 1965. A research study by the authors through interviews with 437 American men and women who were designated as elites, top influentials, or upper-middle-class.

Finkelhor, David, and Yllo, Kersti. *License to Rape: Sexual Abuse of Wives.* New York: Holt, Rinehart, and Winston, 1985. A very readable and comprehensive survey of marital rape including types of rape, who does it, the impact of marital rape, and the like.

Lawson, Annette. *Adultery: An Analysis of Love and Betrayal.* New York: Basic Books, 1988. An extensive overview of adultery (a term chosen to dramatize the greater punishment inflicted on the married woman) using a snowball sample and replies to newspaper articles of men and women in Great Britain.

Mahoney, E. R. *Human Sexuality.* New York: McGraw-Hill, 1983. A multidisciplinary research-based textbook written by a professor of sociology.

Maltz, Wendy, and Holman, Beverly. *Incest and Sexuality: A Guide to Understanding and Healing.* Lexington, Ma.: Lexington Books, 1987. With a focus on female incest survivors, this book examines the effects on self-concept, relationships, and sexuality with concluding chapters on getting help.

Masters, William H.; Johnson, Virginia E.; and Kolodny, Robert C. *Human Sexuality.* Boston: Little, Brown, 1982. The founders and directors of the Masters and Johnson Institute in St. Louis and the authors of *Human Sexual Inadequacy* and *Human Sexual Response* provide an introductory textbook integrating the biological, psychosocial, and cultural elements of human sexuality.

Murdock, George P. *Social Structure*. New York: The Free Press, 1965. Although recommended reading for a general and excellent cross-cultural perspective on family structure, the book also extensively analyzes sexual patterns and incest.

Offir, Carole Wade. *Human Sexuality*. New York: Harcourt Brace Jovanovich, 1982. A textbook on human sexuality, covering a wide range of topics including the psychobiology of sex, sexual behavior and relationships, sexuality across the life span, and sex as a social and medical issue.

Richardson, Laurel. *The New Other Woman: Contemporary Single Women in Affairs with Married Men*. New York: The Free Press, 1985. The author dispels old stereotypes of the "other woman" based on interviews with single women who were involved in relationships with married men.

Russell, Diana E. H. *Rape in Marriage*. New York: Macmillan, 1982. A study involving more than 900 interviews of wives in San Francisco to discover the incidence and circumstances surrounding rape by husbands.

Schulz, David A. *Human Sexuality*. Englewood Cliffs, N. J.: Prentice-Hall, 2nd ed., 1984. A textbook covering sexuality issues from many perspectives: cross-culturally, gender roles, love, commitment, fantasy, anatomy, problems, disease, the law and others.

Shell, Marc. *The End of Kinship: "Measure for Measure," Incest, and the Idea of Universal Siblinghood*. Stanford, Ca.: Stanford University Press, 1988. A calling into question the distinction between kin and nonkin or between chastity and incest and an exploration of the ending of kinship or the doctrine of Universal Siblinghood.

Shepher, Joseph. *Incest: A Biosocial View*. New York: Academic Press, 1983. Combining biological theory and ethnographic data, the author presents a genetic and mathematical model of a sociobiological theory of incest.

Weg, Ruth B., ed. *Sexuality in the Later Years: Roles and Behavior*. New York: Academic Press, 1983. A multidimensional exploration of human sexuality and sensuality among the elderly and the widespread destructive stereotypes associated with this age group.

# CHAPTER TWELVE

# THE MARITAL SYSTEM

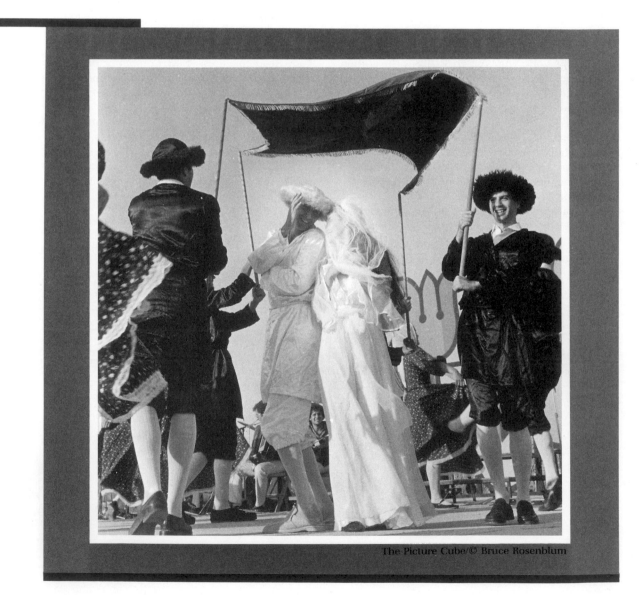

The Picture Cube/© Bruce Rosenblum

$A$lthough this chapter concentrates more exclusively on marriages, with particular emphasis on the dominant husband-wife patterns and roles in the United States, each previous chapter included discussions of selected aspects of the marital system. The first chapter included census data on marriage and issues within U.S. marriages. Subsequent chapters differentiated marriages from families; presented a wide range of nontraditional marital life-styles including those with multiple spouses and dual careers; and provided information on Chinese and African-American marital practices, social-class differences, interfaith and interracial situations, structures and processes in the selection of a mate, and sexual relationships in marital contexts. Included within this chapter are data on the functions of marriage, marriage trends and characteristics, a discussion of conjugal power, and some factors associated with marital adjustment.

## FUNCTIONS OF MARRIAGE

Today marriage is popular. Despite conflict, divorce, delays in marrying and a changing marital scene, most U.S. citizens marry. Normative expectations include marriage as an appropriate and desirable state, and with rare exceptions this end is accomplished. Despite the complex tasks of mastering mate selection interactions, celebrating the rituals and ceremonies that accompany the act of marriage, and fulfilling the requirements of domestic life, few avoid these rounds of activity and remain unmarried. Obviously, marriage fulfills various functions for the individual and society.

Marriage, as an institutionalized relationship within the family system, fulfills many functions attributed to the family in general. As suggested in earlier chapters, family functions include basic personality formation, status ascriptions, nurturant socialization, tension management, replacement of members, economic cooperation, reproduction, stabilization of adults, and the like. Many of these functions, while not requiring marriage for their fulfillment, are enhanced by the marital system. In fact, evidence suggests marriage to be of great significance for the well-being of the individual. Compared to the unmarried, married persons are generally happier, healthier, less depressed and disturbed, and less prone to premature death, with some evidence suggesting the differences in well-being between unmarried and married persons are becoming greater rather than smaller.[1] Weingarten as well, in a national study comparing first married, currently divorced, and remarried

---

1. Ruut Veenhoven, "The Growing Impact of Marriage," *Social Indicators Research* 12(January 1983): 49–63; and Ofra Anson, "Marital Status and Women's Health Revisited: The Importance of a Proximate Adult," *Journal of Marriage and the Family* 51 (February 1989): 185–194.

## Marriage vows: before and after

He married her because among other things, her hair looked so beautiful.

He divorced her because she spent so much time fixing her hair.

She married him because his muscles rippled so much when he swam.

She divorced him because he spent more time in the bedroom doing sitting-up exercises than anything else.

He married her because she was such an adept conversationalist, never at a loss for a word.

He divorced her because she never got off the telephone.

She married him because he loved to take her dancing.

She divorced him because he was "tired" most of the time.

He married her because she was so "vivacious."

He divorced her because she was too restless.

She married him because he could support her in lavish style.

She divorced him because he had too firm a hold on the purse-strings.

He married her because their families shared a common background.

He divorced her because her family kept interfering in their affairs.

She married him because he had a robust masculine appetite and appreciated her cooking.

She divorced him because he never wanted to take her out to eat.

He married her because she was quick, neat, and intelligent.

He divorced her because she had absolutely no patience with the children, who were sometimes slow, slovenly, and stupid.

She married him because he was a "real sport."

She divorced him because he refused to give up the sporting life.

He married her because they shared the same intellectual and political beliefs.

He divorced her because she wasn't interested in anything but the house and the kids.

She married him because he was so courteous and attentive in all the little things that matter so to a woman.

She divorced him because he was so punctilious about little things, and so oblivious to important things.

He married her because all the other men were so impressed with her magnificent figure.

He divorced her, after the third child, because she had "let herself go."

*Source:* Sidney Harris, copyright Publishers-Hall Syndicate.

adults found the currently divorced less exuberant about life than either of the married groups.[2]

Norval Glenn and Charles Weaver, however, using national survey data, show a rather steady decline from 1972 through 1986 in the positive relationship between being married and marital happiness.[3] The change

---

2. Helen R. Weingarten, "Marital Status and Well-Being: A National Study Comparing First-Married, Currently Married, Currently Divorced, and Remarried Adults," *Journal of Marriage and the Family* 47 (August 1985): 653–662.

3. Norval D. Glenn and Charles N. Weaver, "The Changing Relationship of Marital Status to Reported Happiness," *Journal of Marriage and the Family* 50 (May 1988): 317–324; and Norval D. Glenn, "Continuity Versus Change, Sanguineness Versus Concern," *Journal of Family Issues* 8 (December 1987): 348–354. *See also:* Andrew Greeley, "The Declining Morale of Women," *Sociology and Social Research* 73 (January 1989): 53–58; and James A. McRae, Jr. and Charles J. Brody, "The Differential Importance of Marital Experiences for the Well-Being of Women and Men: A Research Note," *Social Science Research* 18 (1989): 237–248.

occurred primarily through an increase in the reported happiness of never-married males and a decrease in the reported happiness of married females. These changes, they suggest, may relate to the increase in similar circumstances of the married and unmarried. A substantial proportion of unmarried persons, for example, have available regular sexual relations without stigma and since divorce can be obtained rather easily by any spouse who wants it, marriage no longer provides the security, financial or otherwise, it once did. In other words, in the context of this discussion, the functions that marriage fulfills may be increasingly found in contexts other than marriage. Given the evidence that Americans are becoming increasingly individualistic and less committed to social groups of all kinds, Glenn and Weaver call for a reassessment of the belief that the institution of marriage in the United States is as strong as ever.

When marriage is examined cross-culturally, the consequences of marriage differ as the structure of marriage differs. For example, where marriage is specifically an extension of the kin and extended-family system, then procreation, passing on the family name, and continuation of property become a basic function. Thus, to not have a child or, more specifically, to not have a male child, is sufficient reason to replace the present wife or add a new wife. In the United States, while most children are born of a married couple and while most married couples want children, to not have children is rarely a sufficient reason to remarry. Nor is the undesirability or impossibility of having a child, as with a career-oriented woman, sterile persons, or older women, a sufficient reason for not marrying. Thus why marriage?

The chapter on mate selection processes mentioned that, for arranged marriages, important factors include the bride's price, the reputation of the potential spouse's kin group, levirate and sororate arrangements, and traditions of prescribed marriage arrangements. Where marriage is based on "free choice," individualistic forces are accorded greater significance. Thus in the United States, marriage has many functions and involves many positive as well as negative personal factors: establishment of a family of one's own, children, companionship, happiness, love, ego support, economic security, an approved sexual outlet, affection, escape, elimination of loneliness, pregnancy, ad infinitum. The greater the extent to which the perceived needs of marriage are met, and the fewer the alternatives in the replacement of the unmet needs, the greater the likelihood of marriage and the continuation of that marriage. Why marriage? At a personal level, any perceived reason may explain marriage; but at a social level, all societies sanction certain reasons and renounce others. Thus personal factors operate within the confines of social boundaries; the functions that marriage performs are determined and qualified by the social and cultural context.

The social and cultural context of the United States is currently witnessing a variety of marital forms other than the traditional monogamous, sexually exclusive marriage pattern for the fulfillment of individuals' perceived needs. A familiar pattern is sequential or *serial monogamy*: the marriage, divorce, remarriage, divorce pattern. Another familiar pattern is *adultery*, the maintenance of the marriage with a secret satisfaction of sexual and emotional needs outside the conjugal relationship. *Nonmarital cohabitation*, a relatively common practice today, involves a male and a female sharing a common residence. These and other nontraditional patterns have been examined previously. In the United States, as around the world, marriage or some alternative exists to fulfill basic functions generally attributed to the husband-wife relationship.

## MARRIAGE TRENDS AND CHARACTERISTICS

As just shown, the reasons for marriage and the functions it performs vary extensively when viewed in a global perspective. So too is there variation in marriage rates: the proportion of people who marry in a given population. For example, one investigation of 111 countries showed that high sex ratios (i.e., a relative undersupply of women) are positively associated with the proportion of women who marry and inversely associated with women's average age at marriage.[4] That is, the fewer women relative to men, the higher proportion who marry and the younger the age at which marriage takes place. The number and proportion of people who marry are influenced by other factors as well: economic conditions, wars, male-female roles, and so forth. Let us take a specific look at marriage trends in the United States.

In 1988, of the 188.4 million persons age fifteen and over in the United States, 105.2 million or 59.1 percent were married. As can be seen in Figure 12–1, the percentages married differed considerably by sex and race. More than 63 percent of white males, but only 41 percent of black females age fifteen and over, were married.

Why the extreme differences? Broadly viewed, marriage results from two factors: composition and propensity to marry. Composition refers to the availability of potential marriage partners with certain characteristics while propensity to marry refers to the mutual attraction for marriage between males and females with specific characteristics, independent of the composition of the population. A composition of black and white marriage rates suggested that propensities play a major role in accounting for black-white differences and for change over time in black marriage rates.[5] The suggestion is that irrespective of population composition, the marriage relationship is less central to blacks as seen in the greater likelihood of consensual unions, ties outside the nuclear family, and of children born out of wedlock and reared in

---

4. Scott J. South, "Sex Ratios, Economic Power, and Women's Roles: A Theoretical Extension and Empirical Test," *Journal of Marriage and the Family* 50 (February 1988): 19–31.

5. Robert Schoen and James R. Kluegle, "The Widening Gap in Black and White Marriage Rates: The Impact of Population Composition and Differential Marriage Propensities," *American Sociological Review* 53 (December 1988): 895–907.

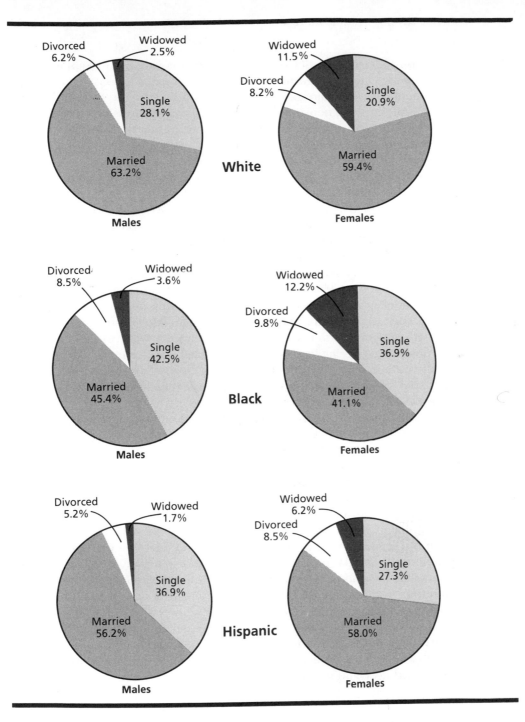

*Figure 12–1*
*Marital status of persons fifteen years old and over by sex, race, and Spanish origin, 1988.*
*All figures represent percentages* (*Source:* U.S. Bureau of the Census, *Current Population Reports*, Series P-20, no. 433, "Marital Status and Living Arrangements: March 1988" [Washington, D.C.: U.S. Government Printing Office, 1989], Table 1, pp. 4–8.

single-parent households. Blacks, especially women, are more skeptical of the value of marriage than are whites; they hold lower expectations for realizing a stable monogamous marriage where husbands provide much financial support; and they have negative expectations about relationships that they see as exploitative. Again, irrespective of composition, rather than enter a marriage from which little is expected and which holds the promise of exploitation, many lower-income black women prefer to remain unmarried.

For the population as a whole, in spite of the increasing delay in marriage, a divorce rate perceived as very high, a dramatic increase in cohabitation, and the talk of a declining popularity of and propensity for marriage, 2.4 million marriages occurred in 1988, a marriage rate (number of marriages per 1,000 population) of 9.7.[6] This rate has varied widely over the past fifty years (see Figure 12–2). It has fluctuated under the influence of wars, changing economic conditions, sex ratio of the marriageable population, and the number of potential brides and grooms present in the general population. Characteristically, the marriage rate has risen at the outset of a major war, declined during the course of the conflict, and increased sharply in the immediate postwar years. This was the experience for World Wars I and II and was probably true during the Civil War. Economic recessions and depressions generally have had an inhibiting effect on marriages, as have shifts in the age distribution of the population resulting in a smaller proportion of the population at the young adult ages.

In 1932, at the depth of the Depression, the rate plunged to a low of 7.9, probably unprecedented in this country except perhaps during the Civil War. The influence of World War II is unparalleled in the history of marriage rates in the United States. Just before and immediately after the United States' entry into the war, the rate rose sharply as young men sought to avail themselves of the deferred status granted to married men or simply wanted to marry before going overseas. The end of the war and the return of millions of men to civilian life precipitated an upsurge in marriages. In 1946 the marriage rate reached 16.4, an unprecedented and to date unsurpassed peak. By 1949 the rate had returned to the pre–World War II level, dropping as rapidly as it had climbed. This marked the end of twenty years of the most frequent and pronounced fluctuations in the history of United States marriage rates.

Dropping back to rates below 9.0 in the late 1950s, the marriage rates increased through the 1960s to a level of between 10 and 11 and fluctuated between these levels for nearly 20 years. The 1988 rate of 9.7 is the lowest rate since 1967. A number of recent changes in family life have been attributed to declines and delays in marriage. These include increases in sexuality among

---

6. National Center for Health Statistics, "Annual Summary of Births, Marriages, Divorces, and Deaths: United States, 1988," *Monthly Vital Statistics Report*, Vol. 37, No. 13 (Hyattsville, Maryland: Public Health Service, July 26, 1989): 2.

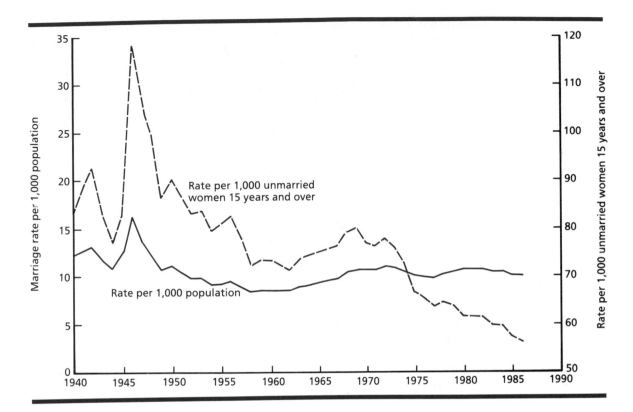

*Figure 12–2*
**Marriage rates: United States, 1940–1986.** (*Source:* National Center for Health Statistics, "Advance Report of Final Marriage Statistics, 1986," *Monthly Vital Statistics Report*, Vol. 39, No. 3, Supplement 2[Hyattsville, Maryland: Public Health Service, July 13, 1989], Figure 1, p. 2.)

the unmarried and an accompanied increase in out-of-wedlock births, an increase in the independence of young people, nonmarital cohabitation, labor-force participation of women, a reduction in fertility, a temporary shortage of eligible males in the marriage market (a marriage squeeze), and the trend over the past few decades of an increase in divorce.[7] Although these represent dramatic changes from the past that could suggest further declines in marriage, strong evidence exists that people in the United States continue to value marriage. Marriage is viewed as important among both young and old and remains a popular choice for most U.S. citizens.

---

7. Willard L. Rodgers and Arland Thornton, "Changing Patterns of First Marriage in the United States," *Demography* 22 (May 1985): 265–279; Thomas J. Espenshade, "Marriage Trends in America: Estimates, Implications, and Underlying Causes," *Population and Development Review* 11 (June 1985): 193–245.

### Variations in marriage rates

In the United States, marriages have a distinct *seasonal* pattern: a higher number of marriages typically occur in June than in any other month, with August and July being the next most popular months. The seasonal low for marriage tends to occur in January, February, and March. Monthly variations are also greatly affected by holidays, the ending and beginning of school years, climatic conditions, and religious holy periods such as Lent.

Marriages also vary widely by *day* of the week. Over half of all marriages take place on Saturday, three times as many as are performed on Friday, the next most popular day. Tuesdays, Wednesdays, and Thursdays, the least popular days, have less than one-tenth the number as occur on Saturdays.

Marriage rates in the United States consistently show distinct differences by state. In 1988 the highest marriage rates were in Nevada (114.5), Hawaii (15.8), and South Carolina (15.7), all favored states for nonresidents to marry. The lowest marriage rate was in Illinois (6.8), where a new law required that both applicants for a marriage license have a blood test for human immunodeficiency virus (HIV) infection. Other states with low rates (under 8.0 per 1,000 population) were New Jersey, Pennsylvania, Minnesota, North Dakota, Nebraska, West Virginia, and Louisiana.[8]

Marriages are reported by, and subject to laws of, the state where the ceremony is performed. Lenient marriage laws attract couples from out of state, particularly if the adjoining states have more restrictive laws. The major attractions are laws that do not require a waiting period between the date of application for a license and issuance of the license or between license insurance and the ceremony, or laws that do not require a medical examination or a blood test. These factors have a two-pronged effect—they lower the rates of the states from which the couples are drawn and raise the rates of the states to which they are attracted.

## POWER IN CONJUGAL RELATIONSHIPS

One important aspect of the marital system is the power positions of husband and wife—as individuals and in relation to each other. There appears to be considerable agreement that power refers to the ability to influence others and affect their behavior. Conjugal power would refer to the ability of the husband and wife to influence each other. It is often measured by determining who makes certain decisions or who performs certain tasks.

Power involves the crucial dimensions of authority and influence. Social norms determine who has *authority*, in that the culture designates the positions that have the "legitimate" and prescribed power (authority). In some

---

8. *Monthly Vital Statistics Report*, Vol. 37, No. 13, pp. 4–5, and Table 2.

societies, authority is invested in the husband; in others, it rests with the oldest male in extended-family situations, and in some it goes to the mother-in-law. Other family members can *influence*, that is exert pressure upon, the person with authority. The president of the United States has the prescribed authority to make a wide range of decisions, but he can be influenced by the press, the public, or his own family, none of whom are given the authority to make political decisions. The husband may have authority over his wife and children, but he is greatly influenced by them.

## Characteristics of conjugal power

Mary Rogers makes several key points about power.[9] First, she argues that power is a capacity or an ability to influence others, *not* the exercise of that ability. Ability does not denote social action. The perceived or real ability to influence can affect outcomes even when the exercise of that ability is not undertaken. Second, an individual's power must be viewed relative to specific social systems and the positions (statuses) a person occupies within a given social system. Note that power is not inherent within a person. Power must be viewed in dynamic terms; one must note that the power of individuals to influence others is linked to the social statuses and social roles they occupy and perform within special social systems. Third, if power is an ability to influence others, resources are the primary determinants of that ability. A *resource* is "any attribute, circumstance, or possession that increases the ability of its holder to influence a person or group."[10] Attributes might include age, sex, race, health, and level of energy; circumstances might include location, friendships or acquaintances, flexibility, or access to information; possessions might include money, land,[11] property, goods, and so on. The contention is that persons with greater resources have an advantage over those without those resources. In a social-exchange perspective, they can bargain with others from a position of strength.

Rebecca Warner and others make a strong case for broadening the conceptualization of resources to include selected features of family and kinship structures (family organization).[12] It was argued, for example, that wives will have more power in marriages in societies with nuclear rather than extended family structures and in societies with matrilateral rather than patrilateral customs of residence and descent. Ethnographic data on over one

---

9. Mary F. Rogers, "Instrumental and Infra-Resources: The Base of Power," *American Journal of Sociology* 79 (May 1974): 1418–1433.

10. Ibid., p. 1425.

11. Support for control over land as a source of women's power can be seen in Sonya Salamon and Ann Mackey Keim, "Land Ownership and Women's Power in a Midwestern Farming Community," *Journal of Marriage and the Family* 41 (February 1979): 109–119.

12. Rebecca L. Warner, Gary R. Lee, and Janet Lee, "Social Organization, Spousal Resources, and Marital Power: A Cross-Cultural Study," *Journal of Marriage and the Family* 48 (February 1986): 121–128.

hundred nonindustrial societies provided support for these propositions, highlighting the fact that organizational resources may be as important as material and personal resources in understanding conjugal power.

## Processes of conjugal power

The processes in the use of power within marriage are dimensions often overlooked. Since marriage involves two or more people, and since social power involves the ability of one person to influence others, it becomes necessary to ask questions that involve persons in relation to each other. For someone to influence, someone else must be influenced. And in being influenced, how does this affect the use of power by the influencer? Jetse Sprey indicates that in any reciprocal power relationship, compliance itself must be considered a potential source of influence.[13] If there is total compliance by one spouse to the demands of the other, such an event must be seen as part of a reciprocal exchange of power from which it is not logically possible to determine who is the most powerful. For example:

> A wife may threaten her husband with divorce unless he stops his heavy drinking. If we assume that she has the ability to carry out her threat, the fact remains that it is up to her spouse to accept or reject her demand. By refusing to comply, he will force her to either carry out the threat or to retreat. In both instances her conduct would be influenced by his. If he decides to stop his drinking she indeed did influence his conduct, but his decision to comply in turn determines her course of action. There is an additional aspect to this case: in a marriage, a threat to divorce affects *both* its sender and its receiver, since each must face the consequences if it is carried out. Both spouses presumably are aware of this and can be expected to perceive a threat of this nature within this shared context. To interpret, therefore, the outcome of the above confrontation as a mere "win" for the wife, and to code it as an indication of her "power," seems rather unrealistic, to put it mildly.[14]

This illustration and others that could be given clearly demonstrate the complexity of understanding power processes. The use of power is often indirect; the outcome may have no "winner" or finality; and the nature of the interaction will vary from one group and system to another and from one social context to another.

## Conjugal power and decision making

One of the ways in which conjugal power has traditionally been measured is to determine which spouse makes the major decisions and how the husband

---

13. Jetse Sprey, "Family Power and Process: Toward a Conceptual Integration," in *Power in Families*, ed. by Ronald E. Cromwell and David H. Olson (New York: Wiley, 1975).

14. Ibid., p. 68.

> The Woman who will not be ruled must live without marriage.
>
> Susan B. Anthony, 1877

and wife decision-making patterns vary by area of concern. One of the most widely cited studies and one that served as a major stimulant to many studies that followed was done by Robert Blood and Donald Wolfe.[15] In an attempt to measure the balance of power between husbands and wives, they interviewed 731 city wives in metropolitan Detroit.

They selected eight situations that they felt would include both masculine as well as feminine decisions about the family as a whole. These included: (1) what job the husband should take, (2) what kind of car to get, (3) whether or not to buy life insurance, (4) where to go on vacation, (5) what house or apartment to take, (6) whether or not the wife should go to work or quit work (7) what doctor to have when someone is sick, (8) and how much money the family can afford to spend per week on food.

The wives' answers to the eight situations revealed that two decisions were primarily the husband's province (his job and car), two were primarily the wife's province (her work and food), while all the others were joint decisions in the sense of having more "same" responses than anything else. Even the wife's working turned out to be quite a middling decision from the standpoint of the mean score, leaving only the food expenditures predominantly to the wife.

Even though published more than thirty years ago, perhaps the responses of the wives to these eight decision-making questions are not surprising even today. In the United States, it is expected that the male is responsible for the economic support of his wife and children. His job and his work are his primary exertions in both time and energy. Factors related to automobiles might also be expected to be primarily the concern of the husband; although most wives in our society have operators' licenses, when the husband and wife travel together it is likely to be the husband who does the driving. Traditionally, it has also been the husband who cares for repairs and upkeep of the automobile.

Whether or not to buy life insurance, where to go on a vacation, and what house or apartment to take are decisions that are more likely to be shared equally by husband and wife than by either spouse separately. It could be assumed that both have equal competencies in these choices. Furthermore, these areas affect both partners more equally than do the other decision-making areas.

---

15. Robert O. Blood, Jr. and Donald M. Wolfe, *Husbands and Wives: The Dynamics of Married Living* (Glencoe, Ill.: The Free Press, 1960): 20.

*Basic to all marriages are communication and decision making: about money, children, sex, and division of labor among other things. Both are influenced by the partner who has the legitimate authority, the resources available to either person, and the social context in which the communication and decision making take place.*

Blood and Wolfe's theoretical explanation of why husbands make certain decisions, wives make others, and there is joint involvement in still others is based on resource availability. That is, the source of authority and power lies in the comparative resources each spouse has available. The balance of power is weighted toward the partner who has the greater resources as perceived by the spouse.

Joint decision making, sharing of marital power, perceptions of both self and spouse as doing a fair share of family work, and a feeling of equity appear to be positively related to marital satisfaction and negatively related to depression.[16] Findings such as these lend support to social exchange theories and equity models that suggest personal happiness and the highest levels of satisfaction with a marriage occur in the context of each partner defining his

---

16. Sara Yogev and Jeanne Brett, "Perceptions of the Division of Housework and Child Care and Marital Satisfaction," *Journal of Marriage and the Family* 47 (August 1985): 609–618; John Mirowsky, "Depression and Marital Power: An Equity Model," *American Sociological Review* 91 (November 1985): 557–589; and Bernard Davidson, "A Test of Equity Theory for Marital Adjustment," *Social Psychology Quarterly* 47 (1984): 36–42.

or her spouse as contributing a fair share to housework and child care and perceiving equity in the exchange. Evidence shows less depression among spouses who share marital power. For many married persons, particularly wives, an inequitable balance of marital power is a serious problem.

## Differences in wife-husband responses

Considerable criticism has been made of studies of decision making and task performance that elicit responses from wives only (such as the Blood and Wolfe study). Evidence suggests that when husbands respond, they report less power for themselves than their wives claim for them, that wives tend to overestimate the power of their husbands, and that discrepancies exist in the reports of husbands and wives about their respective roles. Interviews with nearly 500 married couples in the midwest, for example, revealed that spouses accurately perceive their partner's expectations about half the time. Also, spouses think they carry more responsibility for household duties than their partners think they do.[17] In spite of twenty years of repeated warnings about husband-wife discrepancies and "wife only" research, recent data report a continued reliance on these methods.[18]

In addition to methodological concerns such as a one-spouse response, a number of writers have questioned the theoretical accuracy of explaining power based on resources. The theory of resources (in reality a proposition rather than a theory) contends that the more a partner controls resources of value to him- or herself and the mate, the greater his or her relative power. Here data show some mixed and inconsistent results. To understand why we will examine the theory of resources issue more intensely.

## The theory of resources issue

Sprey makes several interesting points in regard to the "resource" argument.[19] One, he questions how individuals without authority or other resources manage to influence the family process. Housewives in patriarchal families and children in most households fit into this category. Second, he suggests that while the availability of a given resource will be a necessary condition for its use, the *absence* of a resource among other members may serve to limit, or even neutralize, its usefulness for those who have access to it. A child, for

---

17. Dana V. Hiller and William W. Philliber, "The Division of Labor in Contemporary Marriages: Expectations, Perceptions, and Performance," *Social Problems* 33 (February 1986): 191–201.

18. Janet Bokemeier and Pamela Monroe, "Continued Reliance on One Respondent in Family Decision-Making Studies: A Content Analysis," *Journal of Marriage and the Family* 45 (August 1983): 645–652. Also, Szinovacz illustrates how couple data can be used as a methodological tool. *See* Maximiliane E. Szinovacz, "Using Couple Data as a Methodological Tool: The Case of Marital Violence," *Journal of Marriage and the Family* 45 (August 1983): 633–644.

19. Sprey, "Family Power and Process," pp. 76–78.

example, may use ignorance or lack of knowledge to counteract a parent's expertise in a given dispute. Third, he suggests that the distribution of resources is relative; it is defined and guided by the rules and role prescriptions of the system in question. Yet, while systems provide boundaries and rules, they do not determine outcomes. Outcomes, influenced by resources as related to the system involved, are a result of reciprocal influencing.

This "theory of resources," which I've been discussing, provides the conceptual core around which many of the later studies have been built. Several authors have stressed that power is not merely based on an individual's resources but on the comparative contributions (resources) and exchange processes of the husband and wife relative to each other. Hyman Rodman, for example, developed a "theory of resources in a cultural context" that takes into account the "theory of resources," the "theory of exchange," the comparative contributions of both husband and wife, and the cultural context in which the interaction occurs. [20] His argument is that one must not only be aware of resources in attempting to explain conjugal power, but must consider as well the cultural context in which decision making takes place. Thus, in certain societies it is the upper and middle status groups, the highest income, educational, and occupational groups, that first accept norms of marital egalitarianism. This in effect diminishes the impact of resources upon power in marital settings.

This idea not only had support in Greek and Yugoslavian families tested by Rodman, but among husbands in United States families as well. Mark Rank[21] found that increments in wives' resources correlated positively with wives' influence, supporting the theory of resources argument. But increments in husbands' resources correlated negatively with husbands' influence, thus not supporting the greater resources leading to greater influence and power argument. The explanation is that as husbands gain higher levels of income, education, or occupational prestige, they come in contact with sets of egalitarian norms regarding spousal relations. In brief, as both husbands and wives gain resources, women become less economically dependent upon their spouses while men become socialized into an egalitarian ethic.

The power dimension of marriage is too complex and vast to cover adequately in a portion of one chapter. Interested persons may want to examine an overview of power in families with some guidelines for future research by Maximiliane Szinovacz.[22]

---

20. Hyman Rodman, "Marital Power in France, Greece, Yugoslavia, and the United States: A Cross-National Discussion," *Journal of Marriage and the Family* 29 (May 1967): 320–324; Hyman Rodman, "Marital Power and the Theory of Resources in Cultural Context," *Journal of Comparative Family Studies* 3 (Spring 1972): 50–69.

21. Mark R. Rank, "Determinants of Conjugal Influence in Wives' Employment Decision Making," *Journal of Marriage and the Family* 44 (August 1982): 591–604.

22. Maximiliane E. Scinovacz, "Family Power," in *Handbook of Marriage and the Family* by Marvin B. Sussman and Suzanne K. Steinmetz, eds. (New York: Plenum Press, 1987): 651–693.

### Meaningful conversation and marriage don't mix

At a party the other evening, people were discussing marriage. Marilyn turned and looked at her husband lovingly (as if she had just popped a Geritol tablet) and said, "Dan and I have a good marriage because we have meaningful conversations with one another."

I couldn't get it off my mind. On the way home I asked my husband, "Have we ever had a meaningful conversation?"

"I don't think so," he said.

"That's hard to believe," I persisted. "In 26 years we've never had one?"

"Not that I can remember."

We drove along in silence for about 20 minutes. Finally I said, "What is a meaningful conversation?"

"You're kidding! You actually don't know?"

"No. What is it?"

"Well," he said, "it's a conversation with meaning."

"Like the oil embargo and Paul Harvey?"

"Exactly."

"What about them?" I asked.

"What about who?"

"The oil embargo and Paul Harvey."

"It doesn't have to be a conversation about the oil embargo and Paul Harvey," he said. "It could be a discussion on anything in your daily schedule that is pertinent."

"I shaved my legs yesterday."

"That is not pertinent to anyone but you."

"Not really. I was using your razor."

"If you read the paper more," he said, "your conversations would be more stimulating."

"Okay, here's something meaningful I read just yesterday. In Naples—that's in Italy—police were searching for a woman who tried to cut off a man's nose with a pair of scissors while he was sleeping. What do you think of that?"

"That's not meaningful," he said.

A few minutes later I offered, "Suppose it was the American Embassy and the woman was a spy, and the nose belonged to Henry Kissinger which held secret documents about an oil embargo between Saudi Arabia and Paul Harvey?"

He drove in silence. "How long have Dan and Marilyn been married?"

"Twelve years," I said.

"They must pace their meaningful conversations."

*Source.* From *At Wit's End* by Erma Bombeck. Reproduced through the courtesy of Field Newspaper Syndicate.

# ADJUSTMENT IN MARRIAGE

Marital adjustment, marital well-being, happiness, satisfaction, or a number of variables that attest to the quality of a marriage may be the most frequently studied dimension in the marriage and family field.[23] Many attempts have been made to assess the quality of marital relationships, using such concepts as "marital adjustment," "success," "satisfaction," "stability," "happiness," "consensus," "cohesion," "adaptation," "integration," "role strain," and the like. Sometimes these terms are used interchangeably; other times each denotes something different. Sometimes the terms are used in a psychological sense, referring to the state of one of the marital partners; sometimes they are

---

23. Graham B. Spanier and Robert A. Lewis, "Marital Quality: A Review of the Seventies," *Journal of Marriage and the Family* 42 (November 1980): 825–839.

used in a social-psychological sense, referring to the state of the relationship; and sometimes they are used in a sociological sense, referring to the state of the group or system. In addition, there are times the terms are used to refer to the achievement of a goal and other times they are used to refer to a dynamic process of making changes. All the concepts emphasize a dimension that contrasts with maladjustment, dissatisfaction, instability, unhappiness, and so forth.

As indicated, irrespective of the label and the diversity of operational definitions, research on this issue attempts to assess marital quality. Johnson and others, while agreeing that marital quality is a useful umbrella term for summarizing the literature, question its utility as a research tool since it is so multidimensional.[24] It may include marital happiness, interaction, problems, disagreements, or instability, for example, all of which appear to be empirically distinct concepts. They cannot fruitfully be combined into a single measure, and as such, the concept of marital quality is not well-suited for research purposes. For our purposes, and perhaps due to the lack of any single concept that incorporates the multiple dimensions of quality, the general concept of adjustment will be used.

The adjustment of married mates is unlike any other human relationship. It may share many conditions of friendship groups, peer groups, work groups, or religious groups, but the husband-and-wife relationship differs. Marriage, involving two sexes in physical propinquity, is public and binding in nature. Being publicly sanctioned, marriage becomes more difficult to break. Being binding, the members must act as a unit and cooperation becomes essential. Every decision must take into account the desires and wishes of the spouse. These forces determine the level of adjustment, the nature of the interaction, and the degree of conflict.

A social conflict frame of reference, as described in the second chapter, includes the basic assumption that conflict is natural and inevitable in all human interaction. This is true of marital interaction as well. As couples interact, as they define and redefine their relationship to one another, and as they perform daily activities and fulfill role expectations, conflict is inevitable: conflict over one's work, over children, over criticism, over in-laws, over expenditures, over sex, and, as stressed in popular literature prior to the days of the pump, even matters such as how one should squeeze the toothpaste tube. The "adjustment" of a marriage is not therefore based on whether conflict exists but on how conflict is managed in a way mutually satisfactory to the marital partners. Let us examine more fully the dimensions of marital adjustment and how it is measured.

---

24. David R. Johnson, Lynn K. White, John N. Edwards, and Alan Booth, "Dimensions of Marital Quality: Toward Methodological and Conceptual Refinement," *Journal of Family Issues* 7 (March 1986): 31–49.

## Dimensions of marital adjustment

From the introductory statement it should be clear that **marital adjustment** or marital well-being is a varied concept that lacks a general consensus of definition. A general concept is likely to include a relative agreement by husband and wife on issues perceived to be important, the sharing of similar tasks and activities, and the demonstration of affection for one another. *Marital success*, as distinguished from marital adjustment, generally refers to the achievement of one or more goals: permanence, companionship, fulfilling the expectation of the community, and so forth. *Marital happiness*, distinguished from either adjustment or success, is an emotional response of an individual. While happiness is an individual phenomenon, marital success and adjustment are dyadic achievements or states of the marriage.

One study asked newlyweds to evaluate the quality, that is well-being, of their marriage.[25] Four dimensions of marital well-being emerged from a factor analysis of responses. These were identified as happiness, equity, competence, and control. Happiness was more clearly associated with all aspects of well-being than any other, but feelings of equity in the relationship, a person's feelings of competence in the marital role, and feelings of control over marital outcomes were important and separate dimensions of marital well-being.

Probably still true today are major dimensions of marital adjustment that Jessie Bernard listed more than twenty-five years ago. These included: (1) the degree or extent or nature of the *differences* between or among the parties involved, (2) the degree or extent or nature of the *communication* between or among the parties, and (3) the *quality of the relationship* between or among them—that is, its positive or negative affectivity, friendliness, or hostility.[26]

Differences may be a matter of degree or they may be categorical: no flexibility, no leeway. Often matters of principle are categorical and thus the most difficult to resolve. Thus "we will never miss Mass" or "oral sex is wrong," if taken categorically, do not permit flexibility in dealing with a mate or spouse who feels differently. On the other hand, differences of degree permit give-and-take, bargaining, and negotiation.

One specific example of how differences as well as the nature of those differences affect the quality of marriage involves sex-role attitudes. A study done of military couples on sixteen bases in Europe and the United States examined sex role congruency and assessed how these attitudes were related to the marital relationships.[27] The marriages they found to have the lowest

25. Susan E. Crohan and Joseph Veroff, "Dimensions of Marital Well-being among White and Black Newlyweds," *Journal of Marriage and the Family* 51 (May 1989): 373–383.

26. Jessie Bernard, "The Adjustment of Married Mates," in *Handbook of Marriage and the Family*, ed. by Harold T. Christensen (Chicago: Rand McNally, 1964): 690.

27. Gary Lee Bowen and Dennis K. Orthner, "Sex-Role Congruency and Marital Quality," *Journal of Marriage and the Family* 45 (February 1983): 223–230.

### What keeps a marriage going?

Jeanette Lauer and Robert Lauer reported in *Psychology Today* (June 1985) the responses of 351 couples who had been married for 15 years or more as to why their marriages had lasted. Men and women showed remarkable agreement on the keys to an enduring relationship. The top seven reasons that both men and women gave, in order of frequency were:

My spouse is my best friend.
I like my spouse as a person.
Marriage is a long-term commitment.
Marriage is sacred.
We agree on aims and goals.
My spouse has grown more interesting.
I want the relationship to succeed.

Other reasons, in differing order of importance

for men and women, included things like laughing together; agreeing on a philosophy of life, on how and how often to show affection, and on their sex life; being proud of the spouse's achievements; discussing things calmly; and having a stimulating exchange of ideas.

These couples were not blind to each others' faults but believed their strengths more important than their deficiencies and the difficulties. Some said they would stay together no matter what, thus, divorce was not an option. The authors suggest that for most of these couples, "till death do us part" is not a binding clause but a gratifying reality.

*Source:* Jeanette Lauer and Robert Lauer, "Marriages Made to Last," *Psychology Today* , 19 (June 1985): 22–26.

level of marital quality were those with a traditional husband and a modern wife. Interestingly, however, the modern husbands and traditional wives had a quality of marriage similar to marriages where both spouses were modern or both were traditional. Apparently nontraditional men who honor the rights of the wife to pursue independent interests and who jointly share household tasks find it acceptable to have wives who behave traditionally. The point is that differences as well as the nature and extent of those differences affects dyadic or interpersonal adjustment.

The second dimension, communication, of necessity involves interaction. Few people would doubt or question the importance of communication to successful relationships of any kind. Yet communication is an extremely complex factor in marital relationships: it may be verbal or nonverbal, it may be explicit or tacit, it may clarify or mislead, or it may draw relationships closer together or tear them apart. To not talk at all, to talk constantly, to order, to nag, to scold, to praise, may each be used to convey a certain message. Yet a review of research over the past twenty years revealed strong support for the relationship between communication and marital satisfaction.[28] This relationship held true for both the content and the process of communication. Findings consistently replicated were that couples with higher rates of

---

28. Joseph P. Boland and Diana R. Follingstad, "The Relationship between Communication and Marital Satisfaction: A Review," *Journal of Sex and Marital Therapy* 13 (Winter 1987): 286–313. *See also:* Mary Anne Fitzpatrick, *Between Husbands and Wives: Communication in Marriage* (Newbury Park: Sage Publications, Inc. 1988).

self-disclosure and expressions of love, support, and affection tended also to experience greater satisfaction. Research on process variables suggested that positive forms of nonverbal communication, such as laughter, voice tone, touching spouse, and body position, were found more frequently in happy couples. Nondistressed couples were more likely to show better listening skills and clarity of speech, and to positively interpret their partners' behavior.

The quality of the relationship is a third major dimension of adjustment. A friendly and loving spouse does not automatically mean adjustment, but it makes accommodation easier. Making sacrifices or changes in plans becomes easier when spouses have a love and genuine concern for one another. If the quality of the relationship is affection, results are far different than if it is hatred or hostility. These three dimensions—differences, communication, and quality of the relationship—are each important for understanding the process of adjustment.

### Evaluating marital adjustment

The measurement of marital adjustment began in a serious way in the late 1920s. Each decade since then, an extensive body of literature that tries to predict marital success or determine factors, psychological or social, associated with marital adjustment has been accumulated.

Today, it is likely that the most widely used measurement of marital or interpersonal adjustment is the Dyadic Adjustment Scale developed by Graham Spanier.[29] The scale consists of thirty-two items centering around four basic components: dyadic satisfaction, dyadic cohesion, dyadic consensus, and affectional expression. *Satisfaction* is measured by asking questions such as "Do you confide in your mate?" "Regret that you married?" and inquiring into the degree of happiness in the relationship. *Cohesion* focuses on whether the couple does things together and exchanges ideas. *Consensus* measures the extent of agreement on issues such as finances, friends, religious matters, or household tasks. *Affectional expression* refers to the extent of agreement regarding demonstrations of affection, sex relations, and showing love.

Two researchers from Australia, in testing Spanier's Dyadic Adjustment Scale, suggest Spanier's thirty-two items are unnecessary and that, for quick screening purposes, one global self-rating item is sufficient.[30] This item presents seven degrees of happiness in the marital relationship, ranging from extremely unhappy to perfect; each partner is to indicate the one best describing their relationship.

---

29. Graham B. Spanier, "Measuring Dyadic Adjustment: New Scales for Assessing the Quality of Marriage and Similar Dyads," *Journal of Marriage and the Family* 38 (February 1976): 15–28; and Graham B. Spanier and Linda Thompson, "A Confirmatory Analysis of the Dyadic Adjustment Scale," *Journal of Marriage and the Family* 44 (August 1982): 731–738.

30. C. F. Sharpley and D. G. Cross, "A Psychometric Evaluation of the Spanier Dyadic Adjustment Scale," *Journal of Marriage and the Family* 44 (August 1982): 739–741.

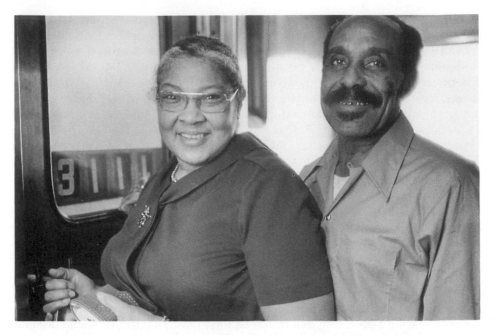

*Marital adjustment appears to be highly related to doing things together, agreeing on issues such as friends and finances, and demonstrating love and affection. As long as rewards are greater than the costs and an existing marriage is preferable to any other alternative, marriages are likely to remain intact.*

Other measures of marital or relationship adjustment, satisfaction, or well-being focus on related issues. Susan Hendrick, using a seven-item relationship assessment scale, asks each partner the following questions: How well does your partner meet your needs? What is your level of satisfaction with the relationship? How good is your relationship compared to most? How often do you wish you hadn't gotten into it? What is the extent to which the relationship meets your original expectations? How much do you love your partner? What are the problems in the relationship?[31] She claims her seven-item scale is easily administered, is highly correlated with the longer Dyadic Adjustment Scale, plus it effectively discriminates between partners (married couples, cohabitors, gay couples, friends) who stay together versus those who split apart.

Jessie Bernard makes a different point for evaluating marital relationships. She says a criterion should be set up in terms not of the best imaginable relationship but of the best possible one.[32] Thus a marriage may be said to be successful to the extent that it provides the highest satisfaction possible, not

31. Susan S. Hendrick, "A Generic Measure of Relationship Satisfaction," *Journal of Marriage and the Family* 50 (February 1988): 93–98.

32. Bernard, "The Adjustment of Marital Mates," p. 732.

the highest imaginable. However unsatisfactory it may be in terms of happiness, it may still be judged better than the alternatives.

From this relativistic and exchange point of view, a marital relationship is successful (1) if the satisfaction is positive, that is, if the rewards to both partners are greater than the cost, and (2) if it is preferable to any other alternative. Two examples follow:

1. A and B do not like one another; they get on one another's nerves; the costs of remaining married are great in frustration and loneliness. But the rewards are great also; together they can afford a lovely home; they have high status in the community; the children are protected from scandal; the church approves of them; etc. This relationship is "successful" or "good," not because it is the best imaginable, but only because it is the best possible in the sense that the satisfactions are greater than the costs.

2. An example in which a marital relationship is successful only because it is better than any alternative would be the marriage of a dependent woman to, let us say, an alcoholic, in which the costs in misery were much greater than the rewards in security or status; but the spread between costs and satisfactions would be much greater if she left him. She would then be alone; she would not have the protection of the status of marriage; she would not even have the occasional sober companionship of a husband, etc. Bad as it is, therefore, her marriage seems better to her than any alternative she has.[33]

Udry suggests that the dimension of marital alternatives appears to be a better predictor of marital disruption than are measures of satisfaction.[34] Using longitudinal data of married couples from sixteen United States urban areas, he measured the respondents' perceptions of how much better or worse they would be without their present spouse and how easily that spouse could be replaced with one of comparable quality. Marital alternatives were found to correlate positively with resources of the self and negatively with the spouse's resource. In the ensuing year or two after these resources were measured, couples in which spouses were high in marital alternatives had several times the disruption rate of couples low in alternatives.

## Factors related to marital adjustment

Many statistical studies have been geared to find factors associated with marital adjustment that couldn't be explained by chance alone.[35] But often the

---

33. Ibid., pp. 732–733.

34. J. Richard Udry, "Marital Alternatives and Marital Disruption," *Journal of Marriage and the Family* 43 (November 1981): 889–897.

35. For eighty-seven propositions dealing with marital quality and a list of more than one hundred fifty references on this subject, *see* Robert A. Lewis and Graham B. Spanier, "Theorizing About the Quality and Stability of Marriage" in *Contemporary Theories About the Family*, vol. 1, ed. by Wesley R. Burr et al. (New York: The Free Press, 1979): 268–294.

findings quoted in texts and popular literature are those that support the opinions of the writer, and contradictory evidence is frequently discounted or ignored completely. Many writers are prone to a Pollyanna-like view of marriage characterized by a tendency to view consistently nonargumentative discussions, agreements, similarity, and the like as good or positive and conflict, anger, disagreements, or differences as negative. Conflict is generally viewed in the context of divorce and not as inevitable to a marriage. The literature traditionally has tended to lack research data on conflict and conflict management as crucial aspects of marriage (note conflict theory in Chapter 2).

In a chapter entitled "Marital Conflict as a Positive Force," Scanzoni argues that, in understanding the dynamics of husband-wife interaction, the first step is to divest ourselves of the notion that equilibrium or stability for all is a necessary ideal; the second step is to rid ourselves of the idea that conflict is ipso facto bad or unhealthy within marriage.[36] Conflict brings into the open the issues that one or the other partner considers unjust or inequitable. If disagreement is brought into the open, bargained over, and resolved in a way that is satisfactory to both partners, the outcome may be a new, more positive level of marital adjustment or solidarity. In contrast, failure to engage in conflict when injustice is perceived may result in a less beneficial, less rewarding situation for both marital partners and may actually increase the chances for dissolution of the marriage.

Conflict, when viewed from this perspective of injustice, should not be confused with difficulties and discord brought about by factors such as economic hardship or facing unexpected income constraints. These too produce conflict and change in marital relations. Longitudinal data of couples who suffered income loss during the major depression (1929–1933) showed marked decline in marital quality and an increase in marital discord.[37] Men who lacked adaptive resources became more difficult to live with, more tense, irritable, and explosive. This behavior in itself produced conflict but appeared to be related less to interpersonal inequities than to disrupted patterns of social interaction and adverse psychological changes brought about by economic loss.

Norval Glenn and Charles Weaver analyzed data from three national surveys to estimate the direct effects of each of ten independent variables on the reported marital happiness of white males and females aged 18 through 59.[38] Contrary to predictions based on theory and previous evidence, all of the estimated direct effects were weak or nil. For example, socioeconomic status, years of schooling, duration of marriage, age at marriage, church attendance,

36. John Scanzoni, *Sexual Bargaining: Power Politics in the American Marriage,* 2d ed. (Chicago: The University of Chicago Press, 1982): 61–102.

37. Jeffrey K. Liker and Glen H. Elder, Jr., "Economic Hardship and Marital Relations in the 1930s," *American Sociological Review* 48 (June 1983): 343–359.

38. Norval D. Glenn and Charles N. Weaver, "A Multivariate, Multisurvey Study of Marital Happiness," *Journal of Marriage and the Family* 40 (May 1978): 269–282.

the presence of children, or wife's employment outside of the home all indicated little or no positive relationships to marital happiness. Many of these findings are inconsistent with textbook generalizations and earlier evidence. These differences may be due to differences in measurement, sampling, and methods of analysis but, as suggested by Glenn and Weaver, they may also reflect changes associated with the steep increase in marital instability since the early 1960s. In their words:

> If, as we suspect, the persons most likely to enter into unsuccessful marriages are generally the same people who are most likely to terminate unsatisfactory marriages, then even the strongest predictors of the success of marriages may bear little or no relationship to the happiness of individuals in intact marriages. In other words, to the extent that marital "mistakes" are quickly rectified by divorce, they may contribute little in the long run to marital unhappiness.[39]

What the previous paragraphs are suggesting is that the high divorce rates of the 1970s may have been the results or "solutions" to unhappiness in many marriages that would have remained intact in earlier decades. Getting divorced means these unsatisfactory marriages are no longer available to substantiate findings that were supported earlier. These statements do not mean that all unsatisfactory marriages terminate in divorce or that all satisfactory marriages remain intact. But marital quality, happiness, satisfaction, and the like do seem to be highly interrelated. Let's see what happens when we examine marital satisfaction over the life cycle.

## Marital satisfaction over the life cycle

The developmental concept as applied to adjustment in marriage has stimulated interest in changes over the life cycle. This approach, which deals with changes over time, has been used to test equity in marital roles (which appeared to increase for both husbands and wives over the life cycle),[40] variations in the life course of U.S. women (with blacks having greater variation than whites in factors such as having more children and having them sooner),[41] and perceived marital quality (which supported a curvilinear, U-shaped trend).[42]

---

39. Ibid., p. 280.

40. Robert B. Schafer and Patricia M. Keith, "Equity in Marital Roles Across the Family Life Cycle," *Journal of Marriage and the Family* 43 (May 1981): 359–367.

41. Graham B. Spanier, "Marital Trajectories of American Women: Variations in the Life Course," *Journal of Marriage and the Family* 47 (November 1985): 993–1003.

42. Stephen A. Anderson, Candyce S. Russell, and Walter R. Schumm, "Perceived Marital Quality and Family Life-Cycle Categories: A Further Analysis," *Journal of Marriage and the Family* 45 (February 1983): 127–139; Walter R. Schumm and Margaret A. Bugaighis, "Marital Quality over the Marital Career: Alternative Explanations," *Journal of Marriage and the Family* 48 (February 1986): 165–168.

What does happen to marriages over long periods of time? Most studies seek answers to this question by comparing groups that are at different points in the life course or at different stages of a family life-cycle. That is, newlyweds are compared with families with preschool children, who are compared with those with adolescents in the home and so forth. One unique exception to this approach took place at the Institute of Human Development at the University of California in Berkeley.[43] Seventeen marriages that lasted for fifty to sixty-nine years were the survivors of an original study of 250 couples which were first studied in 1928 and 1929 and interviewed from time to time since then. In all of these surviving marriages, there were both shared and separate interests and the partners had both a commitment to the marriage and an acceptance of each other. Husbands tended to be more satisfied with the marriage than the wives. Of the authors' model of six types of very long-term marriages,[44] the greatest number exhibited a curvilinear pattern, starting at a high level of affect and satisfaction, dipping with young children until the children left, and increasing in their later years to a point as high as at the beginning. All of the other couples were categorized as stable (positive, neutral, or negative) with no couples showing a continuous increase or a continuous decline (these may have previously divorced).

Numerous other studies have attempted to discover how families manage their lives, what explains their relative success and failure, and how their relationships change over time. One major study asking "what makes families work" examined 1,140 families using a seven-stage family life-cycle model.[45] Their results confirm the findings of numerous other studies[46] indicating that adults' satisfaction with marriage and family life tends to have the shape of a U-curve (*see* Figure 12–3). From young couples without children (stage 1) to families with preschool age children (stage 2), to families with school-age children (stage 3), to families with adolescents in the home (stage 4), there was a decline in family satisfaction for both husbands and wives. The decline continues for wives through the launching period (stage 5), but increased slightly for husbands. A sharp increase in family satisfaction occurred at the empty nest stage (stage 6) and increased more or remained high through retirement (stage 7). One explanation for the dramatic increase in

43. Sylvia Weishaus and Dorothy Field, "A Half Century of Marriage: Continuity or Change?" *Journal of Marriage and the Family* 50 (August 1988): 763–774.

44. These six types were classified as stable/positive (5 couples), stable/neutral (3 couples), stable/negative (2 couples), curvilinear (7 couples), continuous decline (no couples), and continuous increase (no couples).

45. David H. Olson, Hamilton I. McCubbin, and Associates, *Families: What Makes Them Work* (Beverly Hills: Sage Publications, 1983).

46. David M. Lawson, "Love Attitude and Marital Adjustment in the Family Life Cycle," *Sociological Spectrum* 8 (1988): 391–406; and Boyd C. Rollins and Harold Feldman, "Marital Satisfaction Over the Family Life Cycle," *Journal of Marriage and the Family* 32 (February 1970): 20–28. Canadian data as well show a curvilinear relationship. *See* Eugene Lupri and James Frideres, "The Quality of Marriage and the Passage of Time: Marital Satisfaction Over the Family Life Cycle," *Canadian Journal of Sociology* 6 (1981): 283–305.

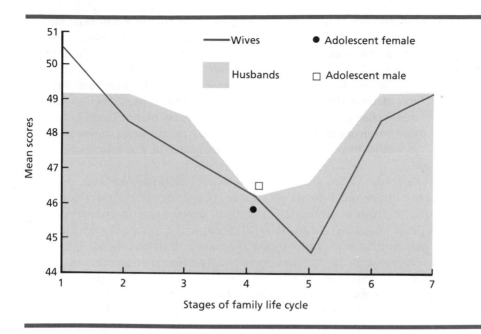

*Figure 12–3*

**Family satisfaction.** (*Source:* David H. Olson, Hamilton I. McCubbin, and Associates, *Families: What Makes Them Work* [Beverly Hills: Sage Publications, 1983], Figure 10.5, p. 181 Copyright © 1983 by Sage Publications, Inc. Reprinted by permission of Sage Publications, Inc.)

satisfaction found following the launching stage is interpreted as a result of the relaxation of sex roles between the parents. Women see themselves as freer to look for work and organizational roles outside the home, and men find themselves with decreased financial responsibility and more ability to be passive and dependent. Gary Lee suggests that marital satisfaction is higher in the later stages of the life cycle because of diminishing demands of other nonmarital roles as well as interaction with friends. These friendship relations typically involve couples as couples, thus solidifying the marital relationship rather than distracting the spouses from the performance of marital roles.[47]

Results of studies showing the effects of children on the marital happiness of parents appear to be highly consistent. Overwhelming evidence suggests that in American society the presence of children in the family lowers marital happiness or satisfaction for the parents. This is true as well for subpopulations delineated on the basis of sex, race, level of education, religious preference, employment status, and other groupings. Glenn and

---

47. Gary R. Lee, "Marital Satisfaction in Later Life: The Effects of Nonmarital Roles," *Journal of Marriage and the Family* 50 (August 1988): 775–783.

McLanahan, in their own national surveys and reviewing many others, find no evidence for distinctly positive effects, and strong evidence for negative effects, of children on marital quality.[48] Given this highly consistent evidence, they suggest it is ironic that most U.S. citizens want to have and do have children and may serve as an example of the social function of ignorance. That is, people are motivated to perform the essential functions of reproduction and child care by the false belief that the psychological rewards of having children outweigh the costs or penalties. Perhaps there are perceptions of rewards, but the research evidence does not find them in terms of the effect of marital satisfaction.

The Olson-McCubbin study *Families*, as well as other research, provides some precautionary notes to the life-cycle data presented. First, while consistent variation from stage to stage is found, the amount of change may be neither as great nor as significant as is often implied in textbooks such as this. For example, adding data from those marriages that had dissolved would reduce the increase in satisfaction reported by most studies. Second, while male-female husband-wife differences are found in most studies, these differences tend to be overplayed. Often the sex differences were even less pronounced than were differences across the life cycle. Third, Spanier and Lewis, in reviewing studies in the 1970s of marital quality over the career of the marriage, argue that reliance on cross-sectional data for the study of trends can be very misleading.[49] That is, comparing groups who are at different stages in the life cycle (cross-sectional comparisons) rather than by following the same group over time through stages (longitudinal) does not adequately account for cohort effects, age-correlated effects, social desirability, or the tendency found in longitudinal studies to report as happy those marriages which survive over time.

A fourth precautionary note alluded to in the third point just described raises a question common to all marital adjustment research, that of marital conventionalization. Marital conventionalization is seen as the extent to which marriages are appraised in terms of social desirability, idealization of the spouse, and conservatism. Indicators of conservative orientations often include measures of traditional family morality, religious activity, premarital sexual abstinence, and general conservative ideology. Gary Hansen made an attempt to test the relationship between marital adjustment and conventionalization and concluded that conventionalization and adjustment measures

48. Norval D. Glenn and Sara McLanahan, "Children and Marital Happiness: A Further Specification of the Relationship," *Journal of Marriage and the Family* 44 (February 1982): 63–72. *See also* Jay Belsky, Mary E. Lang, and Michael Rovine, "Stability and Change in Marriage Across the Transition to Parenthood: A Second Study," *Journal of Marriage and the Family* 47 (November 1985): 855–865 and Laurence Steinberg and Susan B. Silverberg, "Influences on Marital Satisfaction during the Middle Stages of the Family Life Cycle," *Journal of Marriage and the Family* 49 (November 1987): 751–760.

49. Graham B. Spanier and Robert A. Lewis, "Marital Quality: A Review of the Seventies," *Journal of Marriage and the Family* 42 (November 1980): 829.

each contaminate the measure of the other but not to the extent that they invalidate their use.[50] That is, marital adjustment measures are not so hopelessly contaminated by social desirability and conventionality that they must be cast aside.

Similar findings are suggested by Anderson et al., who tested whether the relationship between perceived marital quality and family life-cycle categories was an artifact of marital conventionalization.[51] They found it was not. Clearly, the curvilinear trend of the family life cycle over time could not be attributed to an artifact of marital conventionalization. Conventionalization was no more influential during later life-cycle stages than for any other stage.

Having examined selected aspects of the marital system, including trends, characteristics, power, and adjustment over the total life cycle, let us return to earlier stages and investigate the parental system. The next two chapters take a look at the transition to parenthood, including unwed parenthood and factors such as family size and birth order followed by parent-child interaction and socialization up to the launching stage.

# SUMMARY

1. The marital system fulfills many functions that differ as the structure of marriage differs. Where marriage is an extension of the kin-group or the extended-family system, individualistic factors become relatively unimportant. In contrast, where marriage exists primarily for the individual and the conjugal relationship, the functions that marriage fulfills for the kin group decrease in importance. In either case, the functions that marriage performs will, to a large extent, be predictable on the basis of the social and cultural context that surrounds marriage.

2. In the United States, marriage rates have increased significantly since the end of the Civil War. These rates fluctuate under the influences of war, changing economic conditions, sex ratio of the marriageable population, and the number of potential brides and grooms present in the general population. The rate of marriage varies by season, day of the week, and region of the country.

3. An important and widely researched area of marriage deals with the power positions of husband and wife as individuals and in relation to each other. Power refers to the ability to influence others and to affect their behavior. Power, often measured by determining who makes certain decisions, includes the crucial dimensions of authority (legitimized power) and influence. The processes of family power focus on the interaction and dynamic aspects of decision making or conflict management. The outcomes of family power deal with the product, decision, or results of the process.

4. Studies of decision-making outcomes indicate that certain decisions are made primarily by the husband, others primarily by the wife, and others jointly. Who

50. Gary L. Hansen, "Marital Adjustment and Conventionalization: A Reexamination," *Journal of Marriage and the Family* 43 (November 1981): 855–863.

51. Anderson, Russell, and Schumm, "Perceived Marital Quality and Family Life-Cycle Categories," p. 134.

makes which decision has been widely explained by a theory of resources—the one with the information, education, income, and so forth makes the decision. This theory has been the topic of considerable debate and criticism but has led to a further development of resource exchange, resources in a cultural context, or a theory of comparative resources.

5. As with power, many attempts have been made to measure adjustment in marriage. Although lacking a general consensus of definition, adjustment generally includes relationships that are high in husband-wife agreement and high in the sharing of activities, tasks, and affection. Only infrequently has conflict been viewed as a basic aspect of marriage, the management of which is crucial in adjustment.

6. A number of writers suggest that marital alternatives may be a better predictor of marital disruption than are measures of adjustment or satisfaction.

7. When marital adjustment and satisfaction are examined throughout the life cycle, satisfaction appears to be highest at the beginning of marriage, with low points coming when families have teenagers. Studies indicate a curvilinear relationship throughout the life cycle—the beginning and the end of marriage are points of highest satisfaction.

8. Several notes of precaution are extended in dealing with the satisfaction—life-cycle data. First, differences, while existing, are often not as dramatic as often presented. Second, while sex differences exist as well, these too should not be overplayed. Third, reliance on cross-sectional data can produce misleading conclusions. Fourth, the issue of conventionalization must be recognized although studies suggest the issue is not serious enough to invalidate marital adjustment criteria.

9. Generally, it is the marital system that precedes and is basic to the parental system to which we direct our attention in the chapter that follows.

## KEY TERMS AND TOPICS

## DISCUSSION QUESTIONS

1. Why do people marry? What functions for the individual or society does marriage perform? Are any of these universal?

2. Check marriage rates in your state or community. How do they compare with other states and with national data? What variations occur by month and day of week?

3. Differentiate power, authority, and influence. How can each be determined and measured?

4. Make a list of ten decision-making areas. Take a brief survey among friends to determine whether their father, mother, or both jointly made these decisions. Are certain decisions consistently made by one or the other sex?

5. What is your theory of conjugal power? Can you think of instances where the person with the greatest resources does not have the most power? Are there instances where persons

with very few resources still have a high degree of power?

6. Women's movements are striving for more power. What types of power issues relate to the role of wives, mothers, and marriage? What are some recommended changes and means of attaining these changes?

7. What is the significance of conflict in a marriage? Can it be beneficial?

8. Describe the nature of marital success, i.e., What is it? How can it be measured? Is success the same as adjustment, happiness, and compatibility?

9. Select two or three of the most "ideal" marriages of which you are aware. What factors tend to make those marriages "ideal"? Do the same features exist in each marriage?

10. What factors indicate conventionality and conformity? Is the conventional marriage the "adjusted" or "successful" marriage?

11. How would you explain the curvilinear relationship between marital adjustment and the family life cycle?

## FURTHER READINGS

Blumstein, Philip, and Schwartz, Pepper. *American Couples*. New York: Pocket Books, 1983. An intensive look at money, work, sex, and the lives of couples in the United States: married, cohabitors, gays, and lesbians.

Fitzpatrick, Mary Anne. *Between Husbands and Wives: Communication in Marriage*. Newbury Park: Sage Publications, Inc., 1988. A book that establishes typologies of different types of marriage, styles of communication, and patterns of happiness.

Galvin, Kathleen M., and Brommel, Bernard J. *Family Communication: Cohesion and Change*. Glenview, Ill.: Scott, Foresman, 1982. A family textbook using a communication perspective in dealing with the development of relationships, intimacy, roles, power, decision making, and conflict.

Kammeyer, Kenneth C. W., ed. *Confronting the Issues: Sex Roles, Marriage, and the Family*. 2d ed. Boston: Allyn and Bacon, 1981. A collection of readings built around controversies within marriage and the family. Section I deals with attacks, defenses, and alternatives to marriage as an institution.

Olson, David H., and McCubbin, Hamilton, I. *Families: What Makes Them Work*. Beverly Hills: Sage Publications, 1983. More than 1,100 couples and nearly 2,700 individuals in intact marriages and families from 31 states were studied at seven stages of the family life cycle on five dimensions: family types, family resources, family stress and changes, family coping, and family satisfaction.

Scanzoni, John. *Sexual Bargaining: Power Politics in the American Marriage*. 2d ed. Chicago: University of Chicago Press, 1982. Sexual bargaining deals with motivations to marry, marital conflict as a positive force, and marital change in the past and future.

Scanzoni, John; Polonko, Karen; Teachman, Jay; and Thompson, Linda. *The Sexual Bond: Rethinking Families and Close Relationships*. Newbury Park, Ca.: Sage Publications, Inc., 1989. A stimulating and innovative process approach to examining close, primary, sexually based relationships that extend beyond marriage and family to characterize the reality of relationships in the U.S. today.

Szinovacz, Maximiliane E. "Family Power" in *Handbook of Marriage and the Family* by Marvin B. Sussman and Suzanne K. Steinmetz (eds.). New York: Plenum Press, 1987, Chapter 24, pp. 651–694. A look at family power studies including methodological and conceptual issues, an explanatory analysis, and guidelines for future research.

Wells, J. Gibson. *Current Issues in Marriage and the Family*. 4th ed. New York: Macmillan, 1988. A collection of readings dealing with the following issues: to marry or not; marriage versus cohabitation; marital and family roles; having children; childbearing alternatives; abortion, divorce and remarriage; and child care, family policy, and the future outlook.

# CHAPTER THIRTEEN

# THE PARENTAL SYSTEM

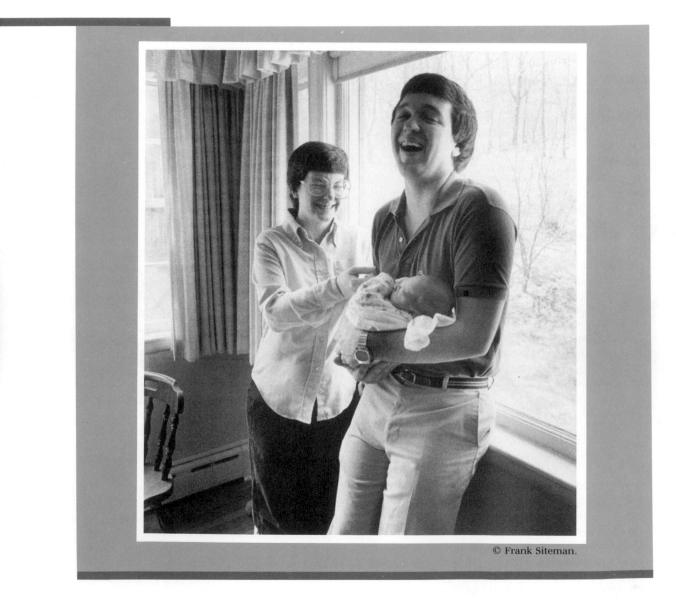

© Frank Siteman.

The parental system centers primarily around the interrelated statuses of parents and children. All societies have normative restrictions on appropriate and inappropriate behavior for both, and all societies have sets of role expectations accorded to the parent and child statuses. Some of the parent-child norms are nearly universal; others are relatively unique to a particular society or subculture. For example, no society is known to place the primary responsibility for the rearing of children on men; no society is known in which the young children customarily are dominant over the parents; and almost all societies place restrictions and taboos on the eating of certain foods by pregnant women.

Wide variations occur from one society to another in family size, methods of child rearing, extended family sharing in child-related tasks, rates of out-of-wedlock births, and the like. On the other hand, certain similarities exist in the norms and consequences of particular structural patterns within the parental system. Lower classes rear children differently than do the upper classes. Children born to unwed mothers do not begin life on an equal footing with children born in wedlock. First-born children appear to differ from later-born children in a wide variety of adult activities. The parental system and selected structural patterns are the focus of description and analysis in this chapter. The next chapter, while dealing with some organizational characteristics, focuses more on interactional and social-psychological dimensions of the parent-child relationship.

## THE TRANSITION TO PARENTHOOD

Becoming a parent, according to family development theorists, is one of the most significant family life-cycle transitions. Many writers do not consider a married couple a "family" until they have children. Others consider parenthood to be the final recognition of reaching adulthood or the culmination of the adult socialization process.

What is involved in the transition to parenthood? What must be learned and what readjustments of roles must take place in order to move smoothly from a childless state to parenthood? What is the effect of parenthood on the adult? What are the distinct roles and responsibilities of fathers and mothers toward infants and young children?

The social realities of parenting in the United States and much of the world stress the wife and mother as the primary caretaker and responsible person. Parenting tends to be viewed as primarily a maternal duty and is often referred to as "mothering" because of the assumption that the birth, the nurturing, and the primary responsibility of rearing children belongs to women.

Mothers in the Detroit metropolitan area, when asked about ideal caregivers for preschool age children, gave clear priority to the maternal role.[1] In their own lives this maternal role held priority over the worker role. Although substantial numbers regarded nursery schools and day care centers as ideal for older preschool children, the majority of mothers of preschool-aged children believed that "mother is best" until a child enters first grade.

What about fathers? In the previously mentioned study, many working mothers cited the father as the ideal daytime caregiver, and they often arranged their work schedules so that the father could, in fact, take care of their children. But generally, when compared to mothers, the role of the father in parenting is de-emphasized. The implied message is that fathers are not important in the parenting process or, if they are important, they tend to be too busy, indifferent, incompetent, or derelict in their parental role.

This neglect and indifference of fathers does not seem to be empirically supported. Data from ninety nonindustrialized societies indicate that in many of them, men assume substantial responsibility for child rearing, with a majority being classified as having close father-child relationships. Findings revealed that societies with high levels of father-child proximity enhance the public status of women, giving them more participation in public decision making and access to positions of authority.[2]

A more limited study covering five countries (United States, Ireland, Spain, Japan, and Mexico) showed that men in the United States do not associate or interact with children much differently from men in the other countries.[3] Men were found to associate with children less than women, but in the United States when societal norms allowed them access to children, the men associated with children in large numbers and responded to their children rather actively. The authors concluded that on balance, there is no compelling reason to assume paternal deprivation by U.S. men toward their children. Changes in society are offering men new contexts for fathering activities. This is particularly evident in nontraditional contexts such as dual-earner families, househusband fathers, stepfathers, fathers in the military, adolescent fathers, single custodial and noncustodial fathers, widowers as single fathers, and gay fathers.[4]

In most countries of the world, married couples in general and women in particular face considerable social pressures to become parents. In the

1. Karen Oppenheim Mason and Karen Kuhlthau, "Determinants of Child Care Ideals among Mothers of Preschool-Aged Children," *Journal of Marriage and the Family* 51 (August 1989): 593–603.

2. Scott Coltrane, "Father-Child Relationships and the Status of Women: A Cross Cultural Study," *American Journal of Sociology* 93 (March 1988): 1060–1095.

3. Wade C. Mackey and Randal D. Day, "Some Indicators of Fathering Behaviors in the United States: A Crosscultural Examination of Adult Male-Child Interaction," *Journal of Marriage and the Family* 41 (May 1979): 287–299.

4. Shirley M. H. Hanson, "Fatherhood: Contextual Variations," *American Behavioral Scientist* 29 (September/October 1985): 55–77.

## Meet your parents

I am the man who raised you. I was assisted by the woman who lived with me. She is not related to you or me by blood, marriage, or adoption but was an influential person in our lives. Now I would like you to meet your surrogate mother, your sperm donor father, their physician, the lawyer of your surrogate mother, the lawyer of your sperm donor father, your godmother, your godfather, your day care teacher, and all of our friends. These wonderful people, my child, are your family.

United States and other highly industrialized countries, these cultural and social pressures appear to have decreased, as evidenced in the delay in first pregnancies, the increased ability to control conceptions and births, the declining birth rates, the movement of increasing numbers of women into the labor force, and the emphasis on two-child or childless families. There are, of course, many unplanned conceptions that result from a sexual act that was recreative rather than procreative in intent or from rape or other involuntary coital encounters. These unplanned and often undesired pregnancies lead to personal and social concerns over pregnancy termination, abortion, or having the child and raising it alone or placing it for adoption.

In spite of nearly 4 millions births each year, interest in parenthood training seems to hold a relatively low priority in the United States. Most public school systems require courses in history, science, and mathematics, but seldom demand training in areas relevant to family life: marriage, child care, interpersonal competence, sex education, and so forth. Does this matter? Specifically, is parenthood education necessary or even beneficial? Is experiential learning from life experiences sufficient for adjustment to parenthood and successful parenting? Questions such as these led a number of researchers to determine if parenthood is a crisis event.

### Parenthood as a crisis or a transition

"Everybody" loves a newborn infant. Some love them more when they belong to someone else. But what effect does that "lovable" newborn and later the young child have upon parents? Several decades ago, E. E. LeMasters began what was to result in a series of studies by hypothesizing that the birth of a couple's first child is a critical event.[5] He claimed that parents in our society have a romantic notion about child rearing and that they tend to suffer from a process of disenchantment after they become parents. In his study of forty-six middle-class couples, he reported evidence that supported his

---

5. E. E. LeMasters, "Parenthood as Crisis," *Marriage and Family Living* 19 (November 1957): 352–355.

hypothesis of disenchantment: 83 percent of the couples reported an "extensive" or "severe" crisis in adjusting to the birth of their first child.

Unconvinced that LeMasters and several other writers were correct, a series of studies was done that questioned the advisability of labeling the arrival of the first child as a *crisis*. Writers noted that a crisis perspective places the emphasis on negative outcomes and overlooks the positive and gratifying aspects of parenthood. Over several decades the emphasis shifted from crisis to difficulties to transition. Reports suggested only slight amounts of difficulty in adjusting to the first child, with mothers reporting greater amounts of difficulty than fathers, and black parents reporting greater difficulties than white parents. Few findings existed to warrant the label of crisis, and it became more appropriate to refer to beginning parenthood as a *transition* rather than a *crisis*.

Whether it should be termed *crisis* or not, there is little doubt that when a dyad (husband and wife) becomes a triad (parents and child), or when a single person becomes a parent, a major reorganization of statuses, roles, and relationships takes place. The effect of the birth of a child and the preschool years of the children on the adjustment of the parent or parents seems fairly well established. As noted in the previous chapter, general marital satisfaction of couples tends to decrease after the birth of their children through the preschool and school years until the children are getting ready to leave home. LaRossa suggests that when you ask parents how their lives have changed after their babies were born—rather than asking whether they were bothered or gratified—the one consistent response deals with time.[6] Both parents report that sleep time, television time, communication time, sex time, and even bathroom time are in short supply as the result of a child. The "crisis" earlier writers made reference to may realistically be a need to adjust to the additional time it takes to do all the additional tasks that accompany the presence of children.

## The value of parenthood

Apparently not all children are problematic, produce a crisis situation, or are viewed negatively. In spite of unplanned pregnancies, a decreasing birth rate, a decrease in the average family size, and an increase in childless marriages (all discussed later in this chapter), women continue to want and voluntarily have children. In fact, nearly half of all currently married women over the age of thirty who had never borne a child and who were sterile for noncontraceptive reasons were found to have adopted at least one child.[7] In addition, given the

---

6. Ralph LaRossa, "The Transition to Parenthood and the Social Reality of Time," *Journal of Marriage and the Family* 45 (August 1983): 579–589. Similar time problems are reported in Julie A. Kach and Paul E. McGhee, "Adjustment of Early Parenthood," *Journal of Family Issues* 3 (September 1982): 375–388.

7. Christine A. Bachrach, "Adoption as a Means of Family Formation: Data from the National Survey of Family Growth," *Journal of Marriage and the Family* 45 (November 1983): 859–865.

## Adoption patterns in the United States

According to a report in *Family Planning Perspectives* (January/February 1987), slightly more than two percent of ever-married women aged 15–44 adopt a child. Those most likely to adopt are older women, sterile women, and women who have never had their own children. Both the proportion of U.S. women who adopt a child and the proportion of U.S. women who place their babies for adoption appear to have remained relatively stable since the mid-1970s. This apparently ended the sharp downtrend in adoptions prior to 1975 that reflected the wider availability of abortion as a means of resolving an unwanted pregnancy.

Who places their child for adoption? Eighty-eight percent of the mothers have never been married. White women are much more likely to place their babies for adoption (12 percent) than black women (less than one percent). Unmarried women who place their babies for adoption are less likely to be receiving some form of public assistance, less likely to be poor, and more likely to have completed high school than unmarried women who keep their babies.

What are the material consequences for adopted children? They have overwhelmingly greater economic advantages than do children who remain with their never-married mothers. Only two percent of adopted children were living below the poverty level compared with 62 percent of children who remained with their never-married mothers.

---

fights over child custody and the estimated 500,000 to 750,000 incidents of child snatching (the abduction of a child by one parent from another) each year,[8] it must be assumed that children are of value, satisfy certain needs for individuals and couples, and fulfill basic functions for society.[9]

Data from a random sample of 600 couples in the early years of marriage revealed that the couples felt the primary advantages of children were derived from seeing them as necessary for "having a real family life" and from regarding them as "sources of love and affection."[10] Children were also seen as buffers against loneliness and impersonality. Only a few couples regarded children as being very important for the fulfillment of sexual love, for the establishment of oneself as a mature person, or for spiritual fulfillment. These data indicated that by only a small margin did couples rate children as more valuable than having extra money to save, invest, or spend; having a neat and orderly household; and finding new interests and hobbies. Values such as freedom of movement, leisure time, and employment opportunities of the wife were rated by nearly half of the couples as equally or more valuable than children. For both husbands and wives, "being alone with my spouse" clearly emerged as having greater reward value than children.

---

8. Richard J. Gelles, "Parental Child Snatching: A Preliminary Estimate of the National Incidence," *Journal of Marriage and the Family* 46 (August 1984): 735–739.

9. For a review of research on satisfaction with parenthood and parenting, *see* Ann Goetting, "Parental Satisfaction: A Review of Research," *Journal of Family Issues* 7 (March 1986): 83–109.

10. Arthur G. Neal, H. Theodore Groat, and Jerry W. Wicks, "Attitudes about Having Children: A Study of 600 Couples in the Early Years of Marriage," *Journal of Marriage and the Family* 51 (May 1989): 313–328.

While the value of children occupies a central place in the lives of men and women around the world, it is evident that changes are taking place in children's perceived value when compared to other options and choices. Compared to older parents and perhaps to most countries of the world, young couples in the United States place a greater emphasis on personal freedom, rational choice, and hedonistic values. From a cross-cultural perspective, values of having children include factors such as attaining adult status and a social identity; attaining immortality by "carrying on the family name"; or satisfying a desire for love, primary group ties, and a feeling of being part of a family group.

Other values include a feeling of achievement and competence, power, social comparison, and economic utility. Some of these values are more prevalent in cultures outside the United States. Power, for example, is a significant value in certain villages in India where the new bride moves into the household of her husband's family where she lives in a subservient role to her mother-in-law. By having sons, she gains some control over her own life and over her childless sisters-in-law. Eventually, when her sons bring home brides, she becomes the powerful and dominating mother-in-law. In the United States, power can be seen in the control and influence parents hold over other human beings—their children. A value like economic utility tends to have greater significance in rural areas or in certain countries. Children provide inexpensive labor and, in addition, are often viewed as important to care for parents in their old age.

## SOCIAL CONSEQUENCES OF PARENTHOOD

Parenthood and its consequences cannot be evaluated apart from the society in which it functions. In the United States, for example, the majority of ever-married women have jobs prior to pregnancy. Waite and others note that most leave these jobs as the pregnancy progresses, with only one in five women remaining employed in the month that the child is born. Many of these mothers return to work, but by two years after the birth, employment rates were found to rise to about 60 percent of their previous levels. Thus, one major social consequence of parenthood in the United States is the withdrawal of women from employment. In contrast, fathers showed higher levels of work activity than would be expected of them at the time of the first birth.[11]

Another consequence of parenthood, at least in the short run, relates to marital stability. In spite of the data presented in the previous chapter on how

---

11. Linda J. Waite, Gus W. Haggstrom, and David E. Kanouse, "Changes in the Employment Activities of New Parents," *American Sociological Review* 50 (April 1985): 263–272. *See also* Ellen Hock, M. Therese Gnezda, and Susan L. McBride, "Mothers of Infants: Attitudes Toward Employment and Motherhood Following Birth of the First Child," *Journal of Marriage and the Family* 46 (May 1984): 425–431.

marital satisfaction drops with the presence of children and data presented later in this chapter showing how childless marriages have higher levels of marital adjustment than couples with children, a national longitudinal study shows strong, positive effects of the first birth on the marital stability of young adults. It was estimated that by the time the first child reaches age two, more than 20 percent of the parents would have been divorced or separated if the child had not been born compared to actual disruption rates of 5 to 8 percent.[12]

Lynn White and Alan Booth refer to this factor as the "braking hypothesis." They suggest that although children do not prevent divorce, they may cause couples to approach the divorce decision more slowly.[13] In spite of a persistent negative correlation between the presence of children and marital happiness, they too found that new parents were significantly less likely to divorce over a three-year period than those who remained childless. Their explanation for these seemingly inconsistent findings was not that persons in more stable marriages have children (a selectivity argument) and was only partially based on the argument that a new baby causes major negative changes in marital structure. Rather, their argument focused on a differential propensity to divorce. Childless couples, they suggest, give greater selectivity to marital happiness than parents. The result is a greater willingness of childless couples to divorce when unhappy. Whatever the reason, fewer divorces seem to occur when very young children are present. Studies reported in Chapter 17 indicate how older children do not provide the same deterrent to divorce.

The social consequences of parenthood may be either positive or negative and, of course, affect far more than female employment, marital stability, and divorce. The concern over young and unwed parenthood, for example, often centers around its negative consequences. Let us examine each of these briefly.

## The concern over young parenthood

The concern over young parenthood is closely linked to the discussion in Chapter 8 entitled "The Concern over Young Marriage" which greatly overlaps with the section that follows entitled "The Concern over Unwed Parenthood." To be married young (generally meaning in adolescence or in one's teens), to be a young parent (meaning to have a child as a teenager), or to be an unwed parent (meaning to have a child apart from marriage irrespective of age) are three interrelated social structural patterns that involve processes often

---

12. Linda J. Waite, Gus Haggstrom, and David E. Kanouse, "The Consequences of Parenthood for the Marital Stability of Young Adults," *American Sociological Review* 50 (December 1985): 850–857.

13. Lynn K. White and Alan Booth, "The Transition to Parenthood and Marital Quality," *Journal of Family Issues* 6 (December 1985): 435–449.

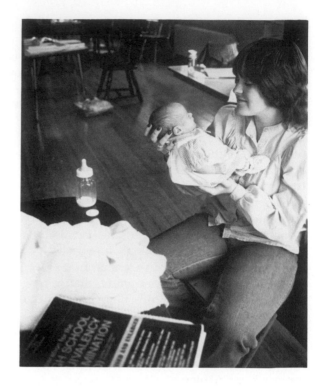

*Teenage or young parent-hood often means unwed parenthood as well. The concern over these is related to the negative effects on health, occupa-tional or educational at-tainment, and sufficient assets and resources to adequately care for par-ent and child.*

perceived as not planned, desired, or preferred. All three result in social consequences defined as difficult and negative. Yet, for some, any of the three may result from consciously planned and preferred decisions, and under certain conditions they may have positive outcomes.

Why do teenagers get pregnant, thus becoming young parents? One in six teenage pregnancies were found to be planned and intended. On the other hand, 92 percent of those conceived premaritally (unwed) and half of those conceived in marriage (by teenagers) were found to be unintended.[14] This high incidence of unplanned teenage pregnancies is explained by a minority (one in three) of sexually active young women using contraceptives and only one in two of these relying on the most effective methods. The two most common reasons for not using contraceptives are the belief that the risk of pregnancy is small and the failure to anticipate intercourse.

It is clear that U.S. teenagers are far more likely to become pregnant than are comparable women in other developed countries. The teenage pregnancy rates in six other Western countries (Canada, England and Wales, Finland, Netherlands, Norway, and Sweden) range from only 13 to 53 percent of the U.S. rate.[15] While teenagers in the U.S. appear to be no more likely than their

14. James Trussell, ''Teenage Pregnancy in the United States,'' *Family Planning Perspectives* 20 (November/December 1988): 262–272.

15. Charles F. Westoff, ''Unintended Pregnancy in America and Abroad,'' *Family Planning Perspectives* 20 (November/December 1988): 254–261.

Canadian or European contemporaries to marry or engage in intercourse, they do seem less likely to practice contraception.

Why are U.S. teenagers so distinctive, even when compared to countries very similar to the United States, such as Canada and Great Britain? The Westoff source just cited suggests that U.S. teenagers may not have the same access to contraceptives, they face different costs in family planning services from countries with national health care systems, they comprise a large underclass of ethnic diversity and unequal income distribution that alienates them from middle-class values, they are greater risk-takers (even teenage auto accident rates are two to eight times as high), and they have an ambivalence toward sexuality. That is, although sex saturates American television programs, movies, and advertisements, the media fail to communicate responsible attitudes about it, with birth control being for the most part a taboo subject.

We might ask "so what" that we have higher rates of teenage pregnancies and young parents? There are tremendous costs: educational, social, and economic consequences for the individuals involved and for society at large. One way to determine the impact or cost of being a young parent is to compare adolescents who relinquish (put up for adoption) their children with those who raise them. One source showed that when background and other characteristics were controlled, relinquishers were more likely to complete vocational training and to have higher educational aspirations.[16] They were more likely to delay marriage, be employed six and twelve months after the birth, and live in higher income households. The child rearers were more likely to become pregnant again sooner and to resolve subsequent pregnancies by abortion. It was noted that adolescents who relinquished their children did not suffer more negative consequences than did those who raised their children.

Young parenthood magnifies the general issues surrounding parenthood in general that have been discussed thus far. When parenthood, and more specifically motherhood, occurs at an early age, it is likely to have a negative effect on occupational attainment, marital stability, asset accumulation, and the woman's health.[17] When compared to women in the twenty- to thirty-five-year age group, teenage mothers are most likely to postpone prenatal care, have a child of low birthweight, and experience a higher rate of infant mortality.[18] The evidence strongly suggests that the bulk of the adverse

---

16. Steven D. McLaughlin, Diane L. Minninen, and Linda D. Wingers, "Do Adolescents who Relinquish Their Children Fare Better or Worse Than Those who Raise Them," *Family Planning Perspectives* 20 (January/February 1988): 25–32.

17. Jay D. Teachman, "Early Marriage, Premarital Fertility, and Marital Dissolution," *Journal of Family Issues* 4 (March 1983): 105–126; and John O. G. Billy, Nancy S. Landale, and Steven D. McLaughlin, "The Effect of Marital Status at First Birth on Marital Dissolution Among Adolescent Mothers," *Demography* 3 (August 1986): 329–349.

18. Michael K. Miller and C. Shannon Stokes, "Teenage Fertility, Socioeconomic Status and Infant Mortality," *Journal of Biosocial Science* 17 (1985): 329–349; and Richard A. Davis, "Adolescent Pregnancy and Infant Mortality: Isolating the Effects of Race," *Adolescence* 92 (Winter 1988): 899–908.

## Vatican condemns birth from frozen embryo

On April 17, 1984, the Associated Press in Rome reported that the Vatican newspaper condemned the process used to conceive a child from a frozen embryo. The report was in response to an announcement one week earlier by scientists that a healthy girl named Zoe had been delivered by doctors at Monash University in Melbourne. Zoe was the first birth announced in Australia resulting from that method.

In an editorial appearing in *L'Osservatore* Romano, Gino Concetti, a theologian, said that one understands the desire of sterile couples to have children, but one must realize that not everything one desires can be right. He said the new technique is unacceptable because it requires the act of masturbation to obtain sperm and, according to the Roman Catholic Church, masturbation is "a deviation and a grave sin." Thus the condemnation of artifical insemination and the use of a frozen embryo.

consequences of teenage childbearing may be of social and economic origin, particularly poverty, rather than attributable to the effects of young age per se. At the macro-level, trends in the age at first birth have important effects on the pace of social change, period fertility trends, and the state of the economy.[19] It affects as well the milieu in which children are raised, the kinds of opportunities available to them, and their intellectual development.

In a study of 400 young adolescent mothers, their partners, progeny, and parents, Frank Furstenberg explored when, how, and why childbearing before the age of eighteen jeopardizes the life prospects of the young mother and her child.[20] Four out of five of the adolescent mothers became pregnant within two years following the onset of intercourse, which typically occurred at age fifteen. Fewer than one in four of the teenagers' mothers admitted that they had known that their daughters were having sexual relations prior to the pregnancy. While most of the adolescents had some limited knowledge of birth control, they tended to be most aware of those forms to which they had the least access, and their control was confined largely to "getting the boy to use something." Contraception was much more likely to be practiced by couples who had a stable romantic relationship.

As might be expected, the pregnancies were greeted by both adolescents and parents with astonishment. Three-quarters of the expectant mothers wished they had not become pregnant and half could not tell their parents for several months. Those women who married were more likely than those who did not to indicate positive feelings toward the pregnancy.

Furstenberg's results, consistent with other studies, found that premarital pregnancy greatly increased the probability of eventual marital dissolution.

---

19. Ronald R. Rindfuss and Craig St. John, "Social Determinants of Age at First Birth," *Journal of Marriage and the Family* 45 (August 1983): 553–565.

20. Frank F. Furstenberg, Jr., "The Social Consequences of Teen-age Parenthood," *Family Planning Perspectives* 8 (August 1976): 148–164. The data presented in this section came from this report.

A comparison group of classmates who married but had not conceived premaritally had one-half the probability of the marriage breaking up after two years than that for the adolescent mothers. Although unplanned pregnancy may not *cause* the breakup of the marriage, it is an important link to a weak economic position of the male who fathers a child out of wedlock. Most of the men—young, inexperienced, and unskilled—had a low earning potential before they wed. Again, like other studies, economic resources are strongly linked to marital stability.

The problems of young parenthood are further compounded by additional unwanted pregnancies. Estimates vary, but Furstenberg indicates that most published studies show that at least half of the teenage mothers studied experience a second pregnancy within thirty-six months of delivery. In his sample, one-fourth of the women became pregnant within twelve months of the birth of the first child, and by three years, half of the women with two children had become pregnant a third time.

Pregnancy, marriage, or both was a principal reason for leaving high school. One-fourth of the adolescents never returned, and half never graduated, this in contrast to 18 percent of the comparison group who did not graduate.

One-quarter of the respondents had obtained most, if not all, of their income from working. Welfare barely edged out income from spouse as the second most common source of support. Welfare was not, however, a contributing factor in the encouragement of childbearing out of wedlock. The welfare mother was not significantly more likely to become pregnant after she went on relief than the young mother who was not receiving support. In any case, nearly half of all adolescent mothers were living below the poverty level.

What happened to these adolescent mothers seventeen years later? Furstenberg and some colleagues, engaging in a longitudinal study spanning almost two decades, located about three-fourths of the mothers from the original study.[21] While space does not permit adequate coverage of their results, several findings appear of interest. For example, a substantial majority of these mothers completed high school, found regular employment, and, even when they had been on welfare, eventually managed to escape from public assistance. Relatively few ended up with large families. Compared to twelve years earlier (from a five-year follow-up), the young mothers were in almost all respects better off than a decade earlier.

These findings modify the stereotype of the adolescent mother, but do not refute it. That is, while many teenage mothers managed to get out of poverty, finish high school, and so forth, the authors suggest the majority did not make out as well as they probably would have had they been able to postpone parenthood. An early pregnancy does affect the life-course path, but

---

21. Frank Furstenberg, Jr., J. Brooks-Gunn, and S. Philip Morgan, *Adolescent Mothers in Later Life* (Cambridge: Cambridge University Press, 1987).

it does not destroy it. Upon reaching older adulthood, marriage, voluntary sterilization, employment, and degrees were significant life-course transformers. The authors argue for social programs that are preventive as well as ameliorative and focus on contraceptive, medical, educational, and vocational programs. These programs need to focus on disadvantaged males as well as on teenage mothers, and they need to be geared specifically to the client. One principal reason so many young mothers encounter problems is that they lack the resources to adequately cope with a poorly timed birth.

One major resource available to the young parent comes from their nuclear families: parents and siblings. This is often in the form of free room and board and partly or wholly subsidized child care. This assistance can significantly alter the life chances of the young mother, enhancing her prospects of educational achievement and economic advancement. Were it not for the increased poverty and dependency, the social isolation, less schooling, and the increased levels of childbearing (much of which is unwanted and out of wedlock), there would be far less concern over young parenthood.[22]

## The concern over unwed parenthood

Closely related to and often simultaneous with the concern over young parenthood is the issue of unwed parenthood with the attached label of *illegitimacy* placed upon the child. Illegitimacy or legitimacy is only characteristic of the human family since no other animal grouping has regulations that define who has the right to procreate and rear a fully accepted member of society. It is the family and marital system that universally fulfills the function of giving legal status and social approval to the birth of a child. To be born outside the family is to be illegitimate, a label generally defined as a social problem and an economic burden. Legal changes granting equal rights to children born in or out of parental wedlock are in process, but the unwed parent is still viewed with less approbation than the approval and congratulations granted to the married parent and the child born into a conjugal family unit.

A family unit requires someone to assume the roles of sociological father and sociological mother. Even though some degree of premarital sexual license exists in about 70 percent of the societies for which information is available, childbirth outside marriage is not approved in those societies. The

---

22. You may want to note Gina Adams, Sharon Adams-Taylor, and Karen Pittman, "Adolescent Pregnancy and Parenthood: A Review of the Problem, Solutions, and Resources," *Family Relations* 38 (April 1989): 223–229; Catherine S. Chilman, "Social and Psychological Research Concerning Adolescent Childbearing: 1970–1980," *Journal of Marriage and the Family* 42 (November 1980): 793–805; and Frank L. Mott, "The Pace of Repeated Childbearing Among Young Mothers," *Family Planning Perspectives* 18 (January/February 1986): 5–12.

suggestion is that marriage bestows legitimacy on parenthood more than on sex. That is, most societies are more concerned with illegitimacy than with sexual intercourse outside marriage.

This greater concern for unwed parenthood than for unwed intercourse may be the key to understanding the emphasis and attention given to the mother and the relative lack of attention given to the father. Despite his obvious involvement in the pregnancy, the male is studied far less frequently and is assigned a less deviant label. Data from a nationally representative survey show that 7 percent of young males age twenty to twenty-seven had fathered a child while they were teenagers.[23] One-third of those who were responsible for a nonmarital conception married within twelve months of conception and half of the young men lived with their child shortly after the child's birth. Young black men were more likely to have been responsible for a nonmarital first birth than were males of other racial backgrounds, but only 15 percent of black teenagers lived with their first child compared with 48 percent of Hispanics, 58 percent of disadvantaged whites, and 77 percent of nondisadvantaged whites. Teenage fathers, compared to other male teenagers, were more likely to be high school dropouts, to be from low-income families, and to face distinct disadvantages in the labor market. These are factors that hamper their ability to contribute financially to the support of their partner or child and that provide low incentives for either mothers or fathers to marry. All information on unwed parenthood suggests that a double standard, while operative in sexual behaviors, is much more in evidence with regard to the pregnancy consequences that result from sexual behavior.

Some antecedents of out-of-wedlock adolescent pregnancy come from over 2,000 young adults first surveyed as seventh-grade students and followed up ten years later. Among the males, having a girlfriend become pregnant was associated with school difficulties, low parental socioeconomic status, and high popularity. Among females, pregnancy risk was related to race, low socioeconomic status, father absence, number of siblings, school difficulties, family stress, and popularity.[24] Sexual differences in experiencing pregnancy were attributed to the possibility that some males were unaware they had impregnated girls, the greater ease males have in the denial of causing a pregnancy, and the tendency of adolescent girls to date older males.

As of 1986, nearly one-fourth of all births were to unmarried women (15.7 percent for white women, 61.2 percent for black women) with 33 percent of

---

23. William Marsiglio, "Adolescent Fathers in the United States: Their Initial Living Arrangements, Marital Experience and Educational Outcomes," *Family Planning Perspectives* 19 (November/December 1987): 240–251. *See also:* Jacqueline Smollar and Theodora Ooms, *Young Unwed Fathers: Research Review, Policy Dilemmas and Options* (Rockville, Md.: Shared Resource Center, 1988).

24. Cynthia Robbins, Howard B. Kaplan, and Steven S. Martin, "Antecedents of Pregnancy Among Unmarried Adolescents," *Journal of Marriage and the Family* 47 (August 1985): 567–583.

## Do welfare benefits encourage early childbearing?

When unmarried teenagers become pregnant, they can choose abortion, adoption, marriage, or welfare. Some people say it is that last option, the government dole, that is encouraging the tremendous upsurge in children having children.

Two Harvard researchers, David Ellwood and Mary Jo Bane, examined the impact of welfare, and, in particular, the Aid to Families with Dependent Children (AFDC) program, on family structure and living arrangements. As reported in *Family Planning Perspectives* (September/October 1985), they did their study because of widespread concern that the availability of AFDC—which supports mainly single women and their children—encourages out-of-wedlock childbearing and is destructive of family relationships.

What they found was that the level of welfare

benefits in a state seems to have *little* impact on the decisions of unmarried women to have children. It does, however, appear to have a substantial effect on the living arrangements of young single mothers. In states where benefit levels are high, unmarried mothers are considerably more likely to move out of their parents' home and set up their own households. Also, young married mothers are somewhat more likely to become divorced or separated.

The authors conclude that a dramatic cut in welfare would change the lives of poor women. It would reduce the income of single mothers and influence where many young single mothers live. But welfare (AFDC alone or AFDC plus food stamps) would do little to slow the growth of single-parent families and early childbearing.

---

these births to teenagers.[25] Thus, still relevant is a question Kingsley Davis posed more than fifty years ago, "Why doesn't society solve the problem of illegitimacy by requiring the use of contraceptive methods and, when these fail, abortion?"[26] His answer was that to break the normative relations between sexuality and the family, so that adults would as a matter of course decide rationally whether they would enjoy sex within or outside the family, would also reduce the strength of the motive to marry and found a family. The radical changes necessary to eliminate illegitimacy would very likely come close to eliminating the family system too. If this is true, the concern over childbirth in or out of wedlock is well understood.

One central element in understanding unwed parenthood is the class status of the child, family, and community. In fact, one study claimed that 81 percent of the variance in predicting state teenage birthrates could be explained by state poverty rates, low school completion rates, low state per capita expenditures for public welfare, and high unemployment rates.[27] These

25. U.S. Bureau of the Census, *Statistical Abstract of the United States: 1989*, 109th ed. (Washington, D.C.: U.S. Government Printing Office, 1989), no. 93, p. 66. On black teenage pregnancy *see:* Joyce A. Ladner, "Black Teenage Pregnancy: A Challenge for Educators," *Journal of Negro Education* 56 (1987): 53–63; and on black-white differences on unmarried motherhood *see:* Larry Bumpass and Sara McLanahan, "Unmarried Motherhood: Recent Trends, Composition, and Black-White Differences," *Demography* 26 (May 1989): 279–286.

26. Kingsley Davis, "Illegitimacy and the Social Structure," *American Journal of Sociology* 45 (September 1939): 221–222.

27. Shirley Zimmerman, "State Level Public Policy Choices as Predictors of State Teen Birthrates," *Family Relations* 37 (July 1988): 315–321.

*Table 13–1*
**Births to unmarried women, by race and age of mother, 1950–1986**

| Race and age | 1950 | 1960 | 1970 | 1980 | 1986 |
|---|---|---|---|---|---|
| Total live births (in thousands) | 141.6 | 224.3 | 398.7 | 665.7 | 878.5 |
| White | 53.5 | 82.5 | 175.1 | 320.0 | 466.8 |
| Black and other | 88.1 | 141.8 | 223.6 | 345.7 | 411.7 |
| Percent of all births | 4.0% | 5.3% | 10.7% | 18.4% | 23.4% |
| Total rate (# per 1,000) | 14.1 | 21.6 | 26.4 | 29.4 | 34.3 |
| White | 6.1 | 9.2 | 13.8 | 17.6 | 23.2 |
| Black and other | 71.2 | 98.3 | 89.9 | 77.2 | 80.9 |
| Number (in thousands) by age of mother | | | | | |
| Under 15 years | 3.2 | 4.6 | 9.5 | 9.0 | 9.4 |
| 15–19 years | 56.0 | 87.1 | 190.4 | 262.8 | 280.7 |
| 20–24 years | 43.1 | 68.0 | 126.7 | 237.3 | 316.2 |
| 25–29 years | 20.9 | 32.1 | 40.6 | 99.6 | 165.7 |
| 30–34 years | 10.8 | 18.9 | 19.1 | 41.0 | 74.9 |
| 35 years and over | 7.7 | 13.6 | 12.4 | 16.1 | 31.6 |
| Percent 19 years and under | 41.8 | 40.9 | 50.2 | 40.9 | 33.1 |

*Source:* U.S. Bureau of the Census, *Statistical Abstract of the United States:* 1989, 109th ed.
(Washington, D.C.: U.S. Government Printing Office, 1989), no. 93, p. 66.

class-related factors illustrate how economic factors and educational and occupational opportunity structures influence the prevalence of both teenage and unwed parenthood. In addition, it might be predicted that unwed parenthood among the lower classes would be of less concern to a society than would unwed parenthood among the higher classes. With less property to protect or to inherit and with lineage and family honor less a focus of attention in the lower classes, families have less to lose if a birth out of wedlock occurs. The expected result of this would be more frequent unwed births among the lower classes.

Among the higher classes, since property and family name is at stake to a greater degree, some expected results are likely to include pressure on the couple to marry, to turn over the child to an adoption agency, or to leave home to bear the child. Births can be avoided altogether via abortion, which is more accessible to the educated and financially able.

*Rates of birth outside of marriage*    At the very time that birth rates are steadily declining or leveling off (to be discussed later in this chapter), the **rates of birth outside of marriage** are showing a dramatic increase. The number of births to unmarried women approached 900,000 in 1986 (*see* Table 13–1). That represents more than a 620 percent increase in the number of such births since 1950. Equally dramatic is the change in the *percentage* of all births to unmarried women. In 1950, the percentage was 4.0. By 1986, the same figure was 23.4, an increase of 585 percent.

The rate varies widely by race, with much of the difference explained by social class. The differences in stigma attached to unwed births, the likelihood of reporting, and the access to, and use of, contraceptives and abortion account for a major proportion of the white–non-white difference.

The incidence of live births by age of mother shows a profound change. Unwed mothers are getting older. In 1970, 50.2 percent of births were to teenage mothers compared to 40.9 percent in 1980 and 33.1 percent in 1986. The *number* of mothers under age fifteen remained about the same in the same time interval. While teenage unwed mothers ages fifteen to nineteen increased by 90,300 or 47 percent between 1970 and 1986, the increase in those ages twenty to twenty-four was 189,500 or 150 percent. Even greater increases occurred among the twenty-five to twenty-nine and thirty to thirty-four age categories (up 308 and 292 percent respectively).

Unwed parenthood is no longer most prevalent among teenagers when compared to other age categories. Most unwed births in 1986 were to mothers in the twenty to twenty-four age category and older. These age changes might suggest fewer problems related to emotional immaturity, dropping out of school, and skills to care for the child, but whether it means fewer income and employment problems is unclear. Let's examine if having a child out of wedlock matters.

## Does birth out of wedlock make a difference?

Again we return to the question relating to the concern over unwed parenthood. Does it really make a difference that nearly 900,000 births each year are outside of wedlock? Do these children experience more social, economic, and health handicaps than children born in wedlock? Is the presence of both a male and a female parent essential to the growth and development of a child? Does the unmarried mother face increased emotional and economic difficulties that seriously affect both the mother and the child? Some of these specific questions are discussed elsewhere (note the section on the single parent in Chapter 7 on social class, Chapter 6 on the African-American family, and Chapter 14 on parent-child socialization in particular); however, several research studies are worthy of consideration here.

Empirical research indicates that birth outside of wedlock does have an impact on the child, the parent, and society as evidenced in studies completed in California and elsewhere.[28] Information from a sample of two-year-old legitimate and illegitimate children indicated that despite significant social

---

28. Beth Berkov and June Sklar, "Does Illegitimacy Make a Difference? A Study of the Life Chances of Illegitimate Children in California," *Population and Development Review* 2 (June 1976): 201–217.

changes, illegitimate children continue to face poorer life chances than legitimate children. They were found to have a higher infant mortality rate, and the unadopted illegitimate children fared quite poorly on a number of measures including school performance. Unmarried mothers were less likely to marry within three years after the birth than the general population of unmarried women and were more likely to separate from their husbands if they did later marry. It is of interest to note that adopted children born to unwed mothers did as well or better than legitimate children.[29] It would appear from the data in the Berkov and Sklar study that, despite a decrease in the degree of stigma attached to birth out of wedlock and the proliferation of services and programs for these children and their mothers, these children do not begin life on an equal footing with legitimate children, and their handicaps persist beyond the hazards of infancy.[30]

Other data clearly support negative and long-lasting repercussions of teenage and/or unwed childbearing. Young parents acquire less education than their contemporaries; they are often limited to less prestigious jobs and, in the case of the women, to more dead-end ones. From the moment of pregnancy awareness, both young parents and unwed mothers have difficult decisions and adjustments to make. Little toleration is extended to the young unwed mother who wishes to keep her child as her own, although greater toleration does exist in the lower-class strata where the commitment to the norm of legal marriage is less.

In 1935, the United States Congress established a national policy of providing financial aid to a mother and her children when they did not have financial support. This Aid to Families with Dependent Children (AFDC) program enabled a mother to keep her children with her. Programs such as these receive constant protests from taxpayers who argue (falsely) that mothers want more children to increase their aid (*see* insert, Do Welfare Benefits Encourage Early Childbearing?). Increased aid is seldom a central motivational factor in the birth of additional children.

## FAMILY SIZE AND RELATED FACTORS

### Birth rates and birth expectations

Most married couples want, have, or expect to have children. In 1987, there were 3.83 million births in the United States, a rate of 15.7 births per 1,000

---

29. Similar findings are reported in Christine A. Bachrach, "Children in Families: Characteristics of Biological, Step-, and Adopted Children," *Journal of Marriage and the Family* 45 (February 1983): 171–179.

30. Berkov and Sklar, "Does Illegitimacy Make a Difference?" p. 215. *Also see* Wendy Baldwin and Virginia S. Cain, "The Children of Teenage Parents," *Family Planning Perspectives* 12 (January/February 1980): 34–43.

population.[31] The same year, 18.6 percent of all ever-married women aged fifteen to forty-four, either by choice or circumstances, were childless.[32]

The birth rate is one of the best documented series of descriptive social data available today. Census data show quite clearly the increase and decrease in number and rate of births in the United States. In 1910 the birth rate was 30.1 per 1,000 population, decreasing to 18.7 during the Depression years of the mid-thirties, increasing to 25 in 1955, steadily decreasing until the mid-1970s when it reached a low of 14.6, and varying between 15.5 and 15.9 in the decade of the 1980s. The decline in the fertility rate for American women was especially sharp in the early 1970s, but this was a continuation of the drop in the level of fertility since the peak year of the baby boom in 1957.

What do demographers and journalists mean when they talk about a "baby boom"? Simply stated, the baby boom was a post–World War II "disturbance" that upset what had been a century-long decline in the U.S. fertility rate. It was an unanticipated, pronounced, and consequential rise in the United States birth rate during the late 1940s and 1950s (see Figure 13–1). Theories as to its cause include increases in normative pressure on women to have children, the disruption and dislocation brought about by war, the postwar economic prosperity, and the longterm psychological effects of growing up during the Depression. Bean suggests that social and cultural conditions during the era supported having families, while at the same time increasing the cost of having large families.[33] This postwar spurt in annual births did not represent a return of the large family of the nineteenth century. What happened was a movement away from singlehood, childless marriage, and one-child families, and a bunching together of births. Only a minor part of the baby boom could be attributed to increases in the proportions having three or more births.[34]

In 1988, the average number of lifetime births *expected* by currently married women aged eighteen to thirty-four was 2.21, a slight decline from a 2.27 average exactly ten years earlier in 1978, but well below the 3.05 average reported in 1967. About 10 percent said they expected to be childless, 14 percent expected one child, 48 percent expected to have two children, and 29 percent expected three or more.[35] A comparison of the average number of lifetime births expected by currently married women versus the never-married women indicated that single women expect a lower average number of births than wives (1.86 versus 2.21 in the eighteen to thirty-four age group). The

31. U.S. Bureau of the Census, *Statistical Abstract of the United States: 1989*, 109th ed. (Washington, D.C.: U.S. Government Printing Office, 1989), no. 83, p. 61.

32. Ibid., Table 98, p. 68. (Comparable figures for 1940 were 26.5; 1950, 22.8; 1960, 15.0; 1970, 16.4; and 1980, 18.8 percent.)

33. Frank D. Bean, "The Baby Boom and Its Explanations," *The Sociological Quarterly* 24 (Summer 1983): 353–365.

34. Leon F. Bouvier, "America's Baby Boom Generation: The Fateful Bulge," *Population Bulletin* 35 (1980): 4. Published by The Population Reference Bureau, Inc., Washington, D.C.

35. U.S. Bureau of the Census, *Current Population Reports*, Series P-20, no 436, "Fertility of American Women: June 1988," (Washington, D.C.: U.S. Government Printing Office, 1989), Table 5, p. 30.

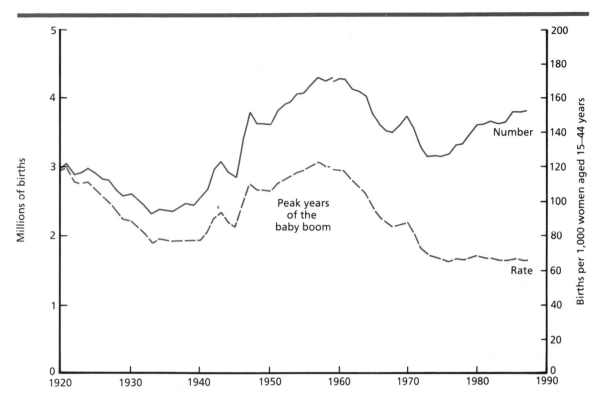

NOTE: Beginning with 1959, trend lines are based on registered live births; trend lines for 1920–59 are based on live births adjusted for underregistration.

*Figure 13–1*
***Live births and fertility rates: United States, 1920–1987.*** (*Source:* National Center for Health Statistics, "Advance Report of Natality Statistics, 1987," *Monthly Vital Statistics Reports*, vol. 38, no. 3 [Public Health Service, Hyattsville, Md., June 29, 1989], Figure 1, p. 2.)

difference in lifetime birth expectations between married and single women decreases with age, indicating both a reduction in the remaining number of reproductive years and a decrease in marriage prospects at later ages for single women. If women now in their late teens and twenties live up to their expectations for the future, the number of persons who come from "large" families will be a small proportion of the population.

There seems to be some disagreement as to whether the fertility rate and average family size will continue a downward trend or level off at no more than two children. Due to factors such as improved methods of birth control, liberalized abortion laws, and increased acceptance of birth planning by Catholics, we might anticipate a decrease in the number of unplanned and unwanted births. We do know that since the early 1960s there has been a trend to delay first births. Women who delay childbearing have fewer children and

## Baby boomers having children

Fertility rates during the 1980s have been quite stable. The Census Bureau recorded 3.85 million births or 15.8 births per 1,000 people in 1988. That's up from 14.6 in 1975. But it's below 1970's 18.4 births per 1,000 and 1960's 23.7. Since 1979 the number of births per 1,000 population ranged between 15.5 and 15.9.

The increase in number of births since the mid-1970s (see Figure 13–1) is an echo of the past. More children are being born because there are so many women of childbearing age—women born during the post-war baby boom. But births per 1,000 population vary widely by region and state.

The Northeast and Midwest are regions with a birth rate below the national average, while the South and West are above average. Figures for 1987 show the West with 17.6 births per 1,000 whereas the Northeast had 14.6 births per 1,000.

Alaska at 21.8 and Utah at 21.4 top the nation in births per 1,000 population, with third place going to New Mexico with 20.1 births per 1,000 population. The high rate in Utah reflects the Mormon high fertility rate. Non-Mormons in Utah have a rate close to the nation as a whole (Journal of Marriage and the Family, May 1985: 459). At the low end of the scale, West Virginia had the lowest birthrate in the nation, at 12.4 per 1,000 people. The bottom quartile were all in the Northeast and Middle Atlantic area of the United States.

are significantly better off economically than either average-age childbearers or the childless. And by retirement age the delayed childbearer with only one or two children appears better off than all other women.[36]

36. Sandra L. Hofferth, "Long-Term Economic Consequences for Women of Delayed Childbearing and Reduced Family Size," Demography 21 (May 1984): 141–155; and Jane Riblett Wilkie, "The Trend Toward Delayed Parenthood," Journal of Marriage and the Family 43 (August 1981): 583–591. For a study that suggests few differences between delayed and younger childbearers in other than demographic characteristics see: Mark W. Roosa, "The Effect of Age in the Transition to Parenthood: Are Delayed Childbearers a Unique Group?" Family Relations 37 (July 1988): 322–327.

## Breakdown of live births per 1,000 residents by state, 1987

| | | | | |
|---|---|---|---|---|
| 1. | Alaska | 21.8 | 26. Montana | 14.8 |
| 2. | Utah | 21.4 | 27. Nebraska | 14.8 |
| 3. | New Mexico | 20.1 | 28. South Carolina | 14.8 |
| 4. | Arizona | 18.7 | 29. Rhode Island | 14.7 |
| 5. | Texas | 18.4 | 30. Tennessee | 14.7 |
| 6. | California | 17.9 | 31. Virginia | 14.7 |
| 7. | Hawaii | 17.2 | 32. Wisconsin | 14.7 |
| 8. | North Dakota | 17.2 | 33. North Carolina | 14.6 |
| 9. | Georgia | 16.9 | 34. Oregon | 14.6 |
| 10. | Louisiana | 16.9 | 35. Alabama | 14.5 |
| 11. | Colorado | 16.5 | 36. Connecticut | 14.5 |
| 12. | Washington | 16.3 | 37. Florida | 14.5 |
| 13. | Nevada | 16.2 | 38. New Jersey | 14.5 |
| 14. | South Dakota | 16.2 | 39. Ohio | 14.5 |
| 15. | Idaho | 16.0 | 40. Wyoming | 14.5 |
| 16. | Delaware | 15.6 | 41. Maryland | 14.3 |
| 17. | New Hampshire | 15.5 | 42. Arkansas | 14.0 |
| 18. | Mississippi | 15.4 | 43. Indiana | 14.0 |
| 19. | Illinois | 15.3 | 44. Oklahoma | 13.9 |
| 20. | New York | 15.2 | 45. Pennsylvania | 13.9 |
| 21. | Minnesota | 15.1 | 46. Iowa | 13.7 |
| 22. | Kansas | 15.0 | 47. Kentucky | 13.7 |
| 23. | Missouri | 14.9 | 48. Maine | 13.6 |
| 24. | Massachusetts | 14.8 | 49. Vermont | 13.2 |
| 25. | Michigan | 14.8 | 50. West Virginia | 12.4 |

*Source:* U.S. Bureau of the Census, *Statistical Abstract of the United States: 1989,* 109th ed. (Washington, D.C.: U.S. Government Printing Office, 1989), no. 86, p. 63.

Thus, with delayed childbearing, we not only get fewer children who are better off economically, but a lengthened time until the new generation reaches childbearing age. The consequence is a decrease in population growth over the longer term but an upturn in growth in the short run. This appears to be happening. Increases in first-order birth rates have been substantial in the baby-boom cohorts of women now aged twenty-five to thirty-nine who have delayed births. This is combined with the older women who had the high fertility and earlier timing patterns of the 1950s and 1960s who already had all the children they wanted when they were younger.

Related to the delay in first births is the spacing of births. Child-spacing patterns have not received the research attention given to number of births and family size, but it is an important issue for consideration. Particular child-spacing factors are likely to influence the labor force participation and education of women as well as to affect the health of the child. For example, low birth weight, a condition strongly associated with morbidity (sickness and

## The season of birth paradox

Joseph Lee Rodgers and J. Richard Urdy, writing in *Social Biology* 35(Fall–Winter 1988): 171–185 examine the seasonality of U.S. birth patterns. They note that over the past fifty years there has been a remarkably consistent seasonality in birth patterns with a major peak occurring in the late summer (August–September) and a minor peak in the winter (December–February). The depth of the birth valley occurs in April and May.

The paradox occurs in that when asked about preferences for birth seasons, respondents said that the best month in which to give birth to a child would be April and May. The worst months were December–January and July–August. The seasonal preference, usually spring, was chosen because of moderate weather. The "worst month" choices, late summer and winter, had weather that was too hot or too cold. Thus the paradox is apparent. The most frequent births occur at the times least desired and the fewest births occur at the most preferred time.

The authors suggest that one explanation for the paradox is due to a lag between attempts at pregnancy and success. That is, women will stop contracepting with a pattern that predicts seasonal preferences. However, a lag exists in the time of actual pregnancy occurrence. Biological explanations are not rejected, but fail to explain the different seasonal birth patterns found in other geographical and cultural settings.

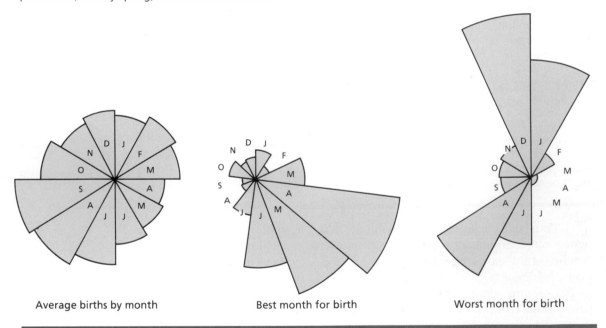

Average births by month          Best month for birth          Worst month for birth

disease) and mortality (death) among infants, is highest among children born very shortly after the end of their mothers' last pregnancy.

One study of child spacing concluded that younger women are less likely to experience short birth intervals than are older women.[37] While both groups

37. Howard Wineberg and James McCarthy, "Child Spacing in the United States: Recent Trends and Differentials," *Journal of Marriage and the Family* 51 (February 1989): 213–228.

of women are likely to have a second birth, the interval is longer for younger women. It was also concluded that group differences in spacing of births have decreased. That is, groups that in the past were most likely to have short intervals (those with less education, those who married young and began childbearing early, etc.) are now much like others. These reductions in short birth intervals are suggested to be a result of an increase in effective contraceptive use among women in these groups and a reduction in birth timing failures. As fertility in the United States remains low, it is suggested that it will become more uniform throughout the population.

In spite of trends toward delayed childbirth, greater control of spacing, fewer births, and a convergence of group differences, many variables continue to be related to marital fertility: socioeconomic status, more than one marriage, religion, race, education, urbanization, female income, child-care arrangements, gender roles, age at marriage, age at first birth, interval since last birth, age of women, and others.[38] Even the size of the family of origin (number of brothers and sisters) appears to influence marital fertility. And, of course, many couples make a conscious choice to have no children or for some reason, fail to have them. Let us examine briefly these childless marriages.

### Childless marriage

For many years the myth existed that because of a maternal instinct, all women wanted children. This "instinct" even went one step further and assumed that once a child was born, the mother would "instinctively" love and care for him or her. These assumptions were given major blows as statistics, research reports, newspaper accounts, and gossip networks revealed the widespread termination of pregnancies through legal and/or illegal abortions, the commonality of mothers abusing and even killing their children, and the discovery that women who never had children—in or out of marriage—did not suffer physical or emotional damage. These and other factors tended to dispel the notion of the biological linkage between being female and a natural desire for and love of children.

There is little doubt that children place enormous demands on parents in terms of emotional and financial costs. Yet, most married couples, either voluntarily or involuntarily, have children. It is possible that many of these couples have children because they were never socialized to believe that not having them is a viable alternative to marriage and family life. Since marriage

38. For example, *see* Sandra L. Hofferth, "Childbearing Decision Making and Family Well-Being: A Dynamic Sequential Model," *American Sociological Review* 48 (August 1983): 533–545; Jay D. Teachman, "Historical and Subgroup Variations in the Association Between Marriage and First Childbirth: A Life-Course Perspective," *Journal of Family History* 10 (Winter 1985): 379–401; and William D. Mosher, David P. Johnson, and Marjorie C. Horn, "Religion and Fertility in the United States: The Importance of Marriage Patterns and Hispanic Origin," *Demography* 23 (August 1986): 367–379.

legitimizes the sexual union and the birth of children, voluntary childless marriage may not have been viewed as a realistic choice.

Most cultures and societies impose social pressures upon couples to be "fruitful," meaning "to bear children." The marriage is not complete or socially mature until children are born of the union. One study asked respondents to describe their perceptions of fictitious individuals assigned one of six family size statuses. Voluntary childless couples and parents of one child were found to be viewed most negatively.[39]

Census material shows that in 1988, 11.1 percent of ever-married women aged thirty-five to forty-four were childless. This figure increases to 22.3 percent among twenty-five to thirty-four-year-old married women and to 42.8 percent among those eighteen to twenty-four years of age. These younger age groups have not, however, completed their childbearing years and most expect to have children at some time in their lives. Only approximately 10.1 percent of all women and 5.4 percent of currently married women age eighteen to thirty-four do not expect to have any children in their lifetimes.[40]

The rate of childlessness has increased over the past few decades. The most important demographic predictors of childlessness were found to be fecundity status, (inability to have children), marital status (the never-married), age (older persons), labor force status (working and temporary unemployed), education (higher) and race (Asians and Native Americans).[41] But childbearing remains a dominant role in most segments of American society and it is doubtful that large groups of women will choose not to have any children in the near future. For example, U.S. census data show that the proportions of women eighteen to thirty-four years old expecting no lifetime births by education is 9.2 percent for women who are high school graduates. This increases to 10.5 percent for those with one to three years of college, 12.2 percent for those with four years of college, and 14.0 percent for women with five years or more of college.[42] This data indicates that with an increased level of educational training comes an increased proportion of women who never expect a child. That some of these may later decide to have children will lower these rates of actual or expected childlessness even more.

Voluntarily childless women, whether married or single, rate the costs of a child higher and the satisfactions lower than other groups of women (such as parents or those who desire to become parents).[43] In particular, educated

39. Denise F. Polit, "Stereotypes Relating to Family-Size Status," *Journal of Marriage and the Family* 40 (February 1978): 105–114.

40. U.S. Bureau of the Census, *Current Population Reports*. Series P-20, no. 436, "Fertility of American Women, June 1988," (Washington, D.C.: U.S. Government Printing Office, 1989), Table 2, p. 17 and Table 10, pp. 46–47.

41. Cardell K. Jacobsen, Tim B. Heaton, and Karen M. Taylor, "Childlessness Among American Women," *Social Biology* 35 (1988): 186–197.

42. *Current Population Reports* Series P-20. no. 436, Table 8, p. 36.

43. Victor J. Callan, "The Impact of the First Birth: Married and Single Women Preferring Childlessness, One Child, or Two Children," *Journal of Marriage and the Family* 48 (May 1986): 261–269.

professional women, who have lived with and enjoyed an adult-centered life-style, gave high ratings to the restrictions and disruptions of children and to general life-style costs. They gave low ratings to the emotional satisfactions and personal fulfillment a child might give them, but felt their current life-style choices—especially careers—did meet such needs.

If parenthood seems to interfere with personal happiness and one's freedoms, it seems to interfere with marriage and family life as well. As is noted in several chapters, children impose a strain on marriage. Does this also mean or suggest that couples without children have higher levels of health and marital adjustment and satisfaction than do couples with children? Apparently it does. When voluntarily childless wives, undecided wives, and postponing wives were compared with mothers, the results from one study indicated that all three groups of childless wives have higher mean levels of marital satisfaction than do mothers.[44] Karen S. Renne found that childless marriages were more likely to be happy ones that tended to improve with time while parental marriages tended to deteriorate.[45] Sharon Houseknecht also lent support to the relationship between childlessness and enhanced marital adjustment, although the differences between the voluntarily childless wives and the mothers in her survey were small in magnitude.[46] This finding led her to suggest that it may not be the presence or absence of children per se but rather education, employment, religion, or some combination of these that has the major impact on marital adjustment. In any case, the available evidence on the consequences of voluntary childlessness to persons or marriages does not appear to be negative.

Is this satisfaction true among involuntarily childless women and among older persons as well? In other words, what about women or couples who want children and can't have them, or older persons who, either by choice or necessity, have no children? As will be evident in later chapters, children serve as an important source of gratification to many married couples and as a source of support to older persons. For both the involuntary childless and the elderly, some limited data indicate less marital or personal satisfaction among those without children. Choice may well be one of the most significant determinants of a satisfaction with a particular life-style.

Results from northern Nigeria showed a higher level of marital adjustment among mothers than among *involuntarily* childless women.[47] And four surveys by the National Opinion Research Center of the University of Chicago asked males and females aged sixty-five and over how much satisfaction they

44. Karen A. Polonko, John Scanzoni, and Jay D. Teachman, "Childlessness and Marital Satisfaction," *Journal of Family Issues* 3 (December 1982): 545–573.

45. Karen S. Renne, "Childlessness, Health, and Marital Satisfaction," *Social Biology* 23 (Fall 1976): 183–197.

46. Sharon K. Houseknecht, "Childlessness and Marital Adjustment," *Journal of Marriage and the Family* 41 (May 1979): 259–265.

47. Daniel I. Denga, "Childlessness and Marital Adjustment in Northern Nigeria," *Journal of Marriage and the Family* 44 (August 1982): 799–802.

got from family life.[48] The findings indicated that childlessness had an overall significant negative effect on family satisfaction, with the effect most pronounced among the oldest age cohort and more pronounced for females than for males. Whether the current cohorts of childless women under ages forty and thirty will be negatively affected by the absence of children when they reach ages sixty-five and seventy-five remains to be seen.

The reproductive technology available today can decrease the number of involuntarily childless situations. Until recently, involuntarily childless women and couples who wished to comply with societal norms would resort to adoption. With the decline in the availability of infants for adoption, many infertile women are seeking alternative solutions such as artificial insemination with the sperm of the husband (AIH); artificial insemination with the sperm of an anonymous donor (AID); in vitro fertilization where an artificial environment outside the living organism is used; or surrogate motherhood, in which another woman is used to conceive, carry, and give birth to "your" child (*see* surrogate mother insert). These alternative methods of reproduction have led to heated debates over their social, legal, and moral implications.[49]

## Effects of large or small families

There is little doubt that the number of people in a group influences the interaction and behavior of the members of that group. If you have one roommate and you agree, a decision is unanimous. If you have two roommates, both of whom agree with each other but differ from you, you have the unhappy choice of accepting their decision, trying to change the decision of at least one, or going your own way. Clearly, the number of interactions, the probability of dissensus, the attention given to any one person, and the like are influenced by the number of members in the group. The same factors hold true within a family system. One-child families are conducive to certain patterns of life that differ from two-, three-, or four-child families.

One-child families have, in general, not been viewed positively for either the parents or the child. The "only" child has been described as spoiled, selfish, overly dependent, maladjusted, and lonely. Parents have been described as selfish, self-centered, immature, cold, and abnormal. National surveys over the past thirty years have consistently showed a majority of respondents indicating that being an only child is a disadvantage. Very few

---

48. B. Krishna Singh and J. Sherwood Williams, "Childlessness and Family Satisfaction," *Research on Aging* 3 (June 1981): 218–227. *See also:* Arthur L. Greil, Thomas A. Leitke, and Karen L. Porter, "Infertility: His and Hers," *Gender and Society* 2 (June 1988): 172–199; and Victor J. Callan, "The Personal and Marital Adjustment of Mothers and of Voluntary and Involuntary Childless Wives," *Journal of Marriage and the Family* 49 (November 1987): 847–856.

49. Readers may be interested in seeing Charlene E. Miall, "Reproductive Technology vs. the Stigma of Involuntary Childlessness," *Social Casework* 70 (January 1989) 43–50; and Shirley Zimmerman, "Alternatives in Human Reproduction for Involuntary Childless Couples," *Family Relations* 31 (April 1982): 233–241.

## Surrogate mothers

In the past few years surrogate motherhood has provided a controversial alternative for an increasing number of marriages in which the woman is infertile. A surrogate mother is a woman who, for a fee, contracts to be impregnated through artificial insemination, to carry the child, and after delivery, to relinquish the child, as well as all parental rights, to the biological father. Usually the biological father is married to an infertile woman who hopes to adopt the child. The increased demand for newborn white babies and the decrease in their supply has led a number of infertile couples to seek alternative ways to obtain a baby. One of these ways is to locate and hire a surrogate mother.

Who are these surrogate women? Dr. Philip Parker, a psychiatrist at the School of Medicine at Wayne State University, interviewed more than 200 white women applying for surrogate motherhood. These women were referred to him by a well-known attorney in Dearborn, Michigan who has negotiated numerous contracts between surrogate mothers and couples. Dr. Parker found that the mean age of interested surrogate mothers was twenty-five. More than half were married, about one in five were divorced and about one-fourth had never been married. About 40 percent were Catholic and nearly 60 percent were Protestant. About 40 percent were unemployed at the time of the interviews or were receiving some form of financial aid or both. Among the 60 percent of those working or with a working spouse the total family income ranged from $6,000 to $50,000. More than half had at least a high school education. More than 90 percent had at least one previous pregnancy; 80 percent had at least one birth. About 90 percent of these women said they required a fee for their participation and most wanted at least $5,000.

Not all surrogate mothers were applying strictly for the money, however. Other factors included the perceived degree of enjoyment and desire to be pregnant, the desire to "give" a baby, and to resolve feelings they had regarding a previous voluntary loss of fetus or baby through abortion or relinquishment.

Of the more than 200 surrogate mother applicants interviewed by Dr. Parker, followup interviews were conducted with 25 who since had given birth or become pregnant. Of these, 22 did receive or are receiving a $10,000 fee. Twelve of them had already delivered, received the fee, and did not seem to have any adverse psychological consequences relating to this fee. One surrogate mother who had delivered changed her mind during the pregnancy and refused the $10,000 fee once she established a relationship with the parental couple. Dr. Parker reported that, in general, the fee became less important as the pregnancy developed and as the surrogate established a relationship with the parents-to-be.

Most surrogates felt very contented with the special attention given them, described the pregnancy as doing and producing something (a baby) that only a woman could do, and experienced a sense of accomplishment in giving the gift of a baby to a needy couple. This giving, Dr. Parker suggests, appeared to help many surrogates deal with prior unresolved voluntary losses of a fetus or child. He states that no evidence has been found to support the notion that surrogate motherhood, with or without a fee, leads to serious adverse psychological consequences. Therefore, in spite of descriptions by opponents to surrogate motherhood as baby-buying, slavery, or black marketeering, Dr. Parker feels that all parties involved can benefit if properly selected. Surrogate motherhood should not be prohibited.

people say they want to have just one child or that the ideal number of children for a family is one. The popular stereotype of the unhappy, maladjusted only child and the view that one child is neither a preferred nor desirable family size, calls for an empirical look at this "small" family.

## Grandparents only hope for today's only child?

Only children are in again. I keep reading that teachers and shrinks and other double-domes now say that only children are not a disadvantaged minority cursed with multiple neuroses after all. Instead, only children tend to be bright, well-adjusted high-achievers who usually grow up to be self-reliant adults. The secret is out. Too bad.

I feel a special kinship with only children. That's because I am one. Unlike this present crop, however, I grew up at a time when being an only child was definitely out. You were considered odd and a little pathetic. Everybody worried about you, and this made for a splendid life. I am saddened to think that the only children in contemporary society may not enjoy the advantages I had, surrounded by worry worts.

The feeling back when we were hacking McClure Street out of the wilderness of Peoria was that every house ought to have at least three or four kids in it. Most did. Some had five or six. Ours had me.

My parents fretted that because I had no brothers or sisters (or cousins either) I was not growing up with a proper sense of normal family life.

If someone had suggested to Mom or Dad that our life was abnormal, there would have been a rhubarb, no doubt. Secretly, however, they felt something was missing from my life.

My parents also fretted that through dearth of siblings I was not learning the all-important concept of sharing. This was nonsense. I had to share chalk and crayons and books and half my lunch with the kids at school. Actually, I didn't have to share my lunch. I just did that so that I could get a banana-flip in trade for my apple. I also learned very quickly in the empty lot that if you don't share your stuff with the other kid, they just cut you out of the game, or they clobber you. Kids work these things out. They never care whether you are an only child or the eighth in a string of 14.

Anyway, the guilt and worry my parents felt whenever somebody said, ''Oh, she's an only child, poor thing,'' worked to my distinct advantage. I got to take tap dance lessons at the YWCA on Saturdays.

I also got to spend one month every summer on a farm. My parents found this family with eight kids and cut some deal so that I could join the group. I gathered eggs and fed chickens, milked cows (not

In looking at only children as adults, data from seven U.S. national surveys were used to establish the effects of a number of siblings on eight dimensions of well-being.[50] Without exception, all the effects of having siblings were negative, or stated differently, all were positive effects of being an only child. Only children were more likely to say they were very happy, find life exciting, see their health as excellent, get satisfaction from where they live, from their non-working activities, from their family life, from their friendships, and from their physical condition. The evidence most clearly contradicts the popular stereotype of the unhappy, maladjusted only child.

Some research on adult only children in Boston indicated that when compared with first borns of siblings and with individuals of higher birth orders, only children were found to have higher educational levels, higher occupational status, smaller families, and to be more secularly oriented.[51]

---

50. Norval D. Glenn and Sue Keir Hoppe, ''Only Children as Adults,'' *Journal of Family Issues* 5 (September 1984): 363–382.

51. Denise F. Polit, Ronald L. Nuttall, and Ena V. Nuttall, ''The Only Child Grows Up: A Look at Some Characteristics of Adult Only Children,'' *Family Relations* 29 (January 1980): 99–106.

well), slopped pigs and got to swing on a rope in the hay mow like Tarzan. Yahooo! At night after supper everybody used to gather around the piano in the parlor to sing hymns and hillbilly songs. We did not sing hymns or hillbilly songs at my house. I liked the farm a lot.

None of the kids with brothers and sisters got to do these things. They got to stay home and play with each other which was considered the normal American way. They didn't have my disadvantage. I was pathetic and required special education. Ha!

Grandparents were especially aware of the deprivation of an only child. They were always sure you would be bored and lonely on a rainy day, so they sent lots of toys through the mail even when it wasn't your birthday. They also took you to the circus and the movies or to Forest Park Highlands in St. Louis to ride the roller coaster as many times as you wanted because you were a poor, lonesome, only child. Ha, again!

What nobody noticed back in the olden times was that I had just as many neighborhood playmates as any other kids and did all the same things they did. The only difference I could see was that I had a

room of my own while most of my friends shared space with a brother or sister. I didn't see this as a disadvantage.

Still, it was necessary for me to have all of this special attention in order to make up for this terrible deficiency in my life, perceived only by adults. You can see why I feel sorry for all the sprouting only children today. They are not going to be considered unusual. No one is going to consider them pitiful, so they won't get to go to the farm. Born too late, poor babies.

Grandparents may be the only hope. They will still be convinced that an only child is lonely, despite scientific evidence to the contrary.

If today's kids are lucky, one or another of their grandparents will own a farm or know somebody who does. Maybe Granddad will insist that poor, pitiful Pauline will spend half the summer there with an army of farm kids and a flock of chickens. I wonder if farmers still have hay mows and pianos in the parlor. I hope so. Pauline will love it.

*Source:* Nickie McWhirter, *Detroit Free Press*, October 25, 1978, p. 1-C. Reprinted with the permission of the Detroit Free Press.

Female onlies were more likely to be working, to have planned their families before marriage, and to have been more autonomous in deciding to work. All groups were similar in terms of perceived happiness or satisfaction with life, in their social activities, and in the ways their children viewed them as parents. The researchers concludes that onlies, that is, one-child adults, were not emotionally or personally handicapped by their lack of siblings.

Similar results come from Blake,[52] who concludes that research findings on the only child do not support the negative stereotypes that still persist about singletons. She claims they are intellectually superior, have no obvious personality defects, tend to count themselves happy, and are satisfied with important aspects of life, notably jobs and health. The position of the single child only becomes problematic or has increased problems with health and achievement when that child comes from a broken family with its attendant

---

52. Judith Blake, "Family Size and the Quality of Children," *Demography* **18** (November 1981): 421–442; and Judith Blake, "The Only Child in America: Prejudice versus Performance," *Population and Development Review* 7 (March 1981): 43–54.

*Some families are large because a couple wants children and has the number they desire or because they had more children than they wanted. Other families are large because they adopt additional children. A third type of large family may result from the joining (remarriage) of two smaller families.*

loss of income or when mothers were young enough at birth to continue childbearing, but due to difficulties of their own failed to do so. When parental background is controlled, only children do better than children from any other sibsize.[53]

What the research of Blake shows very clearly is the overwhelming effect of family size on achievement. An increased number of siblings had negative effects on both child and adult achievement outcomes. For example, the larger the family the fewer years of completed schooling. Even after controlling for major parental background differences, there was approximately a two-year difference in educational attainment between small and large families.

Why does this occur? Blake proposed a "dilution hypothesis" that, in effect, suggests a dilution of familial resources available to children in large families and a concentration of such resources in small ones.[54] These diluted resources include the parents' time, emotional and physical energy (including

53. Judith Blake, *Family Size and Achievement* (Berkeley: University of California Press, 1989).
54. Ibid., pp. 10–12.

that of a mother who is frequently pregnant), attention, personal interaction, and material resources that enable personal living space and privacy, living in better neighborhoods, specialized medical and dental care, travel, and specialized instruction such as music lessons. The idea that in large families the older children function as "parents" to the younger ones, she suggests, assumes too much about sibling goodwill and maturity. Youngsters are not adults and are seldom the emotional and intellectual equivalent of parents.

To perceive a family as large or small is relative. In the United States four or more children may be viewed as a "large family." In many countries, and perhaps in the United States at the turn of the century, a family of four would lead to a reaction such as "only four?" Irrespective of the cutoff point as to what is a large or small family, a small family is such for one of two primary reasons: either the parents wanted a small family and achieved their desired size or they wanted a large family but were unable to attain it. In both cases, there is a low probability of unwanted children. In contrast, a large family is such because the parents achieved the size they desired or because they had more children than they in fact wanted. The probability is therefore greater that larger families include unwanted or unloved children.

Particularly in large families, last-born children are more likely to be unwanted than first- or middle-born children. This idea is consistent with what is known of abortion patterns among married women. That is, married women are most likely to resort to abortion when they have achieved the number of children they want or feel they can afford to have.

A substantial body of evidence exists concerning the relationship between family size or number of children and factors such as discipline, achievement, and health. One review of family size effects[55] showed that in larger families, child rearing becomes more rule ridden, less individualized, with corporal punishment and less investment of resources. Persons from smaller families tended to have higher IQs, academic achievement, and occupational performance. Large families produce more delinquents and alcoholics. In regard to health, in large families perinatal (surrounding birth) morbidity and mortality rates are higher, and mothers are at greater risk of several physical diseases. In the words of the authors:

> Women who have many children more frequently develop hypertension, stress symptoms, gall bladder disease, diabetes, and postpartum depression. Women with many children are at higher risk for cancer to the cervix, digestion organs, and peritoneum, but are at less risk for breast cancer.
>
> Fathers of large families are at greater risk of hypertension and peptic ulcers.[56]

---

55. Mazie Earle Wagner, Herman J. P. Schubert, and Daniel S. P. Schubert, "Family Size Effects: A Review," *The Journal of Genetic Psychology* 146 (March 1985): 65–78.

56. Ibid., p. 72.

## Fallout from excess kids

There has been a dramatic decrease in big families. Today 48 percent say 2.1 children is the ideal family.

Where does that leave me? Somewhere between the propagation of the faith, the population explosion and 1.1 surplus kid at my dinner table.

And don't think I haven't paid dearly for my 1.1 overflow. To begin with, he fouled up the family vote. We used to vote even, at two-all, which left some room for persuasion. Since he arrived, my husband and I haven't won a decision in 15 years. Whether it is a vote on a vacation site, what TV show we are going to watch, or whether or not parents are to be impeached, the vote is always the same: Kids, 3—Parents, 2.

I am not being dramatic when I say this is a two-child-geared society. If the Good Lord had meant for people to have more than two children, he would put more than two windows in the back set of the car. We once threatened to put one on the front fender and the other two cried because they each wanted one.

A popsicle can only be divided two ways. There are two pairs of shoelaces in a package, so that one child always goes around with gym shoes that flop off his feet when he walks. There are only four chairs to a dinette set (so that one never matches) and four breakfast sweet rolls to a package.

We always had one too many for a rowboat, and when we rode the Ferris wheel, it was two to a seat and the odd one always rode alone like an only child.

Few people realize this, but did you know that a No. 2 can of fruit cocktail contains only two maraschino cherries? This means when you divide two maraschino cherries between three children, two are happy and the other one runs right out and retains F. Lee Bailey to fight a cherry custody suit.

Chores are geared toward twos—one washes dishes and the other dries, but what does the third child do? He becomes a useless bum and grows up to steal hubcaps.

Bunk beds come in twos. There are two sinks to a bathroom, two Hostess Twinkees to a package and free circus tickets come in pairs.

I mentioned this to the kids the other night and half-kiddingly said, "You know what this means, don't you? One of you has to go. Just for kicks, let's take a vote on it."

When the votes were counted, it was 4—1. I had been phased out of the family.

Somehow, I expected more from a full-grown man who has his own car window.

*Source:* From *At Wit's End* by Erma Bombeck. Reproduced through the courtesy of Field Newspaper Syndicate.

While a number of studies revealed no effect, positive or negative, to be associated with family size, very few exist that substantiate positive consequences associated with large families. The consequences of a large family size, as with most social structural variables, will tend to vary by factors such as educational level, social class, or religious subculture.

One prime example of this can be seen in a study of Mormon women who had at least seven children, were all college graduates, and were married to college graduates.[57] In this highly atypical sample, the basis for the mothers' commitment to large families was rooted in religious beliefs such as that the number of children is destined by God, birth control is wrong, and good families have many children. Even in this context, the mothers perceived

---

57. Howard M. Bahr, Spencer J. Condie, and Kristen L. Goodman, *Life in Large Families: Views of Mormon Women* (Washington, D.C.: University Press of America, 1982).

pressure from relatives to slow down their childbearing and encountered situations of prejudice and discrimination. Most of the mothers had difficulties meeting the various demands of the wife and mother role, had self-doubts, and felt they had many faults and weaknesses. Yet, on balance, they felt the rewards of the struggle were worth the costs. While admitting that rearing a large number of children was no easy task, their religious commitment and a wide repertoire of techniques for coping with stress made them effective mothers.

It should be emphasized that it is not family size per se that creates varied systems of family living. Rather, it is the life factors and personal values that arise in relation to a certain size of group. Large families heighten the complexity of intragroup relations, pose additional problems in the fulfillment of family needs, and are likely to influence the amount of parental comfort or praise available per child.

## Birth order and sibling relationships

Birth order (sibling position) has been found to have a major influence on a wide variety of behavioral and attitudinal phenomena. A frequently reported and well-documented lineage is between first-born status and superior intellectual achievement. That family structure and interaction rather than any innate factor explains this relationship is evident in research findings of Pfouts, who found that family socialization shapes first-borns' academic achievement relative to second-borns even when second-borns are more intellectually gifted.[58]

The complexity of the birth order issue is evident in articles such as one which questions whether the consequences of birth order are real, artifactual (produced artificially), or both.[59] Steelman and Powell, in using two nationally representative samples, find no significant relationship between birth order and academic performance but do find a highly positive relationship between birth order and social skills, with later born children being more outgoing, able to get along with others, more popular, and able to make friends easier. Leadership skills were found to contradict the stereotype of the eldest child, with the younger males exhibiting greater leadership skills. Females exhibited no differences in leadership by birth order. The authors stress the need in birth order research to control for variables such as sex (male or female) and family size (number of siblings).

An additional dimension, beyond sex and family size, that may be important in birth order research is a combination of size and sex. How many

---

58. Jane H. Pfouts, "Birth Order, Age-Spacing, IQ Differences, and Family Relations," *Journal of Marriage and the Family* 42 (August 1980): 517–531.

59. Lala Carr Steelman and Brian Powell, "The Social and Academic Consequences of Birth Order: Real, Artifactual, or Both?" *Journal of Marriage and the Family* 47 (February 1985): 117–124.

siblings are of the same or different sex? For example, one study showed that among male adolescents, first-borns and last-borns perceived their father's educational goals more accurately than did the middle-borns. But female adolescents most likely to perceive their mother's goals accurately were those in families where male children were in the majority. Apparently the accuracy of paternal educational goals is affected both by the sex composition of one's siblings as well as birth order.[60]

Returning to the research that is less complex than that which controls for family size, sibling composition, or interaction effects, most research has tended to suggest that, in general, first-borns tend to be intellectual achievers and higher in self-esteem. Female first-borns, in particular, tend to be more religious, more sexually conservative, more traditionally oriented toward feminine roles, and more likely to associate with adults. The last-born or youngest children, like the one-child family, tend to be more sexually permissive, more likely to engage in social activities, visit with friends more frequently, make use of the media, and be consistently less traditional. Explanations for these differences often focus on the older child being a role model for the younger, having more responsibility for other children, and receiving less attention as siblings enter the scene.

Even middle-borns appear to differ from first-borns and last-borns. An analysis of a national sample of several thousand adolescent males found middle-borns to have a significantly lower self-esteem than the first or last born.[61] A one- or three-year spacing between siblings was more positive for self-esteem than a two-year spacing, as was having siblings who were female as opposed to male or both brother and sister siblings. The explanation of a lower self-assessment of the middle-born may be based on a theory that first- and last-borns have a uniqueness that facilitates status recognition and attention by parents and siblings. The middle child lacks this inherent uniqueness.

Judith Blake found no birth order effects for small families, but in large families being a middle-born child early in the sequence of offspring had its problems.[62] These children experienced the full negative force of large "sibsize" by having older siblings close in age with whom to compete for resources while also experiencing a long period during which younger siblings are born and are dependent.

The role and significance of siblings is often underrepresented in family textbooks. Yet, it is clear siblings have a major impact on the socialization process (described in the next chapter), on each other as friends and

60. Jeannie S. Kidwell, "The Neglected Birth Order: Middleborns," *Journal of Marriage and the Family* 44 (February 1982): 225–235.

61. Thomas Ewin Smith, "Sex and Sibling Structure: Interaction Effects Upon the Accuracy of Adolescent Perceptions of Parental Orientations," *Journal of Marriage and the Family* 46 (November 1984): 901–907.

62. Blake, *Family Size and Achievement*, pp. 300–301.

## Choose the sex of your child

As reported in the *New York Times* (May 29, 1984), a technique has been developed that enhances the chances of sex determination. It was developed by Dr. Ronald Ericsson, a specialist in reproductive physiology in California. How is this done?

In a laboratory the husband's semen is washed in a tissue medium and the sample then is run through first one, and then a second glass column containing an increasingly viscous layer of human serum albumen. Sperm cells containing the Y chromosome, which have the genes for males, are heavier, stronger, and swim faster than sperm containing the X chromosome, but the sperm may contain either X or Y. Since a Y chromosome is necessary for the conception of a male, the chances are enhanced by an artificial concentration of Y's. After the sperm have descended to the bottom of the second glass column they are withdrawn, separated from the liquids that surround them, concentrated, and injected directly into the wife's cervix shortly after ovulation.

Dr. Ericsson said sperm that are immature or abnormal in some other way are almost completely screened out through the use of this procedure, thus, reducing the eventual risk of spontaneous abortion as well as of the birth of babies that are either physically deformed or mentally retarded. In addition, the technique may be used to increase the sperm concentration for men with a low sperm count.

Sex selection for females is more complicated, involving not only the sifting out of X chromosomes but also the use of a drug that both induces ovulation and, for some unknown reason, skews the sex ratio toward females.

The technique is not foolproof, and some specialists have expressed skepticism about claims for its success rate. But a study of about 250 births that involved the procedure shows that it appears to raise the chances of having a child of the desired sex from the ratio that might be expected by chance (about 106 male per 100 females) to more than 75 percent in cases in which a boy is desired.

companions, and on parents. Based on a review of research, Ann Goetting illustrates how the sibling bond typically persists over the life cycle.[63] Some sibling relationships are relatively constant, such as companionship and emotional support, while others, such as specific types of caretaking and sibling rivalry, stand out as unique to specific stages in the life cycle. Sibling relationships are unique in their duration, their common genetic and social heritage, and their common early experiences with the family.

## *Sex control and gender preference*

An interesting question to ponder at the end of a chapter dealing with the parental system is "What will be the consequences as parents can increasingly control whether to have a boy or a girl (sex control) and can choose a male or a female (gender preference)?" The day is at hand when parents will be able to choose the sex of their children using either of two basic procedures: (1) by controlling the type of sperm that will fertilize the egg, or (2) by prenatally determining the sex of an embryo and then aborting it if it is of the undesired

---

63. Ann Goetting, "The Developmental Tasks of Siblingship Over the Life Cycle," *Journal of Marriage and the Family* 48 (November 1986): 703–714.

sex. Amniocentesis and ultrasound photography are becoming low-risk, routine ways to both diagnose the health of fetuses already conceived and to confirm their sex months before birth occurs. In brief, it is no longer unrealistic to foresee the ability to guarantee the reproduction of offspring of the chosen sex.

Will sex control result in an unbalanced sex ratio? It has been estimated that choosing the sex of the child will increase the proportion of male births by 7 to 10 percent. Also, a series of research reports seems to indicate that boys are preferred over girls in much of Africa, Asia, and the Middle East, among the Swiss, Belgians, and Italians in Europe, and among Jews and Catholics in the United States, to mention a few. If this excess of males were to occur, would it increase the number of males who never marry due to a marriage squeeze, delay their age at marriage, force an increase in homosexuality and prostitution, or even force the introduction of polyandry?

Would a consequence of choosing the sex of a child be a reduction in the birth rate because some parents would not have to bear additional children in order to have one or another of a particular sex? Studies indicate that the desire for more children is closely correlated with the number of sons.

Would a consequence be an increased proportion of first-born males? Some of the consequences of birth order have already been shown. Thus, the result may be children who have more friends, are more conservative, or are more eminent scholars.

Finally, would a consequence of choosing a boy or a girl be improved family relationships by avoiding births of the undesired sex, by having fewer resented or rejected children, or by the elimination of gender-role confusion?

We are living in a "biological revolution" of which sex control is one aspect, yet such control is one biological "advancement" that could have a far-reaching social impact on the parental system in the United States and around the world.

# SUMMARY

1. The previous chapter examined various aspects of the marital system. Continuing through the life cycle, children follow shortly after the beginning of most marriages. This chapter examines structural factors relating to the parental system: a system of interrelated statuses of parents and children.

2. The transition to parenthood and parenting requires a major reorganization of statuses, roles, and relationships. Parenting tends to be viewed primarily as a maternal duty and is often referred to as "mothering," but fathers have been found to assume substantial responsibility as well.

3. Early studies labeled parenthood as a crisis event; however, more recent studies focused on the transition to new responsibilities and duties. Time appears to be a major problem for most mothers. Although children are valued as necessary for a "real family life," as buffers against loneliness, or as sources of self-esteem and self-fulfillment, many couples in the United States place a great emphasis on

personal freedom, leisure time, and employment opportunities, all of which become more restricted with the arrival of children.

4. Young parenthood and unwed parenthood are issues of specific concern, both in terms of the parents and the children. Parents are often at a disadvantage in terms of the marriage, education, income, employment, and training in general. Unwed parenthood does appear to make a difference in the child's ability to get started on an equal footing with children born in wedlock and to avoid disadvantages after infancy as well. While the birth rate within marriage is dropping, the number of births outside of marriage is increasing sharply. The greatest increases are not among teenagers but among women who are older.

5. Most couples want, have, or expect to have children. The rate of births varies by wars and periods of economic depression and prosperity. Over the past few decades, women have been delaying their first births with the consequences of having fewer children and being better off economically.

6. Some couples have no children by choice. Many of these women choose a career path and marital style that rejects mothering and parenthood. These couples appear to have higher levels of health and marital satisfaction than do couples with children. Other involuntarily childless couples turn to adoption or alternative solutions such as surrogate mothers, artificial insemination, or other means of conceiving and/or having a child.

7. Family size does make a difference. Research evidence tends to support the "dilution hypothesis" that suggests a dilution of familial resources available to children in large families and a concentration of such resources in small ones. Most of the negative stereotypes about the small family or single child family find little, if any, support.

8. As with family size, differences exist by order of birth. First-borns appear to be more traditionally oriented, less sexually permissive, more achievement-oriented, and differ from later-born children in a variety of ways. But researchers warn against ignoring sex and family size in these considerations.

9. Some evidence suggests that gender preferences exist within the population of many countries for male children. Perhaps within the near future parents can choose to have a child of one sex or the other. This ability to choose could result in dramatic changes in the sex ratio, in birth rates, and in family relationships in general.

10. This chapter covered a range of topics dealing with parents and parenthood. Some attention was devoted to both young and unwed parenthood and to an examination of factors related to family size. The next chapter continues with the parenthood issue, but focuses more specifically on parent-child interaction, socialization patterns, and gender role differences.

## KEY TERMS AND TOPICS

# DISCUSSION QUESTIONS

1. Discuss the likely effects of the following structural dimensions on parenthood: age of parents, length of marriage, number of children, spacing of children, and sex of children.
2. In what ways do urbanization and industrialization affect parental roles in U.S. society? Are there advantages for farm families in rearing children?
3. What conditions are likely to increase the probability that parenthood will be a "crisis" event?
4. Why are young parenthood and unwed parenthood considered social problems? If they are social problems, why doesn't society make birth control, abortion, sterilization, and the like available for the unwed teenage males or females?
5. A number of states have passed legislation that requires Planned Parenthood clinics to notify parents that their teenage children have requested contraceptive or abortion information. What do you predict to be some of the consequences of this type of action?
6. Discuss the myth of the "maternal instinct." How do you explain the widespread acceptance of it? What factors disprove its existence?
7. Examine the birth rate data presented. Explain: (1) why the birth rate dropped sharply in the 1930s, (2) how it was accomplished without the pills, abortions, and sterilizations more prevalent today, and (3) the drop in the birth rate in the 1960s and then its recent upturn.
8. Why are childless marriages not likely to become the norm? Are there advantages to marriage without children?
9. Discuss the implications of the slogan "stop at two" in regard to family size. Why two? What if everyone had two? What means should be used to accomplish this if it is perceived as a desirable goal?
10. Itemize advantages of large and small families. What are the consequences of being an only child? What types of factors are likely to influence the size of a family?
11. Discuss the implications of being an oldest, middle, or youngest child. Does spacing make any differences?
12. If sex of the fetus could be determined accurately within a few weeks following pregnancy, what effect, if any, would this have on birth rates? Would most parents in the United States choose boys, girls, or have no preferences? What about other countries, particularly outside of the Western world?

# FURTHER READINGS

Blake, Judith. *Family Size and Achievement*. Berkeley: University of California Press, 1989. An examination of what the author calls the *sibsize revolution* with a focus on the cognitive and educational consequences of coming from families of different sizes.

Campbell, Elaine. *The Childless Marriage*. New York: Tavistock, 1986. A sympathetic and humanistic account of the childless careers of seventy-eight people in a Scottish city.

Elster, Arthur, B., and Lamb, Michael E. (eds.) *Adolescent Fatherhood*. Hillsdale, N.J.: Lawrence Erlbaum Association, 1986. A compilation of eleven writings on adolescents, including topics such as risking paternity, stresses and coping strategies, parent behavior, and others.

Falbo, Toni (ed.) *The Single Child Family*. New York: Guilford Press, 1984. A collection of papers that dispels traditional notions about the disadvantages of being an only child.

Fox, Greer Litton. *The Childbearing Decision: Fertility Attitudes and Behavior*. Beverly Hills: Sage Publications, 1982. A multidisciplinary collection of eleven articles summarizing connections between fertility decision making and factors such as socialization, sex roles, work, motivational variables, and divorce.

Furstenberg, Frank F. Jr.; Brookes-Gunn, J.; and Morgan, S. Philip. *Adolescent Mothers in Late Life*. Cambridge: Cambridge University Press, 1987. A study describing long-term variations in the careers of teenage mothers and a look at the situation of their children as they encounter adolescence a generation later.

Hanson, Shirley M. H., and Bozett, Frederick, W. (eds.) *Dimensions of Fatherhood.* Beverly Hills: Sage Publications, 1985. An interdisciplinary compilation of nineteen articles that view fathers and fatherhood in a variety of social roles presented in a life-span perspective.

LaRossa, Ralph. *Becoming a Parent.* Beverly Hills: Sage Publications, 1986. A look at becoming a parent. fertility decision-making, pregnancy, birth, and infant care, with an emphasis on how these experiences differ between the sexes.

LeMasters, E. E., and DeFrain, John. *Parents in Contemporary America: A Sympathetic View.* 4th ed. Homewood, Ill.: Dorsey, 1983. An overview of parents in the United States today, including an analysis of parenthood and folklore, roles, social class, minority groups, parents without partners, social change, and counseling.

Lewis, Charles, and O'Brien, Margaret, (eds.). *Reassessing Fatherhood: New Observations on Fathers and the Modern Family.* Newbury Park, CA.: Sage Publications, Inc., 1987. A compilation of fifteen writings dealing with fathers, fatherhood, and paternal roles in a range of contexts.

Mackey, Wade C. *Fathering Behaviors: The Dynamics of the Man-Child Bond.* New York: Plenum Press, 1985. A cross-cultural observation study of interaction between adults (especially males) and children in public places.

Rindfuss, Ronald R.; Morgan, S. Philip; and Swicegood, Gray. *First Births in America: Changes in the Timing of Parenthood.* Berkeley: University of California Press, 1988. An examination of the changes in parenthood timing in the U.S. in the twentieth century, the determinants of such changes, and the process that unfolds in conjunction with other aspects of the life course.

Robinson, Bryan, E., and Barret, Robert L. *The Developing Father: Emerging Roles in Contemporary Society.* New York: Guilford Press, 1986. A comprehensive view of fathers, based on both research and personal accounts of men describing their own fathering experiences.

# CHAPTER FOURTEEN

# PARENT-CHILD INTERACTION AND SOCIALIZATION

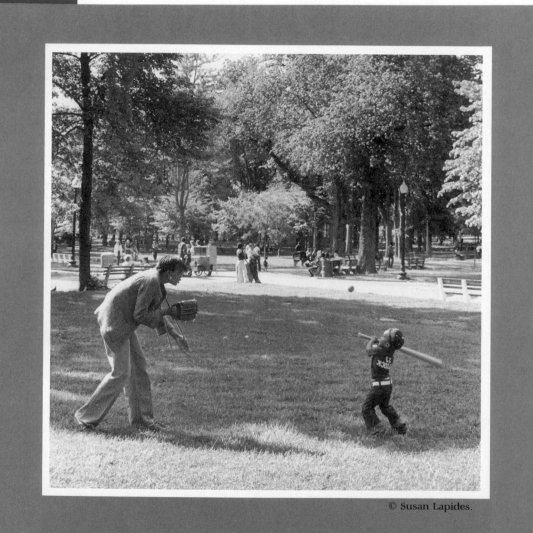

© Susan Lapides.

The previous chapter examined selected structural arrangements of the family system: norms and values surrounding parenthood, young parenthood, unwed parenthood, birth rates and birth expectations, effects of large or small families, birth order, and the like. This chapter as well looks at selected social structural patterns such as gender (male-female) differences, but it focuses primary attention on interactional and social psychological patterns in parent-child relationships. Of central concern are theoretical frames of reference that vary in their explanations of the socialization process.

## THE SOCIALIZATION OF PARENTS AND CHILDREN

The helplessness of human infants is perhaps unequaled among newborns. They cannot walk, feed themselves, know where danger lies, seek food or shelter, or even roll over. Infants may grow up to be criminals, teachers, or athletic superstars, but first they must learn to care for basic needs, learn to interact with other humans, and learn what behavior is expected and accepted. In short, they must learn to be human.

The process of acquiring these physical and social skills to become a social being and a member of society is called **socialization.** Socialization, the central concept of this chapter, is a never-ending process of developing the self and of learning the ways of a given society and culture. While the focus of attention in the socialization literature is generally upon the newborn and the young child, teenagers, middle-aged, and older people as well are in a continual process of learning skills, developing the self, and becoming a participant in the groups and social systems of society. Parents too need to be socialized to parenthood. Parents not only influence and shape the behavior of children, but children do the same to parents.[1]

Socialization, particularly of the young infant, may be the single universal function of the family.[2] There may be others—such as social placement—but every society appears to link people by affinity (marriage) or consanguineous (blood) ties to the nurturant socialization of persons. This does not imply that families do not fulfill other functions, that socialization only occurs among infants, or that the family is the only socializing agent. Rather, the key implication is that the basic function of the family in all societies is nurturant socialization.

---

1. Note: John F. Peters, "Adolescents as Socialization Agents to Parents," *Adolescence* 20 (Winter 1985): 920–933.

2. Ira L. Reiss, "The Universality of the Family: A Conceptual Analysis," *Journal of Marriage and the Family* 27 (November 1965): 443–453.

## Sect parents who don't "spare the rod"

The Northeast Community Church, a 400 member religious sect group in Vermont, was under investigation by state officials in the mid-1980s because of child beating. A public meeting was called after the state seized 112 children of church members to have them examined for signs of physical and psychological abuse. They were released within hours after a judge ruled there was not enough evidence to warrant the emergency detention.

Newspaper accounts of the public meeting gave comments of the seven church elders in attendance. One told the angry townspeople that a lost generation would result unless youngsters, even babies, were "properly spanked." When asked at what age children should be spanked, a response was that if you wait until a child is able to reason, you have waited too long. Another said that even little babies have a fallen nature and needed strict discipline.

A Mr. Wiseman, who faced charges that he beat a 13-year-old for seven hours, quoted the Book of Psalms by saying "Serve the Lord with fear." He argued that strict discipline is part of the standard of God. Strict discipline included the use of slender wooden rods for reasons ranging from lying to asking for second helpings at meals.

## Preconditions for socialization

Frederick Elkin and Gerald Handel state that there are two preconditions for adequate socialization:

1. Children must have the requisite biological inheritance.
2. There must be an ongoing society.[3]

The first precondition for socialization is a biological inheritance that is adequate to permit learning processes to occur. Thus a brain, a digestive system, and a beating heart are clearly prerequisites for socialization. These prerequisites, however, while necessary, are not sufficient. A "perfect" biological system, while influencing the socialization process, will not be the determinant of what is internalized mentally. Factors such as brain damage, deafness, extreme tallness or shortness, shape of nose and chin, or a wide variety of other physical conditions may hinder or influence interaction and socializing processes. But it should be made extremely clear that the biological inheritance, while influencing learning processes and necessary for their occurrence, are never sufficient conditions for socialization. Certain needs such as food, drink, and sleep are basic to survival, but they can be satisfied in a wide variety of ways. And while temperaments and intelligence may be basically biological, the development or direction that they take is influenced and modified by the society in which the infant exists. In brief, while biological requisites are necessary for adequate socialization, they alone are not determinants of socialization.

---

3. Frederick Elkin and Gerald Handel, *The Child and Society: The Process of Socialization* 5th ed. (New York: Random House, 1989): 8–25.

The second precondition for socialization is an existing society that has values, norms, statuses, roles, institutions, and a wide variety of social structures that are highly regular and patterned but in constant change. The unsocialized infant has no knowledge of these changes, structures, or processes. The patterns of thinking, feeling, and acting of that society are what the socializing agents must pass on to the newcomer. This is the task of socialization.

# THEORIES OF SOCIALIZATION PROCESSES

As previously defined, *socialization* refers to the process by which the infant and adult learn the ways of a given society and culture and develop into participants capable of operating in that society. A number of relatively comprehensive theories have been developed to explain various aspects of this process. Let's examine several of them.

## A learning-behaviorist frame of reference

Learning theory, also recognized as reinforcement theory, stimulus-response theory, and behaviorism, assumes that the same concepts and principles that apply to lower animals apply to humans. Thus it is logical and rational to spend time in the laboratory experimenting with rats, cats, dogs, pigeons, monkeys, or other animals to learn more about humans. Although there are many variations of learning theory, as with the other theories that follow, basic assumptions and common lines of agreement do exist.

Learning, or socialization as applied to the newborn infant, involves changes in behavior that result from experience. (This is opposed to changes in behavior that result from physiological maturation or biological conditions.) Learning involves conditioning that may include classical conditioning or instrumental (operant) conditioning. *Classical conditioning* links a response to a known stimulus. Most students are already familiar with Pavlov's dog experiment, which provides a good example of classical conditioning. The hungry dog, placed in a soundproof room, heard a tuning fork prior to receiving meat. When repeated on several occasions, the dog salivated upon hearing the tuning fork prior to receiving, or even without receiving, the meat. The tuning fork, a conditioned stimulus, produced the response (salivation). In the classical conditioning experiment, the focus of attention is largely on the stimulus. If this works with dogs, the same principle should hold true with an infant upon hearing his mother's approaching footsteps. The footstep stimulus, with repeated occurrences, should elicit a response from the child.

Instrumental conditioning, or what Skinner calls *operant conditioning*, places the focus of attention on the response. The responses are not related to any known stimuli but rather they function in an instrumental fashion. We learn to make a certain response on the basis of the consequences the response produces. It is the response, rather than the stimulus, that is correlated with reinforcement. Let's return to the example of the hungry dog. Under classical conditioning the dog salivated upon hearing the tuning fork, the stimulus. Under operant conditioning, the hungry dog may sniff, paw, and chew whatever is around. If upon pawing, the dog opens a door behind which is food, the sniffing and chewing will soon decrease and the pawing on the door will occur whenever food is desired. Thus instrumental conditioning is a response followed by a reward (reinforcement).

How does this apply to an infant? Suppose the infant utters sounds like "da-da-da." Father, who is convinced the child is saying *daddy*, rewards him or her by picking up, feeding, or rocking. As a result, the response (da-da-da) soon becomes used by the infant all day long. The infant has learned to make a certain response on the basis of the consequence or result the response will produce; hence it is the response that is correlated with reinforcement.

These same general principles, refined by behaviorists with reference to intermittent reinforcement, partial reinforcement, negative and positive reinforcement, discrimination of stimuli, differentiation of response, and the like are said to apply in the learning of any kind of behavior. Socialization results from stimulus-response conditioning and from positive and negative reinforcements. The conditioning stimuli (classical conditioning) and the consequences of responses (operant conditioning) are both external to the animal or human.

Many of these processes are most readily observed in early childhood when parents use rewards and punishment as deliberate techniques for teaching the child approved forms of behavior. As individuals mature, sanctioning becomes increasingly complex, and candy, weekly allowances, spanking, or other forms of rewards and punishments lose their ability to either eliminate undesirable behavior or increase desirable behavior.

Within the learning theory–behaviorist framework, symbols, language, reasoning, internalized meanings, and other internal processes play a minimal role. This is in sharp contrast to the symbolic interaction framework (described in Chapter 2 and later in this section) where the socialized being can create his or her own stimuli and responses, can define and categorize, can distinguish between self and nonself, can separate inner and outer sensations, and can take the role of the other. As a result, this basically mechanistic approach to socialization is rejected by most sociologists to whom the self, roles, reference groups, and symbolic processes are viewed as central to an understanding of human behavior. Although learning theory has been extremely illuminating in research with animals and infants, it has been less successful in explaining social situations, group norms, or the learning of language itself.

From the biased perspective of this author, it is largely a waste of time, effort, and expense to attempt to understand the behavior of socialized humanity, capable as we are of dealing with symbolic processes, reasoning, shared meanings, and the like, by studying nonhuman forms. Behaviorism does, however, add greatly to our understanding of the human who (1) has not learned to share meanings—the infant, the isolate, or the severely retarded—or (2) has once learned but no longer has the capacity to share meanings—the more severe cases of aphasia or the extreme cases of schizophrenia where words may exist but the meanings are not shared with others.

This brief, minimal treatment of learning theory may seem unfair to the disciples of behaviorism. The same can be said for the minimal treatment of the psychoanalytic theory that follows. Both are intended to illustrate some contrasting views on the nature of socialization.

## A psychoanalytic frame of reference

Classic psychoanalytic theory, developed by Sigmund Freud and his adherents, stresses the importance of biological drives and unconscious processes. This is in sharp contrast to the behaviorist theory just described. The process of socialization, according to this framework, consists of a number of precise though overlapping stages of development. What happens at these stages from birth to age five or six, although unconscious, becomes relatively fixed and permanent. These stages are referred to as the *oral, anal,* and *phallic* stages, followed later by a period of *latency* and a *genital* phase. Attention is focused around three principal erogenous zones: the mouth, the anus, and the genitals, which are the regions of the body where excitatory processes tend to become focalized and where tensions can be removed by some action such as stroking or sucking. Each region is of extreme importance in the socialization process because they are the first important sources of irritating excitations with which the baby has to contend and upon which the first pleasurable experiences occur.

The first stage of development, the *oral stage*, occurs during the first year of the child's life. The earliest erotic gratifications come from the mouth and, as a result, the child forms strong emotional attachments to the mother who supplies the source of food, warmth, and sucking. During the first year, the child is narcissistic with the self-gratification derived via the oral source, namely the mouth. The modes of functioning of the mouth include taking in, holding on, biting, spitting out, and closing, all prototypes for ways of adjusting to painful or disturbing states. They serve as models for adaptations in later life.

The *anal stage* of development follows and overlaps with the oral stage. This phase is so called because the child experiences pleasure in excretion and because toilet training may become a major problem. At this point, two functions become central: retention and elimination. Since the mother is still the predominant figure, her methods of training the child and her attitudes about such matters as defecation, cleanliness, and control are said to determine the impact that toilet training will have upon the development of the person. Carried to the extreme, the mother who praises the child for a large bowel movement may produce an adolescent or adult who will be motivated to produce or create things to please others or to please himself or herself, as he or she once made feces to please mother. On the other hand, if the mother is very strict and punitive, the child may intentionally soil himself or herself and, as an adolescent or adult, be messy, irresponsible, disorderly, wasteful, and extravagant.

The *phallic stage* is the period of growth during which the child is preoccupied with the genitals. Prior to this stage, the first love object of both the boy and girl is the mother. But with the arrival of this stage, the sexual urge increases, the boy's love for his mother becomes more intense, and the result is jealousy of the father who is his rival. The boy's attachment to his parent of the opposite sex is widely known as the *Oedipus complex.* Concurrently, the male becomes fearful that his father will remove his genitals and develops a fear known as *castration anxiety.* This anxiety increases upon observation of the female who has, in his unconscious mind, "already been castrated." A similar or reverse process is in operation for the female. She forms an attachment to her father, the *Electra complex,* but has mixed feelings for him because he possesses something that she does not have. The result is *penis envy.* According to traditional Freudian psychology, penis envy is the key to feminine psychology. Located here are the roots of male dominance and female submissiveness, male superiority and female inferiority.

The oral, anal, and phallic stages taken together are called the *pregenital period* and occupy the first five or six years of one's life. These are the important years when the basic personality patterns are established and fixed. Following this time, for the next six or seven years until the onset of puberty, the male and female egos go through a *latency phase* when the erotic desires of the child are repressed and he or she forms attachments to the parent of the same sex.

Finally, with the arrival of puberty, the *genital phase* of development begins. This period is less a stage than the final working out of the previous stages, particularly the oral, anal, and phallic that occurred during the pregenital period. At this time, group activities, marriage, establishing a home, developing vocational responsibilities, and "adult" interests become the focus of attention. Given the importance of the early years, one can readily understand why factors such as bottle or breast feeding, nursing on a regular or self-demand time schedule, weaning abruptly or gradually, bowel training early or late, bladder training early or late, punishment or nonpunishment for toilet accidents, or sleeping alone or with one's mother, serve as crucial items of attention to the psychoanalyst.

The claims of the Freudians regarding the importance of infant training to personality adjustment have received mixed empirical support. The support that has been received has, in general, been derived from clinical studies of emotionally disturbed individuals. Other studies show different results. For example, one attempt to test empirically the crucial role of infant discipline in character formation and personality adjustment was published about forty years ago and has since become a somewhat classic article on the

## No hitter can hold a candle to mom

Everybody says motherhood is the toughest game in the world, a grueling physical, psychological contest. Winners and losers shape the entire future of our society, perhaps worldwide. Motherhood makes pro baseball, football and basketball look like child's play.

So, where are the stats? Where's the rule book? Where are the coaches and fans, the amateur and pro leagues, pennants, trophies and those fat TV contracts? Nowhere, and that's a crock.

So far, motherhood is considered a sissy sport, even a non-sport. Not one high school or college has a varsity team. There are only neighborhood pickup games, so to speak. Everybody is an amateur player, all ages, all levels of talent, all unsung. And when their playing days are over, there's no Motherhood Hall of Fame.

Not one aging mother has been hired as a greeter in Las Vegas, or a manufacturer's rep. Oh, some ex-mothers are employed, for sure. Lots of them hold down full-time jobs even while they're playing the game at full potential, which is frequently awesome. But nobody hires any player just because she's a world-class mother. Mothers get hired because they can type or do neurosurgery.

The interest is there, but there's no money and no organization. There's no pro tour to watch on Wide World of Sports. Motherhood is ignored by the International Olympic Committee.

### The competition is on

All that has to change. If there's room on the sports pages for the USFL (ho-hum), there has to be room for the National Motherhood League. I can see it now . . .

Detroit Matriarch players and fans breathed a collective sigh of relief Tuesday night. Mary Smith's elbow is healthy again.

In Detroit's decisive 28–25 victory over the Chicago Mummies, Smith was in top form, high-scorer with 14 points, and voted MVP. All Smith's points came in the critical diapering and burping phase of this best-of-seven preliminary to the conference semifinals. Detroit's D&B specialist, Smith has been plagued with recurring bursitis of the left elbow since spring training, when she attempted to hoist a four-year-old out of a sandbox while simultaneously balancing a two-year-old on her right hip.

"I've done that maneuver a million times," she said. "Maybe I tried to do too much too fast."

Coach Crusty McCrea agreed and took Smith out of the lineup until last night. That hasn't been easy for the plucky player from Petoskey. While Smith was out, the Matriarchs barely managed to squeak out victories over the Baltimore Mamas and the Los Angeles Mommie Dearests. But Smith was at the top of her form again on Tuesday.

"I couldn't let the fans down tonight," Smith said after the game in the locker room. "This was one we had to win. I can score from the inside and the outside, and that's what we needed. I gave it everything I had. The elbow felt fine. I'm just glad I had the stuff."

A capacity crowd of 27,325 wildly cheering Matriarch fans were more than glad. They were ecstatic. "Goldang! I wish I had a mother like that 'un!" shouted one enthusiastic Matriarch booster as he tipped over a police car on Michigan Avenue after the game. Don't we all pal? Don't we all!

*Source:* Nickie McWhirter, *Detroit Free Press,* May 12, 1985, p. 16. Reprinted by permission of the Detroit Free Press.

---

subject.[4] That study set up a series of null hypotheses concerning the relationship of specific infant disciplines to subsequent personality adjustments. The general hypothesis was that the personality adjustment and traits

---

4. William H. Sewall, "Infant Training and the Personality of the Child." *The American Journal of Sociology* 58 (September 1952): 150–159.

of children who had undergone varying infant training experiences would not differ significantly from each other. These infant training experiences included the self-demand feeding schedule, gradual weaning, late bowel training, and similar factors. The results indicated support for the null hypothesis, that is, there were no significant differences in the personality adjustments of children who had undergone varying infant training experiences. Of 460 Chi-square tests, only eighteen were significant at or beyond the .05 level.[5] Of these, eleven were in the expected direction and seven were in the opposite direction from that expected on the basis of psychoanalytic writings. Such practices as breast feeding, gradual weaning, demand schedule, bowel training, and bladder training, which have been so emphasized in the psychoanalytic literature, were almost barren in terms of their relationship to personality adjustment.

## Child development frames of reference

The ideas of Erik Erikson and of Jean Piaget are of interest in dealing with the socialization issue. Both, like Freud, focus their attention primarily on stages of development. Both, unlike Freud, extended their stages beyond the early years and place more importance on social structure and reasoning.

*Erik Erikson's ideas*   Erikson, one of Freud's students, was a psychoanalyst who saw socialization as a lifelong process, beginning at birth and continuing into old age. He developed and is well-known for his eight stages of human development.[6] Each stage constitutes a crisis brought on by physiological changes and the constantly changing social situation. In infancy (the first year), the crisis centers around *trust versus mistrust*. Being totally dependent on adults, the feelings of the child are developed in response to the quality of maternal care as dependable or undependable, accepting or rejecting. In early childhood (the first two to three years), the issue centers around *autonomy versus shame and doubt*. Again the feelings of the child are developed in response to the actions of parents who allow the child to accomplish new things and govern himself or herself (autonomy) or receive constant supervision, indicating he or she cannot reach, walk, control bowels, and the like without ridicule and shame.

The play stage (age 4 or 5) involves the issue of *initiative versus guilt*. As children master their own bodies, as they play and fantasize and act out adult roles, they develop feelings of self-worth. Ridicule and disinterest lead to guilt feelings, while encouragement to explore may lead to personal initiative. By school age and up to adolescence, the issue centers around *industry versus*

5. The .05 level means that these relationships would occur simply by chance less than 5 times in 100.
6. Erik K. Erikson, *Childhood and Society* 2d ed. (New York: Norton, 1963), Chapter 7.

*inferiority.* Parents become less the focal point as the school and the community take on greater importance. Recognition is received by achieving success in physical and mental skills and producing things (industry), while failure in school, disapproval of race or family background, and inability to achieve may be negative experiences that result in feelings of inferiority.

By adolescence, the issue becomes one of *identity versus role confusion.* Identity, the focal concern of Erikson,[7] is being able to achieve a sense of continuity about one's past, present, and future. An inability to integrate the many and varied roles into a clear identity leads to role confusion. Peers at this point are of prime importance.

Young adulthood, another major turning point in life, involves the issue of *intimacy versus isolation.* Friendship, love affairs, and intimacy require the risk of rejection, losing the friend or lover, and being hurt. Only with a clear sense of ego identity and an ability to trust can one avoid isolation. In young adulthood and middle age the issue centers around *generativity versus stagnation.* People can feel they are making contributions to society, working creatively, rearing children for the next generation, and in general being productive, or they may find life boring, painful, and dull. Childish self-absorption and "early invalidism, physical or psychological, are signs that a person has not found generativity."[8] Old age, the last stage of development, is one of reflection and evaluation and focuses on the issue of *integrity versus despair.* Integrity involves coming to terms with life and death. Despair involves seeing life as a series of missed opportunities and realizing it is too late to start over.

Erikson sees the social order as resulting from and in harmony with these eight stages of development. As people work out solutions to these developmental concerns, the solutions become institutionalized in the culture.

*Jean Piaget's ideas*   Piaget, a Swiss social psychologist, spent more than thirty years observing and studying the development of intellectual functions and logic in children.[9] His work has stimulated an interest in maturational stages of development and in the importance of cognition in human development. Differing dramatically from the views of the learning and psychoanalytic frames of reference, Piaget sees development as an ability to reason abstractly, to think about hypothetical situations in a logical way, and to organize rules (which he calls *operations*) into complex, higher order structures. Children invent ideas and behaviors that they have never witnessed or had reinforced.

---

7. Erik K. Erikson, *Identity: Youth and Crisis* (New York: Norton, 1968).

8. Erikson, *Childhood and Society*, p. 267.

9. Jean Piaget and Barbara Inhelder, *The Psychology of the Child* (New York: Basic, 1969); and Piaget's theory in P. H. Mussen, ed., *Carmichael's Manual of Child Psychology*, 3d ed. (New York: Wiley, 1970): 703–732.

Piaget believes that there are four major stages of intellectual development: *sensorimotor* (0 to 18 months), *preoperational* (18 months to age 7), *concrete operations* (ages 7 to 12), and finally *formal operations* (ages 12 onward). The stages are continuous and each is built upon and is a derivative of the earlier one.

The *sensorimotor stage*, further differentiated into six developmental stages,[10] involves for the child a physical understanding of himself or herself and his or her world. The unlearned responses such as sucking and closing one's fist become repetitive but with no intent, purpose, or interest in the effect this behavior has on the environment. Later activities in this first stage become more intentional. A child may kick his or her legs to produce a swinging motion in a toy hung on the crib. A child may knock down a pillow to get a toy behind it. A primary cognitive development at this stage is the discovery of object permanence: toys and mother do not dissolve when they are not visible. Early development includes the coordination of simple motor arts with incoming perceptions (sensorimotor arts).

The *preoperational stage* involves language and its acquisition. Objects are treated as symbolic of things other than themselves. Dolls may be treated as babies or a stick may be treated as a candle. At this stage, overt actions and the meaning of objects and events are manipulated, but the child has difficulty taking the point of view of another child or adult. Unlike the next (operational) stage, the child does not have a mental representation of a series of actions. For example, a child may be able to walk to a store several blocks away but cannot draw the route on paper. Nor can the child at this stage grasp the notion of relational terms (darker, larger), reason simultaneously about part of the whole and the whole, or arrange objects according to some quantified dimension such as weight or size.

The *operational stage* involves the ability to do things such as those just mentioned. Children learn to manipulate the tools of their culture. They learn that mass remains constant in spite of changes in form. They learn to understand cause and effect, to classify objects, to consider the viewpoints of others, and to differentiate between dreams and real things. By approximately age twelve the child enters the adult world and the stage of formal operations.

The *formal operations stage* includes the ability to think in terms of abstract concepts, theories, and general principles. Alternate solutions to problems can be formulated. Hypothetical propositions can be formulated and answered. Preoccupation with thought is the principal component of this stage of development.

Piaget's insights into cognitive development are unsurpassed. His stages take into account both social and psychological phenomena. Like Freud,

---

10. These stages Piaget refers to as *reflexes, primary circular reactions, secondary circular reactions, coordination of secondary reactions, tertiary circular reactions,* and *internal experimentation.* Jean Piaget, *The Construction of Reality in the Child* (New York: Basic, 1954).

## Traditional child-rearing in the kibbutz

The kibbutz has been and continues to be extremely child centered. Children represent the future. The traditional manner in which child rearing occurred followed a collective pattern from infancy to adulthood. In that context the infant was born of a kibbutz couple who generally married just before or soon after the first child was born. This was done in accordance with the laws of Israel and gave the child legal rights. Upon return from the hospital, the infant was placed in the infant house. During the first year of the infant's life, his or her mother came to this house to breast-feed the infant as long as she physically could. Young fathers participated at this period in bottle-feeding and diapering. In a radical departure from child rearing in most of the world, neither an infant nor any older children lived with or were directly supported by the biological father and mother. The socialization and education of kibbutz children were functions of nurses and teachers.

During the first year, the general pattern of child care emerged. Most of the child's time was spent with peers in the children's house. In the afternoon, two or three hours could be spent with parents in their flat or room, meeting with other families or engaging in some joint activity. On the Sabbath, only the essential chores were performed, and children of all ages spent much time with their parents. In addition to these hourly and Sabbath visits, the child frequently saw the parents while they worked or by attending this weekly assembly of the kibbutz. Thus parents were extremely important in the life of the child but were, in a sense, junior partners.

Training occurred, for the most part, separate from the residence of the parents. For the first year, the infant was in the nursery. The child was then moved to a toddler's house, each of which had approximately two nurses and eight children. This was where toilet training, learning to feed oneself, and learning to interact with age-mates occurred. When the children reached the ages of two or three, a nursery teacher replaced one of the nurses. By the fourth or fifth birthday, the children moved into the kindergarten. This involved a different building, sometimes a new nurse and teacher, and an enlargement of the original group to approximately sixteen members. This enlarged group remained together as a unit until age twelve and the completion of sixth grade. At this point they entered high schools where for the first time they encountered male educational teachers and began to work directly in the kibbutz economy. Their work varied from one to three hours per day, depending on age, and was done in one of the economic branches under the supervision of adults (not parents). Upon completion of high school, the students were expected to live outside the kibbutz for approximately one year. Membership in the kibbutz followed this experience.

While the children did not sleep with, did not have their physical needs cared for, were not taught social, book, or economic skills by, and were not—for the most part—disciplined or socialized by their parents, most writers stress the importance of parents in the development of the child. They serve as the object of identification and provide a certain security and love not obtained from others.

Piaget has a specific conception of the goals of maturity and adulthood. Also like Freud, Piaget believes that the child passes through stages. But where Freud emphasized emotional maturity and the unconscious as extremely important, Piaget emphasizes reasoning and consciousness. While Freud focused on bodily zones, Piaget focuses on the quality of reasoning.

The frames of reference covered up to this point can be summarized by suggesting that the learning theorists are concerned with overt behavior, the

Freudians with motives and emotions (often unconscious and rooted early in childhood), and the child developmentalists with motor skills, thought, reasoning processes, and conflicts. Let's now turn our attention to a symbolic interaction frame of reference that shares many assumptions of Erikson and Piaget in the importance given to language, reasoning, and societal influences.

### A symbolic interaction frame of reference

Contrasting considerably with the learning and psychoanalytic frames of reference is the symbolic interaction frame of reference. Within this framework, although the first five years are important, personality does not become fixed; socialization becomes a lifelong process. Although mother is an important figure, so too are fathers, siblings, grandparents, teachers, and many others who are perceived as significant to the child or adult. While internal needs and drives are important as energy sources and motivating devices, greater significance comes from interactions with others and the internalized definitions and meanings of the world in which one interacts. Although erogenous zones may be sources of pleasure and gratification, the significance of these zones depends on the learned internalized meanings attached to them. While unconscious processes may be at the core of socialization (purely speculative), conscious processes relating to perceptions of self and others take on prime importance. Although rewards and punishments influence behavior, these too can only be understood in the light of the meanings attached to them. While conditioning (classical or operant) is significant and basic to learning, internal processes cannot be ignored. To understand socialization as explained within a symbolic interaction frame of reference (*see* Chapter 2), it is necessary to review in more detail the basic assumptions and meaning of key concepts such as "social self," "significant others," and "reference groups."

*Basic assumptions of symbolic interactionism*   As summarized in Chapter 2, the interactionist frame of reference, when applied to the study of the family and to an understanding of socialization, is based on several **basic assumptions.** Four of these have been delineated by Sheldon Stryker.[11] The initial assumption is that *humans must be studied on their own level.* Symbolic interactionism is anti-reductionistic. If we want to understand socialization, infant development, and parent-child relationships among humans, then we must study humans and not infer their behavior from the study of nonhuman or infrahuman forms of life.

---

11. Sheldon Stryker, "The International and Situational Approaches," in *Handbook of Marriage and the Family*, ed. by Harold T. Christensen (Chicago: Rand McNally, 1964): 134–136; and Sheldon Stryker, "Symbolic Interaction Theory: A Review and Some Suggestions for Comparative Family Research," *Journal of Comparative Family Studies* 3 (Spring 1972): 17–32.

The basic difference between human and infrahuman is not simply a matter of degree but a basic difference of kind. The evolutionary process involves quantitative difference in species, not merely qualitative ones. The human-nonhuman difference centers around language, symbols, meanings, gestures, and related processes.

Thus, to understand a person's social development and behavior, relatively little can be gained by observing chimpanzees, dogs, pigeons, or rats. Social life, unlike biological, physiological life, or any nonhuman form, involves sharing meanings and communicating symbolically. Due to language and the use of gestures, human beings can respond to one another on the basis of intentions or meanings of gestures. This assumption is in direct contrast with the behaviorist assumption, which suggests that humans can best be understood by studying forms of life other than humans. Psychologists who assume that the difference between human and animal is one of degree have relatively good success in explaining and controlling those who do not share meanings or communicate with one another at a symbolic level: infants, extreme psychotics, isolated children, the severely retarded, the brain damaged, people with more severe forms of aphasia, and the like. To the interactionist, the possession of language has enabled humans alone to deal with events in terms of the past, present, or future and to imagine objects or events that may be remote in space or entirely nonexistent.

The differences between socialized human beings and the lower animals, or between human families and nonhuman families, may be summarized by saying that the lower animals do not have a culture. They have no system of beliefs, values, and ideas that are shared possessions of groups and are symbolically transmitted. They have no familial, educational, religious, political, or economic institutions. They have no sets of moral codes, norms, or ideologies. Much stress and emphasis is placed on similarities between the animal and human worlds, but an equal amount of emphasis needs to be given to understanding and focusing on that which is different in humans. Recognizing these differences, the symbolic interactionists assume that to understand humans one must study humans. Thus very little can be learned about socialization, husbands, wives, children, in-laws, grandparents, or family life-styles of the upper class, native Americans, or the Amish by studying nonhuman forms.

A second assumption is that *the most fruitful approach to social behavior is through an analysis of society.* One can best understand the behavior of a husband, wife, or child through a study and an analysis of the society and subculture of which they are a part. Personal behavior is not exclusively or even primarily an individual phenomenon but is predominantly a social one. The assumption is not made that society is the ultimate reality, that society has some metaphysical priority over the individual, or that cultural determinism explains all behavior. Neither does it exclude biogenic and psychogenic factors as important in explaining or understanding behavior. However, these factors are not salient variables. They are viewed as constants in a social setting and as random variables in a personality system.

Being born into a given society means that the language one speaks, the definitions one gives to situations, and the appropriateness or inappropriateness of any activity are those learned within a social and cultural context. Thus, the behavior of couples from rural areas in the Philippines who would not be seen holding hands in public, or the behavior of a U.S. couple kissing and caressing in a public park can only be understood by analyzing the society in which these behaviors take place.

A third assumption is that *the human infant at birth is asocial*. Original nature lacks organization. The infant is neither social nor antisocial (as with original sin in certain religious organizations or the id within the psychoanalytic scheme). The equipment with which the newborn enters life does, however, have the potential for social development.

It is the society and the social context that determine what type of behavior is social or antisocial. A newborn infant does not cry all night to punish or displease a parent nor does she or he sleep all night to please them. Only after these expectations become internalized do social or antisocial acts take on meaning. Although the newborn infant has impulses—as does any biological organism—these impulses are not channeled or directed toward any specific ends. But the human infant, having the potential for social development, can, with time and training, organize these impulses and channel them in specific directions. This process, by which the newborn infant becomes a social being, is the main concern of social psychologists, who are interested in the process of socialization, and of family sociologists, who are interested in child rearing.

A fourth assumption is that a *socialized human being*, meaning one who can communicate symbolically and share meanings, *is an actor as well as a reactor*. This does not simply mean that one person acts and another person reacts. The socialized human being does not simply respond to stimuli from the external environment. Rather, humans respond to a symbolic environment that involves responses to interpreted and anticipated stimuli.

That humans are actors as well as reactors suggests that investigators cannot understand behavior simply by studying the external environment and external forces; they must see the world from the viewpoint of the subject of their investigation. Humans not only respond to stimuli but select and interpret them. As a result, it becomes crucial and essential that this interpretation and meaning be known. It is this assumption that most precisely differentiates symbolic interactionists from the positivists in sociology and the behaviorists in psychology.

The assumption that humans are both actor and reactor suggests that humans alone can take the role of the other—that is, they can view the world from the perspective of the other person. Thus we can "put ourselves in the shoes of another person." We feel sad over the misfortune of a friend; we share the joys of our children even though the experience did not happen to us. A

### Should parents be punished when their child breaks the law?

When children break the law, should parents be punished? The assumption supporting this action is based on the notion that parents are the sole and primary sources of socialization and control of their children. It gained increasing attention when in 1989, federal drug czar William Bennett said in a speech that parents and live-in boyfriends and girlfriends should face stiffer legal liability in drug-related juvenile crimes. Bennett said that parents who have turned their juvenile offenders loose must learn why the social contract demands that they oversee and control the impulses of their children.

The *Charlotte Observer* reported (May 15, 1989) that the Charlotte Housing Authority told a 34-year-old mother that her Fairview Homes public housing lease would be terminated because her 16-year-old son was convicted of dealing cocaine in the complex. The previous week the Los Angeles police, using a ground-breaking California law that holds parents responsible for the crimes of their children, arrested the mother of a 17-year-old rape suspect and gang member. She was charged with "failure to exercise reasonable care, supervision, protection, and control" of her son. She was freed on $20,000 bail pending arraignment on the charge, which carries a penalty of up to one year in jail and a $2,500 fine.

Are these laws fair, reasonable, or workable? Can parents be responsible for the behavior of teenagers and older children, the ones most likely to commit the crimes? Should we not go a step further and punish their siblings and friends as well—or maybe teachers who may spend more time with a child than a parent? What do you think?

professor can take the role of the student and anticipate the response to a three-hour lecture or a certain type of exam without giving either the lecture or the exam. A wife can anticipate the response of her husband to an embrace or to inviting friends to dinner. The responses of the professor and the wife may be inaccurate but the perception and the meaning or definition attached to the situation will influence and direct behavior. In short, a person's behavior is not simply a response to others but is a self-stimulating response: a response to internal symbolic productions.

*The development of a social self* "Self" is a key concept in understanding socialization and personality. Self, although often seen in psychological and personal terms, is a social phenomenon. It is developed in interaction with others. The process of socialization, a primary concern of child rearing and that which makes humans social beings, is the development of a social self: the organization of internalized roles.

A woman may occupy the statuses of wife, mother, sister, student, executive, Methodist, and many others. Each status has expectations (roles) assigned to it. A person must know how each role is related to the others. All these roles need to be organized and integrated into some reasonable, consistent unity. This organization of internalized roles is the **social self.**

This organization of roles and the internalization of them occurs in interaction with others; the social self is never fixed, static, or in a "final" state. George Herbert Mead used *self* to mean simply that a person is the object of his or her own activities; he or she can act toward him- or herself as he or she acts toward others.[12] Thus, we can talk to ourselves, be proud of ourselves, be ashamed, or feel guilty.

Who we are, how we feel, what we want, and so on constitute our social self. It consists of our self-concepts, our perceptions of who we are, and our definitions of self-worth and self-esteem. Our personalities then, consist of these definitions of self with the predisposition to act and behave in ways that are consistent with these self-concepts. If you are convinced you are not capable of passing the exam, are not attractive enough to meet that special person, or are unable to fulfill the expectations of your job, a self-fulfilling prophecy becomes operative. That is, you fail at the very things you knew you couldn't do. The opposite is equally true. Knowing you can do it increases the probabilities you can or will.

These self-concepts, definitions of who we are, senses of self-worth, and so forth develop in interaction with others. They do not exist at birth, but must be internalized; that is, they are learned. It does not take much imagination to assess the central role a spouse, sibling, parent, or grandparent—that is, family members—plays in the development of the social self. Documentation exists to show that parent support and behavior affects the self-esteem of children and adolescents and reciprocally, the self-esteem of children affects how much support their parents give them.[13] Perceived parental rejection was found to be a potent cause of depressive symptoms and low self-esteem among young people.[14] Mothers with higher self-esteem were more likely to provide their children with greater decision-making freedom, to communicate better with them, and to be less concerned about their children's behavior. Fathers with higher self-esteem were less likely to report using a physical form of punishment.[15]

Many other examples could be given. Note again the futility of studying nonhumans in dealing with issues such as these. Animals and any other form of life (including newborn infants) who have neither language nor any internalized role definitions or sense of self-worth have no social self. They cannot take the position of others and cannot view themselves as objects. Neither can they judge past, present, or prospective behavior. Among humans, where potential exists for sharing meanings, a social self can develop.

---

12. George Herbert Mead, *Mind, Self and Society* (Chicago: University of Chicago Press, 1934).

13. Viktor Gecas and Michael L. Schwalbe, "Parental Behavior and Adolescent Self-Esteem," *Journal of Marriage and the Family* 48 (February 1986): 37–46; and Richard B. Felson and Mary Z. Zielinski, "Children's Self-Esteem and Parental Support," *Journal of Marriage and the Family* 51 (August 1989): 727–735.

14. Joan F. Robertson and Ronald L. Simons, "Family Factors, Self-Esteem, and Adolescent Depression," *Journal of Marriage and the Family* 51 (February 1989): 125–138.

15. Stephen A. Small, "Parental Self-Esteem and Its Relationship to Childrearing Practices, Parent-Adolescent Interaction, and Adolescent Behavior," *Journal of Marriage and the Family* 50 (November 1988): 1063–1072; and David H. Demo, Stephen A. Small, and Ritch C. Savin-Williams, "Family Relations and the Self-Esteem of Adolescents and Their Parents," *Journal of Marriage and the Family* 49 (November 1987): 705–715.

*The importance of significant others and reference groups*   Significant others and reference groups are of central importance in understanding the development of the child and the modification of the social self. Not all persons or groups are of equal importance to us. Certain persons and groups, again in processes of interaction, come to be perceived as more important, as more significant, and as a source of reference. These persons and groups with which we psychologically identify are termed respectively, **significant others** and **reference groups.**

To most infants and young children, mother is a significant person, that is, an object of emotional involvement, especially in the child's development. Note that "mother," in terms of interaction and involvement, is a social not a biological concept. As a result, an adoptive foster parent, grandparent, or other person—male or female—can fulfill the expectations (roles) of mother. And mother (socially or biologically) is not the only significant other, as is seen in the influence of the father, siblings, peers, teachers, athletes, or movie stars. These are persons who are important and with whom one psychologically identifies. To identify with them is to attempt to conform to the expectations one perceives they have toward oneself. An attempt is made to please and receive approval from those others who are significant.

There are two essential ways in which significant others present themselves: (1) by what they do and (2) by what they say and how they say it. The doing and saying is organized in terms of roles. Mothers (traditionally, at least) change diapers, cook meals, clean houses, offer tenderness, and the like. Fathers read newspapers, complain about bills, watch football games, and so on. As a child or an adult interacts with others, he or she becomes interested in some, attached to others, and shares certain expectations and behaviors with them. Significant others are perceived as role models. Personal behavior and thinking is patterned on the conduct of these persons. Uncle Pete the pilot, Sally the movie star, or Marcia the teacher, as a significant other, may each play a decisive part in the socialization and development of our social self. A sister or brother, a boyfriend or girlfriend,[16] or a television figure may become a role model, a significant other, and a person with whom we psychologically identify.

In addition to persons who are viewed as significant, groups (real or imaginary) are used as a frame of reference with which a person psychologically identifies. These groups are generally termed *reference groups:* any group from which an individual seeks acceptance or uses as a source of comparison. A church, a club, or a company may serve as a point of reference in making comparisons or contrasts, especially in forming judgments about

---

16. Luther B. Otto, "Girl Friends as Significant Others: Their Influence on Young Men's Career Aspirations and Achievements," *Sociometry* 40 (September 1977): 287–293; and Jan F. Brazzell and Alan Acock, "Influences of Attitudes, Significant Others, and Aspirations of How Adolescents Intend to Resolve a Premarital Pregnancy," *Journal of Marriage and the Family* 50 (May 1988): 413–425.

### Resocializing the severely deprived: a case example

I could write volumes about this foster child we've raised. When he came to us he was two years and four months old and was really a basket case. I had read about children from deprived backgrounds, but I had never seen one. It was really a cultural shock for all of us.

The child didn't seem to know what people were for. He could ignore a person like he ignored a piece of furniture. He apparently had never had any interpersonal relations with another human. He did not want anybody near him and he was only two years old. Our way was to hold our children, cuddle them, tell them bedtime stories and carry them around. The older children played with him but he had no idea what they were doing. Everything terrified him. It was a lot more than I miss my mother. In fact, he did not know the words *mama, daddy.* He didn't miss anybody 'cause he didn't know what anybody was for. He had no language in that he didn't understand like our two-year-olds understood everything. He had no understanding of the difference between *yes, go ahead and do it,* or *no, you can't do that. No* was a concept he never heard.

Apparently he never sat at a table and ate a meal. He was more like an animal. I really hate using that word when we are talking about humans. But, you could not sit him at a table; he didn't know what it was for. I recall the first breakfast we had— that he had with us. He drank orange juice for as long as I gave it to him. Like he had four or five glasses of orange juice. He gobbled up toast and ate huge bowls of cereal. First I thought, "Gee, the kid is starved." But then I realized that he ate like that probably because that's his pattern. You eat all you could get when you could get it because you didn't know where the next meal was coming from. But we ate three times a day. It was years, and I mean years, before he could really sit at the table with us, eat a meal, and then leave without creating a major disturbance. By major, I mean he thought he could get his jollies by just sweeping everything off the table or grabbing the table and making things spill or taking his own food and throwing it around. You would think that in a few weeks this will all go away.

But it didn't and we started bringing him around to psychologists and the agency was very helpful. He was seen by neurologists and psychologists and he had EEGs, intelligence tests, and all of the support that seemed to be available in the community. They would all just say that as far as they could see he had no brain damage; his intelligence was maybe low normal.

For a long time he was as rigid as a door. He would not bend an inch. Like here's an example of what I mean. At our house the children play outside in the summer. We have playground equipment in the backyard and the children have bikes. I raised a bunch of kids who really love the outdoors. But I don't think he had ever been outside his little apartment or whatever it was they lived in. So, I would put him outside in the morning and his hands would go up to his eyes like he couldn't stand the light. I'd stay out there with him, but unless I was holding his hand, he would spin right around and go into the house again. So I'd take him out and put him outside again. We actually had to physically hold him out there. You could not walk him. You couldn't put him in the sandbox. He didn't know what a sandbox was for. He didn't know what toys were for. He had no idea what you did with a toy. We had to very patiently teach him all of this.

Eventually he began to show that it became important to him that he start pleasing us. But now this didn't happen until he was almost school age. Prior to that he couldn't care less whether he pleased us or pleased anybody else. He had not been socialized that way and I think that kind of socialization happens really early. I'm even more aware of it with my own grandchildren. They're sensitive. They cry if they are corrected. He never cried. We still laugh about the time I broke the pingpong paddle on him and he got up and said, "That didn't hurt." He went back and started doing exactly the same thing he was spanked for. I just had to take a deep breath and sit back and let him do it. Or I would have killed him that day, I'm sure I would have.

*Source:* Personal interview with a mother of a severely damaged foster child.

self. In some instances, a person may attempt to gain membership or acceptance in the group, although this is not always the case. These groups, like significant others, serve as standards for conduct, as bases for self-evaluation, and as sources of attitude formation.

To most adolescents, peers rather than parents are said to be key groups of reference. They serve many functions once fulfilled by parents. Peers, who understand the adolescent and share his or her world, become his or her reference set for sizing up problems, strivings, and ambition. The inclusion of peers as a source of reference may help us understand why the values of adolescents appear to be more like other age-similar youth than like those of parents. A widely held assumption is that the family, and particularly parents, is so central to the primary socialization of children that it can be taken for granted that children's values and parent's values are alike, similar, or at least positively related. Yet, in line with earlier findings, Les Whitbeck and Viktor Gecas show a poor correlation between the actual values of parents and children.[17] More strongly correlated were parents' personal values and the values they were attempting to socialize in their children as well as the children's personal values and their perception of their parents' socialization values. But there were considerable differences between parents and children with regard to the values they respectively held. Each assumed much greater congruence between their own values and those of the other family members than in fact existed.

Peers as a source of reference may also help us understand that behavior defined as deviant by parents may be given social approval by peers. Using drugs or alcohol, engaging in sexual intercourse, dating interracially, espousing political liberalism, and the like may be conforming behavior to peers. The antisocial behavior of adolescents, as viewed by parents, may simply mean that the adolescent is "in step with a different drummer" (peers).

In Chapter 10, a reference group framework was used to explain an increase in personal sexual permissiveness when the behavior of friends was viewed as permissive. Wilbur Bock and others[18] use reference group theory to explain the anomaly that exists between sexual morality, socioeconomic status, and religiosity. SES and religiosity are related to each other yet SES is related to liberal sexual attitudes and religiosity is related to conservative sexual attitudes. Specifications of reference group theory help to pinpoint the conditions under which particular choices are made. Thus, reference groups serve as sources of comparison, decision making, and as influential sources of behavioral and attitudinal change for children, youths, and adults.

---

17. Les B. Whitbeck and Viktor Gecas, "Value Attributions and Value Transmission between Parents and Children," *Journal of Marriage and the Family* 50 (August 1988): 829–840.

18. E. Wilbur Bock, Leonard Beeghley, and Anthony J. Mixon, "Religion, Socioeconomic Status, and Sexual Morality: An Application of Reference Group Theory," *The Sociological Quarterly* 24 (Autumn 1983): 545–559.

*Socialization stages and interaction processes*    The importance of the early years cannot be denied. Very early experiences provide the infant with his or her first sense of self, other persons, and social relationships. It is usually the mother who becomes the first, primary, and most significant other. But rather than specific priorities such as breast or bottle feeding, or toilet training early or late, the significant dimensions in the socialization process become attention, love, and warmth, or their absence. More important, the nature of the social relationships with mother and others influences the image that the infant or child has of himself or herself. Scolding, slapping, pampering, or praising may not be crucial per se, but their repetitive nature leads to the internalization of a sense of self-worth and an image of one's self. Although mother is crucial in the development of these images, so are father, siblings, other kin, and friends. Although mother carries out most of the infant care functions, the socialization experiences of most infants include interaction with other members of the nuclear family, extended family, and others. Since relationships with different persons signify statuses and roles in relation to kin, each provides a unique and different contribution to the socialization process.

In the development of the self, Mead postulated that children go through three continuous stages of observation: preparatory, play, and game.[19] In the *preparatory stage*, children do not have the ability to view their own behavior. Actions of others are imitated. As described under the learning frame of reference and also under the interaction frame of reference, certain sounds like "da-da-da" bring attention and a response from others. This operant conditioning leads the child to repeat and learn the sounds.

The second stage, overlapping with and continuing the preparatory stage, is the *play stage*. At this point, children take roles of others, that is, they play at being the others whom they observe. They may sweep the floor, put on their hat, and pretend to read a book. Elkin and Handel described a four-year-old "playing daddy" who put on his hat and coat, said "goodbye," and walked out the front door only to return a few minutes later because he did not know what to do next.[20]

Later, children enter the *game stage*. At this point, they do not merely play or take the role of another; they now participate in games involving an organization of roles, involving the development of the self. At this point they have to recognize the expected behavior of everyone else. This involves a process of responding to the expectations of several other people at the same time. This is termed the **generalized other.** In Mead's famous example of the baseball game, the child

---

19. Mead, *Mind, Self and Society*, p. 150. For a comparison of Piaget and Mead regarding play and games, *see* Norma K. Denzin, "Play, Games and Interaction: The Contexts of Childhood Socialization," *The Sociological Quarterly* 16 (Autumn 1975): 458–478.

20. Elkin and Handel, *The Child and Society*, p. 57.

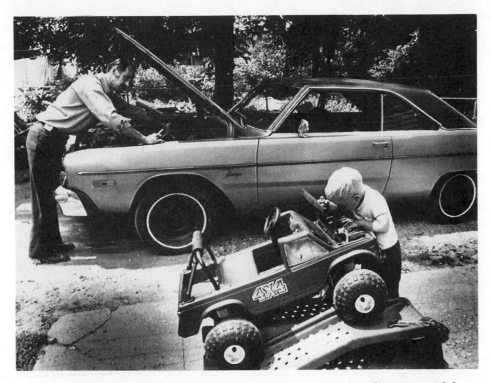

*Like father, like son. Mead postulated that in the process of socialization to adulthood, children go through a play stage where they take the role of others by "playing" or imitating others whom they observe.*

must have the responses of each position involved in his own position. He must know what everyone else is going to do in order to carry out his own play. He has to take all of these roles. They do not all have to be present in consciousness at the same time, but at some moments he has to have three or four individuals present in his own attitude, such as the one who is going to throw the ball, the one who is going to catch it, and so on. These responses must be, in some degree, present in his own makeup.[21]

The concept of "generalized other" enables us to understand how given individuals may be consistent in their behavior even though they move in varying social environments. We learn to see ourselves from the standpoint of multiple others who are either physically or symbolically present.

In light of this perspective of socialization, it should be recognized that any behavior results less from drives or needs, less from unconscious

---

21. Mead, *Mind, Self and Society*, p. 151.

## What do children fear most?

As reported in the *New York Times* (March 17, 1988), the thing that children fear the most is that of being humiliated and incidents that make them seem "bad." Among their biggest concerns are being caught stealing or being sent to the principal's office.

Dr. Kaoru Yamamoto at the University of Colorado has done research on children's perceptions of stress in six countries: the United States, Australia, Canada, Egypt, Japan, and the Philippines. He found that children share similar fears and concerns, even across national boundaries. In general, these concerns pointed to the prominence of school life and peer opinions in their world. His findings suggest that many seemingly trivial moments in a child's life, such as being sent to the principal, may loom among the more daunting, and that parents, teachers, and even child counselors are likely to miss their emotional import for the child.

From the children's point of view, the possibility of a parent's death was a haunting one. Also rated high was a fear of going blind. Other particularly troubling events in their view were being kept back a grade, wetting their pants in class, or seeing their parents fight. One of the sharpest differences between adults and children was in how traumatic they felt it was for a child to have a new sibling. Both clinical wisdom and most children's therapists rate a new baby in the family as one of the most stressful events in a child's life. The children, however, rated having a new brother or sister as the least troublesome of twenty listed events.

processes, and less from biological or innate characteristics than from interaction processes and internalized meanings of self and others. As a result, the behavior appropriate to whites or blacks, royalty or outcasts, Jews or gentiles, or males or females is dependent less upon skin color, genital makeup, or biological facts than upon the internalized meanings and definitions that result from interaction with others. These interactions, viewed in their broadest context, include schools, peers, the mass media, and all involvement of daily living.

Now the concern over latchkey children, day care centers, neglected or abused children, foster children, and the extensive violence portrayed on television can be viewed in a different light and be more fully understood. Traditional norms continue to relegate child care responsibility and childrearing to women and mothers.[22] But with the changes taking place in society in the roles of men and women, the increasing proportion of mothers in the paid labor force, ad infinitum, there seems to be a weakening link between marriage and the care of children.[23] Perhaps research becomes more important than at

---

22. For an excellent overview of child care, the role of women in it, and social responses to the child care dilemma, *see:* Greer Litton Fox and Jan Allen, "Child Care," in Josefina Figueira-McDonough and Rosemary Sarri, (eds.), *The Trapped Woman: Catch 22 in Deviance and Control* (Newbury Park: Sage Publications, Inc., 1987), Chapter 5, pp. 112–142.

23. Andrew J. Cherlin, "The Weakening Link Between Marriage and the Care of Children," *Family Planning Perspectives* 20 (November/December 1988): 302–306.

any time in our history in assessing the impact of "parental substitutes" and nontraditional patterns of interaction on the development of children. And these interactions and socializing influences, both within families and external to them, are not only important to infants and preschool children but also continue beyond early childhood, through adolescence and middle age, into old age.

## SOCIALIZATION IN ADOLESCENCE AND AFTER

Most books on socialization, most chapters on child-rearing, and the greatest public interest in both focus generally on the young child. Perhaps this is readily understandable since, to the newborn child, the entire world is new. Even the most common and routine events must be learned. But if socialization is role learning, if socialization refers to learning the ways of a given society and culture, and if socialization means the development of members who are capable of operating in society, then how can anyone argue that socialization is complete after five or six years of life? Particularly in a rapidly changing society such as exists in the United States, persons are newcomers to unfamiliar events almost daily. Without a doubt, early socialization experiences will have a major influence and impact on the type of events and experiences that are acceptable or unacceptable. But socialization is a continuous process, and learning experiences after the early years not only mean incorporating the new but discarding much of the old.

It is a rare society in which the individual can be prepared during childhood for the complex roles he or she will undertake at a later time. This in no way denies the fundamental importance of socialization experiences in the childhood years but only asserts that role learning is a continuous process. The emphasis placed on education at the junior high, high school, and college levels represents formalized attempts at changing adolescents' perceptions about the world in which they live.

Many studies indicate clearly the significance of socialization during the adolescent years.[24] During the teen years, the school and the peer group are powerful and pervading socializing forces. Learning processes similar to those in early childhood are in operation. The adolescent is actively engaging in sex-role identification, learning the norms and expectations of the opposite sex, participating in new and different types of social activities, gaining insights

---

24. Irving Tallman, Ramona Marotz-Baden, and Pablo Pindas, *Adolescent Socialization in Cross-Cultural Perspective* (New York: Academic Press, 1983); Greer Litton Fox, "The Mother–Adolescent Daughter Relationship as a Sexual Socialization Structure: A Research Review," *Family Relations* 29 (January 1980): 21–28; and Lloyd B. Lueptow, "Social Influence, Social Change and Parental Influence in Adolescent Sex-Role Socialization: 1964–1975," *Journal of Marriage and the Family* 42 (February 1980): 93–103.

and skills for the future occupational world, attempting to become emancipated from parents, and developing a new sense of self-reliance.

Socialization does not end at adolescence, but when attention shifts from adolescents, the available research data on adult socialization, even at a descriptive level, are minimal. From age twenty through sixty a mythical assumption seems to be that socialization to new roles, tasks, and activities either doesn't exist or is unnecessary. The social self, it seems, is believed to be relatively stable or even fixed in these adult years, thus, it is not an exciting or vital area for research. This idea seems to change somewhat at retirement with some literature making reference to the need for resocialization to the new life-styles associated with aging and the aged (*see* Chapter 15).

Socialization, whether for young children, adolescents, mid-life adults, or the aged, follows similar interaction processes. The same is true in terms of content: socialization to violence (Chapter 16), sexual socialization (sexualization—Chapter 10), or socialization to gender-sex roles. Our attention turns to this issue of sex-role socialization for the rest of this chapter.

## GENDER IDENTITY AND SEX-ROLE SOCIALIZATION

Confusion often exists over concepts such as sex, sex roles, gender roles, and gender identity. But more precisely, one's sex, irrespective of behavior, refers to a biological condition of being male or female. Sex roles, therefore, refer to the expectations associated with being biologically of one sex or the other. Gender, rather than sex, is the umbrella term that refers to the totality of being male or female, masculine or feminine. Gender roles thus become the expectations associated with being masculine or feminine and may or may not correspond precisely with one's sex. Doesn't he (biological male) act feminine (gender expectation)? is one example of how sex and gender can be differentiated. **Gender identity** refers to the way one defines or perceives oneself in terms of one's sex, as male or female, and as masculine or feminine.

Roles, differentiated both by sex and gender, are discussed frequently throughout this book, particularly those of male-female and husband-wife. Chapter 1 includes a discussion of the issue of marital and gender role differentiation, including the psychological concept of androgyny. Chapter 2 describes various approaches to roles consistent with a structural-functional and an interactional theoretical orientation. Chapter 3 examines differential treatment given to male and female members of kin groups. The entire fourth chapter focused on family and work, particularly the employment of women and male-female roles in the home. Other chapters look at gender-role differences among the Chinese and blacks, in mate selection, in sexual behavior, in marriage, in child rearing, and throughout the life cycle, with a particular focus on sexual differences in mid-life and old age, in crisis, and in remarriage.

## Women are the superior sex

Writing in *The New York Times* (September 19, 1986) Anna Quindlen argues that women are the superior sex. She claims that she can't think of any jobs that women can't do—or for that matter that women don't do, including lawyers, doctors, editors, interior decorators, or garbage slingers.

Reading about sanitation workers convinced her of the inherent superiority of women. That New York City has finally hired women to pick up the garbage seemed to make sense since she feels that a good bit of being a woman consists of picking up garbage. But of particular interest was the male sanitation workers' responses of how women were incapable of doing the job. The comment of one worker was that this wasn't their kind of job since women were designed to do dishes and men were designed to do yard work. This type of comment peeved Ms. Quindlen because personally, not only

has she done dishes, yard work and tossed Hefty bags, but also because she would fight for a laid-off sanitation worker to work, for example, at a gift-wrap counter "even though any woman knows that men are hormonally incapable of wrapping packages or tying bows."

For men to say that women are the superior sex means they are "too wonderful to enter courtrooms, enjoy sex, or worry our minds about money." For Ms. Quindlen to say that women are the superior sex means that "what passes as a terrific man would only be an adequate woman." She expects men to be polite and clean. But from her female friends she expects unconditional love, their ability and willingness to pour their hearts out to her, and even their ability to inform her why the meat thermometer isn't supposed to touch the bone. Who can doubt which sex is superior?

## *Female-male differences*

There is no denying that normatively, attitudinally, behaviorally, and physically, males and females differ.[25] Anthropologists provide clear evidence that in a worldwide perspective, certain activities such as hunting, trapping, herding, and fishing are predominantly the province of men. Other activities such as care of infants and children, grinding grain, carrying water, gathering herbs, and preserving food are predominantly the province of women.

These divisions are found both in the most primitive as well as in the most egalitarian societies. Even in Finland and Sweden where sex roles are deemphasized, wives in the majority of families feed the family, do the cleaning and washing, and serve as primary caretakers for the children.[26] Likewise, in the Israeli kibbutz, which was founded on sex-egalitarian terms, most of the men are in agricultural and industrial roles and most of the women are in service or educational roles. Similar household and child care patterns are said to exist today in the Soviet Union and mainland China (*see* Chapter 5) even though the overwhelming majority of the women are employed outside the home.

---

25. A fascinating accounting of these differences can be found in Cullen Murphy, "Men and Women: A Survey of the Research," *The Wilson Quarterly* 6 (Winter 1982): 63–80.

26. Linda Haas, "Domestic Role Sharing in Sweden," *Journal of Marriage and the Family* 43 (November 1981): 957–967.

Beyond these male-female task differences, who would deny that physical differences exist between males and females? Probably no one. But who among us would argue that differences in the behavior of males and females are rooted in the genes, in the innate, in the hormones, in the biological, or in the anatomy? Probably some would, others wouldn't be so sure, and still others would deny it forcefully. Maybe all three groups are partially correct. For centuries, it was assumed that male-female differences in behavior were inborn or "natural." Females had "maternal instincts" and were submissive; males were aggressive and dominant. More recently, certain social scientists—particularly anthropologists who discovered societies where men are passive and women domineering—have questioned any relevance of biological factors in behavior. They have argued that all behavior is learned. While I tend to lean more toward the latter position, the most accurate answer probably lies between the two positions and is far more complex than suggested by a nature-nurture, biology-culture argument.[27]

It had been argued (and tested) that irrespective of the extent of *actual* inborn differences between the sexes, a belief that they are innate provides a major ideological justification for a system of stratification by sex. Since men and husbands are in the advantaged power position, it could be expected that they would believe in innate, inborn sex roles more than women and wives. This was found to be true. Within a marriage however, disagreement about the origin of sex roles was reduced by the mutual influence of husband's and wife's beliefs on each other, resulting in higher similar beliefs.[28]

The biological argument is deeply rooted in a number of theories of socialization, including the psychoanalytic frame of reference discussed earlier in this chapter. It is further enhanced by research into hormones (such as progesterone and estrogen secreted by the ovaries in females and testosterone and the androgens secreted by the testes in males) that initiate sexual differentiation in the fetus and later at puberty activate the reproductive system and the development of secondary sex characteristics. Research has shown that if a female fetus is given testosterone, she will develop male-like genitalia. If a male is castrated (testes removed) prior to puberty, he will not develop secondary sex characteristics such as a beard. But do these chemical substances known generally as hormones determine or predict behavior?

The strength of cultural factors is overwhelming in our understanding of gender identity and sex-role socialization. One prime example comes from cross-cultural data that have shown great diversity in the attitudes, values, and behavior of both men and women. Margaret Mead's classic study of three primitive tribes in New Guinea found both men and women among the

---

27. *See*, for example, Lois Wladis Hoffman, "The Changing Genetics/Socialization Balance," *Journal of Social Issues* 41 (1985): 127–148.

28. John Mirowsky and Catherine E. Ross, "Belief in Innate Sex Roles: Sex Stratification versus Interpersonal Influence in Marriage," *Journal of Marriage and the Family* 49 (August 1987): 527–540.

Arapesh to be cooperative, mild-mannered, gentle, and unaggressive (sex-typed feminine behavior). Among the Mundugumor, both men and women were hostile, aggressive, combative, individualistic, and unresponsive (sex-typed masculine behavior). Among the Tchambuli, the typical sex roles found in the Western cultures were reversed: women were dominant, powerful, and impersonal; men were emotionally dependent and less responsible.[29] If it can be assumed that the biological makeup and hormonal balance of men and women in these tribes and men and women in the Western world are similar, then how is the difference explained? It is not necessary to go to New Guinea in the 1930s to note the strength of cultural factors in gender differences and sex-role socialization. Data from Utah in the 1980s, for example, show that the attitudes toward appropriate roles for men and women are strongly affected by religious affiliation.[30]

Another, and even more convincing, line of research comes from studies of hermaphrodites, persons who possess complete sets of both male and female genitalia and reproductive organs. Infants who were assigned one sex at birth and were later found to belong biologically to the opposite sex, behaved as they were assigned and taught. Biological females, defined and reared as males, grew up developing fantasies typical of males, enjoyed sports assigned generally to males, fell in love with girls, and the like. Biological males, defined and reared as females, had the "maternal instinct," preferred marriage over a career, and were oriented toward dolls and domestic tasks.[31] Thus, when socialization contradicts the biological, hormonal, or genetic, the learned and interactional experiences prove to be powerful determinants of current gender roles (*see* "Brother Becomes Sister" panel).

## Sex-role socialization

Socialization to sex (female-male) and gender roles follows basic socialization processes described earlier in this chapter. Gender role socialization begins at birth and continues throughout one's lifetime.[32] As Lenore Weitzman indicated, "from the minute a newborn baby girl is wrapped in a pink blanket and her brother in a blue one, the two children are treated differently."[33] From that point on, socialization as to appropriate roles for males and females

---

29. Margaret Mead, *Sex and Temperament in Three Primitive Societies* (New York: Mentor, 1950). Originally published in 1935 by Morrow.

30. Moshe Hartman and Harriet Hartman, "Sex Role Attitudes for Mormons and Non-Mormons in Utah," *Journal of Marriage and the Family* 45 (November 1983): 897–902.

31. John Money, *Sex Research: New Developments* (New York: Holt, Rinehart and Winston, 1965). *See also* John Money, "Sex Assignment in Anatomically Intersexed Infants," in M. A. Watson, ed., *Readings in Sexology* (Dubuque, Ia.: Kendall/Hunt, 1984).

32. Peter I. Rose, ed., *Socialization and the Life Cycle* (New York: St. Martin's Press, 1979); and Rhoda E. Estep, Martha R. Burt, and Herman J. Milligan, "The Socialization of Sexual Identity," *Journal of Marriage and the Family* 39 (February 1977): 99–112.

33. Lenore J. Weitzman, *Sex-Role Socialization* (Palo Alto, Cal.: Mayfield Publishing Co., 1979): 1.

## Brother becomes sister: The alteration of masculine-feminine behavior

A young rural couple took their identical twin boys to a physician to be circumcised. During the first operation, performed with an electric cauterizing needle, a surge of current burned off the baby's penis. Desperate for a way to cope with this tragedy, the parents took the advice of sex experts: "Bring the baby up as a girl." The experiment has apparently succeeded. Aided by plastic surgery and reared as a daughter, the once normal baby boy has grown into a nine-year-old child who is psychologically, at least, a girl.

This dramatic case, cited by Medical Psychologist John Money at the Washington meeting of the American Association for the Advancement of Science, provides strong support for a major contention of women's liberationists: that conventional patterns of masculine and feminine behavior can be altered. It also casts doubt on the theory that major sexual differences, psychological as well as anatomical, are immutably set by the genes at conception. In fact, says Money, there are only four imperative differences: women menstruate, gestate, and lactate; men impregnate. Many scientists believe that crucial psychological imperatives follow from these biological facts, limiting the flexibility of sexual

roles. Money, however, is convinced that almost all differences are culturally determined and therefore optional. The Johns Hopkins psychologist further spells out his views on sex-role learning in a book titled: *Man & Woman, Boy & Girl.*

In the normal process of sexual differentiation, Money explains, if the genes order the gonads to become testes and to produce androgen, the embryo develops as a boy; otherwise it becomes a girl. Androgen not only shapes the external genitals but also "programs" parts of the brain, so that some types of behavior may come more naturally to one sex than to the other. For instance, both men and women can mother children—the necessary circuits are there in every brain—but the "threshold" for releasing this behavior is higher in males than in females. The same phenomenon is demonstrated by laboratory animals. If a mature female rat is put into a cage with newborn rats, she begins mothering them at once. In a similar situation, a male rat does nothing at first, but after a few days he too begins to display maternal behavior.

Money believes that hormones secreted before and after birth have less effect on brain and behavior

---

constitutes one of life's most important learning experiences. In interaction with others, in words, deeds, films, and books, the child is taught what behavior is appropriate for each sex.[34] As one writer indicated:

> We throw boy babies up in the air and roughhouse with them. We coo over girl babies and handle them delicately. We choose sex-related colors and toys for our children from their earliest days. We encourage the energy and physical activity of our sons, just as we expect girls to be quieter and more docile. We love both our sons and daughters with equal fervor, we protest, and yet we are disappointed when there is no male child to carry on the family name.[35]

In regard to relative status, boys are more highly valued than girls. In regard to personality differences, most boys are active and achieving whereas most girls are passive and emotional.

---

34. Spencer E. Cahill, "Reexamining the Acquisition of Sex Roles: A Social Interactionist Approach," *Sex Roles* 9 (March 1983): 1–15.

35. Florence Howe, "Sexual Stereotypes Start Early," *Saturday Review* (October 16, 1971): 76.

in human beings than the "sex assignment" that takes place at birth with the announcement: "It's a boy!" or "It's a girl!" This exultant cry tells everyone how to treat the newborn baby, and sets off a chain of events, beginning with the choice of a male or female name, that largely determines whether the child will behave in traditionally masculine or feminine ways.

Money's evidence for this familiar thesis comes largely from cases in which accidents before or after birth made it impossible to raise children according to their genetically determined sex. In each of his examples, youngsters learned to feel, look, and act like members of the opposite sex.

For the little boy who lost his penis, the change began at 17 months with a girl's name and frilly clothes. An operation to make the child's genitals look more feminine was done, and plans were made to build a vagina and administer estrogen at a later age. The parents, counseled at the Johns Hopkins psychohormonal research unit, began to treat the child as if he were a girl. The effects of the parents' changed attitude and behavior were marked. "She doesn't like to be dirty," the mother told the clinic in one of her periodic reports. "My son is quite different. I can't wash his face for anything. She seems to be daintier. Maybe it's because I encourage it. She is very proud of herself when she puts on a new dress, and she just loves to have her hair set."

The experience of two hermaphrodites, from different families, further bolsters Money's view. Each was born with the female chromosome pattern, and each had internal female organs but a penis and empty scrotum outside. One set of parents believed they had a boy and raised their child accordingly; the other set assigned their offspring as a girl. (Surgery and hormones made the youngsters' appearance conform to the chosen sex.) According to Money, the children's "antithetical experiences signified to one that he was a boy and to the other that she was a girl." The girl therefore reached preadolescence expecting to marry a man; in fact, she already had a steady boy friend. The boy, by contrast, had a girl friend and "fitted easily into the stereotype of the male role in marriage," even though "he and his partner would both have two X chromosomes."

*Source: Time Magazine*, January 8, 1973, p. 34. Reprinted by permission from TIME, The Weekly Newsmagazine. Copyright Time Inc.

Lenore Weitzman and others concentrated on one aspect of sex-role socialization: the socialization of preschool children through picture books.[36] They chose eighteen children's books identified as "the very best": the winners of the Caldecott medal, given by the Children's Service Committee of the American Library Association for the most distinguished picture book of the year. Their analysis was concentrated on winners and runners-up for a period of five years. To ensure representativeness of the study, the authors examined three other groups of children's books: the Newbery Award winners, the Little Golden Books, and the "prescribed behavior or etiquette books." Their findings make interesting reading. They noted that it would be impossible to discuss the image of females in children's books without first noting that, in fact, women are simply invisible. They found females underrepresented in the titles, central roles, pictures, and stories in every sample of books examined.

36. Lenore J. Weitzman, Deborah Eitler, Elizabeth Hokada, and Catherine Ross, "Sex-Role Socialization in Picture Books for Preschool Children," *American Journal of Sociology* 77 (May 1972): 1125–1150.

*From birth, girls are taught to be feminine and boys are taught to be masculine. But they have to be "carefully taught" or boys will mother and girls will play football and fix cars.*

Most children's books were about boys, men, and male animals, and most dealt exclusively with male adventures. Where there were female characters, they were usually insignificant or inconspicuous.

What were the activities of boys and girls in the world of picture books? Weitzman et al. found that not only were boys presented in more exciting and adventuresome roles, but also they engaged in more varied pursuits and demanded more independence.[37] In contrast, most of the girls in the picture books were passive and immobile. Girls were more often found indoors than were boys. The girls in the stories played traditional feminine roles directed toward pleasing and helping their brothers and fathers.

Most books clearly implied that women cannot exist without men. That is, the role of most of the girls was defined primarily in relation to that of the boys and men in their lives and was not defined primarily in relation to girls working or playing together.

What about adult role models? Weitzman's study found the image of the adult women to be stereotyped and limited.[38] Again, the females were passive

---

37.  Ibid., pp. 1131–1138.
38.  Ibid., pp. 1139–1144.

## Sex-role differentiation and the draft

How far should we carry the idea that no sex or sex-role differentiation should exist? We don't have to search long for contemporary issues that confront this question. For example, take the issue of draft registration or the draft itself. Assuming a draft registration is necessary (which many youths have difficulty doing), are there biological, psychological, or social grounds on which to logically include one sex and not the other? Should men be included but not women? Should husbands be included but not wives? Should fathers be included but not mothers?

In July 1980, draft registration for men was revived. All 19- and 20-year-old men were required to register at their local post offices. Failure to register was considered a felony punishable by up to five years in prison and a $10,000 fine. Immediately the American Civil Liberties Union sued to block the plan, alleging sex discrimination.

The ACLU charge was that it is unconstitutional to register men and not women. The suit said that solely because they are not female, the plaintiffs, all men, are burdened with the requirement of registering for the draft. Imposition of this burden on men while exempting women denies men equal protection under the law.

---

while the males were active. Men predominated the outside activities and women the inside ones. While inside, the women almost exclusively performed service functions, taking care of the men and children in their families. When men lead, women follow. When men rescue others, women are the rescued.

One interesting finding of particular significance for this chapter was that not one woman in the Caldecott sample had a job or profession. Motherhood was presented in the picture books as a full-time, lifetime job, despite the reality that about 90 percent of the women in this country will be in the labor force at sometime in their lives and that the average woman has completed the main portion of her child rearing by her mid-thirties. Most of the stories portrayed the woman as a mother or a wife, although she also played the role of fairy, fairy godmother, or underwater maiden. The roles that men played were highly varied: storekeepers, housebuilders, kings, spiders, storytellers, gods, monks, fighters, fishermen, policemen, soldiers, adventurers, fathers, cooks, preachers, judges, and farmers.[39]

You may note that these findings by Lenore Weitzman and others were published in 1972, and understandably predict that with the women's movement and the heightened awareness of sex stereotyping and the changing roles of women, children's books have changed since then. But have they?

About ten years later, a study attempted to replicate the Weitzman study and found that the number of books containing stories about females had not changed much, although the rates of male to female pictures (human and

---

39. Ibid., pp. 1140–1141.

nonhuman) had changed.[40] Female characters continued to be cast as passive and dependent and to be placed in traditional nonsignificant and stereotyped roles. The activities engaged in by females continued to consist of service and helping roles. Women continued to be portrayed as engaged in indoor ventures. The stereotyping was as evident in female-authored as it was in male-authored books, suggesting that female writers are not changing the status quo.

If it is assumed that children's books are one influential factor in the sex-role socialization of children and do influence children's attitudes and behavior, we can predict a continuation of sex-role stereotyping in this and the future decades. This is particularly true when it is recognized that these sex-typed portrayals are not confined to children's books or the preschool years. Throughout the school years, the educational system tends to stereotype males and females. Textbooks, achievement tests, athletic emphases, vocational counseling, and parental and peer pressures all tend to reinforce stereotypical expectations and behaviors. Beyond the school, the mass media, the religious and work worlds, and most of our social institutions tend quite consistently to put men in selected occupations, to put women in others, and to stress "appropriate" behavior for women that is not identical to that stressed for men.

In the socialization of males and females, empirical evidence suggests a continuation of sex-role stereotyping and gender segregation in spite of tremendous shifts in sex-role attitudes.[41] Current conceptions of femaleness and maleness have marked similarities to earlier conceptions. A contemporary view of men as aggressive, work minded, and capable of leadership resembles characteristics similar to those attributed to men in earlier research. Current conceptions of femaleness as stressing sensitivity, affection, and consciousness of appearance are also similar to earlier stereotypes of women.[42] Socialization to sex-gender roles, in spite of shifts in attitudes, continues to emphasize a differentiation between males and females, with a heavy concentration on the perpetuation of traditional expectations and behaviors for each sex.

# SUMMARY

1. The central concept in dealing with parent-child relationships is socialization— the process by which the infant and adult learn the ways of a given society and

---

40. Richard Kolbe and Joseph C. LaVoie, "Sex-Role Stereotyping in Preschool Children's Picture Books," *Social Psychology Quarterly* 44 (December 1981): 369–374.

41. Barrie Thorne and Zella Luria, "Sexuality and Gender in Children's Daily Worlds," *Social Problems* 33 (February 1986): 176–190; Andrew Cherlin and Pamela Barnhause Walters, "Trends in United States Men's and Women's Sex-Role Attitudes: 1972 to 1978," *American Sociological Review* 46 (August 1981); 453–460; and Raymond J. Adamek and Mike Miller, "Changes in Coeds' Sex Role Concepts: 1969 and 1980," *Sociological Spectrum* 4 (1984): 71–87.

42. Patricia A. Smith and Elizabeth Midlarsky, *Sex Roles* 12 (1985): 313–328.

culture and develop into participants capable of operating in that society. Socialization of the young infant may be the single universal function of the family. Preconditions for socialization include biological inheritance and an ongoing society.

2. Several frames of reference were examined to explain various aspects of socialization: a learning-behaviorist theory, a psychoanalytic theory, two theories of child development, and a symbolic interactionist theory. Learning or reinforcement theory assumes that the same concepts and principles that apply to lower animal forms apply to humans. The conditioning processes may be classical or operant. The former links a response to a known stimulus, the latter links a response of the consequence produced by the response. Child-rearing and socialization processes result from conditioning and positive or negative reinforcements.

3. Classic psychoanalytic theory contrasts sharply with the behaviorist theory. Internal drives and unconscious processes are of central importance. Socialization takes place according to precise, though overlapping, stages of development. These include the oral, anal, and phallic stages, followed later by a period of latency and a genital phase. What happens in these early stages from birth to age five or six, although unconscious, becomes relatively fixed and permanent, serving as the basis for responses in later life.

4. Child development theories focus on the individual and the manner in which motor skills, thought, and reasoning develop. Erikson described eight stages of human development, each constituting a crisis brought on by changing social situations as the individual moves from infancy through old age. Piaget focused more on the cognitive development of the child and described four major stages of intellectual development.

5. Symbolic interaction theory contrasts considerably with the theories already described. Infants, who are not born social, develop through interaction with other persons. As interaction occurs, meanings are internalized and organized and the self develops. The social self enables a person to consciously and purposively represent to him- or herself what he or she wishes to represent to others.

6. A social being can take the role of others, can interpret and define, and can have and use symbols. In interaction with others, the child learns to define him- or herself and the world in certain ways. These definitions and meanings in turn predispose him or her to behave in ways consistent with these self-concepts. Interaction, the social self, significant others, reference groups, and the generalized other are concepts basic to the socialization process.

7. Socialization does not end at any given age, but is a lifelong process. For teens, school and peer groups serve as important sources of reference, interaction, and identity. Minimal research exists on adult socialization with an increased amount focusing on resocialization for the elderly.

8. Gender identity and gender roles refer to one's identity and the expectations associated with being masculine or feminine. Male-female and masculine-feminine differences are universal. Debate continues over the extent to which sex and gender roles have their roots in biology, culture, or a combination of the two.

9. Sex role socialization follows the principles of any type of socialization. In interaction with others, children learn about gender-sex roles very early in their lives. This is heavily reinforced in schools, particularly through childrens' books. While some change in sex role attitudes has taken place, current conceptions of femaleness and maleness fit earlier stereotypes and highly traditional expectations.

10. The previous chapter on the parental system and this one on parent-child interaction follow a life course sequence that generally, but not always, follows marriage. The next chapter continues this time sequence by turning to families in the middle and later years.

## KEY TERMS AND TOPICS

## DISCUSSION QUESTIONS

1. Discuss ways in which parents need to be socialized. What role does the infant play in this process?
2. Review the preconditions for adequate socialization. What would happen if either of them were absent? Would socialization be possible? Why or why not?
3. What do you perceive to be the most important factors in producing stable, healthy adults?
4. Contrast the learning-behaviorist, the psychoanalytic, the child development, and the symbolic interaction frames of reference in regard to socialization. What are the contributions each makes? What are some of the drawbacks of each?
5. Take a pencil and paper to a nearby park, a preschool setting, or somewhere where you can observe the interaction between adults (preferably a parent) and children. Record what is said and done for a five- or ten-minute period. What inferences can you draw about social class, language patterns, childrearing practices, discipline, and the like?
6. Interview three mothers or fathers of preschool children. Find out whether the arrival of their first child was a crisis; whether they toilet-trained their babies early, breast-fed or bottle-fed them, etc., and whether they believe it

makes any difference; what means of punishment they use; what role the father plays in child-rearing; how other children assist or hinder the socialization process; and so forth.

7. In what ways and areas are you being socialized? To what extent are you a victim of early childhood experiences, a father-absent family, a lower-class background, or a home with marital conflict? When will you be "fully" socialized?
8. What influence did early adolescence, dating, friendship relationships, siblings, or teenage experiences have on your personality? To what extent is your personality today a product of your early, as opposed to more recent, socialization experiences?
9. Is a marriage with no sex or gender role differentiation (androgyny) possible? Explain and give examples.
10. To what extent does your biological sex determine your behavior? Do you believe that you could be socialized to think and act like the opposite sex?
11. In spite of women's movements, an increasing number of women entering the paid work force, decreasing family size, and so forth, why do school materials, the mass media, the work world, etc. continue to differentiate and segregate people by sex?

# *FURTHER READINGS*

Balswick, Jack. *The Inexpressive Male.* Lexington, Ma.: Lexington Books, 1988. An extensive investigation of expressiveness in men covering theoretical explanations, role types, gender differences, marriage, and friends.

Belsky, Jay; Lerner, Richard M.; and Spanier, Graham B. *The Child in the Family.* Reading, Mass.: Addison-Wesley Publishing Company, 1984. A life-span and ecological perspective of the reciprocal relations between infant, child, and adolescent development and changes in the family.

Davis, Kingsley. "The Sociology of Parent-Child Conflict." *American Sociological Review* 5 (August 1940): 523–535. Although published several decades ago, this classic paper on parent-child conflict is still widely reprinted today.

Elkin, Frederick, and Handel, Gerald. *The Child and Society: The Process of Socialization.* 5th ed. New York: Random House, 1989. A coherent treatment, from a sociological standpoint, of how children are socialized in modern society.

Epstein, Cynthia Fuchs. *Deceptive Distinctions: Sex, Gender, and the Social Order.* New Haven, Ct.: Yale University Press, 1988. Deceptive distinctions reveal how differences between the sexes, widely believed to be inherent, are largely the social products of a sexist society.

Eshleman, J. Ross, and Clarke, Juanne N. *Intimacy, Commitments, and Marriage: Development of Relationships.* Boston: Allyn and Bacon, 1978. Part II—"Becoming a Human Being"—includes chapters on gender identity and development, sex-role socialization, and socialization and child-rearing patterns.

Kimmel, Michael S. (ed). *Changing Men: New Directions in Research on Men and Masculinity.* Newbury Park, Ca.: Sage Publications, Inc., 1987. Contributions in this volume deal with issues such as reformulating the male role, men in domestic settings, men/women relationships, sexuality, race and gender, and future directions for men's studies.

Lewis, Robert A., and Salt, Robert E., eds. *Men in Families.* Beverly Hills: Sage Publications, 1986. A collection of sixteen writings, several of which deal with men's involvement as fathers and socializing agents.

Peterson, Gary W. and Rollins, Boyd C. "Parent-Child Socialization" in *Handbook of Marriage and the Family* by Marvin B. Sussman and Suzanne K. Steinmetz (eds.), New York: Plenum Press, 1987, Chapter 18, pp. 471–507. A review and integration of the social mold, bidirectional, and systemic literatures within the parent-child area.

Robinson, Bryan E.; Rowland, Bobby H.; and Coleman, Mike. *Latchkey Kids: Unlocking Doors for the Children and Their Families.* Lexington, Mass.: Lexington Books, 1986. An exploration of children ages five to thirteen, involved in self-care before and after school.

Rossi, Alice A. *Gender and the Life Course.* Hawthorne, N.Y.: Aldine Pub. Co., 1985. An interdisciplinary collection of original essays on the lives of men and women as they are affected by processes that attend maturation and aging.

Tallman, Irving; Marotz-Baden, Ramona; and Pindas, Pablo. *Adolescent Socialization in Cross-Cultural Perspective.* New York: Academic Press, 1983. The authors provide a theory of socialization and an empirical examination of how families and adolescents in Mexico and the United States deal with the social changes in their countries.

Weitzman, Lenore J. *Sex Role Socialization.* Palo Alto, Cal.: Mayfield Publishing, 1979. A brief, easy-reading paperback covering socialization to sex roles from early childhood through the school and college years, with a concluding chapter on where socialization fails to help women to achieve.

# CHAPTER FIFTEEN

# MARRIAGES AND FAMILIES IN THE MIDDLE AND LATER YEARS

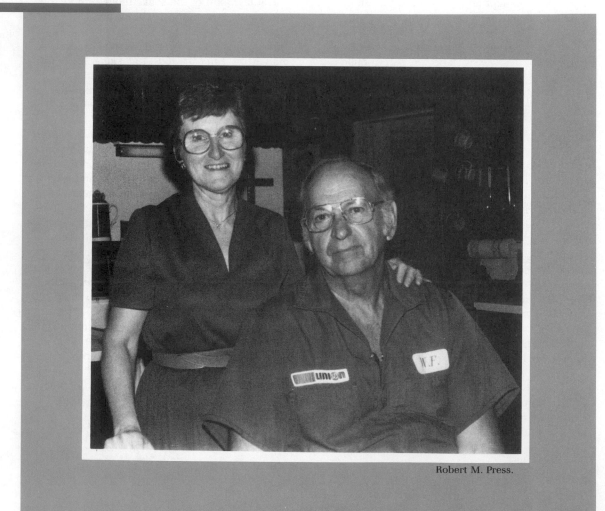

Robert M. Press.

Chapters 13 and 14 examined some selected aspects of families with children. But marriage and family life do not end when children enter adolescence or, in later adolescence, when the children leave home for marriage, employment, school, or some other reason. Family structure, interactions, and life-styles change considerably at this period of the family life cycle: the second half. A prime example of this change was shown in Chapter 12 in dealing with marital satisfaction over the life cycle. Studies indicated a process of disenchantment and a decrease in satisfaction at this time, followed by increases in the later years.

It is the intent of this chapter to examine two major periods in the life course: the middle years from approximately age forty to retirement and the later years from approximately age sixty or sixty-five. This includes general descriptions of families at these periods plus a consideration of grandparents, retirement, socialization of the aged, and social conditions and problems surrounding the aged.

## THE POSTPARENTAL PERIOD: THE MIDDLE YEARS

In order to capture the experience of the period after children leave home, a number of phases have been used. Among these are the *stage of the empty nest*, the *launching stage*, the period of *contracting family size*, and the term used here, the **postparental.** Technically, the term postparental is a misnomer, for parents do not stop being parents or become ex-parents. Postparental suggests that the children are now legally and socially recognized as adults and assume a greater independence from their parents and greater personal autonomy and responsibility. While the "launching" stage entails periods of child "reentry" into the parental home for many families, it involves the return of the conjugal family to a two-person, married-couple household and many nuclear one-parent units to a one-person household. The periods of family life from this point until the death of one or both parents can be classified as: (1) families launching their oldest children: ages forty-five to fifty-four; (2) families of preretirement: ages fifty-five to sixty-four; (3) the "young-old" retired families: ages sixty-five to seventy-four; and (4) the "old-old" families in the later years: age seventy-five and after. This section examines families in the middle years as they launch their children and approach retirement, the age period of approximately forty-five to sixty-five.

### Marital status and the length of the middle years

In 1988, of those persons in this age period, about 80 percent of the men and 70 percent of the women were married (*see* Table 15–1). Compared with other age categories, the percentage married is high with relatively low percentages of single, separated, widowed, or divorced. For women, the percentage who

*Table 15–1*

**Marital status of men and women, ages 45–64, March 1988, (percentage distribution)**

| Marital status | Age of men | | Age of women | |
|---|---|---|---|---|
| | 45–54 | 55–64 | 45–54 | 55–64 |
| Single | 5.6% | 4.9% | 5.1% | 4.9% |
| Married | 79.6 | 81.7 | 71.6 | 67.3 |
| Separated | 3.7 | 2.8 | 4.5 | 3.4 |
| Widowed | 1.3 | 3.7 | 5.9 | 16.7 |
| Divorced | 9.8 | 6.9 | 12.9 | 8.6 |
| Total | 100.0 | 100.0 | 100.0 | 100.0 |

*Source:* U.S. Bureau of the Census, *Current Population Reports*, Series P-20, no. 433, "Marital Status and Living Arrangements, March 1988" (Washington, D.C.: U.S. Government Printing Office, 1989), Table 1, p.3.

are widowed begins to climb sharply at ten-year intervals after age fifty-four. The figures change from 6 percent (ages forty-five to fifty-four) to 17 percent (ages fifty-five to sixty-four), to 36 percent (ages sixty-five to seventy-four), to 66 percent (age seventy-five and over).[1]

The period after the children leave home lasts longer than any other stage in the marital life cycle. Interestingly, this factor is unique to the twentieth century. At the turn of the century, men married at age twenty-six, had their last child at age thirty-six, saw their last child marry at age fifty-nine, but lost their spouses at age fifty-seven. Women married at age twenty-two, had their last child at thirty-two, saw their last child married at fifty-five, and lost their spouses at fifty-three.[2] The result for both sexes was no postparental period, since the typical or average couple survived two years short of the time their last child (which on the average was their fifth) was expected to marry.

In contrast, today both sexes marry in their early or mid-twenties, have their last child in their late twenties or early thirties, see their last child launched in their mid-to-late forties, but do not lose their spouse until the early or mid-seventies. The result is a postparental period of twenty to twenty-five years. Although marriage occurs at a similar age, children are fewer in number and parents gain an earlier release from child rearing. These factors, combined with a longer life expectancy for both sexes, give the average couple several decades together prior to retirement or the death of one spouse.

There are, of course, many exceptions to parents gaining an early release from child rearing. Recent demographic indicators show that more young

---

1. The first two figures are taken from Table 15–1. The last two are taken from Table 15–3 presented later in the chapter.

2. Figures taken from Paul C. Glick, "The Life Cycle of the Family," *Marriage and Family Living* 17 (1955): 3–9.

adults now than a few years ago are residing with their parents.[3] Most young adults leave their parental homes during their late teens or early twenties, some linger while they continue schooling or hold jobs, while others return to their parents following a job loss, a disrupted marriage, unwed motherhood, or when hardships arise.

There are as well many exceptions to a return to the two-person husband-wife family even if all children are "launched." In addition to the return of children, some evidence suggests an increase in extended households due to the taking in of aged parents.[4] Traditionally, the common pattern was adult children moving into the homes of parents. The situation today is usually reversed with the aged parents moving into the home of adult children. The effect of either children or parents returning to the family in the middle years is to modify the nature of the postparental period as one that returns to the two-person marital unit.

## The significance of the middle years

What is the significance of being a quadragenarian (age forty or more but less than fifty)? To many couples, the middle years are the "prime of life." Business and professional men in particular are likely to hold their top positions, women are likely to be in the paid labor force, and family total income is at its peak. For example, in 1987, the mean earnings of married-couple families where the husband was between the ages of forty-five and fifty-four was $44,086 compared to $16,773 for those sixty-five and over and $21,975 for those of ages eighteen to twenty-four.[5]

Debate exists over whether the middle years are depressing and strain-filled or whether they are the prime time as family income data suggest. The one argument suggests that combined with the physical processes and changes, it is the time of pressure to be successful and to "get ahead." For many, "it's now or never." The prestigious position they were going to attain, the book they were going to write, the children they were going to have, or the stardom they were going to achieve may become a reality or may become a dream never to be fulfilled. A man's "handsome ladies' man" image of ten to twenty years earlier may turn into a need to convince himself of his virility. A woman's ability to "make men look twice" and the loss of her reproductive

---

3. Paul C. Glick and Sung-Ling Lin, "More Young Adults are Living with Their Parents: Who are They?" *Journal of Marriage and the Family* 48 (February 1986): 107–112; and David M. Heer, Robert W. Hodge, and Marcus Felson, "The Cluttered Nest: Evidence That Young Adults are More Likely to Live at Home Now Than in the Recent Past," *Sociology and Social Research* 69 (April 1985): 436–441.

4. Scott H. Beck and Rubye W. Beck, "The Formation of Extended Households During Middle Age," *Journal of Marriage and the Family* 46 (May 1984): 227–287.

5. U.S. Bureau of the Census, *Current Population Reports*, Series P-60, no. 165, "Earnings of Married-Couple Families: 1987," (Washington, D.C.: U.S. Government Printing Office, 1989), Table 4, p. 16.

capacity may challenge her self-perception of attractiveness and worth. The expenses of weddings or college and the departure of the child may produce restless nights. This argument suggests, then, that the middle years are rough—physically, socially, and emotionally.

The opposite argument suggests that this is a period of life when things are brightest. Income is highest, leisure time is the greatest, childbearing responsibility is past, and opportunities exist as never before. Which view is correct—or is it possible that both are?

Contrary to their expectations, Farrell and Rosenberg, in comparing 300 men entering middle age to men in their late twenties, did not find evidence for a universal *midlife crisis* or of signs of increased alienation or social disconnection.[6] The exception was among men in the lowest socioeconomic class. Men who were unskilled laborers gave evidence of personal disorganization and psychopathology as they approached middle age. Lower-middle-class men (skilled workers, clerical workers, small businessmen) showed a remarkable ability to ignore, distort, or deny information that challenged their world views. Professionals and middle-class executives exhibited neither denial patterns nor identity problems but reported satisfaction with work, family, and their positions in the community.

Some social scientists refer to a *midlife transition* for men around age forty. This transition may go relatively smoothly or may involve considerable turmoil. The transition to an empty nest for men may or may not be an important factor. For example, the vast majority of fathers do not report distress or unhappiness when they approach an empty nest and their children leave home. Some research does, however, suggest greater distress and unhappiness among fathers when the youngest child leaves home, particularly among farm families.[7] But most research finds that the majority of families, farm or nonfarm, are not affected negatively when their children leave home. A greater stressor may be the unexpected return of a young adult to the home.

What about women? Is the "empty nest" or postparental stage of the family life cycle a traumatic and unhappy period? According to data from six U.S. national surveys, middle-aged women whose children have left home report, as a whole, somewhat greater happiness and enjoyment of life than women of similar age with a child (or children) living at home, and the former also report substantially greater marital happiness than the latter.[8] Thus, the children's leaving home does not typically lead to an enduring decline in the

---

6. Michael P. Farrell and Stanley D. Rosenberg, *Men at Midlife* (Boston: Auburn House, 1981).

7. Robert A. Lewis, Robert J. Volk, and Stephen F. Duncan, "Stresses on Fathers and Family Relationships Related to Rural Youth Leaving and Returning Home," *Family Relations* 38 (April 1989): 174–181; and Pauline Boss, Debra Pearce-McCall, and Jan Greenberg, "Normative Loss in Mid-Life Families: Rural, Urban, and Gender Differences," *Family Relations* 36 (October 1987): 437–443.

8. Norval D. Glenn, "Psychological Well-Being in the Postparental Stage: Some Evidence from National Surveys," *Journal of Marriage and the Family* 37 (February 1975): 105–110.

## Empty nest syndrome must have flown the coop

We can forget all about the empty nest syndrome. What a relief!

The empty nest syndrome was in the news a lot about 10 years ago. It was said to be the inescapable scourge of women in their tragic middle years. Husbands were advised to be especially understanding of and sympathetic to their wives' symptoms. Shrinks everywhere stood ready to help with counsel and advice, at $75 an hour and up.

Empty nest syndrome symptoms were alleged to include depression, restlessness, loss of identity, loss of self-confidence and a general feeling of being worthless. It was awful, worse than menopause. (No one had invented Herpes II yet.)

Women whose children had grown up and left home were supposed to be victims of the syndrome. Without babies to burp, women were supposed to feel they had no useful function. Without kids at home to mess up the kitchen, throw wet towels around the bathroom, or have tomato fights in the garage, women were supposed to become lumps of quivering insecurity.

Some of these suffering women just couldn't stand it and went ahead and got pregnant all over again, at age 45. That's what the magazine articles said. Some of them had nervous breakdowns, got divorces, looked for jobs or otherwise behaved peculiarly. The magazine articles said that, too.

Altogether, the empty nest syndrome was something dreadful, greatly to be feared. I kept looking for symptoms in myself as soon as all my kids were in college. I was still looking when they graduated, when Sue got married, when the boys moved into their own house and apartment. Nothing.

I figured even if I had no immediate symptoms, the empty nest syndrome was only delayed. It would get me. It would strike as soon as I reached my tragic middle years.

I asked local experts, such as my friends, to pinpoint the tragic middle years of a woman's life. They couldn't agree. Men said somewhere around age 27. Women said it was closer to age 82. I developed my own guidelines, based on maturation, not years.

I decided the tragic middle years of a woman's life must occur when . . .

the cellulite spreading in all directions from her thighs finally reaches her dewlap

she can no longer remember the last time she wore a bikini bathing suit, or if she ever wore a bikini bathing suit

she has no interest in frisbee games, beach parties, roller skating, wind surfing, or becoming a Pepper

she thinks Willie Nelson is cute

she gives up saying, "I'll have whatever you have, Darling," to her dinner partners in restaurants, shamelessly puts on her coke bottle glasses, reads the menu, and orders for herself—liver and onions!

There were some other things. Anyway I figured I had just about reached the perigee of my tragic middle years, and I hadn't recognized a single symptom of the empty nest syndrome yet. I was obviously in for it, any day now. Then, deliverance!

I read about a recent survey of more than 200 women, aged 35 to 55. Grace Baruch and Rosalind Barnett, a couple of Wellesley College psychologists, did it. They called these women middle aged, although they didn't mention cellulite or Willie Nelson testing. Anyway, Baruch and Barnett found that 74 percent of the women whose children had grown up and left home were not depressed at all. There was no tragedy in their middle years. In fact, they were relieved, happy, even delighted.

The women said such things as, "I've never felt better," and "I'd never go back to being 20 again!" The researchers found that these women also had greater feelings of self-worth now than they ever had when they were younger with houses full of children to tend.

Baruch and Barnett labeled the empty nest syndrome a cruel myth and hoax. I wouldn't count on such good luck with Herpes II.

*Source:* Nickie McWhirter, *Detroit Free Press,* June 6, 1982, p. C-1. Reprinted with the permission of the Detroit Free Press.

psychological well-being of middle-aged mothers. Rather, on balance, the effects seem to be moderately positive.

A study of the passage of U.S. women through thirteen years of midlife demonstrated a significant diversity in the occurrence of life events, as well as their sequencing and spacing.[9] A large portion of these women experienced no transitions, at least with respect to marriage and the presence of children in the home. Two events, however, had detectable and important effects on their employment patterns and economic well-being: the launching of the last child and marital dissolution. These two events were found to have opposite effects. The empty nest transition (launching of the last child) increased both labor market involvement and economic well-being, while marital dissolution (divorce and widowhood) decreased well-being. Sequencing made a difference as well. If marital dissolution occurred first, the woman suffered a reduction in income while maintaining custody of the child. Recovery from this was difficult even when benefits of an empty nest transition were forthcoming. If the empty nest occurred first, the women benefited economically as long as their marriages were kept intact.

For females, the notion of the **empty-nest syndrome** as a period of depression, identity crisis, role loss, and a lowered sense of well-being that occurs when the last child leaves the parental home has little research support. The extent of its existence is likely to vary by factors such as socioeconomic level or employment status. Dolores Borland hypothesizes that if the empty-nest syndrome occurs, it may occur to a greater degree in a particular cohort of white middle-class women because of a unique set of social circumstances in which they live and a unique set of family values and social norms concerning women's "proper" roles.[10] These are women who dedicate their lives selflessly to their families' needs and believe that to be feminine and happy is to be married and to be mothers. Lower- and upper-socioeconomic status women, she argues, are less likely to experience this syndrome because the former have had to work throughout their lives to help support the family and the latter have developed other community roles, have resources to find parental role substitutes, and have smaller families, which leads them to the empty-nest stage at a younger age.

The absence of children symbolizes the children's new independence. Since the children are gone, many mothers form new nonfamilial relationships to fill the void. Many women in this age category become more active in civic and religious affairs, an increasing number of wives and mothers become employed (*see* Chapter 4), and this is the time period when mothers become grandmothers and fathers gain the status of grandfather.

---

9. Ken R. Smith and Phyllis Moen, "Passage Through Midlife: Women's Changing Family Roles and Economic Well-Being," *The Sociological Quarterly* 29 (1988): 503–524.

10. Dolores Cabic Borland, "A Cohort Analysis Approach to the Empty-nest Syndrome Among Three Ethnic Groups of Women: A Theoretical Position," *Journal of Marriage and the Family* 44 (February 1982): 117–129.

# *THE GRANDPARENT STATUS*

Grandparenting has become a middle-age as well as an old-age phenomenon with the potential of spanning three or four decades of life. With the majority of men and women in U.S. society marrying in their early or mid-twenties, and with many of them having children within the first year or two of marriage, parents are becoming grandparents in their forties. The rocking chair and the cane-carrying grandfather images seem grossly inappropriate. The reduction in family size, closer spacing of children, and the fact of women having their last child at a younger age leads to the transition into grandparenthood as a distinct status of the middle years, separate from and with less overlap with one's own parenting.

After prolonged neglect, grandparenthood is now receiving greater attention in the literature on adulthood, family development, and intergenerational relations.[11] Two key demographic changes have shaped modern grandparenthood in U.S. society: increased life expectancy and changed fertility patterns. With more people reaching old age, more people experience grandparenthood as well as great- and great-great-grandparenthood. As with grandparenthood, interviews with great-grandparents revealed that most found the role to be significant and emotionally fulfilling, providing a sense of personal and familial renewal, diversion to their lives, and a mark of longevity.[12]

Marion Crawford suggests that the role of grandparent can be seen as instrumental for the family as a social institution.[13] First, it can bring together the two adult generations that may tend to drift apart during the postparental phase of the family life cycle. Grandchildren provide a common focus of interest, activity, and affection. Second, the family can benefit materially from grandparents, both in terms of financial and other services while the grandparents are alive and also in terms of capital and property after their deaths. In the transfer of property, children and grandchildren are expected to receive first priority. Third, while the role of grandparent has been seen by some writers as an essentially maternal or feminine role, it may also ease the transition into retirement for men. She suggests that in these three ways, grandparenthood, while not occurring in old age, may be a useful preparation for both sexes for old age by reintegrating the middle-aged person into the family unit and by anticipatory socialization into the role of retired persons.

Perhaps the role of grandparent, like that of parent, differs considerably by social class. It has been suggested that the middle-class grandparent role is

11. Gunhild O. Hagestad, "Grandparenthood, Life Context, and Family Development," *American Behavioral Scientist* 29 (March/April 1986): 471–484.

12. Kenneth J. Doka and Mary Ellen Mertz, "The Meaning and Significance of Great-Grandparenthood," *The Gerontologist* 28 (1988): 192–197.

13. Marion Crawford, "Not Disengaged: Grandparents in Literature and Reality, An Empirical Study in Role Satisfaction," *The Sociological Review* 29 (1981): 499–519.

*To children and grandchildren, grandparents often serve as a valuable family resource: as custodians of family history, as conflict mediators, as gift givers, as providers of child care, and as significant others.*

one which is "ideological" rather than "real." That is, there is a kinship position of grandparent, but there are no normative rights and obligations attached to it, so grandparenthood could be described as a "roleless role."[14] Thus, middle-class parents, on becoming grandparents, must construct a role for themselves as babysitter, surrogate parent, gift giver, crisis intervenor, and the like. In contrast, the lower-class grandparent is one who is far more integrated into ongoing daily family life. The lower-class maternal grandmother frequently socializes and nurtures her grandchildren, engages in more regular interaction, and feels a sense of obligation far more than simple contact between generations.

Grandparenthood appears to have different meanings for grandmothers and grandfathers. Sometimes the grandparent role is depicted as a maternal role with women feeling greater responsibility to and intimate involvement with their grandchildren. One study, for example, concluded that the grandfather role was perceived by older men as less important than other

14. Sylvia Clavan, "The Impact of Social Class and Social Trends on the Role of Grandparent," *The Family Coordinator* 27 (October 1978): 351–357.

social roles, such as worker, church participant, and leisure user. A second conclusion pointed to the moderate to low levels of interaction and mutual assistance between grandfathers and grandchildren.[15]

In contrast to grandfathers, the relationship between grandmothers and grandchildren is less likely to be one of low levels of interaction and mutual assistance; grandmothers are more likely to be regular providers of day care. National data of a youth cohort, for example, show that over one-half of young mothers with children rely upon relatives for child care when they are employed, and the primary relative is the grandmother.[16] The number of hours of child care provided per week by grandmothers was substantial even though one-third of these middle-age grandmothers were also employed. Like employed husbands and wives who were shown to juggle their work schedules to care for children, so too were grandmothers and their children shown to juggle their work schedules to participate in child care. One underlying assumption of these patterns is that a relative, particularly the grandmother, is more emotionally committed to the child and will provide more loving care than nonrelatives. This assumption continues at a time when the availability of grandmother care seems to be on the decline while the need for infant and toddler care is increasing.

Given the frequency of divorce/remarriage patterns, stepgrandparents are taking on a new significance. If grandparenthood can be described as a "roleless role," the description is even more apt for the grandparent by marriage rather than birth. Unlike the grandparent tie, stepgrandparents have no biological tie and a shorter relationship time to a newly acquired grandchild. Factors such as these might suggest greater contact, more social involvement in personal and social roles, and a stronger relationship with grandparents than stepgrandparents; one source found this to be the case.[17] The divorce/remarriage pattern not only affects the stepgrandparent, but it also has a major impact on the grandparent as well. Many grandparents experience frustration in maintaining contact and frequent interaction with their grandchildren. This is particularly true when the grandchildren reside with the son- or daughter-in-law rather than the son or daughter. A relatively new and increasingly frequent phenomenon are the legal and court cases involving grandparent-grandchild visitation rights.

With the changes that take place over the life course, great-grandparenthood rather than grandparenthood, is emerging as the familial status associated with old age. It is likely that this status, like the described middle-class grandparent status, is more "ideological" than "real" and that

15. Vira R. Kivett, "Grandfathers and Grandchildren: Patterns of Associations, Helping, and Psychological Closeness," *Family Relations* 34 (October 1985): 565–571.

16. Harriet B. Presser, "Some Economic Complexities of Child Care Provided by Grandmothers," *Journal of Marriage and the Family* 51 (August 1989): 581–591.

17. Gregory F. Sanders and Debra W. Trygstad, "Stepgrandparents and Grandparents: The View from Young Adults," *Family Relations* 38 (January 1989): 71–75.

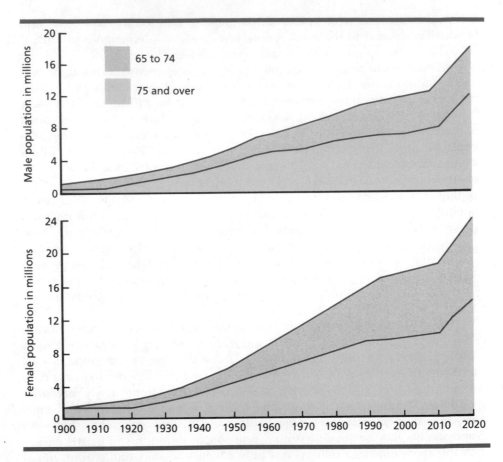

*Figure 15–1*
**The growth of the population 65 years and over, 1900–2020.** (*Source:* U.S. Bureau of the Census, *Current Population Reports.*)

great-grandparents need to construct the type of role they wish to perform in their ascribed great-grandparent status.

## *THE FAMILY OF LATER LIFE*

Since the turn of the century, one of the more significant changes in family and marital relationships has related to life expectancy. People are living longer and more people are living, both of which increase the number of older persons (*see* Figure 15–1). An early age at marriage, the absence of divorce, and a longer life combine to increase the length of marriage, the number of generations of family members living, and the extension of the kin network. In 1988, at birth the infant could expect to live 74.8 years. For white males, this

*Table 15–2*
**Life expectancy, by race, age, and sex, United States, 1988**

| Age | Total | White Male | White Female | Black Male | Black Female |
|---|---|---|---|---|---|
| At birth | 74.8 | 72.0 | 78.8 | 65.2 | 73.5 |
| 5 | 70.7 | 67.8 | 74.6 | 61.7 | 69.9 |
| 10 | 65.8 | 62.9 | 69.2 | 56.8 | 65.0 |
| 15 | 60.9 | 58.0 | 64.7 | 52.0 | 60.1 |
| 20 | 56.2 | 53.5 | 59.9 | 47.3 | 55.3 |
| 25 | 51.5 | 48.8 | 55.0 | 42.8 | 50.5 |
| 30 | 46.8 | 44.2 | 50.1 | 38.5 | 45.7 |
| 35 | 42.1 | 39.5 | 45.3 | 34.3 | 41.1 |
| 40 | 37.4 | 34.9 | 40.5 | 30.3 | 36.6 |
| 45 | 32.9 | 30.4 | 35.8 | 26.8 | 32.2 |
| 50 | 28.5 | 26.1 | 31.2 | 22.7 | 28.0 |
| 55 | 24.3 | 21.9 | 26.8 | 19.3 | 24.0 |
| 60 | 20.4 | 18.2 | 22.6 | 16.1 | 20.3 |
| 65 | 16.8 | 14.8 | 18.7 | 13.4 | 17.0 |
| 70 | 13.6 | 11.7 | 15.1 | 10.8 | 13.9 |
| 75 | 10.7 | 9.1 | 11.8 | 8.7 | 11.1 |
| 80 | 8.1 | 6.9 | 8.8 | 6.8 | 8.5 |
| 85 and over | 6.0 | 5.1 | 6.4 | 5.5 | 6.7 |

*Source:* U.S. Bureau of the Census, *Statistical Abstract of the United States: 1989*, 109th ed. (Washington, D.C.: U.S. Governmental Printing Office, 1989), no. 109, p. 73.

figure was 72.0 years and for white females, 78.8 years (*see* Table 15–2). Those who reach age sixty-five can expect to live 16.8 more years (14.8 for white men; 18.7 for white women; 13.4 for black men; and 17.0 for black women).

There has been relatively little increase in the life expectancy of older persons since the turn of the century. In 1900, the person who reached age sixty-five could expect to live until age 76.9. In 1988, the person who reached age sixty-five could expect to live until age 81.8 or slightly less than five years longer than his or her counterpart of more than eighty years earlier. More people are living, however, as fewer people are dying in infancy or childhood. In 1986, approximately 73 percent of the men and 85 percent of the women reached age sixty-five.[18] In 1900, only 39 percent of the men and 44 percent of the women reached age sixty-five. Thus, although a much higher percentage of

18. U.S. Bureau of the Census, *Statistical Abstract of the United States, 1989*, 109th ed. (Washington, D.C.: U.S. Government Printing Office, 1989), no. 107, p. 72.

people are living longer, there has been a relatively small increase in the life expectancy of older persons.

In 1987 there were approximately 29.8 million U.S. citizens age sixty-five and over.[19] This number makes up about 12.3 percent of the population of the United States, and the rates have been expanding far more rapidly than the nation's population as a whole. While the number of U.S. citizens has increased by 19.8 percent since 1970 (203.2 million to 243.4 million), the number of people age sixty-five and over has increased by 49 percent (20 million to 29.8 million) in seventeen years. The increase in these figures is not due to an increase in the life span (the biological age limit), or due to the fact that older individuals are living much longer but rather to the larger number of people living. With birth rates declining or remaining stable, the aged will likely constitute an even larger proportion of the population for decades to come.

Throughout history older persons have played significant roles, particularly men who, with increasing age, often received increasing status, prestige, and deference. In the United States, and apparently in modernized societies in general, old age does not bring increased prestige and status but rather brings negative perceptions and definitions.[20] Frequently, old age is defined as a time of dependency and declining productivity and vitality. The socioeconomic status held is generally determined by the achievement of earlier periods of life; if the achievements were limited and provisions for these years were inadequate, opportunities for a full, meaningful life are limited.

It is not difficult to remain sensitive to the older person and aging. In tomorrow's community newspapers will be pictures of couples who are celebrating their fiftieth wedding anniversaries, announcements of community and business leaders who are retiring, polls showing attitudinal differences between the old and the young, and of course the obituary notices. All these serve as reminders of the social dimension of aging and of the position of the older person in society.

Social gerontology, the study of older persons and the aging process, as well as the closely related field, the sociology of aging, have both been concerned with the social definition of who is thought to be old, their interaction patterns and behaviors, the expectations that are imposed upon them, the age, sex, place of residence, and other demographic factors about them, as well as the problems and needs that older members within a society face. Within this framework, the family of later life has come to take on a particular significance in dealing with, and understanding, these other factors of concern to the aged.

---

19. Ibid., no. 21, p. 17.
20. Donald O. Cowgill, "Aging in Comparative Cultural Perspective," *Mid-American Review of Sociology* 6 (1981): 1–28; and Carol Seefeldt, "Children's Attitudes Toward the Elderly: A Cross-Cultural Comparison," *International Journal of Aging and Human Development* 19 (1984): 319–328.

*Table 15–3*
**Marital status of men and women, aged 65 and over, March 1988**
*(percentage distribution)*

| Marital status | Men | | Women | |
| --- | --- | --- | --- | --- |
| | Age 65–74 | Age 75 and over | Age 65–74 | Age 75 and over |
| Single | 4.8% | 4.2% | 4.6% | 6.2% |
| Married | 79.5 | 66.8 | 51.5 | 23.6 |
| Separated | 2.3 | 2.9 | 1.8 | 1.3 |
| Widowed | 8.7 | 23.7 | 36.3 | 66.1 |
| Divorced | 4.7 | 2.4 | 5.8 | 2.7 |
| Total | 100.0 | 100.0 | 100.0 | 100.0 |

*Source:* U.S. Bureau of the Census, *Current Population Reports*, Series P-20, no. 433, "Marital Status and Living Arrangements, March 1988" (Washington, D.C.: U.S. Government Printing Office, 1989), Table 1, p. 3.

## Marriages and families in the later years

In 1988, there were an estimated 12.1 million men and 17.7 million women in the United States who were sixty-five years old and over. Eighty percent of the men and 52 percent of the women aged sixty-five to seventy-four were married. At age seventy-five and over, 67 percent of the men and 24 percent of the women were married (*see* Table 15–3).

Relatively few men and women in these age categories are divorced, separated, or single (*see* Figure 15–2). This is a time when the widowed status becomes increasingly frequent. While less than one in ten men aged sixty-five to seventy-four and less than one in four of the men aged seventy-five and over are widowers, nearly four in ten women aged sixty-five to seventy-four and two-thirds aged seventy-five and over are widows. This factor will be discussed later in this chapter.

Married couples in this over-sixty-five group comprise a high proportion who have been married a long time. Of those in first marriages, most of them previously celebrated silver wedding anniversaries, and many have or will celebrate their golden anniversaries. Over the years they have shared many joys and weathered many crises. Although it exists, rarely does one read about divorce or incompatibility among these couples. Even when unhappy in their marriage, the experiences of their years, the lives and activities of their children, and perhaps the lack of realistic alternatives to the marriage keep the couple together.

Marital and family relationships are often proclaimed to be the primary sources of social involvement, companionship, fulfillment, and happiness for the elderly. Existing studies suggest that marriage has a positive effect on psychological well-being among the elderly (particularly when compared to

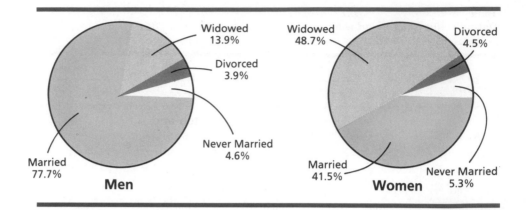

*Figure 15–2*

*Marital status of persons 65 years and over, by sex: 1988* (*Source:* U.S. Bureau of the Census, *Current Population Reports*, Series P-23, no. 162, "Studies in Marriage and the Family," [Washington, D.C.: U.S. Government Printing Office, 1989], Figure 4, p. 9).

the divorced and widowed)[21] and, as shown earlier, that marital satisfaction may be higher for the elderly than for married people in the intermediate stages of the family life course.

As at any point in the life course, intergenerational relationships maintain their importance among adult children and their aging parents. Mancini and Blieszner, in presenting an overview of the dominant themes between these two groups, suggest that after years of investigation there is no evidence that older people are alienated from their children.[22] By now we should be convinced that adult children and their older/aging parents are characterized by patterns of reciprocal support. These groups have frequent face-to-face contacts (three-fourths on a weekly or semi-weekly basis), keep in touch by phone and correspondence, exchange care during illness, give money and gifts, run errands, prepare meals, give emotional support and affection, and in general promote the well-being (happiness, satisfaction, morale) of family members. Again note that the exchange patterns are mutually supportive. Contact, support, and so forth are seldom "one-way," but are characterized by reciprocal interactions.

The belief that adult children abandon their elderly relatives or fail to meet their needs is basically a myth. Another myth appears to be that high levels of conflict will exist if the generations live together. While certain circumstances may produce family discord, research reports surprisingly low

21. Walter R. Gove and Hee-Choon Shin, "The Psychological Well-Being of Divorced and Widowed Men and Women," *Journal of Family Issues* 10 (March 1989): 122–144.

22. Jay A. Mancini and Rosemary Blieszner, "Aging Parents and Adult Children: Research Themes in Intergenerational Relations," *Journal of Marriage and the Family* 51 (May 1989): 275–290.

THE FAMILY OF LATER LIFE

levels of conflict between parents and their resident adult children.[23] Even the parents' health and the parents' dependency were not found to be related to parent-child conflict. Most parents and adult children, including those who live together, get along quite harmoniously.

What about the childless elderly? The value of children to their elderly parents in providing emotional, material, financial, and other support is widely asserted and empirically supported. However, one study of the childless elderly demonstrated levels of well-being that match and sometimes exceed those of parent elderly.[24] The childless were more financially secure (*see* Chapter 13 on the childless as well) and in better health, while parents tended to be surrounded by a greater number of friends and have more general satisfaction with life. By and large, this study and others show that the elderly, whether parent or childless, are very satisfied with family, friendships, and life, while less satisfied with health and income, two problems discussed in the pages that follow.

What about the unmarried elderly who never married, are divorced, or widowed? These groups comprise a sizable proportion of the aged population. How important are families to them? Studies show that geographic proximity to siblings, particularly same-sex siblings, exerts a positive influence on life satisfaction and well-being.[25] Another study based on two national samples concluded that men and women were more isolated from neighbors and friends than from family. Men were somewhat more likely to be isolated from family than were women.[26] Women were more likely than men to see relatives and maintain contacts with them by phone.

Interestingly, one hedge against loneliness for the unmarried was found to be dating.[27] While older women were said to derive increased prestige from dating, older men stressed the importance of dating as a means for self-disclosure. For most persons, greater emphasis was placed on the companionate nature of such relationships. As one 73-year-old woman stated:

> It was a lot harder when my boyfriend, Ted, died than when my husband of 40 years passed away. I needed Ted in a way I never needed my

23. J. Jill Suitor and Karl Pillemer, "Explaining Intergenerational Conflict When Adult Children and Elderly Parents Live Together," *Journal of Marriage and the Family* 50 (November 1988): 1037–1047; and J. Jill Suitor and Karl Pillemer, "The Presence of Adult Children: A Source of Stress for Elderly Couples' Marriages?" *Journal of Marriage and the Family* 49 (November 1987): 717–725.

24. Judith Rempel, "Childless Elderly: What Are They Missing," *Journal of Marriage and the Family* 47 (May 1985): 343–348. For the impact of children throughout the life course, *see:* Masako Ishii-Kuntz and Karen Seccombe, "The Impact of Children upon Social Support Networks Throughout the Life Course," *Journal of Marriage and the Family* 51 (August 1989): 777–790.

25. Jerrie L. McGhee, "The Effects of Siblings on the Life Satisfaction of the Rural Elderly," *Journal of Marriage and the Family* 47 (February 1985): 85–91; and Shirley L. O'Bryant, "Sibling Support and Older Widows' Well-Being," *Journal of Marriage and the Family* 50 (February 1988): 173–183.

26. Pat M. Keith, "Isolation of the Unmarried in Later Life," *Family Relations* 35 (July 1986): 389–395.

27. Kris Bulcroft and Margaret O'Connor, "The Importance of Dating Relationships on Quality of Life for Older Persons," *Family Relations* 35 (July 1986): 397–401.

husband. Ted and I spent so much time together; he was all I had. And at my age I know it will be hard to find someone else . . . but, well, let's face it; how many men want a 73-year-old woman?[28]

## Living arrangements among the elderly

As persons reach age sixty-five and over, an increasing number retire, suffer decreases in income, and experience the loss by death of spouses and siblings. Where do people of this age category live? Are they institutionalized? Do they live with children? Do they live alone? The answer to this will greatly depend on the sex to which you are referring.

In 1987, three-fourths of the men were living with their spouses compared to less than 40 percent of the women (*see* Table 15–4). Women were far more likely than men to be living alone (41 percent vs. 16 percent) or to be living with someone other than spouse (20 percent vs. 9 percent). Many of these people were living with children or other relatives. A situation of this nature may be a matter of choice or of necessity. Where both parents and children elect to live together, the arrangements frequently work out to the satisfaction of both the older members and the children. If a wife is employed, the mother or mother-in-law is likely to assume much of the major responsibility of the household. Babysitting, lawn care, cooking, and fulfilling the daily needs of the home are often functions that older persons can satisfactorily perform. If, however, the arrangement is not one of choice but of necessity, the probability of difficulty is likely to increase. Frequently the relationship is unsatisfactory both for the aging parents and for the children, and in some instances for the grandchildren.

Another living arrangement that is frequently satisfactory is for the aging parents and the married children to have separate but geographically close residences where they can maintain close relationships. Many parents like to be independent and want their children to allow them to remain so. This permits both generations to give favors or suggestions with fewer threatening feelings. In addition, it permits both to share interests and life-styles without the constant physical presence of the other. Unfortunately, census data are not available on the number or percentage of persons in the later years who maintain residences separate from their children but live close to them.

The men and women sixty-five years of age and over who live in long-term care institutions, primarily nursing homes, represent an estimated 5 percent of the population. This would total 1.5 million persons, a relatively small proportion of the total aged population. About 20 percent of all persons eighty-five years of age or older live in institutions and it is suggested that, over a lifetime, about one in four older persons will spend some time in an institution.[29] As a result of differing mortality between the sexes, women not

---

28. Ibid., p. 401.

29. James E. Montgomery, "The Economics of Supportive Services for Families with Disabled and Aging Members," *Family Relations* 31 (January 1982): 21.

*Table 15–4*
**Characteristics of persons 65 years and over, by sex, 1970 and 1987**

| Characteristics | 1970 | | 1987 | |
|---|---|---|---|---|
| | Male | Female | Male | Female |
| Total (in millions) | 8.3 | 11.5 | 12.1 | 17.7 |
|   Percent of population | 8.5% | 11.1% | 10.2% | 14.2% |
| Percent below poverty level | | | | |
|   Family householders | 16.6% | 23.5% | 6.1% | 13.0% |
|   Unrelated individuals | 40.0 | 49.9 | 19.6 | 26.8 |
| Family Status (by percent) | | | | |
|   In families | 79.2% | 58.5% | 81.9% | 56.7% |
|   Non-family householders | 14.9 | 35.2 | 16.6 | 41.8 |
|   Secondary individuals | 2.4 | 1.9 | 1.6 | 1.5 |
|   Residents of institutions | 3.6 | 4.4 | (n/a) | (n/a) |
| Years of school completed | | | | |
|   8 years or less | 61.5% | 56.1% | 34.4% | 31.8% |
|   1–4 years of high school | 25.0 | 32.0 | 41.5 | 49.8 |
|   1 or more years of college | 13.5 | 11.9 | 23.2 | 18.4 |
| Labor-force participation (by percent) | | | | |
|   Employed | 25.9% | 9.4% | 15.9% | 7.2% |
|   Not in labor force | 74.1 | 90.6 | 84.1 | 92.8 |
| Living arrangements (by percent) | | | | |
|   Living in household | 95.5% | 95.0% | 99.7% | 99.5% |
|   Living alone | 14.1 | 33.8 | 15.6 | 40.9 |
|   Spouse present | 69.9 | 33.9 | 74.9 | 39.2 |
|   Living with someone else | 11.5 | 27.4 | 9.2 | 19.4 |
|   Not in household | 4.5 | 5.0 | .3 | .5 |

*Source:* U.S. Bureau of the Census, *Statistical Abstract of the United States: 1989*, 109th ed.
(Washington, D.C.: U.S. Government Printing Office, 1989), no. 41, p. 36.

only greatly outnumber men among the older population generally, but among the population living in institutions particularly, at a ratio of about two to one.

These figures tend to lend support to the ideas that: (1) most of the elderly are not in nursing homes or in long-term care institutions, and (2) most elderly are not abandoned by their families. Even those who are institutionalized are disproportionately drawn from those who are childless, widowed, and living alone. Gordon Streib argues for alternative living arrangements for older persons which include, for many, living in their own homes, in families with a spouse, with children, or with other relatives. But an increasing number of elderly people encounter problems in these arrangements. For these, he suggests a continuum of living arrangements from living independently to a full-care institution with twenty-four-hour nursing care. These arrangements may include retirement communities, retirement hotels, cooperative housing arrangements, or "Share-A-Home."[30] The latter involves a "family" of nonrelated senior adults who share their own household, employ a manager, and share expenses. A board of directors of community citizens provides leadership and guidance. This concept blends in one location both familial and bureaucratic functions.

Other alternatives that could be considered include a partial institutionalization plan in which the member could participate in group recreational or work activities during the day and sleep at home or a night institutional plan where persons would sleep at the institution but be free to participate in community programs and activities during the day. Or older persons could live in "foster homes" in which they would be given the opportunity to actively participate in the activities of the host family. Thereby, a person could maintain healthy social interactions, gain a feeling of usefulness, and have physical needs provided for as well. The host family would be paid for the services they provided, either by the person or by the state (as is frequently done with young children).

## PROBLEMS FACING THE AGED

As already suggested, the aged are not without problems. One problem focuses on health and care. It is a time of life when a disproportionate number are isolated, disabled, sick, or in poor health. For example, some type of health problem almost invariably accompanies old age. Sometimes hospitalization is required, which raises a range of issues involving medical payments, visiting patterns, care for the residence of the hospitalized, and, on occasion, legal matters. Yet, in a nationwide sample of the noninstitutionalized elderly over age sixty-five, Shanas[31] found there were twice as many old people who were housebound and bedfast at home (10 percent of the elderly) as were living in all kinds of institutions (approximately 5 percent). She found the majority of the frail and sick were taken care of at home, with the main source of help for the homebound invalid to be the spouse or an immediate family member. Wives took care of the men who were ill while women, more apt to be widows, were cared for by their children. Family members not only assumed the care of the bedfast but prepared meals and did the housework and shopping.

Other research as well confirms the preference for and the importance of family members and adult children, particularly daughters, as caregivers for the noninstitutionalized elderly. It is widely believed that families are becoming less willing than families were historically to care for their elderly

---

30. Gordon F. Streib, "An Alternative Family Form for Older Persons: Need and Social Context," *The Family Coordinator* 27 (October 1978): 413–420.

31. Ethel Shanas, *National Survey of the Elderly*, Report to the Administration on Aging (Washington, D.C.: Department of Health and Human Services, 1979).

*For the noninstitutionalized elderly, family members, particularly wives and daughters, serve as primary caregivers for husbands and fathers. For the institutionalized elderly, family visits and calls are primary sources of support and caring.*

impaired family member at home. This belief, referred to as the "myth of abandonment," has little scientific evidence to support it, and, indeed, much evidence to the contrary. National surveys show that informal caregiving by families is currently the dominant mode, by far, of providing care services to the aged in general and the functionally disabled more specifically.[32] These functionally disabled may require assistance with personal care (bathing, eating, toileting), mobility (from room to room or in and out of chairs or beds), or daily living tasks (shopping, cleaning, cooking).

A second problem focuses on income and standard of living. In economic terms the aged remain a sizable segment of the nation's poor, particularly if they are not in family households. Yet, the percentage of elderly below the poverty level is less than half of what it was in 1970 (*see* Table 15–4). Social security, retirement plans, tax allowances and other benefits have been successful at reducing poverty for this segment of our population over age

---

32. Pamela Doty, "Family Care of the Elderly: The Role of Public Policy," *The Milbank Quarterly* 64 (1986): 34–75; and Kathryn Beckham and Jeffrey A. Giordano, "Illness and Impairment in Elderly Couples: Implications for Marital Therapy," *Family Relations* 35 (April 1986): 257–264.

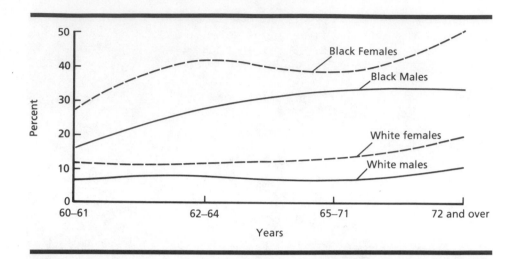

*Figure 15–3*
**Poverty rate in 1981 of persons 60 years and over, by age, race, and sex.** (*Source:* U.S. Bureau of the Census, *Current Population Reports*, Series P-23, no. 128, "America in Transition: An Aging Society" [Washington, D.C.: U.S. Government Printing Office, 1983], Figure 14, p. 11.)

sixty-five. As can be seen in Figure 15–3, the poverty rate varies dramatically by race and sex. Black females in particular, while having a poverty rate nearly four times that of white males or white females in the sixty to seventy age category, show the largest increase in the percentage in poverty after age seventy.

In spite of these figures and a decline in income after age sixty and seventy, the quality of life of the elderly in the United States has improved dramatically. A report in *Family Planning Perspectives* (July/August 1984:186) in reference to an address of demographer Samuel H. Preston, noted that a growing number of elderly are demanding and getting what they need, whereas the needs of many children are being ignored. As a result, the incidence of poverty among children under fourteen in 1982 was 56 percent greater than that of the elderly. In 1970, the opposite was the case. This switch in economic well-being was attributed to the expansion of social security and noncash benefits such as medicare. Preston claimed that federal expenditures for the elderly in 1983 equaled $7,700 per person, while expenditures for all the major child-oriented programs combined (AFDC, Head Start, food stamps, and education) were approximately $700 per child. The politics of this major switch reveals the power of special interest groups determined by wealth and size. Children don't vote nor do they have much financial clout.

David Cheal, as well, reminds us that old people in the United States are, overall, not as deficient in economic resources as the image generally presented would suggest.[33] While average income declines sharply, so do average expenditures. The ownership of domestic assets, such as the family home, makes it possible to enjoy a certain standard of living with a lower income than would otherwise be required. In fact, he suggests that young adults are major beneficiaries of familial transactions, that gift giving by old people is more significant than might be expected, and that financial aid is given by the elderly to relatives more frequently than received.

A third problem facing the elderly is that of abuse and neglect. This may be one of our "newest" social problems in that little or no information prior to the late 1970s was published about domestic mistreatment of the elderly in their homes by relatives or other domestic caregivers. This issue is examined more thoroughly in the next chapter.

Extreme caution must be taken in the categorization of the aged as a homogeneous population. Although dependency, sickness, isolation, and abuse are frequent, a sizable proportion of these people have few health problems, carry on active lives with families and friends, and continue to make major economic and social contributions to their communities and society.

## Socialization of the aged

The tremendous emphasis given to children and youth in socialization literature largely ignores and overshadows the resocialization needs of the aged. In contrast to the aged, children receive much of their socialization within the family, from peers, schools, jobs, or the community. But what socializing agents exist to direct the aged? Where is the training for retirement? Where is the training for widowhood? Where is the training or preparation for illness or death? Where is the training for the narrowing of social relationships?

In many ways U.S. society overlooks the fact that persons over sixty-five are social beings, that their world is maintained and meaning is found through interaction with others. As should have become very clear in the previous chapter, of primary importance to the socialization process and to the defining and redefining of the self is the extent and nature of friendship ties, association with significant others, involvement in groups of reference, and social interaction in general. Why should these factors be less important to persons over age sixty-five than to those under age twenty? It could be argued that these social relationships take on increased importance as persons move outside of their occupational spheres and as they experience the deaths of their age-peers.

When compared with younger adults, older persons as a group are removed from primary social roles. Society has provided few role definitions

---

33. David J. Cheal, "Intergenerational Family Transfers," *Journal of Marriage and the Family* 45 (November 1983): 805–813.

for older persons that would attach them to or keep them active in the social system. While students, parents, and persons in the business or professional world speak with glee of the day when they will be relieved of social responsibility, older persons often find their new "freedom" carries with it grave consequences. Simply providing a variety of recreational activities does not serve as an adequate functional substitute for the responsibilities of gainful employment.

Intimacy and familiarity characterize the family system and make it highly suitable to fulfill many of the needs, services, and interaction patterns of the individual members. However, it should be noted that family factors do not operate independently of the culture in which families operate. To avoid having the aged become "socially disabled," there needs to be a congruity between the cultural goals and structural opportunities that a society provides. The effectiveness of the family as a resource is largely contingent upon the values and services of the larger society: job opportunities, leisure time activities, health care, clarity of role, perception of the aged as fulfilling valuable functions, and socializing and resocializing opportunities appropriate to the later stage of the life cycle.

## RETIREMENT

The problem of retirement involves the resocialization of men and women to new roles and life-styles. Traditionally, men assumed the major economic responsibility for their families, and men's lives revolved heavily around work-employment roles. Thus it could be expected that the literature on retirement would focus heavily on the husband. Women's retirement was less studied because it was not perceived to constitute a salient social issue. With the dramatic increase in the labor force employment of women and the growing proportion of women retirees, studies of the preparation for and effect of retirement on both sexes are appearing with increasing frequency.

Robert Atchley suggests that the retirement process involves three major periods: preretirement, the retirement transition, and postretirement.[34] The first, *preretirement*, looks ahead to retirement: when to retire, what to expect, and the like. The *retirement transition* involves leaving one's job and taking up the role of retired person. The *postretirement* period involves life without the job or employment that occupied a major focus of time and attention in the preceding years. Retirement is thus viewed as a process that can occur over many years rather than a time-specific event.

To see what happens in the retirement process, Atchley received responses to mailed questionnaires in 1975 from more than 1,100 persons of

---

34. Robert C. Atchley, "The Process of Retirement: Comparing Men and Women," in Maximiliane Szinovacz, *Women's Retirement: Policy Implications of Recent Research* (Beverly Hills: Sage Publications, 1982): 153–168.

both sexes in a small town near a large metropolitan area. These respondents were resurveyed again in 1977, 1979, and 1981. About 350 respondents were in the *preretirement* period and employed full-time. About 50 of these did not plan to retire, due to self-employment, good health, and for women, an unmarried status. Those who planned to retire gave a mean planned retirement age of sixty-four. Women were much more likely than men to plan to retire before age sixty as well as at age seventy or after. The early retirees tended to have high social status and to be married while the late retirees tended to have low social status and to be unmarried. This reinforces the notion of important class differences in retirement and cautions against relying too heavily on general statements about women's retirement. Less than 1 percent of either sex in this preretirement period had negative attitudes toward retirement.

The *retirement transition* period included about 170 persons who retired between 1975 and 1979. Those who had a negative attitude toward retirement (17 percent of the women and 11 percent of the men) were more likely to have poorer health and a low social status and to see their income as inadequate. But retirement turned out better than expected and attitude scores went up significantly following retirement. For both men and women in the total sample, retirement tended to improve life satisfaction slightly, irrespective of marital status, health, income adequacy, social status, or living arrangements. Retirement reduced the activity level for both sexes, although the reduction was much greater for women than for men due to their much higher level of activity before retirement.

The *postretirement* period included nearly 300 persons who were retired in 1975. Attitudes toward their retirement were very positive, activity levels were relatively high, and life satisfaction scores were positive for both sexes. Activity level was a strong predictor of morale among retired men and health was more important among retired women. Interestingly, the older the retired woman, the more positive her attitude toward retirement was likely to be. It should be noted that the findings reported in this particular study occurred with generally healthy people in one small community that offered many opportunities for participation. In this context at least, people look forward to retirement, go through the transition smoothly, and find life in retirement satisfying.

Studies on the effects of retirement on marriage have tended to focus on the reactions of wives, changes in role differentiation, and the sharing of household tasks. Satisfaction of wives in retirement was highly related to joint decision making by husbands and wives.[35] Brubaker and Hennon, in comparing household tasks between dual-earner and dual-retired marriages,

---

35. Lorraine T. Dorfman and Elizabeth A. Hill, "Rural Housewives and Retirement: Joint Decision-Making Matters," *Family Relations* 35 (October 1986): 507–514; and Lorraine T. Dorfman and D. Alex Heckert, "Egalitarianism in Retired Rural Couples: Household Tasks, Decision Making, and Leisure Activities," *Family Relations* 37 (January 1988): 73–78.

found few differences.[36] Husbands had the primary responsibility for lawn work, car maintenance, and earning money. Wives were responsible for cooking, washing clothes and dishes, writing letters, and cleaning house. The only differences in task allocation were in shopping (retired couples were more likely to share) and earning money (retired couples were more likely to assign responsibility to the husband).

As indicated previously, with the increased employment of women, retirement for women is likely to take on increased significance and in many ways parallel the experiences and issues traditionally faced by men. This seems to be true already. One study of 1,530 retired residents of Washington state found that retirement is not materially different for women than for men.[37] No support was found for the idea that retirement is a less stressful event for women. In fact, women reported somewhat lower levels of satisfaction with retirement than men. Reasons given for this included their lower incomes and, to a lesser degree, their lower probability of being married. Regardless of gender, those in better health and those with higher incomes were most likely to express satisfaction with retirement.

Irrespective of the reasons for retirement, it seems likely that major role readjustments will be necessary for both sexes. Health, income, status, and feelings of self-worth often tend to decrease at the time of retirement, with the problems compounded upon the death of a spouse.

## HOW FAMILIES DEAL WITH DYING AND DEATH

Two adages that come to mind in relation to death are "Two things are certain in life: Taxes and Death," and "Don't love and you won't get hurt." In the application of these to the family, the first would suggest that, pleasant or unpleasant, death is an inescapable event that will occur within all family or kin networks. The second suggests that the loss of those one loves most intensely is likely to cause tremendous pain. For most family members, while death may be certain, the loss of a parent, spouse, child, or other family member is a painful experience. Few relationships are more intimate and few groups more primary than those of marriages and families.

Terminal illness, dying, and death are separate but interrelated events or processes. The application of interaction theory to these events would suggest that definitions and meanings attached to illness and death would greatly

36. Timothy H. Brubaker and Charles B. Hennon, "Responsibility for Household Tasks: Comparing Dual-Earner and Dual-Retired Marriages," in Maximiliane Szinovacz, *Women's Retirement* (Beverly Hills: Sage Publications, Inc., 1982): 205–219.

37. Karen Seccombe and Gary L. Lee, "Gender Differences in Retirement Satisfaction and its Antecedents," *Research on Aging* 8 (September 1986): 426–440. *See also* Fred C. Pample and Sookja Park, "Cross-National Patterns and Determinants of Female Retirement," *American Journal of Sociology* 91 (January 1986): 932–955.

influence the ability to accept, cope, or adjust to them. A recognition of significant others may help explain why many persons choose to endure illness and death at home rather than in a hospital or institutional setting. An understanding of reference groups may help us understand the relevance of the church, friends, or the kin network as support systems in facing these circumstances. While death may be a physical process, it is the cultural, social, and interpersonal processes that influence and affect it. To mourn, to wear black, to commit suicide by burning following the death of a spouse, to build mausoleums, or to bury in air-tight vaults are dependent upon cultural, class, and other social conditions.

Widows and widowers, described in the section that follows, are said to be a group perceived to be carriers and transmitters of the realities of death.[38] The word *widow* itself forces persons with this social status to respond as if they have an infectious disease. People want to know when—if ever—they will "get over it." They want to know if anyone ever "completely recovers." The death of a spouse is consistently seen as a major source of stress requiring more readjustment than any other event in life. The loss of any loved one is likely to result in consequences that include grief, loneliness, depression, and economic difficulties. The economic difficulties may not be associated solely with the loss of income but from illness and funeral expenses as well.

In the United States as well as in most cultures, in times of illness, the immediate family and the immediate kin network has been found to be a major social support. Among the elderly, the presence of relatives makes it possible for bedridden persons to live outside institutions. Elderly people turn first to their families for help, then to neighbors, and, finally, to the bureaucratic replacements for families. Thus, it is not surprising that surveys indicate most people say they would like to die at home. In spite of this, medical attention, nursing care, and social-work help for the dying is hospital-based. And while four people would prefer to die at home for every one who would like to die in a hospital, in actual practice the ratio is reversed.[39]

Movements seem to be in process to make family-kin interaction with the terminally ill or dying patient more possible. One plan, called *hospice*, is a therapeutic environment designed from the patients' point of view. Unlike a regular hospital, which stresses privacy, hospice programs deemphasize this, emphasizing instead space for interaction with staff, family, and friends. Instead of subordinating the patient to the needs of the institution with families waiting in the hall, hospice programs are designed to provide as much care in the patient's home as possible; when medical facilities are needed, they involve a team of medical, nursing, psychiatric, and religious people, social workers, and family members as the need indicates. The concern is on

---

38. Carol J. Barrett, "Women in Widowhood," *Signs: Journal of Women in Culture and Society* 2 (Summer 1977): 856.

39. Virginia H. Hine, "Dying at Home: Can Families Cope?" *Omega* 10 (1979–80): 175.

increasing the quality of the last days of life and on making humane care synonymous with good medical practice. As a result, the family of the institutionalized patient is encouraged to be involved: bring in "home cooking," bathe the patient, supply medication, or bring along the family dog. Hours or visits are unlimited and interaction is permitted with young children or grandchildren.

The significance of family ties takes on an added dimension when one looks at the relationship between marital status and mortality. Mortality is lower for married persons with children than for those without children, and lower for nonmarried persons who are household heads than for those who are not heads.[40] These findings tend to suggest that protection against death itself may be afforded by different kinds of social ties, particularly marital, parental, and kin ties. These same ties, or severance of them, may explain some of the difficulties of the widow or widower.

## THE POSTMARITAL FAMILY: THE WIDOW AND WIDOWER

The postmarital family, consisting of the widow or widower, is not unique to the aged family but is disproportionately represented after age sixty-five (*see* Figure 15–4). In 1988, there were 11.2 million widows and 2.3 million widowers with 72 percent of them age sixty-five and over.[41] Facing the loss of a spouse and making the shift from a married to a widowed status may present extreme emotional and financial difficulties.

Society compounds the difficulty of adjusting to the widowed status by placing an unstated taboo on the discussion of death between husband and wife or parents and children while they are alive. As a result, the widow or widower is often unprepared for the decisions that need to be made. Even if discussions preceded the death, the likelihood is great that loneliness, social isolation, and a need for major readjustments in living patterns will result. There is probably no other period in one's life when there is a greater effort at self-awareness. Feelings of inadequacy and guilt, which lead to depression, are frequent occurrences after the death of a spouse.

Readjustment processes may be less difficult if widowhood follows a major illness or some type of major role change on the part of the spouse. Widowhood is often surmounted best when a person has already built some autonomy of personality, close continuing friendships, a realistic philosophy of life, economic security, and some meaningful personal interests.

While studies indicate a high degree of contact between older people and younger family members, especially adult children, this contact is not directly

40. Frances E. Kobrin and Gerry E. Hendershot, "So Family Ties Reduce Mortality? Evidence from the United States, 1966–1968," *Journal of Marriage and the Family* 39 (November 1977): 737–745.

41. U.S. Bureau of the Census, *Current Population Reports*, Series P-20, no. 433, "Marital Status and Living Arrangements, March 1988" (Washington D.C.: U.S. Government Printing Office, 1989), Table 1, p. 3.

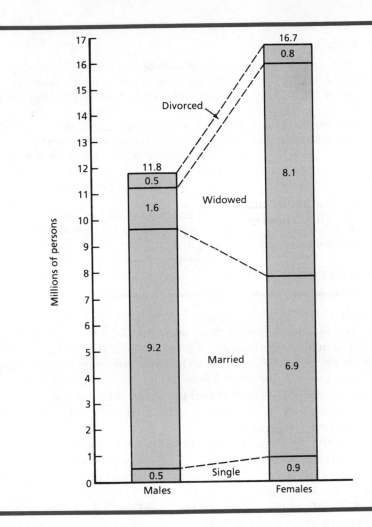

*Figure 15–4*
**Number of males and females over age 65 by marital status, 1988.** (*Source:* Adapted
from U.S. Bureau of the Census, *Current Population Reports*, Series P-20, no. 433,
"Marital Status and Living Arrangements, March 1988" [Washington, D.C.: U.S. Government Printing Office, 1989], Table 1, p. 3).

associated with higher morale or greater personal satisfaction.[42] In contrast to
family members, friendship-neighboring is clearly related to less loneliness

---

42. Norval D. Glenn and Sara McLanahan, "The Effects of Offspring on the Psychological
Well-Being of Older Adults," *Journal of Marriage and the Family* 43 (May 1981): 409–421; and
Elizabeth A. Bankoff, "Social Support and Adaptation to Widowhood," *Journal of Marriage and the
Family* 45 (November 1983): 827–839.

## Casserole Women

The *Wall Street Journal* (April 22, 1986) reported that in South Florida's retirement communities, the women in pursuit of husbands are called "casserole women" because they descend on newly eligible men bearing food and sympathy. Men who live to an old age and want to date have little trouble finding partners.

One 75-year-old retired speechwriter said he has lots of fun and to prove it pulled from his wallet photographs of a woman leaning on his shoulder and another of a blond woman talking on the telephone. A 78-year-old ex-chef spurns women his own age and says he doesn't take to the old because they have no pep, no sex life.

Yet, the intense shortage of unmarried older men is not without its difficulties. Unattached men report periods of intense loneliness while women often find a supportive community of other women in similar situations. The chairman of a governing board of one of the retirement communities says that there are two basic social units in retirement communities—couples and widows. The single men aren't a viable entity as a group. Widowers are so scarce that the single man becomes the odd man out in retired life.

An attorney who often draws up pre-nuptial agreements to preserve the separation of assets, says the aged date and marry with few illusions. They come in holding hands, saying, "Dearie this" and "Dolly that"—but "Don't touch my money."

and worry, to a feeling of "usefulness," and to individual respect within the community. Friendship relationships are voluntary and are often based upon common interests and a common life-style, while family ties are often marked by dissimilar concerns, different interests, formal obligations, and a role reversal between the elderly parent and the adult children. Certain intergenerational difficulties may be inevitable and be increased by factors such as ill health and economic dependency.

One problem, believed to be widespread among elderly persons in general but particularly among the widowed, is that of social isolation and loneliness.[43] Social isolation is the objective condition of having few contacts with family, friends, or both. Loneliness is a subjective condition which includes feelings of emptiness, aimlessness, and lack of companionship and involves a dissatisfaction with the present level of social interaction. One study of widows found that loneliness was listed by almost half of the respondents as their most serious difficulty: another third listed it as second.[44] Social norms for the United States and numerous other countries stress independence, but independence apart from frequent social interaction, marriage, employment, or adequate income leads to an increased vulnerability toward loneliness and low levels of mental and physical health.

---

43. Helena Znaniecki Lopata, *Widowhood in an American City* (Cambridge, Mass.: Schenkman, 1973); Philip G. Clark, Robert W. Siviski, and Ruth Weiner, "Coping Strategies of Widowers in the First Year," *Family Relations* 35 (July 1986): 425–430; and Marilyn J. Essex and Sunghee Nam, "Marital Status and Loneliness Among Older Women: The Differentiated Importance of Close Family and Friends," *Journal of Marriage and the Family* 49 (February 1987): 93–106.

44. Lopata, *Widowhood in an American City*, p. 70.

The extreme outcome of conditions such as those just mentioned can be seen in examining the frequency of suicides. Within a given age group, the suicide rates of the widowed are consistently higher than those of the married, and the rate of completed suicides is significantly higher for males than for females. A study of aged persons in Florida reported the following major findings:

> (1) The widowed exhibit higher suicide rates than the married; (2) this differential is partially explained by the greater social isolation of the widowed, particularly the widowers; (3) the widowed can find in other types of relationships meaningful alternatives to marriage which help prevent suicidal behavior; (4) widowers have greater difficulty than widows in making effective substitutions for the loss of spouse; and (5) there appear to be limits to the effective mitigation of these alternatives for the widowed, especially the widower.[45]

These problems do not exist independently of retirement—discussed previously—and may be aggravated by it. The widow and widower are removed from their major sources of self-identity: job and the relationships with co-workers. The result of losing a spouse in old age, particularly among males, is therefore characterized by unhappiness, low morale, mental disorders, high death rates, and high suicide rates. All these seem to be related to the social isolation the widower faces. Not only has he lost a significant other in his spouse, but he also becomes isolated from other persons significant to him: friends, neighbors, kin, and those connected with formal organizations. On the other hand, the widow has a greater opportunity for role continuity: housekeeping, interacting with relatives, going to church, and participating in various other kinds of formal and informal relationships.

Some widows and widowers remarry, but the chances of remarriage are, of course, higher for widowers than for widows. With women outliving men, the sex ratio (about 71) is very unbalanced in the later years. Of those not married, the ratio is even more unbalanced. In 1988, the ratio of unmarried males over age sixty-five to unmarried females over age sixty-five was 27 to 100 (*see* Figure 15–3 and note 2.6 million unmarried men versus 9.8 million unmarried women). Programs to encourage remarriage among widows and widowers could not be successful, at least in a monogamous system. The problem is further compounded in our society by the norm that suggests that women should marry men of their own age or older. The remarriage problem for widowers is less severe since there is both an excess of women their own age as well as a social approval given to marriage to women younger than themselves.

The questions centering around the remarriage of widows and widowers are often different from the questions centering around the remarriage of

---

45. E. Wilbur Bock and Irving L. Webber, "Suicide Among the Elderly: Isolating Widowhood and Mitigating Alternatives," *Journal of Marriage and the Family* 34 (February 1972): 24.

divorced persons. The persons are generally older and face different circumstances surrounding the ending of the previous marriage. A remarriage after the death of a spouse is likely to lead to a comparison of the new spouse with the memory of the deceased. It has been suggested that the perceived quality of marriage improves after the death of a spouse; the tendency is to recall the pleasant experiences and be keenly aware of the spouse's absence. Lopata's sample of Chicago widows showed a strong tendency to idealize the late husband and life with him, often to the point of sanctification.[46] This was less likely to happen among young and black women, those with a lower education and income, and those who had a difficult time in marriage. Older white widows in particular were apt to sanctify their husbands. Perhaps it is not accidental that saints exist primarily among the deceased.

## SUMMARY

1. This chapter included an examination of two major periods of the life cycle: the middle years from approximately age forty to retirement, and the later years from approximately age sixty or sixty-five until the end of the life span.
2. The middle years, after the departure of children and prior to retirement, is a period when most men and women are married, with small percentages of single, widowed, or divorced people. It is one of the longest periods of the marital life cycle, covering a span of twenty to twenty-five years.
3. The significance of the middle years appears to differ somewhat for men and women. While family income approaches its peak, mixed evidence exists as to the extent to which this period of life for men and women is bright or difficult. Writers talk of a midlife crisis or transition for men and an empty-nest syndrome for women. It appears likely that family-work changes lessen the negative impact of this period for both sexes.
4. Grandparenting has become a middle-age in addition to an old-age phenomenon. It may be an instrumental role for family systems in linking generations, in financial and service support functions, and in assisting the transition to other life-cycle stages. It appears to be a positive status for most respondents, although the roles vary considerably by social class and cultural context.
5. In the United States, later life is often viewed as an undesirable period, accented by dependency relationships and declining productivity. This stands in contrast to much of the world where older persons receive increasing status, prestige, and deference.
6. In the United States, nearly 80 percent of the men but only about one-half of the women aged sixty-five to seventy-four are married. After age seventy-five, more than two-thirds of the men but less than one-fourth of the women are married. Marriages that do exist are perceived as favorable when compared to preceding periods of the life course. Most of the men and women of this age are living in

---

46. Helena Znaniecki Lopata, "Widowhood and Husband Sanctification," *Journal of Marriage and the Family* 43 (May 1981): 439–450.

families or living in geographical proximity to their children. Relatively few are in long-term care institutions such as nursing homes.

7. The problems facing the aged population are many, but this chapter focused briefly on three: health, money, and abuse. Most health problems are handled in the home rather than hospitals, with primary care coming from spouses or children. Money income drops in old age but most families cope quite well and even give more than they receive.

8. Retirement, widowhood, changing relationships, and the like create a need for resocialization to new roles and definitions of self in relation to society.

9. Retirement has been described as a process involving periods of preretirement, the retirement transition, and postretirement. For both sexes it appears to be positive. Marital and household roles appear to change relatively little in retirement over the traditional patterns established during years of employment. The increased employment of women appears to be lessening the difference between the sexes in significance of retirement.

10. Dying and death are processes and events of major importance and significance to family members. Family members have been found to be major support systems both to the dying persons as well as to one another following death. The recognition of this seems to be encouraging movements in treating terminally ill and dying patients in home settings or in family-focused medical settings.

11. The postmarital family, particularly as represented by the widow or widower, while not unique to the aged family, is disproportionately represented after age sixty-five: more women occupy a widow status than any other marital status. With the unbalanced sex ratio, remarriage is out of the question for a large number of women. For men, although the availability of a new spouse is less of a problem, the problems may be equally severe. Suicides are high among this marital status group, particularly among the very old.

12. The family life cycle, while ending for a particular nuclear family grouping, continues for the multigenerational extended family. Each stage or category of the life cycle has circumstances that are both unique to, and different from, the other stages. This chapter examined selected factors relating to the postparental periods: middle years, retirement, and old age. Conflict, crisis, and marital disorganization, although present at these periods of the life cycle, are not confined to them. The next chapter explores social patterns surrounding crisis and disorganization with a particular focus on abuses and violence.

## KEY TERMS AND TOPICS

# DISCUSSION QUESTIONS

1. What is unique about the middle years or the empty-nest period? How is the period of adjustment different for women and for men?

2. Discuss the midlife transition and the empty-nest syndrome. Do they exist and, if so, how serious are they? How might sex-role socialization patterns affect the middle years for both sexes?

3. Indicate changes in the grandparent role over the last thirty years. How might this role affect generational relationships? How might the grandparent status differ by class and subculture?

4. How true is the argument "you can't teach an old dog new tricks" when applied to the middle-aged or aged couple?

5. Health, money, and abuse were stated as problems facing the aged. What other problems exist? How might a society establish programs, tax structures, and social policies that lessen the negative impact of these problems?

6. Discuss changes in husband-wife roles that are likely to accompany illness, retirement, grandparenthood, remarriage, and so forth. How can resocialization be facilitated?

7. What are the implications of retirement at age seventy, sixty, or fifty? Note marital status and male-female differences in adjustment patterns after retirement.

8. What advantages or disadvantages exist to the widow or widower: if living alone, if living with kin, if living in a private home with other than kin, if living in an institution? What types of conditions make one more favorable than another?

9. Explain the incidence of suicide among widowers versus widows, and single versus married persons.

10. Invite several persons over age seventy-five to your class or to a "bull-session" to discuss such topics as the empty-nest syndrome, grandparenthood, retirement, widowhood, or facing death. Examine the significance of having children and their importance as systems of support.

# FURTHER READINGS

Bahr, Stephen J., and Peterson, Evan T., (eds.). *Aging and the Family*. Lexington, Mass.: D.C. Heath and Company, 1989. An examination of aging from a family perspective: transition to the empty nest and widowhood, family relationships, health and economic well-being of families.

Blau, Zena Smith ed. *Current Perspectives on Aging and The Life Cycle*. Greenwich, Conn.: JAI Press, Inc., 1985. This volume, the first in an ongoing series, focuses on work, retirement, and social policy viewed from a life-course perspective.

Brubaker, Timothy H. *Later-Life Families*. Beverly Hills: Sage Publications, 1986. An intensive look at marriages, generational relationships, widowhood, and the future of persons and families in later life.

Brubaker, Timothy H. *Married for Fifty Years*. Lexington, Mass.: Lexington Books, 1986. Interviews with fifty couples who were married for fifty years reveal how they view marriage, mortality, and themselves.

Cherlin, Andrew, and Furstenberg, Frank F., Jr. *The New American Grandparent*. New York: Basic Books, 1986. Based on a nationwide study, two family sociologists provide a portrait of grandparenthood in U.S. society.

Giele, Janet Zollinger. *Women in the Middle Years*. New York: John Wiley and Sons, 1982. A look at women in adulthood: their health, development, work, and family roles. The book includes an appendix that summarizes longitudinal and cross-sectional data sources on this age-grouping of women.

Lopata, Helena Znaniecki. *Women as Widows*. New York: Elsevier North Holland, 1979. A theoretical and descriptive study of widows that focuses on the societal, community, family, and personal resources available to them.

Peterson, Warren, A., and Quadagno, Jill, eds. *So-*

*cial Bonds in Life: Aging and Interdependence.* Beverly Hills: Sage Publications, 1985. Twenty readings dealing with the interdependence of intimate relationships, social support systems, and health and social services.

Szinovacz, Maximiliane, ed. *Women's Retirement: Policy Implications of Recent Research.* Beverly Hills: Sage Publications, 1982. A compilation of fifteen original publications of research specifically devoted to women's retirement.

Treas, Judith, and Bengtson, Vern L. "The Family in Later Years" in *Handbook of Marriage and the Family* by Marvin B. Sussman and Suzanne K.

Steinmetz (eds.). New York: Plenum Press, 1987, Chapter 23, pp. 625–648. Macrosocial, microsocial, and intervention perspectives on aging families are presented.

U.S. Bureau of the Census. "America in Transition: An Aging Society," *Current Population Reports.* Series P-23, no. 128. Washington D.C.: U.S. Government Printing Office, 1983. One of the special studies published by the Bureau of the Census, giving a wide variety of statistics covering the numerical growth, income and poverty, health status, and social characteristics of older persons.

# CHAPTER SIXTEEN

# FAMILY CRISIS AND VIOLENCE AMONG INTIMATES

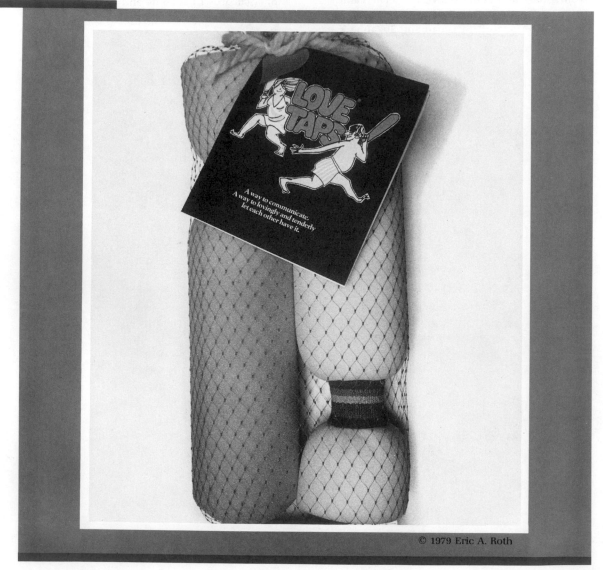

© 1979 Eric A. Roth

Marriages and families have been examined throughout the life course. No period in life is without the potential for **marital crisis.** You may recall references to parenthood as crisis, low levels of marital satisfaction ten to fifteen years after marriage, role conflicts, and the like. Each refers to some event or process that produces or produced stress, conflict, crisis, or reorganization to the marital or family unit or intimate relationships.

If eyewitnesses to the family in the United States are to be believed, this institution and the interpersonal relationships within it have been in a state of decline for the past several hundred years. Preachers, teachers, philosophers, political leaders, commentators, and others have recorded their beliefs, irrespective of the generation in which they lived, that parental authority was becoming more lax, sexual taboos were weakening, spouses were rebelling against one another, and so forth. This was usually contrasted to the "old days" when authority was respected, sexual taboos were observed, and spouses were more understanding and tolerant. That each generation makes reference to weakness and decline may indicate dissatisfaction with present events, whatever these events may be, and sentimentality over the past, or it may indicate that actual conditions are never equal to the ideal. In either case, marital and family life is seldom "perfect" either for a given marriage or family as it covers the life course or for the marital and family system at any given time within a society. Stressor events produce crises and a need for family reorganization. Let's examine some of these social stresses on the family.

## SOCIAL STRESSES ON FAMILIES

In a widely quoted article, now more than thirty years old, Reuben Hill speaks of *stressor* or crisis-provoking events.[1] These are situations for which families have little or no prior preparation. They are never the same for any given family but vary in striking power by the hardships that accompany them. Hardships are those complications in a crisis-precipitating event that demand competencies from the family that the event itself may have temporarily paralyzed or made unavailable.

Closely related to this idea is Pauline Boss's usage of *stress* to mean "pressure or tension in the family system."[2] She says that it is a disturbance in the steady state of the family. With change comes disturbance, pressure— what we call stress. It is normal, inevitable, and even desirable at times. The family's degree of stress results from events or situations that have potential to cause change.

---

1. Reuben Hill, "Social Stresses on the Family," *Social Casework 39* (February/March 1958): 139–150.
2. Pauline Boss, *Family Stress Management* (Newbury Park, Ca.: Sage Publications, Inc. 1988).

Why do different families respond so differently to change? Why is a pregnancy a blessing to some and a curse to others? Why is a geographical move a thrilling event to some family members and a severe disruption to others? Why does unemployment, divorce, or death severely cripple some persons while others seem to "take them in stride"? A key to answering questions such as these was provided by Hill in what today is widely referred to as the **ABCX model of stress.** This formula refers to A (the event) $\rightarrow$ interacting with B (the family's crisis meeting resources) $\rightarrow$ interacting with C (the definition the family makes of the event) $\rightarrow$ producing X (the crisis).[3] The two key dimensions are B and C in the formula. If both are adequate, the level of stress will be low or nonexistent. If one or both are inadequate the level of stress will be high. Let us examine this ABCX formulation more closely.

Stressor events (A) may come from a wide variety of sources both within and outside the family. The consequences are likely to differ considerably depending on the source. For example, a general principle in sociology indicates that certain events outside a group such as war, flood, or depression tend to solidify the group. Thus, although stressful, certain external events may tend to unify the family into a more cohesive unit rather than to lead or contribute to its breakdown. These same events may not be defined as critically stressful because other persons are in the same situation or worse. For example, it is disappointing to professional researchers to have their writings rejected by editors of journals. The pain may be less severe if it is recognized that a given publication has a 90 percent rejection rate. To know that many others submitted articles and were rejected, did not get their research funded, lost their homes, had premature births, or were unemployed often makes the event appear less critical. That is, others share similar misfortunes.

Events within the family that are defined as stressful may be more disruptive because they arise from troubles that reflect poorly on the family's internal adequacy. These events may be nonsupport, mental breakdown, violence, suicide, or alcoholism, among others. The range of events, either within or outside the family, that disturb the family's role patterns is numerous. Not only do they involve losses of persons, jobs, or incomes, but additions as well. The arrival of a child, grandmother, or mother-in-law may be as disruptive as the loss of any of those three. Sudden fame or fortune may be as disruptive as loss of either. Any sudden change in family status or conflict among family members in the conceptions of their roles may further produce family crisis.

The dimensions that characterize any given stressor or crisis-provoking event extend far beyond whether it occurs internally or externally to the family. A crisis-producing event may affect the entire system or only a limited part, may occur gradually or suddenly, may be intense or mild, may be a short- or

---

3. Hill, "Social Stresses on the Family," p. 141.

long-term problem, may be expected and predicted or random, may arise from natural conditions or artificial and technological man-made effects, may represent a shortage or overabundance of vital commodities, may be perceived to be solvable or insolvable, and may vary in substantive content. The nature of the crisis event will influence the specific response of an individual or family system.

Again, what factors make for crisis proneness and freedom from crisis proneness? The explanation lies in B and C in the formula presented earlier. That is, to what extent do families have resources to meet the event (factor B) and to what extent do families define the event as a crisis (factor C)? Crisis-meeting resources (factor B) may include many factors: family adaptability, family roles, kin support systems, money income, insurance, friends, religious beliefs, education, good health, and the like. Problem families are often those without adequate resources to meet the stressor events. The extent to which families define the event as a crisis (factor C) reflects the value system of the family and previous experience in meeting crisis. This definition of the event refers to the meaning attached to it, the interpretation as to its seriousness, and the perception of the event as enabling (making other things possible) or disabling (weakening or destroying possibilities). Crisis proneness (X), that is, the level or degree of stress, is therefore a function of both a deficiency in family organization resources (factor B) and the tendency to define hardships as crisis producing (factor C). These two factors are combined into one concept of family inadequacy or family adequacy.

McCubbin and others, in an attempt to build on Hill's ABCX model, have proposed a **double ABCX model** that differentiates the precrisis and postcrisis variables.[4] The model now becomes a longitudinal one and the factor of time differentiates the precrisis from the postcrisis situation. The initial stressor event becomes a double "A" by separating the changes that occur irrespective of the initial stressor from those changes that are consequences of the family's efforts to cope with the hardships of the situation. The resources become a double "B" by differentiating those resources already available to the family from those coping resources strengthened or developed in response to the crisis situation. The perception and meaning become a double "C" by likewise differentiating the definition prior to the event of how stressful it may be from the postcrisis perceptions of the level of stress. Combining the pre- and postcrisis ABC factors leads to family adaptation (or maladaptation) as a possible outcome. This double model was put to an empirical test using data on army families' adaptation to the crisis of relocation.[5]

---

4. Hamilton I. McCubbin and Joan M. Patterson, "Family Adaptation to Crisis," *Family Stress, Coping, and Social Support,* ed. by Hamilton I. McCubbin et al. (Springfield, Ill.: Charles C Thomas, 1982): 44–46.

5. Yoav Lavee, Hamilton I. McCubbin, and Joan M. Patterson, "The Double ABCX Model of Family Stress and Adaptation: An Empirical Test by Analysis of Structural Equations with Latent Variables," *Journal of Marriage and the Family* 47 (November 1985): 811–825.

Alexis Walker makes a case for expanding the ABCX model of stress and crisis to incorporate new dimensions.[6] These include a recognition that (1) all levels of the social system are interdependent and (2) stress occurs in a unique and influential sociocultural context. The interdependence of levels incorporates individual factors with dyadic, family, non-family, and community ones. That is, levels more macro than individuals and families need to be incorporated into the model.

Individual resources may be very different from family, community, or societal ones. Definitions or perceptions may vary for multiple members of a family. Whose definition is more important? If members don't agree, will the crisis be unresolvable?

The sociohistorical context recognizes how perceptions of stressful circumstances and resources available vary considerably over time. The differing contexts, and the unique perspectives and resources related to a given context, need to be recognized. In brief, in examining the process of adjustment to stress, it becomes necessary to focus, over time, on individual changes, dyadic changes, social network changes, and developments in the wider society that influence the ability of an individual, dyad, or family to respond effectively.

One example of a contextual analysis and the incorporation of the larger society (macroanalysis) into research comes from Kersti Yllo.[7] She attempts to understand violence against wives by looking at the balance of power in marital relationships as they are shaped by women's aggregate economic, political, legal, and educational status. Interpersonal interaction, including stress and violence, does not occur within a social vacuum and needs to incorporate factors such as patriarchal social structures and social inequalities built into marriages.

Another factor to consider is how stress in one area or from one source spills over into other areas. An article on the contagion of stress across multiple roles documented that home-to-work stress occurs more strongly among men than women and that both men and women reduce their involvements in stressful home situations following a stressful day at work.[8] Wives in particular modified their housework efforts to compensate for the work stresses of their spouses. Stresses in one area such as work affect stresses in other areas such as home and stresses experienced by one spouse or partner affect stresses in the other.

While the list of stressor events, family problems, or conflict situations in marriages and families may seem infinite, this chapter focuses only on a

---

6. Alexis J. Walker, "Reconceptualizing Family Stress," *Journal of Marriage and the Family* 47 (November 1985): 827–837.

7. Kersti Yllo, "The Status of Women, Marital Equality, and Violence Against Wives," *Journal of Family Issues* 5 (September 1984): 307–320.

8. Niall Bolger, Anita DeLongis, Ronald C. Kessler, and Elaine Wethington, "The Contagion of Stress Across Multiple Roles," *Journal of Marriage and the Family* 51 (February 1989): 175–183.

selected one: violence. Other potentially stressful events such as mobility, commuter marriages, dual-career situations, sexual or racial inequality, poverty, intermarriage, sexual inadequacies, incest, conjugal decision making, parenthood, father-mother absence, mid-life crisis, widowhood, death, and aging were discussed in some detail in prior chapters. Other issues, like separation, divorce, and stepchildren, are discussed in the next chapter.

## *VIOLENCE IN FAMILIES AND AMONG INTIMATES*

Violence in families and among intimates refers to any act among legally related individuals or those in close primary relationships that is carried out with the intention of causing physical harm. This broad definition would include acts such as spanking a disobedient child, raping a lover, or murdering a spouse. Are you aware that you are more likely to be physically assaulted, beaten, raped, and killed in your own home at the hands of a loved one than anyplace else, or by anyone else in our society?[9]

Despite the pictures of missing children on cards and milk cartons, children are more likely to be kidnapped by their own parents than by strangers. Despite the image of marriage as one of love and affection, more than half of all couples report physical violence by a partner at some time during their marriage. Despite the sensational headlines of "woman raped in public park," "child beaten in day-care center," and "elderly person mugged in parking lot," these events are most frequent in homes by persons "close" to us. Nearly one out of every four murder victims in the United States is killed by a member of his or her own family, and this is also the case in Africa, Great Britain, and Denmark.[10]

It should be noted that violence, while frequent in most societies, is not an inevitable consequence of family life. David Levinson, for example, in examining violence cross-culturally, lists sixteen societies of the ninety in his sample that are relatively free of family violence.[11] Hunter-gatherers (Ona, Andamans, Siriono, Bushman), he suggests, rarely mistreat their children and are overrepresented among the societies without family violence.

Levinson adds that:

> in general, in societies without family violence, husbands and wives
> share in domestic decision making, wives have some control over the
> fruits of family labor, wives can divorce their husbands as easily as their
> husbands can divorce them, marriage is monogamous, there is no pre-
> marital sex double standard, divorce is relatively infrequent, husbands

---

9. Richard J. Gelles and Murray A. Straus, *Intimate Violence* (New York: Simon and Schuster, 1988): 18.

10. Richard J. Gelles, *Family Violence* (Beverly Hills: Sage Publications, 1979): 11.

11. David Levinson, *Family Violence in Cross-Cultural Perspective* (Newbury Park: Sage Publications, 1989): 102–107.

and wives sleep together, men resolve disputes with other men peacefully, and intervention in wife beating incidents tends to be immediate.[12]

The central conclusion reached from these findings is that family violence does not occur in societies in which family life is characterized by cooperation, commitment, sharing, and equality. In contrast, family violence will be more common in societies in which men control women's lives, violent resolution to conflicts is acceptable, and the mother bears the major responsibility for childrearing.

Whether in the United States or other societies around the world, precise data on conjugal and parental abuse and violence are difficult to obtain. Not only do they occur behind closed doors and hidden from public view but also they may not be perceived as improper. Behaviors such as spouse shoving, child spanking, and sibling fighting may be defined as normative, appropriate, and even necessary marital and family behaviors. Given this type of situation, one can only infer and speculate about how much intrafamily violence and/or abuse exists. What is no longer speculative is the idea that violence is a pervasive and common feature between partners, spouses, and among family members in most societies of the world.

## The myth of the U.S. family as nonviolent

Richard Gelles and Murray Straus suggest that intraviolence in the United States may be more common to the institution of the family than love.[13] Their suggestion is based on their own research and a review of other studies. The data indicate that:

1. Between 84 and 97 percent of all parents use physical punishment at some point in the child's life.
2. Conservative estimates of child abuse run to between 200,000 and 500,000 cases per year in the United States.
3. Twenty to 40 percent of all homicides involve domestic relationships.
4. Family fights are the largest single category of police calls.
5. A study of applicants for divorce found that 23 percent of middle-class couples and 40 percent of working-class couples gave "physical abuse" as a major complaint.
6. A national cross section of the population revealed that one in four men and one in six women would approve of slapping a wife under certain conditions, and 26 percent of the men and 19 percent of the women would approve of slapping a husband.

---

12. Ibid., p. 103.
13. Richard J. Gelles and Murray A. Straus, "Determinants of Violence in the Family: Toward a Theoretical Integration," in *Contemporary Theories About the Family*. Vol. 1, ed. by Wesley R. Burr et al. (New York: The Free Press, 1979): 550–552.

7. Within a single year, 62 percent of high school seniors studied had used physical force on a brother or sister, and 16 percent of their parents had used physical force on each other.

These types of data offer a persuasive counterargument to the widespread view that violence within families is a rare phenomenon found in scattered families. To view the family as nonviolent therefore is basically a myth. What about other myths related to family violence?

### Myths of family violence

In a chapter entitled "People Other Than Us: Public Perceptions of Family Violence," Gelles and Straus reveal a number of stereotypes developed about abusive partners and families.[14] These stereotypes about the nature and causes of domestic violence are often more pieces of conventional wisdom than facts or truths. The perpetuation of these myths serves the function of attributing violence to "people other than us" or to mentally disturbed unbalanced people rather than acknowledging that violence and the violent home are an outgrowth of the very structure of our society and family.

The first myth relates to the one just cited, that is, the myth of the family as being nonviolent. This myth is double-sided. One view is that family violence is rare and the other view is that an increase in violence is of "epidemic" proportions. The range of estimates from thousands to millions suggests that no one really knows how much violence there is in families—the conclusion drawn is that the problem is not a problem at all.

Myth number two suggests that abusers are aliens and victims are innocents. The stereotype is that the abuser is mentally disturbed, psychologically unbalanced, or even psychotic while the victim is a defenseless innocent. The authors suggest that only about 10 percent of abusive incidents are caused by mental illness. Not desiring to see our own behavior or that of our friends or relatives as improper, we envision family violence as being committed by horrible persons against innocent people.

Myth number three suggests that abuse is confined to poor minority families. Research does find that intimate violence is more likely to occur in lower income or minority households but that it is not confined to them. Violence cuts across all classes and races but the poor, while having a greater likelihood of being violent, also run the risk of being overrepresented in official statistics. Confining violence to poor or minority families is another way of seeing others as violent and our own behavior as normal.

Myth number four suggests that alcohol and drugs are the real causes of violence in the home. A high association does exist between violence and alcohol and drug usage. But this myth suggests that violence ends when the

---

14. Gelles and Straus, *Intimate Violence*, Chapter 2, pp. 37–51.

drinking/drug problem is eliminated and that alcohol or drugs are the *cause* of the violence. Evidence disputes the claim that alcohol causes violence and supports the claim that certain drugs are rarely associated with violence; in fact, some drugs produce a euphoric effect, reducing the level of violence. In short, curing or eliminating an alcohol or drug problem would not eliminate domestic violence.

Myth number five suggests that children who are abused grow up to be abusers. Again this myth has truth in that abused children *tend* to grow up to be abusive, but *all* abused children do not grow up to be abusive. No evidence supports the claim that people who are abused are preprogrammed to be abusers.

Myth number six suggests that battered women like being hit. Supporting this myth are ideas that since most abused women stay in the home, they must like being hit, or that battered women must do something to provoke the abuse and thus desire to be beaten. The dynamics of family violence and the social position of women in our society explodes this myth while detailing the conflicting double bind in which victims of wife abuse live day in and day out.

The seventh and final myth reported by Gelles and Straus is that violence and love are incompatible. Many battered spouses have strong feelings for their partners and most battered children love their parents. Unlike violence in the streets, violence in the home is linked to bonds of love, attachment, and affection. The authors conclude the chapter by stating:

> It is not only the myths that have to be abandoned, but the social func-
> tion that they serve. The greatest function served by the seven myths we
> have discussed is that collectively they serve as a smokescreen that
> blinds us to our own potential for violence. Moreover, when our explana-
> tions focus on "kinds of people"—mentally disturbed, poor, alcoholics,
> drug abusers, etc.—we blind ourselves to the structural properties of the
> family as a social institution that makes it our most violent institution
> with the exception of the military in time of war.[15]

Why is there so much violence in the family? Drawing upon an earlier work of Gelles and Straus, they suggest that the family has unique character-istics as a social group which contribute to making it a violence-prone setting. The irony of these characteristics is that they also have the potential for making the family a warm, supportive, and intimate environment. These characteristics include: the intense time spent interacting with other family members; the wide range of activities and interests of families; the intensity of involvement; the impinging activities of multiple members wanting differing things at the same time; the right to influence and attempt to change the behavior of others; the sexual and age differences which make the family an arena of cultural conflict; the assignment of roles based on ascription rather

---

15. Ibid., p. 51.

## A worldwide perspective of family violence over the life course

### Infants

Killing babies at birth or when very young

Harsh disciplinary practices such as hitting, pinching, burning, overly hot baths

Deprivational feeding, punitive bladder/bowel training behaviors

Selling or offering for sacrifice

Binding head, feet, or other body parts

### Early childhood

Fights between siblings

Child prostitution, slavery, marriage

Harsh disciplinary practices including spanking, hitting, beating, burning, pinching, etc.

Forced labor

Ridicule, threats, teasing

Mutilating, selling, killing for money or ritual

### Adolescence

Physical punishment as with infants and children

Sibling fighting and abuse

Rape, forced sexual relations with same or opposite sex, between children, or adults and children

Initiation ceremonies that may involve scarring, circumcision, clitoridectomy, bloodletting, or other painful activities

Killing or forced suicide

### Adulthood

Wife/husband beating and abuse

Co-wife beating and abuse

Marital and nonmarital rape

Physical or mental torture

Killing or forced suicide

### Old age

Physical and mental abuse

Abandonment and neglect

Beating, killing, forced suicide

than on interest and competence; the privacy and insulation of the family from both social controls and assistance with conflict; the difficulty in terminating long-term marriage commitments and the impossibility of terminating birth relationships; the high levels of stress brought on by continual family changes associated with births, jobs, aging, and the like; and the social norms which provide parents with the right to use physical violence.[16]

Many theories have been advanced to explain interpersonal violence in general and family violence more specifically.[17] Some theories, as noted, place the explanation within the individual in the form of psychopathologies, alcohol, or drugs. Other theories are social-psychological in nature, with the explanations rooted in social learning, exchange, or social interaction. A third grouping of theories is sociocultural, with the explanations found in societal resources, conflict systems, or the larger culture. Irrespective of cause, let's examine selected forms of family abuse and violence.

---

16. Gelles and Straus, "Determinants of Violence in the Family," pp. 552–554.

17. Fifteen of these theories and conceptual frameworks can be seen in Ibid., pp. 560–568. *See also:* Levinson, *Family Violence in Cross-Cultural Perspective,* pp. 14–20 and 82–88.

### Child abuse and violence

The history of the western world reveals that children have been subject to a range of abuses and cruelties, including the abandonment of infants left to die. While today only isolated incidents of such action are heard, physical punishment of children is legal in every state in the United States. In contrast to Sweden, where a parent can be imprisoned for striking a child, parents in the United States tend to view corporal punishment and spanking as an acceptable and appropriate means of discipline. This "privilege" of spanking is even being extended to school teachers and administrators as a means of punishment and maintaining discipline. Do we not all know what happens if we "spare the rod"?

What about violence in the home? What forms of child abuse occur beyond spanking? One study of a nationally representative sample of 2,143 families in the United States included 1,146 with at least one child between the ages of three and seventeen living at home.[18] Violence was defined as an act carried out with the intention, or perceived intention, of physically injuring another person. The injury could range from a slap to murder, with motives ranging from concern for a child's safety to hostility desiring the death of the child. The results indicated that nearly two-thirds of these families mentioned at least one violent episode during the survey year. The milder forms of violence, as expected, were the most common: slaps, spankings, pushing, or shoving. Twenty percent of the parents reported hitting, and 10 percent reported throwing, as having ever taken place. Least frequent were the most dangerous types of violence. Eight percent reported kicking, biting, or hitting their child with a fist at some point in the raising of the child. Four percent reported "beating up" the child, and three percent said that they had at some time threatened their child with a gun or knife.

The researchers, extrapolating the preceding data to the 46 million children between the ages of three and seventeen who lived with both parents during the year of the study, suggested that between 3.1 and 4.0 million of these children had been kicked, bitten, or punched by their parent at some time, between 1.4 and 2.3 million children had been "beaten up," and between 900,000 and 1.8 million had experienced their parents using a gun or knife on them. These forms of violence, with the exception of the use of a gun or knife, were found to be a pattern of parent-child relations rather than an isolated event. Since the data come from self-reports of "intact" families and from only one of the two parents, they are seen as quite conservative and low estimates of the true level of violence toward children in the United States.

What seems to be happening with time? Is there an epidemic of child abuse that is increasing each year? Apparently not. Murray Straus and Richard

---

18. Richard J. Gelles, "Violence Toward Children in the United States," *American Journal of Orthopsychiatry* 48 (October 1978): 585–586; and Richard J. Gelles and Murray A. Strauss, "Violence in the Family," *Journal of Social Issues* 35 (Spring 1979): 22–26.

*A child has a greater chance of being killed or severely injured by his or her parents than by anyone else. Since much of this behavior is "behind closed doors," most cases of severe spankings, beatings, and violence never become public.*

Gelles compared the rate of physical abuse of children from a 1975 study with the rates from a 1985 replication.[19] Both studies showed an extremely high incidence of severe physical violence against children; however, the 1985 physical child abuse rate (as measured by the number of children who were kicked, punched, bitten, beaten up, or attacked with a knife or gun) was 47 percent lower than the rate ten years earlier.

How can this dramatic drop in violence toward children be explained? Critics argue that the changes may have been due to methodological artifacts—differences resulting from gathering data by telephone rather than in home interviews. But the authors discount that argument and even suggest the anonymity provided by telephone would lead to more, rather than less reporting of violence. A second explanation focused on a greater reluctance to report severe violence following the massive amount of public and media attention paid to abuse over the decade. Again the authors discount this argument and suggest that, if anything, the increase in public attention should have made abused wives and children more likely to report their abuse.

19. Murray A. Straus and Richard J. Gelles, "Societal Change and Change in Family Violence from 1975 to 1985 as Revealed by Two National Surveys," *Journal of Marriage and the Family* 48 (August 1986): 465–479; and Richard J. Gelles and Murray A. Straus, *Intimate Violence*, pp. 109–114. For changes in black families *see:* Robert L. Hampton, Richard J. Gelles, and John W. Harrop, "Is Violence in Black Families Increasing? A Comparison of 1975 and 1985 National Survey Rates," *Journal of Marriage and the Family* 51 (November 1989): 969–980.

### Spanking illegal in Sweden

Sweden has outlawed the old adage "spare the rod and spoil the child." It is illegal for Swedish parents to spank their children or treat them in a humiliating way. A 1979 law passed in the Swedish Parliament by an overwhelming majority of 259 to 6 says that "the parent or guardian should exercise the necessary supervision in accordance with the child's age and other circumstances. The child should not be subjected to corporal punishment or other injurious or humiliating treatment."

A member of the justice ministry in Stockholm said that this law is an attempt to change people's attitudes toward the physical punishment of their children and to show them that society does not approve of this sort of behavior. It is based on the belief that the reaction of children when hit by parents is one of revenge, not one of respect, and that physical punishment of children stimulates fear instead of love.

Despite the critics, the writers are convinced that a decline has taken place in violence toward children and, as reported later, toward wives and women as well.

These changes are reported to be consistent with other changes that have occurred in the family and society over the past decade that most likely served to reduce violence in the home. Changes in family structure, such as increased age at marriage, a later age of having the first child, the decline in number of children per family, and number of unwanted children, are all related to lower rates of child abuse. Changes in the economy, with lower rates of unemployment and inflation in 1985 than 1975, should have helped to reduce the frequency of child abuse. The growth of new and innovative treatment programs, social services, and therapists and therapy approaches has probably helped to reduce intrafamily violence. And finally, deterrence in the form of legal sanctions and a perception of a high probability of getting caught and punished serve as reminders that abusive behavior is inappropriate behavior.

The authors use their findings as a basis for believing that when a national effort is made about some aspects of intrafamily violence (as with child abuse programs), a national accomplishment can result. But they remind us even with the reduction in child abuse, that still leaves a minimum estimate of over a million abused children aged three through seventeen in two-parent households.

Who are these abusive parents? In general, it appears that mothers are slightly more likely than fathers to use violence in parent-child relations. However, male children are more likely to be victims.[20] The first finding may be related to the likelihood of mothers spending more time with children than

---

20. Gelles, "Violence Toward Children in the United States," pp. 588–589.

the fathers, but factors other than time are likely to be operative. The second finding may be explained from a sex-differentiation perspective in which parents may see physical acts toward boys as helping them grow up but a less important character builder for girls. Young children seem to be more frequent victims of parental violence, perhaps suggesting greater interference in parents' activities and a lesser ability to use reason as punishment.

The child abuser, the victim, and the type of abuse all vary by gender and by the type of biological relationship. This seems to be particularly true with sexual abuse. A sample of several thousand cases of "founded" child sexual abuse revealed that nonbiological related caretakers (stepparents, adoptive parents, foster parents, babysitters, institutions) were substantially overrepresented, and biologically related caretakers (parents, siblings, grandparents) were substantially underrepresented in child sexual abuse.[21] Male perpetrators greatly surpassed female perpetrators in all situations: three times as many biological fathers as mothers, nearly five times as many male babysitters as females, and more than twenty times as many males as females in other caretaker roles such as stepparents, paramours or lovers, and institutional staff.

The issue of child abuse, maltreatment, and violence is extremely complex. Concerns relate not merely to the frequency of their occurrence and the types of abuse and the abusers, but extend to neglect, to the availability of services, and to the forms of legal intervention including the questions of custody and placement, decision making, and program coordination. Case identification lags considerably behind the actual rates of abuse, and the increasing levels of reporting place strains upon the limited levels of services available. Listed in the footnotes are other sources for a more extensive treatment of this issue.[22]

## Parent abuse and violence

Violence between parents and children is reciprocal. Children not only are recipients of violence but are perpetrators as well. And while many cases of parental abuse of children go unnoticed and unreported, an assaulted parent (generally the more powerful) may go to great lengths to conceal abuse by his or her child. Severe violence, such as the child who kills a parent, may get publicity, but cases of hitting and biting or threats are likely to remain unnoted by the outsider. Yet, parent assault is common, with attention more focused on adolescents who are abusive than on younger children. Whether by young

---

21. Leslie Margolin and John L. Craft, "Child Sexual Abuse by Caretakers," *Family Relations* 38 (October 1989): 450–455.

22. Michael S. Wald, J. M. Carlsmith, and P. H. Leiderman, *Protecting Abused and Neglected Children* (Stanford, Ca.: Stanford University Press, 1988); and David Finkelhor and Sharon Araji, *A Sourcebook on Child Sexual Abuse* (Beverly Hills: Sage Publications, 1986).

children or by adolescents, violence toward parents is often a neglected dimension.[23]

Data from a national survey of adolescents showed that parent assault is extensive, with roughly 5 percent of the adolescents hitting one of their parents in the past year.[24] Both males and females assaulted parents, but males were less likely to hit mothers and more likely to hit fathers as they got older while females became more likely to hit either parent as they aged. The study reported that adolescents who assaulted parents were more likely to (1) have friends who assaulted parents, (2) approve of delinquency, including violence, (3) perceive the probability of official sanction to be low, (4) hold weak attachments to parents, and (5) be white. More traditional violence factors such as social isolation, drug use, stress, and power differentials were largely unrelated to parent assault.

### Wife abuse and violence

Following the concern over the abuse of children and parents is the abuse of wives. It was previously stated that one in six women expressed the belief that their husbands had the right to slap them under certain conditions. And as women learn that husbands have the right to slap, so do men learn that violence against their wives is acceptable. Data from a national probability sample of about 2,000 men and women revealed that men are more likely to approve of violence against women if they observed their fathers hitting their mothers.[25] Violence begets violence and the cycle of violence continues from one generation to the next.

That violence against women, like much family violence, is not always viewed as improper or deviant has historical precedence. As recently as the late nineteenth century in Great Britain and the United States, it was considered a necessary aspect of a husband's marital obligation to control and chastise his wife through the use of physical force. Violence against wives can be viewed as a logical extension of a patriarchal family system in which the husband, as the dominant ruler and head, uses whatever means necessary to obtain obedience and control. And considerable evidence suggests that irrespective of whether violence toward wives is a carryover of an historical pattern, whether it is a logical extension of a patriarchal system, or whether it

23. Charles W. Peek, Judith L. Fischer, and Jeannie S. Kidwell, "Teenage Violence Toward Parents: A Neglected Dimension of Family Violence," *Journal of Marriage and the Family* 47 (November 1985): 1051–1058.

24. Robert Agnew and Sandra Huguley, "Adolescent Violence toward Parents," *Journal of Marriage and the Family* 51 (August 1989): 699–711.

25. Patricia Ulbrich and Joan Huber, "Observing Parental Violence: Distribution and Effects," *Journal of Marriage and the Family* 43 (August 1981): 623–631; and Debra Kalmuss, "The Intergenerational Transmission of Marital Aggression," *Journal of Marriage and the Family* 46 (February 1984): 11–19.

## Abused women and wives: why do they stay?

The research of Gelles and Straus (*Intimate Violence*, 1988: 143–146) reports a number of factors that distinguish battered or abused wives who stay in the home or relationship from those who leave abusive relationships. They found that: (1) women who leave seemed to have experienced more severe violence; (2) women who grew up in violent homes were more likely to stay with abusive husbands; (3) women who stayed in violent marriages were less educated, had fewer job skills, and were more likely to be unemployed than women who sought help, called the police, or left their violent partners; and (4) women with young children were more likely to stay.

What this suggests is that: (1) the more severe the violence the greater the likelihood of leaving; (2) experience with or exposure to violence seems to make women more tolerant of domestic violence or more lacking in hope of really escaping; (3) women who have few resources are more entrapped in violent homes; and (4) as children get older and perhaps less dependent on them, women are more likely to leave.

Other studies suggest as well that limited educational resources and occupational skills result in wives who are economically dependent and more "forced" to remain with abusive husbands. These studies suggest that other reasons for staying in an abusive relationship include: a commitment to the spouse, a belief their husbands will reform, lower self-concepts, a belief that divorcees are stigmatized, and the difficulty for women with children to get work. These factors all point to social factors entrapping women in violent marriages and explode the myth that wives who remain with violent men are masochistic—seeking or deriving pleasure from mistreatment.

is granted a level of acceptability for some other reason, the practice is common.

Marital conflict is an established and well-known pattern. How these conflicts are resolved takes a wide variety of forms including silence, screaming, withholding services, leaving, throwing objects, homicide, or others. In a review of research in the 1970s that included studies of the extent of violence between marital partners, Gelles noted that 16 percent of those surveyed reported some kind of physical violence between spouses during the past year; 28 percent reported marital violence at some point in their marriage; and a national study revealed that 3.8 percent of U.S. women were victims of abusive violence during the preceding twelve months.[26] Steinmetz as well noted reports of 17,000 wife-abuse complaints brought to New York family courts; 1,125 cases of wife beating reported to Salt Lake City police per year; 2,000 cases of wife beating in Fairfax County, Virginia (estimated to be underreported by 40 percent); and numerous other reports each testifying to the commonality of violence toward women of a nature extreme enough to come to the attention of the police and the courts.[27] Steinmetz's own research in a Delaware sample revealed severe physical abuse received by 7 percent of wives (and 6 percent of husbands). And extrapolating from a national sample

26. Richard J. Gelles, "Violence in the Family: A Review of Research in the Seventies," *Journal of Marriage and the Family* 42 (November 1980): 877.

27. Steinmetz, "Violence Between Family Members," p. 4.

to the total population, as was done with the child abuse data, Steinmetz indicated that 3.3 million wives have experienced severe beatings from their spouses.

The question raised about changes in child abuse will be raised about wife or spouse abuse. Is there an epidemic of wife abuse that is increasing each year? And again the answer is, apparently not. The same Straus-Gelles study mentioned earlier comparing violence rates in 1975 and 1985 showed that wife beating (as measured by the number who were kicked, punched, hit with an object, bitten, beaten up, or attacked with a knife or gun) decreased by 27 percent.[28] Interestingly, similar severe assaults by wives on husbands (*see* next section) decreased only 4.3 percent. Again, even if these rates indicate actual reductions, that still leaves over a million and a half beaten wives each year in the United States.

Most abuse and violence toward wives does not take the form of beating, but rather it takes the form of throwing things, shoving, pushing, grabbing, slapping, or hitting. These events appear to be more common at selected times such as during a wife's pregnancy or following the husband's drinking. Gelles reported that pregnant women for example, while not an especially vulnerable group, did experience higher rates of minor, severe, and overall violence than nonpregnant women, particularly among women under twenty-five years of age.[29] He suggests that these higher rates may be a methodological artifact in that women may be more outraged at violence when pregnant, may feel more vulnerable, or may have violent acts that occur at this time stand out in their memories. It is possible, however, that husbands or partners may increase the frequency and/or severity of their violence toward women during pregnancy and may change the nature of the attacks—more hitting on the abdomen instead of the face or other parts of the body.

Marital rape and sexual abuse by intimates is another common form of violence sustained by women. As noted in Chapter 11, the forcing of sexual intercourse by a husband, technically marital rape, although legally not usually recognized as such, is seldom viewed as rape by wives, who often blame themselves for the incident. That wives blame themselves or learn to accept forced sexual intercourse may be why so little attention has been devoted to this topic in spite of what may be a widespread occurrence.

While abused children cannot readily choose to leave family members who abuse them, wives, it seems, have this choice. Thus a logical question is, Why do abused wives stay? Some answers to this question appear in the panel on abused wives. Other answers stem from two separate research studies that

---

28. Straus and Gelles, "Societal Change and Change in Family Violence," pp. 465–479; and Gelles and Straus, *Intimate Violence* p. 109.

29. Richard J. Gelles, "Violence and Pregnancy: Are Pregnant Women at Greater Risk of Abuse?" *Journal of Marriage and the Family* 50 (August 1988): 841–847.

both emphasize economic dependency.[30] Wives who are highly dependent on marriage were less able to discourage, avoid, leave, or put an end to abuse than women in marriages where the balance of resources between husband and wife was more nearly equal. Dependent wives lacked both alternatives to marriage and resources within marriage to negotiate change.

Of those abused wives who do leave, a number turn to shelters—short-term refuges from violent relationships.[31] It is estimated that over 900 of these shelters exist in the United States alone and represent the result of an international movement that began in England. The emphasis of shelters is placed on separating the victim from the assailant, providing alternate room and board, and providing support services. The effects seem to depend upon the attributes of the victim. For women who actively take control of their lives, a shelter stay was found to dramatically reduce the likelihood of new violence. For others, shelters were found to have no impact or even trigger retaliation or disobedience.[32] Within the context of the ABCX model, shelters represent an important community resource for many physically abused wives.

Another community resource that appears to be effective in wife-battery incidents is that of police response with a follow-up arrest. For over two years in one county in California, researchers explored the deterrent effect of arrests (made in 26 percent of wife-battery incidents) and concluded that (1) on the average, arrests deter new wife-battery incidents, and (2) reductions in wife-battery are greatest and especially effective for batterers whom police would ordinarily be inclined to arrest.[33] This is no guarantee that simply increasing the number of arrests would have the same deterrent effect, but with the more serious incidents where arrest did occur, it had the desired deterrent effect.

## Husband abuse and violence

Existing research data tend to focus attention on child abuse and wife abuse. But overlooked aspects of family violence include the abused husband, abused siblings, and abused elderly.

30. Debra S. Kalmuss and Murray A. Straus, "Wife's Marital Dependency and Wife Abuse," *Journal of Marriage and the Family* 44 (May 1982): 277–286; and Michael J. Strube and Linda S. Barbour, "The Decision to Leave an Abusive Relationship: Economic Dependence and Psychological Commitment," *Journal of Marriage and the Family* 45 (November 1983): 785–793.

31. *See:* Nanette J. Davis, "Shelters for Battered Women: Social Policy Response to Interpersonal Violence," *The Social Science Journal* 25 (1988): 401–419.

32. Richard A. Berk, Phyllis J. Newton, and Sarah Fenstermaker, "What a Difference a Day Makes: An Empirical Study of the Impact of Shelters for Battered Women," *Journal of Marriage and the Family* 48 (August 1986): 481–490.

33. Richard A. Berk and Phyllis J. Newton, "Does Arrest Really Deter Wife Battery? An Effort to Replicate the Findings of the Minneapolis Spouse Abuse Experiment," *American Sociological Review* 50 (April 1985): 253–262.

It has already been stated that many men and women grant social approval to slapping husbands. In addition some general surveys indicate that wives often exceed their husbands in the use of physical violence during a marital conflict and in the frequency with which these acts occur. Murray Straus stated that one of the cruel ironies of marriage is that, although husband-wife relationships are largely male dominant, the use of physical violence seems to be one of the few aspects of marriage that approaches equality between spouses.[34] It should be noted, however, that the *effects* of this violence are far from equal, for the husbands generally cast the last and most damaging blows. The high rate of violence by women, Straus claims, can be accounted for by: (1) retaliatory violence which increases the probability of initiating family violence; (2) implicit cultural norms that make the marriage license also a hitting license; (3) childhood training in the use of violence within the family; (4) child care in U.S. society that involves role practice in violence since over 90 percent of parents use physical punishment; and (5) the high degree of frustration involved in marriage, with wives relatively powerless in comparison with their husbands.

Wife abuse and husband abuse are treated separately here. Yet, it needs to be emphasized that mutual abuse is more common than either alone. Likewise, disparity between husbands and wives in recall of violence is evident. While husbands tend to view their marital relationships as mutually violent, wives view the husbands as violent.[35] Both spouses report more violence for their partner than they are willing to acknowledge for themselves. Also, each spouse tends to be more likely to report their own victimization than their own use of violence.

The effects of family structure on both spouse and child abuse are evident from data on stepfamilies and remarriages. Findings show that spouse and child abuse is more likely in stepfamilies and families in which one or both spouses have been divorced (remarried and reconstituted) than in never-divorced (intact) families.[36] Explanations for this occurrence may relate to carrying on previously learned behavior patterns, to stepparents not having the strong bonding and blood ties, to selecting spouses who dominate or can be dominated, to higher levels of stress in remarried families, or to other reasons. In any case, there is a continuity of abuse in reconstituted families.

The effects of marital violence extend to persons beyond those who are directly abused or battered. Specifically, children who witness a parent being

---

34. Murray Straus, "Victims and Aggressors in Marital Violence," *American Behavioral Scientist* 23 (May/June 1980): 681–704.

35. James Browning and Donald Dutton, "Assessment of Wife Assault with the Conflict Tactics Scale: Using Couple Data to Quantify the Differential Reporting Effect," *Journal of Marriage and the Family* 48 (May 1986): 376–379.

36. Debra Kalmuss and Judith A. Seltzer, "Continuity of Marital Behavior in Remarriage: The Case of Spouse Abuse," *Journal of Marriage and the Family* 48 (February 1986): 113–120; and Jean Giles-Sims and David Finkelhor, "Child Abuse in Stepfamilies," *Family Relations* 33 (July 1984): 403–413.

## Quaker families and marital violence

Among Judeo-Christian religions, perhaps none is better known for their stand against violence and for peace than are the Quakers, known formally as the Religious Society of Friends. They are noted for their emphasis on peaceful means of resolving conflict, on the deep respect for each person's right to conscience, and on their identification as conscientious objectors and participants in peace movements.

Do these principles that operate at the international level carry into Quaker homes as well? Judith Brutz and Craig Allen (*Journal of Marriage and the Family*, August 1986) received questionnaire returns from 159 Quaker wives and 131 Quaker husbands. For both wives and husbands, and for both com-

munication violence and ordinary physical violence, lower levels of marital violence were associated with high levels of religious participation. But they found important gender-related differences in the meanings attached to religious experience and violence. For wives, high levels of peace activism were associated with low levels of marital violence. For husbands, high levels of peace activism were associated with high levels of marital violence. The authors suggest that commitment to Quaker principles is confounded with traditional norms of nonaggressiveness for Quaker wives and aggressiveness for Quaker husbands.

---

abused may be vulnerable to a variety of behavioral and emotional difficulties, including psychosomatic disorders and aggression. Results of students who had viewed parental violence were found to be significantly more anxious than those from satisfactory relationships. Females, in addition, showed elevated levels of depression and aggression.[37] This finding is consistent with a "learned helplessness" model of wife abuse that suggests seeing one's mother in a helpless situation transmits the message that women are helpless to control their own lives. This promotes depression in women most likely to identify with the victim-mother. In contrast, men who witness parental violence might be more likely to identify with the aggressor-father than with the victim, thus avoiding depression. These men in turn are more likely to be abusive husbands themselves.

### Sibling abuse and violence

It seems that the most frequent and acceptable form of violence within families occurs between siblings. Available evidence from the Straus and Gelles studies mentioned previously revealed that 40 percent of children whose parents they interviewed had hit a brother or sister with an object during the preceding year and 82 percent had engaged in some form of violence against a sibling.

This is a form of violence granted a high degree of tolerance. Identical acts between parent and child or husband and wife might well result in

---

37. Barbara Forsstrom-Cohen and Alan Rosenbaum, "The Effects of Parental Marital Violence on Young Adults: An Exploratory Investigation," *Journal of Marriage and the Family* 47 (May 1985): 467–472.

possible criminal charges and social service intervention. It appears that although male sibling pairs outdo female sibling pairs in throwing things, pushing, and hitting, the greatest amount of physical violence occurs between boy-girl pairs.

This type of activity is usually explained in terms of sibling rivalry or jealousy. Supposedly, each sibling resents something the other has: parental attention, privileges, clothes, objects, and the like, or centers around differences over limited resources: use of the bathroom or telephone, what TV show to watch, or who gets the remaining candy bar. These resentments and differences may become aggravated when greater powers (parents) intervene and insist they share or make a decision that favors one over the other. Reacting abusively toward a sibling who is more one's equal in size and age is both more equitable as well as more acceptable than acting abusively toward parents, although as noted later, this does occur as well.

Sometimes sibling discord revolves around the division of labor in the family. Siblings compete in avoiding undesirable tasks or chores: dishes, cleaning rooms, sweeping walks, etc. Age differences may aggravate the situation if younger children are assigned fewer chores. In short, exchange theory is operative and perceived inequalities lead to conflict. While obviously not all inequity leads to abuse or violence, fighting or throwing objects are resources available to most children. And even when one child is outmatched, parental intervention in stopping the fight, protecting the younger sibling, or punishing the older siblings is a realistic possibility.

It is factors such as these that help to explain the common occurrence of sibling abuse and violence. Recognizing the importance of socialization experiences and social contexts would lead us to expect that even among siblings, differences in abuse would exist by sex, ethnicity, and social class.

## Elderly abuse and violence

The battered elderly parent, as noted in the previous chapter, is the subject of recent investigation. A number of investigators agree that a substantial problem exists, with estimates ranging between 700,000 and 2.5 million cases per year.[38] The variety and severity of mistreatment ranges from passive neglect (unintentionally ignored, forgotten) to active neglect (financial exploitation, withholding of medicine, food, assistance) and from verbal or emotional abuse (calling names, threatening, humiliation) to physical abuse (slapping, pushing, injuring). Abuse may take the form of tying the elderly parent to a bed

---

38. Richard L. Douglass, "Domestic Neglect and Abuse of the Elderly: Implications for Research and Service," *Family Relations* 32 (July 1983); Claire Pedrick-Cornell and Richard J. Gelles, "Elder Abuse: The Status of Current Knowledge," *Family Relations* 31 (July 1982): 457–465; and Karl Pillemer and David Finkelhor, "The Prevalence of Elder Abuse: A Random Sample Survey," *The Gerontologist* 28 (1988): 51–57.

or chair, excessive use of medication or drugs to keep the parent more manageable, battering with fists or objects to enforce particular behaviors, or nearly any conceivable activity.

The victims are generally the older elderly persons who are frail, mentally or physically disabled, female, and living with the person responsible for mistreatment. A commonly cited "cause" of the abuse includes becoming over-taxed by the requirements of caring for the elderly adult. This burden for caring often leads to despair, anger, resentment, or violence. In some instances the abuse is clearly malicious and intentional, while other instances involve caretakers with more serious emotional and dependency problems who do not deliberately intend to abuse, but are less able to control their behavior.

Research suggests that the typical abused elder, rather than being a dependent, may be an older woman supporting a dependent child or, to a lesser extent, a physically or mentally disabled spouse.[39] The powerlessness of the abuser who is dependent on an elderly parent may be a critical factor in understanding elderly abuse. This contradicts the common notion that the dependency of the elderly victim on the abuser is a primary cause of abuse. From an exchange perspective, the victims perceived themselves as being on the losing end, or giving much and receiving little. Most did not leave the situation but felt trapped by a sense of family obligation.

The application of the ABCX formula to marital and family violence suggests that the various types of hitting, throwing, biting, and the like that take place within a family may or may not represent crisis events depending upon the resources available and meanings attached to them. It has been clearly shown that many acts between siblings, between parents and children, or between partners are perceived as expected and normal behaviors. While resources have not been covered in detail per se, strength, withholding of money or services, friends and other kin, police, crisis intervention centers, and the like may all be essential resources.

## Violence among other intimates

Abuse and violence may have their origin long before husbands, wives, children, and siblings enter the scene. One key example centers around friendships and intimates involved in the mate selection-courtship process. Most studies that deal with the courtship processes of dating, going steady, or engagement tend to portray these events in a context of love, attraction, affection, mutual disclosure, and increasing closeness and commitment as the courtship process moves toward marriage. Other recent studies, however,

---

39. Karl Pillemer, "The Dangers of Dependency: New Findings on Domestic Violence Against the Elderly," *Social Problems* 33 (December 1985): 146–158.

suggest that dating violence is very prevalent[40] and that the marriage license and what preceeds it in dating and cohabitation is a hitting license.[41]

Exploratory studies of college students were completed by James Makepeace in an attempt to estimate the incidence of courtship violence and gender differences in victimization.[42] As expected, the incidence of courtship violence "known of" by the students in the study greatly exceeded what was directly experienced. Also, as expected, more extreme forms of violence, such as assault with an object or weapon, were less common than the milder forms, such as pushing or slapping. Nearly two-fifths of the students knew of instances of threats, pushing, or slapping. Overall, males and females were about equal in initiating, committing, and sustaining violence. Females, being the principal victims, more often reported serious forms of violence done to them; they also more often reported sustaining sexual assault, physical injury, and emotional trauma. Yet, males rarely reported that sexual assault was attempted or occurred and did not perceive that females sustained greater physical or emotional harm. Attempts to explain these disparities included for males denial, the nonrecognition or recall of details of experiences, and the minimization of the frequency and intensity of the males' abuse.

Results from Oregon students indicated that nearly all of them had been involved in some conflict, including heated discussion, crying, sulking, stomping away, or getting drunk or stoned during dating and courtship.[43] About two-thirds had been involved in some type of abuse including insulting, swearing, spiteful acts, or threats to hit or throw something. Sexuality was an important source of violence in dating and courtship, with males more likely to inflict a variety of forms of sexual aggression and females more likely to experience sexual victimization.

It appears that violence among high-school couples is similar to that found in college couples, with the only difference being that it occurs to a lesser degree. A study of high-school juniors and seniors in Michigan showed that one student in ten had a direct personal experience of dating violence, and three in ten knew someone who did.[44] The authors, in comparing their results of high-school students with studies of college students, suggest that the main causes of violence are the same (jealousy and alcohol), as well as

---

40. David B. Sugarman and Gerald T. Hotaling, "Dating Violence: Prevalence, Context, and Risk Markers," in Maureen A. Pirog-Good and Jan E. Stets, (eds.), *Violence in Dating Relationships* (New York: Praeger, 1989): 3–32.

41. Jan E. Stets and Murray A. Straus, "The Marriage License as a Hitting License: A Comparison of Assaults in Dating, Cohabiting, and Married Couples," *Journal of Family Violence* 4 (June 1989): 161–180.

42. James M. Makepeace, "Courtship Violence Among College Students," *Family Relations* 30 (January 1981): 97–102; and "Gender Differences in Courtship Victimization," *Family Relations* 35 (July 1986): 383–388.

43. Katherine E. Lane and Patricia A. Gwartney-Gibbs, "Violence in the Context of Dating and Sex," *Journal of Family Issues* 6 (March 1985): 45–59.

44. Bruce Roscoe and John E. Callahan, "Adolescents' Self-Report of Violence in Families and Dating Relations," *Adolescence* 20 (Fall 1985): 545–553.

*Friends and relatives, and shelters and counselors, are important sources of help for victims of serious family abuse. But eliminating cultural norms and values that support violence would likely have the greatest impact of all in preventing it.*

where it occurs (places of residence and vehicles), how it is interpreted (anger, confusion, and love), and its effects on the relationship (ranging from termination to improvement). Adolescents who experience violent interaction in dating may be establishing patterns that will continue into subsequent relationships and ultimately into marriage.

The occurrence of violence during adolescence, whether exhibited toward parents or in the courtship process, seems to be a foundation for marital and parental violence. The experience of violence between spouses or toward children is seldom the perpetrator's first experience.

## Treating and preventing family violence

Applying the ABCX model described at the beginning of this chapter to family violence would direct us toward two specific avenues of action: resources (B) and meanings or definitions (C). When Gelles and Straus asked women who experienced violence how they reacted to the most recent incidence, more than half said they cried. This response was followed by yelled, ran to another room, hit back, ran out of the house, and called a friend or relative; the response in last place was to call the police.[45] The first few responses would

_____

45. Gelles and Straus, *Intimate Violence,* Figure 10, p. 258.

suggest immediate and personal responses to being hurt: crying, yelling, and running to get away. Longer term responses tend to be more closely related to personal or social resources, such as calling on friends or relatives or community resources such as the police. Gelles and Straus suggest that an important and beneficial way of helping battered women is to empower them to engage in negotiation with their husbands to end the violence. An important intervention service (resource) would be education in mediation or conflict resolution techniques. Other resources include sources of help such as police, social workers, battered women's shelters, medical services, and so forth. These resources all seem important and are a step in the right direction. But how do we prevent family violence in the first place and modify assumptions that violence is a legitimate solution to conflict?

Gelles and Straus argue that prevention policies and programs must be directed at the two factors that make it possible for people to abuse and maltreat those they love.[46] First is a need to eliminate cultural norms and values that accept violence as a means of resolving conflict and problems in families. Second is a need to develop programs and policies that support families and reduce internal and external stresses and inequalities. How is this accomplished?

It is suggested that the first goal of eliminating cultural norms and values that support violence begins with establishing a moral code that loved ones are not to be hit. This means banning spanking and corporal punishment. Sweden and all other Scandinavian countries, for example, have taken the lead in this regard by banning capital punishment, outlawing corporal punishment of children in schools, and passing legislation prohibiting spanking. Firearm ownership is rigorously controlled. Violent programming on Swedish television is severely restricted. In contrast, most readers in the United States are aware of the controversies over capital punishment; corporal punishment; spanking; control or registration of firearms; and violence on TV, in the movies, and in children's games. Family, marital, parental, or sibling violence, as well as violence in general, will remain high as long as the society in which it occurs glorifies killing, shooting, beating, hitting, and abusing.

The second goal of developing programs and policies that support families is closely related to the first goal of changing norms and values. Some policies and programs have been enacted in many states in relation to child abuse, spouse abuse, and marital rape. Additional efforts to eliminate poverty and unemployment; to provide adequate medical and hospital care to all families; to support effective planned parenthood; to reduce sexual, class, and racial inequality both in the home and community; and to promote kin and community linkages and support networks would likely result in the lowering of family violence.

---

46. Ibid., p. 194.

# SUMMARY

1. The central issues of this chapter, marital and family crisis and violence, are not unique to any given stage of the family life cycle or any particular family structure.

2. Stressor or crisis-provoking events refer to any situation that threatens the status quo and well-being of the system or its members. These events may come from sources both within and outside the family. Certain events may solidify the unit, while others may be very disruptive.

3. The ABCX model refers to some event (A) interacting with the family's crisis-meeting resources (B) and the definition or meaning given to the event (C), resulting in the level or degree of crisis (X). When and if B and C are adequate, the level of stress and crisis will be minimal. If they are inadequate, the level of stress and crisis will be high.

4. Since the original ABCX model was proposed, other writers have expanded it to include a double ABCX model and recommended the incorporation of new dimensions, such as interrelating the levels of various systems and recognizing the sociohistorical context.

5. One common event within families is abuse and violence. Unique characteristics of the family as a social group make it a violent-prone setting for both spouses, for the children, and for the interpersonal relationships among them. The prevalence of violence offers a persuasive counterargument against the myth of the family as nonviolent.

6. Considerable attention is focused on the abuse of children. Traditional modes of discipline grant legitimacy to the spanking and physical punishment of children. Since most of it occurs behind closed doors, most abuse never comes to the attention of the public. Recent data suggest an increasing awareness of this as an important issue and an actual decrease in child abuse.

7. Violence is not merely directed by parents toward children but is directed by children, particularly adolescents, as well. Research shows that parental assault is extensive, occurring among both males and females and being directed at both mothers and fathers.

8. Wife abuse, like child abuse, is not always viewed as inappropriate, particularly in contexts of male authority and dominance. Marital conflict is a well-established phenomenon, and this conflict is often acted out in verbally and physically abusive ways. Like child abuse, we may have witnessed an actual decrease in abusive acts such as wife beating. Many wives do not or cannot leave their violent husband due to economic dependency or lack of alternatives, while others turn to shelters.

9. Husband abuse is granted far less attention than the abuse of children and wives; however, physical violence seems to be one aspect of a marriage that approaches equality between the spouses. Marital violence extends beyond the spouses to children in a way that often has both short- and long-term negative consequences.

10. Sibling abuse is the most frequent and acceptable form of violence within families. Explanations often center around sibling rivalry and jealousy. Supposedly each sibling resents something the other has, or the tensions center around differences over availability of limited resources. Sibling discord often involves the family division of labor as well.

11. Elderly abuse frequently centers around aging parents, particularly the mother. The

typical abused adult, rather than being a dependent, may be an older person supporting a dependent child. The mistreatment ranges from passive or active neglect to verbal and physical abuse.

12. Other forms of violence among intimates include that of adolescents in the dating-courtship process. While this chapter focused on marital and family stress and violence, the next chapter turns to the termination of marriages, particularly via divorce, and the subsequent pattern of remarriage.

# KEY TERMS AND TOPICS

Marital crisis   489
Social stress   489
ABCX model   490
Double ABCX model   491
Family violence   493
Myth of the nonviolent family   494
Child abuse   498

Parent abuse   501
Wife abuse   502
Husband abuse   505
Sibling abuse   507
Elderly abuse   508
Violence among intimates   509
Treating and preventing violence   511

# DISCUSSION QUESTIONS

1. Itemize a list of "stressor events." What ways exist to prepare for events such as these? How is it possible that certain events "strengthen" families whereas others tend to "tear them apart"?

2. What factors make for crisis-proneness and freedom-from-crisis-proneness? Using the formula given in the chapter, show how "resources" and "meanings" lead to family adequacy or family inadequacy in facing potential crisis situations.

3. Select any personal or family problem. How could or does the availability of resources affect the problem? What are these resources? How does your definition of the problem affect the level of stress?

4. Explain the myth of the family as nonviolent. Why are behaviors involving abuse and violence so common and so acceptable within families that would be punishable and unacceptable among nonfamily members?

5. Discuss the likely differences in frequency and type of child abuse based on characteristics of the child: age, sex, retarded, or handicapped. What is the impact of ethnicity or sociohistorical context in explaining differences?

6. Is not marriage an interpersonal private rela-

tionship? If so, should the community or state get involved in what husbands and wives do to each other? Why or why not? What actions should "outsiders" take?

7. Why don't abused wives leave?

8. Is it necessary to pay attention to or do research on violence toward husbands or between siblings? Can't husbands take care of themselves? Aren't fights "natural" among children?

9. Think of personal childhood and sibling experiences of violence. Did they occur? With whom? For what reason?

10. Discuss various forms of abuse that exist within families toward elderly parents. What type of action or programs might lessen the problem or the severity of it?

11. Are you aware of abuse or violence in dating or in nonmarital heterosexual interactions? What form did or does it take? How do you explain its prevalence?

12. What is the relationship of factors such as alcoholism, drug addiction, unemployment, lack of money, and the like to violence and abuse? How might a pregnancy, birthday, or holiday affect the likelihood of violence?

# FURTHER READINGS

Boss, Pauline. *Family Stress Management.* Newbury Park, Ca.: Sage Publications, Inc., 1988. An intensive examination of family stress including theory, barriers to stress management, values and belief systems, and victimization.

Finkelhor, David, and Associates. *A Sourcebook on Child Sexual Abuse.* Beverly Hills: Sage Publications, 1986. A consideration of the prevalence of sexual abuse, children at high risk, offenders, effects, and prevention.

Gelles, Richard, J., and Cornell, Claire Pedrick. *Intimate Violence in Families.* Beverly Hills: Sage Publications, 1985. A comprehensive overview of family violence covering child, courtship, spouse, sibling, parent, and elder abuse with a concluding chapter on prevention and treatment.

Gelles, Richard J., and Straus, Murray A. *Intimate Violence.* New York: Simon and Schuster, 1988. A book resulting from fifteen years of research on family violence and the reporting of results from two national surveys.

Klein, David M., and Aldous, Joan, (eds.). *Social Stress and Family Development.* New York: Guilford Press, 1988. A volume of twelve writings bringing together two orientations often addressed separately: family development and family stress theory.

Levinson, David. *Family Violence in Cross-Cultural Perspective.* Newbury Park, Ca.: Sage Publications, Inc., 1989. An anthropological look at family violence in its various forms and frequencies in societies around the world.

Lystad, M., ed. *Violence in the Home.* New York: Brunner/Mazel, 1986. A compilation of twelve writings covering violence and U.S. society, causes of family violence, and clinical and community intervention programs.

McCubbin, Hamilton I.; Cauble, A. Elizabeth; and Patterson, Joan M. eds. *Family Stress, Coping, and Social Support.* Springfield, Ill.: Charles C. Thomas, 1982. An anthology of thirteen articles divided into two sections, one dealing with stress and crisis theory and the other dealing with stressors, coping, and social support.

Pirog-Good, Maureen A., and Stets, Jan E. *Violence in Dating Relationships: Emerging Social Issues.* New York: Praeger, 1989. A collection of fourteen articles focusing on physical and sexual abuse in dating relationships.

Quinn, Mary Joy, and Tomita, Susan K. *Elder Abuse and Neglect.* N. Y.: Springer Publishing Co., 1986. An investigation of the phenomenon of elder abuse, including diagnosis and intervention.

Steinmetz, Suzanne K. "Family Violence: Past, Present, and Future" in *Handbook of Marriage and the Family* by Marvin B. Sussman and Suzanne K. Steinmetz (eds.), New York: Plenum Press, 1987, Chapter 26, pp. 725–765. Following an historical perspective, attention is focused on the level of violence in families; a wide range of theories is used to explain and understand violence.

Straus, Murray A.; Gelles, Richard J.; and Steinmetz, Suzanne K. *Behind Closed Doors: Violence in the American Family.* New York: Anchor Books, 1980. A report on the experiences of 2,143 families as to the extent, breadth, and meaning of violence within families in the United States.

# CHAPTER SEVENTEEN

# DIVORCE AND REMARRIAGE

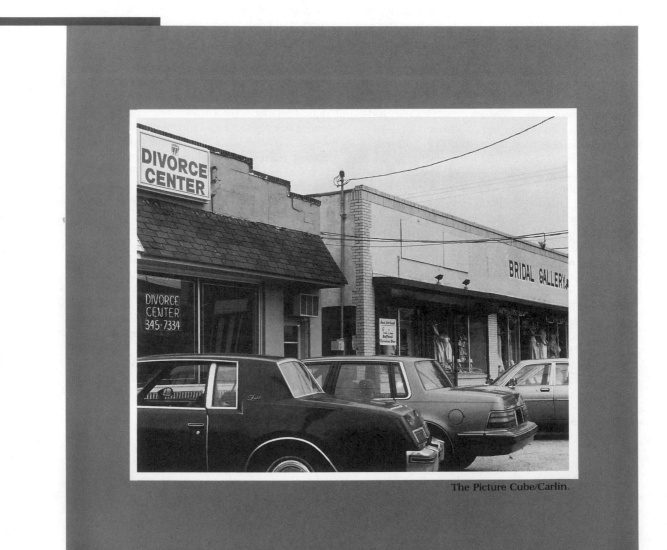

The Picture Cube/Carlin.

$A$ll societies have one or more ways for husbands, wives, or both to deal with unsatisfactory marital relationships. Highly patriarchal, male-dominant societies are likely to permit men mistresses or concubines to co-exist with their marriage. In many societies, including the United States, marriage may be regarded as a civil contract with the state specifying how old people have to be to get married, how many spouses they may have, and the conditions under which marriages can be dissolved.

In some countries, often in conformity with the Canon Law of the Roman Catholic Church, marriage was, until recently, indissolvable except by death. These included countries such as Argentina, Brazil, Chile, and Colombia in Latin America; the Philippines in Southeast Asia; and Italy, Ireland, and Spain in Western Europe. In some countries, such as the United States, France, Switzerland, Russia, Poland, and the Scandinavian countries, a divorce is granted if one or both parties has been guilty of a grave violation of marital obligations or if it is shown that the marriage is completely broken in fact. Finally, the official law of Islam and of Judaism grants free power of the husband to terminate his marriage by repudiation of his wife. In reality, this occurs infrequently and movements exist to provide power to wives to bring about a dissolution of the marriage as well.

In the United States, divorce is the best known and most common means of ending an unsatisfactory marital relationship; thus, most attention in this chapter will be devoted to it. Desertions, legal separations, informally agreed upon separations, and annulments are other means that people use to get out of, at least temporarily if not permanently, a marriage.

## DESERTION AND MARITAL SEPARATION

Desertion refers to the willful abandonment, without legal justification, of one's spouse, children, or both. Compared to divorce, little is known about desertion, and few studies exist on this issue. Traditionally, it has been assumed that desertion applied only to men. Today, reports exist on "runaway wives" as well. Unlike men who may want out of a marriage, deserting women are more likely to seek escape from childrearing and home responsibilities that have become unbearable. For both sexes it appears that desertion is one response or solution to dealing with an issue they define as incapable of being handled: children, marital conflicts, alcoholism, infidelity, inability to support a family, and the like.

Unlike divorce, desertion is not institutionalized, no registration takes place with the courts or any other official body, the deserting and nondeserting spouse cannot remarry, and little clarity exists as to exactly what constitutes desertion and what roles are appropriate in legal, economic, or social situations. For example, how many days' absence constitutes desertion? When a spouse leaves and returns on multiple occasions, do marital and parental role patterns resemble those of the one- or two-parent family? Is one spouse legally responsible for the expenses and activities of the other? Because of the lack of institutionalized norms and the ambiguity of events surrounding desertion, it is believed that desertion has far more negative effects than divorce.

What about marital *separation?* A widely held assumption is that marital separation is a stepping stone to divorce or another marriage. While this is true for many couples, others are separated for reasons other than conflict or marital difficulties; a third group uses separation as a means of reconciliation, and a fourth category remains in married but long-term unresolved separations.

The Bureau of the Census separates the *married, spouse present* from the *married, spouse absent.* These married, spouse absent persons are further categorized as *separated* or *other.* The *separated* include those with legal separations, those living apart with intentions of obtaining a divorce, and other persons permanently or temporarily separated because of marital discord. The *other* group of married, spouse absent includes married persons living apart due to employment, serving away from home in the armed forces, or residing apart for any reason except separation as just described. In 1988, 6.2 million persons or 3.3 percent of the U.S. population were classified as married with a spouse absent. Four and one-half million of these were separated (*see* Tables 15–1 and 15–3 for differences by sex and selected age categories).[1] In cases of *legal separations* the husband and wife are authorized to live apart, and formal agreements specify visiting patterns, support, and so forth. These are sometimes referred to as limited divorce, partial dissolution, or divorce from bed and board.

The majority of separations are not legalized. These **informal separations** are often arrangements between husband and wife where one or both decide to live separately. Unlike desertion, each knows the whereabouts of the other and unlike divorce, the couple is legally married and cannot remarry. These couples seem to be overrepresented among low-income families and have been referred to in literature as the "poor man's divorce."

One of the few studies of marital separations was done in the metropolitan Cleveland area with a random sample of over 1,100 residents.[2] It was found that one in six couples was likely to separate for at least forty-eight hours at some point in their relationship because of arguments or disagreements. Some separations were a step on the way to permanent separation or divorce. Others were used as a conflict resolution technique or a dramatic gesture to force some action on the part of the spouse. Some separated persons remained in relationships because of psychological restraints, such as

---

1. U.S. Bureau of the Census, *Current Population Reports,* Series P-20, no. 433, "Marital Status and Living Arrangements, March 1988," (Washington, D.C.: U.S. Government Printing Office, 1989), Table 1, p. 3.

2. Gay C. Kitson, "Marital Discord and Marital Separation: A County Survey," *Journal of Marriage and the Family* 47 (August 1985): 693–700.

physical abuse, or structural restraints, such as low income or the presence of minor children. Those most likely to separate were blacks, women, and those with low income and minor children. For most, separations were associated with a high sense of emotional distress.

# ANNULMENT

The word *annul*, legally defined, means to reduce to nothing, to obliterate, to make void and of no effect, to abolish, to do away with, to eradicate. To say a marriage has been annulled is to say that a court, acting under the law of the state, found that causes existed *prior* to the marriage that render the marriage contract void. The court is saying that the marriage, when performed, was in fact no marriage at all, and is annulling it as though it had never existed.

Generally, the distinction between divorce and **annulment** revolves around the time of the cause or the time in which certain actions occurred. Divorce generally involves an action that occurred *after* the date of marriage —adultery, incompatibility, cruelty, desertion, nonsupport, alcoholism, and the like. Annulment generally involves an action that occurred *before* the date of marriage—being under age, another existing marriage, insanity, incurable impotence, incestuous relationship, and the like. While the marriage was a social and psychological reality, legally it never existed. If there are children, the "husband who never existed" may be required by the court to support minor children. Socially, relatives and friends are well aware of the once-existing marriage. Psychologically, both the male and female involved are well aware of once "being married" and the mate selection processes that preceded it.

# DIVORCE AROUND THE WORLD

In the Western world, divorce has traditionally been viewed an an unfortunate event for the persons involved and as a clear index of failure of the family system. But over the past few decades, in the United States at least, attitudes toward separation and divorce have changed with a definite trend toward approval. Interviews with mothers over an eighteen year period show that three-fifths believed that divorce is usually the best solution when marital problems cannot be solved.[3]

Not only in the United States, but also around the world, rather than divorce being seen as a personal misfortune or as an index of failure, it has increasingly been viewed as an escape valve, a way out of the tensions of marriage itself. William Goode claims that divorce is permitted in nearly all the world's nations (Spain and Ireland are still exceptions), and has been common

---

3. Arland Thornton, "Changing Attitudes toward Separation and Divorce: Causes and Consequences," *American Journal of Sociology*, 90 (January 1985): 856–872.

## Family law changes in Greece

In 1983, the Greek parliament in Athens approved changes in the country's family law, making divorce easier, guaranteeing equality between spouses, and ending official discrimination against illegitimate children.

The new law also abolished the dowry, a centuries-old tradition, as a legal requirement in marriage.

Couples are now allowed to divorce by consent. Under the old system, one partner had to show that the other was responsible for the marriage's breakdown on strictly defined grounds, including bigamy, adultery, and desertion.

in most tribal societies.[4] In addition, a few nations have had higher divorce rates than the United States at different times in the past, such as Japan in the period 1887–1919; Algeria in 1887–1940; and Egypt in 1935–1945.

At present, the United States may have the highest divorce rate in the world. In 1986, the U.S. rate of divorce per 1,000 persons in the population was 4.8 compared to 3.4 in the USSR, 3.1 in Germany, 2.9 in Cuba, 2.4 in Canada, 2.3 in Sweden, 1.4 in Japan, 1.3 in Poland, 1.2 in Israel, and 0.3 in Italy.[5] Divorce rates are not available, or perhaps even computed, for a number of the highly Catholic countries (Philippines, Spain, Mexico, and others).

How are variations in the rate or frequency of divorce explained? One study sampled 66 countries to investigate the societal-level correlates of divorce.[6] Four variables were shown to bear a significant relationship to the likelihood of divorce. Associated with lower divorce rates were (1) a high sex ratio indicating a relative undersupply of women, and (2) a late average age at marriage for women. Significantly, but nonlinearly related to divorce was (3) level of socioeconomic development, and (4) female labor force participation rate. Both of these variables exhibited U-shaped associations with divorce. This suggests that socioeconomic development and increased female labor force participation in the early stages of industrialization tend to reduce the rate of divorce, but at later stages of industrialization and modernization, they tend to increase the incidence of divorce.

Many societies in the Western world, including the United States, rate high in socioeconomic development and in female labor force participation. Thus, with an erosion of traditional patriarchal patterns and a heavy emphasis on the individual and small nuclear family in contrast to an emphasis on extended kin, we could expect high rates of divorce. Let us take note of how divorce rates are determined and examine trends in the United States.

---

4. William J. Goode, *The Family*, 2nd ed. (Englewood Cliffs, N.J.: Prentice-Hall, 1982): 150.

5. United Nations, *Demographic Yearbook*, 1986 (New York, 1988), Table 19, pp. 470–472.

6. Katherine Trent and Scott J. South, "Structural Determinants of the Divorce Rate: A Cross-societal Analysis," *Journal of Marriage and the Family* 51 (May 1989): 391–404.

## Divorce rates

**Divorce rates** are likely to be calculated in one of three ways: by the number of divorces that take place per 1,000 persons in the total population, by the number of divorces per 1,000 married females aged fifteen and over, and by the ratio of divorces granted in a given year to the number of marriages contracted in that same year. Note the difference in rate depending on the figures used.

The number of divorces that took place *per 1,000 persons in the total population* in the United States in 1988 was 4.8. This means that for every 1,000 persons in the population (men, women, children, adults, married, single, etc.), 9.6 persons became divorced or 4.8 marriages ended in divorce or annulment. Or said another way, if you come from a city of 100,000 population where 480 divorces were granted in 1988, the divorce rate was 4.8. Since our system is monogamous (two persons per divorce), 960 individuals in a city of 100,000 persons were divorced last year. Note how this divorce rate can be influenced by factors such as the age distribution or the proportion of the married or single population. A country or city with a large family size, a low life expectancy, a late age at marriage, a sizable proportion of the population being children or single teenagers, and a disproportionate number of the population unmarried, could have a sizable percentage of those married getting divorces and yet have a seemingly "low" divorce rate.

The number of divorces, again including annulments, that took place *per 1,000 married women aged fifteen and over* in the United States in 1988 was approximately 21. This means that there were 21 divorces per 1,000 (210 per 10,000) married females age fifteen and over. Of the three rates mentioned this one is probably the most accurate. Unlike the first rate described, men, single persons, children, and the like are excluded. It is figured on the basis of the legally married women who constitute the group that is susceptible to divorce. This figure could be used to compare the divorce rate cross-culturally without being influenced by the number, age, or marital status of the total population.

The ratio of *divorces granted in a given year to the number of marriages in that year* was about 49 in 1988. This is the rate used to best illustrate the "breakdown in the U.S. family." See for yourself. Nearly one out of two marriages end in divorce—or does it? Let's assume that your city of 100,000 population issued 1,000 marriage licenses in 1990. The same year, 500 divorces were granted. This would result in a divorce-marriage ratio of 1 in 2 or 50 divorces per 100 marriages. Thus, there was one divorce for every two marriages in your community in the year 1990. Suppose your state modified its divorce law that year and instead of 500 divorces, 2,000 divorces took place while the number of marriages remained constant at 1,000. Now, according to this rate, we have two divorces for every marriage or a divorce rate of 200.

While it may be accurate to speak of twice as many divorces as marriages in a given year, it is not accurate to say that of those marriages one-half will end in divorce. The inaccuracy is due to at least three reasons. First, those marriages are not the ones that ended in divorce. The divorce figures come from marriages which began one, eight, or thirty years ago. These should not be compared with the number of marriages begun in 1990. Second, approximately 40 percent of all marriages that are remarriages of one or both spouses are not taken into account. Persons who divorce and remarry in the same year contribute to both the number of marriages and the number of divorces giving a ratio of 1 to 1: as many divorces as marriages. To redivorce the same year would again produce the impossible result of more divorces than are marriages from which to divorce. The third reason, like the example just shown, results in a number of marriages that is smaller than the number of marriage dissolutions. Note an example using 1988 census figures. In 1988, there were 2.39 million marriages. The same year there were 1.18 million marriages that ended in divorce (49 percent). Also that year there were approximately 2.17 million deaths, giving a ratio of deaths to marriages of 91 (91 percent). Since the majority of these deaths occurred among married persons, the sum of marriages that ended in death or divorce was 140 percent—40 percent more marriages ending than existing.

Irrespective of the manner of calculation, you should be aware that statistics on divorce are not perfect. Even national data reported by the National Office of Vital Statistics are based on estimates obtained from states participating in the divorce-registration area (DRA). As of 1988, thirty-one states and the Virgin Islands participated in the DRA.[7] Thus, actual data from all fifty states are not available. Second, sampling rates vary among the DRA states, depending on the size of their annual divorce totals. All statistics estimated from probability samples have a sampling error. Third, completeness of reporting individual demographic items on divorce records varies considerably among DRA states. For example, some states do not require the reporting of race and others do not require the reporting of the number of this marriage. Fourth, often many items are left blank. This is particularly true of personal characteristics of husband and wife—age, race, and number of this marriage. Although the accuracy of divorce rates and statistics is improving, the divorce data are not perfect. The best available information is presented with the recognition that the figures are based on estimates from selected available data.

## Trends in divorce rates in the United States

The number of divorces and annulments granted in the United States increased from the pre–World War II figure of 264,000 in 1940, to the post–World War II figure of 379,000 in 1954, to 708,000 in 1970, to a peak of 1,213,000 in 1981. The number declined since then to the 1988 figure of 1,183,000. The rate per 1,000 population increased from 2 in 1940, to 2.4 in 1954, to 3.5 in 1970, to 5.3 in 1981 with a decline to 4.8 in 1988. The increase was not as steady as it appears from the selected figures given (see Table 17–1 and Figure 17–1).

---

7. U.S. Bureau of the Census, *Statistical Abstract of the United States: 1989*, 109th ed. (Washington, D.C.: U.S. Government Printing Office, 1989), p. 60.

Table 17–1

*Number of divorces and divorce rates: United States, 1945–1988*

| Year | Number of decrees | Rate per 1,000 | | Year | Number of decrees | Rate per 1,000 | |
|---|---|---|---|---|---|---|---|
| | | Total population | Married women | | | Total population | Married women |
| 1988 | 1,183,000 | 4.8 | 21.0 | 1968 | 584,000 | 2.9 | 12.4 |
| 1987 | 1,157,000 | 4.8 | 21.0 | 1966 | 499,000 | 2.5 | 10.9 |
| 1986 | 1,159,000 | 4.9 | 21.2 | 1964 | 450,000 | 2.4 | 10.0 |
| 1985 | 1,187,000 | 5.0 | 21.7 | 1962 | 413,000 | 2.2 | 9.4 |
| 1984 | 1,169,000 | 5.0 | 21.5 | 1960 | 393,000 | 2.2 | 9.2 |
| 1983 | 1,158,000 | 4.9 | 21.3 | 1958 | 368,000 | 2.1 | 8.9 |
| 1982 | 1,170,000 | 5.0 | 21.7 | 1956 | 382,000 | 2.3 | 9.4 |
| 1981 | 1,213,000 | 5.3 | 22.6 | 1954 | 379,000 | 2.4 | 9.5 |
| 1980 | 1,189,000 | 5.2 | 22.6 | 1952 | 392,000 | 2.5 | 10.1 |
| 1978 | 1,130,000 | 5.1 | 21.9 | 1950 | 385,000 | 2.6 | 10.3 |
| 1976 | 1,083,000 | 5.0 | 21.1 | 1948 | 408,000 | 2.8 | 11.2 |
| 1974 | 977,000 | 4.6 | 19.3 | 1946 | 610,000 | 4.3 | 17.9 |
| 1972 | 845,000 | 4.1 | 17.0 | 1945 | 485,000 | 3.5 | 14.4 |
| 1970 | 708,000 | 3.5 | 14.9 | | | | |

*Source:* National Center for Health Statistics, "Advance Report of Divorce Statistics, 1986," *Monthly Vital Statistics Reports*, vol. 38, no. 2 (Public Health Service, Hyattsville, Md. June 6, 1989), Table 1, p. 4; and *Statistical Abstract*, 1989, no. 83, p. 61.

The 1981 figure of 1,213,000 divorce decrees—that is, more than 2.42 million divorced persons—was the highest national total ever observed for the United States. Over the past decade until that year, the number of divorces increased more rapidly than the total population and the married population of the United States. The 1982 figures, however, show the first annual decrease in several decades. By 1988, an estimated 1.18 million couples divorced, 2 percent fewer than in 1981.

Generally, divorce rates have declined in times of economic depression and risen during times of prosperity (*see* Figure 17–1). The Depression years between 1932–1933 had the lowest rate of divorce per 1,000 married women in the last sixty years. Following the Depression, the rate of divorce moved upward almost steadily until the first postwar year, 1946. After 1946, the rate dropped sharply until 1950. For about fifteen years, until 1965, the divorce rate showed considerable stability, increasing slightly some years and decreasing during the mini-recession years of 1954 and 1958. Since 1965, the divorce trend has again climbed relatively sharply, reaching the highest rate in the history of the United States in 1981. The recessionary period of the early 1980s has again proven to be effective in reducing the number and rate of divorces.

Scott South agrees that the relationship between economic conditions and the divorce rate has changed over time. However, it is his contention that

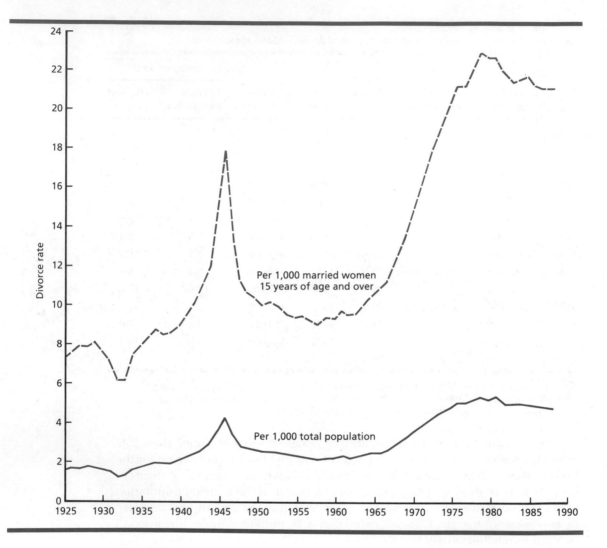

*Figure 17–1*

***Divorce rates: United States, 1925–1988.*** (*Source:* National Center for Health Statistics, "Advance Report of Divorce Statistics, 1986," *Monthly Vital Statistics Reports,* vol. 38, no. 2 [Public Health Service, Hyattsville, Md. June 6, 1989], Table 1, p. 4.)

substantially stronger influences on the divorce rate are changes in age structure and the labor-force participation of women.[8] In regard to age structure, the suggestion is that the rise in divorce rates over the past several

8. Scott J. South, "Economic Conditions and the Divorce Rate: A Time-Series Analysis of the Postwar United States," *Journal of Marriage and the Family* 47 (February 1985): 31–41.

decades is at least partially attributable to the economic pressures faced by the large cohort of the baby boom generation. With the abundance of younger workers, their incomes fall relative to older workers, and their prospects for marital dissolution are increased. In regard to the labor-force participation of women, the suggestion follows that is made at several other places in this chapter. As economic opportunities for women expand, wives become less dependent on husbands (or marriage) for financial support. Wives whose earnings are high relative to their husbands' have a particularly increased probability of experiencing marital dissolution.

## Variations in divorce rates

Divorce is permitted in every state in the United States. With each state having its own divorce code, it could be expected that rates would vary widely by geographic, demographic, and social characteristics. Let's examine several variations and seek explanations for higher or lower rates according to the selected characteristics.

*Geographic distribution*  The geographic distribution of divorce rates in the United States indicates a general trend toward an increase as one moves from east to west. This appears to have been true since the nineteenth century. The divorce rate is highest in Western states, followed by the South, the Midwest, and the Northeast.

Major variation exists by individual states as well. The divorce rate per 1,000 population in 1988 was lowest in Massachusetts (rate of 2.9) and highest in Nevada (a rate of 14.1). States with a rate of 3.5 or less per 1,000 population included Connecticut, Maine, Maryland, Massachusetts, Minnesota, New Jersey, North Dakota, Pennsylvania, and Wisconsin. States with rates of 6.5 or more included Alaska, Arizona, Arkansas, Florida, Nevada, Oklahoma, and Wyoming.[9] Note how the lowest rates generally occur in the Northeast and the highest rates in the South and West.

How can these geographical variations be explained? It is likely that different factors operate in different areas, but it is believed that divorce rates will be lower in culturally homogeneous rather than heterogeneous communities, and in communities with primary face-to-face interactions in contrast to communities with anonymous relationships, segmentalized relationships, or both. In traditional Durkheimian social structural terms, this refers to a social integration hypothesis of lower divorce rates in areas of high consensus on rules of behavior (norms) and effective social controls to ensure conformity. Communities or areas (regions, states) that are highly integrated socially

---

9. National Center for Health Statistics, "Advance Report of Divorce Statistics, 1986," *Monthly Vital Statistics Reports*, vol. 38, no. 2, June 6, 1989), Table 2, p. 5; and *Statistical Abstract of the United States*, 1989, no. 134, p. 88.

would tend to exert stronger social pressures against nontraditional behaviors (as divorce is generally perceived to be) and exert both formal and informal pressure for conformity to community norms.

The level of social integration and pressure toward conformity are likely to be influenced by residential mobility as well. High levels of residential movement are related both to higher levels of divorce and lower levels of social integration. Norval Glenn and Beth Ann Shelton state that the very high level of marital dissolution in the U.S. "divorce belt" (the West, South Central, Mountain, and Pacific census divisions) can be accounted for by a very high level of residential mobility there.[10] Residential mobility and other variables associated with lower levels of social integration would affect variations in divorce rates not only by region of the country and by state but would result in lower levels of divorce in rural than in urban areas as well.

Unique circumstances like those that exist in Nevada are greatly influenced by legal requirements. While Nevada may produce a small fraction of the total divorces granted nationally (about 1 percent), the divorce rate per 1,000 population within that state can be affected significantly by relatively few couples who come into the state from another state. Except for Nevada and a few other states, it is unlikely that migratory divorce has a major effect on divorce rates.

*Age of husband and wife*    The divorce rate is very high among young marriages. Spanier and Glick, analyzing census material, report that women who marry at ages fourteen to seventeen are three times as likely to divorce and women married at ages eighteen and nineteen are twice as likely to divorce as women who married in their twenties. Men who marry in their teens are twice as likely to divorce as men who marry in their twenties.[11] Explanations for this high rate may include emotional, immaturity, inability to assume marital responsibilities, greater incidences of early marriage in lower socioeconomic statuses where divorce is more likely, a longer time period in which to get divorced, more premarital pregnancies (also related to higher incidences of divorce), and similar factors.

Young marriages are not, however, responsible for the dramatic increases in family dissolution witnessed in the United States over the past twenty years.[12] While they manifest higher rates of marital disruption, the typical ages at divorce after the first marriage are twenty-five to thirty-four. More than half of all divorces occur among persons in their late twenties and thirties. Age at divorce has shifted upward over the past several decades reflecting the steady

---

10. Norval D. Glenn and Beth Anne Shelton, "Regional Differences in Divorce in the United States," *Journal of Marriage and the Family* 47 (August 1985): 641–652; and Beth Anne Shelton, "Variations in Divorce Rates by Community Size: A Test of the Social Integration Explanation," *Journal of Marriage and the Family* 49 (November 1987): 827–832.

11. Graham B. Spanier and Paul C. Glick, "Marital Instability in the United States: Some Correlates and Recent Changes," *Family Relations* 30 (July 1981): 333.

12. A. Wade Smith and Jane E. G. Meitz, "Cohorts, Education, and the Decline in Undisrupted Marriages," *Journal of Marriage and the Family* 45 (August 1983): 613–622.

rise in the age at marriage. In 1986, the median age for divorce after the first marriage was 32.4 for men and 30.2 for women.[13]

Although divorce rates are highest in young marriages and occur most frequently in the first few years following a marriage, these factors should not blind us to the reality that divorce is a common occurrence at any age or stage of the life course, including the elderly.[14] Yet, the increasing numbers of older persons, the changes in the perceptions of the roles of women, a shifting social acceptability of divorce, and so forth, present a realistic potential for dramatic increases in the number of divorced older persons.

*Duration of marriage*    The largest number of divorce decrees are granted one to three years after marriage and the number declines relatively consistently with increasing duration. In 1986, 3.8 percent of the divorcing couples had been married less than one year. One-third of divorcing couples (33.6 percent) were married one to four years, and about one-fourth (26.9 percent) were married five to nine years. The remaining third of divorcing couples had been married ten years or more with 14.6 percent married ten to fourteen years and 21 percent married fifteen years or more.[15] Without doubt, the breakup of marriages in all ways except the legal begins well before the actual divorce. Although more divorces occur during the second and third year of marriage (the mode) than at any other time, the first and second year may be the modal ones for marital breakups. Divorces that occur in the seventh or fourteenth year of marriage may simply be a legal break of a marriage severely disrupted years earlier.

In 1986 the median interval between the first marriage and divorce was 7.9 years. For those who remarried and got another divorce, the median interval between the second marriage and redivorce was approximately 5.5 years. For the third marriage or more, the median interval was about 3.9 years. It would appear that the median length of each succeeding marriage that ends in divorce is shorter than the previous one. Some support seems to exist for the idea that the first divorce experience is the most difficult one. Having been through a divorce, accepting the divorce status, and later remarrying may tend to make divorce a more acceptable solution to an unsuccessful second, third, or fourth marital relationship.[16] Perhaps remarriages involve all kinds of relationships that are not covered by established norms: ex-spouses, ex-inlaws, stepchildren, and so on. Perhaps remarriages are composed of people

13. National Center for Health Statistics, "Advance Report of Divorce Statistics, 1986," *Monthly Vital Statistics Reports*, vol. 38, no. 2, (June 6, 1989), Table 7, p. 9.

14. Helen R. Weingarten, "The Impact of Late Life Divorce: A Conceptual and Empirical Study," *Journal of Divorce* 12 (1988): 21–39; and Barbara S. Cain, "Divorce among Elderly Women: A Growing Social Phenomenon," *The Journal of Contemporary Social Work* (November 1988): 563–568.

15. *Monthly Vital Statistics Report*, vol. 38, no. 2 (June 6, 1989), Table 12, p. 13.

16. Frank F. Furstenberg, Jr. and Graham B. Spanier, "The Risk of Dissolution in Remarriage: An Examination of Cherlin's Hypothesis of Incomplete Institutionalization," *Family Relations* 33 (July 1984): 433–441.

who have problems that make stable marriages difficult: alcoholic, abusive, or unstable persons. Whatever the reason (and this issue is discussed further in this chapter), the time span of remarriages that end in divorce is shorter than in first marriages.

As indicated at the beginning of this section, the number of divorces declines relatively consistently with increasing duration. In other words, after the peak years for divorce (years two, three, and four) have been passed, the proportion of divorces by length of marriage gradually diminishes. I know of no evidence that supports an increase in divorce "after the children have grown up." That phase of the family life course is reached at quite varied lengths of time after marriage.

Readers need to be cautioned about differentiating divorce at midlife and later based on age at divorce versus duration of the marriage.[17] The dissolution of a three-year marriage at age fifty is probably quite different from the dissolution of a 25-year marriage at the same age.

Many marriages that never end in divorce are seriously disrupted in fact except for the legal decree. This leads to a point indicated at various times throughout the book: that length of marriage is not necessarily an index of success or adjustment and that divorce is not necessarily a good index of marital breakdown. Divorce may simply provide an indication of the greater willingness or acceptance to acknowledge a legal ending of a previously ended meaningful marital relationship. It is possible that higher divorce rates indicate greater success, greater adjustment, and higher levels of satisfaction among existing marriages in the United States. In other words, the ending of more of the "poor" marriages raises the overall quality level of existing marriages.

*Race, religion, and socioeconomic status*  The success of interracial and interfaith marriages was discussed in Chapter 8. At this point, rather than looking at the success or divorce rate of mixed marriages, the question becomes how rates differ by race, religion, or socioeconomic level in nonmixed or endogamous marriages. Are divorce rates different for blacks or whites, Protestants or Catholics, and lower or higher socioeconomic levels?

Divorce rates by race usually differ within a state as well as for the same racial groupings in different states. For example, for the United States as a whole, in 1987, white males had a divorce rate per 1,000 persons in the population of 10.2 compared to 18.4 for black males. The rate for white females was 14.2 compared to 31.7 for black females.[18] Racial differences may be partly explained by urban residence, mobility patterns, social-class differences, or by differing accessibility to various types of social and economic resources. Generally, the greater the accessibility to these resources, the lower the incidence of divorce.

---

17. Sally A. Lloyd and Cathleen D. Zick, "Divorce at Mid and Later Life: Does the Empirical Evidence Support the Theory?" *Journal of Divorce* 9 (Spring 1986): 89–102.
18. U.S. Bureau of the Census, *Statistical Abstract of the United States: 1989*, no. 53, p. 43.

## Is there ever a winner in a divorce?

WASHINGTON—It was an old story, one I've heard many times before. The woman sitting across the table from me had just been told by her husband that their marriage was over. He wanted out after 15 years.

True to the standards for women of her generation, she had worked his way through college and medical school, carving out no career for herself other than that of wife and mother. In her eyes, she had done everything right. In his, she had gotten boring. Now, in tears, she tried to figure out what would happen next. He had it all figured out—a sensible settlement, then out the door. She was apprehensive about her financial future. What, she asked me, did he owe her? Hadn't she helped make him what he was?

I didn't have the heart to tell her what she would learn soon enough: Parceling out property after divorce is sticky enough; allowing for the intangible investments either partner has made in a marriage is just about impossible.

Now comes a Stanford University study confirming something most divorced women have known for years: After divorce, men in general get richer; women get poorer.

Men often earn high incomes later in life after their wives worked as switchboard operators and filing clerks to launch their husbands' careers; and some courts are beginning to ask what, indeed, is owed beyond a division of tangible property. The answer may well be revolutionary: a piece of the husband's financial future.

That means that a woman could be compensated for the investments of work and energy she makes in a joint future that falls apart. After having lived on a struggling doctor's salary, a woman would get part of what he earns when he becomes a high-paid surgeon—even if she's been replaced.

Stories abound of rapacious women who clean out their husbands at divorce proceedings, but the truth is that most divorced women get very little money. Alimony is rare. And at least half of all divorced men stop supporting their children within a few years.

The Stanford study takes note of the fact that even in equal-property-division states such as California, men get richer and women poorer after divorce. The reason is simple: When judges are forced to divide everything 50-50, that usually means selling the family home. A man who goes on to make more money can reestablish his life-style in a few years. But a woman without the same opportunity gets stuck with the kids in rental housing.

The fact that the courts are taking a harder look at the realities of divorce settlements is heartening. But it doesn't change a basic lesson for women who hope never to be left financially helpless. It's a lesson learned often only through experience, which is why I believe women should teach it to their daughters in the cradle. It is this: Married or single, a woman should have a way of supporting herself.

As my friend who sat across from me will learn, putting a price tag on a marriage is still a no-win game.

*Source:* Patricia O'Brien, *Detroit Free Press*, June 6, 1982, p. 9-A. Reprinted with the permission of the Detroit Free Press.

---

What about religion? What divorce differentials exist by major religious affiliation? Data from seven U.S. national surveys by Glenn and Supancic showed that marital dissolution is moderately higher for Protestants, considered as a whole, than for Catholics, and is lower for Jews than for Catholics.[19] The highest rates are for persons with no religion. This is consistent with the

---

19. Norval D. Glenn and Michael Supancic, "The Social and Demographic Correlates of Divorce and Separation in the United States: An Update and Reconsideration," *Journal of Marriage and the Family* 46 (August 1984): 563–575. *See also* Jay Y. Brodbar-Nemzer, "Divorce and Group Commitment: The Case of the Jews," *Journal of Marriage and the Family* 48 (May 1986): 329–340.

data on frequency of attendance of religious services; religiosity is an important deterrent to divorce and separation.

Contrary to what one might expect, the Glenn and Supancic study as well as others show that Protestant fundamentalists, the most conservative Protestant denominations (Nazarene, Pentecostal, Baptist), have relatively high dissolution rates in spite of their strong disapproval of divorce. Factors associated with conversion to these fundamentalist denominations were found to be important in producing the higher dissolution rate.[20] Conversion may signify the cultural conflict that results from the radical transition from one context to another. It may indicate a lack of normative integration in the anti-separation–divorce doctrine on the one hand, while urging acceptance and tolerance of the converted "sinner" on the other. This higher divorce-separation rate may also reflect the lower than average socioeconomic status of persons in these denominations; the strong demands these groups make on the time, energy, and money of their adherents (which may negatively affect marriages); the inflexibility or rigidity of their theological position; or even the focus and emphasis on the next life rather than the current one.

What about socioeconomic level? The increased incidence of divorce has been occurring at all socioeconomic levels; yet, the proportion of persons ever-divorced remains the highest for relatively disadvantaged groups. Whether education, occupation, or income is used as an index of socioeconomic level, the divorce rate goes up as socioeconomic level goes down. One exception to this relationship exists among professional women who have five or more years of college education. Professional women, compared to women in general of similar age groups, were more likely to never have married, were more likely to divorce if they did marry, and were less likely to remarry if they got divorced. Female lawyers in particular, were found to have markedly higher rates of divorce and lower rates of remarriage than women in other professions such as teachers and physicians.[21] But marital disruption, high among professional women in general, may be due both to their lessened dependence on men and viable alternatives to marriage and to the strain resulting from their efforts to balance both work and family roles.

The greater marital instability and higher divorce rates at the lower socioeconomic levels may stem from a number of factors. First, the frustrations involved in the greater difficulty in meeting expenses and the lesser income may affect other areas of marital life. Second, at higher social strata, satisfaction in work and sexual spheres may less necessitate an escape from marriage. Third, the upper strata are more tied in to long-term investment expenditures

20. S. Kenneth Chi and Sharon K. Houseknecht, "Protestant Fundamentalism and Marital Success: A Comparative Approach," *Sociology and Social Research* 69 (April 1985): 351–375.

21. Teresa M. Cooney and Peter Uhlenberg, "Family-Building Patterns of Professional Women: A Comparison of Lawyers, Physicians, and Postsecondary Teachers," *Journal of Marriage and the Family* 51 (August 1989): 749–758; and Sharon K. Houseknecht, Suzanne Vaughn, and Anne S. Macke, "Marital Disruption Among Professional Women: The Timing of Career and Family Events," *Social Problems* 31 (February 1984): 273–284.

that are less easily stopped or ended in contrast to the immediate daily need expenditures of the lower strata. Fourth, although the income is insufficient at the lower strata for the type of car, house, or fur coat of the higher strata, the desire for them remains. Fifth, the kin and friend network of the upper strata is larger and more tightly knit, making divorce more difficult and giving it far greater consequences.

The alert reader may note what appears to be a contradiction in the data. For example, it was shown in Figure 17–1 and mentioned in the text that divorce rates tend to decrease during an economic depression and rise during times of prosperity. Also, it was just mentioned that the incidence of divorce increases as socioeconomic level goes down. How is it possible that divorce rates decrease during depressions when "times are hard," and increase among the lower strata where "times are also hard"?

Several factors are involved. During depressions, divorce rates drop at all class levels. The lower classes during the Great Depression of the 1930s still had the highest divorce rate. Many of the marriages that "survived" the 1930s contributed to the divorce rate of the 1940s. Also, the total life-style, the sense of loyalty, the linkages with kin, the occupational and income security, and the group support in general affect rates of divorce. These factors were different for Depression families and are different for lower-class families. Once again we note the powerful influence of the social network in something perceived to be so "individualistic and personal" as divorce.

## Legal and social grounds for divorce

The legal grounds for divorce vary somewhat for each state.[22] Apart from "no-fault" divorce, the most widely accepted legal grounds for divorce are breakdown of marriage, incompatibility, cruelty, and desertion. In all states adultery is either grounds for divorce or evidence of incompatibility, irreconcilable differences, or a breakdown of the marriage. Other legal grounds in at least one state include nonsupport, alcohol and/or drug addiction, felony, impotence, insanity, joining a religious order, disbelieving in marriage, treatment that injures health or endangers reason, pregnancy at marriage, fraudulent contract, gross neglect of duty, bigamy, attempted homicide, and the like. California, Colorado, and Oregon have procedures whereby a couple can obtain a divorce without an attorney and without appearing in court provided certain requirements (such as being married less than two years, having no children, no real estate, and few debts) are met.

Under a "fault" or "guilt" system, the wife brings suit in about seven of ten divorce actions. The social norm favors the wife in terms of cruelty, adultery, drunkenness, physical threat, and the like, which makes the entire process

---

22. These can be seen in *The World Almanac and Book of Facts* (New York: Newspaper Enterprise Association, 1989): 801.

easier to finalize. It is also more socially acceptable for the husband to accept the blame even though common sense alone would attest to the infrequency and unlikelihood of one spouse guilty and the other spouse innocent. Under a "no-fault" system, the sex of the filer for divorce shifts drastically. Figures from California, Florida, and Georgia following no-fault divorce show a dramatic increase in the percentage of men who filed for divorce.[23] Men can now proceed without the fear that their wives will contest the divorce or file damaging countercharges leading to protracted court battles.

The adversary divorce system in the United States, in which one party must be innocent and the other guilty, has led numerous states to **no-fault divorce.** The present no-fault trend first reached fruition in California, where traditional fault grounds were abolished January 1, 1970 in favor of dissolution of marriage based on "irreconcilable differences which have caused the irremedial breakdown of the marriage" and incurable insanity. Irreconcilable differences are defined as any grounds that are determined by the court to be substantial reasons for not continuing the marriage and that make it appear that the marriage should be dissolved. In California, the term *divorce* was replaced with *dissolution of marriage*. Community property was to be substantially equally divided. Alimony was to be determined by considering a woman's earning ability and the duration of the marriage. The one-year residence requirement was cut to six months.

Since the first no-fault divorce law was instituted, all states have displaced the traditional grounds for fault (adultery, desertion, cruelty) with the more subjective standards of "irreconcilable differences." Did the no-fault law changes accomplish their intended goals? Regrettably, studies of property settlements have suggested consistently that divorcing mothers are faring more poorly under the no-fault system than they did under the former adversary system.

Divorce proceedings under the no-fault system are relatively routine. Where cases are contested, they can become drawn-out affairs with much bitterness, fighting, and expense resulting. Attempts to decrease this conflict have led to divorce *mediation*. Mediation is a conflict resolution process where the divorcing couple meets with a neutral third-party intervenor (mediator) who helps them negotiate an agreement about property distribution, support, and child custody. The emphasis is on direct communication, openness, attention to emotional issues and the underlying causes of the disputes, and avoidance of blame. Proponents of mediation stress that it relieves court dockets clogged with matrimonial actions, reduces the alienation couples experience in court, inspires durable consensual agreements, helps couples resume workable relationships to jointly rear their children, and translates into savings in time and money. The mediation process works on building and

---

23. Ruth B. Dixon and Lenore J. Weitzman, "When Husbands File for Divorce," *Journal of Marriage and the Family* 44 (February 1982): 103–114.

strengthening relationships, while the adversarial process tends to weaken and destroy them.

Most disagreements and divorce conflicts extend over a period of years. Although conflict is often depicted as resulting from a single event (adultery, pregnancy, drunkenness), most divorces result from a series of minor maladjustments or difficulties, none of which can be singularly listed as the "cause" or "reason."[24] Levinger claims that people stay in relationships because they are attracted to them and/or they are barred from leaving them and that, consciously or not, people compare their current relationships with alternative ones.[25] If internal attraction and barrier forces become distinctly weaker than those from a viable alternative, the consequence is breakup.

While this approach is somewhat different from that adopted by exchange theorists, the decision to divorce still contains important reward-cost considerations. The rewards (attractions) may include love, goods, services, security, joint possessions, children, sexual enjoyment, and so forth while the costs (barriers) may include feelings of obligation or inadequacy, fears of family/friend reactions, religious prohibitions, financial costs, and the like. The key implication is that the probabilities for divorce increase as alternatives are perceived that provide greater rewards or lower costs than exist in marriage.

## Consequences of divorce for adults

Consequences of divorce are evident at both the individual and interpersonal (micro) levels as well as at the organizational and societal (macro) levels. Most research focuses on the former levels. But one macro-level finding in the United States, Norway, and Canada supports the proposition of a direct relationship between divorce and suicide.[26] This is consistent with the work on suicide originally published in 1897 by Emile Durkheim, who theorized that societies with lower degrees of social integration typically share higher rates of suicide.

Apart from suicide, one clearly defined consequence of divorce is its influence on psychological well-being. The newly divorced in particular were found to become significantly more depressed following a change in marital

---

24. *See:* Gay C. Kitson, Karen Benson Babri, and Mary Joan Roach, "Who Divorces and Why: A Review," *Journal of Family Issues* 6 (September 1985): 255–293.

25. George Levinger, "A Social Psychological Perspective on Marital Dissolution," *Journal of Social Issues* 32 (Winter 1976): 43; *see also* John N. Edwards and Janice M. Saunders, "Coming Apart: A Model of the Marital Dissolution Decision," *Journal of Marriage and the Family* 43 (May 1981): 379–389; and Stan L. Albrecht and Phillip R. Kunz. "The Decision to Divorce: A Social Exchange Perspective," *Journal of Divorce* 3 (Summer 1980): 319–337.

26. Steven Stack, "The Impact of Divorce on Suicide in Norway, 1951–1980," *Journal of Marriage and the Family* 51 (February 1989): 229–238; Frank Trovato, "The Relationship between Marital Dissolution and Suicide: The Canadian Case," *Journal of Marriage and the Family* 48 (May 1986): 341–348; and Ira M. Wasserman, "A Longitudinal Analysis of the Linkage Between Suicide, Unemployment, and Marital Dissolution," *Journal of Marriage and the Family* 46 (May 1984): 853–859.

## A portfolio to prepare for a marital bear market

Last week I heard about two marriages of many decades that are heading for the divorce shredder. In both cases the husbands asked out, and the wives were dumbfounded.

Ready or not, however, the women now have to hire lawyers and set about the serious business of dividing up the pots and pans, equitably. They're scared almost speechless.

What is your husband's income? What are the sources of his income, all sources, all income? How is it disbursed, invested?

How much did the house cost? The cottage? The furnishings? Are there any rental properties? What and where? What is fair market value today for all of the above?

Stocks, bonds, trusts, foreign accounts, real property, personal property, coin collections, artworks, retirement funds, pension benefits, who, what, where, when, how, how much? Stop!

Both women said many of the same things: "I never thought it would happen to me." "My husband took care of everything. I don't even know what the gas bill is at our house."

*Get your disaster plan going*

The moral of this story is that even the most happily married woman should not pack her brains away with her wedding gown.

In this era of profligate divorce—a little over 50 percent at present—I would suggest all wives formulate divorce plans right now. Just as we buy car insurance and home-and-contents insurance, praying we'll never need them, women should put together divorce survival insurance, praying they'll never need that either.

Some basics:

*Know what your separate and joint assets are,* where they are, how they are accessed and by

status from married to divorced.[27] This increase in depression following divorce closely reflected greater economic problems, the perception that one's standard of living had deteriorated, and the lesser availability of close, confiding relationships.

Continued attachment to the ex-spouse appears to impede emotional adjustment for both men and women.[28] This appears to be true whether the attachment is positive or negative. Negative attachment was found to be exacerbated by the strain of conflict with the ex-spouse while positive attachment was reduced by the development of an active social life and, for men, a new intimate relationship.

The economic consequences of divorce differ dramatically for males and females. The economic situation improves for men and declines for women. California data show a radical change in the standard of living just one year after a legal divorce. Men experienced a 42 percent improvement in their postdivorce standard of living while women experienced a 73 percent loss.[29]

---

27. Elizabeth G. Menaghan and Morton A. Lieberman, "Changes in Depression Following Divorce: A Panel Study," *Journal of Marriage and the Family* 48 (May 1986): 319–328.

28. Jeanne M. Tschann, Janet R. Johnson, and Judith S. Wallerstein, "Resources, Stressors, and Attachment as Predictors of Adult Adjustment after Divorce: A Longitudinal Study," *Journal of Marriage and the Family* 51 (November 1989): 1033–1046.

29. Lenore J. Weitzman, "The Economics of Divorce: Social and Economic Consequences of Property, Alimony, and Child Support Awards," *UCLA Law Review* 28 (August 1981): 1251.

whom. How do you find out? I guess you'll have to ask your spouse. Tough. Do it anyway.

*Know what your living expenses are.* Some women don't even know if the family home has a second mortgage, if the car or cars are paid for, if husband has personal or home-improvement loans outstanding, all kinds of things.

*A woman who does not work outside her home* should seriously think about a paying job she would enjoy. Prepare for it. Study for it. Work at it, if possible—part-time, perhaps, or as a volunteer. You may never need or want to do this work for a living, but if you must, you can.

*Choose a highly qualified divorce lawyer* based on experience and track record, not personal friendship or because he's your cousin. You don't have to contact him or her at all. Sober, cool-headed research in advance of need is all that is required. It's like knowing the name and phone number of a fine doctor, all the while you hope never to need the doctor's services.

*Consider where you might live* should you be unable to live in the family home after a divorce. Do you know a qualified real estate broker? Find one. Consult. Think of temporary and permanent locations, neighborhoods, housing types. What are the advantages or disadvantages of each? What do they cost? Are you sure, or guessing?

Imagine yourself divorced and you will know what other information to put into your survival insurance portfolio. It's the same information any widow needs and often doesn't have.

A wise person is not caught in the rain without an umbrella. You have to think about that in advance, too. Sensible. Prudent, and a comfort.

*Source:* Nickie McWhirter, *Detroit Free Press* September 8, 1986, p. 1-C. Reprinted with the permission of The Detroit Free Press.

National longitudinal surveys as well show that 40 percent of widows and over one-quarter of divorced women fall into poverty for at least some time during the first five years after their divorce.[30] Little wonder that more divorced women report that they are in constant financial crisis, are perpetually worried about not being able to pay their bills, have more stress, and feel less satisfied with their lives than any other group in the United States. In contrast, men who divorce or separate are immediately better off. They retain most of their labor incomes, typically do not pay large amounts of alimony and child support to their ex-wives, and no longer have to provide for their former families.[31] While writers frequently refer to *his* and *her* marriages, those differences appear minor when comparing *his* and *her* divorces.

Findings consistently show trauma and stress following marital disruption and divorce to be significantly greater for the female than for the male. The Wallerstein longitudinal study of sixty divorcing families shows significant differences between former spouses in the quality of their lives.[32] Among women, persistence of anger and widespread loneliness was prevalent. This

30. Leslie A. Morgan, "Economic Well-Being Following Marital Termination," *Journal of Family Issues* 10 (March 1989): 86–101.

31. Greg J. Duncan and Saul D. Hoffman, "A Reconsideration of the Economic Consequences of Marital Dissolution," *Demography* 22 (November 1985): 485–497.

32. Judith S. Wallerstein, "Women After Divorce: Preliminary Report from a Ten Year Follow-up," *American Journal of Orthopsychiatry* 56 (January 1986): 65–77.

was particularly true among women over age forty. Even ten years after the divorce, many of these women felt angry, lonely, and rejected and were living in economic, social, and psychological conditions well below that which they had achieved during their marriage. Younger women were more likely to exhibit greater economic and emotional progress. Wallerstein indicates that the capacity to replace failed relationships is neither a psychological nor social given. In two-thirds of the families, only one of the former spouses was able to make use of the divorce to significantly improve the quality of his or her life. In only 10 percent of the couples did both former spouses do so. Apparently there are few victimless divorces even among adults and fewer still when children are involved.

In reviewing the literature on the possible long-term effects of divorce on the adults involved, Ann Goetting suggests that physical and mental health are best among the happily married, worst among the unhappily married, and between the two extremes are the divorced.[33]

### Children of divorced parents

The existence of children of divorced parents is increasingly common. Data from a national survey discovered that nearly a third of all children have experienced family disruption by the time they reach the age of fifteen. When children of never-married parents and those not currently living with a biological parent are included, the authors expect "that close to half of all children living in the United States today will reach age eighteen without having lived continuously with both biological parents."[34]

The number of children involved in divorce has exceeded 1 million every year since 1971. The average number of children per decree granted has generally been falling since 1964 when it peaked at 1.36. By 1986, this measure had fallen to 0.90 children per decree, meaning that today there are more divorces than children involved (see Figure 17–2). One reason for the decline is the drop in the birth rate. Other reasons include a slight increase in the proportion of childlessness at divorce and a decline in the estimated interval between marriage and divorce.

Are children a deterrent to divorce? The answer appears to be both yes and no. Data show that children serve as a deterrent to both separation and divorce only when they are at the preschool ages. Once all the children in a family are in school, they do not seem to influence the probability of separation and divorce.[35]

---

33. Ann Goetting, "Divorce Outcome Research: Issues and Perspectives," *Journal of Family Issues* 2 (September 1981): 350–378.

34. Frank F. Furstenberg, Jr., Christine Winquist Nord, James L. Peterson, and Nicholas Zill, "The Life Course of Children of Divorce: Marital Disruption and Parental Contact," *American Sociological Review* 48 (October 1983): 667.

35. Andrew Cherlin, "The Effect of Children on Marital Dissolution," *Demography* 14 (August 1977): 265–272.

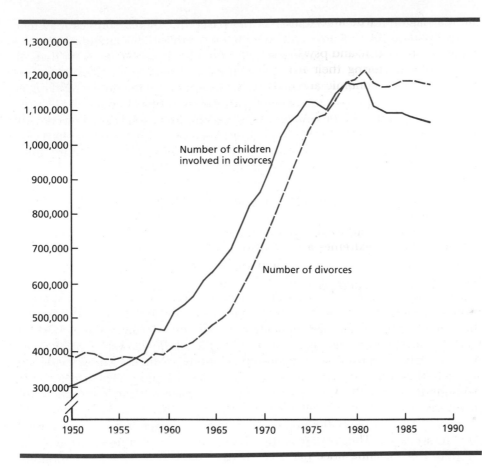

*Figure 17–2*
***Divorces and children involved: United States, 1950–1988.*** *(Source:* National Center for Health Statistics, "Advance Report of Divorce Statistics, 1986," and "Annual Summary of Births, Marriages, Divorces, and Deaths: United States, 1988," *Monthly Vital Statistics Reports,* vol. 37, no. 2 and vol. 38, no. 2 [Public Health Service, Hyattsville, Md., June 6, and July 26, 1989], pp. 4–6.)

Data from over 11,000 divorcing families in northern California clearly support the relationship between the length or duration of marriage and the presence of children.[36] Explanations for children delaying (not preventing) divorce include the presence of children making divorce more costly than continuation in the marriage, the cost in having the wife confined to the home and less free to take employment, the articulation of older children about their feelings, the possibility that people who have children may be more secure in

36. Robert P. Rankin and Jerry S. Maneker, "The Duration of Marriage in a Divorcing Population: The Impact of Children," *Journal of Marriage and the Family* 47 (February 1985): 43–52.

the marriage than their childless counterparts, the stigma couples may feel toward parents who divorce, and anticipated complications attending divorce action: child custody, co-parenting, or single-parent problems. Note that all the couples in this study got divorced, thus, it provides no support for the myth that "children prevent divorce." What it supports is the notion of a longer duration of marriage before a divorce with the presence of children.

Given that there are more than 1 million children each year involved with divorced parents, the question of greater concern is, What are the effects or consequences on these children? Should couples, although unhappily married, stay together for the sake of the children? The presumed effect of divorce on children is usually negative. That is, the assumption is that divorce is always traumatic for the children who will suffer psychologically, socially, and economically.

Very few of us would quarrel with the notion that children are better off in happy, stable families than in divorced or unhappy, unstable families. Evidence does suggest that divorce diminishes the economic and social resources available to children. And these fewer resources seem to have negative consequences for educational attainment, marital timing, marital probability, and divorce probability.[37] That is, for children of divorced parents, the relative gain over mother's educational attainment is lower; these children tend to marry at an earlier age, have a lower probability of ever marrying, and have a higher probability of themselves getting divorced. Other evidence suggests that adolescents from divorced homes are more prone to commit delinquent acts, they experience problems in peer relations, and they are highly associated with family-related offenses such as running away and truancy.[38] This confirms the popular notion that divorce is bad for children.

In spite of findings such as these, rarely do research results suggest or support the idea that, for the sake of the children, partners in unhappy marriages should stay together, that is, not divorce or separate. For example, one national sample of 1,400 children aged twelve to sixteen showed that conflict in intact homes, especially if persistent, was as harmful as disruption itself.[39] Thus, we are faced with two "less than optimal" choices. Both the intact home with persistent conflict and the divorced home are likely to result in varying degrees of stress, pain, and difficulties. The impact of divorce on

37. Verna M. Keith and Barbara Finlay, "The Impact of Parental Divorce on Children's Educational Attainment, Marital Timing and Likelihood of Divorce," *Journal of Marriage and the Family* 50 (August 1988): 797–809; Norval D. Glenn and Kathyrn B. Kramer, "The Marriages and Divorces of the Children of Divorce," *Journal of Marriage and the Family* 49 (November 1987): 811–825; and William R. Catton, Jr., "Family Divorce Heritage and Its Intergenerational Transmission," *Sociological Perspectives* 31 (October 1988): 398–419.

38. David H. Demo and Alan C. Acock, "The Impact of Divorce on Children," *Journal of Marriage and the Family* 50 (August 1988): 619–648; and Joseph H. Rankin, "The Family Context of Delinquency," *Social Problems* 30 (April 1983): 466–479.

39. James L. Peterson and Nicholas Zill, "Marital Disruption, Parent-Child Relationships, and Behavior Problems in Children," *Journal of Marriage and the Family* 48 (May 1986): 295–307.

*Children are frequently innocent victims of parental separation and divorce. Some children are known to run away while others experience severe depression, bitterness, guilt, loneliness, and loyalty conflict.*

children will probably vary considerably according to the age of the children and many other factors.

One of these factors relates to custody and the level of economic support. Joint custody is generally perceived to be the most ideal arrangement, and research does show joint-custody fathers to be more involved in making parental decisions, sharing responsibility, and making contact and participating in activities with their children than non-custodial fathers.[40] However, most custody is not joint. It is estimated that in about 90 percent of divorces that involve minor children, the mothers gain custody. The impact of being a female-headed single parent and the likelihood of being at a poverty level is very great (review Chapter 7).

One primary reason for this poverty status following divorce is the father's non-compliance with child support awards. The severity of this problem is well documented by U.S. census and other reports that show only about one-half of all children for whom child support has been decreed actually receive it. Another one-fourth of the children receive less than the

---

40. Madonna E. Bowman and Constance R. Ahrons, "Impact of Legal Custody Status on Fathers' Parenting Postdivorce," *Journal of Marriage and the Family* 47 (May 1985): 481–488.

specified amount, and the remaining one-fourth receive no support at all.[41] Reasons for this non-support extend well beyond court enforcement or even ability to pay to interpersonal reasons such as the level of attachment between former spouses, the quality of their relationship, and even the frequency of visits by the noncustodial parents to their children.[42] But the inescapable conclusion is that poverty, in general, and nonsupport, more specifically, have effects on the welfare of children.

An in-depth study by Judith Wallerstein and others of 60 families with 131 children in California over a ten and fifteen year time period concludes that divorce produces not a single pattern in children's lives but multiple patterns with many variations.[43] The authors were surprised to discover that the severity of a child's reactions at the time of the parents' divorce did not predict how that child fared five, ten, and even fifteen years later. Earlier reports by Dr. Wallerstein indicated that five years after the marriage breakup, 34 percent of the children were said to be happy and thriving. Their self-esteem was high, and they were coping competently with the tasks of school, playground, and home. Twenty-nine percent were doing reasonably well; they were considered average by teachers, learning at grade level, and scoring in the middle range of psychological health. The final 37 percent were found to be consciously and intensely unhappy and dissatisfied with their lives; they experienced moderate to severe depression, felt intense loneliness, and complained of coming home to empty houses. Ten and fifteen years after the divorce, Dr. Wallerstein found among these children continuing strong feelings of sadness, bitterness, guilt, loyalty conflict, and loneliness. As they entered young adulthood, all of the children expressed fears of repeating their parents' failure to maintain a loving relationship, as well as fears of rejection and betrayal.

Perhaps it is understandable that research has shown very mixed results on the consequences of divorce on children. Clearly many structural variations such as custody arrangements, remarriage of parent, presence of grandparents or other kin, age of children, educational and neighborhood influences, economic resources, presence of siblings, and the like tend to influence the consequences of a shift from a marital to a divorced parental status. Thus, taken alone, findings comparing the adjustment of children from broken homes with children from unhappy, unbroken homes do not produce results that are nearly as detrimental as is often believed to occur.

---

41. U.S. Bureau of the Census, *Current Population Reports*, Series P-23, no. 154, "Child Support and Alimony: 1985," (Washington, D.C.: U.S. Government Printing Office, 1989): Figure 2, p. 1.

42. Judith A. Seltzer, Nora Cate Schaeffer, and Hong-Wen Charng, "Family Ties after Divorce: The Relationship between Visiting and Paying Child Support," *Journal of Marriage and the Family* 51 (November 1989): 1013–1032.

43. Judith S. Wallerstein and Sandra Blakeslee, *Second Chances: Men, Women, and Children a Decade After Divorce* (New York: Ticknor and Fields, 1989).

# REMARRIAGE AND RECONSTITUTED FAMILIES

The United States is recognized as practicing monogamy. Yet it is likely that a greater number, as well as proportion, of people in the United States experience a multiple number of spouses than in many, if not most, countries recognized as polygamous. This would be especially true for women since polyandry occurs rarely. While the marriage of one man to several women is common, the marriage of one woman to several men is infrequent. Thus, it is possible that in the United States, more than anywhere in the world, women are likely to experience multiple husbands. About one out of five households maintained by a married couple include one or both spouses who have been divorced, and one-sixth of all children under eighteen in the United States live in these households.[44] Remarriages and reconstituted families are common.

Like first marriages, couples are likely to marry for reasons of love, be monogamous, and expect the marriage to last until death. Yet the remarried couple faces life experiences and engages in life-styles that in many ways differentiate them from a couple in their first marriage. Those who remarry are older on the average than those marrying for the first time, presumably more mature, and more likely to have a child upon entering the marriage.

## Remarriage rates

There are over 11 million remarried families including more than 4 million stepfamilies in the United States.[45] Persons whose marriages end in divorce are more likely to renounce a particular marriage partner rather than the institution of marriage. An estimated two-thirds of all divorced persons remarry. A life-course analysis of divorce and remarriage revealed that at least 60 percent of women and 70 percent of men who became divorced were subsequently remarried.[46] The chance of remarrying following widowhood was substantially smaller, especially for women, for whom the probability was less than 15 percent. Interestingly, the mean age at remarriage after widowhood for women was ten years *less* than the mean age at widowhood. This paradox suggests that even though the probability of remarriage following widowhood is small for females, it is the youngest widows who are most likely to remarry. Remarriage among older widows is compounded by the declining supply of potential husbands due to higher male mortality rates.

---

44. Andrew Cherlin and James McCarthy, "Remarried Couple Households: Data from the June 1980 Current Population Survey," *Journal of Marriage and the Family* 47 (February 1985): 23–30; and Paul C. Glick and Sung-Ling Lin, "Remarriage After Divorce: Recent Changes and Demographic Variations," *Sociological Perspectives* 30 (April 1987): 162–179.

45. Paul C. Glick, "Remarried Families, Stepfamilies, and Stepchildren: A Brief Demographic Profile," *Family Relations* 38 (January 1989): 24–27.

46. Thomas J. Espenshade and Rachel Eisenberg Braun, "Life Course Analysis and Multistate Demography: An Application to Marriage, Divorce and Remarriage," *Journal of Marriage and the Family* 44 (November 1982): 1032.

Similar patterns of remarriage were found to exist in Japan, but with some interesting differences. Like in the United States, Japanese men are more likely to remarry than are women (although in far greater proportions) and the supply of available husbands decreases with age (a declining sex ratio). But unlike the United States, the percentage of women who say they "do not want to remarry" is high even among younger women and it increases with age. A result is that Japanese women are actually much less likely to remarry than are their American female peers.[47] This was explained by suggesting that in a society where there is little divorce and where marriage is treated more as a practical relationship than as a romantic one, divorced women are more likely to be completely disenamored with both their partner and the institution of marriage itself. When asked why they have not remarried, both widows and divorcees frequently responded, "I'm fed up with it."

It is assumed that in all countries where remarriage occurs at all, the likelihood of it varies depending on social and demographic characteristics.[48] In the United States, by race, remarriage is both more likely and more quickly experienced for white than for black women. By age, remarriage is more likely for those who are married at a relatively young age and for those who are under age thirty at the time of divorce. By children, remarriage is more likely for those who have no children or only a small number of children in their first marriage. By education, remarriage is greater for those who have less than a college education. By employment, remarriage is more likely if the woman is not in the labor force. By income, remarriage is more likely for women with lower income.

In analyzing remarriage according to the financial condition of women, Anne-Marie Ambert suggests that financially secure women display behavior that is dysfunctional on the remarriage market.[49] While they have more opportunities to meet men, have more dates, and have more steady relationships, they are also more likely to break up relationships that do not suit them, they are less likely to tolerate abusive male behavior toward them, and they are less likely to flatter a man's ego. In brief, consistent with an exchange theory model, high status women have less to gain from remarriage than lower status women.

The 1986 census data show the median age at divorce after the first marriage to be 32.4 for males and 30.2 for females.[50] The median age at remarriage is about 36.2 for males and 32.9 for females. Accordingly, the time lapse between the median age of divorce for first marriages and the median age

---

47. Laurel L. Cornell, "Gender Differences in Remarriage after Divorce in Japan and the United States," *Journal of Marriage and the Family* 51 (May 1989): 457–463.

48. Paul C. Glick, "Remarriage: Some Recent Changes and Variations, *Journal of Family Issues* 1 (December 1980): 455–478; and Paul C. Glick and Sung-Ling Lin, "Recent Changes in Divorce and Remarriage," *Journal of Marriage and the Family* 48 (November 1986): 737–747.

49. Anne-Marie Ambert, "Separated Women and Remarriage Behavior: A Comparison of Financially Secure Women and Financially Insecure Women," *Journal of Divorce* 6 (Spring 1983): 43–54.

50. U.S. Bureau of the Census, *Statistical Abstract of the United States: 1989*, no. 1301, p. 86.

of remarriage is 3.8 years for males and 2.7 years for females. Thus, while remarriage rates are higher for men than for women, the women who do remarry do so more quickly than the men. Useful predictors of early remarriage for women include not being employed and, to a lesser extent, not having any children.[51]

## Marriage among the remarried

Earlier in this chapter it was stated that the length of remarriages that end in divorce is less than that of first marriages. Perhaps this is because remarriages include many persons who have already proved they will divorce rather than remain unhappily married. Perhaps these second and third marriages are characterized by more ambiguous norms and more complex family structures. But when married, is there a difference in marital satisfaction for those in first marriages compared with remarriages? The answer from a review of sixteen studies that addressed this question was yes. People in first marriages reported greater satisfaction, but the difference appeared to be minuscule and certainly not substantial.[52]

By gender, remarried men were found to be more satisfied with their marriages than remarried women, but only slightly so. One explanation for the slight difference has been related to the complexities of stepmotherhood—a common event of marrying men who are noncustodial fathers.

Do factors such as the greater willingness to divorce, the slight difference in satisfaction, or the presence of stepchildren mean that remarriages are more conflict-ridden and unsuccessful than first marriages? One test of this is to compare the present marriage of remarried persons with their own first marriage. In a study of 369 remarried persons living in eight western states, respondents rated their marriages as much better than their previous marriages, as better than the marriages of others they knew, and as better than they had anticipated them to be prior to their occurrence.[53]

Helen Weingarten compared remarried adults with first-married and currently divorced adults.[54] When comparing the remarried with the divorced, similarities existed in levels of self-esteem, perceived internal control, levels of dissatisfaction, perceived shortcomings, worry, anxiety, immobilization, physical health symptoms, and substance use. But the divorced were significantly more likely to report that they are "not too happy," less likely to report that the present is the happiest time of life, and more likely to view the past as much

---

51. Frank L. Mott and Sylvia F. Moore, "The Tempo of Remarriage Among Young American Women," *Journal of Marriage and the Family* 45 (May 1983): 427–435.

52. Elizabeth Vemer, Marilyn Coleman, Lawrence H. Gonong, and Harris Cooper, "Marital Satisfaction in Remarriage: A Metaanalysis," *Journal of Marriage and the Family* 51 (August 1989): 713–725.

53. Stan L. Albrecht, "Correlates of Marital Happiness Among the Remarried," *Journal of Marriage and the Family* 41 (November 1979): 857–867.

54. Helen R. Weingarten, "Marital Status and Well-Being: A National Study Comparing First-Married, Currently Divorced, and Remarried Adults," *Journal of Marriage and the Family* 47 (August 1985): 653–662.

*As many as one-third of all marriages taking place today are remarriages. Many of these marriages involve legal consultation prior to the ceremony.*

happier than the present. When comparing the remarried with the currently married, similarities existed in reporting they feel "very happy," consider the present to be the happiest time of their lives, and are optimistic about the future. But the remarried were more likely to answer "a lot" when asked how frequently difficult events have occurred in their lives, they more frequently reported feelings of having a nervous breakdown, and they were more likely to report ill health and use of alcohol and medicine, measures sensitive to chronic stress. It does appear that first marriage, divorce, and remarriage are distinctive "institutions" with both similarities and significant differences between them.

Remarriages alone show tremendous variations as well. For example, considerable research over the past decade has noted the special problems of remarriage when an adolescent child from a prior marriage is present. These children appear to have a destabilizing effect on the husband-wife relationship. Remarriages with adolescent stepchildren experience higher rates of divorce than other remarriages and these stepfamilies move teenagers out of the home faster than first-married families.[55] In addition to the adolescent

---

55. Lynn K. White and Alan Booth, "The Quality and Stability of Remarriages: The Role of Stepchildren," *American Sociological Review* 50 (October 1985): 689–698. Note also: Jean Giles-Sims and Margaret Crosbie-Burnett, "Adolescent Power in Stepfather Families: A Test of Normative-Resource Theory," *Journal of Marriage and the Family* 51 (November 1989): 1065–1078.

having a destabilizing effect on the parent and stepparent, the adolescents too report that divided loyalty and discipline are particularly stressful problems for them. Let us look at remarried couples with stepchildren more closely.

## Remarried couples with stepchildren

Stepfamilies have been classified as a high-risk setting with more pathological behaviors and higher rates of child sexual abuse than among first families.[56] Traditionally, remarriages and stepfamilies were formed primarily as a result of the death of a spouse; today the formation results primarily from divorce. These "remarried," "reconstituted," "binuclear," "blended," and "stepparent" families constitute significant nontraditional marital and family arrangements that present unique circumstances and relationships. Stepfamilies may include a stepfather, mother, and her children; a stepmother, father, and his children; or a mother and father joining two sets of children. Unique circumstances arise when the stepparent couple is not married but live together or when two separated parents living in separate households both attempt to provide financial and emotional support to their children.

Many structural variations of remarriage have the potential for boundary ambiguity—the uncertainty of family members as to who is in or out of the family and who is performing or responsible for certain roles and tasks within the family system. This uncertainty of boundaries is likely to increase both family stress and the risk of behavior problems in children.[57] This is true not only in cases with an alcoholic parent or a husband missing in action, but also in cases where it is not clear who *really is* a member of the family and what roles or tasks should be performed (e.g., between a stepmother and her nonresidential children or a grandparent with the children of their stepson).

Ambiguity and difficulty with children may be heightened when children visit rather than live with the stepparent. The stepparenting experience, particularly for stepmothers, was found to be more positive with live-in stepchildren.[58] Most research suggests the role of stepmother is a more difficult one than that of stepfather, and this difficulty seems to stem in large part from the fact that most stepmothers do not have live-in stepchildren. In contrast, most stepfathers do. When stepchildren visit, it is usually the stepmothers and not the children's fathers who have the extra housecleaning, shopping for food, and cooking. This work is often perceived as a burden

---

56. For a good overview of research on stepfamilies *see:* Marilyn Ihinger-Tallman, "Research on Stepfamilies," *Annual Review of Sociology* 14 (1988): 25–48.

57. B. Kay Pasley and Marilyn Ihinger-Tallman, "Boundary Ambiguity in Remarriage: Does Ambiguity Differentiate Degree of Marital Adjustment and Integration," *Family Relations* 38 (January 1989): 46–52. Note also: Charles Hobart, "The Family System in Remarriage: An Exploratory Study," *Journal of Marriage and the Family* 50 (August 1988): 649–661; and Pauline Boss, *Family Stress Management* (Newbury Park, CA: Sage Publications, Inc., 1989): Chapter 4.

58. Anne-Marie Ambert, "Being a Stepparent: Live-in and Visiting Stepchildren," *Journal of Marriage and the Family* 48 (November 1986): 795–804.

because they receive little benefit emotionally from the visits. And like stepparenting, stepsiblings' relations were found to be more positive when they lived together rather than visited.

Stepfamilies differ structurally from first families in a number of ways. First, there is one biological parent not presently living in the household. Second, the parent and child relationship predates the new marriage. And third, while a legal relationship binds the remarriage, no legal relationship binds the stepchildren and stepparents. In fact, Sarah Ramsey reports that only fourteen states have statutes that even obligate the stepparent to support stepchildren, and typically even in those instances, the obligation is more limited than that imposed on a natural parent.[59]

These structural elements have been found to alter parenting practices in a major way. One national sample of children between the ages of seven and eleven revealed that in a majority of families, marital disruption effectively destroyed the relationship between children and the biological parent living outside the home.[60] Nearly half of all children had not seen their nonresident fathers in the past year. Unlike that suggested in the media, children of divorce rarely have two homes and only a minority have ever slept over at their fathers' houses. It was suggested that perhaps a majority have never set foot into the houses of their non-resident fathers. In addition, the contact that does exist with the outside parent tends to be a social rather than an instrumental exchange. That is, the non-resident parent may take the children to dinner or on trips but rarely helps with schoolwork or daily projects.

The unique structural elements of stepfamilies raise a variety of questions and problem situations not likely to be found in the traditional nuclear unit. For example: How does the "ex-spouse" affect the relationship with the "new" spouse? Which parent "gets" the child for birthdays, holidays, and special events? Do parents compete in giving the more expensive gift? Does the gift come equally from the parents and stepparents? Is discipline likely to be equal and consistent coming from a mother and stepmother or father and stepfather? Do incestuous relationships become frequent issues of concern, particularly between stepfathers and stepdaughters? Are children the messengers or communication link between the mother and father who may or may not be on cordial terms? Do children living in homes with stepparents experience increased emotional and behavior problems? What socialization difficulties occur in the process of stepparenting? Clearly the list could be extended considerably.

---

59. Sarah H. Ramsey, "Stepparent Support of Stepchildren: The Changing Legal Context and the Need for Empirical Policy Research," *Family Relations* 35 (July 1986): 363–369.

60. Frank F. Furstenberg, Jr. and Christine Winquist Nord, "Parenting Apart: Patterns of Childrearing After Marital Disruption," *Journal of Marriage and the Family* 47 (November 1985): 893–904. *See also:* Judith A. Seltzer and Suzanne M. Bianchi, "Children's Contact with Absent Parents," *Journal of Marriage and the Family* 50 (August 1988): 663–677.

# SUMMARY

1. In the United States, divorce is the best known and most common means of ending an unsatisfactory marital relationship but desertion, marital separation, and annulments exist as well. Desertion shares with marital separation the condition that the spouses are married and cannot remarry. Separation may be formally and legally arranged or informally agreed upon. Annulment, due to conditions existing prior to the marriage, eradicates it so that in theory, at least, it never existed.

2. When viewed cross-culturally, higher divorce rates appear to be associated with a high sex ratio and a late average age at marriage. A curvilinear relationship appears to be related to the level of socioeconomic development and the rate of participation of females in the paid labor force.

3. The rate of divorce is likely to be calculated in a number of ways such as per 1,000 persons in the total population, per 1,000 women age fifteen and over, or the ratio of divorces to the number of marriages in a given year. Irrespective of how the rate is calculated, the trend has been upward with a leveling off or slight decrease in the last few years.

4. Within the United States, divorce rates vary by a wide range of geographic, demographic, and social characteristics. Rates vary considerably by state as well as by metropolitan areas within the state. Teenage marriages have higher divorce rates than marriages begun when the couple were in their twenties. Persons who are married more than once have a higher likelihood of divorce than those married only once. By race, divorce rates are higher for blacks than for whites; by religion, divorce rates are higher for Protestants than for Jews and Catholics; and by socioeconomic level, divorce rates tend to go up as educational level, income, or occupational positions go down. One exception to this relationship exists among educated professional women.

5. The legal grounds for divorce vary somewhat for each state, with the most widely accepted grounds being marital incompatibility or evidence of irreconcilable differences. In the past decade, no-fault divorce has been adopted in most states to resolve many of the difficulties associated with proving "fault." Studies suggest, however, that women are faring more poorly under no-fault than under the former adversary system.

6. Social grounds for divorce often differ considerably from the legal grounds. Divorce mediation as a conflict resolution process has grown rapidly as a means of diminishing the bitterness and divisiveness that accompanies divorce. Reasons for staying in or leaving a marriage are viewed as attractions (rewards) and barriers (costs) and take on significance in light of alternatives available.

7. The consequences of divorce for adults are evident at both macro- and micro-levels, as reflected in factors such as higher rates of suicide and depression. The economic consequences differ dramatically for males and females, with men doing better and women much worse following divorce.

8. Children are a primary concern to those interested in divorce. While research would not lend support to the idea that unhappy or unsuccessful marriages should remain intact for the sake of the children, neither does it lend support to the idea that children of divorced parents do not go through periods of stress and periods of major readjustment. Mothers tend to get custody of children and the under-

    payment or nonpayment of child support creates hardships for many women and children.

9. Most persons who end one marriage enter another. The remarriage rate climbs as the divorce rate climbs. Men are more likely to remarry than women, divorcees are more likely to remarry than widows, and younger persons are more likely to remarry than older persons. Although people may have failed in their first marriage, the remarriage was generally perceived to be better than the former.

10. The complexities of remarriage are compounded by the presence of children. The stepparenting experience is most difficult for the stepmother but is more positive with live-in stepchildren. Structural elements such as one biological parent not living in the home, the child predating the new marriage, and the lack of legal, binding relationships between stepchildren and stepparents alter parenting in dramatic ways—even to the extent of destroying many relationships between children and the biological parent living outside the parental home.

11. This chapter focused on divorce and remarriage. To have "strong" families and to offer programs and establish policies that lend support to marriages and families is, at least in terms of rhetoric, the goal of governmental and community units. Our attention in the final chapter is directed to this issue of the family and social policy.

# KEY TERMS AND TOPICS

# DISCUSSION QUESTIONS

1. What are some of the reasons for desertion, separation, or annulment rather than divorce? How does each affect husbands, wives, or children?

2. Compare the divorce rates of different countries. Why are some much higher than others? What types of social factors might cause the likelihood of divorce to increase or decrease?

3. How are divorce rates determined? In this chapter, three different divorce rates were given for the same year. How is this possible? What does each mean? What factors influence rates even when the number of divorces remains constant?

4. Divorce rates were found to differ by duration of marriage, race, religion, socioeconomic status, and the like. What were the differences and how are these variations explained?

5. In regard to religion, explain why conservative or fundamentalist Protestant religious groups that oppose divorce tend to have high divorce rates.

6. Visit a local court that handles divorce cases. Arrange to meet with the judge to discuss the legal process, the legal grounds for divorce compared to the nonlegal reasons for divorce, and his or her views on divorce mediators, joint custody, grandparents' rights, and other

legal issues. What legal changes does he or she view as necessary?

7. Discuss the implications and consequences of no-fault divorce. What are its pros and cons? What effect is it likely to have on rates, long-term trends, and the like?

8. What do you define as the primary reasons that marriages end? Are these reasons that can be predetermined or influenced prior to marriage? Why do many "poor" marriages not end?

9. Examine some of the consequences of divorce for adults. Why are the consequences so different for males and females?

10. Discuss the relationship between the presence or absence of children, the number of children, and divorce. What are the consequences of divorce on children? Compare with children from unbroken but unhappy homes.

11. How do remarriages differ from first marriages? Explain.

12. How do stepchildren affect a marriage? Discuss some advantages and difficulties that accompany reconstituted or binuclear families.

# *FURTHER READINGS*

Ahrons, Constance R., and Rodgers, Roy H. *Divorced Families: A Multidisciplinary View*. New York: W. W. Norton and Company, 1987. A view of divorce as a normal process of family change with a focus on sociological, psychological, and therapeutic perspectives.

Cherlin, Andrew J. *Marriage, Divorce, Remarriage*. Cambridge, Mass.: Harvard University Press, 1981. An examination of the trends in marriage, divorce, and remarriage; explanations for these trends; and the consequences.

Furstenberg, Frank F., Jr., and Spanier, Graham B. *Recycling the Family: Remarriage After Divorce*. Beverly Hills, Cal.: Sage Publications, 1984. The results of an eight-year study examining aspects of adjustment unique to the marriage-divorce-remarriage transition.

Maglin, Nan Bauer, and Schniedewind, Nancy, (eds.). *Women and Stepfamilies: Voices of Anger and Love*. Philadelphia: Temple University Press, 1989. An anthology of letters, journals, poems, stories, and essays by women as stepmothers, stepdaughters, and stepgrandmothers.

Pasley, Kay, and Ihinger-Tallman, Marilyn, (eds.). *Remarriage and Stepparenting: Current Research and Theory*. New York: Guilford Press, 1987. An excellent collection of writings and studies dealing with a range of historical, theoretical, and conceptual issues of stepfamily living.

Price, Sharon J., and McHenry, Patrick C. *Divorce*. Newbury Park, CA: Sage Publications, Inc., 1988. An overview of divorce: why people divorce, adjusting to divorce, children of divorce, legal aspects of divorce, the economics of divorce, and interventions to divorce.

Raschke, Helen J. "Divorce" in *Handbook of Marriage and the Family* by Marvin B. Sussman and Suzanne K. Steinmetz (eds.). New York: Plenum Press, 1987, Chapter 22, pp. 597–624. A review of trends, correlates, consequences for adults and children, and legal aspects of divorce.

Spanier, Graham B., and Furstenberg, Frank F. Jr. "Remarriage and Reconstituted Families" in *Handbook of Marriage and the Family* by Marvin B. Sussman and Suzanne K. Steinmetz (eds.). New York: Plenum Press, 1987, Chapter 16, pp. 416–434. An overview of demographic factors of American remarriage with a summary of literature on well-being, children, and generational ties.

Spanier, Graham B., and Thompson, Linda. *Parting: The Aftermath of Separation and Divorce*. Beverly Hills, Ca.: Sage Publications, 1984. The results of a study that examines the complex transition from marriage to divorce.

Walczak Yvette, with Burns, Sheila. *Divorce: The Child's Point of View*. New York: Harper and Row, 1984. A brief paperback about children and divorce based on "conversations" with children of divorced parents.

Wallerstein, Judith S., and Blakeslee, Sandra. *Second Chances: Men, Women, and Children a Decade After Divorce*. New York: Ticknor and Fields, 1989. A ten-year follow-up study of sixty families looking at the long-term consequences of divorce.

# CHAPTER EIGHTEEN

# *F*AMILY AND SOCIAL POLICY

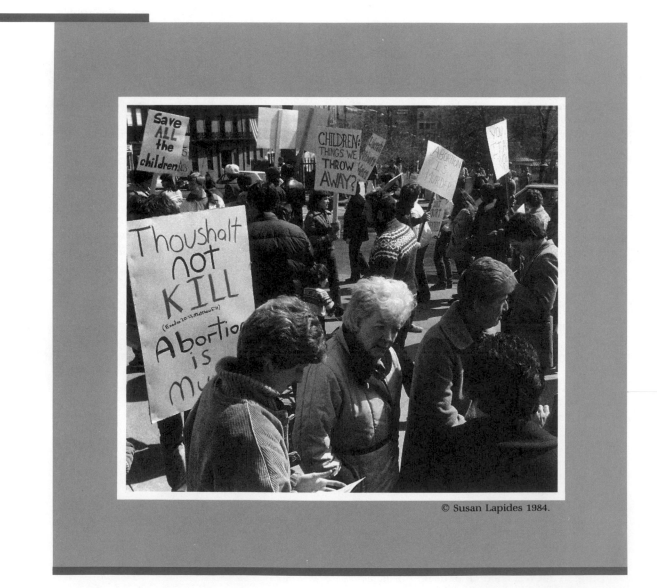

© Susan Lapides 1984.

Few persons, married or single, are willing to dismiss the family as insignificant and unimportant to their own lives or to the lives of others. In fact, one could make an argument for the value-laden position that, across cultures and throughout history, no single institution has had a greater influence in shaping the lives of persons, in affecting interpersonal relationships, or even in determining national stature. Yet the United States has no explicit national policy (or policies) for families. The United States, with all its agencies overseeing education, health, commerce, labor, energy, transportation, defense, agriculture, and the like, has no agency devoting its attention directly to families. The government, while professing the importance of the family, is disruptive of kin networks in programs related to labor and defense, and punishes persons or groups who don't conform to a particular marital and family life-style.

Perhaps a "national family policy" is both unnecessary and unwanted. First, United States citizens have gotten along without an explicit family policy for centuries; thus, why now? Second, a family policy is an unrealistic goal since no one family policy could meet the needs of the many family life-styles in the United States (*see* Chapters 4–7). And no single policy would be able to deal with premarital, nonmarital, and marital interactions ranging from mate selection to sexual relationships (*see* Chapters 8–11). Nor could one policy be made equally relevant to families at all stages of the marital and family life cycle (*see* Chapters 12–15). Thus, no one policy could answer questions that affect everything from crisis to abuse to divorce (*see* Chapters 16–17). For these reasons we should begin with an examination of what is meant by "family policy" and how this concept can profitably be explored in this chapter.

## *THE MEANING AND USE OF FAMILY POLICY*

Family policy can mean very different things to different people. It can be defined broadly enough to incorporate everything that touches the lives of family members or it can be defined so narrowly that it includes very little or nothing because specific policies can be subsumed under policy headings such as health, taxation, employment, or education. In terms of government action, "family policy" seems minimal, for persons, not families are the directed targets.

Phyllis Moen and Alvin Schorr, two leading family policy scholars, use the term *family policy* to mean a widely agreed-on set of objectives for families, which the state and other major social institutions try to realize through deliberately structured programs and policies.[1] This definition incorporates

---

1. Phyllis Moen and Alvin L. Schorr, "Families and Social Policy," in *Handbook of Marriage and the Family* by Marvin B. Sussman and Suzanne K. Steinmetz (eds.). (New York: Plenum Press, 1987): Chapter 28, p. 795.

*Research is an effective way to determine the success of various policies or programs, as well as their impact, positive or negative, on families.*

the sense that family policy is coherent and more or less deliberate or intended.

A continuing difficulty in family policy is determining who is and what is *family?* Must members be related economically, morally, or social-psychologically rather than by birth or law? Moen and Schorr suggest that rather than settling for one particular definition, it seems more appropriate to define families according to the particular issues involved. For example, if the issue involves the socialization of children, use a definition including households with children. If the issue involves a property settlement with cohabiting adults, use a definition that includes intimate primary relationships. The definition should not become so rigid and sacred that it defeats the program or action.

The range of programs and policies affecting families is very broad. Some programs and policies support a *nurturance* function: child care, health care, and services to the elderly or handicapped. Other programs support the *economic* functions of the family by providing welfare benefits or stimulating employment. *Social* functions are served by programs that promote helping arrangements, social networks, and the exchange of services. The interest here is to deal with family policy in general terms both in our definition of *family* and in our definition of *policy.* Prior to dealing with major issues surrounding family policy, let us first direct our attention to family policy research.

## FAMILY POLICY RESEARCH

Within the social sciences, an issue that frequently emerges is the extent to which social research can or should be value-free. This issue becomes particularly acute when dealing with family policy research. One side of the issue argues for value neutrality, objectivity, and basic research apart from any policy objective. The opposite side of the issue argues that value-free research is impossible even if desired and that trained social researchers need to provide their expertise in constructive ways. One solution to these dichotomous positions is to do both by "wearing two hats": one of researcher and one of citizen. The researcher provides empirical evidence of what *is*, the citizen works for goals she or he deems important. Nye and McDonald,[2] for example, distinguish between **family policy research** and **family policy advocacy.** The researcher attempts to maintain objectivity throughout the research endeavor. The advocate endorses and actively works for a course of action that improves family life and hopefully enhances the well-being of its members. They argue that individuals who choose to be both researcher and advocate need to state which role they are performing at any given time.

Scanzoni makes a case for both positions.[3] His research and theory in *Shaping Tomorrow's Families* is basically positivistic because it describes and analyzes *what is.* Yet it is stimulated by policy and normative considerations of *what should be.* His position is that research itself should be conducted under the strictest positivist procedural canons possible. Yet researchers should not be deluded into thinking they have no vested interest in the outcome of the investigations any less than a medical researcher has an interest in finding some cure or solution to a sickness or disease. That empirical research must simultaneously be kept distinct from and yet connected with practical applications, Scanzoni recognizes as a difficult tightrope to walk. Yet this sort of "balancing act" is required because family *research* has often been devoid of practical application on the one hand and because family *policy* has been devoid of basic research and organizing principles on the other.

## Research to establish family policy

One type of research is done to establish family policy. Research to establish policy typically starts with a general hypothesis that some kind of social actions may be desirable. It does not assume a problem exists, does not evaluate an existing policy or program, and does not assess the consequences of a policy or program. Rather, given some "nontraditional" life-style (cohabitation, dual-career marriages, female-headed households, reconstituted families, never-married parents, and so forth) research for family policy examines certain categories of persons who have a particular structural arrangement or life-style and seeks to discover the outcome of that way of life for the individuals involved as well as for society as a whole. The result of the research

2. F. Ivan Nye and Gerald W. McDonald, "Family Policy Research: Emergent Models and Some Theoretical Issues," in F. Ivan Nye, ed., *Family Relationships: Rewards and Costs* (Beverly Hills: Sage Publications, 1982): 195.

3. John Scanzoni, *Shaping Tomorrow's Family: Theory and Policy for the 21st Century* (Beverly Hills, Cal.: Sage Publications, 1983).

## Policy research: State welfare expenditures and rates of teen births, poverty, divorce, and suicide.

Spending for public welfare is a frequent issue in political campaigns. The message is that spending for such "worthless" causes is a waste of taxpayers' money, a public dole, and an anti-work incentive. But what does research show to be related to state welfare expenditures?

Shirley Zimmerman (*Understanding Family Policy*, 1988) looked at state per capita expenditures for public welfare and a range of other variables. Examining all fifty states, the following inverse relationships were found. Lower state per capita expenditure for public welfare was related to:

1. Higher state teen birthrates
2. Higher state poverty rates
3. Higher state divorce rates
4. Higher state suicide rates

For those with political interests, each of these relationships is directly opposite those implied by conservatives who argue that welfare is the culprit that causes teen parenthood, poverty resulting from a desire not to work, and family breakup. The added belief that welfare is a key cause of high state taxes led many states to reduce their welfare budgets sharply in the 1980s.

to establish family policy may be that all is well and nothing needs to be done, or it may be that laws need to be changed, programs developed, or action taken to fulfill specific needs.

An example of research to establish family policy can be seen in a study aimed at discovering the socioeconomic processes that determine the use of welfare and its accompanying dependency, and the impact of labor market conditions on the determinants of dependency.[4] The life-style at issue was low-income female-headed households dependent on welfare. Data were gathered from more than 300 of these women in New Jersey at three different time periods. One of the hypotheses was that the most immediate economic trade-off faced by low-income single female parents was between the expected return from labor supplied to the formal labor market, and the need for her at home. Findings provided basic support to the idea that welfare can be reduced by making the expected value of work outside the home greater than home-related work. The policy implication is not to merely expand jobs or provide work of any kind, but to provide jobs that maximize the potential for financial independence. In other words, producing fewer, but relatively better, jobs may be a more useful strategy than producing poor jobs for a broad cross-section of the low-income population. The research suggests that welfare dependency among low-income women can be reduced by jobs that possess internal job ladders, the possibility of advancement, on-the-job training, and the job protection afforded by unionization. Unfortunately, federal support has largely been withdrawn for these types of training and

---

4. Robert F. Kelly, "Welfare Dependency Under Depressed Labor Market Conditions: Lessons from the 1970s for the 1980s," *Journal of Urban Affairs* 5 (Fall 1983): 331–348.

job experiences. And workfare, as this research suggests, if it is only an administrative requirement that some job be found regardless of the job's quality, is unlikely to have a long-term positive impact.

## Family evaluation research

A second type of policy research is done to evaluate existing policy. *Family evaluation research* is conducted at a programmatic level to determine the degree to which social programs have achieved or are achieving the stated goals of a public policy or resultant program. For example, Aid to Families with Dependent Children (AFDC) policy is intended to encourage the care of dependent children in their own homes or those of relatives in ways that maintain and strengthen family life, retain personal independence, and provide parental care and protection. Family evaluation research would attempt to determine if these basic goals are being met and address such issues as whether eligible families are being serviced, whether the financial aid contributes to greater family stability, or whether the level of assistance is greater than necessary or inadequate to achieve the goals.

Shirley Zimmerman, using a family perspective, examined research findings and other data dealing with government policies and programs to determine their effectiveness or lack thereof.[5] Effectiveness was viewed as a fit between the goals or objectives of a program and their actual outcomes. Drawing upon other studies as the source of her evaluation attempts, she assessed the effectiveness of income guarantee experiments, AFDC, Supplementary Security Income (SSI) and social security, deinstitutionalization policies in relation to the mentally ill and retarded family members, compensatory preschool education, and abortion services. While her conclusions cannot be considered definitive given the limited number of studies and the various interpretations of different criteria, she claims that from a family perspective, government programs seem to have promoted family well-being under conditions that take family variables into account. When programs do run counter to family interests, the negative effects of such policies and programs on affected families tend to reflect the absence, rather than the presence, of supportive service policies and programs. Her evaluation research provides evidence that changes or reductions in public programs and government's involvement in them cannot be justified on the basis of ineffectiveness. Those changes rest more on ideological grounds than on empirical evidence.

## Family impact analysis

A third type of policy research is *family impact analysis*. Here the attempt of the research is to assess the intended and unintended consequences of public

---

5. Shirley L. Zimmerman, "Public Policies and Family Outcomes: Empirical Evidence or Ideology?" *Social Casework* 64 (March 1983): 138–146.

policy and social programs. For example, what is the impact of mortgage interest deductions on those who cannot afford to purchase a home? What are the effects of a program like Head Start on the mothers as well as on the children? What are the employment and income consequences of a policy that prohibits a woman from terminating a pregnancy?

Unlike evaluation research that is focused on whether the goals or objectives are being met, family impact analysis looks at how families are affected beyond the explicit intentions or goals of the policy or program. As a result, evaluation research may show the intended goals are being met but impact analysis may show the goals are counterproductive by having negative consequences for families in unintended ways. In our previous example of AFDC families, evaluation research may show the level of funding is adequate to feed, clothe, and house the dependent children, yet an impact analysis may show the funding and support has negative consequences as well.

In fact, Patricia Spakes examined the impact of the AFDC mandatory work registration policy on AFDC clients.[6] The mandatory work registration requirement is intended to insure that AFDC recipients register to work through the Work Incentive Program (WIN). The purpose was to move families off welfare through employment, thus reducing welfare dependency, enhancing clients' self-esteem, and establishing the parent as a positive working role model for children in order to break the welfare cycle. In studying 102 welfare clients in Wisconsin, the data suggested that the mandatory work registration requirement had no effect on the majority of individuals or their families. However, 28 percent reported negative individual effects and 24 percent reported negative family effects (compared to 5 percent who reported positive effects).

Negative individual impacts were most often described in terms of the strain of having to look for work in addition to performing other duties, lowered self-concept as a result of failure to obtain employment, and disappointment with the failure to get training or a better job. Negative family consequences included expensive and inadequate child care, behavior problems of unsupervised children, and concern regarding children left at home to care for themselves. In brief, a family impact analysis of the policy that required welfare parents to register for work showed negative consequences for adults and children alike and an increase in family problems. These findings lead to questioning whether the psychological benefit to society in seeing welfare mothers work is worth the millions of dollars it costs to implement the program and the negative social psychological consequences to its recipients.

Effective family policy is highly dependent upon all three types of research: research to determine what type of policy is needed, research to

---

6. Patricia Spakes, "Mandatory Work Registration for Welfare Parents: A Family Impact Analysis," *Journal of Marriage and the Family* 44 (August 1982): 685–699.

evaluate programs or policies in existence, and research to assess the impact or consequences of programs or policies beyond their specific intent. Let's turn our attention to some key issues, presented again in ideal-type terms, that surround the formulation and enforcement of policies directed toward or affecting families.

# ISSUES SURROUNDING FAMILY POLICY

Policy matters seldom exist without a divergence of ideas, conflicts over positions, or opposing recommendations. Policy matters seldom satisfy all interest groups or get the endorsement of all social and political organizations. At times these differences relate to basic philosophies of life, perceptions of the role of government, or images of what the family is or should be. Following is an examination of several of these differences. While they are presented in dichotomous or "either/or" terms and often as polar extremes, both views do exist simultaneously. Rarely can they be resolved into either/or positions.

## Policy for the status quo or as a force for change?

The first issue addresses questions related to the type of family or families desired and the goals or objectives of family policy. Should policy be directed toward "the family" or toward a diversity of life-styles, relationships and "families"? Is policy directed at preventing the family from change and maintaining the status quo or at supporting change, flexibility, and creativity? This issue is at the heart of Scanzoni's differentiation of conventionals from progressives.[7]

**Conventionals** are those that believe the normal family is conjugal. A male as husband is head of the household and the sole economic provider. A female as wife and mother is a helpmate to the husband and a homemaker who is responsible for household duties, domestic care, and the socialization of the children. Children are helpless and dependent. Conventionals, represented by political and religious conservatives, want to save this traditional image of what families should be. Groups representing this perspective view family change as a breakdown of morality and disintegration of *the* family. They have demonstrated substantial political power in crippling sex education programs, halting the Equal Rights Amendment, and electing persons who oppose abortion. They have influenced legislation such as the Family Protection Act that provides that parents be notified when an unmarried minor receives contraceptive devices or abortion services from a federally supported organization. They have restricted the federal government from

---

7. Scanzoni, *Shaping Tomorrow's Family*, and John Scanzoni, "Reconsidering Family Policy: Status Quo or Force for Change?" *Journal of Family Issues* 3 (September 1982): 277–300.

interfering with state statutes pertaining to child abuse and changed the definition of abuse to exclude corporal punishment (spanking). They have opposed legal services for homosexuals and educational materials that "do not contribute to the American way of life as it has been historically understood" (*Family Protection Act*, Section 301). The function of policy from the perspective of conventionals is to maintain the status quo or return to some idealized image of what the family once was and should be.

*Progressives* are those that believe a normal family can take many forms. The view is not of *the* family but of families and of close relationships. A progressive model is a pluralistic one that allows many options. At the core of this model is the notion that involved adults should strive to become equal partners and should seek to achieve equity among family members. Scanzoni states that "given their pluralistic view of society, progressives accept the notion that alternative views of family should be allowed to 'compete' in the marketplace, with nonaligned persons being allowed to gravitate toward those patterns suiting them best.[8] Conservatives cannot accept this notion.

Theoretically, Scanzoni links the functionalist approach with the conventionals. The emphasis is on structure and stability. Thus couples who stay together are successful and those who divorce are failures and represent breakdown. Out-of-wedlock births and female-headed households represent disorganization. In contrast, progressives are linked more closely with the conflict approach. Here the emphasis is on process and change. A wide variety of goals are legitimate and result from complex negotiations between interest groups, each with preferred patterns and relationships. Thus childless marriages; equalitarian relationships; divorce; marriage in middle or old age; diverse family forms among minorities or the poor; cohabitation without marriage; homosexual relationships; abortion; women, wives, and mothers in the employed labor force; or males as housekeepers and childrearers all become acceptable intimate relationships and life-styles.

Scanzoni notes that in spite of the unified and influential efforts of the conventionals, the major weakness of their model is that it is out of sync with the times. It does not conform to what is actually happening on the current scene. Society is not static, families are not uniform, and goals are not unanimous. As Scanzoni states:

> To be sure, the progressive vision includes order, but the order is not maintenance of the status quo. Instead, order emerges out of the ongoing development of satisfactory equity as well as intimacy: Creativity replaces conformity and flexibility supersedes fixed duties.[9]

From the progressive perspective, intimate relationships, including marriage, are not entered to carry out predictable, predetermined duties

---

8. Ibid., p. 153.
9. Ibid., p. 159.

where males do certain things and females do others; rather, they are entered as a context for the facilitation of interests held by both persons. Children are not helpless and dependent but can be effectively trained in the dynamics of equitable decision making. Individuals may choose to not marry, to cohabit, to have no children, and to find employment that was traditionally defined as inconsistent with their gender. Policy is aimed not at maintaining past traditions or the status quo that the majority of citizens have already discarded, but at looking ahead and coming up with fresh ideas molded around an equal partner framework. The function of policy is first to recognize and accept the reality of changes already apparent in Western society.[10] A second function is to implement further change in a fashion that is responsive both to the question of social order and to the preferences of the persons involved. Other related issues surround this task.

## Policy at a federal or local level?

A second issue is whether federal, state, or local units should assume responsibility in the formulation and enforcement of family policy. Under the Reagan administration this issue was central to funding activities. The federal government position has been that states, in the form of block grants from the federal government, should determine how and for what purposes the money should be spent. Opponents of this position argue that family-related concerns will be ignored even more than at present and that policies that are established will reflect the views of the most conservative segments of the population. Evidence does suggest that the thrust of state family laws continues to support the conventional family model described in the first issue.

There is evidence as well that family legislation within states mirrors the political cultures of those states. For example, a comparative analysis of the legislative summaries of three states: Nevada—individualistic; Minnesota—moralistic; and South Carolina—traditionalistic, revealed that an individualistic state such as Nevada enacted much less legislation with explicit family content than a politically moralistic state such as Minnesota.[11] At the same time, a traditionalistic state such as South Carolina enacted less legislation than either of the other two states. The content and topics of legislation differed as well. Minnesota had the most breadth of legislative topics vis-à-vis families covering economic benefits and assistance, domestic violence and abuse, followed by marriage, divorce, and family obligations. Nevada focused

---

10. *See* Sanford M. Dornbusch and Myra H. Strober, (eds.), *Feminism, Children and the New Families* (New York: The Guilford Press, 1988). Note particularly Chapter 14 on "Public Policy Alternatives," pp. 327–355.

11. Shirley L. Zimmerman and Phyllis Owens, "Comparing the Family Policies of Three States: A Content Analysis," *Family Relations* 38 (April 1989): 190–195.

more on marriage, divorce, and family obligations while South Carolina focused on health.

As indicated elsewhere, the United States has no federal family policy as such. As noted in previous chapters, the legal control of marriage and divorce in the United States currently resides with the states rather than the federal government.[12] All states designate the husband as the head of the family and require him to support his family. While no state permits polygamy per se, the states differ considerably as to grounds for divorce and ease of remarriage. While no state permits the marriage of pre-teenage children, states vary as to the age that youth may legally marry. Involvement at the federal level becomes evident when one notes how certain restrictions set at the state level, such as the prohibition of miscegenation (marriage between members of different races), abortion, and the distribution of contraceptives, were ruled unconstitutional by the Supreme Court. So, while marriage laws are formulated and enforced by the state, federal courts have at times declared various practices to be unconstitutional. Also at the federal level, the United States Congress has established both explicit and implicit civil rights policies that have an impact on every facet of marriage and family life.

This issue, like all others, is not an either/or question. There are both advantages and disadvantages to the establishment of family policies at either a national or a state level. Robert Leik and Reuben Hill[13] illustrate advantages of family policy at the federal level as including:

1. The family per se would not be lost in local obscurity but would become visible as the major unit of concern, which may be as much a symbolic advantage as a practical one.
2. Many major influences on families, such as the military, labor, business, or agriculture, occur primarily at the national level and only at this level can significant power be obtained for families.
3. Standards can be set at a national level which minimize local prejudices, indifference, or economy-minded legislative concerns.
4. Large-scale funding and the establishment of priorities are possible at a national level, but impossible at a state or local level.
5. Only at the national level can a vision for families be created which transcends regions and localities.

While there are distinct advantages of family policy at the federal level, there are also inherent problems. One problem centers around how policies can be maximally adapted to the special needs of racial, ethnic, regional, or other cultural groups. A second problem centers around how to make policies

---

12. For an overview of many of these state laws, *see* Doris Jonas Freed and Timothy B. Walker, "Family Law in the Fifty States: An Overview," *Family Law Quarterly* 19 (Winter 1986): 331–441.

13. Robert K. Leik and Reuben Hill, "What Price National Policy for Families?" *Journal of Marriage and the Family* 41 (August 1979): 458–459.

### How about a tax-free family lunch?

Those familiar with our basic social institutions are well aware of the tax breaks afforded them. All church property and religious holdings, amounting to billions of dollars, are free of federal and state taxation. Educational expenses relating to employment such as books, supplies, professional meetings, or additional training to improve skills in a current position are tax-deductible items. Gifts to politicians, their travel expenses, postage costs, office space and supplies, and entertaining costs are at the taxpayers' expense. Business expenses such as food, lodging, travel, supplies, labor, gifts, or entertainment done on behalf of a business become legitimate pre-profit expenses and are not subject to taxation when they exceed a certain percentage of one's income.

Is marriage and the family of lesser social importance? Can dinner with a wife be considered as worthwhile as a dinner with a business associate? Is taking a son or daughter to one baseball game not as valid for society as the block of season tickets the company writes off as an expense? Is the home and shelter provided for families not as important to society as the elaborate churches, synagogues, and cathedrals of religious groups? Is a family vacation not equal in importance to the political junkets of a small town official or a U.S. Congressman or/-or/-woman? Should the husband pay taxes at a higher rate because his wife takes on a part-time job to supplement the family income? How about a tax-free family lunch? What do you think?

maximally responsive and accountable to clients. This requires local control. A third problem centers around assessing the adequacy of monitoring services provided. Leik and Hill suggest that there are appropriate roles for the participation of the national government, state or regional government, local government, and the private sector in an overall set of policies aimed at helping and strengthening families.[14] According to this view, money alone cannot do the job; nor can one level of government.

## Families and intimate relationships as a public or private institution?

A third issue revolves around the extent to which intimate relationships and families are *public* or *private* institutions. Many times the family is seen, even reverenced, as a private institution that is separate from and closed to public scrutiny. Family policy, in contrast, demands an openness to public view and public scrutiny. The privacy position argues that the family or an intimate relationship is a matter of personal concern, a haven for privacy, a place of unconditional affection and love, a network for sharing fears, anxieties, or joys, and a source of protection and security free from "big brother" and public dominance. Can't husbands and wives decide for themselves when, where, and how they desire to "make love"; the number of children they want or don't want; the manner in which they control that number; and how they discipline, educate, clothe, or feed these children?

---

14. Ibid., p. 459.

The public position argues that the state and community have the right (and even obligation) to establish boundaries on what happens in private. If children are hungry, wives are raped, or families are homeless, should not the state or public agencies intervene? But intervene when, to what extent, and on what issues? Minimum income? Day care? Discipline or corporal punishment? Abortion? Alcohol or drug dependency? Health care? Housing?

Advocates of the privacy position argue for minimal intervention of the state into family and intimacy matters. Advocates of the public position argue that laws must be written and enforced to protect all group members and enhance equal rights and opportunities for all citizens. Interestingly, advocates of the privacy position on certain issues such as child care and a minimum family income often take a public position on governmental intervention in sex role behavior or the prohibition of abortion. For example, right-wing religious and political groups led organized efforts in the past two decades against the passage of an Equal Rights Amendment but for the passage of anti-abortion laws.

Alvin Schorr sees the resistance to government intervention in private affairs of individuals to be one of the key factors against ever seeing an explicit family policy in the United States. In his words:

> As citizens, we are profoundly suspicious of and opposed to government. Despite all the power that government has come to have, we perennially oppose its spread—and, most particularly, where we believe it to be interfering in matters private, sentimental, or sexual.[15]

The fact that no explicit national or governmental family policy exists should not lead you to believe that the government is totally uninvolved in or neutral to families. A wide range of public policies deal with social security, health and medical care, child welfare, education, day care, and most areas of interest to family members. The lack of a coherent plan, set of services, or national policy may be testimony to the fact that families have no organized or powerful lobby groups to influence family legislation and oversee the impact of any legislative matters on marriages and families. By contrast, business, religious, and medical groups have many organized efforts to protect their vested interests.

The difficulty of family policy formulation may also reflect the wide range of nontraditional forms, functions, and processes of families and relationships in the United States. As indicated previously, perhaps a first step in the formation of family policies relates to the need to recognize that families do not all fit one monolithic stereotype with a husband as wage earner, a wife as homemaker, and two children (one girl and one boy, of course) as future replicates of their parents. This is one component of the next issue as well.

---

15. Alvin L. Schorr, "Views of Family Policy," *Journal of Marriage and the Family* 41 (August 1979): 465.

## How about tests for marriage and parenthood—renewable if passed?

Anyone who has attended school is familiar with tests. They follow a course of training and are intended to measure familiarity and competence in that area. If you pass them, you get certain rewards such as higher grades, course or class advancement, degrees, and the like. If you fail them, some alternatives may be to drop out, take them again, or find some substitute for the course or exam. Anyone who drives an automobile at one time received instructions, took a driving test, a written exam, or both, and if passed, received a license. Anyone who has a life-saving certificate received it after a period of training and evidence of knowledge and competence. Are marriage and parenthood less important? Do persons who marry and become parents have no need for training? Should couples receive licenses or endorsements for marriage or parenthood only following the passing of a test showing competence?

Evidence surrounding divorce, abuse, alcoholism, crime, or mental illness suggests that many persons should not marry, or if married, should not have children. Evidence shows that many married couples and parents say they were not fully aware of what they were getting into, had no formal and explicit training, and were not prepared financially or emotionally to cope adequately. Some would not have married or have had children at all. Others would have delayed both marriage and parenthood.

As a possible remedy, one suggestion could be to require training for marriage and parenthood and require the passing of tests (other than age and blood) for entrance into these new status positions. A more radical suggestion could be to require periodic retesting. These ideas are not suggested as cure-alls to marital and family problems, but they could be considered a service to many would-be spouses and parents and might serve as a deterrent to or constraint on certain persons who are not prepared for or equipped to handle these situations. What are the implications of such suggestions? Everyone has heard cases of couples who decided to end "serious" premarital relationships after one or both became aware that a marriage with that particular individual couldn't work. Should this situation be established into a more formal process? Should training and testing be required for obtaining a marriage license, for entrance into parenthood, or both? Who would write the requirements? What do you think?

### Policy for all close relationships or just for "families" with "problems"?

Assuming certain policies are necessary, a fourth issue is whether these policies should be directed toward all close relationships or toward those "families" with "problems"; toward any intimate life-style or toward marriages, families, or groups with "pathologies." This is a basic question of *entitlement* versus *need*. And if the need exists, it adds a dimension of *deserving* or *undeserving*. The deserving have a need through no fault of their own, such as the ill elderly or poor children. The undeserving too have a need, but they could have done or should do something about it. Thus social security becomes a legitimate deserving income support program without stigma because it was "earned and deserved." Welfare and AFDC as income support programs carry a connotation of disrepute. These are undeserving people who should be able to support themselves and could have prevented the unintended pregnancy.

A policy for all families or intimate relationships focuses on issues that affect everyone: employment, health, minimum wages, housing, sexual and racial equality, tax equity, and the like. The *need* position focuses on "problem"

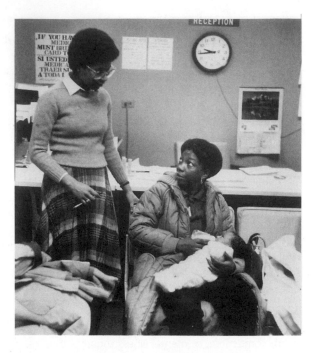

*Are single parents a problem or an acceptable family structure? Should local, state, or federal agencies intervene? Answers to these and other questions affect what type of programs and policies, if any, are put into effect.*

areas: unwed parenthood, abortion, abuse, single parents, divorce, and the like. Perhaps a medical analogy is relevant. Traditionally, medical care in the United States was directed toward the sick. Physicians were to be seen only when colds, disease, or broken bones "created" the need. An emerging view is directed at prevention, as a holistic orientation to care, or toward an emphasis on health and how to maintain it.

To label specific types of relationships or structures as *problems*, *pathological*, or *ill* may in itself affect the type of policy directed toward it. Consider single parenthood as an example. If this form of structure—one parent with children—is "pathological," then policy is likely to be couched in terms of preventing the formation of single-parent family structures and providing services designed to facilitate reconstitution of these "less than complete" families. On the other hand, if one-parent families are one of many accepted family life-styles, the policy is likely to be couched in terms of what is necessary for all families: minimum incomes, adequate housing, inexpensive child care, employment opportunities, support services, and the like.

This issue of single parenthood, like most others, is not an either/or situation. But it may focus attention on three questions. One is the key issue just described of whether we focus on all close relationships or on "families" with problems. The second is the issue of how the definition of a particular behavior pattern or structure may affect the type of policies suggested. The third issue is the question of what effect any specific policy may have for families or persons in primary relationships. It seems safe to assume that policies are rarely established in response to this question, but rather they seem to be directed at some specific "problem" area of concern, either in general social policy or in solving some problematic aspect of family policy. This question of what a given policy means to families or persons in primary close relationships needs to be asked continually if the family is to be an institution of importance and concern to our policy making.

## Policy for family groups and systems or for individuals?

The fifth issue is whether policy should be directed at *family* groups and systems or at *individuals*. This involves a difference between one perception of the family unit as a system in which all parts (statuses) are interrelated and interdependent, versus another perception of the family unit as a collection of separate and isolated individuals. The individual perspective focuses on the person as the unit of analysis, with little attention devoted to the unit of which that individual is a part. Today, the individual reigns supreme in the United States. The interests of the individual, his or her happiness, development, or achievement, are emphasized. Families are apt to be regarded as a vehicle for individual satisfaction.

As a result of this emphasis, family policy as well is heavily oriented toward individuals and persons rather than toward families or groups. To deal with a marital problem, counsel the husband or wife. To deal with the elderly, the ill, unwed mothers, the mentally retarded, delinquent youths, abused children, and the like, provide housing (or institutionalization), personal counseling, and individual attention. In contrast, the family-group-system perspective recognizes the relationship, the marriage, the nuclear family, or the extended kin network as a composite unit, rather than as collections of individuals. In dealing with marital or family problems, the system focus would be directed toward the whole system or unit, recognizing that all components of that unit affect all other components.

The advocates of the individualistic position might argue that the sick person, the unwed mother, or the mentally retarded person is the one with the problem and needs the "treatment" and the attention. They may also argue that one is never sure of exactly what comprises the family unit. Advocates of the family-group-system position might argue that persons never exist in isolation from a larger social order and society. According to a systems view, statuses are reciprocal. Husbands only exist in relation to wives, children in relation to parents, and brothers and sisters in relation to other siblings. Thus, the proponents of a systems approach will argue that social policy needs to include a recognition that all social beings are parts of, and are affected by, other parts, and that the welfare of any given individual is greatly affected by the persons, groups, and community with which that individual identifies. While the family unit may not consist of one mother, one father, and two children, various organizational structures fulfill similar functions.

From a systems viewpoint, policies directed at families are not anti-individual—nor are they intended to be. The needs of children, husbands,

### How about divorce insurance?

In the United States people are encouraged to protect themselves against future difficulties by insuring themselves. We buy automobile insurance to protect us from the economic loss of the automobile and the possibility of suit against loss of life and property. We buy health insurance to protect us from the possibility of major medical bills. We buy dental insurance to protect us from major costs associated with tooth decay, removal, or correction. We buy property insurance to protect us from destruction or loss of our homes. We buy disability insurance to protect us from an inability to work and maintain an income. We pay dues or taxes to cover unemployment compensation as protection against the loss of a job. We pay into a social security system to (hopefully) provide income for our retirement years. Should we not be covered by divorce insurance?

As shown in Chapter 17, more than one million divorces occur annually. An overwhelming number of female-headed households and some male-headed households face a serious problem of inadequate income. While welfare and child support payments are available to many persons, it can be argued that a welfare dollar is different from an insurance dollar and child support payments are different from social security payments. Divorce insurance, involving largely the private sector of the economy, may for many parents, provide them with the freedom and autonomy to plan for their own lives and those of their children with assurance and certainty.

Let's consider how such a system might work: Divorce insurance premiums, unlike most health and life insurance premiums, could be large during the early years of the policy and decrease with the length of time married. Benefits could work inversely: small benefits for brief marriages and increasingly larger benefits for longer-term marriages. If the benefits are paid over time rather than in one lump sum, divorce for the purpose of insurance collection could be minimized. The basic principle behind this type of insurance, like any other insurance, would be to provide guaranteed financial resources to single parents, particularly those with children. Would newly married couples be motivated to invest in such insurance? If not, how would the insurance be funded? What do you think?

---

wives, adolescents, or the elderly may be equally important to the needs of the group. A systems approach suggests that individuals are components of social networks, and that those individuals can be served best by a recognition of the others involved. A systems approach looks at the tasks and functions of families, the interdependence of family roles, the maintenance of boundaries, and the adaptive propensities that ensure their viability.[16]

### Policy at a micro- or macro-level?

A sixth issue is whether policy should operate at primarily a *micro-level* or a *macro-level*. Micro-level policy focuses on patterns of personal interactions that characterize everyday life. Macro-level policy focuses on the social patterns and forms of social organization that shape an entire society. These patterns are beyond the control of any given individual, yet they play a powerful role in affecting families and influencing personal lives.

---

16. *See:* Shirley L. Zimmerman, *Understanding Family Policy: Theoretical Approaches* (Newbury Park, Ca.: Sage Publications, Inc., 1988): Chapters 5 and 8, pp. 74–85 and 126–144.

Many social policies at a macro-level are related to areas such as taxation, medical care, employment, housing, education, or leisure. While policies in these areas may not be established directly for the benefit of families, they affect them greatly. If poverty status is characterized by lowered levels of commitment to marriage, and if high rates of marital dissolution are related to frequency of unwed parenthood, child abuse, and low levels of mental and marital health, then it seems imperative that social policy be directed not merely at counseling the mother or the abused wife or child, but at the conditions maintaining poverty. If welfare policies force men to live separately from their mate and children, or if federal tax laws or social security requirements impose penalties on marriage, then these policies, operating at a macro-level, need to be reexamined. If sexual or racial inequality in society prevents wives from establishing credit or owning property and prevents black families from living in certain neighborhoods or attending certain schools, then these practices and conditions need to be addressed at a level beyond any given individual or family.

One example of this can be seen in a paper dealing with the consequences of unemployment for families in the 1980s.[17] Phyllis Moen, using data from several depression periods, notes that: (1) most families of the unemployed who suffered financial hardship received no government income support; (2) unemployment benefits are an important coping mechanism for families of the long-term unemployed; (3) limiting the duration of unemployment appears to be as important a strategy for preventing financial hardship as is the availability of income support; and (4) families with more than a single wage earner are much more able to avoid economic privation. The differential distribution and unequal sharing of the costs of unemployment across families highlights the plight of black families, single parents, and parents of young children, and highlights how unemployment and its financial repercussions are shaped by broad social, economic, and political forces operating at a macro-level. Even with a healthy economy with "full employment," some portion of the labor force remains jobless. With major cutbacks in social programs plus the lag in governmental response, the financial toll on families experiencing unemployment can be traumatic. Note how events at a macro-level increase or decrease the level of unemployment and how macro-level policies lessen or heighten the negative impact of being unemployed.

Moen suggests as well that public policies facilitating the employment of women (flexible work patterning, day care, nondiscriminatory hiring and wage practices) could help both two-earner families and single-parent women make ends meet.[18] The policies are, however, slow in being developed and implemented.

---

17. Phyllis Moen, "Unemployment, Public Policy, and Families: Forecasts for the 1980s," *Journal of Marriage and the Family* 45 (November 1983): 751–760.

18. Ibid., p. 758.

Scanzoni[19] presents the argument that macro-level family-related objectives have rarely addressed fundamental issues, since it is impossible to define a family in concrete terms and not exclude many of the nontraditional forms as described throughout this text. Likewise, micro-level responses have been inadequate because a gap often exists between the demands of contemporary society and the capabilities of conventional families and individuals to grapple with those demands. Thus he argues for policy at a **meso** level, an alternative model that supplies a fit between the macro- and micro-levels. The meso-level involves "mediating structures," that is, groups and organizations that extend beyond the person or family but don't encompass an entire state or nation. These include community groups, agencies, churches, local chapters of national organizations such as the National Organization for Women (NOW), the American Civil Liberties Union (ACLU), Planned Parenthood, Family Service Associations, veterans' associations, unions, political action groups, and so forth. These groups could mediate, provide training, and offer support to the diverse range of family structures and concerns found in our pluralistic society.

## THE FUTURE OF THE FAMILY SYSTEM

The underlying issue in this chapter dealing with family policy related issues is that of the future of the family system. Will it survive? What types of sexually-bonded relationships, families, and societies will exist in the next ten, fifty, or one hundred years? How do we prepare for them? What type of training do we need to provide for our children and grandchildren (assuming they will be "our" children)? What types of structures will exist in the family realm? What functions will be expected of this institution? Will families be necessary? Will marriages exist? Will women have equal status with men? Will heterosexual partners be necessary for marriage or for children? These are a sampling of the questions that can be raised. The answers may depend on who gives them, the basis or theory on which the projection is based, the length of time projected, the types of family and social policies instituted, and, perhaps, the personal wishes of the projector.

That families and close relationships are changing and will continue to change is perhaps, although not necessarily, a definitive statement and one on which we could find widespread agreement. But comments on decay and breakdown or on progress and advancement must be approached cautiously. The following observations are made in relation to predicting the future. First, changes that take place and will take place in the society or in intimate relationships are not necessarily pleasing or regrettable, good or bad, or constructive or destructive per se. Changes are likely to be welcomed or rejected depending largely on one's own frame of reference, the groups with

---

19. Scanzoni, *Shaping Tomorrow's Family*, pp. 97–118 and 225–227.

which one identifies, and the value orientations to which one adheres. Rising divorce rates can be viewed either as a problem or as a solution to other problems. Homosexuality may be viewed as an illness or as a right to love whomever one chooses. War may be viewed as vital to national defense or as an immoral destruction of life and property. This is not meant to imply that there are not changes that are disruptive to the social order; rather, it is meant to imply that social matters must be seen in the context in which they occur. It is a rare issue that cannot be interpreted in various ways.

Second, although many people see the family at the core of society and as the most basic of all institutions, it should be made clear what has been stated time and again: the family cannot be understood as an isolated phenomenon. It must be viewed in relation to economic, educational, religious, and political institutions. In addition, factors such as population density, mobility patterns, and stratification divisions must be taken into account. It is not by chance that agricultural societies will tend to emphasize extended families, parental involvement in mate selection, and, often, plural marriage. Neither is it by chance that the United States places an emphasis on romantic love, separate households, and monogamous marriages. The central point is that, if accurate predictions are to be made, it is essential to have an understanding of what is going to take place in other social systems. A change in any element of a social system will likely lead to changes in other elements, including this institution we refer to as "family."

Third, the family is not a uniform entity. That change will occur is almost without question. But to speak of the changing family, or even of families in the United States, as if they were uniform entities can be misleading. From the very beginnings of U.S. society, the cultural base of its population was diverse and varied. Then, as today, one could expect to find variations in intimate relationships and family patterns by factors such as rural-urban residence, region of the country, religious affiliation, racial and ethnic identity, social-class background, or age. And yet, despite the diversity that comprises family life in the United States, one significant change has been the assimilation of quite different cultural heritages. One must recognize the manifest differences that exist in social class, race, and religious background and at the same time recognize that within this diversity there are strands of unity that belie heterogeneous origins.

Fourth, any type of social projection into the future is hazardous. Some trends are short-term ones, tied to the economic climate of prosperity that so drastically affects marriage, birth, and divorce rates. Some trends are not necessarily linear or even directional and may be highly or basically unpredictable. Other changes may be internal to the system or external to it, accidental or planned, behavioral or attitudinal, material or nonmaterial, actual or ideal, patterned or nonpatterned, peaceful or violent, continuous or spasmodic, rapid or slow, due to single causes or many causes. This suggests that predictions should be made cautiously—no one can predict the future without error.

Having provided all these qualifications—that change is not equal to decay, breakdown, or destruction; that what happens to the larger social order and other systems affects families; that families and relationships are extremely diverse; and that projection into the future is hazardous—permit me to brave this hazard and state, unequivocally, that as long as a society exists, some form of family system will survive. It is more difficult to state with equal conviction what forms the family will take, the meaning it will have for its members, the structure of relationships, and how or what specific functions it will perform.

The passing of the traditional conventional family has left a great many traumas, a great deal of suffering, and a great many loose ends. But the rebuilt pieces in their many variations will include sexually bonded, primary, intimate, close relationships that fulfill family type functions. Most Americans will continue to find marriage and family type interactions as a basic source of emotional and psychic stability. Families will continue to be primary sources of socialization, primary sources of security and affection, and primary sources of meaning. Families are likely to remain the largest social service agency in the nation and world—responsible for the care of children, the sick and disabled, the aged, the economic welfare of its members, and so forth. Partners within a relationship or marriage may change, the expectations of men and women may change, the sexual codes and practices may change, and the general family life-styles may be vastly different. These changes are not necessarily to be equated with decay, immorality, or a general deterioration of U.S. families. If our society is destroyed and the family has a hand in this destruction, it is not likely to be because of change but rather because of an inability to change.

# SUMMARY

1. All areas of marriage and family life are affected by certain economic, political, or other social policies. It seems safe to assume that while most social policies have an effect on families, few of these policies were developed or formulated with marriages and families in mind. As used in this chapter, *family policy* refers to definite methods of action directed at marriages, families, or kin groups with the intent of guiding, influencing, or determining their form, their functions, or the behavior, ideas, or values of their members.

2. This chapter deals with three family and change topics. First, family policy research is examined and three specific types are presented. Second, six issues that surround family policy are discussed. Third, the chapter concludes with some comments on the future of the family.

3. Family policy research, perhaps even more than most, is confronted with the issue of whether or not the researcher permits a personal value stance or policy objective to influence the research. It raises anew the research issue of focusing on what is as opposed to what should be.

4. Three types of family policy are discussed. Research for establishing family public policy examines some particular family structure or life-style to determine if certain

policies or programs are necessary and to make recommendations as to what they should be. Family evaluation research attempts to determine the degree to which social programs achieve the stated goals. Family impact analysis assesses the intended and unintended consequences of public policy and social programs.

5. Policy matters seldom exist without a divergence of ideas, conflicts over positions, or opposing recommendations. At a general level of analysis, six of these issues or differences are examined. These include:

   a. The extent to which policies are aimed at maintaining the status quo or serve as forces for change. Conventionals seek the status quo as idealized in *the* traditional conjugal family while progressives seek change and multiple family forms more consistent with a pluralistic society.

   b. The extent to which policies should be established or controlled at the *federal, state,* or *local* level—that is, national in scope and control or in the hands of regional, state, or local communities.

   c. The extent to which families and intimate relationships are a *public* or *private* institution, meaning basically the extent to which there should be a separation of family and governmental or legal intervention.

   d. The extent to which policies should be directed toward all close relationships or toward *families with problems*—that is, toward all intimate relationships irrespective of life-style or toward families with "pathologies."

   e. The extent to which policies should be directed at *family groups* or at *individuals*—that is, focusing on the social unit or system or focusing on persons as our unit of attention.

   f. The extent to which policies should operate at primarily a *micro-level* or *macro-level*—that is, focusing on small-group or interpersonal relationships or focusing on social patterns or forms of social organization that shape entire societies.

6. What about the future of families? Our social policies will, without doubt, affect the future directions families and their members take. The family is changing and will continue to change. We should take note that, first, these changes are not good or bad, per se. Second, the future of the family cannot be understood separate from other institutions and systems. Third, the family of the future will not be a uniform entity. And, fourth, any type of social projection into the future must be made cautiously. Given these qualifications, I predict unequivocally that as long as a society exists, some form of family system will survive. It will have many differing structural arrangements, perform a variety of functions, and fulfill a range of personal and social needs. Whether your interest in the family is at a professional level of teaching, research, or social action or at a personal level of dating, child rearing, or caring for aged parents, it will be impossible not to affect or be affected by families.

# KEY TERMS AND TOPICS

## DISCUSSION QUESTIONS

1. How would you differentiate among policy, social policy, and family policy? Can you think of
examples of social policy that exist independently of or have no impact on families?

2. Can, or should, family policy research be value-
free? Can, or should, policy research be separated from policy advocacy? How can family
policy researchers integrate or combine finding
out *what is* with a concern over *what should
be?*

3. Describe the different goals or intents of research to establish family policy, family evaluation research, and family impact analysis.

4. What arguments exist for establishing policy to
maintain the status quo as opposed to policy
that permits or forces change and diversity? Is
it possible to talk about *the* family in the Western world? Why or why not?

5. Contrast the stances taken by conventionals
and progressives. How do these stances translate into policy directives on issues such as
teenage sexual behavior and contraceptive usage, sex education, abortion, day care facilities,
cohabitation, divorce, remarriage, the employment of mothers of young children, and so
forth?

6. List some arguments for family policy to be
established at a federal as opposed to a state
or local level. What are arguments against this
idea? Is a national family policy possible or
realistic? Why or why not?

7. Discuss some of the arguments for or against
the separation of family and state. List areas in
which the government clearly has no "right" to
get involved and areas in which its involvement
is mandatory.

8. One issue differentiated policy directed at all
intimate relationships from policy issues directed at families with problems. Explain. What
are some effects of labeling certain life-styles or
structural arrangements as "problems"?

9. How might policies for children, unwed
mothers, the terminally ill, or the elderly differ
depending on whether they are directed at individuals or directed at marital, family, or kinship units?

10. Do you believe effective family change can occur within a society by directing programs and
policies exclusively at individuals or interpersonal relationships, that is, at a micro-level?
Explain.

11. Examine the three panels that end with "What
do you think?" What do you think about tests
for marriage and parenthood, divorce insurance, or a tax-free family lunch? Explain.

12. What predictions can you make about "families" and marital life-styles in the twenty-first
century? Describe their structures, functions,
the impact of new technologies, changing parent-child relationships, the division of marital
roles and tasks, the status of women, and sexual norms. What areas are most likely to remain static, stable, and relatively unchanged?

## FURTHER READINGS

Bane, Mary Jo. *Here to Stay: American Families in
the Twentieth Century*. New York: Basic Books,
1976. A book divided into two distinct parts: the
first deals with contemporary U.S. families in the
perspectives of change during this century; the
second explores policy areas illuminated by data
presented in Part I.

Dempsey, John J. *The Family and Public Policy*. Baltimore: Paul H. Brooks, 1981. An historical overview of developments leading to the emergence of the family as a public policy issue.

Giraldo, Zaida I. *Public Policy and the Family: Wives and Mothers in the Labor Force.* Lexington, Mass.: D. C. Heath, 1980. An examination of the impacts of employment on family life, tax policy on employed women, and the Equal Rights Amendment on families.

Huttman, Elizabeth Dickerson. *Introduction to Social Policy.* New York: McGraw-Hill, 1981. An introduction to social policy issues. Chapter 8 deals with AFDC and the poor, Chapter 9 with child welfare services, and Chapter 10 with the aged.

Kelly, Robert F. "Poverty, the Family and Public Policy: Historical Interpretations and a Reflection on the Future," in Patricia Voydanoff and Linda C. Majka (eds.) *Families and Economic Distress.* Newbury Park, CA.: Sage Publications, Inc., 1988, Chapter 13, pp. 261–284. Identification of three models of public policy toward poor families: a laissez-faire model, a clinical model, and a family support model.

Moen, Phyllis, and Schorr, Alvin L. "Families and Social Policy" in *Handbook of Marriage and the Family* by Marvin B. Sussman and Suzanne K. Steinmetz (eds.). New York: Plenum Press, 1987, Chapter 28, pp. 791–813. The authors look at approaches to family policy, cite a number of case studies, look at the role of social science research, and present forecasts and opportunities for the future.

Moroney, Robert M. *Shared Responsibility: Families and Social Policy.* Hawthorne, N.Y.: De Gruyter Aldine, 1986. A development of the notion of shared responsibility between the family and the state in the delivery of social care through social services.

Sawhill, Isabel V. (ed.). *Challenge to Leadership: Economic and Social Issues for the Next Decade.* Washington D.C.: The Urban Institute Press, 1988. Twelve chapters on domestic priorities including family incomes, the family, and poverty and the underclass.

Scanzoni, John. *Shaping Tomorrow's Family: Theory and Policy for the 21st Century.* Beverly Hills: Sage Publications, 1983. An insightful analysis of the struggle between "conventionals" and "progressives" in determining the type of family or families appropriate for U.S. society.

Steiner, Gilbert Y. *The Futility of Family Policy.* Washington, D.C.: Brookings Institution, 1981. A commentary on the family policy developments of the 1970s, with the central theme that not only is a comprehensive family policy futile, it simply does not exist.

Zimmerman, Shirley L. *Understanding Family Policy.* Newbury Park, CA.: Sage Publications, Inc., 1988. A book that provides the conceptual tools for understanding policy/family connections and the frameworks for application.

# GLOSSARY

**ABCX model**   A model of family crisis in which A (an event or situation) interacts with B and C (the resources available and the definition or meaning of the event) to produce X (the level or degree of crisis).

**Abortion**   The termination of a pregnancy either spontaneously (miscarriage) or induced.

**Achieved status**   A social position that is obtained through one's own efforts, such as husband or teacher.

**Adoption**   The process of legally becoming parents of a child not biologically one's own.

**Affiliated families**   A variation of an extended family in which a nonrelative (often an older person) becomes recognized as a part of the nuclear family network.

**AIDS**   (Acquired Immune Deficiency Syndrome) A sexually transmitted disease where white blood cells that hinder resistance to viruses and bacteria are broken down.

**Androgyny**   A society with no sex-role differentiation. Androgynous individuals are those who are capable of expressing both or either masculine or feminine behavior.

**Annulment**   The ending of a marriage because of conditions that existed prior to the marriage. The result makes the marriage nonexistent.

**Arranged marriage**   When marital partners are selected by persons (parents, matchmakers, etc.) other than the couple themselves.

**Ascribed status**   A social position that is assigned to persons by society or by birth such as age, race, or sex.

**Assortive marrying**   The idea that people marry those like themselves more often than could be due to chance.

**Authority**   Legitimate power.

**Baby boom**   The dramatic rise in the number of births following World War II until about 1960.

**Behaviorism**   A theory of learning that focuses on actual behavior believed to be the result of conditioning through rewards and punishments.

**Bigamy**   The marriage of one person to two persons of the opposite sex (like polygamy but restricted to two).

**Bilateral system**   A family system that traces descent and inheritance through both the male and female lines.

**Biological predispositions**   The idea that certain biological or genetic characteristics predispose people toward a certain kind of behavior.

**Birth order**   Sibling position based on the order of birth.

**Blue-collar families**   The "working class" or the upper-lower class of semiskilled, service, and other workers with some sort of manual skill.

**Bourgeoisie**   The "class" or grouping of people who control the means of production and use capital, natural resources, and labor for profit.

**Child abuse**   Overt acts of physical, sexual, or verbal aggression against a child.

**Childless marriages**   Couples who either voluntarily or involuntarily have no children.

**Child neglect**   The failure to provide for adequate physical or emotional care of a child.

**Cohabitation**   An arrangement where an unmarried male and female share a common dwelling.

**Coitus**   Sexual intercourse.

**Common-law marriage**   A recognition of cohabiting couples as legally married if they meet certain requirements (such as time living together or recognition of each other as husband and wife) as specified by the state in which they reside.

**Commune**   A group of people holding collective ownership and use of property.

**Complementary marriage**   A traditional type of marriage where the husband and wife perform interdependent but different tasks: he is employed outside the home and she does the domestic tasks.

**Complementary needs**   A theory of mate selection based on the idea that people marry those who provide the maximum need gratification. Needs tend to be complementary rather than similar.

**Concept**   Tools or symbols by which one can share meanings and enable a phenomenon to be perceived in a certain way.

**Conceptual frameworks**   A cluster of interrelated concepts used to describe and classify phenomena.

**Conflict frame of reference**   A perspective of society that views conflict as natural, permanent, and inevitable and as a significant source of social change.

**Conjugal family**   A nuclear family which always has a husband and wife (the conjugal unit) and may or may not include children.

**Conjugal power**   The ability of husbands and wives to control or influence the behavior of one another.

**Consanguine families**   Extended families based on blood relationships as the basis of descent from the same ancestors.

**Conventionals**   Groups and persons who want to maintain the status quo and adhere to a traditional image of what families should be.

**Courtship**   The process that couples go through in developing a close relationship or commitment to marriage.

**Crisis**   A disturbance in the state of the family that leads to tension or pressure (see ABCX model).

**Dependent variable**   A variable that is changed or influenced by the effect of another variable (termed the **independent variable**).

**Developmental frame of reference**   A perspective that emphasizes the life cycle and various stages of transition with specific tasks to be accomplished at each stage.

**Displaced homemaker**   A full-time housewife, who through widowhood or divorce, loses her means of economic support.

**Double standard**   The use of one set of norms and values for females and a different set for males.

**Dowry**   A sum of money, property, or possessions brought to the marriage by the female.

**Dual-career marriages** Employment by both husband and wife in careers with levels of commitment and continuous developmental sequences.

**Ecology** The relationships between the physical environment and the human population that lives in that environment.

**Egalitarian family** Equal authority of husband and wife in family matters.

**Electra complex** The unconscious desire of the female to marry her father.

**Empty nest** A postparental stage of family life when children leave the "nest" and the family household contracts in size to the couple or individual member.

**Endogamy** A marriage pattern requiring persons to marry someone within their own social group.

**Evaluation research** As applied to families and family policy, evaluation research is conducted at a pragmatic level to determine the extent to which the stated goals are being achieved.

**Exchange frame of reference** A perspective that seeks to explain personal and social behaviors based on a reciprocity of rewards and costs.

**Exogamy** A marriage pattern requiring individuals to marry outside their own group.

**Extended family** A family in which two or more generations of the same kin live together (extension beyond the nuclear family).

**Extramarital coitus** Nonmarital sexual intercourse between a man and a woman, at least one of whom is married to someone else.

**Family** A kinship-structural group of persons related by blood, marriage, or adoption, usually related to the marital unit and including the rights and duties of parenthood.

**Family life cycle** The social sequence of events such as marriage, children, empty nest, retirement, and death that are repeated by successive generations of families.

**Family networks or clusters** A circle of families who live separately but meet regularly to share ideas, services, and supports.

**Family of orientation** The nuclear family into which one was born and reared (consists of self, siblings, and parents).

**Family of procreation** The nuclear family formed by marriage (consists of self, spouse, and children).

**Fecundity** The biological potential of a woman to bear children (in contrast to fertility, the actual number of births).

**Fertility** The actual number of births to women of childbearing age.

**Fictive kinship** Exchange patterns in which non-related friends offer services, support, and goods as if they were kin.

**Fraternal polyandry** The marriage of one woman to two or more men all of whom are brothers.

**Function** As related to a structural-functional frame of reference refers to what a system does (the functions it performs) or the consequences of a given form of structure.

**Gender** The cultural concepts of masculinity and femininity that society creates around sex (the biological fact of being male or female).

**Gender identity (sexual identity)** The sex of which one considers oneself to be a member.

**Group marriage** The marriage of two or more women to two or more men.

**Heterosexuality** Sexual acts or feelings directed toward members of the opposite sex.

**Homeless** Families, couples, and children without a dwelling in which to live that provides a stable place of residence within a community.

**Homogamy** Marriage to a person with similar social characteristics.

**Homosexuality**   Sexual acts or feelings directed toward members of the same sex.

**Homosexual marriage**   A couple of the same sex who share a common residence and a sexual and emotional commitment, and who recognize one another as united in marriage.

**Horizontal mobility**   A change from one social status to another that is roughly equivalent.

**Household**   The persons who occupy a housing unit.

**Househusbands**   Husbands who stay at home and perform the domestic tasks and care of the children while their wives are engaged in full-time employment.

**Hypergamy**   Marriage wherein the female marries upward into a higher social stratum (male marries down).

**Hypogamy**   Marriage wherein the female marries downward into a lower social stratum (male marries up).

**Hypothesis**   A statement of a relationship between variables that can be put to an empirical test.

**Ideal-type constructs**   Hypothetical models of polar extremes which provide contrasting (opposite) points with which to compare any social phenomenon.

**Illegitimacy**   The birth of a child to an unmarried woman.

**Impact analysis**   Research aimed at an assessment of the intended and unintended consequences of family policy and programs.

**Incest**   Socially forbidden sexual relationships or marriage with certain close relatives.

**Independent variable**   A variable that causes a change or variation in another variable (termed the **dependent variable**).

**Influence**   The ability to model the thinking and behavior of persons who hold authority.

**Institution**   A stable cluster of values, norms, statuses, and roles that develop around a basic need of society.

**Intergenerational mobility**   A change in the social status of family members from one generation to the next.

**Internalization**   The process by which one makes the society's values part of one's personality.

**In vitro fertilization**   The conception of a baby outside a woman's body (as in a laboratory dish); the fertilized egg is then placed within a woman's uterus for development.

**Joint custody**   The situation where divorced or legally separated parents assume mutual responsibility for the care and upbringing of their children.

**Joint family**   One type of extended family in which brothers share property but do not always live in a single household.

**Kin**   A network of persons who are related by common ancestry (birth), adoption, or marriage.

**Latchkey children**   Children who are unsupervised for part of the day. This is often linked to the time between the end of a school day and the time an employed parent gets home from work.

**Legal separation**   A legally married couple who maintain separate residences, but with established (legal) responsibilities of support and rights of visitation.

**Legitimate birth**   Birth to parents who are married to each other.

**Levirate**   The marriage of a widow to the brother of her deceased husband.

**Life expectancy**   The average number of years that a person in a given population can expect to life.

**Lifespan**   The maximum length of life possible in a given society.

**Life-style**  As related to families, the shared patterns of marital and family relationships, childbearing, dress, eating, recreation, etc.

**Macro-level policy**  Policies that focus on large-scale units such as social categories, systems, and forms of social organization that affect families: taxation, medical care, employment, housing, education, laws, and so forth.

**Marriage**  A socially approved sexual union of some permanence between two or more persons.

**Marriage squeeze**  The effects of an imbalance between the number of males and females in the prime marriage ages due to rising or falling birth rates and the median age difference at marriage.

**Mating gradient**  The tendency for high-status women and low-status men to be less likely to date and marry.

**Matriarchal family**  A family in which the wife rules or has dominance over the husband.

**Matrilineal system**  A family system that traces descent and inheritance through the mother's line.

**Matrilocal residence**  A family system in which a newly married couple is expected to live with the wife's family.

**Mediation**  A conflict resolution process where a divorcing couple meets with a third-party intervenor who helps them negotiate an agreement on property settlement, child support and custody, and other important matters.

**Mésalliance**  Marriage with a person of an inferior position.

**Meso-level policy**  Policies that focus on groups and organizations as mediating structures between the large-scale macro units and the small-scale micro units.

**Micro-level policy**  Policies that focus on small-scale units such as individuals and small-group interaction.

**Midlife transition**  The changes that take place in men and women at about age forty or forty-five as they reassess where they have been and what lies ahead (traditionally referred to as the midlife crisis).

**Minority group**  Any group that is subordinate to another group.

**Miscegenation**  Marriage and interbreeding between members of different races, as in the United States between blacks and whites.

**Modified-nuclear, modified-extended family**  Nuclear families which retain considerable autonomy and yet maintain a coalition with other nuclear families where they exchange goods and services.

**Monogamy**  The marriage of one male to one female.

**Neolocal residence**  A family system in which a newly married couple is expected to establish a new place of residence separate from either parent.

**No-fault divorce**  The dissolution of marriage based on irreconcilable differences where neither party is "at fault."

**Norm**  A rule that tells members of a society how to behave in particular situations.

**Nuclear family**  Any two or more persons of the same or adjoining generation related by blood, marriage, or adoption sharing a common residence.

**Oedipus complex**  The unconscious desire of the male to marry his mother.

**Orderly replacement**  The idea of having successive generations being duplicates or similar to the preceding generation.

**Ordinal position in birth order**  The position of birth among siblings, such as being the oldest or youngest child.

**Parallel marriage**  A type of marriage where the husband and wife perform similar tasks on an equitable basis: both are employed and both share child care and domestic tasks.

**Patriarchal family**   A family in which the husband rules or has dominance over the wife.

**Patrilineal system**   A family system that traces descent and inheritance through the father's line.

**Patrilocal residence**   A family system in which a newly married couple is expected to live with the husband's family.

**Peer group**   A group of people with similar or equal status and usually of similar age.

**Policy**   In reference to families, these are definite courses or methods of action with the intent of influencing or determining present and future forms of family organization, behaviors, or decisions.

**Polyandry**   The marriage of a woman to more than one husband.

**Polygamy**   The marriage of one man or one woman to more than one wife or more than one husband at the same time.

**Polygyny**   The marriage of one man to more than one wife at the same time.

**Poverty**   A classification of families below a specified income level based on a sliding scale of money income that is adjusted for factors such as family size, composition, and farm-nonfarm residence.

**Power**   The ability to control or influence the behavior of others, even in the absence of their consent.

**Primary group**   A small group of people who interact in a personal, direct, and intimate way.

**Principle of least interest**   The proposition that the partner with the least interest in a relationship is in a position to be exploited by the other.

**Progressives**   Groups and persons who view families as pluralistic and accept change and nontraditional life-styles as legitimate.

**Proletariat**   The "class" or grouping of people who labor and serve as the instrument of production for the bourgeoisie.

**Propinquity**   The marriage of persons who live close to one another.

**Proposition**   A statement of the relationship between two or more concepts or variables.

**Random sample**   A selection of persons in a way in which every member of the population has an equal chance of being chosen.

**Rape**   Sexual intercourse by force or threat of force without the consent of the victim and involving vaginal, anal, or oral penetration. Marital rape refers to the same conditions occuring between spouses.

**Reciprocity**   Two-way exchange of goods and services. Basic to a social exchange frame of reference.

**Reference group**   A group with which persons psychologically identify and to whom people refer when making evaluations of themselves and their behavior.

**Remarriage**   Marriage by anyone who has previously been married.

**Role**   The social expectations or behaviors that accompany a particular status.

**Role conflict**   The situation in which incompatible expectations or behaviors accompany a given status or set of statuses.

**Role taking**   The ability to assume the status of persons with whom one interacts and see the world from their perspective.

**Secondary group**   A group whose members interact in an impersonal manner, have few emotional ties, and come together for a specific, practical purpose.

**Separation**   Individuals who are legally married but are not sharing a common household or residence.

**Sequential monogamy**   Marriage to a succession of partners but always to only one at a time.

**Sex**   The biological fact of being male or female.

**Sex ratio**   The number of males per one hundred females in a population.

**Sex role**   Learned patterns of behavior expected of males and females in society.

**Sexualization**   Sexual socialization. The process by which individuals acquire their sexual self-concepts, values, attitudes, and behaviors.

**Sexual scripts**   A learned designation of the who, what, when, where, and why of sexuality.

**Sibling**   One's brother or sister.

**Significant other**   A person with whom one psychologically identifies and whose opinions are important.

**Single parent**   Generally used in reference to a mother-child or father-child nuclear family unit.

**Social class**   An aggregate of individuals who occupy broadly similar positions on the scale of prestige.

**Socialization**   The process of learning the rules of and expectations for behavior for a given society.

**Social self**   The organization of internalized roles which were developed in interaction with others.

**Social system**   A set of interrelated social statuses (positions) and the accompanying expectations that accompany these positions.

**Society**   A group of interacting individuals sharing the same territory and participating in a common culture.

**Sociology**   The study of human society and social behavior.

**Sororal polygamy**   The marriage of one man to two or more women all of whom are sisters.

**Sorate**   The marriage of a widower to the sister of his deceased wife.

**Status**   A socially defined position that a person occupies which may be ascribed (age, race, sex and so forth) or achieved (husband, father, teacher and so forth).

**Stem family**   An extended family type consisting of two families in adjacent generations based on economic and blood ties.

**Stepchildren**   The children by a former marriage of one's husband or wife (stepmother, wife of one's father by remarriage; stepbrother, son of one's stepparent by a former marriage; etc.).

**Stepfamily**   A family including a man and a woman, at least one of whom has been previously married and often including children from that previous marriage.

**Stratification**   The differential ranking of people into horizontal layers (strata) of equality and inequality.

**Structural-functional frame of reference**   A perspective that emphasizes the units of organization plus the consequences of that particular structural arrangement.

**Subculture**   A group of persons that shares in the overall culture of a society but also has its own distinctive values, norms, and life-styles.

**Surrogate mother**   A woman who conceives, carries, and bears a child for another couple.

**Swinging**   A type of extramarital coitus in which the couple openly and willingly engages in sexual relationships with other married persons. Sometimes referred to as *co-marital sexual mate sharing* or *consensual adultery*.

**Symbolic interaction frame of reference**   A perspective that stresses interaction between people as well as the social processes that occur within individuals made possible by language and internalized meanings.

**Symmetrical family**   Families as consumption units rather than production units where marital roles based on gender are eliminated.

**Theory**   A set of logically and systematically interrelated propositions that explain some particular process.

**Traditional family**   Patterns of family organization, customs, life-styles, or behaviors that are passed down from prior generations and maintained or valued because of an idealized image of how things once were and should be today.

**Underclass**   Families within the poverty population that are characterized by persistent poverty and a variety of associated problems such as welfare dependency and crime.

**Unilineal system**   A family system that traces descent and inheritance through either the male line *or* the female line.

**Universal permanent availability**   The idea that any individual is a potential mate or available for marriage with any other individual.

**Values**   Ideas and beliefs about what is worthwhile and important. A value theory of mate selection suggests that people select partners who share similar values.

**Variable**   A characteristic such as age, class, or income that can vary from one person or context to another.

**Vertical mobility**   Social mobility that involves movement toward a higher or lower social status.

**Violence**   Any act that is carried out with the intention of physically hurting someone else. Family violence focuses on behaviors among and between parents, spouses, children, siblings, and the elderly.

**White-collar families**   The middle-class category of professionals, clerical workers, salespeople, and other employees who have traditionally worn white shirts in their work. Often differentiated from blue-collar or working-class families.

**Widowhood**   The loss of a spouse by death.

# Name index

# Subject Index